The New South Creed

THE
NEW
SOUTH
CREED

A Study in Southern Mythmaking

PAUL M. GASTON

 VINTAGE BOOKS

A Division of Random House, New York

Library of Congress Cataloging in Publication Data
Gaston, Paul M.   1928–
    The new South creed.
    Reprint of the 1st ed. published by Knopf, New York. Bibliography: p.
    1. Southern States—Civilization. 2. Southern States—Race question. I. Title.
[F209.G3 1973]   917.5'03   73-6647
ISBN 0-394-71936-0

for my father
and the memory of my mother

Acknowledgments

My interest in the New South movement began a long time ago in the seminar of Fletcher M. Green at the University of North Carolina. Professor Green subsequently directed my dissertation on the subject and this book is an extension and refinement of that study.

Many persons and institutions have helped me in the interval between dissertation and book, and it is pleasant finally to be able to acknowledge their assistance. I have received financial aid from the Southern Fellowships Fund, the Social Science Research Council, the American Council of Learned Societies, the Old Dominion Foundation, and the Wilson Gee Institute for Research in Social Science of the University of Virginia. To all of them I reiterate my gratitude. Two research assistants, John Boles and Holt Merchant, helped more than I had a right to expect. Mr. Boles, with an unerring eye for the relevant, collected a large stack of notes which I have used profitably; Mr. Merchant checked most of the footnotes and offered valuable criticism and welcome enthusiasm. Several friends and colleagues have read all or portions of the manuscript. For their suggestions, encouragement—and time—I thank William W. Abbot, George H. Callcott, John Hammond Moore, Willie Lee Rose, and C. Vann Woodward. My reading of Professor Woodward's essay,

"The Search for Southern Identity," led me to the framework for the study.

My wife types badly and her spelling, punctuation, and proofreading are unreliable; but she persuaded me to pursue the subject in the first place, let few of my paragraphs escape revision, and wrote the passages I like most.

P.M.G.

Contents

The New South Creed

Prologue

The New South Symbol

Surely the basis of the South's wealth and power is laid by the hand of the Almighty God, and its prosperity has been established by divine law.

—HENRY W. GRADY, 1887[1]

Who can picture the vast, illimitable future of this glorious sunny South? . . . Here is a land possessing in its own matchless resources the combined advantages of almost every other country of the world without their most serious disadvantages. . . . It is beyond the power of the human mind to fully grasp the future that is in store for this country. . . . The more we contemplate these advantages and contrast them with those of all other countries, the more deeply will we be impressed with the unquestionable truth that here in this glorious land, "Creation's Garden Spot," is to be the richest and greatest country upon which the sun ever shone.

—RICHARD H. EDMONDS, 1888[2]

In the spring of 1865 momentous decisions awaited the American people. The old Federal Republic, sundered by the secession of the principal slaveholding states, had existed barely more than seventy years under the Constitution. With victory won, it now had a second chance to vindicate the faith of the Founding Fathers. But the task of mending its torn fabric and revitalizing the principles of which Lincoln had spoken on the Gettysburg battlefield would not be easy. That fabric and those principles had been strained at one time or another before the war by every section of the country, but in 1865 only the memory of the South's apostasy was recalled. Tension caused by the peculiarities of the slaveholding region had been an omnipresent source of national disquietude and, according to the Northern view, the South's determination to perpetuate its anachronistic way of life had been, in some ultimate sense, responsible for disruption of the Union, discredit to the cause of democracy everywhere, and bloody civil war. In the aftermath of Appomattox, then, citizens of the victorious Union believed that the future of the Republic and the success of its mission as exemplar of free government would depend heavily on the extent to which the South could adjust, or be made to adjust, to the national viewpoint.

Meanwhile, the conquered Southerners abandoned

forever their dream of separate nationhood, and having
to share with Northerners the desire to restore the Union,
they wished keenly for that result to come about quickly.
Cherishing memories of the Republic, and proud of their
conspicuous role in creating it, they likewise wished to
see it regain its former glory, and to share in its fame.
But in the agony that arose from their collapse they could
hardly agree that the injuries it had sustained and the
calamity the nation had suffered were all of their doing.
Rather, they expressed reverence for the civilization that
had existed in the South, but conceded that it had passed
irrevocably into history, had become an "Old South" that
must now be superseded by a new order. In time, the
words "New South" became the symbol that expressed
this passage from one kind of civilization to another.

This book is about that symbol. It deals with the
meaning that spokesmen for a new South gave to their
rallying cry, analyzes their program for making it a
reality, discusses the outcome and significance of their
movement in the nineteenth century, and concludes with
an appraisal of the legacy they bequeathed to the twentieth century.

I

Almost from the beginning of its popularity, the term
"New South" has had a blurred and ambiguous meaning.
Historians have not had much success with their efforts
to bring it into sharp focus. For one thing, they have
never agreed on the central characteristics of Southern

history itself, so that different interpretations of the region's past necessarily lead to conflicting accounts of what is new in the New South. Other factors have similarly complicated the historians' job of clarifying the image. For some, New South signifies a doctrine or point of view, not always clearly defined, that has been characteristic of certain groups of Southerners. For others, it has been used to delimit a period of time, with little agreement on beginning or terminal dates. It may mean the South since 1865; since 1877; from 1877 to 1913; since 1900; or simply the South of the present. And some compound the ambiguity by using it to designate both a doctrine and a period of time.

Another reason for ambiguity is that the concept of a New South, unlike the picture of the Old South, has always been a contemporary one, useful as a propaganda device to influence the direction and control of Southern development. Various groups have seized upon the term to symbolize their particular programs and name their publications. A nineteenth-century New South journal championed industrialism, high tariffs, and social Darwinism. A twentieth-century one was the voice of Southern communism.[3] Since its creation in 1944, the Southern Regional Council has published a magazine called *New South* which advocates a South free of racial discrimination; and in Nashville, the Southern Student Organizing Committee's *New South Student* joins to the movement for racial equality a militant antimilitarism and a vaguely defined program for the restructuring of Southern society. Used in these and other ways, "New South" may stand for whatever kind of society adopters of the term believe will serve the region's interests best or promote their own ambitions most effectively.

The common ingredient in these variations is the concept of a *South*—of whatever kind or period it may be. Southerners have shared experiences and circumstances which seem to make it natural, perhaps necessary, for their memories, new ideas, and aspirations to be arranged to fit coherently into some concept of Southernness. The spokesmen for a new South after the Civil War were as influenced by and responded as naturally to this tendency in their society as other Southerners. For this reason it is important in understanding their "New South" to see their ideas not only as a program or new departure but also as elements in a total mythic configuration with a history of its own.

Perception of the reality of both the past and the present is greatly determined for most people by the myths which become part of their lives. Defeat in the Civil War and humiliation in the Reconstruction that followed provided an atmosphere for the growth of two images of the South that, on the surface at least, appeared to have little in common. The defeat and despondency called forth a collection of romantic pictures of the Old South and a cult of the Lost Cause that fused in the Southerner's imagination to give him an uncommonly pleasing conception of his region's past. Increasingly, he came to visualize the old regime as a society dominated by a beneficent plantation tradition, sustained by a unique code of honor, and peopled by happy, amusing slaves at one end of the social spectrum and beautiful maidens and chivalric gentlemen at the other—with little in between. That this noble order had been assaulted and humiliated by the North was a source of poignancy and bitterness for Southerners; but, in the bleak aftermath of defeat, the recollection of its grandeur was also—and more importantly—a wellspring of intense satisfaction and the basis for an exaggerated regional pride.

No amount of nostalgia, however, could gainsay the fact that the South in the generation after Appomattox was desperately poor, alternately despised, ridiculed, or pitied, and saddled with many unwelcome burdens. To find a way out of this syndrome, optimistic young Southerners like Henry W. Grady and Richard H. Edmonds began to talk hopefully of a new scheme of things that would enrich the region, restore prestige and power, and lay the race question to rest. The term "New South" in their lexicon bespoke harmonious reconciliation of sectional differences, racial peace, and a new economic and social order based on industry and scientific, diversified agriculture—all of which would lead, eventually, to the South's dominance in the reunited nation.

Unlike though they were, the picture of the Old South and the dream of a New South were both expressions of the hopes, values, and ideals of Southerners. In time, both became genuine social myths with a controlling power over the way in which their believers perceived reality. The mythic view of the past, already beyond the embryo stage in the antebellum period, was fully articulated in the 'eighties. The New South creed, born to inspire a program of action, expressed faith in the South's ability to bring about its own regeneration in partnership with sympathetic Northerners; but in the 'eighties it began to undergo a metamorphosis and soon came to be a description not of what ought to be or would be, but of what already was.

The presence of myths in and about the South does not, of course, mark the region off as different either from the rest of the country or from other parts of the world, for every nation or group can be identified in some measure by the myths upon which it rests. What does distinguish the South, at least from other parts of the United States, is the degree to which myths have been spawned and the extent to which they have asserted their hegemony over the Southern mind. George B. Tindall, in a recent essay on the mythmaking penchant of the South, has prepared a kind of genealogical guide to Southern mythology which abundantly supports his conclusion that its "infinite variety . . . could be catalogued and analyzed endlessly."[4] One of the reasons for the superabundance of Southern myths is that Southern life has involved such a high degree of failure and frustration that intellectual and emotional compensations have been at a premium. Myths have been equally important as means of making some sense and order out of the complex, ambivalent patterns of the Southern experience. The South, as David M. Potter observes, "has been democratic as well as aristocratic, fond of 'flush times' and booms as well as of tradition; it has lusted for prosperity, bulldozers, and progress, while cherishing the values of stability, religious orthodoxy, and rural life." Caught in a painful dilemma, Southerners "could not bear either to abandon the patterns of the Old South or to forego the material gains of modern America."[5]

To harmonize these conflicting ambitions and experiences, Southerners have nurtured their myths to perform something closely akin to the function of religion—to unify experience, as Mark Schorer has remarked in another context, "in a way that is satisfactory to the whole culture and to the whole personality." Myths, Schorer writes, "are the instruments by which we continually struggle to make our experience intelligible to ourselves."

A myth, he continues, "is a large controlling image that gives philosophical meaning to the facts of ordinary life; that is, which has organizing value for experience."[6] For their believers, as C. Vann Woodward writes, myths are "charged with values, aspirations, ideals and meanings";[7] and for the individual involved, as Robert Penn Warren puts it, the myth "defines the myth-maker's world, his position in it, his destiny, and his appropriate attitude."[8] Myths, as these comments attest, are not polite euphemisms for falsehoods, but are combinations of images and symbols that reflect a people's way of perceiving truth. Organically related to a fundamental reality of life, they fuse the real and the imaginary into a blend that becomes a reality itself, a force in history. The distinction between creed and myth, which is important to this study, is one of emphasis. Both concern beliefs, but the former is a conscious statement concerned primarily with how things ought to be, while the latter is more a generalized, unconsciously held belief in how things actually are or were.

Historians have long been aware of dynamic myths in the Southern past but, with a few notable exceptions, they have not focused their studies on myth as a subject of historical investigation. Rather, they have produced a lush and stimulating interpretive literature designed to identify the central theme or themes of Southern history. Fruitful though this approach has been, it is beset by serious limitations. In ordering and simplifying their materials—and investing their conclusions with value judgments—most practitioners of this genre of historical writing have fashioned interpretations that have become little myths themselves, subject to endless critiques by other historians. For example, William E. Dodd wrote early in the twentieth century that the normative South was the South of Jefferson, which he presumed to be liberal and agrarian, not intolerant and hierarchical.[9] But, as Potter observes, Dodd "reconciled his love for his native South and his commitment to democracy, and with very little disclosure of the wishful thinking which was involved, identified the land he loved with the values he cherished."[10] Similarly, in 1930 a group of young Nashville intellectuals, the Vanderbilt Agrarians, projected their hostility to modern industrial America into a generalized picture of the Southern past which portrayed agrarianism as the decisive factor in the region's development. In their view agrarianism had produced a traditional style of life characterized by order, rootedness, and respect for the individual.[11] In literal form, neither Dodd's picture of a democratic agrarian society nor the Nashville group's image of a conservative agrarian society fits with what historians now know about the Southern past, and "the whole idea of the South as an agrarian society," Potter notes, "seems more and more an illusion, nourished by a wish."[12]

Less illusory, and somewhat more durable, is Ulrich B. Phillips's thesis that the central theme of Southern history has been the white man's determination to maintain a biracial society. Southernism, Phillips wrote in 1928, arose from "a common resolve indomitably maintained" that the South "shall be and remain a white man's country." And, he continued, "the consciousness of a function in these premises, whether expressed with the frenzy of a demagogue or maintained with a patrician's quietude, is the cardinal test of a Southerner and is the central theme of Southern history."[13] But even the Phillips thesis has appeared outmoded of late because of the rapid and profound changes in race relations. These and altera-tions of other aspects of Southern life have caused many scholars to doubt the continuing distinctiveness of the region and have stimulated a new round of assessments of the Southern experience. They have led to C. Vann Woodward's "Search for Southern Identity," to the invocation of Harry Ashmore's epitaph for Dixie, to a reconsideration of the validity and usefulness of the concept of regionalism, and to one writer's proclamation of the "happy truth" that the South has lost its "regional integrity," so that the "writer of tomorrow must take into account another South, a South already born and growing lustily, a rich South, urban, industrialized, and no longer 'Southern,' but rather northernized, Europeanized, cosmopolitan."[14]

Changes, in both the region and the nation, have transformed the reality as well as the image of the South in recent years, but as Edgar T. Thompson remarked a short time ago, "before and since Henry W. Grady used the expression in 1886, every generation of Americans has been told that the South of its day was a 'New South.' "[15] This ongoing concern to discover and explain the significance of a new South, suggested by Thompson's observation, has nearly always required the would-be discoverer to distinguish between the civilization of the Old South and the emerging, or presumably emerging, New South. Deprecating this tendency, W. J. Cash wrote more than a generation ago, in what is probably still the most widely read study of the Southern mind, that "the extent of the change and of the break between the Old South that was and the South of our time has been vastly exaggerated," and he urged his readers to disabuse their minds "of two correlated legends—those of the Old and the New Souths."[16] But Cash's popular theory of historical continuity, as later parts of this study will suggest, was constructed by misjudging the significance of key elements in the Southern experience; and the Old South–New South dichotomy which he minimizes is in fact a crucial one with which every search for the "central theme" of Southern history must come to terms at one point or another.

II

Quests for the essence of Southernism have been greatly aided by the appearance of numerous excellent works on the values and ideals of the antebellum South so that we have today a rich literature in that field.[17] Unfortunately, the same cannot be said for the intellectual history of the postwar South, and because the subject has been neglected generalizations about the ideology of the period and attempts to portray convincingly the Old South–New South dichotomy rest on inadequate monographic foundations.[18] In part, then, this study of the New South creed is designed to narrow one of the gaps that must be closed to permit further advances in the interpretive literature of Southern history. It is also conceived as a study in the history of Southern mythology, a largely unexplored field. As Tindall notes, myths have profoundly influenced the shaping of the Southern character and have had much to do with "unifying society, developing a sense of community, of common ideals and shared goals, making the region conscious of its distinctiveness." Whether he is accurate in predicting that historians may "encounter the central theme of Southern history at last on the new frontier of mythology" remains to be seen, but the prospects are inviting enough to encourage exploration of that frontier.[19]

Neither Southern mythology nor Southern history can be studied intelligently in a regional vacuum. The South, to be sure, has been different from the nation, but to explain the nature and significance of its distinctiveness the successful historian must transcend regional perspectives. For example, Woodward's influential essay, "The Search for Southern Identity," explains how Southern peculiarities appear to be unique only because the South is part of America. American history, unlike the history of other parts of the world, has been characterized by economic abundance and opportunity, success and invincibility, and a legend of moral innocence. The Southern experience, on the other hand, has been shaped by the obverse of these endemically American characteristics: poverty, frustration and defeat, and an ever-present moral dilemma.[20]

To the men of the postwar period who proclaimed the New South creed, these differences were real and painful; and their program, product of a subtle interaction between national ideals and achievements on the one hand and regional aspirations and failures on the other, was designed to obliterate them. How the New South creed was first articulated; how it inspired a program to make the South rich, triumphant, and morally innocent; how it adjusted to and manipulated the myth of the Old South; and how, in the end, it became itself a powerful and enduring social myth are the subjects of the chapters that follow.

1

Birth of a Creed

The pride which we might have felt in the glories of the past is rebuked by the thought that these glories have faded away. It is rebuked by the thought that they were purchased at the expense of the material prosperity of the country; for men of wealth and talents did not combine their fortunes, their energies, and their intellects to develop the immense resources of the land of their nativity.

—DANIEL HARVEY HILL, 1866[1]

The Old South . . . has gone "down among the dead men," and on its head-stone we see not the word "Resurgam." For that vanished form of society there can be no resurrection. . . . But the New South—its child and legitimate successor—sits in the seat of the dethroned king, exhibiting a lustier life, and the promise of greater growth and strength, than did its predecessor.

—EDWIN DELEON, 1870[2]

We can live neither *in* nor *by* the defeated past, and if we would live in the growing, conquering future, we must furnish our strength to shape its course and our will to discharge its duties. The pressing question, therefore, with every people is, not what they have been, but whether and what they shall determine to be; not what their fathers were, but whether and what their children shall be.

—BENJAMIN HARVEY HILL, 1871[3]

Henry W. Grady, the young and ebullient editor of the Atlanta *Constitution*, appeared before the New England Society of New York in 1886 to make a speech that subsequent generations of Southern schoolboys would be required to commit to memory. Surrounded by imposing men of affairs, Grady announced that an Old South of slavery and secession had passed away to be replaced by a new South of union and freedom. The national press reacted jubilantly to the occasion, hailing the optimistic orator from Georgia as the personification and chief spokesman of his region's dynamic movement of regeneration. When he died three years later, still a young man, the New York *Times* lauded him as the "creator of the spirit" that animated the once despondent region. Other contemporaries, in all parts of the country, were similarly impressed by Grady's evangelistic mission and golden words and were extravagant in their praise of him as the first and foremost New South spokesman.[4]

Later generations of Southerners, seldom corrected and sometimes abetted by their historians, continued to look upon Grady not only as the chief apostle of the New South movement—a title he probably deserved—but as its originator as well. It was not so many years ago, for example, that a president of the Southern Historical Association lent his authority to the popular belief that the term "New South," if not actually invented by Grady, was "first put into circulation by him."[5] Grady himself, however, never claimed either to have coined the phrase or to have been the first to popularize it. He had used it as early as 1874, in an editorial in the Atlanta *Daily Herald*, but he knew that others had used it before; and by the time of his widely publicized New York address the term was already household knowledge.

I

Twenty-four years before the New York speech, and three years before Lee surrendered to Grant, the term New South made its debut. A Union officer, exhilarated by his army's capture of the sea islands of South Carolina and Georgia, apparently had visions not only of victory but also of a new and better order to come. On March 15, 1862, Captain Adam Badeau edited the first number of *The New South*, a newspaper designed to serve the Federal troops in the Port Royal area. Less than a year after the war had begun, at nearby Fort Sumter, Port Royal was the scene of a rehearsal for the later reconstruction and it seemed appropriate that the newspaper serving the lush and once opulent sea islands should adopt a name symbolizing the inauguration of a new era.[6]

Despite the title, however, the journal gave little indication of what shape the postwar order might take, for neither Badeau nor his editorial successor, Joseph H. Sears, spelled out a comprehensive program for the region. The newspaper was heavily military in tone and coverage, exuding contempt for the South's aspiration to independence and frequently emphasizing Badeau's declaration in the maiden issue that the Federals were able and determined to restore the "civil union at any cost." Partly because of wartime circumstances and partly because of its peremptory, hostile tone, the Port Royal newspaper was read by relatively few Southerners and even fewer looked to it for instruction and encouragement. Not surprisingly, then, the first effort to introduce the term "New South" into the lexicon of Southerners faded from memory and Badeau's creation earned no place in the movement that was to adopt its name.

It would be five years after Appomattox before the term was to be used positively as the symbol for a specific and indigenous movement of social, economic, and intellectual regeneration. During the first half-decade after the war Southerners responded in a variety of ways to the crushing defeat they had sustained and to the revolutionary consequences of emancipation which suddenly faced them. Some, filled with hatred and belligerence, hoped to restore the old order as perfectly as possible by assigning the Negro to a status of near-slavery and by refusing to abandon their agrarian economic and social order and the static value system it had spawned. Others, despairing of all programs to save the region, proposed mass emigration, convinced that the Confederate ethos could be preserved only in a foreign land, untainted by the progressive doctrines of the nineteenth century. Persuaded that the society they cherished could never be revived, these fatalists spoke naturally of an "old" South that now belonged to history. To most Southerners, however, total resistance to change or flight from their country were unsatisfactory solutions. They, too, recognized the passing of an era and undoubtedly many of them used the term "new" South to suggest, however vaguely, the inevitability of change.

Gradually, out of the attempt to give form and direction to a new order, the New South movement of the next decade emerged.

The need for a new material basis and a new intellectual rationale for Southern society was obvious and acute in the early postwar period. Before the Civil War the South had worked out an intricate material and social system, elaborately rationalized by an intellectual and moral creed that viewed the Southern way of life as fundamentally different from and superior to that of the North. When cotton culture spread across the older regions of the South and then into the newer lands of the Southwest, staple-crop agriculture became more firmly established than ever before. At the same time, and as a product of the same dynamic, a new and more aggressive plantation aristocracy was grafted onto the older one to dominate society and dictate the course of its development. Slavery, which had shown some signs of being moribund before the cotton revolution, rapidly came to be regarded as a vital and immutable condition of both staple-crop agriculture and plantation aristocracy. These three intertwining economic and social interests—staple-crop agriculture, plantation aristocracy, and Negro slavery—produced a formidable defense mechanism that frustrated industrial and urban developments capable of undermining their foundations. The value system that grew naturally out of this order was inevitably hostile to the increasingly pragmatic and utilitarian cast of mind of nineteenth-century liberal development and suspicious of its notable shibboleths and achievements: economic individualism, urbanism, industrialism, and mass culture.

During the three decades prior to the war all facets of the Southern system were bitterly attacked as a consequence of the crusade against slavery. Attack produced response, and the best minds of the South labored for more than a generation to fashion a damning critique of free society and an ingenious rationalization of slavery as the only sound basis for the development and preservation of republican virtue, constitutional rectitude, and class harmony. Hostility to the forces of industrialism and urbanism was greatly augmented, and in the contest with anti-slavery polemicists the planters and their theoreticians identified the North, and especially New England, with virtually all of those evils inimical to the peace and prosperity of the South. Hostility combined with fear quickly led to the erection of a "cotton curtain" to diminish the flow of hostile ideas from the outside and to protect the orthodox viewpoint from erosion within.

By the time Lincoln called for 75,000 troops to suppress the disorders at Fort Sumter, the most popular slogan in the South was the exuberant cry, "Cotton is King." The boast meant not only that the Confederacy was unbeatable, but also that the Southern monarch had produced a near-idyllic society ready to prove its superior quality in warfare. Enthusiasm for the Confederate cause burgeoned into euphoria at the outset of the conflict, and for this reason the frustrations and defeats that soon came struck with unusual force. The war completely destroyed the myth of invincibility and made it increasingly difficult to retain the corollary myth of superiority, for failure to meet the test of endurance inevitably raised doubts about the quality of the defeated society. To many Southerners, then, sober second thoughts came in 1865; the result was dissipation of the antebellum unity of mind that had unquestioningly accepted the social, economic, and intellectual structure of Southern civilization.[7]

There was, to be sure, no mass repudiation of Southernism in 1865, or at anytime thereafter. On the contrary, nostalgia, despair, pride in the defeated soldiers, and pathos—mixed with a generous measure of relief—combined to produce a mood of ambivalence. Few Southerners neatly sorted out their conflicting sentiments and certainly few of them suffered a real crisis of faith. Their mental dilemmas were resolved simply by paying homage to the gallantry and honor of the old regime without letting that ritual interfere excessively with an examination of the problems of the present and the future—even when that examination led them, as it must, to search for the flaws in the old closed system of staple-crop agriculture, planter domination, and Negro slavery.

Although it never appeared with clarity in the first years after the war, what the South set off in search of was a new modus operandi with a harmonizing rationale to supply the same kind of fraternal unity that the creed of the Old South had furnished. The task was formidable. For one thing, it could not be achieved without substantial material and spiritual aid from the North; and yet pride could be restored and confidence built only if the movement were, or at least appeared to be, indigenous in origin and control. Moreover, with the power of the planter destroyed, there was no group within the region that could wield the kind of moral and social power that the deposed class had enjoyed. For this reason proposals for self-reconstruction often lacked focus and authority and crystallized slowly. Finally, the more violent and dramatic contest over Congressional Reconstruction, centered on the status of the Negro and the locus of political power, both diverted energies from programs of self-reconstruction and virtually eliminated the possibility of intersectional harmony necessary to their achievement.

Nevertheless, during the immediate postwar years a beginning was made. Dozens of proposals, having little or nothing to do with the more publicized issues of the main Reconstruction, appeared in speeches, newspapers, magazines, and reports; and, despite the turmoil, a program began to take shape. Increasingly, hope was expressed that old errors could be corrected and new courses charted. A former Confederate colonel, member of an aristocratic South Carolina family, put the necessity simply: "We must," said Ben Allston, "begin at the beginning again. We must make a new start."[8]

II

No more likely place for launching the new start that Allston called for could be found than *DeBow's Review*, the journal which published his speech. Before the war, J. D. B. DeBow's New Orleans magazine had combined an intense Southern nationalism with an equally fervent call for industrialization. The journal ceased publication during the war, but DeBow revived it in 1866. In the maiden issue of the "After the War" series, he roamed broadly over the problems of the South. "The vast mineral resources which geological surveys have divulged," he wrote, were as yet untouched by the "hand of industry," and the limitless number of rich manufacturing sites dazzled the imagination, so that the South now faced her moment of greatest opportunity. "If there ever was, then, a period in the history of a people, when it became necessary for them to be aroused as one man into action," DeBow declared, "and to put their shoulders to the wheel, and with energy and spirit and determination to make a giant and master struggle, that period has come for the South." Meeting the challenge and seizing the opportunity which now lay before her, he promised, the South would quickly resume "her place in the mighty empire of States" and "no son of hers will have reason to be ashamed of her place in the picture."[9]

In June 1866, DeBow published an essay by Matthew Fontaine Maury, promoter of a Confederate colonizing effort in Mexico.[10] DeBow understood the sense of despair which had caused the exodus, but though he confessed that "the clouds are dark," he wrote in the introduction to Maury's article that he was "not yet despondent. We have the nerve yet to endure and wait."[11] This cautious mood, based largely on his suspicions of the Radical element in Congress, was but a minor motif in the *Review*. Characteristically, like the New South prophets who would follow him, DeBow wrote extravagantly of the boundless resources whose exploitation would make emigration a senseless surrender. Typical of the pieces he published—and a striking contrast to Maury's somber article—was an ecstatic essay by A. P. Merrill, who believed that the unparalleled advantages of the South would make "Nineveh, Babylon, Rome, and Britain, with all their boasted wealth and dominion, sink into insignificance."[12]

In an essay on South Carolina, DeBow confessed that much had been said and written about the underdeveloped resources of the South, "but there are very few who are informed as to the peculiar advantages or special aptitudes of any particular section." He therefore proposed, as "one of the first and most practicable steps that can be adopted to revive the former prosperity of these States," a project "to disseminate reliable information regarding the opportunities for profitable employment offered by the specialities of each section."[13] The present flow of population was westward, DeBow noted, but he believed that this could not continue indefinitely. Once the true possibilities of the South were understood a mighty immigration movement would begin. Happily, he believed the South was now ready to remove the "dykes and barriers and invite the inundation."[14]

To seize the opportunities that lay before them, Southerners were told by *DeBow's Review* that the region must industrialize, diversify its staple-crop agricultural system, seek immigrants and capital from the North and from Europe, and infuse the region with a new spirit of business enterprise. DeBow saw, perhaps more clearly than some of the later New South prophets, that the shortage of capital and skilled labor, combined with difficult marketing problems, presented severe obstacles; but he wrote confidently that they would be overcome once a genuine effort got underway. Industrial development was the first necessity. Designating manufacturing as the South's "true remedy," he wrote:

We have got to go to manufacturing to save ourselves. We have got to go to it to obtain an increase of population. Workmen go to furnaces, mines, and factories— they go where labor is brought. Every new furnace or factory is the nucleus of a town, to which every needed service is sure to come from the neighborhood or from abroad. Factories and works established establish other factories and works. Population, we repeat, is one of the sorest needs of the South; immigration only can supply this. We can surely obtain that by providing our labor with diversified employment.

Capital, to the extent that the South shall have occasion to borrow, will, by a law of economy that never fails, flow here to erect, equip, and start every manufacturing establishment as fast as it can profitably be run.[15]

DeBow's plea for manufacturing was supported by numerous contributors to the *Review*. Robert M. Patton, a former governor of Alabama, writing in 1867 of a "New Era of Southern Manufacturers," stressed the importance of cotton textile development. With increasing uncertainties in the cotton field, owing, he thought, to the unreliability of Negro labor, Patton argued that a shift of capital from cotton growing to cotton manufacturing would provide employment for thousands of war widows and orphans. Moreover, the advantages of the South in textiles—favorable climate, abundant water power, nearness to the raw material—especially suited the region to the industry.[16] Another contributor, repeating many of Patton's arguments, added the happy thought that the textile industry could be built on the cheap labor of poor whites. Housed in mill villages, where common schools would be practicable, they would become better educated, more industrious, happy, and responsible citizens.[17] So important was industrial development to the material welfare of the region that another contributor pleaded for support from the region's state legislatures. "The capital of the State and its credit," he wrote, "should be employed to aid in establishing certain leading manufactures of iron and cotton." State aid to manufacturers was necessary and justifiable, he argued, "on the same principle that States aid [is] . . . in building ways of transportation. The reasoning is precisely the same, with this special and conclusive reason. The State must build a poor-house and a prison, or a cotton factory in every county or parish."[18]

DeBow's main emphasis was on industrial development, which he believed would go far toward bringing balance to the Southern economy. But his analysis also led him to attack vigorously the notion that the South should continue to place most of its agricultural capital into production of staple crops. Farming, he recognized, would continue to be the backbone of the economy for some time, but the region would not prosper until it created a new, diversified agriculture. Farmers, he frequently wrote, should take advantage of the long growing season to produce numerous and varied crops for ever widening markets. A contributor from New Orleans stated the dogma of the *Review* when he wrote that cotton was no longer king, that a revolution of "great magnitude" had taken place, and that it would be the essence of folly to attempt to resurrect an agricultural system that had caused such woe.[19]

The attraction of capital and skilled labor from the North and from Europe was a critical element in DeBow's program. To lure them he proposed, first, that the South begin its industrial development earnestly, using the resources immediately at hand; and, second, that the leaders of the region undertake a massive campaign to advertise its rich potential. With a faith that capital would come in naturally as a result of proper dissemination of information, and despairing of the reliability of Negro labor, DeBow and his contributors devoted most of their energies to designs for attracting non-Southern whites to supply the shortage of skilled labor. Proposals were made for the promotion of immigration societies and states were urged to form immigration bureaus. One contributor, like DeBow, urged that the state take the leadership in breaking up large plantations in order to make land available to immigrants. The hope was that such a scheme would offset the competitive advantage which the Homestead Act had given the West.[20] To assure potential non-Southern investors and laborers of a friendly reception, the *Review* ran several articles in 1866 on the theme of sectional reconciliation. One optimistic contributor, writing in the first issue, pronounced the end of sectionalism. Sectional questions, he wrote, "are *settled;* and settled forever. We all, North, South, East, and West, have *one country, one destiny, one duty.*"[21]

DeBow died in 1867, and his magazine survived him only a short while. William M. Burwell, the new editor, was a loyal disciple and the *Review* continued, until its demise in 1870, to develop the program DeBow had worked out in 1866. In his statement of purpose, Burwell summarized the goals to which his predecessor had been committed and pledged his support to them. He would oppose sectionalism, advocate protection of Negro rights, encourage programs to entice labor and capital into the region, and impress upon all Southerners their "paramount duty" to work "silently, resolutely, honorably for the social and industrial reconstruction of the South."[22]

In the same year that DeBow revived his *Review,* former Confederate general Daniel Harvey Hill had published the first number of his new magazine in North Carolina. The name Hill chose, *The Land We Love,* suggests nostalgia and recrimination rather than optimism and innovation; and editorial pronouncements from a former Confederate general—even one as irascible as Hill—might well be expected to excoriate prophets of a new order. But, in the beginning at least, Hill offered his readers a fare strikingly similar to DeBow's. In May 1866 he began his personal crusade to remake the South, warning that Southerners had better change their "minds upon many subjects, else our very name and nation will be taken away."[23] To begin with, Hill called into question the pride which blinded men to the deficiencies of the old regime:

The pride which we might have felt in the glories of the past is rebuked by the thought that these glories have faded away. It is rebuked by the thought that they were purchased at the expense of the material prosperity of the country; for men of wealth and talents did not combine their fortunes, their energies, and their intellects to develop the immense resources of the land of their nativity. What factories did they erect? What mines did they dig? What foundries did they establish? What machine shops did they build? What ships did they put afloat? Their minds and their hearts were engrossed in the struggle for national position and national honors. The yearning desire was ever for political supremacy, and never for domestic thrift and economy. Hence we became dependent upon the North for everything, from a lucifer match to a columbiad, from a pin to a railroad engine. A state of war found us without the machinery to make a single percussion cap for a soldier's rifle, or a single button for his jacket.[24]

Hill's first editorial, a broad-ranging survey of the South's problems, was entitled "Education." The title was revealing because Hill believed that the planters' failure to produce a flourishing and balanced economic system was intimately related to a value system that scorned material progress. Thus, the educational task of the postwar South was to retrain its people and particularly to educate them in the ways of thrift and industry and instill in them a respect for manual labor. Men needed to learn that the effete, aristocratic educational values of the Old South were both cause and consequence of the economic failures the South had sustained. The needs of the present, he felt, were clear:

Is not attention to our fields and firesides of infinitely more importance to us than attention to national affairs? Is not a practical acquaintance with the ax, the plane, the saw, the anvil, the loom, the plow, and the mattock, vastly more useful to an impoverished people than familiarity with the laws of nations and the science of government? What will a knowledge of the ancient classics, of metaphysics and belles-lettres do to relieve our poverty? What will it add to our prosperity? We want practical learning, not scholastic lore. We want business men with brain and hand for work, not the recluses of the library or convent.[25]

Building on a new appreciation of the value of work, inculcated by an educational system attuned to the needs of the region, the South's next step in regeneration, Hill believed, led to a broadly diversified agricultural system to replace the old regime of staple-crop agriculture, and an imaginative, aggressive industrial system that would fully exploit the rich natural resources of the region. For two years the magazine developed these themes. In contrast to DeBow, whose emphasis was on industrial growth, Hill was more interested in diversified, scientific farming. Successive issues not only exhorted farmers to break away from the old system, but also supplied abundant practical and technical advice on such subjects as soil types, fertilizers, truck farming, and the economic management of small enterprises.

In 1868, Hill's tone changed abruptly. For reasons that are not entirely clear—but which probably relate to his growing enmity toward the unfolding program of Congressional Reconstruction—he began to retreat from many of his previously expressed views. He continued to preach agricultural reform, as he would throughout the rest of his life, but he said no more about the benefits of industrialism. Instead, he wrote vehemently about its evils. By May 1868 he was in full attack on the grasping drive for material success which he felt abounded in the nation. In this vein he wrote that rapid industrialization was producing a new industrial oligarchy "a hundred-fold less respectable and venerable, than the landed aristocracy which the spirit of the age has swept away."[26] Never returning to his early views, he was scornful of the New South movement when it materialized. Speaking to a veterans group in 1887 he referred sarcastically to the movement that had built on his own early ideas. Southerners, he said, are proud of the label New South; they "brag about it, and roll it as a sweet morsel under their tongues." For his part, he told the veterans, he would rather talk about the Old South.[27]

If D. H. Hill retreated from the New South movement before it had fairly begun, there were other Southerners with an audience who showed more tenacity, less squeamishness. Across the region the ideas expressed by DeBow and Hill were repeated with increasing emphasis. In Charleston in 1869, William Lee Trenholm told the city's Board of Trade to accept the fact of defeat, banish animosities toward the North, and turn to new patterns of development. Respect for the Old South, he said, was natural and proper, but the economic theories of that era should be abandoned so that the region might pursue the "Northern ideal" (by which Trenholm meant industrial development) while at the same time cultivating the best that was indigenous.[28] In Virginia, in the same year, the Richmond *Whig* declared that nothing was more important to the South than the establishment of factories and workshops. The editor had a vision of Richmond as the region's leading manufacturing center and pledged the newspaper "to hasten the realization of that destiny."

He closed with an admonition to the people of the South to cast aside "all men wedded to old systems, dogmas and prejudices, and take up progressive men, with enlarged and liberal views, who draw their inspirations from the present and the future, and not from the past."[29]

III

Until 1870, the "progressive men, with enlarged liberal views," to whom the Richmond *Whig* looked for leadership, had set forth their program of regeneration without the benefit of an appropriate and inspiring slogan. In April of that year Edwin DeLeon published what may have been the essay that gave the name "New South" to the incipient movement which he attempted to define and encourage. A native South Carolinian of good lineage, DeLeon was an author, diplomat, and former Confederate propagandist.[30] The title of his article, published in *Putnam's Magazine*, was "The New South: What It is Doing, and What It Wants." The Civil War, DeLeon wrote, marked a great divide in the history of the South. "Four years of war wrought mighty changes internally on the society," he wrote, "and Reconstruction completed what the war [had] begun, utterly overturning the old system." Out of the debris of the old order, he continued, there arose "a New South, whose wants and wishes, ends and aims, plans and purposes, are as different from those of 1860, as though a century instead of a decade only, divided the two."[31] No despondent prophet of gloom, DeLeon surveyed the developments of the previous half-decade, with special emphasis on Virginia, to find that the South was turning to constructive measures of reform, despite the turmoil of Reconstruction.

Encouraged by industrial and railroad developments and by immigration movements into the region, DeLeon foresaw two related prospects which augured well for the South's future. First, he was convinced that increasing numbers of Southerners were coming to realize that a New South program of industrial progress, diversified agriculture, and cooperation with the North was the only hope for the region. Second, he believed that the opportunities in the South were now sufficiently recognized by those outside the region that the influx of labor and capital already in evidence would inevitably be multiplied many times in the next few years. "Whatever the case may be as regards the political affinities of the two sections," he noted, "there can be no doubt of the rapid fusion and assimilation of the social and material elements," for "each successive day blends and binds more intimately together the lives and fortunes of the two, owing to the movement of Northern men and capital southwards."[32] The outcome of this new union was bound to be mutually beneficial, he believed:

> The Northerner will carry South his thrift, his caution, his restless activity, his love of new things; the Southerner will temper these with his reckless liberality, his careless confidence, his firey energy, and his old-time conservatism; and both will be benefited by the admixture.[33]

Three years later DeLeon made an extended tour of the region and published his observations in a series of long articles in *Harper's Magazine*, *The Southern Magazine*, and *Fraser's Magazine*. The *Harper's* piece, the only one entitled "The New South," was widely read, and after its publication the term "New South" appeared regularly as the recognized name of the emerging movement.[34]

A year after the appearance of DeLeon's first New South essay, Benjamin Harvey Hill told the Alumni Association of the University of Georgia that "thought is the Hercules of this age," and he urged his listeners to turn their minds to the task of "cleaning out the Augean stables of accumulated social errors." In strong, bold fashion Hill recounted those social errors which had made the civilization of the Old South a terrible failure. Certain that it would be foolish to attempt to resurrect "theories and systems" that had been "swept down by the moving avalanche of actual events," he declared that Southerners could "live neither *in* nor *by* the defeated past." The overriding question for his generation, Hill warned, was not what Southerners had been, "but whether and what they shall determine to be; not what their fathers were, but whether and what their children shall be." The South stood at one of those rare moments in history when "one civilization abruptly ends and another begins." The test of greatness for the new civilization, he said, would lie in men's ability and courage to "correct the real cause of this, our failure in the past."[35]

Like Daniel Harvey Hill, to whom he was not related, B. H. Hill was a former Confederate general. He had opposed secession, but served loyally once Georgia had left the Union. After the war he was one of the state's leading opponents of Congressional Reconstruction. By 1870, however, he had moderated his stand and in July 1871, when he spoke to the Alumni Association, he was under suspicion as a man much too friendly with the invading Republicans.[36] Partly for this reason the speech, which was widely circulated, produced a mild storm of controversy in the Georgia press. Outside the state, in the national magazines, it gave rise to extended discussion and analysis of the emerging New South doctrine. And Henry Grady, soon to become the major spokesman of the doctrine, read and admired the speech and later declared that Hill, more than anyone else, had provided him with the ideas and the inspiration which he carried into his crusade.[37]

For the most part, Hill's speech dwelt on the baneful effects of slavery on the South. Combining simple analysis with extravagant language, Hill declared that a thoughtful observer of 1787 would have foreseen greater material advancement for the South than for any other part of the country. This reasonable prediction was not borne out, Hill felt, because of the total commitment the region subsequently made to a system that demanded the perpetual ignorance of the laboring class. For two generations, he declared,

> Southern progress, Southern development, and Southern power have been in bondage to the negro; and Southern failure, Southern dependence, and Southern sorrow are the heavy penalties we suffer for that bondage. For more than thirty years Southern genius, with all its glorious natural spirit of Promethean daring and venture, has been chained by some offended god of jealous vengeance to this solid rock of slavery, and vultures have preyed upon it.[38]

In the closing section of his address, and in subsequent speeches and essays, Hill challenged his fellow Southerners to look upon emancipation primarily as the opportunity to free the white South from the bondage of an outmoded, stultifying economic system. The region now had the chance, he believed, to exploit fully its many resources by constructing a balanced industrial system to be complemented by a diversified, scientific agriculture. Essential to the success of this program, he stressed, would be the proliferation of new institutions of learning to train men in the ways of industry, and the strengthening of established universities to impart the new doctrine. The educated men of the South, he told the university alumni audience, must be responsible for the future of the South. Should the South's leaders respond to the challenge, Hill promised, "we shall soon find that only our fetters have been broken, and the day of unequaled greatness and prosperity will dawn and brighten to glorious and lasting noon in the South."[39]

Hill did not use the term "New South" in his 1871 speech, but the ideas he expressed would, in time, form the nucleus of the New South ideology. One of his reviewers, William D. Trammell, wrote ecstatically of the speech in *The Southern Magazine* and, two years later, published a trite novel, entitled *Ça Ira*, in which he applied the term "New South" to Hill's program.[40] One of his characters took words almost directly from the Hill address, asking "why should we look back? We have neither time nor strength to waste in defense of theories and systems that have been forever swept away by the progress of actual events. They must learn that we cannot live by the defeated past."[41] Making its way into fiction, the new doctrine also began to appear in poetry, once the stronghold of the romance of the Old South.[42] Margaret J. Preston, another Hill enthusiast, intoned:

> *Not a word of the Past! It has perished,*
> *Gone down in its beauty and bloom:*
> *Yet because it so proudly was cherished,*
> *Shall we sigh out our years at its tomb?*

Entitling her poem "Gospel of Labor," the poetess admonished Southerners to be done with the effete ways of the past, to give honor to the laboring man, and to cherish "the clink of the artisan's hammer."[43]

IV

In 1874, DeLeon published his extensive series of New South articles. The immediate and enthusiastic response to them, far surpassing the reception his 1870 article had received, indicates that both the term and the movement were catching hold. Their rising popularity, in fact, increased in direct proportion to the declining enthusiasm for the program of Congressional Reconstruction. For Southerners, it was difficult to focus on programs of self-reconstruction when, as so many felt, immediately pressing demands of the duel with the Radicals required all of one's energy. Henry Watterson, whose Louisville *Courier Journal* would soon rival Grady's *Constitution* as an organ of the New South movement, recalled later that "there was in those days but a single political issue for the South. Our hand was in the lion's mouth, and we could do nothing, hope for nothing, until we got it out."[44] To Grady it seemed almost impossible for the movement to gain real momentum until "redemption" from alien rule was achieved. To celebrate restoration of home rule in Georgia he wrote his first editorial under the title New South. "Freed from organized bands of robbers and bayonet rule," he wrote, Georgia and the South would have the opportunity to accept and act on new programs.[45]

Francis W. Dawson's early career as New South editor

further illustrates the delaying influence which Reconstruction had on the movement. As a young man, Dawson left his native England to join the Confederacy. Only twenty-five when the war ended, he moved to Charleston, where he soon became the city's leading newspaper editor —first of the *News* and then of the combined *News and Courier*. Continuing to pay fealty to the honor and justice of the Confederate cause, Dawson nonetheless scored those who let memories of the past interfere with programs for the future. "Respect for ourselves and our fathers requires us to reverence the past," he wrote in criticism of a fellow editor, "but we cannot rebuild the fallen structure, and it would be simply foolish in our people to spend the fleeting years of opportunity in lamentation."[46]

To make the postwar South better, Dawson was an early advocate of all those ideas advanced by DeBow, the two Hills, and DeLeon. He invented the slogan "Bring the Cotton Mills to the Cotton" and used it effectively in numerous editorials in the 'seventies. Campaigning for any factory "which would turn the South's natural resources into finished products in their native environment," he was also an avid promoter of the commercial development of Charleston, which he hoped would one day become the "Liverpool of America."[47] But Dawson was also an intensely political editor, and the files of the *News and Courier* reflect his absorbing interest in the issues of Reconstruction. The most articulate critic of Radicalism in his state, he labored first to moderate the impact of Reconstruction and later to overthrow Republican rule. As a consequence, his advocacy of agricultural and industrial reform was partially sacrificed to the cause of Reconstruction politics.

While not all of the advocates of change were as

deeply involved in Reconstruction politics as Dawson, they were inescapably bound up in the antagonisms which it engendered. Fully aware that reconciliation between the sections, based on a liquidation of the Reconstruction program and the spirit that undergirded it, was essential to their movement, they naturally applauded the triumph of each new home-rule movement. With equal pleasure they noted the waning enthusiasm in the North for Radicalism as a happy portent for the New South movement.

Coincidentally with the waning of enthusiasm for Reconstruction, and a major reflection of it, was a new image of the South that began to be projected to Northern readers by a spate of journalists who traveled through the region, beginning in the early 'seventies. *Scribner's Monthly* played a leading role by sending Edward King on trips which resulted in a series of widely read articles, later assembled in a large book entitled *The Great South*. When the last of the articles in the series appeared, *Scribner's* editor Josiah G. Holland commented:

> It is with no ordinary pride and satisfaction that we thus record the completion of a task undertaken with the desire to enlighten our country concerning itself, and to spread before the nation the wonderful natural resources, the social condition, and the political complications of a region which needs but just, wise, and generous legislation, with responding good will and industry, to make it a garden of happiness and prosperity.[48]

Other books which had originally appeared in Northern periodicals or newspapers included Robert Somers, *Southern States Since the War* (1870); James S. Pike, *The Prostrate State* (1874); and Charles Nordhoff, *The Cotton States in the Spring and Summer of 1875* (1876). These and numerous other works began to revise drastically Northern opinions of the former enemy. They argued that sectional bitterness was on the wane in the South and would vanish as soon as unreasonable and hostile legislation ceased to come from the North. Much sympathetic understanding of the South's allegedly cruel plight was expressed, and hope was voiced that Northerners would come to realize that Southerners understood the Negro question and, if let alone, would deal fairly with the former slave. Finally, these journalistic outpourings were highly optimistic in reporting the abundant resources of the region and in designating the South as the section of the country in which great economic advances of the future were to be made.

Despite the growing popularity of the New South idea and the optimistic paeans to reconciliation there were still many persons in all parts of the country who remained skeptical. Albion W. Tourgee, removed from Ohio after the war to become a North Carolina jurist and author of political novels, was exceedingly dubious about the prospects for change in the basic character of the South. As Tourgee viewed the situation, the South was in the process of winning the peace despite defeat in war. Rallying together with greater unity than they had shown in the war itself, Southerners were dedicated to the one "great and holy aim" of expelling all Yankee influence. They desired, Tourgee wrote, to perpetuate Southern isolation from the mainstream of American development, protect white supremacy from all attacks, and preserve the old social order with as little alteration as possible.[49] Reconstruction, despite all the grand designs in the beginning, was nothing but "a fool's errand," based on the disastrously false assumption that defeat would cause the South meekly to mend its ways and adopt a Northern view of life. Nothing, says the hero of one of Tourgee's novels, could be more wrong: "The sick man cannot cure himself. The South will never purge itself of the evils which affect it."[50]

Tourgee's bitter complaints, though inaccurate in some particulars, correctly forecast the abandonment of Reconstruction. As the North became wearied of its experiment and increasingly attuned to the music of the New South prophets, it chose to ignore the warnings from Tourgee and others like him. Increasingly it appeared that Northerners were searching for a suitable rationale to justify the end of an era of Yankee reform in the South, and the New South movement appeared perfectly tailored to meet that need. It promised respect for the rights of the Negro and, more important, invited an invasion of Northern men and capital into the region on terms that seemed to be unusually advantageous to the invaders. To the Southerners, the process of self-reconstruction could begin only when the alien Reconstruction ended. Their obvious preference for the former included the ironic invitation to a new kind of Northern invasion, but at the outset the prospects for mutual benefit seemed too bright to cause them to wonder if a New South reconstruction might, in time, bring them to a point of subjugation quite as serious as the one they were trying to escape.

None of these long-range issues was in focus in the mid-'seventies, however, and the infant movement was still struggling for a wider acceptance. The withdrawal of federal troops and the official end of Reconstruction in 1877 made the struggle easier, but the movement experienced no sudden triumph. For one thing, the South —along with the rest of the nation—was still in the grip of a severe depression, and hard times did not disappear until the end of the decade. The depression over, some contemporaries felt that the election of 1880, involving the "honest" defeat of a Democratic presidential candidate, acted as a catalyst. Josephus Daniels of North Carolina drew the moral that "out of political defeat we must work . . . a glorious material and industrial triumph."[51] Both he and Grady, convinced that the South had put too many false hopes in politics as a salvation, urged their fellow citizens to work more and politic less. Grady's editorial comment on the election results opened with the opinion that "the defeat of Hancock will be a blessing in disguise if it only tends to turn our people from politics to work." In a passage that would be quoted frequently in the future, he declared that the South needed "fewer stump-speakers and more stump-pullers." The old order was passionately devoted to politics, Grady wrote, but the power and plenty of the new order must be based on hard work and a single-minded devotion to business enterprise. "Let us let politics alone for a while," he admonished, so that a new orientation might make the South "thrill and swell with growth until it has compassed the full measure of the destiny for which God intended it."[52]

With Grady's rhetoric and boundless enthusiasm the program outlined over a decade earlier by DeBow and D. H. Hill began to take on the aspects of a creed of salvation. As older men passed from the scene, Grady would shortly be joined by a band of young men with an evangelistic commitment equal to his so that the New South doctrine would become, in the 'eighties, the South's major intellectual and moral issue. The subject of numerous books and pamphlets, endless articles, commencement addresses, and sermons, it finally came into its own. By the time Grady made his address before the New England Society of New York, in 1886, it had outdistanced all of its rivals and was on the verge of achieving the hegemony once enjoyed by the creed of the Old South.

2
The Opulent South

The record of the south for the past ten
years is equal to that of the west. We
predict that for the next ten years it will
surpass the record made by the west.
The time will come when there will be an
amendment to the shibboleth "Westward
the star of empire holds its sway."

—HENRY W. GRADY, 1884[1]

Wealth and honor are in the pathway of the
New South. Her impulses are those which
are impelling the advance of civilization
and the progress of wealth and refinement
throughout Christendom; and as her
resources . . . are greater and more
diversified than those in the possession of
any other people of equal numbers . . .
[she will soon] resume her once proud
position in the van of civilization's advancing
column. She is the coming El Dorado of
American adventure.

—WILLIAM D. KELLEY, 1887[2]

It is the young men . . . who are making
the South of today. They ask no favors.
Worthy sons of worthy sires, gifted with
the best treasures of Anglo Saxon brawn,
brain, courage and energy, they are resolved
to make "Dixie" the Canaan of the new
world. They are filled with an enthusiasm
that cannot be dampened. They are bold,
earnest, energetic, and above all, they have
a faith in the South's future that
cannot be weakened. All honor to the
young South.

—RICHARD H. EDMONDS, 1889[3]

Perhaps you know that with us of the younger generation in the South," the poet Sidney Lanier wrote to his brother, "pretty much the whole of life has been merely not-dying."[4] Lanier's melancholy estimate of his own postwar experience echoed the lament of a generation of Southerners, including the young New South spokesmen who grew to maturity in the circumstances he decried. Their world was one of crushing poverty and heartbreaking disillusionment—powerful reminders that the inherently weak and static civilization of the Old South was no match for the dynamic and powerful North that had smashed the Southern bid for independence and saddled the region with unwelcomed burdens. Moreover, the victors had devised no modern Marshall Plan to spark economic recovery and soon "The Prostrate South" became a common nomenclature for the region, popularized by the hordes of observers who came to report on life in the former Confederacy.

The poverty and industrial lethargy that hung over the South in the years after the war were sufficient in themselves to cause despair and lead to programs for self-reconstruction. They take on added significance, and indeed can only be understood properly, when one recalls that they existed in a country envied for nothing more than its fabled wealth and opportunity. As David M.

Potter has shown in his brilliant study of the effects of economic abundance on the national character, Americans had been a people of plenty from early colonial days. This happy circumstance shaped their institutions and beliefs and made possible the success of their democratic experiment.[5] Widespread poverty, coupled with and reinforced by fettered opportunity, seemed a strange anomaly in mid-nineteenth-century America; and thoughtful Southerners, as they pondered their own misfortune, could scarcely help but reflect that they were plagued by what C. Vann Woodward would later call a "quite un-American experience with poverty."[6]

The striking and enduring contrast between Southern poverty and American opulence dates most obviously from the devastation of the Civil War era. But even before the war the peculiar structure of the Southern economy had put the South at a disadvantage within the union. Plantation slavery made fortunes for many men, of course, but, as Douglas C. North points out, the income received in the South from the export of staple crops had "little local multiplier effect, but flowed directly to the North and West for imports of services, manufactures and foodstuffs."[7] Whether or not Eugene D. Genovese is correct in characterizing plantation slavery as technologically backward, self-defeating, incapable of reform, and incompatible with genuine industrialism,[8] there is no doubt that Southerners became increasingly aware of their dependence on—and inferiority to—the North. This awareness was revealed in the frantic and abortive campaigns to achieve economic independence and in the bitter denunciation of special economic legislation presumed to favor Northern interests at the expense of the South. As Thomas Prentice Kettell correctly saw, Southern wealth was systematically converted into Northern profits.[9]

One of the purposes of secession was to invigorate Southern economic growth and destroy the colonial dependence on the North. Not only, of course, were these objectives not realized, but the smashing victories of the Union troops seemed to symbolize the hopelessness of the venture in the first place. Concentrating on the development of their own strength, Union leaders greatly expanded productive capacity and appeared almost to ignore manpower losses, instead of playing cautiously on their enemy's weaknesses. In many ways it seemed to be a story of the rich beating the poor; or so it appeared, in any case, to many disillusioned Southerners in 1865.

The lesson of the war, then, seemed clearly to demand the reconstruction of the Southern economy. Postwar developments reinforced this lesson by widening even more the disparity between the two sections. As the South languished during the Reconstruction era, the North boomed ahead. The war had wrecked Southern productive capacity while vastly stimulating and advancing Northern development and after the war, as Eric F. Goldman vividly portrays it, "everybody and everything certainly seemed on the move"—except "in the battered South." "In the East, a rampant prosperity touched every venture with the magic of anything-is-possible. In the West, the tide of migration swept out in proportions unequaled in all man's restless history. West and east, virtually every index of activity . . . showed a wild surge upward."[10] But in the South, as Lanier recorded, "merely not-dying" was the major concern of the day. Thus it became increasingly and painfully clear that the South did not share in the historic American experience of opulence; and, as that experience was on the verge of becoming fantastic beyond belief, fear mounted that the South might be forever left out.

1

The principal spokesmen for the emerging New South movement, with but one notable exception, were all born in the 1850's. Too young to serve in the war, they passed through childhood and adolescence under its influence and reached maturity during the Reconstruction era.[11] Thus their formative years coincided with the period of their region's greatest failure. Quite naturally, the perspective which this experience gave them sharpened their criticisms of the Old South and led them to look to the North in their search for those variables which accounted for Southern poverty in a land of plenty.

Henry Woodfin Grady, the most famous of the New South spokesmen, was born in Athens, Georgia, in 1850. The Athens of Grady's youth was the trading center for surrounding farms and plantations and Grady's father was a prominent local merchant, co-owner of the firm of Nicholson and Grady, a notable mercantile establishment in the community. On the eve of the Civil War the elder Grady sold his share in the firm, invested heavily in real estate, and retained half-ownership in the store building, a gas works, and a saw mill.[12] It was an environment admirably suited for the future New South prophet. Commercial in its essence, young Grady's world was built on bustle, energy, and shrewdness, and he experienced none of the genteel leisure allegedly characteristic of the planter class which had led his region into war.

In the wake of the havoc wrought by the war, Grady secured a college education at the University of Georgia, followed by a year of postgraduate study at the University of Virginia. When he left Virginia he began the career in journalism that was to be his life work. During the 1870's he was associated with several Georgia newspapers and served as Georgia correspondent for a number of Northern papers, beginning with the New York *Herald* in 1876. It was also in 1876 that he joined the staff of the Atlanta *Constitution*, the journal that he would mold into the major organ of the New South movement. Four years later, on the strength of a $20,000 vote of confidence from Cyrus W. Field, he bought a quarter-share in the *Constitution*. From then until his death in 1889 he preached the gospel of the New South in editorial columns and in frequent public addresses in both the South and the North.[13] When he died, the nation's press hailed him as the most effective leader of the New South movement and the New York *Times* declared that he was both the symbol and the creator of the dynamic spirit in the South.[14]

Born a year after Grady, in 1851, Daniel Augustus Tompkins had roots in the plantation South. One of his grandfathers, a first cousin of John C. Calhoun, lived in a "fine country home," while the other, who had been a captain during the Revolutionary War, owned a North Carolina plantation. His father was a wealthy South Carolina planter, owning two thousand acres of land and forty slaves.[15] The war, and Tompkins's restless spirit, severed his connection with the plantation, and he rapidly began to plan a career as publicist and industrialist.

After undergraduate training at the South Carolina College, Tompkins studied in the Rensselaer Polytechnic Institute at Troy, New York, and worked later as a machinist at the Bessemer Steel Works in Troy and then with the Bethlehem Iron Works in Pennsylvania. While employed by Bethlehem Iron he traveled to Germany to

take part in the construction of an iron plant there. He was
in Missouri next, with the Crystal Plate Glass Works and
Crystal Railway Company, but he moved to Charlotte,
North Carolina, in 1882, where he was to make his reputation as a promoter and exemplar of the New South creed.
As an industrialist he quickly rose to prominence as the
principal proprietor and president of three large cotton
mills, director of eight others, and stockholder in many
more. In addition to his conspicuous role in the cotton-mill
industry, and as the father of the cottonseed oil industry,
he became a chief publicist of the New South movement
as owner of three newspapers—of which the Charlotte
Observer was the most influential—author of innumerable
pamphlets, contributor to manufacturing journals, and
popular after-dinner speaker.[16]

The longest-lived of all the New South prophets, and
a man who was still writing fervent New South editorials
during the administration of Herbert Hoover, was Richard
Hathaway Edmonds. Born on a Virginia farm in 1857,
Edmonds later claimed that his boyhood experience there
had exercised a direct influence upon his mature thinking.
The farm was small, he recalled, and there was too little
money for hired help to free the youngster from heavy
labors. "I worked, and worked hard," he said, "and it was
in my opinion the best experience which I ever had, and
it has influenced my life for good ever since." It was from
this experience, Edmonds believed, that he derived the
"gospel of work" that was to form a central part of his
later teachings.[17] In fact, Edmonds was probably captured
by his own later propaganda and consequently exaggerated
the significance of his boyhood labors. His uncle recalled
Edmonds as a fragile youth on whom even the slightest
amount of work would have made a profound impression.

Later in life the uncle observed that Edmonds was "totally unable to drive a nail," and in the uncle's opinion Edmonds's program derived from his keen and inquiring mind rather than from his farm experience.[18]

In 1871 the Edmonds family moved to Baltimore, where the future New South spokesman was to distinguish himself. During the next decade he pondered the economic problems of the South, traveled widely in the region, and concluded that the depressing poverty of a people living in a land richly endowed in natural resources was the greatest scandal of his day. Determined to reorient what he considered the misguided economic policies of the region, he wrote that the South's basic problem was its lack of industries and cities; the way to create them, he believed, was to organize an informed and effective movement of enlightenment. He rejected politics as the least hopeful approach and put his faith in journalism. The journal that he founded, the *Manufacturers' Record*, began its career in 1881 and soon was widely recognized as the leading industrial periodical of the South. Edmonds turned it into a missionary journal, and its pages fairly bristled with glowing descriptions of the industrial future of the region.[19]

Of all the New South spokesmen, Walter Hines Page was easily the most gifted and the most complex. Born in Cary, North Carolina, in 1855, Page came from a respected family of self-reliant small proprietors, leaders in their community, but not dominant figures in the state. From his mother he learned to love books and from his father he learned to respect enterprise and honesty. He also learned from his father to be suspicious of Southern shibboleths, for the elder Page had had misgivings about slavery, was an opponent of secession, and even during the war had spoken openly of the inevitability of the restoration of the Union. But it was Page's grandfather who made the most lasting impression on him. The ideas he gathered from the patriarch of "The Old Place" were those he later described as "the background of my life." "My grandfather," he once wrote, "did not even know the sectional feeling that the war had aroused." With memories running back to the first years of the Republic, the grandfather instilled in Page the image of a South innocent of bitter sectionalism, dedicated to a broad, optimistic nationalism. This was a vision Page never lost, and he always referred to the civilization of the Jeffersonian era as the authentic Southern heritage.[20]

At fifteen, Page left home to begin his college training, first for a short stay at Trinity College and then for a longer period at Randolph-Macon College. At Randolph-Macon his interest in the classics was intensified and he made the decision to pursue them further in graduate study. The Johns Hopkins University was a natural choice and Page studied there for two years under the direction of Basil Gildersleeve. But, disenchanted with the prospects of an academic career, he left Hopkins in 1878 and within a short time had started on a career as a journalist. Soon he would be back in North Carolina, editing a newspaper and launching his mission as one of the region's most persistent and intelligent critics.[21]

The only one of the major New South spokesmen who grew to maturity in the prewar years of sectional strife was Henry Watterson, born in Tennessee in 1840. The Wattersons came to Tennessee when the state was in its infancy, and Henry's grandfather shortly became a wealthy planter. Harvey, his father, turned to law and then to politics. In addition to imbuing his son with the virtues of the Democratic Party, Harvey Watterson was an advocate of Southern industralization and preached to his son many of the "New South" ideas which Henry himself was later to popularize. Lacking sympathy for slavery, the Wattersons were almost as hostile to the Southern fire-eaters as they were to Northern abolitionists. As the crisis of the 1850's wore on, both father and son stood out as strong Union men and Henry Watterson, remaining in Washington until after First Bull Run, was torn in his loyalties by the outbreak of war. His decision to join the Confederacy was not easily reached, but, like many others in his plight, he was resolute once the choice had been made.[22]

As a youth Watterson developed a flair for journalism that aided him well during the war. He served only briefly in various military capacities, making his primary contribution as editor of *The Rebel*, the most widely read newspaper of the Confederacy. In editorial columns he paid homage to Southern nationalism, but the nation of which he dreamed was one which would repudiate plantation agriculture to dedicate itself to diversified farming and industrial upbuilding. "Smoky cities and blue overalls," his biographer writes, "promised more for the South, he believed, than white Grecian porticoes and crinolines."[23] At war's end, Watterson took up the editorship of the Nashville *Banner*, urging reunion and forgiveness. Before long he was in Louisville, and in the 1880's his *Courier-Journal* became second in importance only to Grady's Atlanta *Constitution* as a daily organ of the New South movement.

II

As they grew up in, and pondered, the depressed state of the South in the postwar years—and as the burgeoning wealth of the North was incessantly thrust before them as evidence of their backwardness—the New South prophets were early persuaded that their plight was not the result of the war itself (as so many Southerners believed) but that it was a natural consequence of those conditions which had led to defeat in the first place. The essential lesson which they learned and then translated into the first plank of the New South program was that wealth and power in the modern world flowed from machines and factories, not from unprocessed fields of white cotton. To make the region rich, then—to bring into existence the opulent South—they became in the first place proponents of industrialism and urbanism.

In an ironic sense, they welcomed the desolation and poverty that confronted them, for it created inescapably the necessity of rebuilding the Southern economy; and, in rebuilding, they would persuade the region to reconsider its ancient prejudices and redirect its energies into new paths. Edwin Lawrence Godkin, assessing the chances of the program from his perspective as editor of *The Nation*, wrote in 1880 that the conversion of the South to the "industrial stage of social progress" would not be a more difficult task than that which the abolitionists had undertaken, ultimately with success. For one thing, Godkin pointed out, there was in the new situation a large body of indigenous opinion sympathetic to the conversion. But Godkin recognized that there would be difficulties in prying the Southern mind from its agricultural precepts.[24]

Among the New South advocates themselves there was also a keen awareness of the weight of tradition that would be against them, and as late as 1900, when their ideology had captured large segments of the population, Tompkins sadly acknowledged that "long training as an agricultural people has brought to us a certain abiding degree of prejudice against manufactures and commerce."[25]

To dislodge this "prejudice" and to enlist public spirit and funds in their program, the spokesmen of the New Order knew that more was required of them than a positive program of regeneration. Before they could feel secure in advancing the industrial argument, they had to elaborate a damning critique of the institutions of the Old South. It was not enough, they reasoned, that the old system had been wrecked; it had to be so thoroughly discredited that no one would wish to revive it, in however altered a form.

One of the most outspoken critics of the old regime—a man who played a major role in formulating the New South creed—was a Pennsylvanian whose first desire to reform the South found outlet in the abolition movement. William Darrah ("Pig Iron") Kelley, congressman and industrialist, traveled widely in the South, urging, scolding, and advising the region. During his first visits, shortly after the war, his life was threatened at least once.[26] But, as time passed and as native Southerners began to praise the work of this radical Republican and erstwhile abolitionist, increasingly sympathetic audiences listened to his devastating critique of the old regime.

As he reflected on the poverty of the South, he dismissed the common view that the war had caused it. That it may have been the "proximate cause," he conceded, but the fundamental reason lay in the "economic opinions and industrial system" that had dominated the South before

1860. The root of the difficulty, Kelley explained, was to be plainly seen in the way the "peculiar institution" had enslaved the South. With the perfection of the cotton gin, slavery had become so embedded in Southern life that to challenge it was regarded as a treasonable act. The real disloyalty to the region, though, lay in perpetuating the institution, for slavery wedded the South to a staple-crop agrarian system that ruthlessly militated against the growth of industry and urban centers. Cities were regarded by the leaders of the Old South as "great sores"; and yet, without urban development, there could be no stimulus to develop the bountiful natural resources of the land.[27]

Kelley regarded the "aristocrats" who perpetuated the central institutions of the old regime as conspirators involved in "darkening the minds" of the South's laborers and "protecting her borders from innovations of every kind." Worst of all, he felt, the "fatally vicious economic and agricultural theories" of the old regime had not died with the war. Writing in the 1880's, he hailed the advance of industry where he saw it but called attention to the large areas where the spirit of the Old South persisted. In these places, he wrote, the people were as poverty-stricken as ever—"Yes, the poverty and ignorance that characterized the 'poor whites,' the 'low downs,' the 'clay eaters,' and the 'crackers' of the Old South still prevail" and would continue to exist until the South fully purged itself of past sins and redirected its thinking along the lines charted by the New South program.[28]

The native Southerners in the movement praised Kelley's colorful analysis and eagerly solicited more of it. Edmonds, in particular, was especially obliging in opening to him the columns of the *Manufacturers' Record*, where he became a frequent contributor. The Southerners added an abundance of detail to Kelley's critique, but the essential pattern was the same. The starting point in all arguments was the institution of slavery and the evils it had engendered. Tompkins, lamenting the "estrangement" that slavery had caused between the sections, believed that the failure of Southerners to abolish it themselves had been responsible for the Civil War and the violent, unplanned termination of the institution. The subsequent paralysis of Southern society, it followed, was not due primarily to the war itself but to the errors inculcated by slavery and to the shock of its sudden disappearance.[29]

The shock, however, was necessary to bring the region to its senses, and one of the happiest discoveries of the New South spokesmen was the finding that the destruction of slavery was a great event not because it freed the blacks, although that was important, but because it liberated the whites. As Grady put it, "the shackles that held . . . [the South] in narrow limitations fell forever when the shackles of the negro slave were broken." The Old South, he explained, "rested everything on slavery and agriculture, unconscious that these could neither give nor maintain healthy growth."[30] Emancipation—the first requisite of "healthy growth"—was thus the white man's passport to prosperity.

No one put the new dogma more succinctly than a Virginia contributor to Edmonds's *Manufacturers' Record*. The white man of the Old South, declared John W. Johnston, "was a slave" and "the chains that encumbered him were as inexorable as those that bound the colored race." Contemplating the full extent of the white man's bondage, Johnston waxed eloquent:

The negro was a slave to him [the white man], and he was a slave to the situation. He could not abandon it

without disastrous results to himself, to the negro, to the
State and the world. If ever man were impelled by an
irresistible force, it was the Southern white man. What
did it matter to him if the earth beneath his feet was
loaded with all the minerals which contribute to the
wealth, convenience or enjoyment of mankind, or that
the stream running by his door had waterpower enough
to turn a thousand wheels? He could not utilize them;
he was bound hand and foot—bound to his slaves, bound
to his plantation, bound to cotton, to his habits of life,
to the exigencies of the situation.[31]

In the light of these sentiments, it was no wonder that
Kelley should dedicate his vigorously New South book
to "The Emancipated South."[32]

To document the baneful effects of slavery on Southern
economic growth, Tompkins turned to the census data
of 1810. According to his interpretation of those data, the
South of 1810—not yet fully committed to cotton and still
willing to doubt the wisdom of slavery—was in the process
of sound economic development. The census data, he
wrote, showed that "the manufactured products of Virginia, the Carolinas and Georgia exceeded in value and
variety those of all New England." As late as the 1820's
the South Carolina railway, "one of the most important
engineering enterprises in the world," demonstrated again
the "relative advantage" which the South enjoyed over
the North. But all of the South's advantage was swept
aside when the impetus to cotton culture, made possible
by the perfection of the cotton gin, extended slavery
westward, firmly embedded the institution in Southern
life, and brought to an end the burgeoning sentiment for
industry as well as the notable antislavery sentiment that
had previously existed. The result, Tompkins felt, was

catastrophic, not only because of the destruction and loss of life, but because those things were made inevitable by the adoption of erroneous policies in the first place.[33]

Like Tompkins, Edmonds stressed the encouraging features of the Southern economy in the early nineteenth century. He was also convinced that the slavery and cotton combination had worked powerfully to thwart healthy economic growth, but he believed that the appeal of industry had been too great even for slavery to frustrate it entirely. He pointed out, for example, that the falling price of cotton in the 1840's caused Southerners once again to pay attention to industrial pursuits, and he paid homage to the band of industrial publicists who struggled for that cause in the twenty years before the war. The results of their efforts, he believed, were not negligible. Between 1850 and 1860, he observed, the railroad mileage of the South more than tripled, iron production increased markedly, $12,000,000 was invested in cotton mills, and the manufacture of steam engines and other machines increased notably. The war, he felt, interrupted this work —a work that was already revealing the grave defects of slavery and staple-crop agriculture.[34]

To reinforce their sweeping condemnation of the old regime, the New South prophets carried their analysis into the present to argue, first, that those who continued to hold to old ideas and old systems courted personal ruin and, second, that those who resisted the new appeals to reason and progress were guilty of a great disservice to their region. Tompkins spoke frequently to the first point. In a piece published in the *Manufacturers' Record* he noted that "the condition of civilization" that had grown up on "the basis of the institution of slavery is dying and fading away." But not everyone recognized his good fortune because of the change. "There are tenacious people of fine education who are living in the dying conditions of ante-bellum life," Tompkins lamented. "They are as a rule growing poorer day by day and will continue to grow poorer until the most tenacious of them pass out of life, and with them will go the system to which they persist in adhering."[35]

To hasten the day of their departure, and with it the system they wished to perpetuate, no New South spokesman was more mercilessly critical than Walter Hines Page. The disenchanted classics scholar began his career as critic of the opponents of progress with an article in the *Atlantic Monthly* in 1881. Fixing on Hillsborough, North Carolina (which was but thinly disguised in the essay), as a "typical" Southern borough, Page drew a picture of the community that none of its first citizens could have been expected to admire. In Europe, Page began, one observed both old and new civilizations, side by side, through architecture. In the South two distinct civilizations existed, but the difference was social, not architectural. "It lies at the very heart of the people," he wrote, "and comes to view only after a study of their history and their life." In Hillsborough the new elements in society were powerless to effect change, so entrenched were the powers of the old regime. The typical Southern community, he wrote, was all but completely out of touch with modern science, art, and thought—and yet the local inhabitants felt it was God's chosen place on earth. It was a discouraging sight to a young reformer, and the prospects for change appeared dim.[36]

A few years later Page expanded his "Southern Borough" attack into a full-scale assault. After some absence from the region, he turned homeward in 1883 to become editor of the Raleigh *State Chronicle*. Aware of the weight of tradition that faced him, he was bolstered by a youthful enthusiasm and apparently expected to remain permanently in North Carolina as a crusading editor. Riding southward on the train, he reflected on the region that unfolded before him and pondered its difficulties. Ironies abounded. Those who had built the South and fought for its independence in 1861–1865 had regarded it as "the crown of civilization." But Page saw only worn-out land, poverty-stricken inhabitants, and directionless Negroes. White men were caught up in "hopeless inertia" and "the earth itself seemed to revolve slowly."[37]

Taking up his editorial cudgels, Page flailed North Carolina for two years with a brand of criticism and prodding that was fresh and novel. "Pungently, wittily, mercilessly," and in English that was "scholarly, clear and dignified," he jarred, instructed, and, on occasion, entertained the state.[38] But the inertia would not yield, at least in his judgment, and he despaired of breaking the hold of the past on the present. Writing years later of his experience in Raleigh, he recalled his view that efficiency, thrift, and imaginative thought were stifled because "only old thoughts were acceptable." There was no change, he wrote, because "society's chief concern was to tolerate no change." For the young crusader it was a "smothering atmosphere."[39]

After two years of crusading, filled with frustration and discouragement, Page resigned from the *State Chronicle* and left the South. His last contribution to the newspaper was a series of "Mummy Letters," published by the new editor, Josephus Daniels.[40] More a Jeremiah than an optimistic prophet of change at this stage of his career, Page was "utterly discouraged" in his hope for the regeneration of North Carolina and of the South. Control of all phases of life, he wrote, was in the hands of

those who looked through rose-tinted glasses to the past—
the Mummies, he called them—and allowed their idealized
vision of the old regime to stand in the way of progress.
There was no intellectual stimulation; it was forbidden.
The gifted men (like Page himself) were driven into exile.
Granting that there had been some "material advancement" since the end of Reconstruction, Page wrote that
it was accompanied by "no appreciation of scholarship, no
chance for intellectual growth." The cause "at the bottom
of all this," he believed, was "the organization of society,
of trades, of professions—of everything—against improvement." Was there hope for a change? Page did not
think so:

> It is an awfully discouraging business to undertake
> to prove to a Mummy that it is a Mummy. You go up
> to it and say, "Old Fellow, the Egyptian dynasties crum-
> bled several thousand years ago: you are a fish out of
> water. You have by accident or the providence of God
> got a long way out of your time. This is America. The
> Old Kings are forgotten, and this is the year 1886, in the
> calendar of a Christ whose people had not even gone to
> Egypt when you died." The old thing grins that grin
> which death set on its solemn features when the world
> was young; and your task is so pitiful that even the
> humour of it is gone.
>
> Give it up! It can't be done. We all think when we are
> young that we can do something with the Mummies.
> But the Mummy is a solemn fact, and it differs from all
> other things (except stones) in this—it lasts forever.[41]

Sixteen years later, with the emotional trials of the
State Chronicle days well behind him, Page retained es-
sentially unchanged his criticism of the party of reaction.
Writing in 1902, he singled out three historic deterrents

to progress in the South. The first was slavery, which had "pickled" Southern life at about 1830. The second was the politician; and the third, the preacher. "One has for a hundred years proclaimed the present social state as the ideal condition," he wrote, "and, if any has doubted this declaration, the other has told him that this life counts for little at best." Thus "gagged and bound," Page concluded, "Southern rural society has remained stationary longer than English-speaking people have remained stationary anywhere else in the world."[42]

Page was more pessimistic in his appraisal of the forces of progress than were most of the New South spokesmen. Grady, for example, reprinted some of the North Carolinian's pieces on the tradition-bound and priest-ridden South but then disagreed strongly with the emphasis of Page's criticisms, arguing that his examples were scarcely typical now that the New South crusade was fully launched. Progress, Grady said, was evident more frequently every day.[43] But if Page was less convinced of the reality of progress than were typical New South spokesmen, his essential message was not fundamentally different from theirs: slavery and a spirit of anti-industrialism and anti-urbanism had been responsible for the South's great failure; the New South must root out all remnants of that heritage.

III

Assailing the errors of the past and denouncing their perpetuation in the present, the New South spokesmen turned confidently to the positive aspects of their blueprint for an opulent South. The commanding feature of their plan, of course, was the design for an industrial society. But the South in the 1880's continued to be overwhelmingly rural and agrarian, and it required no great insight to see that a program for the reconstruction of the Southern economy could not neglect agriculture. Despite their passion to erect an industrial utopia, then, the New South spokesmen also drafted a program for a renovated agricultural system infused with the values of business enterprise. Moreover, the vital connection between a sound farm economy and dynamic industrial growth was quickly perceived and assiduously worked out. The spirit of Hamilton and Clay was much alive in Edmonds when he wrote that a "harmonious relationship between industry and agriculture would make the South, with its vast natural resources and human power, 'the garden spot of the world.' "[44]

Sidney Lanier, the pre-eminent poet of the region, was especially hopeful about the future of Southern agriculture. In a famous essay entitled "The New South," published in *Scribner's Monthly* in 1880, he acknowledged and saluted the revolutionary changes which he believed had taken place since the war. The New South which he saw emerging was characterized by political, social, moral, and aesthetic developments that augured well for the future of the region. But, most important of all, he believed, "The New South means small farming." As he interpreted the statistics of land tenure, Lanier concluded that plantations were giving way to farms and staple-crop agriculture to diversified pursuits. An economic democracy in the countryside was in the making.[45]

In "Corn," one of his better poems, Lanier turned his views into a meter-making argument for the new agriculture. The farmer whose life he depicts is driven to ruin by his persistent dependence on cotton. The soil becomes depleted and the farmer impoverished; escape from this vicious circumstance can be found only by migrating, and so he leaves the South, finding a new home in the West. Thus, the tyranny of cotton drives the sturdy men out of the region, depleting not only the land but the human resources as well. To diversify the crops and divide the land, Lanier implies, would solve the problems of the farmer and of the region.[46]

Cotton's dominion was the great *bête blanche* of the New South spokesman and its tyranny occupied a central position in their economic and promotional writings. Edmonds filled column after column in the *Manufacturers' Record* with blasts at "the all-cotton curse" and Grady railed against the "all-cotton plan" with dependable regularity in his editorials and elsewhere.[47] "It is time for an agricultural revolution," Grady announced in one editorial. "When we once decide that southern lands are fit for something else besides cotton, and then go to work in earnest to multiply and diversify our products and industries, independence and wealth will be the certain reward of our intelligent and industrious farmers."[48] Cotton's tyranny, according to the New South view, was all-pervasive. For the region as a whole it retarded economic growth and thus per capita income by frustrating industrial development. It put the farmer at the mercy of a capricious international market and tied him to a credit system that drove him deeper into debt each year. With a lien on his crop and a mortgage on his home he failed to realize that much of the profits from the cotton crop went out of the region, never to return, and it never occurred to him to grow crops which might be marketed locally;

or, if it did, he lacked either the knowledge or the credit, or both, to undertake new systems.

To break this unhappy syndrome, the New South spokesmen early became advocates of agricultural diversification. Over and over again the farmer was told to cut his cotton acreage in half and plant the other half in smaller crops. The possibilities for agricultural diversification were without limit, or so it must have appeared to readers of Grady's optimistic essays on the variety of crops suitable for Southern agriculture. In the North, he noted, farmers concentrated on "small grains, grasses, truck farming, fruit growing, stock raising, and dairy farming," among other things, and all of these enterprises, he believed, were eminently suited for the South.[49] Truck farming held special appeal for him, as it offered profits that were "simply wonderful." The truck farm, Grady wrote,

> should also be a fruit farm, and the fruit that cannot be marketed at good rates should be dried by the new processes. This would give employment throughout the entire season, and at the end of it the fortunate farmer would have before him the assurance that diversified crops and a never-failing market alone afford, with no guano bills to settle, and no liens past or to come to disturb his mind.[50]

The newly diversified farmer, the beau ideal of the New South movement, was to replace the large planter. In the fashion of Lanier, Grady wrote that "the old plantation is a thing of the past." The small farmer, he believed, must press to the front, and "the ambition which covets large areas must be content with a holding small enough for every acre to produce profits. Necessity overrides either sentiment or policy here, and necessity will have its way."[51] Unlike the planter of the Old South, the New South's small farmer was expected to be thoroughly scientific in his application of new agricultural implements and knowedge. More important, he was to be thoroughly businesslike in his planning. The cash nexus would drive out the last remnants of an unprofitable patriarchal system.[52]

With the disappearance of the planter and the "all-cotton plan" which he had created, the New South spokesmen foresaw also the end of the inherited enmity between agriculture and industry. Planter hegemony in the Old South had demanded stringent control of the pace of industrialization and opposition to anything beyond its modest development as an adjunct to the plantation economy.[53] The rise of the small farm and the adoption of diversified pursuits in the new era, according to the New South spokesmen, could be achieved only as the region made a full-scale conversion to industrialism. As Edmonds put it, "every manufacturing establishment planted in the South marks the progress towards the time when diversified agriculture will be the rule throughout the section."[54]

To Grady, the issue was a simple one of markets. The only difference between agricultural prosperity in the North and agricultural poverty in the South was that industrial development in the North provided a substantial market for diversified products.[55] Only by developing a balanced industrial-urban complex could the South hope to provide the foundation for a prosperous farm economy. In an editorial penned shortly before he delivered his famous New York address, Grady wrote that the creation of a home market for truck crops, added to the region's

cotton monopoly, would make the South "the richest agricultural country in the world." But the key element in
agricultural development was industrialization. More
"than all things else combined," Grady wrote, manufacturing would "bring prosperity to the southern farmer
and high value to his lands."[56]

Important as the agricultural renascence was to the
New South spokesmen, it always occupied a minor place
in their blueprint for the future. The crusade for an urban,
industrialized society was their absorbing concern. Indeed,
so extensive was the emphasis on industrial propaganda
that one observer, writing at the end of the century, concluded that "the program of the New South . . . has not
taken the direction of agriculture. It is through its urban
development only that the section has justly earned its
sobriquet."[57]

That the South was ideally suited to lead in the modern
world of industry none of the New South spokesmen
doubted. With endless repetition they asserted that the
rich endowment of natural resources which the region
enjoyed gave it unparalleled advantages. In a piece entitled
"Nature's Wonderful Blessings to the South," Edmonds
rejoiced in his belief that "truly, everything seems to
be combined to add to the wealth of this section."[58]
There was, of course, a painful irony in this realization,
for the resources were nothing new. Grady dwelled on this
point when he declared it a "curious fact" that three
fourths of the manufacturing wealth of the country was
produced in a narrow strip of land between Iowa and
Massachusetts, comprising only one sixth of the nation's
area, "distant from the source of raw materials on which
its growth is based, of hard climate and in a large part
of sterile soil." He could think of only two reasons why

this Northern region prospered while the South languished: the Yankees had early rid themselves of slavery, thus paving the way for enterprise and capital; and, once committed to industrialism, they had benefitted from the salutary influence of protective tariffs. With the South now emancipated from the errors of the past—and blessed with bounteous raw materials, mild climate, and fertile soil—the way was clear for an almost incredibly rapid development.[59]

While they explained the industrial reticence of the Old South purely on institutional grounds, the New South spokesmen apparently saw no inconsistency in believing, as it was often their habit to do, that resources alone would almost automatically ensure the industrial revolution. Writing of Gadsden, Alabama, "one of the most promising towns in that marvelously endowed state," Edmonds called attention to its mineral wealth, agricultural advantages, favorable location on the Coosa River, and concluded that "its future is assured."[60] Kelley, lamenting mismanagement and lack of progress at South Pittsburgh, Tennessee, assured his readers that the setbacks were temporary because "the agricultural and mineral resources" of the community were so great, "and her location so admirable, that no such mistakes as have been permitted to occur . . . can permanently impair the prospects." His faith in the city's prosperous future, he declared, "rests solidly on my knowledge of the abounding supplies of materials for widely diversified manufactures" found there.[61]

"Abounding supplies" was a phrase that was to permeate the literature of the New South movement. Edmonds was one among many in insisting that nature had "more richly endowed the South than any other section of the country," so that it could appropriately be designated " 'Creation's Garden Spot.' "[62] The Reverend John C. Calhoun Newton shared this view and was applauded when he based his faith in the success of the New South crusade on his belief that no other part of the country could rival the South's natural endowments.[63] Not unnaturally, a petty pride entered into the discussion of the South's resources and no opportunity was lost to tell of their extent. One such occasion involved Kelley's story of how a piece of marble sent to contribute to the building of the Washington Monument was initially rejected because its unusual beauty obviously identified it as Italian. Apparently it took the testimony of the governor and several congressmen to prove its Alabama origins.[64]

It was partly to dramatize the abundant supplies of the South and partly to stir Southerners out of their lethargy that Grady conceived his famous "funeral" oration. In different forms the story had been related during the industrial campaigns of the antebellum era, but in the new setting it took on a special significance. Speaking of the burial of a fellow Georgian, Grady wrote:

> They buried him in the midst of a marble quarry: they cut through solid marble to make his grave; and yet a little tombstone they put above him was from Vermont. They buried him in the heart of a pine forest, and yet the pine coffin was imported from Cincinnati. They buried him within touch of an iron mine, and yet the nails in his coffin and the iron in the shovel that dug his grave were imported from Pittsburg. They buried him by the side of the best sheep-grazing country on the earth, and yet the wool in the coffin bands and the coffin bands themselves were brought from the North. The South didn't furnish a thing on earth for that funeral but the

corpse and the hole in the ground. There they put him away . . . in a New York coat and a Boston pair of shoes and a pair of breeches from Chicago and a shirt from Cincinnati, leaving him nothing to carry into the next world with him to remind him of the country in which he lived and for which he fought for four years, but the chill of blood in his veins and the marrow in his bones.[65]

Optimistic about the potential of the resources in the South and anxious to launch the industrial revolution based on them, the leaders of the movement did not fail to recognize disadvantages they suffered. Capital was scarce and labor was largely unskilled. Awareness, however, was never translated into discouragement. On the contrary, certain that others would share their optimism, they fervently proclaimed that the things in which they were deficient would come pouring in from the North and from Europe; and, to facilitate this inward flow, the New South prophets launched a vigorous crusade for outside capital and immigration.

Spending the winter of 1880–1 in New York to advertise the South, Grady wrote back to Georgia that once the industrial program were fairly begun—once the South had shown itself ready to carry out its "platform of liberation and progressive development"—then it was certain that Northern capital would be seen "seeking southern investments with eagerness and the stream of immigration turned toward Georgia."[66] Returning to Georgia, he devoted countless editorials to the subject of Southern opportunity and the advantages it held for Northern capital. In 1883 he announced that "northern capital has been coming into the south very rapidly for several years," but the next year he lamented that "capital has been kept out of the south by prejudice." The prejudice was costly to Northerners who invested their money at 4 per cent in the North while "the south offered 8 per cent with the best security, and opportunities for safe investment that would pay twice as much." Recurrent financial panics on Wall Street, he predicted, would cause money to come South, "where climate, resources and opportunity all invite." By 1885 he was ready to declare that, in so far as Atlanta was concerned, there was no longer real need "of advertising the attractions." And just before he died he proclaimed that "from Virginia to Texas the woods are full of New England capitalists hunting investments, and you can hardly fire a gun without killing one. . . . The whole of New England appears to have stampeded. . . . So it goes, and the good Lord only knows where it will end."[67]

Like Grady, Edmonds painted attractive pictures of the boundless opportunity in the South and then attempted to clinch his case—and attract more capital—by reciting endless stories of successful Northern investments in the region. In 1886 he noted the move of a New York manufacturer to Birmingham and cited the instance as "the strongest evidence that could be given of the unequalled advantages of the South for manufactures." Typical of scores of Edmonds's editorial comments was the statement that "the profits to be reaped from investments in the South . . . appear to be fabulous to all who are not familiar with the logic of experience." Let men of wealth come South, he promised, "and with anything like discretion in the matter of management, returns upon capital ventured will be double, triple, and in many cases quadruple what can be obtained upon equal outlays upon safe ventures in the North and the older sections of the West." There was no disguising the fact, he wrote, "The El

Dorado of the next half century is the South. The wise recognize it; the dull and the timid will ere long regret their sloth or their hesitancy."[68] Striking off a pamphlet in 1890, he announced that "capitalists in Europe and America are looking to the South as the field of investment." Improving on Greeley, he declared that the cry should no longer be "Go West, Young Man," but "Go South."[69]

To translate optimism into reality—to make the Southern mecca a truly hospitable region for Northern capital—the New South spokesmen bombarded state legislatures with requests for the enactment of tax-exemption schemes and, when possible, for the provision of building sites. The press was advised to create a friendly atmosphere by playing down social conflict and radical movements. Edmonds believed that the "disreputable attempts" sometimes used to frighten Northern capital and labor stemmed from purely "demagogical reasons," and he wanted it known that the South was "prosperous and contented, devoting her energies to the development of her unequalled resources, and to the education of her citizens, white and black." Southern editors, he advised, should "reduce to the minimum their record of local crimes and should demand that news suppliers send them other matters," particularly "industrial information."[70]

This "industrial information" was eagerly gathered and disseminated throughout the country and abroad in a gigantic promotional undertaking. The task of promoting the South to outsiders was one that every small chamber of commerce undertook, each vying with the other for success. Pamphlets, articles, brochures, and books by the hundreds were sent out across the land to tell non-Southerners where they should come to make their fortunes.[71]

M. B. Hillyard's *The New South*, a book full of optimistic statistics, was published by Edmonds and, at his direction and expense, copies were placed in hotel reading rooms, public libraries, and on board passenger ships plying the seven seas. The inquiring reader would find a volume "richly bound in the finest Russian leather, with gilt edge and gilt title."[72] Individual cities were often singled out for special attention in the promotional campaign, as in the case of Anniston, Alabama. Edmonds invited Kelley to do an article on this "model city of the South," declaring that it "would be read over the country, and would be worth many thousands and tens of thousands of dollars." Kelley was happy to oblige, and "Anniston: A Romance of the New South" appeared in the 1887 columns of the *Record*.[73]

Another favored device frequently used to advertise the promise of the South was the industrial and agricultural exposition. New South spokesmen reacted with pleasure to Atlanta's International Cotton Exposition in 1881, and the October 5 issue of the *Constitution* was a special, record-breaking thirty-two page edition celebrating its opening. The next month Grady wrote that the South had never previously had such an opportunity to make its advantages known.[74] As the exposition device caught on, national attention focused on it and the leading periodicals published friendly descriptions. A correspondent for the *Century Magazine* reviewed the New Orleans exposition of 1885 in a two-piece article and concluded that everyone could now plainly see that "there are vast and inviting fields to the south of us waiting to be conquered for our industries and our commerce." Impressed by the region's rapid recovery from the ravages of war, this correspondent believed that the South stood "in the portal of a great industrial development."[75] Two years later, Grady pronounced the Piedmont Exposition a great success, explaining that "within its commodious exposition halls are to be found the raw materials side by side with the finished products, all the result of the energy and enterprise of the new south."[76] Energy, enterprise—and opportunity: these were the charming allurements the expositions were designed to reveal to the prospective investor in the South's future.

Outside capital was essential to the inauguration of the Southern industrial revolution and there was, therefore, a compelling logic to the pleas of the New South spokesmen for Northern investments. The expositions and the promotional campaigns of which they were a part were also, however, intended to attract a great influx of labor into the region. And, as one contemporary observer accurately reported in 1883, "there is, indeed, everywhere in the South, the strongest desire for immigration from the North."[77] In fact, the campaign to attract outsiders had begun immediately after the war with German-born John A. Wagener of South Carolina setting future patterns as that state's commissioner of immigration. By the time the New South movement was in full swing, in the 1880's, immigrants were eagerly sought by state immigration agencies, various regional immigration organizations and conventions, and by individual planters, speculators, railroads, and business organizations.[78]

Agreed that their program of agricultural renascence and industrial development required large-scale immigration, the New South spokesmen turned naturally to propaganda as the device for attracting immigrants. Edmonds noted on one occasion that "the outside world may know something of the matchless resources of the South," but he felt that substantial numbers of persons would not come to the region "until by persistent work the matter has been forced day after day upon their attention."[79] The "persistent work" Edmonds desired was enthusiastically undertaken by Southern promoters, who received a favorable hearing in the Northern periodicals. Repeatedly the point was made that the South's opportunities were unmatched by those in any other part of the country, and the promoters were frequently at pains to make invidious comparisons with the West. As Grady asked rhetorically once, "why remain to freeze, and starve, and struggle on the bleak prairies of the northwest when the garden spot of the world is waiting for people to take possession of it and enjoy it?"[80] A Eufaula, Alabama, resident made the same point by insisting that cheap land and guaranteed returns could be expected in the South, "where schools and churches are already established." With these advantages, he asked, "why go to the harder climate and less profitable crops of the West?" The same writer, attempting to woo prospective farmers into the South, extolled the sharecrop system as an ideal device for those who had no capital with which to purchase a farm. "This is a most admirable plan," he wrote. "The tenant's risk is small, support is certain, and almost always there is something besides to begin another year on."[81]

When the New South spokesmen wrote in specific terms about the kinds of immigrants they preferred (which was not frequent) they commonly selected what Grady called "the better class of immigrants."[82] By this they meant Northern farmers and artisans of Anglo-Saxon stock, first of all. When they thought in terms of tapping the growing supply of foreign immigrants into the nation, logic moved them to favor the attraction of any hardworking individual, whatever his nationality; but inherited enmities and prejudices caused them to turn their backs on the mass of immigrants from southern and eastern Europe—the very men who made up the great bulk of the immigration of the late nineteenth century. Grady felt, for example, that the immigration conventions which sought to tap this flow were not seeking "the kind of immigration most desirable for the south."[83] Edmonds was more concrete—and more belligerent. He opposed "all schemes looking toward the colonization of large numbers of ignorant foreigners." He wanted settlers, to be sure; and he believed that there was room "for thousands, even millions of industrious people." But the new arrivals of the late 'eighties were "not composed of the character of people desired by the South." Too many of them were "socialists and anarchists," he explained, and "we do not want that kind."[84]

Thus favoring immigration but reluctant to welcome those immigrants in largest supply, the New South spokesmen were driven increasingly into vague generalizations about the wonders of the region, studding their remarks with assertions that "the need of a tide of immigration is greater in the South than in any other section of the country" in order to make the region "as fruitful and as prosperous as nature intended it should be."[85] This kind of appeal was frustrated by the actual conditions of the region. There were already more farmers in the region than could establish themselves on a self-supporting basis—as witnessed by the growing rate of tenancy. And the paucity of factories combined with the flight of Southern farm whites into the mill villages meant that there were few opportunities in industry. Nonetheless, the cry for immigration continued, based on what one historian has recently called "the illusory belief that factories would follow labor."[86] Somehow, they sensed, men must be attracted to fill up the unoccupied land and develop the generous resources, and so they rested their faith in the future, once again, on the bounty of nature, confident that things would work themselves out once the good news were known.

IV

With bountiful resources, confidence in the acquisition of capital, and faith that labor adequate to develop the region would be attracted, the New South prophets found their greatest pleasure in describing the nature of the future. They envisioned a balanced, diversified, dynamic economy that would produce incalculable riches. Cotton would continue to exert its magical powers, but diversification and the application of scientific, businesslike principles would end its debilitating effects on the region. More important than the agricultural renascence, an industrial and commercial revolution was planned and anticipated as the true salvation of the region. With absolute confidence, Grady wrote, one could expect "the certain and steady shifting of the greatest industrial centers of the country from the north to the more favored regions of the south."[87] The vast forests of the region would support a great lumber and furniture industry; the mineral resources would lead to coal, iron, and steel production unmatched anywhere. Older industries, like tobacco manufacturing, were expected to see great expansion. And, of course, by bringing "the factory to the fields," the New South promoters would create a cotton-mill industry that would become a Southern monopoly. "This," Grady declared, "is a result that cannot long be delayed. Those who oppose such a movement are merely fighting one of the invincible forces of nature."[88] With the expansion of railroad track and the multiplication of banking facilities, the region would have a transportation and commercial system more than adequate to facilitate agricultural and industrial prosperity.

The full fruit of the New South program would be riches such as neither the South nor the nation had ever seen before. A Vanderbilt theology professor looked forward to the appearance of numerous millionaires who would use their wealth to develop the land, and he waited confidently because "the white man of the South . . . has set himself to work in earnest; and on the grave of the Old South, aided now by colored freemen instead of slaves, he is building a New South that will be far grander than ever the Old South was or could have been."[89] Virginia, once the proud "mother of presidents," was to become the "mother of millionaires."[90] Edmonds believed that the South was "simply rising to her manifest destiny of advancement,"[91] while Grady was certain that the Deity himself was on her side. "Surely the basis of the South's wealth and power," he declared, "is laid by the hand of the Almighty God, and its prosperity has been established by divine law."[92] Kelley, foreseeing illimitable wealth and honor "in the pathway of the New South," implored the Almighty to "speed and guide her onward progress."[93] The South, Edmonds knew, "was to be the richest country upon the globe."[94] And those riches would lead to grander victories; would recoup the losses of the past and, in the end, create a triumphant South.

3
The Triumphant South

You wish me to talk to you about the South. The South! The South! It is no problem at all. I thank God that at last we can say with truth, it is simply a geographic expression. The whole story of the South may be summed up in a sentence: She was rich, and she lost her riches; she was poor and in bondage; she was set free, and she had to go to work; she went to work, and she is richer than ever before.

—HENRY WATTERSON[1]

> The South whose gaze is cast
> No more upon the past,
> But whose bright eyes the skies of promise
>   sweep,
> Whose feet in paths of progress swiftly leap;
> And whose fresh thoughts, like cheerful
>   rivers run,
> Through odorous ways to meet the morning
>   sun!

—MAURICE THOMPSON[2]

With a population of 80,000,000 active, virile people, unvexed by the arbitrary laws of differing nationalities as in Europe, the foremost in general education, the foremost in wealth, the foremost alike in manufactures and agriculture of all the nations in the world, man never before conceived of such possibilities as the future holds out to us. Well may the people of the South rejoice that it is in their power to make this section hold a dominating position in this, the dominant power of the world.

—RICHARD H. EDMONDS[3]

As he reflected on the progress of the New South movement, Amory Dwight Mayo related it to major themes in American history, one of which was that "every one who is fit for American citizenship has the right to believe that all things are possible in a republic like our own."[4] The statement raised two questions for which the New South spokesmen were to have ready answers. First was the implied query: Are Southerners fit for American citizenship? Second, if they were, was there anything that should prevent them from sharing in the historic sense of optimism and triumph that rightfully belonged to every American?

Between 1861 and 1865 Southerners had fought to dissociate themselves from American citizenship. When capitulation was forced upon them they renounced their former ambitions, pledged fealty to the Union, and expected to resume the role they had enjoyed prior to hostilities. Their conqueror, however, was reluctant to concede that they were so soon "fit for American citizenship." In the minds of many Northerners, as Paul Buck writes, the South continued to be regarded as a threat to those things for which the Republic stood. It was, in many Northern eyes, a region guilty of manifold sins—"the sin of causing the war, the sin of slavery, the sin of seeking the life of the Union"—and, equally reprehensible, it "was still a South in which the evil consequences of wrong exerted a baneful influence."[5]

Thus rudely excluded from the full benefits of American citizenship, the South was also denied that sense of "anything-is-possible" that was deeply imbedded in the minds of other Americans. "Nothing in all history had ever succeeded like America," Henry Steele Commager writes. "As nature and experience justified optimism, the American was incurably optimistic. Collectively, he had never known defeat, grinding poverty, or oppression, and he thought these misfortunes peculiar to the Old World. Progress was not, to him, a philosophical idea but a commonplace of experience."[6] Clearly, the American of whom Commager writes was not a Southerner, or at least not a Southerner who grew to maturity after 1830. The Southerner's experience in the nineteenth century had been, in many essentials, precisely the opposite of that of other Americans.[7] Rewriting Commager's assessment to make it apply accurately to the South, one would have to say that "as experience did not justify optimism, the Southerner was incurably pessimistic. Collectively, he had known defeat, grinding poverty, and oppression, and he did not think these misfortunes peculiar to the Old World. Progress, to him, was more an illusion than a reality."

It is also clear that the prophets of a New South did not cherish these peculiarities of their region. They did not wish to be cast in the common lot of mankind elsewhere, but they aspired to fulfill the American success story in all of its ramifications. The New South creed was designed to point the way toward that achievement. It embodied a fervent gospel of union and brotherhood, to facilitate full acceptance into the union, and tailored its notions of both individual and collective success to the dominant American pattern.

I

When Edward Atkinson, New England cotton-mill magnate and friend of the New South spokesmen, came to Atlanta in 1881 to promote the International Cotton Exhibition, he told a group of receptive Georgians what they themselves would soon be making standard doctrine. The "greatest need of the present time," Atkinson said, was "that the citizens of the two sections . . . should visit each other, learn the respective methods and opportunities of each State, and become convinced that in this mutual inter-dependence is the foundation of their true union."[8]

In the years before Atkinson's address there were those, including Southern men of prominence, who had similarly pleaded for the cessation of sectional animosities. Lee himself had tried to lead the way by declaring that all was not lost and by insisting that Southerners seek to rebuild their shattered society within the framework of a broad nationalism. Other former leaders of the Confederacy added their authority to Lee's in the 'seventies. Benjamin Harvey Hill urged North and South to "unite to repair the evils that distract and oppress the country" and implored, "let us turn our backs upon the past, and let it be said in the future that he shall be the greatest patriot . . . who shall do most to repair the wrong of the past and promote the glories of the future."[9] L. Q. C. Lamar, in his famous eulogy of the once-hated Sumner, declared: "My countrymen! *Know* one another, and you will *love* one another."[10] Henry Watterson chanted, "war or no war, we are all countrymen, fellow citizens."[11] And Wade Hampton urged that the curtain be dropped on the war and that every citizen "look beyond to the future, when through all time that [American] flag shall float over a true and prosperous and reunited country."[12]

These ringing pleas, while they were supported by men in all sections of the country as the Reconstruction experiment underwent successive failures, made only insubstantial progress before the 1880's. The lingering suspicions and enduring dissensions between the sections made the goal of reconciliation seem almost beyond reach. To convert the effort into a brilliant success became a cardinal ambition of the New South prophets in the 'eighties and 'nineties. They plunged into this mission with the same enthusiasm they had applied to the crusade for economic regeneration and, in the process, they created a gospel of union that became an integral part of the New South creed.

No one was more zealous in the mission than Henry Grady. Early in his career he designated "this miserable sectional strife" as the most formidable obstacle in the way of Southern progress, and for ten years he developed the theme in editorials, feature stories, and speeches.[13] In 1880 he charged that the sectional spirit was kept alive in the North, apparently for selfish reasons, and he maintained that there was not in the South "a single spark of that peculiar sectional madness which is now rampant at the North."[14] In the next year he wrote warmly and sympathetically about President Garfield, praying for his recovery, praising his personal qualities, and finally lamenting his death as the loss of a man who would have been a friend to the South.[15] Later in 1881 he welcomed the arrival of Atkinson to the Cotton Exhibition, praising in particular his nationalist message.[16] By 1884 he was writing that "the better the masses of the north and of the south know each other the better it will be for all," explaining that "we have a common country, which is working out a common destiny and in which we have common pride and interest."[17]

These and other editorials, coupled with Grady's optimistic nature and friendly disposition, brought to him a matchless opportunity to send his message of reconciliation vibrating through the nation. The New England Society of New York, determined to have a Southern speaker for the 1886 banquet at Delmonico's, wanted a man who would speak for reconciliation and who would, at the same time, command the respect of all parts of the country. Grady was a natural choice. Growing up since the war, he had no Confederate background, and he was known primarily as a journalist and not as a politician. His record as a spokesman for progressive economic policies and section reconciliation was already well known, and his oratorical abilities similarly commended him.[18]

The atmosphere at Delmonico's would almost surely have frightened, or antagonized, a man who came without confidence—and a purpose. The 360 seats were filled, for the most part, by wealthy, conservative businessmen eager to hear of a South that had mended its rebellious ways and was prepared to offer a stable and suitable climate for Northern investments. On the speaker's platform General William Tecumseh Sherman sat in prominence. At the end of his short address the band played "Marching Through Georgia." It was then that the young editor from Atlanta was introduced.[19] His opening paragraph was destined to become the most famous passage in the literature of the New South movement:

"There was a South of slavery and secession—that South is dead. There is a South of union and freedom—

that South, thank God, is living, breathing, growing every hour." These words, delivered from the immortal lips of Benjamin H. Hill, at Tammany Hall, in 1866, true then and truer now, I shall make my text to-night.[20]

The Northern businessmen could now relax; the speaker they had imported from the South was apparently going to play his role well.

Appealing further to the theme of national unity, Grady rapidly wove into his speech—which was not made from a prepared text—a criticism of one of the earlier speakers, who had stated that the country still had to look forward to the appearance of the "typical" American. On the contrary, Grady declared, the man who had directed the victory of the Union over the Confederacy was the typical American. Abraham Lincoln embodied the best of the "Puritan" and the best of the "Cavalier"; in his simple, sublime life were all the elements that summed up America. National admiration for the great Lincoln should unify former enemies and still leave ample room for reverence of "your forefathers and . . . mine."[21]

With the tone of his speech thus set in a harmonious chord, Grady invited the audience to consider the plight of the South in the two decades since Appomattox. He described the war-weary veteran coming home from the terror of battle only to find his house in ruins. Ruined homes were symbolic of the condition of the whole region. But the veteran did not fret—he worked. Sherman—a general slightly careless with fire, Grady remarked to the amusement of his audience—had left Atlanta in ashes, but from those ashes was raised a "brave and beautiful city," and "somehow or other we have caught the sunshine in the bricks and mortar of our homes, and have builded therein not one ignoble prejudice or memory."[22] With the stops all out, the audience now alternated between discrete weeping and loud cheering.

Trying next to sum up the essence of the New South that he said had now been built, Grady continued:

> But what of the sum of our work? We have found out that in the summing up the free negro counts more than he did as a slave. We have planted the schoolhouse on the hilltop and made it free to white and black. We have sowed towns and cities in the place of theories, and put business above politics. We have challenged your spinners in Massachusetts and your ironmakers in Pennsylvania. We have learned that the $400,000,000 annually received from our cotton crop will make us rich when the supplies that make it are home-raised. We have reduced the commercial rate of interest from 24 to 6 per cent., and are floating 4 per cent. bonds. We have learned that one Northern immigrant is worth fifty foreigners; and have smoothed the path to southward, wiped out the place where Mason and Dixon's line used to be, and hung out our latchstring to you and yours.[23]

With Mason and Dixon's line "wiped out" the rest could only be anticlimactic. He spoke of the achievements of the South in the previous decade and of the failures of the Old South, of the justice tendered the Negro by Southern whites, and of the unqualified acceptance in the South of defeat in the war. In recognizing misguidance in the past—and in accepting the decision of the sword— he nonetheless made it clear that the South had nothing to take back, no fundamental apologies to make, only promises for the future made credible by the actions of the present. In the tradition of Lee and Grant at Appomattox, he explained, the South was prepared to grasp hands with its Northern brethren and resume the joint task of building a great America.[24]

No isolated and unimportant incident, Grady's address created a veritable "tidal wave of New South sentiment." In the North, South, and West the press was enthusiastic and extensive in its reporting.[25] Grady would live but three years after he returned triumphantly from Delmonico's, but in that time he rode the crest of his fame and fanned the sentiment for reconciliation wherever he went. Speaking before the Boston Bay State Club in December 1889, in his last public address, he told his New England friends that his son, the "promise" of his life, could find no better place to learn "the lessons of right citizenship, of individual liberty, of fortitude and heroism and justice" than on Plymouth Rock.[26] Less than a week later, just short of his thirty-ninth birthday, Grady was dead. Joel Chandler Harris, his close friend and associate on the *Constitution*, had a memorial volume on the market before another year had passed and, in the memory of "our Messenger of Peace," he dedicated the book to the "Peace, Unity and Fraternity of the North and South."[27] It was as a pacificator, more than anything else, that Harris liked to remember his old friend.

In his role as "pacificator" Grady had clearly seen that there were two groups which needed to be pacified: the doubters in the North and the doubters in the South. When he spoke in New York he was concerned primarily to allay Northern fears—hence the wiping out of Mason and Dixon's line. When he spoke to Southern audiences he enlarged on the minor theme introduced in New York —that the South had nothing to take back—and promised

his listeners that the authentic Southern heritage of nationalism was one that guaranteed a bright future to the
region.

The announcement of the death of sectionalism in the
South was present in virtually every discussion of the
New South movement. The literature is cluttered with
overblown phrases like those of Robert Bingham, a North
Carolina educator, who proclaimed that "the past of the
South is irrevocable, and we do not wish to recall it.
The past of the South is irreparable, and we do not wish
to repair it," all because "the greatest blessing that ever
befell us was a failure to establish a nationality."[28] Out-
sider observers incessantly reported the new sentiment.
Charles Dudley Warner noted in 1885 that "the South
has entirely put the past behind it, and is devoting itself
to the work of rebuilding on new foundations."[29] Two
years later he wrote that "if I tried to put in a single sentence the most widespread and active sentiment in the
South today, it would be this: The past is put behind us;
we are one with the North in business and national
ambition: we want a sympathetic recognition of this
fact."[30] The editor of *The Century Magazine*, whose devotion to Southern topics was unrivaled by Northern journalists of the 'eighties, observed in 1885 that "the South
believes no longer in slavery, no longer in secession. Some
ex-rebels said not long ago: 'We are glad we were
whipped, and we are in to stay! Now let us see Massachusetts try to get out of the Union!' "[31]

The reporting by non-Southerners accurately reflected
the New South spokesmen's celebration of defeat and the
arrival of a second chance in a stronger nation. Bishop
Atticus Greene Haygood, florid stylist and orator as well
as energetic supporter of the New South movement,

thanked the "gracious Providence that overrules the nations" for the failure of the Confederacy.[32] The extent of
the sentiment was poignantly confirmed in 1889 when the
University of South Carolina conferred an honorary degree
on Edward Atkinson, the New Englander whose first
contact with the South had been in helping to equip John
Brown's raiders with Sharp's rifles.[33] It was further demonstrated by the candid declaration of a twenty-four-year-
old University of Virginia law student. "I yield to no one
precedence in love for the South," Woodrow Wilson
wrote. "But *because* I love the South, I rejoice in the
failure of the Confederacy."[34]

II

To rejoice in the failure of the South's most absorbing
mission required of the New South prophets not only
that they supply a salve for the bitter wounds of defeat,
but also that they offer a vital substitute for the dream of
independence and self-determination; a substitute that
embodied an even nobler vision of the future than the
abandoned Confederate utopia. Fortunately for the New
South spokesmen, the ingredients of such a vision were
already present, though long dormant, in the Southern
mind. To vitalize them required a new appreciation of
the Jeffersonian era when Southerners had been ardent
nationalists and, at the same time, masters of their own
destiny. Spokesmen like Watterson and Page were guilty
of no hypocrisy and hid no duplicitous motives when they
acknowledged and praised this heritage. When Watterson
wrote that "what we really need in the South, above all

else . . . is identity with things national,"[35] he could recall his opposition to both slavery and secession in the years immediately before the war. Page grew up with the doctrine of nation above section and he never forgot his grandfather's injunction to serve the nation—a nation of which the South was but one part.[36]

Other New South spokesmen were genuinely attached to the creed of nationalism, but their writings reveal motives and values which betray a less unreserved dedication to it than they were willing to admit. Underlying the professions of nationalism, in short, were calculations of concrete gains for the region. To put it another way, the nationalism that the New South prophets preached had as its basic goal the recouping of the losses the South had incurred because of her long commitment to militant sectionalism.

Among the most obvious and distressing of those losses was the self-determination of racial policy that had begun to be eroded in the 1820's. The victorious principle of union completed the process and carried with it not only the abolition of slavery but the constitutional requirement of Negro equality as well. The New South spokesmen were honestly relieved to be done with slavery, but to have the terms of racial equality dictated by the North was more than they would tolerate. The full implications of their racial policy will be explored in the next chapter, but here it should be noted that a vital connection existed between the professions of nationalism, on the one hand, and the calculated policy to achieve self-determination in racial matters, on the other.

George Washington Cable, the New Orleans author and ardent defender of civil rights, perceived this purpose behind the New South posture and ridiculed it in rhyme on the occasion of Grady's New York address:

You've probably heard of one, Grady,
A speech to New Englanders made he.
 They thought it delightful
 Becuz he wa'n't spiteful
And they're what they call "tickled" with Grady.

He was eloquent, also, was Grady;
Patriotic! and bright as a lady.
 But on MEN'S EQUAL RIGHTS
 The darkest of nights
Compared with him wouldn't seem shady.

There wasn't a line, good sirs, bless ye,
Of all that he chose to address ye,
 That touched the one point
 Where his *South's out of joint*
For it wasn't his wish to distress ye.[37]

The pattern that Grady worked out in his New York speech was followed in subsequent addresses, and in all of his forays into the North it was evident that he did not wish "to distress." Asked by the Boston Merchants' Association to discuss the Negro problem, he began by scolding the New Englanders for meddling in Southern racial policies. In their overzealousness for Negro rights—and in their ignorance of the nature and character of the Southern Negro—they had unwittingly created intense and debilitating racial friction. To stop the discussion here might have distressed, but Grady was just warming up to his subject. He noted that the unsettled conditions resulting from these misguided sentiments had alarmed capitalists throughout the North and had frightened them away from Southern investments. Since the end of Reconstruction, however, native white Southerners had taken charge with the result that the Negro prospered and social conditions were peaceful. Moreover, the economic opportunities in the South cried out for Northern capital, offering automatic and stupendous returns. But the North remained suspicious, fearful that abandonment of coercion had been a mistake—hence the recurrent talk of new civil rights legislation. The wise men of the North, however, would realize that the race problem was virtually solved and that conditions could remain peaceful only if the South were left alone. By this reasoning, then, a Northern hands-off policy was insurance for the safety of Northern capital in the South. With these essential points made, Grady moved easily into an eloquent peroration to the Union, looking to the creation of a "Republic compact, united, indissoluble in the bonds of love," a Republic "serene and resplendent at the summit of human achievement and earthly glory."[38]

In addition to the quest for racial self-determination, the nationalist creed was also, as the above examples suggest, inseparably bound up with the industrial argument so that nearly every New South declaration of loyalty to the Union was also an appeal for Northern capital. Watterson, for example, understood the need for Northern participation in the economic development of the South and made it a theme in numerous speeches and editorials. To disarm Southern reactionaries who feared Northern interference of any sort, he commonly made his appeal to reliable conservative interests in the North. Scolding them for harsh judgments imposed on the South, he would, at the same time, invite their sympathy and their capital.[39]

Speaking before the American Bankers' Association in 1883 he began with the assertion that the South was "simply a geographic expression" and no longer the home of militant sectionalists. The old notion that a different species of person lived below Mason and Dixon's line, he said, was a product of "morbid minds." "We are one people," he told them; and that solid fact, he declared, "gives a guarantee of peace and order at the South, and offers a sure and lasting escort to all the capital which may come to us for investment. . . . We need the money. You can make a profit off the development."[40] On another occasion Watterson made clear how important it was to correct false Northern notions about the South in order to encourage a flow of capital into the region. Writing in 1882, he insisted that the "philosophic observer" of the North would see in the South not a "huddle of lazy barbarians, composed in large part of murderers and gamblers," but, rather, "a great body of Christian men and women, who have had a hard struggle with fate and fortune, but who have stood against the elements with fortitude that contradicts the characteristics formerly imputed to them."[41]

The patterns worked out in the early 'eighties by Grady and Watterson were assiduously applied by the other New South spokesmen. Edmonds, for example, when he proclaimed the "unparalleled industrial progress of the South," stressed the interdependence of the sections and noted pointedly that Southern advancement guaranteed Northern wealth.[42] Summing up the mission of his journal in 1924, he wrote that the objective had always been to build up "the nation through the upbuilding of the South," and he repeated with Kelley's authority the belief that "the development of the South means the enrichment of the nation."[43] Examples could be multiplied to the point of tedium, but without them one can readily agree with Buck that the spokesmen's message was designed "to advertise a New South of progress and reconciliation" and that "no concept was more often transmitted to the North in the 'eighties than that the South had buried its resentments and had entered a new era of good feeling based upon an integration of material interests."[44]

Edwin Lawrence Godkin had said in 1880 that the conversion of the South to the "ways and ideas" of the "industrial stage of social progress" was really what was required to make the region peaceful.[45] He did not spell out what he meant by "peaceful," but a fair inference would be that an industrial South would mean the end of a distinctive South and that with the end of distinction rancorous sectionalism would dissolve. Seizing upon this idea, the New South spokesmen fashioned the image of a harmonious nationalism as the direct product of the industrialization and consequent enrichment of the South. Grady put it bluntly in one editorial when he wrote that "sectional and political feeling is not likely to make itself heard when people are busy stuffing their pockets with dollars."[46] Tompkins, somewhat less bluntly, declared in a Fourth of July address that the anniversary of American independence should be celebrated as never before because "for the first time in a hundred years, the institutions and interests of the American people are identical and common." The primary reason for the new identity of purpose, he believed, was that manufacturing was once again spreading itself across the South.[47] And Walter Hines Page, less given to wishful thinking than his fellow New South advocates, wrote that the transformation stimulated by their movement would surely mean the disappearance of the old Southern borough he had described in his youth so that it would soon be "very like a thousand towns in the Middle West."[48]

Reflecting on the nationalist creed in the New South movement early in the twentieth century, the Southern historian Samuel C. Mitchell remarked that "common interest is a strong amalgam in a modern government" and went on to observe that "whatever tends to equalize economic conditions in different sections of our country promotes similarity of view and identity of purpose. The cotton-mill owner in South Carolina and the iron master in Alabama are, perforce, responsive to the laws of trade as they operate throughout the whole republic. To industrialize is, therefore, to nationalize the South." Taking a broad view of the nationalist movement, with particular emphasis on the Italian and German experiences, Mitchell wrote that consolidation was one of the major forces at work in the nineteenth century. Southerners, he believed, had simply found out "God's plan" for their generation and had "fallen in line."[49]

Falling in line with God's plan did not, of course, mean that the South was to embrace the national will only to remain a colonial, dependent stepchild. On the contrary, the nationalism to which the New South prophets subscribed was pictured as the sure road to Southern prominence in the nation. This is especially apparent in the ambivalent quality of the Southern quest for Northern capital. Frantically seeking Northern money to build the Southern industrial utopia, and applauding every new investment that was made, the New South spokesmen resented any suggestion that the South they were creating was a product of foreign or outside elements. It was "southern brains, and southern enterprise, and southern energy and courage" that had "inaugurated and sustained the booming development of southern soil and resources," Grady boasted.[50] Edmonds castigated those who used the term New South to mean "something which has been brought about by an infusion of outside energy and money"; it was, he said, an "improper use of the term, or, rather, an abuse of it."[51] This jealous regard for Southerners' claim to the laurels of creation is indicative of the deeper sentiment and root motivation of the New South movement which Grady pointedly expressed in his New York address. The new departure, he declared, had brought to the South "a fuller independence . . . than that which our fathers sought to win in the forum by their eloquence or compel in the field by their swords."[52] Northern aid and participation, but Southern self-determination —this was, in the last analysis, the *raison d'être* of the New South spokesmen's dedication to American nationalism.

III

James Phelan, a forgotten and unimportant Congressman from west Tennessee, was surprised and embarrassed in the summer of 1886 when a Tipton County farmer approached him and said "I am not certain that I know exactly what is meant by the phrase 'New South.' They say you are a progressive Democrat—a man of the 'New South.' Now tell me what this means."[53] Phelan recovered from his shock, drew on the confidence which being a "man of the New South" was meant to impart and, a few days later, delivered a speech in answer to the farmer's question. The reply he gave is important because it underscores the inclusiveness and breadth of the New South

creed. At its core were the ideas of economic regeneration, national reconciliation, and adjustment of the race
question. But, radiating from these central concerns was a
plethora of other ideas that helped to supply a vision of
regional and individual success substantial enough to
replace the creed of the Old South.

The New South, Phelan began, could not be easily
defined, for it meant no one thing. It embodied the idea
of the "social and industrial changes" that had come since
the war; it meant a "spirit of enterprise" which had per-
fected those changes; guiding it was the "liberalized state
of mind which recognizes that a new order of things has
come." Put succinctly, it was "the manifestation in all
walks of life and in all undertakings of the progressive
spirit. It means new methods and . . . modes of thought
and action."

Turning to the specific application of the broad generalizations, Phelan detailed the meaning of the New
South idea for each individual in Southern society. To the
farmer it meant better tools, improved methods, diversified crops, the reading of agricultural journals, a liberal
treatment of hired labor, education for his children, and
an "honest pride of character." To the lawyer the New
South spirit should impart a sense of the grandeur of
his profession; it should cause him to rise above the
pedestrian study of dull cases, inspire in him a love of the
literature of his profession, and cause him to cultivate its
philosophy and its history. To the doctor the New South
issued a call to break the shackles of the past, keep abreast
of modern discoveries, and turn medicine from a "Black
Art" into a true science. To the merchant the New South
should mean a "strict sense of enterprise," the development of new trades, and the widening of business horizons.

To the Negro the New South meant a recognition of his freedom and the acceptance of him as a "fellow citizen," with rights protected honestly and zealously. Those rights, however, were political and economic, not social. The Negro must be trained in the ways of industry and in court he should be given a fair hearing, but God had put between the social relationships of white and black a wide river that forever prohibited social intercourse. Finally, to the Democrat of the South it should mean all these things and more. "In him it should find its highest and most practical exponent." He should be the "Knight of the New South." His leadership should be that of the "practical" statesman of hard work, free from verbiage and empty promises.[54]

Amory Dwight Mayo, an educator and clergyman, was typical of the new breed of Northern reformers who muted or abandoned whatever abolitionists and radical sympathies they might once have had and allied themselves with the spokesmen of the New South. Born in Massachusetts in 1823, Mayo served the Unitarian Church as both minister and professor of church polity in the Meadville Theological Seminary. In the last two decades of the nineteenth century, as a private citizen, he traveled some 200,000 miles in the South, studying conditions in the region, advising on educational matters, and applauding the work of the New South spokesmen.[55] In an article published in 1893 he took an especially broad view of their work. The New South, he wrote, meant urbanization and industrialization and reconciliation with the North—these things were axiomatic. Beyond this it meant the uplifting of "our brothers in black," a logical and just solution to the race problem. Intellectually, it meant the growth of cosmopolitanism, the renunciation of the intense

Southern provincialism which isolated the South from the nation and the world. For the masses it implied a broadening participation in public life, undergirded by education, economic opportunity, and political equality. These changes assured the downfall of the old aristocracy and would lead the South to prominence in a new America based on a new American nationalism.[56]

Among Southern clergymen and educators who carved conspicuous places in the New South movement none was better known than Atticus G. Haygood. Born in Georgia in 1839, Haygood spent his life there and was a staunch admirer of Henry Grady. His father was an attorney and active lay worker in the Methodist Episcopal Church, South. His mother was a committed school teacher. The son combined qualities of his parents to become president of Emory College from 1875 to 1884 and a bishop in the Methodist Episcopal Church, South, in 1881. From this background he was able to speak with an authority that wide segments of Southern society were accustomed to respect.[57]

In the early 'eighties Haygood was probably best known for his attempt to fit the Negro into the progressive ideology of the New South, a subject that will be discussed in the next chapter. But it was on Thanksgiving day, 1880, that he first came into prominence as a New South spokesman. The sermon he preached on that occasion to the students of Emory—*The New South: Gratitude, Amendment, Hope*—launched him on what Judson Ward has called a "tempestuous and controversial career as a social philosopher of the New South."[58] Ten thousand copies of the sermon were printed, at the expense of a New York financier, to spread Haygood's message.[59] Essentially humanitarian, Haygood spoke in broad, hopeful phrases about the future of the region, while pointing to recent changes to justify his optimism. But as a prophet of progress he listed four ills that required attention. The region was intensely provincial; it did not feel the "heart beat" of the outside world. Isolation, he declared, had been a decisive factor in permitting the war to occur; it must be abolished to bring the South into its full development. Illiteracy was a second ailment; great masses of the population must be elevated by a broad program of public education. Thirdly, he lamented the absence of a flourishing literature and found this subject too "painful to dwell on." Finally, he deplored the backwardness in manufacturing, cited the abundant natural resources of the South and exhorted his fellows to take full advantage of them.[60]

Jabez Lamar Monroe Curry was especially sympathetic to Haygood's plea for an end to illiteracy, and more than any other Southerner of the 1880's he sought to make public education the South's number one concern. Born in Georgia in 1825, Curry was trained in law at Harvard and during his Massachusetts residence he was profoundly impressed by Horace Mann, the nation's leading advocate of universal education. Returning to the South, he practiced law in Alabama and served the Confederacy as both legislator and military officer. He was ordained a Baptist minister in 1866, but education remained his enduring concern. After resigning the presidency of Howard University, in Alabama, he accepted a professorship in Virginia, at Richmond College, and in 1881 was appointed General Agent of the Peabody Education Fund, a philanthropy established in 1867 to improve Southern education.[61]

Already a prominent national figure by the 1880's, Curry spoke widely on the needs of the South and, except for a brief period as ambassador to Spain (1885–8), he regularly recorded his support of the standard New South programs. Unlike the notable New South spokesmen, however, Curry placed primary emphasis on public education, the area in which he worked most actively. In addition to his position as General Agent of the Peabody Fund he became chairman of the Committee on Education of the Slater Fund for Negro education in 1890, and was an officer or moving force in every Southern educational organization of consequence until his death in 1903.

Curry crusaded for education in part because he believed in that way he could best discharge his duty to the region, for "the free school is the corner-stone of any New South."[62] He also looked upon state-supported education as a "universal right" of all citizens and the best means of assuring good government.[63] Relating the need for education to the specific goals of the New South crusade, he wrote on another occasion that "ignorance is the parent of poverty, waste, and crime" and maintained that "an ignorant people can never work out a noble civilization." Education, he insisted, "is the fundamental basis of general and permanent prosperity. Poverty is the inevitable result of ignorance. Capital follows the schoolhouse. Thrift accompanies government action in behalf of schools."[64] No stronger plea could have been made for the utility of education in the New South movement, but Curry had one final—and important—touch to add. Negroes, he argued, needed proper schooling quite as much as whites. Acknowledging a selfish reason for his advocacy of Negro education, he wrote that "we are bound, hand and foot, to the lowest stratum of society. If the negroes remain as co-occupants of the land and co-citizens of the States, and *we* do not lift them up, they will drag us down to industrial bankruptcy, social degradation, and political corruption."[65]

Curry was not alone in adding public education to the list of New South demands. In occasional editorials Grady commended Curry for his work and urged the Georgia legislature to authorize units of local government to levy special school taxes and to extend the school term.[66] Edmonds likewise mentioned the importance of education and by the end of the century was demanding that the South pay as much heed to the need of poor Southern white boys as it did to Negroes. He wanted a "white Booker T. Washington" and asked for the emergence of someone who would "do for the poor white boys of his section the effective work which has already been accomplished at Tuskegee."[67] From time to time, too, the meetings of the National Educational Association would ring with pleas for an attack on the problem of Southern ignorance. In 1884, for example, Robert Bingham, a North Carolina educator, said in his address that "the clash of arms ceased nineteen years ago; but the war will not be really ended till the leprosy of illiteracy is removed from the white people whom the war impoverished, and from the blacks whom it enfranchised."[68]

For the most part, however, education remained a relatively minor part of the New South creed, and it was not until the turn of the century that the "education crusade" began to take hold of the Southern imagination. Walter Hines Page was the only one of the prominent New South spokesmen who eventually provided a link between the ideology of the 'eighties and the public school campaign of the early twentieth century. Speaking in Greensboro, North Carolina, in 1897 on "The Forgotten Man," Page denounced the backwardness of the Southern

educational system, castigated the leaders who refused
to appropriate tax funds for schools, and declared that
the inevitable consequence of Southern policy was a large
mass of people who were not only illiterate, but forgotten
as well. This "forgotten man" was the prey of all the
reactionaries in the region. Duped by the politician and
the preacher, he supported the "mummies," the very
people whose position in society depended upon preservation of the status quo. Ignorance trapped the "forgotten
man" in a vicious circle. He voted into office the very men
who quashed the public-education bills that might lift him
out of oblivion. The only way to break this syndrome,
Page said, was to launch a sustained effort of common
people everywhere in the South.[69]

Within a short time the "forgotten man" had become
part of the "indelible imagery" of the Southern people,
and Page's address "created a sensation" from Virginia
to Texas.[70] In the next decade significant improvements
were made in the field of public education and a galaxy
of leaders earned national reputations as spokesmen for
the new enlightenment. But all of this came after the
heyday of the New South movement and was only indi-
rectly related to its creed. Most of the spokesmen of the
'eighties, while they paid lip service to the notion of public
education, preferred to save the region with what seemed
to them to be the less complicated and more speedy method
of industrialization and agricultural reorganization. According to their faith, these reforms would produce the
necessary wealth that one day would finance a desirable,
but not immediately crucial, system of public education.

IV

One of the most venerable of American faiths is the belief that education is everyman's passport to success in a competitive, free enterprise society. In a limited and ambivalent way the New South prophets shared this belief, but one of the reasons why public education received short shrift in their program was that they believed personal success was but incidentally related to formal education. More important, they argued, were the attitudes and moral character that each individual applied to his struggle in life. As they wrote about the New South, they devoted as much energy to defining the value system and qualities of manhood required by the new regime as they did to drafting their blueprint for economic regeneration, sectional reconciliation, and racial harmony. Indeed, their creed held that the new order of affairs could come into existence only if the scale of values which they believed had existed in the Old South were drastically altered. In short, they preached a new set of values as a primary requisite to both collective and individual success.

To begin with, the New South spokesmen believed that the antebellum ideal of the leisured gentleman who scorned manual labor was a relic that had no place in the new age. In the stead of the Old South patriarch, the New South spokesmen would substitute as their ideal the hardworking, busy, acquisitive individual. The new men would be like those Mark Twain had observed on a Southern tour in the 1880's: "Brisk men, energetic of movement and speech; the dollar their god, how to get it their religion."[71] Edmonds explained why when he wrote that "the easy-going days of the South have passed away, never to return. . . . The South has learned that 'time is money.' "[72] This was a lesson that even the aristocrats of the old regime might learn, he wrote on another occasion. "Take the easy-going Southern planter," he predicted, and "turn him loose in a community like that of Birmingham, and the leopard changes his spots in the twinkling of a corner lot!"[73] Kelley made it clear that money was indeed the first goal when he wrote that the man was "a slave or a fool who toils without hope of profit."[74] In an era in which "fruit, not foliage and flowers,"[75] was demanded, the New South prophets proclaimed a "gospel of work as the South's great need" and sure means of bringing praise and position to the very kind of man who lacked status in the old regime.[76] A Scarlett O'Hara would have earned their respect; an Ashley Wilkes their scorn, for, as Watterson declared, the master of the old era, to succeed, must become "the toiler of today."[77] Agreeing with Grady that "the genteel loafer has little place or position in the new system," and with Charles Brantley Aycock that the "most pitiable object in creation is a man who is always idle," Edmonds laid it down as a law of nature that since "the day when it was decreed that in the sweat of his brow man should earn his daily bread, man's greatest blessing has been work."[78] Finally, Edward Atkinson, the friend from the North, rounded out the doctrine with his pronouncement that no society could hope for success when the man who "earns his daily bread by the work of his own hands is not honored."[79]

Closely linked to the "gospel of work" was the doctrine that nonproductive enterprises must assume secondary positions in society. No longer was there either need or excuse for great statesmen who dissipated their time in finely spun constitutional arguments. "Business above

politics," the Grady slogan that was most frequently used
to express this idea, meant that statecraft was another
relic of bygone days. In 1880 Grady wrote of John H.
Inman, a Tennesseean who had made a fortune in New
York as a cotton broker: "I should be charged with irreverence if I wrote down how many politicians . . . this
one young merchant is worth."[80] Apparently worrying
little about the charge of irreverence, he wrote in 1882 that
politicians appeared "cheap" when compared to successful
men of enterprise; in his speech at Delmonico's he announced that the New South men had "sowed towns and
cities in the place of theories, and put business above
politics"; and in an editorial the next year he wrote that
"the man that gives us a new railroad or a new industry
will readily be pardoned if he is a little backward in the
history of parties and such matters."[81] Politics, the New
South advocates agreed, was essentially irrelevant to their
movement and its lure had to be abolished. Edmonds put
it succinctly when he wrote that:

> Politics won't increase the number of factories in a
> town. Politics won't build stores and houses. Politics won't
> attract investors; on the contrary, it often creates such
> oppressive laws for the benefit of its adherents that capital
> is kept away. Politics seldom increases a man's business
> in a legitimate way. In short, in a section which is only
> in the early stages of its development, like the South, the
> professional politician can do untold injury, and is seldom
> or never a power for good.[82]

The attempt to revise society's concept of the successful and honorable man was early linked to the notion of
the "self-made" man. The truly admirable person, Grady
wrote in 1880, was a man who rose to the top "by no
accident of inheritance, nor by capricious turn of luck,

but by patient, earnest, heroic work." He was a man who had "wrought much out of nothing" and had "compelled success out of failure."[83] Ideas such as these became the stock-in-trade of a raft of "success writers" whose literature swept the Northern states in the last quarter of the nineteenth century and found a congenial home in the ideological baggage of the New South school. W. H. Wallace, for example, told the members of the Eutonian Literary Society of Clinton Academy, South Carolina, what qualities a young man should cultivate in the New South: above all the age called for active, energetic, positive men. In a practical age certain things were especially demanded. "For one thing," he announced, "there is the assurance that we are in no danger of becoming a dawdling or effeminate people. A practical people are a sturdy people—full of life and vigor—energetic and enterprising —not necessarily intellectual or cultivated in a bookish sense, but sensible and shrewd and self-reliant." The society of the Old South was "easy going and oligarchical"; it lacked all sense of the practical.[84] In the new, practical age, success should be man's greatest ambition and three things were required to achieve it:

> A competence in money, a good reputation and a good character are essentials of true success in life, and no man having these need have any fear of failure. And all these elements are within the reach of every young man of even ordinary ability and under whatsoever circumstances his lot may be cast. It is, therefore, possible for every man to make his life a success.[85]

William S. Speer, another of the success writers, published *The Law of Success* (significantly under the imprint of the Southern Methodist Publishing House) to provide a comprehensive list of maxims for successful living. Basing his advice on the lives of "self-made" men, Speer told one everything from how to select a wife to how to succeed in business; nor did he overlook the "commercial value" of the Ten Commandments. Pointing to the future training of the youth, Speer prophesied:

> The educator of the future will teach his pupils what will pay best. He will teach them the art of thinking, which, for the purposes in hand, I may define to be the art of turning one's brains into money. He will not teach dead languages, obsolete formulas, and bric-a-brac sciences . . . which are never used in the ordinary transactions of the forum, the office, the shop, or the farm.[86]

Wallace and Speer were but two of the many popularizers of the new doctrine of success in the South and their writings accurately reflected the basic beliefs of the New South spokesmen. Grady, for example, was critical of the University of Georgia because it laid too much stress on such subjects as rhetoric and classics, and he urged that additional instruction be given in practical subjects so that graduates would turn more frequently to business careers rather than to the traditional professions.[87] And Edmonds, responding to the plea of a young Southerner who could not find work, assured his correspondent that "we are all cogs in the great machine" and that one could be sure that, sooner or later, "the right spot is found."[88]

The gospel of work and the success formulas found full expression and pseudo-scientific justification in the doctrine of social Darwinism that captivated American thought in the last part of the century.[89] The Southern exponents embraced it warmly and stoutly defended laissez-faire (so long as that doctrine did not preclude government aid to business), scorned labor unions (which they said were not desired or needed by Southern labor anyway), and made a fetish of the theory of free competition. Tompkins expressed the common New South view when he declared that "the survival of the fittest is, has been, and will always be the law of progress."[90] An "apostle of privilege for capital invested in business," he saw the state as the protector of "natural rights" and not as an instrument of "human welfare."[91]

There was in the Southern version of social Darwinism virtually no appreciation of the enigma noted by concerned social critics of the period: the association of poverty with material progress. Rather, the New South spokesmen ascribed failure to personal shortcomings in the belief that the opportunity created by their program made it possible for anyone who applied himself to succeed. For those who should somehow fall by the wayside, men like the Reverend John C. Calhoun Newton would have "wealthy capitalists, and prince merchants, and lordly bankers" come to the rescue, acting as "stewards of God."[92] Nor was there in the New South literature more than a modicum of awareness of the dangers of monopoly capitalism. Even Page, more sensitive than most to social injustice, largely ignored the danger signals until the twentieth century. Like the others, he felt that industrial development held the answer to the region's economic problems, and during the 'eighties and 'nineties he wrote little about child labor, poor working conditions, marginal wages, and the concentration of economic power.[93] Grady did speak on one occasion of the "shame of the robber barons of the Rhine" and he warned against a repetition of this shame in the

South,[94] but his actions and his writings were overwhelmingly and consistently sympathetic to the railroads, the industrial promoters, and the bankers. He never wrote a serious critique of the dangers in the New South program as he contented himself with promises of the blessings to be ushered in by the industrial, urban era.

Finally, the New South spokesmen showed little patience with those who opposed their program because of its alleged materialism. To those who argued that "mammonism" and "money-mania" were threatening to destroy Southern values, the New South prophets replied sternly. Edmonds found it impossible to understand why people were "prone to sermonize against the spirit of 'commercialism.' " They forgot, or perhaps did not know, that it was "the unceasing, untiring commercial energy of the American people which has put this country to the forefront not only in finance, trade and manufactures, but in almost everything which looks to the betterment of mankind."[95] From the North came Mayo's equally outspoken rebuttal. "It is a simple stupidity," he insisted, to "exclaim over this inevitable trend of Anglo-Saxon society, and to denounce it as materialistic or in any way a symptom of social degeneracy."[96] But it was the irrepressible Edmonds who had the last word: material prosperity, which could come only by adopting the New South program, "if not the foundation, is at least an essential factor in ethical advancement." Every noble aspect of civilization—religion, art, education, intellectual activity—depended upon it. Thus, far from threatening moral values, the New South spokesmen were "really preaching the gospel of education. Yea, they are really messengers preparing the way for religious advancement itself."[97]

V

Holland Thompson was the first academic historian to write a general history of the postbellum South. In 1919 he published a slim volume, appropriately entitled *The New South*, and he set the tone of the work by stating at the outset that "somehow, somewhere, sometime, a new hopefulness was born and this new spirit—evidence of new life—became embodied in 'the New South.' "[98] Writing like a latter-day New South prophet, he joyously proclaimed the "new spirit" and the "new life" and designated them as the South's greatest blessings. Perceiving the essence of the New South creed, he saw that its totality was more than the sum of the individual parts and that its great appeal derived from its philosophy of progress, brash confidence, and sense of boundless optimism—qualities that had been strikingly wanting in the Southern mentality of the early postbellum years. The creed, in short, furnished young Southerners with an ideology that could rationalize the failure of their fathers and point the way to a future of unlimited glory.

Few things appealed to the New South spokesmen more than describing the nature of that future. Commonly drawing their pictures against the background of the postwar chaos and dislocation, they stressed the contrast of rapid accomplishment and divine assistance. Grady would dwell lengthily on the utter hopelessness that seemed to cover the South in 1865 and then would proclaim that from "defeat and utter poverty were to be wrought victory and plenty."[99] Edmonds declared that the phenomenal strides made by the South, "notable in themselves," were of "unparalleled significance when viewed against the appalling background of a generation ago."[100] Underscoring the missionary nature of the movement, Grady called upon an audience of Texans to "consecrate" themselves to the cause of both the South and the Union and, with such "consecrated service," he asked rhetorically, "what could we not accomplish?"[101] What, indeed! One had only to sample the titles of articles in the *Manufacturers' Record:* "The South's Brilliant Future," "The Wonderful South," "South's Prosperity; Past, Present and Future," "Forward," and "Why Optimism Should Reign Through the South."[102]

Why optimism should reign was explained by everyone. Joseph G. Brown wrote that "there is a law of nature that out of death comes life," and "out of the dead Confederacy came the new life, the new energy, the new spirit" that was the New South.[103] Kelley discovered the secret of the South of the 'eighties in its "animation" and its hopefulness.[104] The Reverend Mr. Newton said that, to him, the transcendent meaning of the New South creed was that the "time is fully come when our people look, not backward *only*, but also forward; that the South is to have a future."[105] And Broadus Mitchell—himself caught up in the spirit of progress—looked back on the movement from the vantage point of 1921 to declare that the South, by 1880, "was ready to be no longer negative, but affirmative; not just the passive resultant of its past, but the conscious builder of its future. From a consequence, the South was to become a cause."[106]

The contrast between "consequence" and "cause" is precisely what Commager suggests, in the passage quoted at the beginning of this chapter, as the distinguishing characteristic of the American as compared with other people. The American of the nineteenth century was purely "cause" and knew nothing of "consequence," according to this view. And so, in the last analysis, this is what the Southerner of the New South movement wished to become, too. He wished to become independent of the North, as Grady remarked in New York, but he wished more than that, for he had the testimony of Edmonds that it was in his power to make the South "hold a dominating position in this, the dominant power of the world."[107] Thus did he dream of a South that would rise again; not an Old South of political leadership but a New South of industrial might. Entering the struggle on the terms of the other contestants, he would win back for his region its confidence and its right to an equal—perhaps dominant—partnership in the Union he was eager to re-enter.

4
The Innocent South

The condition of the Southern Negro is one
of progressive evolution from the darkness
of slavery into the fullness of freedom.
He is not only a man by the law of the land,
but he is rising toward true manhood by
the exercise of his physical and moral
powers. In all history there has been no
similar instance in which a ruling race has
so nobly and unremittingly aided its former
bondsmen to rise to the highest levels of
which they were naturally capable.

—RICHARD H. EDMONDS[1]

And with the South the . . . [Negro
question] may be left—must be left. There
it can be left with the fullest confidence
that the honor of the Republic will be
maintained, the rights of humanity guarded,
and the problem worked out in such
exact justice as the finite mind can measure
or finite agencies administer.

—HENRY W. GRADY[2]

But the supremacy of the white race of the
South must be maintained forever, and the
domination of the negro race resisted at
all points and at all hazards—because the
white race is the superior race. This is the
declaration of no new truth. It has
abided forever in the marrow of our bones,
and shall run forever with the blood that
feeds Anglo-Saxon hearts.

—HENRY W. GRADY[3]

Taking stock of the New South movement in the mid-'eighties, the liberal Southern clergyman Thomas U. Dudley related its significance to the future of race relations. A successful analysis of the subject, he felt, must begin with the hard fact "that the conditions of our life are all changed; that old things are passed away."[4] That much had "passed away," there could be no denying. The abolition of slavery removed the one unmistakable institutional expression of white supremacy and the Reconstruction amendments proclaimed the former slaves to be the civic and political equals of their erstwhile masters. But Dudley implied too much when he wrote "that the conditions of our life are all changed," for the persistence of old problems and old attitudes bequeathed to the New South spokesmen a dilemma that had beset their predecessors. The dilemma sprang from the contrast between a national legend of moral innocence, in which Southerners always claimed to share, and the reality of Southern determination to maintain a white master class. Although the conditions of life were different, the race problem would continue to cause Southern leaders to reconcile incompatible allegiances with ingenious rationalizations and paradoxical beliefs.

The legend of innocence has been one of the most

tenacious and influential features of American history. Frederick Jackson Turner recognized this when he wrote long ago that "other nations have been rich and prosperous and powerful," but added that the peculiar genius of the American democracy arose from the nation's determination to root out the obstacles to liberty and equality that had plagued other countries.[5] More recently, Reinhold Niebuhr has noted how Americans looked upon themselves from the beginning as a people who "came into existence with the sense of being a 'separated' nation, which God was using to make a new beginning for mankind. . . . We were God's 'American Israel.' "[6] C. Vann Woodward, to cite one final example, writes that "American opulence and American success have combined to foster and encourage . . . the legend of American innocence." Skipping the feudal stage of development, Americans left behind in Europe the "tyranny, monarchism, aristocracy, and privilege" which they thought accounted for most of the world's evils. In time they created the image of a morally innocent nation and came to regard themselves as "a chosen people and their land a Utopia on the make."[7]

Americans, of course, have not been alone in fostering the notion of their unique innocence. Many foreign observers, often in different ways, have been fascinated by the theme. Crèvecoeur, the most famous of the eighteenth-century commentators, was followed by de Tocqueville in the antebellum period and Lord Bryce after the Civil War.[8] But it was a twentieth-century Swede who gave the most complete and influential account of the legend. Gunnar Myrdal, in his massive study of American race relations, called it the "American Creed" and wrote that it was the "cement in the structure" of the American nation. According to Myrdal, Americans had the most explicitly stated "system of general ideas in reference to human interrelations" of any western nation, and he found "the unanimity around, and the explicitness of, this Creed" to be "the great wonder of America." Born of the colonists' dream of escape from Old World oppression, refined by the philosophy of the Enlightenment, codified in the Declaration of Independence, the Creed sustained Americans in their fight for separation from Britain and in every subsequent war. Its core ideas, Myrdal wrote, consisted of the "essential dignity of the individual human being, of the fundamental equality of all men, and of certain inalienable rights to freedom, justice, and a fair opportunity." Its "main norms . . . are centered in the belief in equality and in the rights to liberty."[9]

I

Myrdal's overarching purpose was to document and dramatize the dilemma besetting a people who righteously celebrated freedom and equality but who practiced a virulent form of racism. The dilemma, of course, was deeply rooted in the nation's history. In fact, the American ideal which Myrdal used as his yardstick was most eloquently expressed by Southern slaveholders of the Revolutionary era. Led by Thomas Jefferson, the enlightened men of that generation were clearly pained by the trap which ensnared them. Articulate and passionate spokesmen for a new freedom in their own land, they vigorously condemned slavery as a repudiation of the foundation upon which they made their claim to universal liberty.

Their actions, however, reflected their ideals only modestly, and as they failed to find what they considered to be a practical way to end the institution they called it a "necessary evil" and cherished the hope that one day it would be abolished so that the ideal and the real might be harmonized.[10]

Quite the opposite result followed, however. With the spread of cotton culture into the southwest, the apparently rising profitability of slavery, and the appearance of a militant abolitionist movement that helped to isolate the South from the mainstream of American thought, Southerners abandoned the Jeffersonian rationale and came to look upon slavery as a "positive good," the essential foundation of their way of life. The antebellum pro-slavery theorists, however, did not fully escape the disquiet that had troubled the Jeffersonians. Many of them spoke harshly of Jefferson's idealism and most perverted the basic structure of the Enlightenment rationale upon which the American Creed rested. Nonetheless, the pro-slavery argument emphasized the same generalized democratic values that held the allegiance of other Americans. The difference was that Southerners believed in the necessity of slavery to guarantee constitutional liberty, equality of opportunity, and class harmony. This was a convenient way to eliminate the inherited dilemma, but the copious literature of justification, full of obeisance to liberty and equality, betrays their awareness of its existence and their need to confront it.[11]

The Civil War and Reconstruction drastically altered the material basis of Southern social relations, as Bishop Dudley implied and as the New South spokesmen incessantly announced, but the Southern faith in white supremacy heartily endured. To seize the leadership of their region, the New South prophets saw clearly that they must give full support to their faith. At the same time, however, they recognized that their plans for abundance, reconciliation, and success—so heavily dependent upon Northern approval—could not flagrantly repudiate the American image of itself as a just and humane society; nor, it must be added, did the New South spokesmen wish to think of themselves as anything but enlightened, progressive men pointing to a future in which happiness might confidently be expected by black as well as by white Southerners.

To make credible their position as both friend of the Negro and defenders of white supremacy, the New South spokesmen were inadvertently assisted by men whose impassioned arguments on both the right and the left vacated for them the happy middle ground of moderation. Not surprisingly, there were many more persons occupying the reactionary than the radical position. With pseudo-scientific notions of racial differences, some of the reactionaries declared that the Negro could not withstand the strains of civilized life and would retrogress to a savage state and ultimately to extinction.[12] After the census returns of 1880 indicated an increase in Negro population, less was said about the trend toward numerical retrogression, but the belief in cultural retrogression received greater emphasis. Philip Alexander Bruce, a prolific amateur historian from Virginia, wrote a book about the emancipated Negro in 1889 in which he stated that "every circumstance surrounding the Negro in the present age seems to point directly to his future decadence." He was certain that the blacks would, in time, reach "a state of nature"—whatever that might be. Favoring deportation as the best solution to the problem, but despairing of its practicability, Bruce advocated stern repression "to ward off political ruin and to save society from destruction."[13]

The reactionaries' fear of "destruction" was rooted in their unshakable conviction that God had created the Negro to be a slave and nothing else. Charles Colcock Jones, Jr., president of the Confederate Survivors' Association, believed that the natural harmony which had been destroyed by emancipation could not conceivably be restored with Negroes as free men.[14] Thomas Nelson Page, with the authority of a Virginia patrician, dismissed the notion that the Negro was handicapped in the era of freedom because of the heritage of slavery. On the contrary, he wrote, the Negro had come to America as a "savage" and slavery had been his "salvation," for he did "not possess the faculties to raise himself above slavery" and the whites had assumed the responsibility for his welfare.[15] Expanding on these views a few years later in a book on the Negro as "The Southerner's Problem," Page recorded the universal belief of all Southern reactionary thinkers when he declared that through all history the Negro had "exhibited the absence of the essential qualities of a progressive race."[16]

Reacting to the frustrations of the Reconstruction era and unable to discover or implement a suitable substitute for slavery immediately after the winning of home rule, outspoken Southern racists found outlet in a rhetoric of hate and repression and in increasing acts of both individual and group violence. To the New South spokesmen, excessive vituperation and unleashed violence were objectionable retreats from the challenges of the present and future and therefore promised the South more of the same ills from which she had long suffered. The Reverend John C. Calhoun Newton, for example, wrote in 1887 that the race question could be settled in one of two ways, either through repression or through a progressive policy designed to lift up the inferior race.[17] Bishop Atticus G. Haygood, whom Newton praised as the guiding spirit in the New South program of racial progress, agreed that the policy of repression could solve no problems. It had been tried many times, from the days of Pharaoh to the Russia of his own day, and it had met with universal failure. Recognition of the interdependent needs of white and black and a plan to elevate the status of both was the only answer to the South's problems, he declared.[18] Grady tried to state the nature of the task when he said "it is to carry in peace and honor and prosperity two dissimilar races with equal civil and political rights and nearly equal in number, on the same soil."[19]

The New South spokesmen's critique of the reactionary attitude toward race relations was carefully constructed to concede most of the fundamental assumptions about the inherent inferiority of the Negroes, and it similarly included abundant reassurance of the need for white supremacy. Its vaunted realism held, however, that the future prosperity and success of the region depended upon cooperation between the races based on a mutual appreciation of the rewards that lay ahead. In an editorial on the subject, Grady stated his view that it was "impossible for the people of the south, either now or hereafter, to get along without the negro." The black man was necessary to Southern progress, he wrote, "and against this necessity mere prejudice will break in vain."[20] On another occasion he stated the commonly expressed New South doctrine that the race question and economic progress were inseparably bound together; the "glory and prosperity of the South," he declared, depended upon an intelligent understanding of their interconnection.[21] Watterson insisted in one of his editorials that the interdependence of the races meant that backwardness in the Negro would inevitably retard the white man's progress and must therefore be combated. Kelley argued similarly that a large, trained labor force was indispensable to economic growth, that the plentiful supply of Negro labor should be tapped, and that "the expertness and productive power of labor do not depend on the race, color, or previous condition of servitude of the laborer or artisan."[22]

Edmonds, who was less sanguine about the equality of capacity implied in his friend Kelley's argument, placed a different emphasis on the importance of Negro labor when he wrote that it was a key element in Southern development "because what white men plan is executed by the strong muscles of industrious negroes."[23] And, like the other New South spokesmen, Edmonds frequently expressed the faith that a new birth of Southern prosperity would cause the race problem to vanish. Blasting Northern policies during the Reconstruction, and warning against further interference in the racial affairs of the South, he promised that "if the South is left to itself, if no inimical legislation interferes with the existing status, economic 'development' will solve all difficulties, and even the troublesome race question will be consigned to oblivion."[24] Thus grounding their argument in apparent realism, the New South prophets gave assurances that their program would preserve white supremacy, insure prosperity, and "solve" the race question.

If the reactionaries provided a useful foil for the New South program, a tiny band of radicals set it off to even greater advantage with a plea for racial equality that could be attacked in order to prove loyalty to the heritage of white supremacy. George Washington Cable, of New Orleans, was the only nationally prominent radical spokesman in the South of the 1880's. Already recognized as a distinguished author—some compared him favorably to Mark Twain and Henry James—Cable moved cautiously but firmly into the controversial debate over Negro rights. In 1885 he achieved national prominence with an essay on "The Freedman's Case in Equity," which appeared in the widely read *Century Magazine*. Cable's essay, which will be considered in more detail later, vigorously condemned the South's denial of constitutional rights to the Negro and issued a moving plea and a tightly reasoned argument for equal justice.[25] The *Century* editor invited Grady to publish a rebuttal and thus gave the leading New South spokesmen the opportunity to declare that Cable's equalitarian arguments, if heeded, would lead to racial amalgamation, the end of white supremacy, and the destruction of society. At the same time, he was given the opportunity to announce opposition to the reactionaries' desire for ruthless repression and praise the New South program of moderation as one that would guarantee liberty and equality to the Negro without sacrificing white supremacy.[26]

II

In rejecting both the reactionary and the radical assessment of the nature of the race problem, the New South spokesmen hoped to present their own program in such a way that it would satisfy the abstract demands of the

American creed of freedom and equality as well as the specific requirements of the Civil War and Reconstruction amendments to the Constitution. Their solution to the problem of freedom, which will be analyzed first, was in several ways a simpler task for their ingenuity than the problem of equality.

The antebellum philosophy of race relations was built on the concept of permanent slavery and it was on the unyielding conviction that the destruction of slavery had been a catastrophic error that the reactionaries took their stand. In contrast, the New South spokesmen boasted that emancipation was a blessing to both races, and many of them argued that slavery had been an error in the first place. Grady spoke for the entire group when he declared that a "higher and fuller wisdom" than that of the South had judged slavery to be wrong, and he expressed his pleasure "that the omniscient God held the balance of battle in His Almighty hand and that human slavery was swept forever from American soil."[27] Similarly, Haygood praised God for freeing the slaves and explained his own conversion from a pro-slavery apologist to an ardent defender of freedom as the result of an intrusion of "new and purer light."[28] Not all agreed with Watterson that slavery had "precipitated an unwilling people" into civil war, but most conceded that it had been a cancer eating at the national fabric; and the nationalism of the New South crusade, like the quest for economic regeneration, led logically to a condemnation of the institution which separated the sections and retarded Southern progress.[29]

The condemnation of slavery and the warm endorsement of Negro freedom thus formed the starting point of the New South departure in race relations. From this

position the New South men had to come to terms with
the most fundamental expression of the citizen's freedom
in a democratic republic: the right to vote. At the birth
of the nation the "American Creed" postulated that
right in general terms, but it was not until the reforms
of the Jacksonian era that white manhood suffrage became
the common practice. With the Reconstruction acts and
the Fifteenth Amendment racial restrictions were removed
and the constitutional requirement of Negro suffrage,
unaltered by the restoration of home rule, presented to
the New South advocates a specific test of their general
endorsement of Negro freedom. Constantly making a great
point of their realism—of dealing in facts, not theories—
they were nowhere confronted more solidly with a set of
facts than in the case of black suffrage. Writing in 1881,
Haygood brushed aside arguments over the wisdom or
constitutionality of the amendment with the declaration
that "the time is past for such arguments; facts and not
theories must be considered now." The fact, he believed,
was unmistakably clear: the Negro "will never be re-
enslaved; he will never be disfranchised."[30]

Haygood's optimistic assessment was typical of the
spirit of his influential book, *Our Brother in Black*, which
appeared just as the New South movement was becoming
fairly launched by its young advocates and formed a link
between them and the older-generation conservatives. In
a symposium in 1879, L. Q. C. Lamar claimed to know of
"no Southern man of influence or consideration" who believed in the possibility of disfranchisement. "Universal
suffrage being given as the condition of our political life,"
he wrote, "the negro once made a citizen cannot be placed
under any other condition."[31] In the same discussion,
Wade Hampton wrote that "it would be almost impossible

to disfranchise the negro."[32] Moreover, both Hampton and
Lamar seemed to have no serious regrets. Hampton
claimed to have championed limited Negro suffrage during the Reconstruction and Lamar stated that neither he
nor his fellow Mississippians would disfranchise the
Negro if the option were open to them.[33]

The views of men like Lamar and Hampton became
doctrine with the New South spokesmen. An Atlanta
Constitution editorial in 1880 announced categorically that
"the people of the South as a whole . . . recognize the
negro as a citizen and acknowledge his right to vote where
he pleases and for whom he pleases."[34] Five years later
Grady wrote his most serious and responsible essay on
the Negro problem in reply to Cable's *Century* article.
Scolding Cable for most of his views, Grady expressed
displeasure over the manner in which the Negro had
received the vote, but pledged himself and his movement
to the continued defense of Negro suffrage.[35] Grady's
view, like that of all the other New South spokesmen,
was rooted in the belief that nothing could be done to
alter the situation and that the wise and progressive leader
would therefore react positively and creatively to the
world as it was. A contributor to the *Century Magazine*
accurately caught the mood when he damned the racial
views of Southern reactionaries and announced that "opposed to these errors is the spirit of the New South. . . .
The negro must be educated in the responsibilities of
citizenship, and this training must be made practical by
the use of the ballot."[36]

The New South prophets' endorsement of Negro suffrage as an inalienable right of free men was accompanied
by a practical limitation of major significance that drew
a distinction between participation in the political process

and domination of it. The Reconstruction image of "Negro domination" formed the bedrock and justification for the distinction. Like nearly all other Southerners, the New South spokesmen cultivated the myth of Negro rule after the war and chorused their condemnation of the way in which the Negro was thrust into the political life of the region. This view was expressed by the most sincere and articulate spokesmen such as Haygood and Page;[37] it was canonized by the popular Grady, who decried the "great error" of suddenly thrusting an illiterate and inferior people into political responsibility and keeping them there with "the Federal drum-beat" and the glimmer of Union bayonets.[38] In Grady's mind the problem before the New South spokesmen was a staggering one. Inheriting an almost impossible situation, they would stand by past decisions; but, at the same time, they must prevent the recurrence of the previous catastrophe. Never had "such a task been given to mortal stewardship," he wrote.[39] Their assignment was "to carry in peace and honor and prosperity two dissimilar races with equal . . . political rights."[40] To do this, they must discover a formula that would permit the Negro, as a free man, to exercise a free ballot, but to exercise it in such a way that white men would never again be deprived of the control of the region.

The formula was readily discovered in the conviction that political control should rest with men of superior wealth, character, and intelligence—three words that permeate the literature of the Negro question. No one appeared to doubt that Negroes as a group were inferior in all three categories and none felt that a society ruled by what might be regarded as a Jeffersonian "aristocracy of talent" could legitimately be accused of compromising the "American Creed." The formula was especially justified, the New South advocates felt, because it carried with it an attractive quid pro quo. In return for acquiescence in white domination, Negroes could expect to exercise the ballot as a means of developing their sense of responsibility. Page urged upon them the kind of attitude and training made famous by Booker T. Washington at Tuskegee Institute. This approach, he believed, would prepare them for increasing participation in the affairs of government as responsible and intelligent citizens. The road ahead was a hard one, Page warned, but at least it led to the possibility of rich rewards. Reconstruction, with its deceptively charming doctrine of immediate power and authority, had only proved the necessity of a longer training period. Preparing for responsibility under Southern white tutelage (or under Negroes who agreed with the New South creed) was the only realistic course to be followed. In the end, Page promised, whites would come to recognize and reward merit wherever it showed itself, in whatever skin color.[41] The formula which Page spelled out, and which was generally accepted by other New South spokesmen, concluded with the argument that political freedom was not political license and that to be meaningful it must be earned. This, they believed, did no violence to the American commitment to freedom and was the only way to make the Fifteenth Amendment a working reality.

Most of the New South spokesmen were less optimistic about the potential of the Negro than Page, and although they frequently endorsed the advancement-through-training philosophy their fundamental reason for supporting Negro suffrage was rooted in considerations of practical politics. The Redeemer state governments—the groups that engineered the fights for home rule and dominated the region until the Populist uprising of the 1890's—were overwhelmingly oriented toward commercial and industrial interests. Representatives of a new kind of capitalistic class in the South, they created the ideal political environment for the flourishing of the New South creed. Recurrent assaults against Redeemer control were customarily led by men who either distrusted or openly condemned the New South doctrine. The success with which these dissident elements were defeated frequently depended upon the Redeemers' ability to court or coerce, as the case required, the Negro vote. With dependable regularity, that vote came down heavily on their side and thereby helped to keep in power the regimes most likely to forward the New South program.[42] Thus, despite the rhetoric which denigrated the importance of politics, the New South prophets understood that their fate was linked to Redeemed regimes supported by Negro votes.

Candid confessions of their opportunistic reason for support of Negro suffrage do not appear in the speeches and writings of the New South spokesmen, but the literature of the movement disguises them only thinly. Writing in 1879, Watterson declared that "he is a poor judge of human nature, or else very ignorant of the Southern character, who does not know that the well-being of the negro must originate at home."[43] The implications of this statement, made more specific by New South writers in the 'eighties, were twofold: first, Negro political rights could be adequately protected only if Southerners were not coerced by outside forces and, second, with Negroes free to make their own political decisions they would support the Democratic Party—which was a euphemism for the dominant Redeemer wing of that party. Grady expressed the two related arguments well and frequently. In his New York address he promised justice for the Negro when determination of his fate was left "to those among whom his lot is cast, with whom he is indissolubly connected, and whose prosperity depends upon their possessing his intelligent sympathy and confidence."[44] He frequently insisted that the Negro's natural inclination was to support conservative whites, and he believed it unquestionable that "the negro will find that his best friend is the southern democrat."[45]

Throughout the 'eighties there was a latent division in the thinking of the New South spokesmen that portended the bitter clashes of the 'nineties over disfranchisement. A few of the spokesmen, most notably Page and Haygood, sincerely advocated the Tuskegee philosophy of advancement-through-training that promised eventual recognition and influence to Negroes of merit. In this spirit, they appeared to think in terms of temporary political subservience and could imagine a different kind of racial pattern existing at some time in the future. A larger group, however, followed Grady through a maze of ambivalence, paying homage when the occasion demanded to the theory of reward through merit, but more frequently asserting permanent political subservience as the *raison d'être* of Southern politics. Writing for the New York *Ledger* in 1889, Grady justified white domination in the first instance on the basis of the wealth-intelligence-character formula. Next, however, he compromised this rationale by asserting a purely racial justification: the white race was the superior race and would never "submit to the domination of the inferior race."[46] In one of his most outspoken statements, at the Dallas State Fair in 1887, he proclaimed categorically that white domination must be maintained forever; that infallible decree ordained the political subservience of the Negro race and that any attempt to alter or reverse the relationship between the races must be "resisted at all points and at all hazards—because the white race is the superior race."[47]

It is not likely that Grady and his followers ever seriously examined the intellectual contradiction of their arguments. Cable tried to raise the issue, in his rejoinder to Grady's *Century* essay, when he approved the character-intelligence-property formula but revealed its incompatibility with a rigid racial criterion for rulership. "Which are you really for," he asked Grady, "the color line, or the line of character, intelligence, and property that divides between those who have and those who have not 'the right to rule'? You dare not declare for an inflexible color line; such an answer would shame the political intelligence of a Russian."[48] But Cable's effort was largely wasted, and the Grady wing of the New South movement continued happily declaring belief in both the character-intelligence-property formula and the color line. They were aware of the more superficial aspects of Darwinian theory, as Guion Johnson has pointed out, and they sometimes appealed to it to explain that the Negro was on a lower scale in the process of evolution. In this manner they believed they found justification for the doctrine of permanent inferiority by insisting that the Negro could not "jump stages," so to speak, and must therefore remain subservient to the white man.[49] With this added to their other arguments they maintained that freedom, universal manhood suffrage, and white supremacy not only were not incompatible but were mutually bound together.

III

Satisfied that they had resolved the problem of freedom, the New South spokesmen faced the complex issue of equality. Deeply rooted in the American ideology, the concept of equality was made concrete for Negroes by the first section of the Fourteenth Amendment, which draped over them the cloak of federal protection against discriminatory action by state governments. The union of the abstract idea with the mandate of the Constitution raised one more dilemma for the New South men. Anxious to justify their racial policies in a way that would offend neither the spirit of equality nor the requirement to make and enforce state laws in a nondiscriminatory fashion, they were committed by their racial beliefs to prevent what they called "fusion" or "amalgamation" and they believed that racial separation was essential to that purpose. This "duality," Robert Bingham asserted, "is an absolute necessity. The load of the country in the South must continue to be pulled by a double horse team, so to speak, with the white horse 'in the lead' and the black horse on the 'off side,' to use the farmer's phrase."[50]

Cable had agreed with Grady in opposing fusion, which he called "the maxim of barbarous times and peoples," but beyond that the two men found little common ground in their debate.[51] As Cable viewed it, the New South program, clearly "predicated on white supremacy," meant a catastrophic abridgment of human rights.[52] Its proponents regarded the Negro as an alien, a menial, and a reprobate, and allegations to the contrary were but poor attempts to disguise their true objectives. He believed that the New South prophets really intended to establish a caste system, almost as rigid in its denial of Negro rights as slavery had been. Already, he wrote, there was evidence to support his view, for there was "scarcely one public relation of life in the South" where the Negro was "not arbitrarily and unlawfully compelled to hold toward the white man the attitude of an alien, a menial, and a probable reprobate, by reason of his race and color."[53]

Vigorously challenging Cable's charge that they intended to abridge anyone's rights, the New South spokesmen made no attempt to deny their belief that inherent racial differences had to be recognized and accounted for in public policy. The Negro was an inferior being and no realistic program could ignore that fact. At the Dallas State Fair, Grady declared that God, not man, was responsible for the differences between the races. "Behind the laws of man . . . stands the law of God," he announced, and "what God hath separated let no man join together." The special characteristics of each race were divinely ordained and stood as "markers of God's will." No man, then, should "tinker with the work of the Almighty."[54] Of all God's races, Grady continued, the "Anglo-Saxon" had been designated to play the role of superior. Thus, the question before the South was "a race issue. Let us come to this point and stand here."[55]

Carried away by the enthusiastic response of his Dallas audience (they were in tears by the end of the address[56]), Grady lingered on the subject of Anglo-Saxon superiority. The quaintness of his logic was surpassed only by the eloquence of his delivery. The Chinese Exclusion Act, recently passed by Congress, was universally approved, he felt, not because the Chinese were ignorant or corrupt but because their admission in large

numbers would establish an "inferior" race in a "homogenous" country of Anglo-Saxons. At decisive points in
history, he continued, Anglo-Saxon blood had proved its
superiority. It "fed Alfred when he wrote the charter of
English liberty" and it had "humbled Napoleon at Water-
loo." The last boast had interesting implications for the
South which Grady did not pursue: the inference would
seem to be that the French, non-Anglo-Saxons, were
members of an "inferior," and therefore an "alien," race.
Presumably, he did not mean to cast aspersions on those
who traced their ancestry to William the Conqueror, nor
does it appear reasonable to believe that he would deny
"social equality" to the Legares and Hugers of Charleston; but he was certain that America had been "consecrated . . . forever as the home of the Anglo-Saxon, and
the theater of his transcending achievement," and that
challenges from an alien and inferior Negro race must
be understood and defeated.[57]

Anglo-Saxonism was a favorite subject of the New
South spokesmen, just as it was with other Southerners.
What the comments lacked in sophistication they made
up for in fervor. Tompkins declared that as long as there
was "any question as to race supremacy, our duty lies
first in saving for each State Anglo-Saxon control."[58]
Bingham wrote that the "Anglo-Saxon man, God's king
of men, will be and must be ahead of the African man
. . . and any forced change of the relations will be fatal
to the weaker race."[59] Throughout his long editorship of
the *Manufacturers' Record*, Edmonds repeatedly declared
his faith in the "superiority of the Southern people." He
believed the South to be "largely a homogenous population; Anglo-Saxon to a greater extent than any other
large center of the world," and Anglo-Saxonism, he

thought, was "a tremendous factor in the development of . . . [the South's] interests and in safeguarding its political affairs."[60]

Basing their justification of separate societies on the assumed superiority of the Anglo-Saxon "race," the New South spokesmen added a second argument designed to prove that Negroes, no less than whites, preferred segregation. This was the contention that both races had inbred instincts toward separation. Bishop Haygood explained that the Negroes created their own churches after the Civil War not out of fear or coercion, but in response to an inherent instinctive wish. "People who build theories out of facts," he wrote, "will study such a case as this."[61] Following Haygood's admonition, the New South spokesmen pictured a harmonious bi-racial society in which white and black mingled and cooperated in mutual tasks but separated otherwise. The "intelligent and self-respecting negroes," Grady wrote on one occasion, had not "the slightest symptom of a desire to push themselves forward into places where their presence would cause embarrassment or irritation, and the absence of such a desire is perfectly natural. It is the manifestation of the race instinct . . . and it is attended with not the slightest feeling of humiliation."[62] Putting the matter succinctly in a later editorial, he wrote that "the tendency of each race—white and black—is to gather about its own center. The force is centripetal, not centrifugal."[63]

The instinct argument was doubly useful to the New South spokesmen. On the one hand, it helped them to create their desired image of a rational and humane system that rested on consent, not force. It thus served to disguise the unilateral way in which Southern racial policies were determined and, at the same time, reassured suspicious Northerners that the New South's voluntary program of reconstruction looked to the Negro's interests. On the other hand, it made it easier for the whites to justify their desire to limit the areas of movement of Negroes and restrict contacts between the races. According to Grady, instinct performed the most essential function required in race relations: it was "the pledge of the integrity of each race, and of peace between the races. Without it, there might be a breaking down of all lines of division and a thorough intermingling of whites and blacks." Intermingling, he concluded, would lead to amalgamation and amalgamation to internecine warfare.[64]

As Grady defined the New South doctrine of race relations he wrote loosely of the relationship between racial "integrity," on the one hand, and "social equality," on the other. Neither term was ever clearly explained, but the Cable-Grady exchange in the *Century Magazine* and Grady's editorial comments on Cable make it evident that Grady saw no need to distinguish between constitutionally guaranteed civil rights and personal social privileges, lumping both together under the emotionally explosive rubric "social equality." Thus he reacted editorially to Cable's first *Century* article with vehemence, declaring that "we have for a long time feared that Mr. Geo. W. Cable would come to be a mischievous element in the negro problem. He has exhibited a growing wrongheadedness on this subject, that, starting from a rather sentimental admiration for the idealized quadroon, has developed into a confirmed negromania."[65] With only slightly less restraint, Grady wrote in his formal rebuttal that Cable's advocacy of equal civil rights was a demand that "white and black shall intermingle everywhere," a doctrine that Grady called "impossible," "mischievous," and "monstrous."[66]

Cable and a small group of other liberal writers, both white and black, strove energetically to disentangle the confused concepts of social privileges and civil rights and to dismantle the racist assumptions that underlay Grady's case for segregation. They believed that Southern actions, based on a faulty understanding of the real issues, increasingly tended to blunt the Negro's development and would therefore make impossible the realization of the New South dream. To begin with, they dismissed as irrelevant the issues of social equality and amalgamation. J. C. Price, a Negro educator, believed that history disproved the notion "that to grant a man his civil rights is to make him necessarily a social equal and companion." The poor whites of the South, Price observed, enjoyed their civil rights, but despite their "Anglo-Saxon" blood they were not accepted as social equals by the dominant class of whites. To assume that a similar enjoyment of civil rights by Negroes would lead to social equality, Price concluded, "implies too great a compliment to the Negro."[67] Cable called social equality the "huge bugbear" of Southern fears and continued with the argument that "amalgamation" of the races could most effectively be avoided by rigorous protection of civil rights.[68] He believed that there was little or no racial mixture in communities where Negroes were treated as first-class citizens but that in caste societies the opposite was true. In the South, he wrote, amalgamation took place "in proportion to the rigor, the fierceness, and the injustice with which . . . excommunication from the common rights of man has fallen upon the darker race."[69] Social equality and amalgamation, he concluded, were quite beside the point. "We are debating," he insisted, "the Freedman's title to a totally impersonal freedom in the enjoyment of all impersonal rights."[70]

Conceding that Negroes were, by nearly every accepted standard of measurement, inferior to the whites, Grady's opponents rejected the racial explanation of the inferiority. Lewis H. Blair, a white Virginian, dismissed as nonsense the notion of the divine ordination of segregation and argued that the Negro's lowly state was due to imposed circumstances that had "always been adverse to improvement."[71] Amory Dwight Mayo, whose general sympathy for the New South movement was keen, urged Southerners to view the plight of the Negro in the light of world history. He believed that such a perspective would show that the "defects" of the Negro were not "special race qualities." They could, in fact, be "paralleled by the immorality, ignorance, superstition, and helplessness" of oppressed groups of other races.[72] Cable claimed that Southern policy, based on faulty notions of race, tended increasingly toward compulsory segregation—at the "steamer landing, railway platform, theater, concert hall, art display, public library, public school, courthouse, church"—and thereby perpetuated the shortcomings allegedly the products of racial characteristics. It was like prohibiting a man from entering the water until he could swim; and the South, fearing that the Negro might learn, "hangs millstones about his neck."[73] Finally, George Henry White, the last Negro to represent North Carolina in Congress, told the House of Representatives that Southern racist views created a vicious circle out of which there appeared to be no escape:

It is easy for these gentlemen to taunt us with our inferiority, at the same time not mentioning the causes of this inferiority. It is rather hard to be accused of shiftlessness and idleness when the accuser of his own motion closes the avenues for labor and industrial pursuits to us. It is hardly fair to accuse us of ignorance when it was made a crime under the former order of things to learn enough about letters even to read the Word of God.

While I offer no extenuation for any immorality that may exist among my people, it comes with rather poor grace from those who forced it upon us for two hundred and fifty years to taunt us with that shortcoming.[74]

Except for the Northerner Mayo, none of the criticisms above came from New South spokesmen. But there were some members of the movement, notably Haygood, Page, and Watterson, whose views were more liberal than Grady's. For the most part, they regarded social equality as an unreal issue and they were less likely to confuse civil rights with social privileges. Watterson stated his support of equal civil rights on several occasions. He was doubtful about finding a way to "argue away or force down . . . the caste of color," but he wrote that "none more earnestly than the Courier-Journal desires to see this question happily settled."[75] In much stronger language, Page disagreed with the belief that the Negroes were a threat to the whites. "Our civilization menaced by the Negro?" Page asked. "That's a lie and you know it. The only way in which the Negro can be a menace to our civilization is by his ignorance."[76] Haygood wrote that he would not "entangle" his discussion "with the question of the relative capacity of the white and black races" and he found the debate over social equality quite pointless.[77] "There never was in this world, in any nation or community, such a thing as social equality, and there never will be," he wrote in 1889. "The social spheres arrange themselves to suit themselves, and no laws . . .

will change the social affinities and natural selections of men."[78] Both Haygood and Page emphasized the importance of character and training, in contrast to race. "If the negro be a bad man," Haygood wrote, "he is a constant menace to peace and good order. Neither more nor less a menace on account of his color, but a menace on account of his character." On the question of civil rights he was equally outspoken, stating bluntly that "the law does not know color or condition in its definitions; the administrators of the law should not know color."[79]

These qualifications of the Grady doctrine of permanent inferiority—and the recognition of "social equality" as an empty shibboleth—highlight an important aspect of the liberal, minority wing of the New South movement. However, these men agreed with Grady and the majority that the New South would be a dual society with the whites in the role of superiors. Whatever measure of equality the Negro might enjoy—and men like Haygood and Page foresaw more than Grady did— would derive in part from the fact that he was a free man but more significantly from the largesse and judgment of the more fortunate white rulers. Basing their judgments on practical considerations rather than on pseudo-scientific racial theories, the liberal wing, like the larger and louder Grady wing, assigned the Negro to an inferior status which would inevitably compromise his civil rights.

IV

Cable concluded his discussion of "The Freedman's Case in Equity" with the warning that "the South stands on

her honor before the clean equities of the [race] issue."
The moral issue—the question of honor—which Cable
believed lay at the heart of the debate was "no longer
whether constitutional amendments, but whether the
eternal principles of justice, are violated."[80] He despaired
for the future when he could no longer doubt that the
moral issue was being buried under layers of empty plati-
tudes. With a summary judgment of Grady's racial views,
he asked rhetorically: "Could any one more distinctly or
unconsciously waive the whole question of right and
wrong?"[81] The question drove to a sensitive nerve, for
the New South literature was permeated with pronouncements on right and wrong, justice and injustice. From a
variety of sources—dedication to the abstract ideas of
liberty and equality; a strong commitment to nationalism;
and a need to allay Northern suspicion—the New South
spokesmen developed an obvious concern to formulate a
critique of their racial program that would satisfy every
reasonable demand of justice and honor.

One aspect of their method derived from the growing
national dedication to pragmatism, a mode of thought that
came naturally to the New South prophets. The prag-
matist's stress upon the practical results of experience, as
opposed to abstract theoretical considerations, provided
a method of analysis that was admirably suited to the
complex moral situation which the race question created.
Haygood, for example, revealed this clearly when he conceded that segregation in public schools engendered a
"spirit of caste" among the whites and, in a strict sense,
compromised the full rights of Negroes. But these "theoretical" considerations could not stand alone as guides to
action and, in fact, they were offset by experiential knowledge which taught that separate schools were "best" for
both races. The "facts" were, Haygood wrote, that

"1. Southern white children, as a class, won't sit at the same desks with negro children; 2. Southern black children, as a class, don't want to sit at the same desks with white children." This mutual desire for unmixed schools, based on a sound knowledge of reality, should be honored, Haygood wrote, and should give "trouble to no soul of man, except to a small class of fanatics, who feel that all things human must yield to their fancies."[82] The lesson of the school house, as Haygood taught it, was applied by the New South spokesmen to other areas and it became their general guide to peace and prosperity. Negroes would recognize that they could not repeat the proven errors of the Reconstruction period and would cultivate a sense of patience rooted in the understanding that full citizenship could come to them only in a slow, evolutionary process built on tangible accomplishments.

Rising from the bottom—a hackneyed idea before Booker T. Washington immortalized it in 1895—was an essential concept in the New South doctrine, and what it implied fitted well into the pragmatic conception of justice that pictured the New South program as a realistic attempt to provide opportunity for Negro advancement after an era of misguidance. Men like Page could become rapturous when writing of the possibilities:

> To teach the Negro to read, whether English or Greek, or Hebrew, butters no parsnips. To make the Negro work, that is what his master did in one way and hunger has done in another; yet both of these left Southern life where they found it. But to teach the Negro to do skilful work, as men of all races that have risen have worked,— responsible work, which *is* education and character; and most of all when Negroes so teach Negroes to do this that they will teach others with a missionary zeal that puts all ordinary philanthropic efforts to shame,—this is to change

the whole economic basis of life and the whole character of a people.[83]

To "change the whole economic basis of life and the whole character of a people" was a tall order, but the New South spokesmen insisted that their realistic integration of the Negro into the new economic life of the region would do just that. Watterson expressed the faith in a pithy epigram. "Under the old system," he wrote, "we paid our debts and walloped our niggers. Under the new we pay our niggers and wallop our debts."[84] In the columns of the *Manufacturers' Record* Edmonds wrote frequently and optimistically about the reliability of Negro labor, its importance to Southern economic development, and the happiness the Negro found in his new opportunities. Negroes were not the "half-paid, half-starved people that some who have never been South have claimed," he wrote; and if the "cranky sentimentalists and the rascally politicians, both North and South, would let him alone to enjoy the fruits of his labor, he would continue happy and contented, and be what he is, the most important working factor in the development of the great and varied resources of our country."[85] Like Edmonds, Grady derided the "purely sentimental" friendship which Northerners expressed for Negroes and contrasted it with the realistic economic opportunities provided by the New South program.[86] He believed that the Negroes of Georgia, typical of all Southern Negroes, "are prospering and are contented," and argued that the material improvement in the life of the Negro honored the black man's ambitions and vindicated the good intentions of the Southern white.[87] A pragmatic evaluation, then, persuaded the New South spokesmen that the larger demands of racial justice were fulfilled by their program, and they dismissed with injured indignation Cable's allegation that the New South creed waived the issue of right and wrong.

To the more specific demands of the Fourteenth Amendment, the New South spokesmen had a response that satisfied their consciences and, after 1896, met the test of the Constitution as well. Grady marked out the lines of approach in an 1883 editorial, applauding the Supreme Court's decision in the *Civil Rights Cases*. Entitled "Where to Draw the Line," the editorial declared:

The line has been drawn just where it should be. Just where nature drew it, and where justice commends. The negro is entitled to his freedom, his franchise, to full and equal legal rights, to his share in the privileges of government and to such share in its administration as his integrity and intelligence will justify. This he ought to have and he must have. Social equality he can never have. He does not have it in the north, or in the east, or in the west. On one pretext or another he is kept out of hotels, theaters, schools and restaurants, north as well as south.

The truth is, the negro does not want social equality. He prefers his own schools, his own churches, his own hotels, his own societies, his own military companies, his own place in the theater. He is uncomfortable and ill at ease when he is forced anywhere else. Even on the railroads he prefers his own car, if he can be secure from the intrusion of disorderly persons. It is best, for his sake, as well as for general peace and harmony, that he should in all these things have separate accommodation.[88]

The formula that emerged from this editorial was expanded by Grady in subsequent writings and by 1885 it had an attractive name: equal but separate. Commenting editorially on Cable's first *Century* essay, Grady wrote that "the *Constitution* holds that there should be equal accommodation for the two races, but separate. . . . In every theater . . . there should be a space set apart for the colored people, with precisely the same accommodations that are given to the white people for the same price. . . . The same rule should be observed in railroads, schools, and elsewhere."[89] The distinction Cable made between social privileges and civil rights was ignored by Grady, who placed public schools and restaurants as well as street cars and literary clubs in the same category, recommending segregation in all of them and, in one of his last articles on the subject, "separate accommodation everywhere."[90]

In 1896 the United States Supreme Court formally announced its approval of the equal but separate doctrine in the case of *Plessy v. Ferguson.* The decision was restricted to legislation requiring separate facilities on the railroads, but its implications and its subsequent application to other types of segregation were a powerful vindication of the New South doctrine of racial equality within a framework of separate societies. Hammering out the logic of the decision for more than a decade before it was proclaimed by the Court, the New South spokesmen repeatedly emphasized their commitment to the "equal" part of the formula. As Grady put it in 1883, on the occasion of the *Civil Rights Cases* decision, the South would demonstrate that "while she could never have been driven by duress into doing what was clearly wrong . . . she will not be tempted by the removal of all restraint into doing anything that is less than right."[91] Separation, he declared later, would never mean unequal treatment or that the Negro was "outlawed" in the South.[92] Nor would it engender among Negroes a sense of debasement, for it resulted from the ineluctable force of "natural instinct," which the Negroes obeyed "without the slightest ill-nature or without any sense of disgrace."[93]

The racial creed of the New South spokesmen received a full hearing in the newspapers, national journals, and books of the time, and it was advanced with all the moral righteousness necessary to obliterate the vanishing tradition of abolitionism and radicalism and to implant in the national mind the image of a South that would guarantee to the Negro a lasting era of freedom, equality, justice, respect, and opportunity. With sympathy and understanding from the rest of the nation, Grady wrote, the South would bring its program to fruition. Then the race problem, which once threatened to destroy the South, would be seen as a blessing. Accusing fingers could no longer be pointed at the region. It would "stand upright among the nations and challenge the judgment of man and the approval of God, in having worked out . . . this last and surpassing miracle of human government."[94]

5
The Vital Nexus

> *Furl that Banner, softly, slowly!*
> *Treat it gently—it is holy—*
> *For it droops above the dead.*
> *Touch it not—unfold it never,*
> *Let it droop there, furled forever,*
> *For its people's hopes are dead!*
>
> —FATHER ABRAM RYAN[1]

Those who use the word [New South] do not thereby proclaim the history of the South discarded; do not confess themselves "unhung rebels," and that they are very sorry—nothing of the kind do they admit.

— JOHN C. CALHOUN NEWTON[2]

And no history is a matter of record; it is a matter of faith.

— JAMES BRANCH CABELL[3]

The New South spokesmen directed their program to the present and to the future; their purpose was to rectify the errors of the past. At the same time, they understood the attachment which bound Southerners to their historic memories and were aware of the swollen meaning that now inflated the Southern past as a result of defeat. The bitter quarrels that had divided Southern society during the war were stored in the attic of memory during the chastening aftermath of Appomattox, and a new unity of spirit emerged, expressing itself in a deep reverence for the old regime. At the very moment of its death, as Robert Penn Warren writes, "the Confederacy entered upon its immortality."[4] In this situation the New South spokesmen understood instinctively that no program of reform could do violence to a universally cherished past and hope to succeed.

With the death of an old way of life there came naturally to Southerners the conviction that the history of their region would forever be divided into two eras, separated by the war. Walter Hines Page grew up with this sense of the passage from one way of life to another. Dissecting his native North Carolina through the device of an autobiographical novel, he wrote that the death of his grandfather, who for him represented the Old South, made it appear that "the history of the world fell into two periods—one that had gone before, and the other that now began." When the old man was buried, Page recalled, "we seemed to be burying a standard of judgment, a social order, an epoch."⁵ This burial theme, combined with the sense of an unmistakable divide between the two eras, raised difficult problems for the New South spokesmen. How would they inter the past reverently, yet build a civilization drastically different from the old regime? How would they lead their people out of the ashes of one era into the glory of a new one without repudiating those very qualities which had caused the collapse of the Confederacy in the first place? How, in short, could they relate the New South creed to the values and aspirations of the past?

I

John Randolph Tucker, a proud, self-styled son of the Old Order, doubted that it could be done. Sharing his fears with the 1887 graduating class of South Carolina College, he declared: "You look to a future—a new future; I to the past—the old past. Have they no nexus? Is the New South cut off from the Old South? Is the past of our Southern land to be buried, and the new era to forget and wholly discard its memories, its ideas, and its principles?"⁶ Pleading for a remembrance of the old by the new, Tucker nonetheless appeared to fear the worst, and the subsequent notes of lament that he struck in his address were sounded again and again in the last two decades of the nineteenth century. Charles Colcock Jones, Jr., the colorful Georgian and bombastic president of the

Confederate Survivors' Association, assailed every annual gathering of veterans with copious illustrations of the undermining of Southern civilization put in process by the New South movement. "I call you to witness," he exhorted in his Memorial Day address of 1889, "that by false impressions and improper laudations of the new order of affairs, men in our midst have sought to minimize the capabilities of the past, and unduly to magnify the development of the present."[7] Under what he characterized as the "absurd guise of a New South," Jones alleged that the principles of the old regime were being swiftly discarded in favor of the mammonism of the New Order.[8] He pleaded for resistance to the onslaught; he would "covet a remembrance and an observation of the patriotism, the purity, the manhood, the moderation, and the honesty of the days that are gone."[9]

Writing at the end of the 'eighties, Tucker and Jones expressed no novel ideas but gave force and colorful imagery to a theme of doubt and despair that was already two decades old. Indeed, a dominant ingredient in the pattern of Old South idolatry which they expanded with such conviction had been forecast as early as 1866 by Edward A. Pollard, the Virginian whose Richmond *Examiner* achieved fame as a bitter critic of the Davis administration during the war. To a long, tedious, often opinionated history of the war, published in the year after Appomattox, Pollard gave the title *The Lost Cause*. Besides furnishing the name for what would become in time an obsessive Southern cult, Pollard concluded his history with a jeremiad that would echo through the next generation. "It is to be feared," he wrote, "that in the present condition of the Southern states, losses will be experienced greater than the immediate inflictions of fire and sword."[10] The greater losses were not, Pollard made clear, necessarily to be inflicted upon the South by a vengeful and victorious North. Rather, the danger was within. Speaking of his fellow Southerners, he warned:

> The danger is that they will lose their literature, their former habits of thought, their intellectual self-assertion, while they are too intent upon recovering the mere *material* prosperity, ravaged and impaired by the war. There are certain coarse advisers who tell the Southern people that the great ends of their lives now are to repair their stock of national wealth; to bring in Northern capital and labour; to build mills and factories and hotels and gilded caravansaries; and to make themselves rivals in the clattering and garish enterprise of the North. This advice has its proper place. But there are higher objects than the Yankee *magna bona* of money and display, and loftier aspirations than the civilization of material things. In the life of nations, as in that of the individual, there is something better than pelf, and the coarse prosperity of dollars and cents.[11]

Warning against those "time-servers" in the cause of material progress who would "fill their bellies with husks" while the traditions of the region were subverted, Pollard called for a "war of ideas" to recover and perpetuate the ideals of the old regime.[12]

The "war of ideas" for which Pollard called was devotedly waged by a small band of other champions of the Lost Cause in the years after Appomattox. Like Pollard, they found it impossible to conceive of a vital nexus between the ideals of the antebellum era and the emerging New South creed. Albert Taylor Bledsoe, the former University of Virginia professor whose writings

on slavery had earned him a prominent place in the ranks
of pro-slavery theoreticians, took up the editorship of the
Southern Review after the war to damn Yankee civilization.[13] A doctrinaire latter-day agrarian, he declared that
virtue and innocence sprang from close connection with
the soil. Industrialization, urbanization, and "materiality"
—which he designated as the "great defect of Northern
civilization"—undermined the spiritual character of the
people. The "whole spirit of Christianity," he felt, opposed Northern civilization; and for the South to enter
upon a fierce competition for industry would surely invite
the sacrifice of the "fine sense of honor which formed
the beautiful enamel of Southern character."[14]

Another Virginian, Robert L. Dabney, much respected
for his achievements and views as a religious leader, was
similarly depressed by a course of events which seemed
to him to repudiate the principles of the old regime.
Summing up the views he had held since the war, he
warned the students of Hampden-Sydney College in 1882
that a now-decadent country seemed to regard the principles of the Old South as "too elevated" to be of relevance
any longer. He would have the youth of the South think
otherwise. The most pernicious doctrine they could accept, he warned, was the notion that "the surest way to
retrieve your prosperity will be to BECOME LIKE THE CON-
QUERORS." The people who "make selfish, material good
its god," he declared, "is doomed."[15]

Bledsoe and Dabney and others who found the new
age uncongenial thus heaped abuse on what they considered to be the brutal materialism of Northern civilization and, ineluctably, they came to interpret the New
South movement as a new and sinister form of scala-
waggery: a profoundly misguided attempt to install the

god of Yankee civilization in the shaken temples of the land of purity. Thus, by the time Tucker and Jones and others were hurling their epithets at Grady and Edmonds and their allies, the notion of a bitter conflict between the principles of the Old and the New South was well established. According to this view, the progressive triumph of the ideals of the New South was premised upon the repudiation and annihilation of the values of the Old South.

The response which Pollard's somber augury of 1866 found in the years of the New South crusade created a historical tradition that survives in the works of twentieth-century scholars. In 1952, for example, the editors of an anthology of Southern literature declared that between 1870 and 1900 "there arose in the South two conflicting ideological groups" whose views were diametrically opposed.[16] These rival groups engaged in a contest whose essential nature two distinguished historians described as a difference "between those who looked to the past and those who looked to the future."[17] To many historians and especially to those who were part of the Vanderbilt Agrarian movement in the 1930's, those who looked to the future—the New South prophets—cast only glances of derision at a past which they condemned. Frank L. Owsley declared that the New South creed involved the "repudiation, more or less complete, of the Old South";[18] and Herman C. Nixon was persuaded that the " 'New South' came to imply that there had been an 'Old South' deserving of repudiation . . . and that a Southern economic revolution, entirely beneficent, had occurred without any evolutionary background."[19] Writing of the cotton mill development of the 'eighties, Robert S. Cotterill, the 1948 president of the Southern Historical Association, insisted that contemporaries, in their enthusiasm, "all agreed that it was new; it was a revolution, unrelated to the past, barren of ancestry, destitute of inheritance."[20] In a more recent and comprehensive judgment, William B. Hesseltine characterized the New South movement as one that would "abandon its past, forsake its rural folkways, and discard the romantic notions and constitutional theories which led to disastrous defeat—to build a new society on a Northern model."[21]

Two related themes appear in this thesis of a New South–Old South conflict. On the one hand, the New South spokesmen are depicted as realistic, hardheaded men of affairs who, wedded uncritically to nationalism and economic progress, abandoned romanticism, denied the existence of a treasured heritage, and determined to repudiate their past in order to clear the way for an industrial utopia of the future. On the other hand, they are described, with apparent logic, as men who saw neither nationalism nor industrial development in the Old South and therefore advertised their program as "barren of ancestry, destitute of inheritance." The two themes, united in an attractive thesis of total hostility between the old and the new, leave no room for interconnecting values and traditions.

The thesis misleads more than it enlightens. To be sure, it is true that the New South movement was vigorously opposed and that the Lost Cause mystique generally served as the rationale for the opposition. It is also possible to argue, depending upon what one considers to be central to the Southern experience, that the New South program, in its essence, implied the abandonment of critical Old South values. It is not true, however, that the New South spokesmen were, or considered themselves to be, detractors of the old regime. Neither evidence nor common sense will support such a view. On the contrary, one of the major and inescapable concerns of the New South advocates was to emphasize the "Southernness" of their movement and to romanticize the past out of which it came, to which it was related, and whose essential aspirations it was to fulfill.

The literature of the New South movement is permeated with a sense of the organic relationship between the old and the new. Out of this literature two complementary patterns emerge. First, the New South spokesmen fashioned an interpretation of the region's past that was congenial to the New South mentality; that is, they discovered in their history a heritage of nationalism and industrialism which, when properly understood, linked past, present, and future inseparably and harmoniously. Second, they almost invariably committed themselves to the romantic, idealized legend of the Old South—the same legend that was used by Tucker and Jones to excoriate them. Despite mutually exclusive aspects of the two views, most New South spokesmen found no difficulty in subscribing to both and, as will be seen, their double allegiance was crucial to their program.[22]

II

The hold of the Southern past on its sons, whether Old South idolaters or New South crusaders, is strikingly illustrated by a comparison of attitudes toward the old regime held by Northern and Southern advocates of a New South. Daniel A. Tompkins and William D. Kelley, two prominent spokesmen in the movement, shared identical views of the needs of the postbellum South. Both served the cause zealously, and when discussions were limited to the problems of the present one would find it difficult to determine which was the Southerner and which the Northerner. There was, however, a vital and illuminating difference between the two in their attitudes toward the old regime. Kelley, a Northerner whose sympathies had once been with the abolitionists, owed no emotional commitments to the region he proposed to save. He felt no pang of conscience, no reservations, no crisis of identity while developing a devastating critique of the old regime and broadcasting it throughout the South.[23] Tompkins, on the other hand, had roots in the plantation tradition and his emotional ties, whatever his economic theories, were with the land of his birth. A distant cousin of John C. Calhoun, Tompkins found much to admire in the early nationalism of the South Carolinian and often reminded his fellow Southerners that Calhoun, too, had once subscribed to the New South goals of industrialization and nationalism. Thus, while Tompkins happily shared Kelley's critique of the economic aspects of the Old South, he would not follow the Pennsylvanian into a condemnation of the moral values and intellectual qualities of his forebears.[24]

Like Kelley, the Northerner Alexander K. McClure, who made modest contributions to the New South movement, declared that "the Old South is dead. It has passed away; it is buried; it is forgotten."[25] But the Methodist bishop from Georgia, Atticus G. Haygood, ever reverent toward the past, could scarcely agree that "it is forgotten." To ask any Southerner, no matter how committed to change, to repudiate his past would be like asking New Englanders to prove their "intolerance of persecution by declaring Cotton Mather to have been a hypocrite and a villain."[26]

What the Southern leaders in the movement searched for, and quickly found, was a reading of the past which would prove conclusively that, in the words of the clergyman John C. Calhoun Newton, those who stood for a New South "do not thereby proclaim the history of the South discarded; do not confess themselves 'unhung rebels,' and that they are very sorry—nothing of the kind do they admit."[27] Such a historical formula would be of little interest to men like Kelley and McClure; indeed, they would probably consider it a little subversive. But, to the Southerners, it was both an emotional and a strategic necessity.

The formula was found readily enough in the economic history of the institution of slavery. The spread and solidification of slavery in the early nineteenth century, according to the New South view, had bottled up capital in land and slaves, and had precluded the development of manufacturing on a significant scale. Before the perfection of Whitney's cotton gin and the opening up of the lands of the southwest, Tompkins argued, the South was well on the way to a bright industrial future. The natural course of Southern development was disrupted by the "peculiar institution" which was, in Tompkins's opinion, responsible "for the frightful calamity that the South has suffered."[28] Manufactures, he argued, had no chance in the contest with slavery, for "apace with all the growth of the South the institution of slavery was also growing, and the falling off of the development of Southern resources may be observed to have kept pace with the growth of slavery." Once the incubus was removed, "the former spirit of enterprise" began to show itself.[29] By the turn of the century, when manufactures and commerce had once again been established as an integral part of the Southern economy, Tompkins declared that the South had simply returned to its true and ancient ways.[30] Repeatedly, in pamphlets and in the pages of its own journals as well as in Edmonds's *Manufacturers' Record*, Tompkins outlined his method of joining the past with the present: the antebellum years, the years of the spread and dominance of slavery, had been but an interregnum, an interruption of the true course of Southern history. Therefore, those who espoused the cause of industry in the South need feel no sense of repudiation; rather, they were the keepers of the older, authentic tradition.

Edmonds reiterated Tompkins's comments on the state of manufacturing in the early nineteenth century and he likewise stressed the limiting effects that slavery had on industrial development. On one occasion he characterized the role of slavery in the Old South in an analogy to a steam engine. Southerners had wished to utilize the steam engine, he explained, but the Negro slave was forever sitting on the safety valve. Ultimately, an explosion came, in the form of the Civil War and Reconstruction. The New South had not been satisfied with a patched-up engine; a new one was built, and "this engine is now running on a good track, no longer obstructed by the rocks of debt, a disorganized labor system, and all the unmasked problems, political and business, against which the old engine so often bumped."[31]

Unlike Tompkins, however, Edmonds was not inclined to regard the antebellum period as an interregnum, despite the pernicious effects of slavery. Rather, he found in the industrial crusade of the 1840's and 1850's a continuation of the earlier trend as well as the genesis of the postbellum New South movement. Striking off one of his numerous pamphlets, he complained that people of his generation were "too prone to believe that the Old South was a non-progressive, pastoral country." Such beliefs were responsible for the wickedly unfair characterization of the New South as a bastard offspring.[32] Actually, Edmonds wrote on another occasion, a true reading of history would show that the New South was simply "taking up the unfinished work of the Old South so rudely interrupted by the shock of war";[33] it was but seeking, through "vigorous" effort, "to regain the relative position held in 1860."[34]

Tompkins and Edmonds, each in slightly different ways, thus found the nexus between the Old and the New South and both men penned many lines contesting the allegations of repudiation hurled at them by disciples of the Old South. Addressing a pamphlet to the youth of the region, Edmonds warned them against falling in with the "sentiment so industriously cultivated" about the relationship between the Old and the New South. "We are told that the New South is a new creation altogether different from the Old South," he wrote; and, sounding the note of distress, he complained that "verily, we almost believe [it] . . . ourselves." Such teachings, Edmonds averred, were completely false—false alike to the past, "to the present and to the future."[35] "The South of today is no novel creation," he asserted in another pamphlet. "It is an evolution."[36]

One of Edmonds's favorite themes in the pages of the *Manufacturers' Record* was the doctrine of a "revived South." Insisting that the antebellum period had produced "the greatest business leaders of that generation," he could not understand why many men of his day saw in the New South movement a repudiation of the past.[37] In viewing the New South as an "evolution," or as "revival of the Old South,"[38] Edmonds helped to weave a pattern industriously worked by the other New South spokesmen. Grady found that the New South was "simply the Old South under new conditions."[39] Less well-known advocates agreed. One explained that the New South was "the old South asserting herself under a new dispensation," while a second spoke simply of the "Renewed South."[40] Whether renewed, rejuvenated, reborn, or the paradoxical "new," it was always the South; and allegations of alien influence and paternity were bitterly resented.

Walter Hines Page was one of the anomalies in the New South movement. His credentials as a New South spokesman were validated by the Vanderbilt Agrarians in the 1930's, who regarded him as an enemy of the Southern tradition more formidable than Grady. Certainly he was the most intellectually sensitive of the New South prophets. No one reading his bitter "Mummy Letters" would accuse him of dropping a veil of fancy over the Old South, and, as the disillusioned pages of his autobiographical novel show, he regarded the cult of the Lost Cause as a liability of the first order.[41] Yet, in his own special way, Page performed an intellectual operation on the Old South which, in its ultimate significance, served the same purpose as the Edmonds-Tompkins formula.

To Page, the South had abandoned the course of wisdom and justice when it jettisoned the philosophy of Jefferson and substituted the narrow views of Calhoun, Yancey, and Davis. The South of the Age of Jefferson,

Page believed, had been innocent of militant sectionalism
and sensitive to the problems of all its people, including
the slaves. It had also, of course, played a dominant role
in directing the fortunes of the nation. Disaster awaited
at the end of the road from Monticello, which the South
traveled from the 1820's onward. The Jeffersonian dream
was abandoned on the journey. Page's biographer recounts
the tragic contrasts which impressed themselves on Page's
sensitive mind:

> Instead of a system of free white labour, the extension
> of slavery; instead of public schools supported at State
> expense, a system of privately managed instruction,
> shabby and inadequate, usually in the control of religious
> sects; instead of a great body of intelligent citizens, more
> than a third of the white population unable to read and
> write. Thus had the South turned its back on its demo-
> cratic leader![42]

The about-face which Page now urged on Southerners
did not, according to his view of history, constitute a
repudiation of the Southern past. Like Tompkins, Page
could look upon the prewar years as an interregnum and
proclaim that the New South movement would vindicate
the authentic Southern tradition—the tradition of Jefferson. Moreover, like the other New South spokesmen,
Page did not urge, as some have alleged, that Northern
civilization serve as the South's exclusive guide. There
was plenty in the Southern past, he felt, to give sus-
tenance to his movement. He made this clear in an article
published early in his career. "The New South cannot build
up its possible civilization merely by looking backward
and sighing, nor yet by simply passing blindly forward

in the new paths that are now open." To achieve greatness the South needed to fuse reverence for the noble qualities of the past with "vigorous work for the future."[43]

The attempt of the New South spokesmen to link their movement with the Southern past thus involved the development of historical formulas to underscore the degree to which the South had once been both broadly nationalistic and economically progressive. Advanced on the eminently sensible grounds that internal opposition to the movement would diminish in proportion to the degree of "Southernness" that infused it, the argument muted the revolutionary aspects of the New South program. The South, its aspiring leaders realized, had had enough of revolutions; and no sane advocate of change wished to be cast in the role of a revolutionary.

III

One of the ironies of Southern history lies in the simultaneous rise during the 1880's of both the New South creed and the mythic image of the Old South. Sweet "syrup of romanticism," to use Professor Woodward's term, flowed over the Old South in the same decade that the New South spokesmen's ideal of a bustling, rich, and reconstructed South captured the American imagination.[44] Joel Chandler Harris introduced Uncle Remus to the general public in 1880 and Thomas Nelson Page's idyllic old Virginia became a national treasure after the publication of "Marse Chan" in 1884.[45] Grady's landmark address before the New England Society of New York was only two years later. To compound the irony, most of the New South spokesmen accepted the mythic view of the past, rarely failing to preface a New South pronouncement with warm praise and nostalgic sighs for the golden age that had passed. While Old South idolaters such as Charles Colcock Jones, Jr., shuddered with horror at the mention of the New South, its spokesmen showed no such single-mindedness, and the warm reception they gave the emerging legend further emphasizes the attempt to relate their movement to the values and aspirations of the past.

The legend of an Old South whose character was shaped by a noble plantation regime did not, of course, emerge unheralded in the 1880's. Its origins are in the antebellum period itself. In his illuminating study, *Cavalier and Yankee*, William R. Taylor shows that the myth-making first appeared shortly after the War of 1812. William Wirt's biography of Patrick Henry, published in 1818, was the most notable precursor of the later tradition. "It was a utopia set in the past," Taylor writes.[46] Wirt "constructed for himself exactly the kind of legendary Southern past into which successive generations of Southerners were to retreat in full flight from the problems of the present."[47] Wirt's preliminary work was overshadowed in importance in the thirty years before the war by polemics and novels, reflecting the increasing alienation of Southern thought from dominant American values and ideals. From Thomas Roderick Dew in the early 'thirties to George Fitzhugh in the mid-'fifties, Southern pro-slavery theorists lauded a stratified agrarian society in terms which they thought the ancient Greeks might have understood.[48] In fiction, John Pendleton Kennedy inaugurated the plantation tradition in 1832 by idealizing his own times and by presenting much of plantation life at its best.[49] "Doing so," remarks one historian of the plantation in literature, "he gave matter and method for a literary tradition."[50] The tradition was amply exploited by a host of other writers in the next thirty years.

The intensity of the abolition controversy led both defenders and opponents of slavery to enlarge and perpetuate the myth. The defenders, for obvious reasons, exaggerated the grandeur of their civilization, while the abolitionist assault had the ironic outcome of adding credibility to the myth. In drawing pictures of the horror of Southern society, abolitionists invariably had their dramas of exploitation played on enormous estates presided over by wealthy planters who lived life on the grand scale. The contrast between the opulence of the planter and the misery of the slave no doubt served the abolitionist purpose, but it also contributed to one of the rare points of agreement between Southerners and Northerners. As Francis Pendleton Gaines observes, the opponents in the slavery controversy "agreed concerning certain picturesque elements of plantation life and joined hands to set the conception unforgettably in public consciousness."[51] A half-century after Harriet Beecher Stowe outraged the South with *Uncle Tom's Cabin*, Joel Chandler Harris took puckish delight in telling a Northern audience that "all the worthy and beautiful characters in her book . . . are the products" of a slave society, while the "cruelest and most brutal character . . . is a Northerner."[52]

When the war came, both sides entered it with rival myths which succored them during the four years. The North's "Armageddonlike vision," Edmund Wilson writes, directed a "holy crusade which was to liberate the slaves and to punish their unrighteous masters." While Northerners saw themselves as acting out the

"Will of God," Wilson continues, Southerners undertook the equally noble cause of "rescuing a hallowed ideal of gallantry, aristocratic freedom, fine manners and luxurious living from the materialism and vulgarity of the mercantile Northern society."[53]

Neither myth, of course, died with the conclusion of the war. During the Reconstruction era, the rhetoric of the Northern press and the "bloody shirt" campaigns of victorious Republican politicians kept the vision of a holy crusade alive, although it became hopelessly tarnished as time passed. Curiously, however, Northern novelists began in 1865 to develop a theme of reconciliation that dominated fictional treatments of the war and paved the way for the later emergence of Southern writers on the national scene. Examining the works of fifty-five novelists who produced sixty-four civil war books between 1865 and 1880, Joyce Appleby writes that "for the Northerner who wrote a novel simply to entertain, forgiveness was the order of the day." The plantation romance, as it would appear in the 'eighties, was undeveloped in these works, but all of the later themes of honest misunderstanding, purity of motive, and the integrity of Southern civiliz⸱ ⸱n are present.[54]

The sympathetic mood cultivated by the Northern novelists was expanded by the Southern writers of the late 'seventies and 'eighties into a national love feast for the Old South. Southern authors began appearing regularly in the pages of the national periodicals in the mid-'seventies, in the wake of the enthusiasm created by Scribner's "Great South" series, a detailed and sympathetic description of the region by Edward King.[55] By 1881, the editor of Scribner's was noting that a recent number of the magazine had contained seven contributions by Southerners. Hailing the new contributors, he confidently announced that "a new literary era is dawning upon the South."[56] A decade later the same editor would report to Joel Chandler Harris the petulant query of a Northern author, "When are you going to give the North a chance!"[57]

The new development came as no surprise to Albion W. Tourgee, the carpetbag judge of North Carolina whose own fiction had a considerable following in the period. As early as 1865 he had predicted that, within thirty years, "popular sympathy will be with those who upheld the Confederate cause . . . our popular heroes will be Confederate leaders; our fiction will be Southern in its prevailing types and distinctively Southern in its character." Writing in 1888, Tourgee felt that his prediction had been more than borne out, seven years in advance of the deadline. "Our literature has become not only Southern in type," he declared, "but distinctly Confederate in sympathy." Poring over all the popular monthlies of recent issue, Tourgee could not find a single one without a "Southern story" as one of its most "prominent features."[58]

Thus it was that the romantic view of the Southern past achieved what Gaines calls a "complete conquest" in the 'eighties. An enormous number of authors, the most prominent of whom were Harris and Page, "fed to the public fancy some variety of the plantation material."[59] At the same time, the mythic view of the past was achieving the status of an inviolable shibboleth through other means as well. Schoolbooks and educational curricula carefully guarded the old memories. Religious imagery and political rhetoric were built on appeals to former glory. And numerous organizations devoted their full time to perpetuating the correct view of the past. To Jones' Confederate Survivors' Association there were soon added the United Daughters of the Confederacy, for women, and the United Confederate Veterans for men. All basked in the admiration shown them by *The Confederate Veteran*, a reverent journal established in Nashville in 1893 to represent the various memorial groups. One contributor to the *Veteran* stated simply what had now become the orthodox Southern view of the past:

> In the eyes of Southern people all Confederate veterans are heroes. It is you [the Confederate veterans] who preserve the traditions and memories of the old-time South— the sunny South, with its beautiful lands and its happy people; the South of chivalrous men and gentle women; the South that will go down in history as the land of plenty and the home of heroes. This beautiful, plentiful, happy South engendered a spirit of chivalry and gallantry for which its men were noted far and near.[60]

In the mythic image of a chivalric and gallant South there remained no traces of the corrupting influences once imputed by the abolitionists. The descendants of Garrison were ambushed after the war, and by 1880 nothing remained of the abolitionist tradition except the exaggerated accounts of plantation splendor. "Abolitionism was swept from the field," according to Gaines; "it was more than routed, it was tortured, scalped, 'mopped up.' "[61] Remaining was only the enchanting picture of a near-perfect society in which, as Thomas Nelson Page believed, "even the moonlight was richer and mellower . . . than it is now."[62] This rich and mellow moonlight beamed on a country studded with magnolias that offered sweet scents and a becoming background for beautiful maidens. The fathers of the maidens, invariably courtly, noble, and generous, presided over enormous plantations and thousands of lovable, amusing, and devoted slaves. Work was apparently infrequent and leisure was put to constructive and cultivating uses. During the numerous holiday seasons—and especially at Christmastime—the regal splendor of the regime was particularly brilliant, enriching the lives of both white and black. Patriarchal in the extreme—yet underneath wholesomely democratic—the stratified society provided precisely the right niche for each member: each fulfilled his true nature; none was dissatisfied.

The New South prophets had no objection to the beautiful maidens, but their program would amend or replace many other aspects of the civilization cherished in the myth. Whirring cotton mills and crimson blast furnaces were preferred to magnolias and moonlight; the factory with its hired hands was superior to the inefficient plantation; bustle and energy and the ability to "get ahead," rather than a penchant for leisure, should characterize the leadership of the New South. Grady made the difference clear when he told his New York audience: "We have sowed towns and cities in the place of theories, and put business above politics."[63]

Unmindful of paradoxes, the New South spokesmen subscribed with ardor to the mythical conception of the Old South. Grady expressed reverence for the "imperishable knighthood" of the old regime; he admired the leisure and wealth which gave to the Old South an "exquisite culture"; he praised the civilization that produced gentle women, honest and devout citizens—all in that dreamlike time when "money counted least in making the social status." On another occasion, he referred to the sea-island plantations of Georgia as "royal homes: . . . principalities in area, dukedoms in revenue." The man who promised an industrial utopia to his own generation could say of the past that "the civilization of the old slave *regime* in the South has not been surpassed, and perhaps will not be equaled, among men."[64] The reciprocal love between master and slave, a basic foundation on which the society rested, was a thing of beauty which came into glorious blossom during the South's great testing time. Speaking before a group of Boston merchants, Grady related a "vision" of the war:

> The crisis of battle—a soldier struck, staggering, fallen. I see a slave, scuffling through the smoke, winding his black arms about the fallen form, reckless of the hurtling death—bending his trusty face to catch the words that tremble on the stricken lips, so wrestling meantime with agony that he would lay down his life in his master's stead.[65]

Edmonds, among the most versatile of the New South leaders, crusaded tirelessly for the industrial order of his day, traced a continuity of development from the Old to the New South, and urged upon his fellows the romantic view of the old regime. He would never want Southerners to forget, he wrote, "to hold in tenderest reverence the memory of this Southern land; never forget to give all honor to the men and women of ante-bellum days; remember . . . that the Old South produced a race of men and women whose virtues and whose attainments are worthy to be enshrined not only in every Southern, but in every American heart."[66] Moreover, in the midst of the South's industrial development, he warned Southerners never to let it be said "that in the struggle for industrial advancement the South has lost aught of the virtues, domestic and public, aught of the manliness and self-reliance, aught of the charms of her women and the honor of her men which hallow the memory of the Old South."[67]

By the turn of the century, as these examples suggest, it caused no embarrassment for New South prophets to espouse the creeds of both the Old and the New South. A North Carolina bank president was typical of the New South accommodation of both creeds when he began an address before the American Bankers' Association by paying reverential homage to the Old South before praising the New. "Prior to the civil war," the talk began, "our Southern land . . . was the home of culture and refinement. With thousands of slaves to cultivate their broad acres, our people lived in ease and plenty."[68]

The allegiance given to the myth of the Old South by the propagandists for the New Order is in itself evidence of the extent to which the romantic view prevailed in the South. Further evidence is found in unsuspected places, the most notable of which is in the writings of Booker T. Washington. Normally, one would not expect the most influential champion of Negro freedom of his generation to contribute to a romanticized view of the slave regime into which he had been born. And, of course, there are many aspects of Washington's picture of the Old South which do not harmonize with the Thomas Nelson Page version. Washington's picture differed from the stereotype in his emphasis on the miserable living conditions of the slaves, the torturous flax shirt, the unpalatable rations, and the absence of the kind of "civilized" living that he was later to champion. Important, too, is his contention that the slaves he knew understood and desired freedom, receiving it first with great jubilation and later with a sobering sense of responsibility.[69]

However, much of Washington's picture resembles the stereotyped version. He stresses the loyalty of the slaves to their masters and insists that it was based on a genuine love. When young "Mars' Billy" died there was great sorrow in the quarters and it "was no sham sorrow but real." There is no sense of resentment, and when emancipation brought hard times to a former master the slaves rallied and stood by him in his adversity. Washington explained that "nothing that the coloured people possess is too good for the son of 'old Mars' Tom.' "[70] One is reminded of Irwin Russell's famous lines which began by extolling the virtues of "Mahsr John" and conclude:

> *Well, times is changed. De war it come an' sot de niggers free,*
> *An' now ol' Mahsr John ain't hardly wuf as much as me;*
> *He had to pay his debts, an' so his lan' is mos'ly gone—*
> *An' I declar' I's sorry for my pore ol' Mahsr John.*[71]

Washington's account of Reconstruction is equally congenial to the romantic version. In his autobiography he includes the standard comic view of the newly freed Negro, stating that the principal crazes were for Greek and Latin and public office. He is critical of the precipitous way in which the Negro was pulled up from the bottom rung of society, and he has harsh words to say about Negro preachers, teachers, and politicians. Most important of all is what is not said: nowhere in *Up from Slavery* does one find an indictment of the native white Southerners' behavior during Reconstruction. The Negro suffered in the end, Washington felt, in large part because "there was an element in the North which wanted to punish the Southern white men by forcing the Negro into positions over the heads of Southern whites."[72]

IV

The commitment of both black and white New South prophets to the romantic view of the past was not made without purpose. To some extent, to be sure, there was no alternative for many of them, for their own emotional requirements as well as the need for public acceptance dictated that they operate within the intellectual framework of the time and place in which they lived. But however compelling the emotional and strategic considerations may have been, they were matched in appeal to the New South spokesmen by several concrete, useful functions which the myth of the Old South could perform in the cause of the New South movement. Washington, as will appear in the next chapter, had special reasons for mythmaking. The white leaders in the movement quickly perceived and ably exploited the benefits that the myth offered them. For one thing, they would not have agreed with those later historians who saw the romantic legend exclusively as a source of fruitless ancestor worship and rancorous sectionalism. On the contrary, a close examination shows that it was nationalism rather than sectionalism, an identification rather than a separation, of interests that emerged as benefactors of the myth.

The triumph of the romantic legend in the North in the 'eighties was essential to this result. Once before, in the antebellum period, the Southern mythmakers had found allies in the North, although the Yankee authors of the Southern myth were a distinct and largely uninfluential minority in their society. Several Northern writers, disturbed by a rapid social mobility and an accelerating materialism which produced, in Taylor's words, "glowing optimism and expectations of a secular millennium," consciously cultivated the plantation theme to bare the disquieting developments in their own region. To them, the culture of the South had "many of the things which they felt the North lacked: the vestiges of an old-world aristocracy, a promise of stability and an assurance that gentility—a high sense of honor, a belief in public service and a maintenance of domestic decorum—could be preserved under republican institutions."[73] In the New South era similar doubts caused some of the North's finest writers to use the Southern romance to damn the excesses of the Gilded Age. Woodward has recently called attention to the fact that Herman Melville, Henry Adams, and Henry James each wrote works which included a Confederate veteran who "serves as the mouthpiece of the severest stricture upon American society or, by his actions or character, exposes the worst faults of that society." These three authors, Woodward writes, detested the "mediocrity, the crassness, and the venality they saw around them," and they found the Southerner "a useful foil for the unlovely present or the symbol of some irreparable loss."[74]

To most Northern writers and readers of the 'eighties and 'nineties, however, the commitment to the romantic legend masked few disturbing social thoughts and stemmed from simple needs. According to Gaines, the Northerner had a romantic, innate "love of feudalism"

and a yearning to identify vicariously with aristocratic
societies. The plantation, "alone among native institutions," he continues, satisfied "this craving for a system
of caste."[75] Both the craving and the myth that satisfied
it continued long beyond the years of the New South
movement. Gunnar Myrdal, noting the enduring fascina-
tion of the American with the romantic legend, wrote
in 1944:

> The North has so few vestiges of feudalism and aris-
> tocracy of its own that, even though it dislikes them
> fundamentally and is happy not to have them, Yankees
> are thrilled by them. Northerners apparently cherish the
> idea of having had an aristocracy and of still having a
> real class society—in the South. So it manufactures the
> myth of the "Old South" or has it manufactured by
> Southern writers working for the Northern market.[76]

The complex strands that wove together the myth of
the Old South—alienation of the Southerner from national
values and ideals in the antebellum period; alienation of
a few Northerners, both before and after the war, from
the strident pace of material progress; innocent love for
another, grander civilization on the part of most—did not
obscure for the New South spokesmen the incalculably
valuable service it could perform in the cause of sectional
reconciliation, a basic tenet of the New South creed.
If the myth in antebellum days had bespoken alienation
on the part of Southerners from national ways, in the
postbellum period it worked in precisely the opposite direction, uniting the two sections. To the South it gave
a vitally necessary sense of greatness to assuage the bitter
wounds of defeat; to the North it offered a way in which
to apologize without sacrificing the fruits of victory.

Henry Grady has always been regarded as the chief peacemaker among the New South spokesmen, but Joël Chandler Harris, his friend and colleague on the Atlanta *Constitution*, served the reconciliation cause in a more subtle and perhaps more effective manner. Many of Harris's stories are unmistakable attempts to heal sectional wounds and unite former enemies. While Grady was serving the cause as the ever-available orator, the shy Harris worked quietly in the background through Uncle Remus.

How Harris served the cause of reconciliation—and, in a larger sense, how the plantation literature promoted national identification of interests—is tellingly illustrated in the comparison of two versions of one of Harris's early stories. The original version appeared in the *Constitution* in 1877 under the title "Uncle Remus as a Rebel: How He Saved His Young Master's Life."[77] The second version, entitled "A Story of the War," appeared in the first of Harris's books, *Uncle Remus: His Songs and His Savings*, published late in 1880.[78] The plot is similar in both stories. Uncle Remus saves his young master from certain death by shooting a Yankee sniper. In both stories Remus thinks only of his love for his master and mistress. He knew the Yankee was there to free him, but when he saw what was going to happen he "des disremembered all 'bout freedom" and pulled the trigger.[79] In the first version, that intended for relatively local consumption, the Yankee is killed. In the second telling, however, Harris is aware of his national audience. Here the sniper loses an arm, but not his life. He is nursed by Remus and Miss Sally, the plantation belle, regains his health, and wins the hand of his lovely nurse. Clearly, the second version reveals Harris consciously courting the North, as John

Stafford points out, by demonstrating that "a Yankee is good enough to join the Southern aristocracy." Moreover, "the North and the South are symbolically wed; and the North accepts the paternalistic pattern. Thus is the patron flattered and at the same time the self-respect of the South retained."[80]

The intersectional marriage, symbol of reconciliation, was a standard device used by Southern writers of the period. Harris used it to good effect again in "Aunt Fountain's Prisoner." Aunt Fountain, the plantation mammy, says of the Yankee bridegroom: "He ain' b'long ter we-all folks, no furder dan he my young mistiss ole man, but dee ain' no finer w'ite man dan him. No, suh; dee ain'." Cheered by this judgment, New South readers both North and South must have been pleased also to read that this Yankee revived the sagging fortunes of the old plantation by a stern application of "vim and vigor," New South qualities *par excellence*.[81] Thus, as Harris would have it, the marriage of a Yankee to a Southern belle, lovely flower of the old regime, excited Northern sympathy and admiration for the honorable qualities of Southern life and, at the same time, showed Southerners that their future would be prosperous if new concepts of work and organization were accepted.

The role of the Negro and of race relations was of special importance in the romantic legend and, in persuading the North to view the "quaint darky" through Southern eyes, the mythmakers accomplished at least two important results. First, by convincing Northern readers that relations between the races were kindly and mutually beneficial a principal obstacle in the way of sectional harmony was removed. The North had doubted this point, but on the authority of Harris and others it came to accept the Southern point of view.[82] Second, the acquiescence by the North in the Southern scheme of race relations permitted the South to deal with (or to fail to deal with) its race problems unmolested.

Humor was a standard and effective device used by Southern writers to mollify the Northern conscience, for, as Sterling Brown caustically observes, "if the Negro could be shown as perpetually mirthful, his state could not be so wretched."[83] In a more sophisticated vein, Stafford comments that Harris's use of ironic comedy invariably produced the "understanding laugh" which gave emotional release from doubts and guilt feelings and induced whites to tolerate what otherwise would appear to be an evil situation. The "pure humor" of Uncle Remus, then, won "acceptance for the existing class harmony."[84] To humor there was added the element of the essential difference between white and black, the image of the Negro as an exotic primitive, as

> *Original in act and thought,*
> *Because unlearned and untaught.*[85]

To make the ideal of blissful race relations a convincing one, the humorous and primitive Negro is, in hundreds of contemporary stories, the guardian of the old memories and traditions. Far from resenting his life under slavery he finds freedom uncongenial—"I wants ter git shet er dis heah freedom," exclaims a Negro who was freed by his master before the war[86]—or at least not as satisfactory as the "old days," and to every passerby he recounts the glories of yesteryear. Tourgee designated this stereotype the "poor 'nigger' to whom liberty has brought only misfortune, and who is relieved by the disinterested friendship of some white man whose property he once was."[87] In Page's "Marse Chan" and "Unc' Edinbrug's Drowndin'," two of the Virginian's most famous tales, it is the former slave who tells the story, glorifies the past, and laments its passing.[88] In one of Harry Stillwell Edwards's stories the old mammy lives out her years in sight of the grave of her mistress, where she may better preserve the memory of happier days.[89] The longing for the past is everywhere expressed. Old Sam, the faithful body servant in "Marse Chan," declares "Dem was good ole times, marster—de bes' Sam ever see."[90] Chad, the loyal servant in Francis Hopkinson Smith's novel of the Virginia gentleman, feels likewise: "Dem was high times. We ain't neber seed no time like dat since de war."[91] And, in one of the poems of Miss Howard Weeden, the old Negro feels that

> *I ought to think 'bout Canaan, but*
> *It's Ole Times crowds my mind,*
> *An' maybe when I gits to Heaben*
> *It's Ole Times dat I'll find!*[92]

Behind the façade of this pleasant fable of Negro happiness and devotion in the regime of slavery there were, of course, harsh realities. Tourgee admitted that there were some real examples upon which the stereotype was built, "but they are not so numerous as to destroy the charm of novelty." About the Negro "as a man, with hopes, fears, and aspirations like other men," he wrote, "our literature is very nearly silent." Moreover, as John M. Webb observes, "the fable applies only to the house slaves who had intimate contact with the whites."[94] But, as the legend would have it, the pleasant state of affairs was a general, not a particular or isolated, characteristic of antebellum life.

The generality of the situation, of course, was meant to apply to the postwar years as well as to the slavery regime. In addition to promoting sectional reconciliation and, in further removing the North from agitation of the race question, the image of the happy Negro helped to destroy one of the burdensome obstacles in the way of Northern investments in the South. Northern capitalists constantly complained of the unsettling conditions in the South stemming from racial friction. To the New South spokesmen it seemed clear that friction would disappear and capital come rolling in once the race question were left entirely up to Southern determination. This is what Tompkins meant when he wrote that "an excess of zeal in the cause of freedom" on the part of Northerners could serve no useful purpose and was, in the long run, to the disadvantage of the Northern capitalists themselves.[95] The myth of the Old South, with its charming picture of the lovable and loving Negro, served well to jettison the zeal which Tompkins felt was rocking the boat.

Finally, in the South itself the romance of the past was used to underwrite the materialism of the present. The names and signatures of Confederate generals were everywhere in demand by railroad companies and corporations, for the New South prophets were well aware that the blessing of a "colonel" (if there were no generals handy) would do as much to float bonds and raise subscriptions as a dozen columns of optimistic statistics in the *Manufacturers' Record*. In *Colonel Carter of Cartersville*, a successful third-rate novel of the period, one of the characters observes wisely that "in a sagging market the colonel would be better than a war boom."[96] The marriage of the gentle life of the past and the bustling era of the present was perhaps nowhere better symbolized than in the advertising columns of that journal of worship, *The Confederate Veteran*. There one learned that Confederate flags could be purchased from a New York firm and the aspiring capitalist found notices of potentially prosperous factories up for sale.[97]

V

The several specific uses to which the mythic conception of the Old South were put to serve the needs of the New South movement help to make intelligible the paradoxical commitment of the New South prophets to the legendary romance. Professor Woodward, in his skeptical assessment of the movement, feels that the "bitter mixture of recantation and heresy" which infused the New South creed "could never have been swallowed so readily had it not been dissolved in the syrup of romanticism."[98] But the sugar coating of the pill of the New Departure, important though it was, does not fully account for the phenomenon of mythmaking. More profound, more universal and less tangible forces were at work as well. Henry James suggested some of these when he wrote:

> The collapse of the old order, the humiliation of defeat, the bereavement and bankruptcy involved, represented, with its obscure miseries and tragedies, the social revolution the most unrecorded and undepicted, in proportion to its magnitude, that ever was; so that this reversion of the starved spirit to the things of the heroic age, the four epic years, is a definite soothing salve.[99]

That there were deep wounds whose treatment required a soothing salve is abundantly clear. The South had so irrevocably committed its soul to the war that when defeat came it was more than a surrender of ambitions for independence; it was a crippling blow to the most basic assumptions upon which life in the region was lived. Pride and hope were destroyed by defeat, and humiliation was added by the Reconstruction. Under the circumstances, the search for self-confidence and a return of pride quite naturally involved more than a program of building on the ashes. Somehow the ashes themselves had to be ennobled. The myth worked powerfully to achieve this purpose: it gave back those very things which the Yankee had tried to take away—the knowledge of a proud past and a noble heritage. Without that knowledge, Grady once remarked, "the New South would be dumb and motionless."[100]

The search for a noble past, like the attempt to discover a heritage of nationalism and industrialism, engaged Southerners in an emotional and intellectual quest common to other people in other times. Nations that have been either victimized or blessed by profound social upheaval have commonly undergone, in one way or another, the experience of replanting the bared roots to the past; of developing the mythmaking process to satisfy collective needs. And for Southerners of the New South era, should they be charged with distortion of the past, their reply might be, with the Virginia novelist James Branch Cabell, that "no history is a matter of record; it is a matter of faith."[101]

6

The Emperor's New Clothes

What a pull it has been! Through the ashes and desolation of war—up the hill, a step at a time, nothing certain—not even the way! Hindered, misled, and yet always moving up a little until—shall we say it?—the top has been reached, and the rest is easy! . . . The ground has been prepared—the seed put in—the tiny shoots tended past the danger-point—and the day of the mighty harvest is here!

—HENRY W. GRADY, 1889[1]

Twenty-odd years ago . . . I fondly imagined a great era of prosperity for the South. . . . I saw in anticipation all her tribulations ended, all her scars healed, and all the ravages of war forgotten, and I beheld the South greater, richer and mightier than when she moulded the political policy of the whole country. But year by year these hopes, chastened by experience, have waned and faded, until now, instead of beholding the glorious South of my imagination, I see her sons poorer than

when war ceased his ravages, weaker than
when rehabilitated with her original
rights, and with the bitter memories of the
past smouldering, if not rankling, in the
bosoms of many.

—LEWIS H. BLAIR, 1889[2]

The Emperor took off all his clothes, and the
impostors pretended to give him one
article of dress after the other of the new
ones which they had pretended to make.
They pretended to fasten something around
his waist and to tie on something. This
was the train, and the Emperor turned
round and round in front of the mirror.

"How well His Majesty looks in the new
clothes! How becoming they are!" cried
all the people round. "What a design, and
what colors! They are most
gorgeous robes."

"The canopy is waiting outside which
is to be carried over Your Majesty in the
procession," said the master of the
ceremonies.

"Well, I am quite ready," said the
Emperor. "Don't the clothes fit well?" Then
he turned round again in front of the
mirror, so that he should seem to be looking
at his grand things.

—from ANDERSEN'S *Fairy Tales*[3]

Allegiance to both the myth of the Old South and the dream of a New South was but one of several contradictions imbedded in the New South creed. There were many others: an institutional explanation of industrial backwardness in the Old South coupled with the faith that natural resources could not help but assure industrialization in the New; an elaborate propaganda campaign to attract immigrants into the region negated by hostility to the immigration pool easiest to tap; a gospel of economic interdependence and reconciliation with the North as part of a campaign for independence and domination; a lauding of freedom for the Negro in a politics of white supremacy; dreams of equal treatment of allegedly unequal races in separate societies devoted to mutual progress—these are among the most obvious.

Rich in paradoxes, the New South creed also had an ironic outcome. Designed to lead the region out of poverty, it made converts by the thousands in all parts of the country of men who looked forward confidently to a South of abundance. Instead, the expectations were unrealized and the South remained the poorest and economically least progressive section of the nation. The plans for regional and personal success, the restoration of self-confidence, and a position of influence and respect in the nation likewise fired the imagination and gained legions of adherents, but they too were largely unfulfilled and at the end of the New South crusade the region found itself in the uncomfortable, if familiar, role of a colonial dependent. Rid of many of the humiliating frustrations of the early postwar years, it was saddled with new ones that had greater staying power. Finally, the dream of a just and practical solution to the race question appealed to former abolitionists and radicals as well as to long-time racists because it promised that justice and practicality could be balanced, that Southerners themselves could do what Yankee reformers had failed to do, and that a harmonious biracial society would emerge and permit Americans to forget about injustice to the black man. Instead, violence increased in the 'eighties, and disfranchisement and rigid segregation followed later as the Negro reached the nadir of his history as a free man.

Unable to bequeath to the next generation of Southerners a legacy of solid achievement, the New South spokesmen gave them instead a solidly propounded and widely spread image of its success, a mythic view of their own times that was as removed from objective reality as the myth of the Old South. In creating the myth of the New South, they compounded all of the contradictions originally built into their creed, added others, and crowned their professions of realism with a flight of fantasy.

I

In the early stages of its development, the New South idea was essentially a program of action. It promised the future but was candid in its discouraging evaluation of the present. In fact, one of the most important arguments of the New South advocates in the early years was based on a frank and distressing contrast between the South and other parts of America. The contrast gave birth both to the method and the purpose of the program. Never doubting the vitality of the human resources, and convinced of the superiority of natural ones, the New South spokesmen believed that by adopting the ways of the industrial age in the same way other Americans had done their dream would be realized. That dream was essentially a promise of American life for the South. It proffered all the glitter and glory and freedom from guilt that inhered in the American ideal. Sloughing off those characteristics which had marked him as poor, quarrelsome, unprogressive, guilt-ridden, and unsuccessful, the Southerner would—if he heeded the New South prophets—become the American he was entitled to be: prosperous, successful, respected and admired, confident of the future.

In 1880 Atticus G. Haygood declared that the New South meant, above all, that a time would come when "the words 'the South' will have only a geographical significance."[4] He foresaw the end of sectionalism and the integration of the South into the mainstream of American progress. Much remained to be done, Haygood felt, and he predicted that it would take at least twenty years for the New South program to succeed. By 1886, however, Grady was rapturous and confident in declaring to his New York audience that the South had "wiped out the place where Mason and Dixon's line used to be."[5] Elsewhere in the same address, and increasingly in the statements of Grady and other New South prophets, their program began to assume the solidity of accomplished fact. Almost imperceptibly at first the promotional strategy changed from the original emphasis on the gap separating accomplishment from ambition to a parade of "facts" that proved the rapidity with which the gap was being closed. As the strategy changed, a bewildering mixture of fact and fancy, wish and reality, emerged. Writing early in 1887, Wilbur Fisk Tillett, a theologian from Vanderbilt, declared "that such a marvelous advance has been made in the South in the last ten years as has rarely been made in any country or in any part of any country in an equally limited period in the history of the world." The New South, which had first "showed itself in 1880," had by 1886 "proved its name by evidences so powerful and convincing that only the blindest can fail to see them."[6]

As if to prove their clear vision to Tillett, an astonishing number of writers testified to Southern advance; and if proclaiming it to be could make it so, the South after the mid-'eighties was no longer the poverty-stricken, despondent region of old. Charles Dudley Warner reported in 1886 that the South was in the throes of a mighty "economical and political revolution" whose story would be "one of the most marvellous the historian has to deal with."[7] A year later he wrote that in the "New Industrial South the change is marvellous, and so vast and various that I scarcely know where to begin in a short paper." The region as he saw it was "wide-awake to business, excited and even astonished at the development of its own immense resources."[8] Pronouncements from Northern friends like Warner were always especially welcomed and frequently quoted by the New South spokesmen. Kelley was aware of this when he added to his own glowing descriptions of the region the remarks of James M. Swank, general manager of the American Iron and Steel Association. According to Swank the South had "experienced in 1886 a new birth." Proof of this signal event, he wrote, could be seen in any set of industrial statistics as well as in the fact that "even its own journals and public men now speak of it as the New South." The New South child, Swank concluded, was on the verge of achieving "those beneficent industrial results which have made the North so rich, so prosperous, and so aggressive."[9]

Like the Northerners, Grady's friend Marion J. Verdery wrote in 1887 of the "blessed dawn" that brought "new strength, new hope, new energy, and new life, all of which combined in sacred pledge to make the New South."[10] But it was Grady himself who played the most important part in creating the image of a dynamic and successful movement, and in his editorials one can trace the evolution of the process. A few selections will illustrate the transition from a mood of optimism in 1881 to a declaration of triumph in 1886. Reviewing business failures over the previous two years, Grady wrote in the summer of 1881 that, despite the rise in failures that year, "the business of the southern states is now considered sound and promising." The next summer he was happier with his review of recent developments. The agricultural outlook had never been as good and "never before has the material development of Georgia made such rapid progress as during the last twelve months." The mood continued unabated, and at the end of the summer of 1883 he wrote that "very few of us know how rapidly the south is progressing in a material sense. We know that we are getting on well, but we have not taken time to set down and measure the pace or the extent of the recuperative process." Without such measuring, however, it was clear that "the situation is altogether hopeful."[11]

By the end of 1884 it was clear to him that the optimism of the previous years was well founded and that an even more confident position was warranted. "This section is rapidly filling up with manufactories," he wrote, "and industry and enterprise in all forms and shapes are making the south their headquarters, and they have come to stay." In the summer of 1885 he took note of a recession but declared that hard times were not "enough to stop southern enterprise." He then reviewed a set of optimistic reports in the *Manufacturers' Record* and concluded that they showed "a remarkable degree of industrial activity in the south." A year later he was again relying on Edmonds, whose survey of the region led him to remark that "if the most enthusiastic southerner is not satisfied with this bird's-eye view of the progress of his section, he must be one of the impracticables. It seems to us that we are entering upon an almost ideal era of progress." By the end of the year, on the eve of his journey to Delmonico's, he was certain that he had been right: "a tidal wave of prosperity is rushing over this region," he announced, "and we must prepare to size it up and utilize it."[12]

From the time he spoke to the New England Society of New York, in December 1886, until his death three years later, Grady's typical comments, in both editorials and speeches, emphasized the marvel of Southern achievement. To one audience he explained that "the Eldorado of which I have told you" sprang inevitably from the South's monopoly of "the three essential items of all industry—cotton, iron and wool." From this "assured and permanent advantage" there had developed "an amazing system of industries."[13] After reciting the funeral tale to the Boston Bay State Club, he noted that great changes had occurred since his fellow Georgian had been dispatched to his grave so unceremoniously attended by the fruits of Southern industry. Twenty years after the burial

Georgia could boast the biggest marble-cutting establishment in the world in addition to a half-dozen woolen mills in the immediate vicinity of the grove in which the man was put to rest. In the same speech, Grady told of a friend who had returned from the war without a pair of pants to his name. His wife sewed trousers out of an old dress, and with five dollars the man bought old timber with which he built a shack. Now, twenty years later, the same man had a large wardrobe and a good home. He was typical of the whole of Georgia, Grady concluded, for "we have prospered down there."[14] Finally, in one of his last speeches, he reviewed the South's struggle against poverty, the carefully laid plans for a society of abundance, and finished with the good news that "the day of the mighty harvest is here!"[15]

The only New South spokesman whose superlatives were even more extravagant than Grady's was the indomitable Edmonds. Devoting his journal almost exclusively to the promotion of the economic development of the South, Edmonds ground out endless statistics embellished with hortatory comments to support his claim that the region was "throbbing with industrial and railroad activity" and that capitalists "in Europe and America are looking to the South as the field for investment." In 1890 he published a pamphlet called *The South's Redemption*. Revealingly subtitled "From Poverty to Prosperity," it furnished other New South writers with highly quotable copy and summed up the theme of a feverish period of propagandistic activity of the *Manufacturers' Record*.[16]

Between 1886 and 1890 Edmonds never veered from his mission of substantiating the double claim that the South's future was brilliant and that its present was unrivaled. In the same month that Grady spoke in New

York, Edmonds wrote that "never before probably in the history of this country has there been such an era of industrial development as we now see in the South." Every "click of the telegraph" announced a new factory. In a later column he declared that "prosperity seems to reign everywhere," and rejoiced in his belief that industrial growth "extends over the whole section." Another article welcomed the "veritable invasion of the South" by eager Northern and Western investors who came to enrich themselves but, unlike the Union invaders of the 'sixties, came to enrich the South as well. On another occasion he wrote that the "marvelous industrial development" of the South was having extraordinarily good effects on agriculture so that the dream of a balanced economy was in fact coming true. Finally, in 1890 he made it unmistakably clear that the New South was a great and present reality. With allusions to his friend Kelley's statement that the South was the "field of American adventure" and the "coming El Dorado of American adventure," he wrote:

> There is no diminution, no falling off in the South. In all lines of industry the advance is steady and continuous. . . . The old agricultural South has ceased to be. . . . From henceforth the South stands in the front rank as the "field of American adventure" and the exponent of American progress. . . . It is in truth not "the coming," but the existing "El Dorado of American Adventure."[17]

Declarations of the reality of the opulent South made it logical for the New South spokesmen to proclaim the achievement of their other goals of reconciliation with the North and the acquisition of a new sense of power and faith in the future, for the creation of a triumphant

South was premised upon the successful conversion to the industrial age. All of the New South advocates, and countless contributors to the national periodicals, remarked on the vanishing sectional animosities, and the favorite explanation for this happy state of affairs was the economic interdependence which bound North and South together. Watterson thanked God that it was at last possible to say of the South "it is simply a geographic expression" and Tompkins rejoiced in the fact that "the institutions and interests of the American people are identical and common."[18] Telling his New York audience that the South had torn down sectional barriers, Grady made it plain that the new era of harmony emanated from his part of the country. After Sherman had left Atlanta in ashes, he said, the city was rebuilt, and "we have caught the sunshine in the bricks and mortar of our homes, and have builded therein not one ignoble prejudice or memory."[19] It may have been Grady's words, rather than the bricks, that caught the sunshine, but certainly the theme of reunion was a dominant one of the 'eighties.[20] Warner was typical of the Northern observers when he wrote that "Southern society and Northern society are becoming every day more and more alike."[21]

With the end of prejudice and discord and with the advent of industrial might came the sense of power and achievement that was the ultimate goal of the New South movement. "Above all," Grady said in New York, "we know that we have achieved in these 'piping times of peace' a fuller independence for the South than that which our fathers sought to win in the forum by their eloquence or compel in the field by their swords."[22] In response to a critic's suggestion that Northern financial and industrial interests were decisive in the movement and that perhaps the South was not quite as independent as he believed,

Grady replied confidently that such charges were completely erroneous. Citing Fulton County, Georgia—the "capital" of the New South—as typical of the region, he stated that only 774 Northerners were numbered in a total population of 47,588.[23] More to the point, Grady would believe, was the analysis of Kelley, who wrote in 1888 that the magnificent progress taking place in the South could "justly be regarded as the work of Titans."[24] And as others looked on the scene later they declared that these titans had brought into existence a South that was everywhere blessed with "plenty and prosperity"; that the South, at last, had risen "victorious in peace from the desolation of war."[25] The metamorphosis was now complete. During the years of conception—the 'seventies—"New South" meant an idea, a program, a goal; by the end of the 'eighties it denoted a whole region that had acted upon the idea, followed the program, and achieved the goal.

II

Walter Hines Page was the only one of the notable New South spokesmen who believed that failures outnumbered the successes of the movement. A persistent critic of the defects in Southern society, Page participated in one crusade after another to save his native region; in the 'eighties he was at one with Grady and Edmonds in looking to industrialization for the answer to the region's problems; in the later 'nineties he joined the education crusade, hoping that a new enlightenment would bring salvation; still later he put his hopes in elimination of the hookworm and for a while appeared to think that the South could be saved only when the ill health which plagued so many of her people disappeared. More cosmopolitan and sensitive than the other New South spokesmen, Page was always suspicious of the extravagant claims made by Southerners. In his autobiographical novel, for example, he recalled his experiences as a schoolboy and wrote that "nobody tells the whole truth about institutions. They prefer to accept traditions and to repeat respectful formulas."[26] By the 'nineties the New South claims had become "respectful formulas" and Page was losing faith with them.[27] Touring the region in 1899, he had hoped to see a South that would justify the optimistic statistics he read in the *Manufacturers' Record*, a journal of which he was the second largest stockholder.[28] Instead, he saw a land that appeared to him to be "listless, discouraged, poverty-stricken, and backward-looking," and he returned from his journey "infinitely sad."[29]

Ten years earlier, Lewis H. Blair, a native Virginian and former Confederate soldier, had been similarly disillusioned by the contrast between what he called the "real South" and what he read in the New South propaganda sheets.[30] "Judging by the glowing reports in the newspapers for the past three years," Blair wrote, "we must conclude that the South is enjoying a veritable deluge of prosperity." According to the propaganda, the South was "surpassing even the Eastern States," and had become a place "where poverty is unknown and where everybody is industriously and successfully laying up wealth."[31] The irate Virginian traced the source of this "mischievous and misleading" information to the "so-called Manufacturers' Records" that had become so popular in the 'eighties. Commenting on their objectivity, he wrote:

Such journals proceed on the same plan as would the Superintendent of the Census in 1890, should he, instead of actually enumerating the people, start with the population of 1880, and add thereto not only all the births, but also all the stillbirths, all the miscarriages, and all the abortions since that year, and deduct nothing for deaths in the meanwhile.[32]

It was the habit of these journals, Blair claimed, to arrive at figures of total aggregate manufacturing capital in the South by including in their estimates not only established firms but those that were merely in the planning stage as well. Failures and bankruptcies were seldom recorded; the inevitable trend had to be upwards.[33]

Edmonds was a natural target of such criticisms and, though not named, it was probably he in particular whom Blair had in mind. Edmonds was accustomed to such charges and occasionally reprinted them in the *Record* to provide a springboard from which to launch an optimistic picture of Southern achievements. In 1887 the Newberry, South Carolina, *Observer* commented that the statistics in Edmonds's journal "make a fine showing." But the ordinary Southerner "feels something like the penniless boy who stands out on the sidewalk and gazes wistfully through plate-glass windows at the beautiful display of toys and candies within!" Edmonds replied that the boy was penniless because he spent too much time gazing; wealth was there for those who wished to work.[34] On another occasion the Baltimore *Sun* described what it considered to be "The Real Condition of the South" in gloomy terms. Edmonds countered with a long statistical table which he believed proved that "none can question" the industrial advance of the region.[35] Even more pointed was an editorial comment in the Chattanooga *Times* that passed off one of Edmonds's statistical surveys as "about three-fourths moonshine and wind." Edmonds characterized this attack on his veracity as "the insolent snarls of envious curs," the product of an editor who was a "disreputable falsifier . . . moved by enmity and spite."[36] With this background, Blair did not exaggerate when he declared that "to doubt the current charming presentations of Southern growth and prosperity is to bring down anathemas upon one's head. What! the South not prosperous. Impossible, they cry; and the individual who questions is an idiot."[37]

Risking the anathemas, Blair wrote a penetrating analysis of the economic and racial problems of the South. His thesis was that the prosperity of the region depended upon the elevation, not the degradation, of the Negro; and because Negroes were not being elevated and Southern economic advance not planned intelligently, the region sustained one setback after another. "We are," he feared, "making an Ireland of the South, and are digging broad and deep graves in which to bury prosperity and all its untold advantages."[38] To support this view he attacked not only the statistics but the integrity of the New South spokesmen. He also pointedly began his analysis with Georgia—"as she has been held up as a model to all the other States"—and, with what he called reliable statistics, he concluded that "the people of Georgia had not added materially to their wealth during the twenty years preceding 1886."[39] Clearly, this was not Henry Grady's doctrine.

Blair and Page had perhaps let their disappointment cause them to underestimate the material advances that were evident in the South, for it is obvious that impressive forward strides had been taken since the end of the war. Factories had been built where there were none before, boom towns dotted the region, railroad mileage increased substantially, and investors, both foreign and domestic, were genuinely impressed by the future prospects of Southern development. Moreover, there was a romantic quality to the New South quest for riches and power that stirred the souls of observers in all parts of the country. Recognizing all of these factors, however, nothing can gainsay the fact that Blair and Page came closer to describing actuality than Grady and Edmonds did or that the New South writings were that fuzzy medley of strong belief and personal experience out of which social myth emerges.

In his general history of the post-Reconstruction South, C. Vann Woodward shows the gap that separated South from North by using per capita wealth figures. In 1880, when the New South movement was just taking hold, the per capita wealth of the Southern states was $376 and the national average was $870. By 1900 the figure for the South had increased to $509 while the national average had risen to $1,165. Expressed in percentages, the per capita wealth of the Southern states in 1880 was 56.8 per cent below the national average. In 1900 it was 56.3 per cent below. The very slight gain on the North which is reflected in these data is misleading, however, because the figures include valuations of Southern railroads, mines, mortgages, and other properties owned by "outside interests."[40] Estimates of per capita income show a similar pattern. In 1880 the per capita income in the South was $88; the national average was $175. By 1900 the South's per capita income had risen to $102 while the national average had moved to $203. Expressed in percentages, the per capita income of the South in 1880 was 49.7 per cent below the national average; in 1900 it was 49.8 per cent below.[41]

These figures show that the per capita wealth of the South increased by 13.5 per cent between 1880 and 1900 and that per capita income increased by 15.9 per cent in the same period. The gains are significant, of course, and they provided just enough substance to make the myth of the New South credible to many persons. But in truth the industrial evolution of the postwar years was neither extensive enough nor revolutionary enough to make much impact on the standard of living of the great mass of Southerners. In the first place, the movement was extremely limited. In 1900, as in 1880, the overwhelming majority of the population was engaged in the extractive industries of agriculture, forestry, fisheries, and mining. With 67.3 per cent of its labor force employed in these occupations in 1900 the South was a unique section of the country. The comparable figure for New England, the New South spokesmen's primary model, was 17.6 per cent. Only 6.3 per cent of the Southern labor force was employed in manufacturing in 1900, which reflects but a modest rise from the 4.6 per cent that was claimed by manufacturing twenty years earlier.[42] Remaining an essentially raw-material economy, the South suffered "the attendant penalties of low wages, lack of opportunity, and poverty."[43]

In addition to the limited extent of industrial development, the industries that did emerge and expand were largely of the low-wage variety. This was particularly true in the case of the cotton-textile industry, which became to many New South spokesmen the symbol of their movement. The low wages paid by Southern factories were further entrenched by the exploitative nature of the early industrial movement. Dependence on child labor and, for a good period of time, on convict labor as well, scarcely validated the happy images woven into the picture of the New South. William H. Nicholls, an economist who has brooded over the Southern past, sums up the failures of the period by writing that "the rate of industrialization in the South during the post-bellum years of the nineteenth century, while no inconsiderable achievement, was hardly sufficient to make more than a small dent in the low-income problems of its overwhelmingly rural-agricultural population."[44]

As reality failed to bear out the New South dream of opulence so, too, did it fail to record success in the campaign for power and independence. With a few notable exceptions, the New South program produced no real Southern Rockefellers and Carnegies, but only a large number of their liveried servants. It was by adopting the ways of Northern industry—by putting business above politics and sowing towns and cities in the place of theories—that the new power and independence were meant to have been gained. But as the industrial pattern deviated from the Northern model the achievement of these goals became impossible. Instead, as of old, the South remained saddled with the burdens of a colonial economy.

Her railway system fell under the control of Northern financial tycoons like J. P. Morgan and her iron and steel industries, during and after the depression of 1893, succumbed to the control of outsiders, culminating in 1907 when United States Steel achieved effective domination of the Tennessee Coal and Iron Company. Even the proud mills, so many of which were built with local money raised in patriotic subscription campaigns, fell into the colonial pattern. Their chief products were often sent North for final processing and their dependence on Northern capital and Northern commission houses belied the claims of self-determination.[45] Finally, many of the South's natural resources—the most celebrated guarantee of industrial progress and power—came to be controlled by men from outside the region. As Woodward writes, the South's "rich mineral deposits . . . were 'Southern' monopolies only in the sense that the sulphur of Sicily, owned by a British syndicate, was once a 'Sicilian' monopoly. Protected by patent laws, franchises, options, or outright possession of mineral lands, the Melons, Rockefellers, Du Ponts, and other capitalists monopolized 'Southern monopolies.' "[46]

To explain why the New South movement failed to produce the blessings it promised is a task well beyond the scope of this study, but a few observations on the nature of the problem may help to cast light on other questions which are of primary concern. To begin with, the persistent optimism of the New South spokesmen was grounded in an unrealistic conception of the industrial process. Repeatedly they claimed that the region's rich endowment of natural resources was a sure guarantee of industrialization. The falsity of this assumption requires no elaboration. As David M. Potter has observed, "a vital distinction separates mere abundance—the copious supply of natural resources—and actual abundance—the availability to society of a generous quota of goods ready for use."[47] The two are related, of course, but the history of the modern world—including the history of the Old South—shows that the potential does not automatically lead to the actual and that "environmental riches" in fact occupy "a relatively small place in the explanation of economic growth." Much more important are institutional and human factors which increase the capacity of society to produce.[48]

It is probably true that the New South dream of rapid industrialization and urbanization, with the attend-

ant benefits of power and prestige for the region, was
an unrealistic one to begin with because of the plethora
of both economic and non-economic obstacles which had
to be surmounted. Among economic factors which militated against success was the relative lateness of the
Southern industrial movement. Beginning after industrialism was well advanced in other parts of the country,
the South had a critical shortage of entrepreneurial talent,
skilled workers, "and other external economies whose
presence in the already industrially established North
tended to make industrialization there self-generating."
The lack of these advantages in the South, as Nicholls
observes, meant that "it was the old agrarian pattern—
only slightly modified by the development of such low-
skill manufactures as textiles—which tended to be self-
generating."[49] In addition to these economic problems,
cultural, intellectual, and social patterns in the region
also militated against rapid industrialization on the Northern model. Loyalty to an agrarian past and determination
to preserve the value system produced by it as well as an
essentially romantic and static conception of history, class,
and race were not compatible with swift industrialization
and urbanization.

The New South spokesmen were aware of some of
these problems and it would be unfair to say that they
did not try to face up to some of those that they saw.
One is especially impressed by their attempt to revise
attitudes toward the industrial society and its principal
ideological appurtenances. But more striking are their
several failures: they straddled fences, arguing that the
peculiar sense of honor and personal identification of the
slave regime could be maintained and fulfilled in an
industrial age; they rejoiced in the wealth of natural
resources, but were prevented by race and class biases

from developing a program to utilize adequately the human resources; they knew they lacked capital, but their plan for getting it encouraged a colonial relationship that tended to drain the region of its wealth; and, finally, their retreat into mythmaking—the most pervasive feature of the New South movement after the mid-'eighties—betrays the absence of the kind of single-minded realism which they correctly said the situation required but so signally failed to embody in their leadership.

III

The final element in the myth of a New South was the image of a region free from the legacy of racial injustice, and the reality of an innocent South was proclaimed quite as fervently as the existence of an opulent and triumphant South. As early as 1885, Grady outlined all of the principal beliefs that became woven into this part of the New South creed:

> Ten years ago, nothing was settled. There were frequent collisions and constant apprehensions. The whites were suspicious and the blacks were restless. So simple a thing as a negro taking an hour's ride on the cars, or going to see a play, was fraught with possible danger. The larger affairs—school, church, and court—were held in abeyance. Now all this is changed. The era of doubt and mistrust is succeeded by the era of confidence and goodwill. The races meet in the exchange of labor in perfect amity and understanding. Together they carry on the concerns of the day, knowing little or nothing of the fierce hostility that divides labor and capital in other

sections. When they turn to social life they separate. Each race obeys its instinct and congregates about its own centers. At the theater they sit in opposite sections of the same gallery. On the trains they ride each in his own car. Each worships in his own church, and educates his children in his schools. Each has his place and fills it, and is satisfied. Each gets the same accommodation for the same money. There is no collision. There is no irritation or suspicion. Nowhere on earth is there kindlier feeling, closer sympathy, or less friction between two classes of society than between the whites and the blacks of the South to-day.[50]

Other New South writers added illustrative detail to this picture of a harmonious biracial society in order to buttress its credibility, but only one dimension remained to be added to foreclose dispute of Grady's joyful conclusion. Throughout the 'eighties the question of Negro endorsement of the New South creed was debated, but without the commanding authority of a recognized Southern Negro leader to offer his stamp of approval. With the rise of Booker T. Washington all of this changed, and after Washington announced his famous "Atlanta Compromise" in 1895 lingering doubts vanished, consciences everywhere were eased, and the New South program was accepted as an honest, biracial attempt to resolve the race question logically and justly.

Washington's rise to fame and power is part of the folklore of America, but it is also an essential part of the mythology of the New South movement. James Creelman of the New York *World* testified to this when he filed his story on Washington's 1895 address. Nothing since Grady's "immortal speech" before the New England Society of New York, Creelman wrote, had shown "so profoundly the spirit of the New South."[51] That Washington should have been heralded as a new prophet of the New South is hardly surprising. Quite apart from his racial views, the ideas he expressed and the life he lived were wonderful examples of New South precepts put into action. It was not simply that he had risen out of slavery and by industry, frugality, and perseverance had achieved eminence, or that he minimized the importance of politics and stressed economic advance. Equally important in identifying him as a New South man were his views on labor unions, which he distrusted, and his generally conservative position on political, economic, and religious questions. Like the white New South spokesmen and the Northern businessmen they befriended, Washington accepted the social Darwinism of his age and subscribed with conviction to Andrew Carnegie's gospel of wealth.[52]

When Washington came to the Atlanta Exposition in 1895 he found a setting ideally suited to his message. Designed to advertise the material and intellectual progress of the South, the Exposition included displays from the Negro population, attesting to the advance of the race. Washington's invitation to speak, considered by many to have been a bold experiment, seemed fitting testimony to the opportunity which the dominant race provided for the Negro. Washington himself regarded his presence on the speaker's platform as proof of his belief that men of merit, whatever their skin color, would not be denied opportunity in the South.[53]

"One-third of the population of the South is of the Negro race," Washington began his momentous address. "No enterprise seeking the material, civil, or moral welfare of this section can disregard this element of our population and reach the highest success."[54] From this opening assertion of the interdependence of the races, Washington developed a masterly presentation of the New South philosophy of race relations. All of the major concessions demanded of the Negroes were there: admission of the false start of the race during Reconstruction; recognition of the fact that "it is at the bottom of life we must begin"; unabashed faith that the Southern white man was the Negro's best friend; and conviction that it was in the South "that the Negro is given a man's chance in the commercial world."

With disarming concessions to the white man's view of things, Washington spoke with apparent candor on the basic issues of freedom and equality. Freedom should not be confused with irresponsibility, he declared, noting that it was out of ignorance and misdirection that Negroes, in the first years of freedom, wrongly preferred political eminence to industrial pursuits. The great danger to the race, Washington felt, was that "we may overlook the fact that the masses of us are to live by the production of our hands, and fail to keep in mind that we shall prosper in proportion as we learn to dignify and glorify common labour." He issued no threat to the political domination of the white race, promising instead that a continuation of the liberal white views which had brought about the Exposition would lead to the abolition of racial friction in a society in which Negroes "will buy your surplus land, make blossom the waste places in your fields, and run your factories." By continuing to offer economic and educational opportunities to the Negroes, the whites "can be sure in the future, as in the past, that you and your families will be surrounded by the most patient, faithful, law-abiding, and unresentful people that the world has seen."

Washington's comments on equality were likewise

satisfying to his white listeners. He assured them that the Negro wished to have opportunities in education and in industry, but that social equality was beyond the pale. "In all things that are purely social," he said in the passage that was most frequently quoted by the Southern press, "we can be as separate as the fingers, yet one as the hand in all things essential to mutual progress." And to emphasize the point, he added: "the wisest among my race understand that the agitation of questions of social equality is the extremest folly."

Washington's address profoundly strengthened the racial component of the New South myth. Widely reported in the press and the national periodicals, it seemed more than sufficient to vindicate Henry Grady's declarations of the previous decade.[55] Typical of magazine editorial response was the comment in the *Outlook* that no other speech at the Exposition had "so notable an effect" as Washington's, and the editor rejoiced at the "spirit of hearty good fellowship" produced by the affair.[56] More extravagant praise of both Washington and the New South movement came from the *Century Magazine*, long a friend of the South. "No patriotic American could have read the reports of the opening exercises of the Atlanta Exposition," the editor declared, "without feeling a thrill of joy run through his veins." The occasion marked "the jubilee of the new South—a South of industrial development and agricultural progress." Everywhere people were "joyous and confident," and not the least reason for celebration was the fact that the Exposition marked the symbolic "burial forever of the old South and negro slavery," proclaimed by Washington with "impassioned eloquence" and received by his white audience with "a perfect tumult of enthusiasm and delight."[57] Clark Howell, Grady's successor at the *Constitution*, spoke for the New South men: "The whole speech," he declared, "is a platform upon which blacks and whites can stand with full justice to each other."[58]

In the decade before Washington's address, lynchings and other forms of violence directed at the Negro increased sharply; by the time he spoke, the movement to disfranchise all Negroes had succeeded in two states, Mississippi and South Carolina, and was gaining momentum in the others; in the decade after he spoke more Negroes were disfranchised, and the doctrine of segregation espoused by Grady was enacted into law with a vengeance by Southern state and local governments. Humiliated by the Jim Crow system and reduced to a political cipher by the disfranchising conventions, Negroes lacked the economic security which might have permitted them to resist these movements. Industrialism had offered them virtually nothing during the 'eighties and 'nineties, and the great majority of their race continued to find that their lives were "circumscribed by the farm and plantation." Each year there were a few more black men who owned their own land, but in 1900 three out of every four who farmed were croppers or tenants whose livelihood was determined by white men.[59] Despite all this, Washington continued to act the role of a leader who believed that things were getting better. In his autobiography, written at the turn of the century, he declared that "despite superficial and temporary signs which might lead one to entertain a contrary opinion, there was never a time when I felt more hopeful for the race than I do at the present."[60] His faith in progress, as Samuel Spencer writes, "made him continue to insist . . . that race relations were steadily improving."[61]

IV

The figure of Washington on the podium at Atlanta poignantly evokes the inner meaning of the myth which he helped to establish. He both creates it and is himself caught by it. More than any other Southerner, the Negro needed to see progress, prosperity, and racial justice—if not at hand, clearly visible around the corner. But as these goals eluded their pursuers the belief in fulfillment was more fervently stated. This is not to suggest that Washington and Grady and their fellow New South spokesmen believed all they wrote. Much was pure propaganda and they knew it. The white spokesmen were engaged in wooing both Northern capital and Northern approbation and in establishing their own hegemony in the South. And Washington, like them, knew his audience and spoke what it wanted to hear. He, too, was wooing his oppressor and establishing himself as a powerful and exclusive leader of his race. In his testimony is all the strange mixture of wishful thinking and calculated opportunism that gave to the myth of the New South its singular force.

The opportunism is easily understood as a necessary tactic of ambitious men in a difficult situation, but the wishful thinking sprang from more complex sources. In part it derived from the universal need to make experience intelligible and agreeable; and for men deeply committed to a cause, only the most unmistakable jolts of defeat would cause them to abandon the belief in progress. For the New South men there was always enough evidence of advance to escape such a fate: factories were built, some men did accumulate fortunes, the North was more kindly disposed toward and respectful of the South, and life did become better for some Negroes. Perspective, too, is part of the answer. Washington's point of reference was slavery, and he was comforted and encouraged by the fact that at least Negroes had not been re-enslaved. For the white New South spokesmen, the background against which they wrote their accounts heightened the contrasts and exaggerated the images they saw. They saw Southern economic achievements against a scene of grinding poverty, increasing political power and self-determination against an experience of galling powerlessness, attempts at reconciliation against the legacy of hatred and mistrust, and concessions to the Negro against a backdrop of slavery and black codes. It is not surprising that in describing their region's attempt to don the mantle of the American heritage they implored their countrymen to admire the Emperor's new clothes.

Their legacy to the twentieth century was a pattern of belief in which Southerners could see themselves and their section as rich, successful, and just. Uncritically it could be assumed that because their "facts" proved it, opulence and power were at hand; that because men of good will and progressive outlook proclaimed it so, the Negro lived in the best of all possible worlds. It was both comfortable and to one's apparent advantage to accept this picture of society. Just as the fair picture of the antebellum South gave Southerners courage and pride while at the same time offering blandishments to Northern antagonism, so the picture of a New South had the double effect of ameliorating the bleak realities of the present and winning approbation and respect from the world outside.

Epilogue

The Enduring Myth

Seventy-five years after Henry Grady presented his vision of hope and good cheer to the New England Society of New York, a distinguished Texas historian who had spent most of his adult life puzzling over the South's problems launched a modest crusade of his own to fire the ambitions of his people with a vision of unbounded progress and prosperity. "I have turned myself into a propagandist," Walter Prescott Webb announced. His mission, he said, was "to tell my tale to various audiences who would listen, and to give them the evidence I had gathered as to the future prospect."[1] Both the evidence and the prospect sounded familiar to anyone who recalled the rhetoric of the New South men of the nineteenth century. "The story I am going to tell," Webb promised, "differs from much that is said and written about the South." His was to be a story "of cheerfulness, of optimism and hope, a story calculated to lift the spirit, turn the eyes of a Southerner . . . to a future so bright as to be to some all but unbelievable." Lamenting the many wrongs the South had suffered and the unique hardships it had endured, he promised release from the burdens. "As things stand now, as I see the South for the next seventy years," he declared, Southerners should take hope as never before "because it is not only possible but it is also probable that this next century will belong to the South."[2]

Before the decade was out, a United States senator from South Carolina appeared before a Congressional committee to present to its members—and to the nation— a confession that probably came neither easily nor naturally to him. Governor of the state during the early 'sixties, he had embraced Webb's optimistic view of the South's future; and, like the historian, he did his part to attract industry to the state and to infuse its people with a spirit of progress. Now, in 1969, Ernest F. Hollings had decided to bring to a dramatic end his allegiance to the tradition of New South boosterism. Having just completed a personal inspection tour of the state, he told the committee of the widespread hunger, disease, and poverty he saw. "We should be ashamed of this hunger," he said. Adding the further confession that his knowledge of its existence was no recent acquisition, he explained his previous silence on the subject directly and credibly: "We didn't want the vice president of the plant in New York to know the burdens" of locating in South Carolina, he commented. "We told him only of the opportunities." Whites had been victimized by the state's backwardness, but according to Hollings Negroes were the principal sufferers. Lack of adequate nourishment, and not skin color, was sufficient to account for the black man's plight. "He is dumb because we denied him food," the Senator declared. "Dumb in infancy, he has been blighted for life."[3]

Walter Webb was no Henry Grady and Senator Hollings can scarcely be regarded as a modern-day Lewis Harvie Blair or George Washington Cable, but the juxtaposition of their responses to some of the problems of the South in the 1960's is a fair reminder that the legacy of the New South movement has been an enduring one and that efforts to cope with its mythology persist seventy years after the original movement reached its climax.

I

In response to the South's crisis of defeat and despair, the New South spokesmen had designed for their beleaguered region a homegrown plan of reconstruction. To industrialize the South, revive its agricultural prosperity, inject its people with a spirit of confidence and zest, harmonize relations between former enemies, and honor the demands of the war and Reconstruction amendments— all of these were noble and ambitious goals. They were also goals that flattered the nation's image of itself as a land of opportunity, success, and justice and therefore had the special appeal of making the South appear to be ready to undertake on its own, free of outside pressure, the process of dismantling its heritage of dissidence and sectionalism. Used in this manner as a compelling justification for Northern abandonment of the Reconstruction, the New South doctrine also defined for Southerners an attractive substitute. Finally, the new creed of progress was tied from the outset to a relatively small group of merchants, industrialists, and planters. This new ruling class, supported by the New South creed, forged what it supposed was a mutually advantageous partnership with Northern capitalists and fastened its control over the region's destiny in the 1880's.

As the regime tightened its hegemony in the 'eighties, the ideology which had contributed to its acceptance evolved into a powerful social myth, further strengthening the existing order and impressing upon Southerners a pattern of belief that would be increasingly difficult to throw off. In the next decade these beliefs survived their first severe test and emerged stronger and more intimately related to the order they sustained. Throughout the 'eighties discontent with the Redeemer regimes had been apparent, but it was not until the Populist uprising of the 'nineties that a formidable assault was mounted. A potentially erosive force for the New South beliefs, the agrarian revolt instead proved to be crucial in assuring their longevity. Persuaded that the economic and political system established by the Redeemers restricted opportunity and deprived the Southern masses of hope for the future, the desperate agrarians who joined in the Populist movement naturally fixed on the New South doctrine of progress, prosperity, sectional reconciliation, and racial harmony as their principal target. But the frenzy of their attack, far from discrediting the mythology, worked rather to strengthen it. Respectable and conservative Americans reacted with unbridled disdain to what they regarded as the wild schemes and subversive tactics of the agrarian radicals so that the New South view of the world seemed, by contrast, to represent sanity, moderation, and security.

The turbulence of the 'nineties, heightened and brought into focus by the Populist revolt, accelerated the movement of the 'eighties toward racial subordination and resulted in the perfection of a far-reaching program of disfranchisement and segregation. To many it seemed that the Jim Crow system was a natural addition and reassuring guarantee of the safety of those standards celebrated in the New South myth, an institutionalization of ideas already approved as right. Thus, at the opening of the new century several fundamental patterns had been established: the incipient New South creed rationalized the abandonment of Reconstruction and the inauguration of the Redeemer regimes in the 1870's; the mature doctrine undermined the first menacing reform movement designed to overhaul that order in the 1890's; the Jim Crow system was added as an insurance measure; and the New South myth, fully articulated, offered a harmonizing and reassuring world view to conserve the essential features of the status quo. The New South movement itself was simultaneously ended. During the next seven decades Southerners would celebrate the achievements of Grady and his fellow prophets and with the regularity of an inherited ritual they would proclaim the arrival of even newer new Souths; but there never again appeared a cohesive group that could legitimately be called the party of the New South. There was no need for one so long as the mythology created by the first one endured.

II

The use of the New South myth as a foil to Reconstruction, Populism, and later assaults on the socio-economic system shaped by the Redeemers suggests that its tenacious influence may be explained simply by regarding it as essentially an instrument manipulated by interest groups opposed to change; and examples of the way in which opportunism of this sort has kept the myth vital and effective are plentiful. Time and again attempts to expose the poverty and want in the region have been frustrated by appeals to the myth, a fact all the more remarkable because of the continuing failure of the Southern economy—a failure about which there is little argument today. The extensive literature on the breadth and depth of economic want in the South exposes the emptiness of the myth and needs no elaboration here. As Joseph J. Spengler, a Duke University economist, noted recently, "the South has been doing badly for at least a century." Fixing on per capita income as "the best single indicator of the performance of the southern economy," he concedes that the region improved markedly in the period 1929–63, but then explains how "this improvement merely reduced the margin of the South's inferiority; it did not move southern incomes up in the national income structure." As Spengler points out, twelve Southern states fell among the fifteen lowest in per capita income in 1962, and the nine lowest positions were a Southern monopoly.[4]

During the Depression one might have anticipated dissipation of the myth of abundance and opportunity, but the power of the old belief was frequently demonstrated and nowhere more dramatically and characteristically than in the reaction to the President's *Report on Economic Conditions in the South*, published in 1938. Product of a long and searching examination of the region's basic problems, this pamphlet distilled the essence of more than a decade of pioneering research. President Roosevelt, much to the delight of the social scientists on whose work the report was based, supported their analysis and recommendations, and announced in his foreword that he regarded the South as "the Nation's No. 1 economic problem."[5] So frank a remark wounded pride and set off

a violent reaction. But it was the content of the report—
which, if accepted, would totally destroy the bastions of
belief upon which all the comforting ramifications of the
myth could rest—that elicited resistance. In taut language
and authoritative tables it laid bare the economic backwardness and social suffering of the region. "The low
income belt of the South," it declared, "is a belt of sick-
ness, misery, and unnecessary death."[6] As cries of foul
misrepresentation rang out in all parts of the region,
Senator Josiah Bailey of North Carolina declared that the
South had made remarkable progress and argued that
emphasis should properly be placed on the achievements
of "our forefathers who rebuilt the South after the Civil
War." Arkansas Senator John E. Miller said that the
South needed to be left alone, not ridiculed. And the ghost
of Edmonds guided the editorial response of the *Manufacturers' Record*. "This section has been unwisely characterized as the economic problem No. 1 of the nation,"
the journal lamented. "Quite the opposite is true. The
South represents the nation's greatest opportunity for
industrial development."[7]

Important though the myth was as a bulwark against
change, a conscious manipulation cannot fully account for
its vitality and effectiveness. Myths are something more
than advertising slogans and propaganda ploys rationally
connected to a specific purpose. They have a subtle way
of permeating the thought and conditioning the actions
even of those who may be rationally opposed to their
consequences. They arise out of complex circumstances
to create mental sets which do not ordinarily yield to intellectual attacks. The history of their dynamics suggests
that they may be penetrated by rational analysis only as
the consequence of dramatic, or even traumatic, altera-

tions in the society whose essence they exist to portray. Thus, the critique and dissipation of myths becomes possible only when tension between the mythic view and the reality it sustains snaps the viability of their relationship, creates new social patterns and with them new harmonizing myths.

The New South myth has been no exception. In race relations, it formed the intellectual and moral touchstone to which all discussion of the Negro's role in Southern society was ineluctably referred for more than half of the present century. Influential in different ways, it has exerted its power over demagogues and racists as well as liberal reformers and well-meaning paternalists. Negroes and white Northerners have likewise responded to and been shaped by it, and much of foreign opinion has reflected its power. This is not to say that the dominant racial attitudes of the twentieth century all derived from the New South myth or that it was the first universally accepted conceptualization of racial sentiments. The fundamental ambivalences of hate and love, fear and trust, oppression and paternalism, repulsion and attraction underlying race relations have a history as old as the country; and successive institutional arrangements resulting from particular historical circumstances have each rested on their peculiar myths. What is true is that the New South myth perfectly complemented the post-Reconstruction search for a new modus operandi in race relations and came to be the intellectual and moral foundation of the Jim Crow system of the twentieth century.

In the thirty years before the Civil War, the slave regime rested securely on an elaborately structured pro-slavery myth. Emancipation and the subsequent failure of the abolitionist-Reconstruction creed of equality to find expression in a viable social system was followed by a period of uncertainty and flux in which no monolithic pattern of race relations emerged. Disfranchising measures and segregation statutes, beginning in the 1890's, rapidly changed all of this, creating a social system that rivaled the old slave regime in its concreteness and universality. By constitutional mandate and legislative statute Negroes were once again set apart as a distinct group within which individual differences were officially unrecognized as significant considerations of public policy. Accepted widely as the final solution to the conundrum presented by the demands of Negro freedom and the American tradition of equality, this new order was neatly rationalized by the New South myth. Defining each individual's role in life and the expectations placed on him by society, the myth was adopted by the Supreme Court in 1896, attractively encased in the slogan "equal but separate," and began a dominion over the American mind that conditioned and controlled the perception and programs of the most disparate groups so that, in its cumulative effect, it worked as a powerfully conservative force, protecting and maintaining the Jim Crow system to which it was wed.

Providing initially the intellectual and moral basis for the abandonment of sectional quarrels over the Negro's place in American society, the myth enjoyed a remarkably long period of freedom from the kinds of frontal assaults that might have helped to undermine it. The National Association for the Advancement of Colored People, founded in 1909, never accepted the moral ideal on which the myth rested, and its officers, especially W. E. B. DuBois, produced an impressive literature of dissent. But the NAACP attack was blunted by two unyielding obstacles. First, the white North was not to be aroused to any new crusades on the part of the black man and, for the most part, it rested comfortably with the assurance that, after all, equal treatment—even though separate—was more than Yankee reformers had ever been able to institute on a permanent basis. Second, Negro leadership itself was seriously divided. Booker T. Washington had placed his authoritative seal of approval on essential elements of the myth; after his death, in 1915, many Negro leaders who competed for the honor of inheriting his mantle—and especially those who worked in the South in cooperation with white liberals and Northern philanthropists—deemed it wise to give formal approval to the doctrine that separate could be equal and that whatever reforms or modifications of the existing order might be required could be achieved within the framework of separate societies. Such an admission, even if only temporary strategy, inevitably strengthened the hold of the myth.

A potential source of difficulty for the myth was the growing strength and influence of Southern liberalism and the work of one of its chief manifestations, the interracial movement. Liberal Southerners, anxiously addressing themselves realistically to the region's problems and demanding genuine reforms of the status quo had always existed in the South, but their number and influence had been minuscule in the last three quarters of the nineteenth century. During the first two decades of the twentieth century the liberalism of the so-called Progressive Movement in the South had been largely for whites only and, despite a growing concern on the part of a small group of respectable professional men, it concerned itself only incidentally with race relations. After the First World War, however, an enduring interracial reform organization established a foothold, and during the next quarter-century its educational work focused attention on the inequities of the Jim Crow system and its action wing engaged energetically in programs of reform. Directed by the patient and imaginative Will W. Alexander, the Commission on Interracial Cooperation found allies all across the region, enlisted support from most of the professions, and succeeded in making race relations a "problem" suitable for study and an object of regional concern rather than unqualified pride. In these important ways the first steps by which the myth might be eroded were taken with both caution and determination.

But the liberals in the interracial movement, though genuinely distraught by racial injustices, were authentic heirs of the myth and their thought and programs were directed and limited by acceptance of the belief that coercive separation was compatible with genuine equality. The great mass of white Southerners, like complacent and inarticulate Northerners, believed not only in the possibility but in the actuality as well. Liberals were distinguished from conservatives in this regard chiefly by their determined efforts to prove that, in nearly all areas of life, the separate societies were grossly unequal. Devoting most of their thought to long-range programs to ameliorate the situation—Will Alexander once remarked that "this situation will not be very greatly affected by any program or any set of men who do not think about it in terms of twenty-five to fifty years"[8]—the Interracial Commission undertook programs to supply legal aid for intimidated Negroes, agitated for an end to police brutality, urged equal pay for equal work, tried to encourage greater and more accurate reporting of Negro accomplishments, and campaigned vigorously against the most blatant abuses of Negroes, such as lynching. The achievement of these and other objectives of the liberals appeared to pose no threat to the system of segregation—an assumption the reformers themselves apparently shared—and thus by concentrating their energies on making a genuine reality of the ideal of the myth they greatly qualified their potential as forces of its erosion.

The interracial movement was but one manifestation of a general intellectual awakening that occurred during the interwar period, giving birth to a new brand of social criticism and reform agitation. Indigenous in origin, it appeared first in the 1920's as a response to the material stagnancy of the region and the spiritual malaise reflected in such phenomena as fundamentalism, prohibitionism, Ku Kluxery, and other offspring of a backward and depressed society. In the 1930's it assumed new directions and received added momentum and national attention as the New Deal emerged as a sympathetic partner in its endeavors. Journalists and publicists set out on voyages of exploration and came back to produce an impressive literature of discovery that revealed a South quite unlike the region celebrated in the myth. Social scientists in the universities announced the coming of a new critical realism that would free the region of its meretricious images, a first step they believed toward constructive reform. In Chapel Hill, sociologist Howard W. Odum, enjoying the support of reform-minded presidents, directed an academic enterprise that resulted in a staggering number of studies of the region and helped to make the University of North Carolina the intellectual center of the new realism. What Odum and his fellow sociologists did for the Southern present, the historians of the 1930's accomplished for the past. Questioning most of the received truths, these revisionist scholars began to expose the sordid aspects of slavery, dismantled the Cavalier myth, recorded the disaffection and disloyalty that plagued the Confederacy, found Reconstruction to be full of progressive, democratic reforms, questioned the motives and achievements of the Redeemers, and wrote sympathetically of the Populist uprising of the 'nineties.

The outburst of reassessment and scholarly activity during the interwar period was matched, if indeed not surpassed, by a literary awakening that broke with the sentimental plantation tradition, furnished painful and ironic images of the region that shocked and startled those who had been reared in the comfort of the old tradition, and brought unprecedented acclaim to Southern writers. Recalling his own impressions of the early 'thirties, one historian believed that the "awakening of historical scholarship . . . was only a minor aspect of a wider intellectual awakening in the South. The most brilliant manifestation was in the field of letters and literary criticism."[9] James Branch Cabell and Ellen Glasgow had presaged the new spirit in novels published before the 'twenties, but the major authors—Faulkner, Warren, Ransom, Tate, and Wolfe, among others—appeared during the interwar years. Miss Glasgow voiced the concern that permeated their best works. What the South needed, she explained, was blood and irony: blood, "because Southern culture has strained too far away from its roots in the earth"; irony, as "the safest antidote to sentimental decay." The South, she believed, was a region where "a congenial hedonism had established . . . a confederacy of the spirit," where "pride, complacency, . . . self-satisfaction, a blind contentment with things as they are, and a deaf aversion from things as they might be . . . stifle both the truth of literature and the truth of life."[10] It was against this kind of South that the Southern writers revolted, and their novels wrestled with the human dilemma of all mankind in a Southern setting that seemed peculiarly appropriate for the revelation of ruthlessness and compassion, deceit and honor, cowardice and courage, the will to endure and the passion to destroy.

A revolt against the literary traditions and intellectual aridity of the region, the revolution in letters affirmed the faith that to probe honestly, even if devastatingly, was a surer means of honoring and strengthening the worthy qualities of the South than to remain mired in the treacly sentimentality of the past. But the term "revolt" suggests perhaps too much. For the most part, its influence was restricted to a small intelligentsia, Northern as well as Southern. Despite its artistic merit and critical acclaim it failed to mirror the fundamental aspirations and beliefs of the population in the way that Thomas Nelson Page had done for his generation. Thus, while the judgment of literary critics will come down strongly on the side of Faulkner, Warren, and Wolfe, the book-reading public preferred *Gone With the Wind* and treasured it as the best fictional treatment of the South to appear in the twentieth century. Margaret Mitchell's portrayal of the myths of the Old South, the Lost Cause, and the Reconstruction were artistically superior to Page's, but her novel was squarely in the plantation tradition of the previous century, and its immense success, coupled with the sensational reception of the movie version, attests both to the continuing vitality of the romantic view and the apparently impossible task of rooting out comfortable myths without profound social upheaval.

The intellectual awakening was closely related to the

Depression and the crisis of faith which affected all parts of the country. Likewise, just as the New Deal wrought profound changes in the social, economic, and political structure of the nation, so the new realism in the South was accompanied by programs of action that jostled the established order. But other parallels between national and regional developments stand out as more significant. Just as the New Deal failed to disturb the fundamental props of the capitalist structure of the country, so, too, the reform literature and agitation in the South failed to dismantle the main outlines of the Redeemer order established in the post-Reconstruction era. Despite all the enthusiasm for overhauling the Southern system, the changes that in fact came about were relatively minor. Economic power, at the end of the 'thirties, continued to rest where it had been before; impoverished croppers and mill hands continued to symbolize the region's economic failures; the Negro, despite modest improvements in his status, remained ensnared by the ramifying tentacles of the Jim Crow system; and the original burst of enthusiasm for FDR soon gave way to a renewed spirit of sectionalism and an enduring sense of alienation from the reformist tendencies of the New Deal.

Surveying the South's political structure in the mid-'forties, in a work that probed deeply into the mental, social, economic, and racial patterns of the region as well, V. O. Key, Jr., wrote what is probably the most cogent and devastating epilogue to the story of the Southern intellectual awakening that has yet appeared. Viewing politics broadly as the system of relationships and procedures whereby society concentrates, orders, and controls power in such a way that fundamental issues that arise among classes, sections, and interests may be reconciled into a program advancing the general welfare, Key rigorously analyzed the Southern performance and recorded the "cold, hard fact that the South as a whole has developed no system or practice of political organization and leadership adequate to cope with its problems."[11] Key's influential study, though not designed for the purpose, was nonetheless a sobering and exhaustive documentation of the fact that neither the New Deal nor the Depression, neither the Southern realists nor the action programs they sponsored or inspired, had succeeded in destroying the viability between the social order and the mythic representation of it, despite all the strains that had been placed on that relationship.

III

With the coming of the Second World War the strains eased and the relationship was fortified. Wars commonly redefine the nature of domestic concerns and cause old issues to be shelved; this one was no exception. The New Deal reform impulse, which had already begun to weaken, was now replaced by the demands of national mobilization for victory. The Depression had produced a national crisis, but not one that brought unity and a common sense of national identity. The stunning attack on Pearl Harbor and the revulsion at the inhumanity of the Nazi onslaught guaranteed near-unanimous support in this national crisis and thereby re-created a sense of national purpose and identity. Under the circumstances, sectional and class quarrels receded. The evil of Hitler's design and the

desperate nature of the struggle against it revived the
nation's tarnished image of itself as a unique force in
human history: once again entrusted with a special mission, it emerged from its isolation to save its gallant but
hapless allies—and freedom as the western world knew it
—from final destruction. Southern leadership relaxed with
the disappearance of the New Deal demands for further
reform, and all Southerners shared in the sense of urgency
and mission. The war thus worked to affirm the national
myth of a powerful Republic devoted to preserving liberty
and justice and, simultaneously, to strengthen the image
of the South as a fully integrated part of the Republic
and its calling.

Accompanying the revival of this sense of national
mission was a return of prosperity, induced largely by
the demands of war production. Depression conditions
vanished in all parts of the country, but in the South the
arrival of more jobs and higher incomes was especially
remarkable. War plants and shipyards moved into the
region to provide employment for thousands of men and
women who came home every Friday afternoon to cash
checks the likes of which had not been seen before. There
were grumblings, as a cumbersome rationing system inter-
fered with the free expenditure of the new income, but
on the whole the nation's faith in itself as a land of opulence and opportunity was re-established and the South's
share of the new abundance was large enough to absolve
the myth of the New South from the insults and doubts it
had suffered in the 'thirties. Predictions that the war
would be followed by a spiral of inflation and then depression were not borne out, and the South continued on
an upward-bound course of economic development. Pub-
licity focused on the growing occupational diversification

of the region, and although income analyses of 1950 and 1960 showed that the South was still well below national per capita averages the gains were striking, the gap closing, and the augury reassuring. Few observed that perspectives were clouded by the intense recollections of the Depression, against which the advances were measured, and there were few Jeremiahs about to remind optimists that the New South spokesmen of the 'eighties had also reached favorable interpretations of economic development by comparing their present with the misery of the Civil War and Reconstruction. Walter Webb sympathized with this refusal to let a long view undermine more optimistic contrasts, and remarked sourly, "those who teach [Southern] history and those who study it are likely to be so conditioned that they take a somber view of not only the past but also of the future." The historical viewpoint, Webb appeared to be saying in 1960, was unconstructive; what Southerners needed was to see "that the South today is the most thriving" region in the United States.[12]

But disturbing crosscurrents were at work as early as the war period, and by the mid-'fifties the myth would once again be under severe strain. During the war racial tensions had risen alarmingly, partly as a result of the unevenness of the new prosperity and partly because of the unavoidable contrast between the reality of Jim Crow at home and the war propaganda image of democratic virtue struggling to destroy a racist Behemoth in Europe. Southern liberals, with increasing uncertainty, had maintained their position that separate could be equal; but now they began to question that assumption more frequently. Appropriately, Alexander was among the first and clearest prophets of a new attitude. Writing in *Harper's* late in the war, he confronted the inherently incompatible elements in the Southern—and American—racial credo. Americans believed, Alexander wrote, that the Negro should be educated, but that he should also be segregated. The sticking point in this policy was that segregation "tends to defeat the inspiring work of Negro education." Education of Negroes had not been a mistake, he wrote, for "here we see American faith and American idealism at its best." But education for Negroes had proceeded along self-defeating lines because "segregation . . . is rooted in fear and in doubt as to whether our democratic principles will really work. It remains to be seen whether or not our faith in democracy is strong enough to overcome our fears as to what may become of its consequences." Whatever the outcome, Alexander was sure of the approach that would determine it. "Unless the problem of segregation can be solved," he warned, "there is no hope of any alleviation of the race problem in America."[13]

In the first decade after the war there was little reason to believe that the problem of segregation would be solved, but Alexander's concern accurately reflected changing attitudes toward the race problem that would cause liberals as well as conservatives to confront the equal-but-separate doctrine in ways they had not dreamed of before. The liberals, uncertain of the consequences of dispensing with an assumption that had increased their numbers and guided their constructive reform work for a generation, quarreled among themselves and eventually suffered a rupture when the Southern Regional Council, successor to the old Interracial Commission, declared segregation to be incompatible with the achievement of equality. Former friends of the liberal movement—typified by Richmond editor Virginius Dabney—now parted company, unable to believe that their old ideas could no longer serve as progressive guidelines. Many of the former liberals joined the conservatives and supported their attempts to save the equal-but-separate doctrine from destruction. Since the late 'thirties the Supreme Court had appeared increasingly likely to qualify or perhaps even strike down the doctrine. Faced with this possibility, Southern conservatives adopted a new strategy. Conceding now that Negro schools were inferior to white schools, they started a massive building campaign to make them equal in all tangible respects, hoping that such a demonstrable effort to equalize facilities would deter the Court from making a frontal assault on the doctrine itself. South Carolina Governor James F. Byrnes was candid about it: "To meet this situation we are forced to do now what we should have been doing for the last fifty years."[14]

New schools were built, but the strategy failed and the Supreme Court decision of May 17, 1954, striking down the fifty-eight-year-old Plessy doctrine of equal but separate, ushered the South and the nation into a new era of history whose course is as yet unspent. For the myth of the New South the events of the Second Reconstruction have been more devastating than any previous assault. From the beginning of the South's program of massive resistance to school desegregation to the Selma–Montgomery march a decade later the nation was overwhelmed with the most graphic evidence of racial injustice and brutality. Obsessively caught up with the drama of the South's turmoil, the nation saw more clearly and more eagerly than ever before the protective coloring stripped from the Southern ethos and the stark form of its racial bedrock revealed. Moreover, the dynamics of this reconstruction ran differently from those of the first. The course of change, especially after the beginning of the nonviolent direct action movement in 1960, was heavily influenced by Southern Negroes. Inspired by the young leaders of the Student Nonviolent Coordinating Committee and by Martin Luther King and his Southern Christian Leadership Conference, they proved both their desire for change and their determination and ability to bring it about. With the Negro revolt as the driving force and the excesses of white Southern response as the catalyst, the national government became increasingly active so that by the summer of 1965 virtually every piece of federal legislation desired by civil rights leaders had become law and the nation seemed assured of vigorous executive support and favorable judicial interpretation.

With such legislation and such pressures taking the limelight, a third influence contributing to the erosion of the myth was the subtle shift in thought that began to affect white Southerners. Despite recurrent attempts to picture the Negro revolt as a product of the communist conspiracy or another sinister form of outside agitation, the widening arc and undiminished force of the revolution made these comforting explanations less and less plausible so that, haltingly and reluctantly, more of them began to believe that Negroes, after all, were not happy in the South in their present conditions. And as those conditions were altered by legislation, judicial and executive actions, and concessions wrung by the demonstrators, white Southerners found themselves in situations they had never believed possible. One after another, old customs and institutions were revised or eliminated and situations abounded for which the myth could by no stretch of imagination remain instructive. At each stage of the social revolution Southerners, horrified by new demands placed upon them, found themselves frequently accepting, by contrast, the latest change—not always as reasonable and just, but at least as one the region had found it could live with—so that each year saw more unprecedented racial patterns at variance with "equal but separate" and a widening acceptance of those new patterns.

Exposing the claims of racial justice and harmony as a hollow sham, the events of the Second Reconstruction also put other parts of the New South doctrine in a harsh light. Regional publicists continued to praise the allegedly increasing benefits of a dynamic economy, and typical of scores of journalistic reminders was the boast that "the once-sleeping South has taken off like an inter-planetary missile. . . . The New South has come in with a clap of thunder."[15] But as national faith in the region's claims to racial justice crumbled under bright exposure, so too did the South appear to the nation as a region in which poverty was widespread, incomes shamefully below the national average, and job opportunities—especially for Negroes—severely limited. The situation was in many respects a novel one for Southerners. In the 1880's, when economic advances were modest in comparison with the 'fifties and early 'sixties, the nation welcomed Southern claims and accepted them at face value. During the 1930's, when all parts of the country were in tight straits, analyses of the South's economic backwardness, while arousing sectional hostility later in the decade, did not compare with the way in which the criticism during the Second Reconstruction aroused indignation and rekindled the flames of sectionalism. Now it was the South alone that offended the national dream of opulence and opportunity, and that offense was part of a larger pattern of crimes that everyone appeared to agree was peculiarly Southern.

The myth of national harmony and regional triumph

was another casualty of the Second Reconstruction. More than at any time since the 1860's, disharmony, virulent sectionalism, and an unending series of frustrations and defeats characterized the Southern experience. To some observers it seemed as though a spiritual malaise had seized the region. To others, with an historical bent of mind, it appeared that the South was determined to relive the most disastrous period of her history. Reacting to assaults from columnists and television pundits, clergymen and college professors, black and white demonstrators, and all branches of the federal government, Southerners revived the old rhetoric of interposition, nullification, and secession, issued ringing manifestos of warning and defiance, and in the heat of resistance to the civil rights movement spawned hate groups, a supercharged literature of Negrophobia, and instituted repressive measures to stifle internal dissent. Believing themselves to be under siege from a hostile nation determined to destroy them, they joined to their ritual of oppression stratagems of defense that could scarcely have been better calculated to stiffen the national will, bring on greater displays of federal power—including armed force—and thus assure the collapse, one after the other, of each new measure of defiance and the fateful creation of changes in their society they had sworn could never be made.

The irrationality and violence of the Southern response to the civil rights movement poignantly evoked memories of the calamitous dispute over slavery a century earlier; and in both national crises the South's mythic view of itself powerfully influenced its actions. The myth of the Old South furnished slaveholders with a comprehensive world view in which they could see themselves and their region as guardians of liberty, defenders of republican virtue, protectors of Negroes, and keepers of a gentlemen's code of honor. Accused by the nation of being enemies of liberty, subverters of republican virtue, oppressors of Negroes, and perpetrators of snobbish values, their behavior was hardly surprising. A century later, the myth of the New South expressed the Southerner's view that his was a land of riches, that it accepted and exemplified the American credo of bountiful opportunity, defended the nation's honor, and provided (or was on the point of providing) equally bountiful but harmoniously separate opportunity for the Negro. All of these views were now ridiculed during the Second Reconstruction: the new affluence and success so apparent on the surface hid a class system that exploited the masses of whites and restricted wealth to the few; the South's nationalism was a stranglehold on Congressional committees; and its oppression of the Negro caused it to be a stain on the nation's honor. Incredulity and wounded pride, mixed with a measure of fear, were the inevitable products of these assaults; and incredulity, offended pride, and fear are the handmaidens of irrational thought and violent action.

IV

With bewildering rapidity, however, the perspective of the mid-'sixties was lost in the kaleidoscopic swirl of events that followed in the last half of the decade. As so often before, the race problem made the difference and caused Americans to see both the nation and the South in a new light. After the victories in the spring and summer of 1965, the civil rights movement, partly because of its successes, splintered and lost direction. As it searched for a new focus the South continued the slow process of absorbing the changes that had already taken place. Demands made upon the region became fewer or took less dramatic forms. Integration proceeded in orderly fashion in more schools each year. Negroes were seen in greater numbers in occupations and public places previously barred to them. The tension and fear which had made racial change electric in the previous decade receded and Southern claims of progress toward racial justice assumed a superficial plausibility impossible to imagine in the recent past.

Simultaneously, the dynamic patterns set off by the Negro revolt in the South now spread outside the region—and the tactic of nonviolence was left behind. Starting with the Watts riot in 1965, non-Southern urban centers were hit with racial violence and police overkill on a grand scale. Earlier, the nation's anxious moments had come in the late summer in anticipation of the violence that would attend school openings in the South. Now, anxiety heightened during the spring in expectation of summer turmoil in Northern cities. The country witnessed the irony of Dr. King leading his Southern Christian Leadership Conference workers into Chicago in a vain effort to find solutions. A puzzled and frustrated people began to reorient their research programs and redirect their philanthropy outside the South. The blue-ribbon Kerner Commission, instructed to study the virulence and ubiquity of racial discord, reported in 1968 that "our nation is moving toward two societies, one black, one white—separate and unequal."[16] Incredible though it seemed, bigotry and oppression of blacks almost overnight ceased to be regarded as a Southern monopoly. Public leaders, including Southerners, spoke fervently of their determination to root out the racist cancer and pointed to the remarkable achievements of the past decade as proof of their good intentions. But the cancer spread. In the ghettoes and on the college campuses racial confrontations, charged with the electricity of black power, became almost a way of life in the last half of the 'sixties, and progress toward alleviation of their causes was uneven and unimpressive. In these circumstances the nation's image of itself as a land of moral innocence became a fragile inheritance, in more danger than ever before of being shattered.

The events of the late 'sixties threatened not only to dissipate the idea of racial justice but to dissolve other components of the nation's historic myth as well. Repudiations came from all directions, and for increasing numbers of persons faith in the old ideas was weakened or destroyed. The myth of American abundance and economic opportunity was attacked not only as an inaccurate reflection of reality but also as an unworthy ideal. Critics declared that the ideal rationalized an economic system whose excessively materialistic value premises promoted acquisitiveness and impersonality of the kind that led straight to a grasping, automated society undeserving of pride and loyalty. Lacking in novelty, this argument nonetheless gained added force because of other critiques of the nation's economic system. Wealthier than ever before in history, America was paradoxically afflicted with a more acute awareness of poverty than at any time since the Depression. Worse yet, the new discovery of poverty seemed especially enigmatic—precisely because of the generally high level of productivity—and for that reason doubly noxious. Other ironies abounded: a society of abundance institutionalized anti-poverty programs; a land of opportunity created head-start and upward-bound programs for youngsters deprived of opportunity; and manpower retraining schools were conducted for men and women lacking in skills that a free enterprise society would employ.

Criticism of the American record and ideal of economic progress was met by persuasive counterargument, and could be regarded as but another phase in a creative tradition of dissidence that always before had strengthened the nation. But only the most ingenious twists of imagination could keep alive the old idea of national invincibility. Mightier than ever before, the country was less able to wield its power to achieve its ends than it had been during the presidency of Theodore Roosevelt. This paradoxical and frustrating situation had been in the making for two decades. With Russia as a dedicated and successful antagonist and the atomic bomb a threat of annihilation, foreign policy since the onset of the Cold War was based on acceptance of the fact that single displays of decisive might to produce once-for-all solutions— so long an American characteristic—were no longer tenable. The Korean War, with its limited objectives, institutionalized the new foreign policy and President Truman's dismissal of General MacArthur—a warrior of the old school—was its most pointed symbol. Frustrations stemming from the new situation heightened throughout the 'fifties and early 'sixties, with important repercussions in domestic affairs, but it was not until the escalation of the war in Vietnam, in the last half of the decade, that the meaning of the nation's loss of power was driven home with a kind of terrible finality. Applying to the Vietnamese conflict the limited-war concepts which had been successful in Korea, the nation met discouragement and failure. No matter how many men were sent into battle or how many bombs were dropped, the prospects of military victory would not brighten. Productive of deep fissures at home and mounting abuse from friends abroad, the war dragged on—a disturbing testimony to the ironic outcome of America's historic conception of itself as master of its own fate, exemplar of the democratic faith, and beacon of liberty for the rest of mankind.

V

An ironic history—like the evil of race prejudice—was once thought to be something from which all Americans except Southerners were immune. But now that the nation as a whole was caught up in a maelstrom of contradictions its differences from the South appeared to be less significant than ever before. Since the Civil War most Americans had believed that the South would be absorbed into the mainstream of national development when its socio-economic system and moral views became standard "American." Hearteningly, the region made impressive material progress during the years after the Second World War, and in the later 'sixties it adjusted its attitudes toward the Negro remarkably. But the importance of these developments was undercut by the ironic twist of the national experience itself. In the final analysis, regional distinctions receded because of the infiltration into the total American experience of the elements of pathos, frustration, and imperfection that had long characterized the South.

As America entered a new era of history and as national images were undermined, the myth of the New South appeared to be losing its *raison d'être*. Southerners accepted new racial patterns that gave to the black man more dignity and greater opportunity than he had ever known before—only to see sharply highlighted the inadequacies of integration and the immensity of the problems caused by a heritage of oppression. The region's continuing economic progress, more substantial than ever before, was beset by the same kind of critiques that confounded national advances. Its growing identity with the national viewpoint, made possible initially by the nationalization of the race problem, was unrewarded by a sense of relief and achievement because the nation itself appeared to have lost a sense of destiny. Thus deprived of the larger frame of reference which had always conditioned its character and given it its special appeal, the myth paradoxically pictured a regional way of life in harmony with a mirage.

Admirable in its vision, the New South creed had been manipulated through most of its history by men who served the region poorly, and the hold it gained over the American mind had obstructed more frequently than it had promoted achievement of its ideals. In the end, it was the force of outside pressure combined with the Negro revolt that made a reality of at least part of its ideal. Study of the history of the New South creed should contribute to greater understanding of the special mental and material forces that have shaped the Southern experience—an important end in itself. But reflection on its relationship to the American faith in opulence, triumph, and innocence may also illuminate the ways in which rigidification of even noble human aspirations can result in powerful myths that shroud and institutionalize abhorrent realities. The dynamics of mythmaking suggest that resolution of the nation's dilemmas cannot be accomplished by clinging doggedly to its old myths—but also that rediscovery of their core of nobility could yet result from the contemporary turbulence caused by pressures from without and revolt from within.

Notes

PROLOGUE: The New South Symbol

1. Joel Chandler Harris, ed., *Life of Henry W. Grady, Including His Writings and Speeches* (New York, 1890), p. 109.
2. *Manufacturers' Record*, March 17, 1888.
3. The industrial journal *The New South* was published in Birmingham in the 1880's. *New South* (titles vary) was an organ of the Communist Party of the U.S.A., published in Chattanooga and Birmingham in the 1930's; it was a successor to *Southern Worker*.
4. George B. Tindall, "Mythology: A New Frontier in Southern History," in Frank E. Vandiver, ed., *The Idea of the South: Pursuit of a Central Theme* (Chicago, 1964), p. 10.
5. David M. Potter, "On Understanding the South: A Review Article," *Journal of Southern History*, XXX (November 1964), 460.
6. Mark Schorer, "The Necessity of Myth," in Henry A. Murray, ed., *Myth and Mythmaking* (New York, 1960), p. 355.
7. C. Vann Woodward, "The Antislavery Myth," *American Scholar*, XXXI (Spring 1962), 325.
8. Quoted in Everett Carter, "The 'Little Myth' of Robert Penn Warren," *Modern Fiction Studies*, VI (Spring 1960), 3.
9. William E. Dodd, *Statesmen of the Old South; or, From Radicalism to Conservative Revolt* (New York, 1911).
10. David M. Potter, "The Enigma of the South," *Yale Review*, LI (Autumn 1961), 144.
11. Twelve Southerners, *I'll Take My Stand: The South and the Agrarian Tradition* (New York, 1930).
12. Potter, "Enigma of the South," 150.

13. Ulrich B. Phillips, "The Central Theme of Southern History," *American Historical Review*, XXXIV (October 1928), 31.

14. C. Vann Woodward, "The Search for Southern Identity," in his *The Burden of Southern History* (Baton Rouge, 1960), pp. 3–25; Harry Ashmore, *An Epitaph for Dixie* (New York, 1958); George B. Tindall, William B. Hesseltine, Cleanth Brooks, and Rupert B. Vance, "The Status and Future of Regionalism—A Symposium," *Journal of Southern History*, XXVI (February 1960), 22–56; John T. Westbrook, "Twilight of Southern Regionalism," *Southwest Review*, XLII (Summer 1957), 234.

15. Edgar T. Thompson, ed., *Perspectives on the South: Agenda for Research* (Durham, 1967), p. xi.

16. W. J. Cash, *The Mind of the South* (New York, 1941), pp. ix–x.

17. The following works are especially helpful: Clement Eaton, *The Mind of the Old South* (Baton Rouge, 1964); Clement Eaton, *The Freedom-of-Thought Struggle in the Old South* (New York, 1964); William Sumner Jenkins, *Pro-Slavery Thought in the Old South* (Chapel Hill, 1935); William R. Taylor, *Cavalier and Yankee: The Old South and American National Character* (New York, 1961); Rollin G. Osterweis, *Romanticism and Nationalism in the Old South* (New Haven, 1949); and Eugene D. Genovese, *The Political Economy of Slavery: Studies in the Economy and Society of the Slave South* (New York, 1965). For a survey of the literature see Herbert J. Doherty, Jr., "The Mind of the Antebellum South," in Arthur S. Link and Rembert W. Patrick, eds., *Writing Southern History: Essays in Historiography in Honor of Fletcher M. Green* (Baton Rouge, 1965), pp. 198–223.

18. There has also been a relative paucity of articles on the postwar period. David Potter's study of articles appearing in the *Journal of Southern History* from 1935 through 1949 shows that, of those that could be classified by period, 48.8 per cent were written on the period 1830–65 while only 16.3 per cent were devoted to the entire period since the Reconstruction; David M. Potter, "An Appraisal of Fifteen Years of the *Journal of Southern History*, 1935–1949," *Journal of Southern History*, XVI (February 1950), 25–32. During the period 1950–63, the proportion on the era since

1877 went up slightly, to 21.9 per cent of the total classifiable by period, but studies in intellectual history are remarkably few; Paul M. Gaston, "The 'New South,'" in Link and Patrick, eds., *Writing Southern History*, p. 332.

19. Tindall, "Mythology," in Vandiver, ed., *The Idea of the South*, p. 15.
20. Woodward, *Burden of Southern History*, pp. 16–22.

1 Birth of a Creed

1. Daniel Harvey Hill, "Education," *The Land We Love*, I (May 1866), 8.
2. Edwin DeLeon, "The New South: What it is Doing and What it Wants," *Putnam's Magazine*, XV (April 1870), 458.
3. Benjamin H. Hill, Jr., *Senator Benjamin H. Hill of Georgia: His Life, Speeches and Writings* (Atlanta, 1893), pp. 335–6.
4. Joel Chandler Harris, ed., *Life of Henry W. Grady, Including His Writings and Speeches* (New York, 1890), p. 449; Raymond B. Nixon, *Henry W. Grady: Spokesman of the New South* (New York, 1943), pp. 243–53.
5. Robert S. Cotterill, "The Old South to the New," *Journal of Southern History*, XV (February 1949), 3.
6. Port Royal [S.C.] *The New South*, March 15, 1862. The story of the sea-islands is told in Willie Lee Rose, *Rehearsal for Reconstruction: The Port Royal Experiment* (Indianapolis, 1964).
7. The standard monograph on the pro-slavery philosophy is William S. Jenkins, *Pro-Slavery Thought in the Old South* (Chapel Hill, 1935). Southern attempts to stifle dissent are the subject of Clement Eaton, *The Freedom-of-Thought Struggle in the Old South* (New York, 1964).
8. Ben Allston, "Address . . . Before the Winyah Indigo Society," *DeBow's Review*, VII (August 1869), 669.
9. J. D. B. DeBow, "The Future of the South," *DeBow's Review*, I (January 1866), 8–14.
10. Matthew Fontaine Maury, "The American Colony in Mexico," *DeBow's Review*, I (June 1866), 623–30.

11. *Ibid.*, p. 623.

12. A. P. Merrill, "Southern Labor," *DeBow's Review*, VI (July 1869), 592.

13. J. D. B. DeBow, "The Future of South Carolina—Her Inviting Resources," *DeBow's Review*, II (July 1866), 38.

14. DeBow, "Future of the South," p. 14.

15. J. D. B. DeBow, "Manufactures, the South's True Remedy," *DeBow's Review*, III (February 1867), 176–7.

16. Robert M. Patton, "The New Era of Southern Manufactures," *DeBow's Review*, III (January 1867), 56–69.

17. Charles J. James, "Cotton Manufactures—Great Field for the South," *DeBow's Review*, I (May 1866), 504–15.

18. "Exodus," *DeBow's Review*, V (November 1868), 983. See also S. H. Gilman, "Cotton Manufacturing in or near the Cotton Fields of Texas Compared with the Same at any Point Distant Therefrom," *DeBow's Review*, V (September 1868), 837–40.

19. John C. Delavique, "Cotton," *DeBow's Review*, IV (December 1867), 571. See also H. T. Moore, "The Industrial Interests of the South," *DeBow's Review*, V (February 1868), 147–55.

20. John A. Wagener, "European Immigration," *DeBow's Review*, IV (July and August 1867), 94–105.

21. E. C. Cabell, "White Emigration to the South," *DeBow's Review*, I (January 1866), 92.

22. William M. Burwell, "To the Patrons of DeBow's Review," *DeBow's Review*, V (March 1868), 332–3.

23. D. H. Hill, "Education," p. 2.

24. *Ibid.*, pp. 8–9.

25. *Ibid.*, p. 9.

26. D. H. Hill, "Industrial Combinations," *The Land We Love*, V (May 1868), 31.

27. D. H. Hill, "The Old South," *Southern Historical Society Papers*, XVI (1888), 425. Hill's magazine is appraised briefly in Ray M. Atchison, *"The Land We Love:* A Southern Post-Bellum Magazine of Agriculture, Literature, and Military History," *North Carolina Historical Review*, XXXVII (October 1960), 506–15.

28. William Lee Trenholm, *The South: An Address on the Third Anniversary of the Charleston Board of Trade* (Charleston, 1869), p. 1 and *passim*.

29. Richmond *Whig*, "The Industrial Policy of the South," in *DeBow's Review*, VI (November 1869), 929.

30. Harry Simonhoff, *Jewish Notables in America, 1776–1865* (New York, 1956), pp. 378–81; *Who Was Who in America: Historical Volume, 1607–1896* (Chicago, 1963), p. 144.

31. DeLeon, "New South," p. 458.

32. *Ibid.*, p. 459.

33. *Ibid.*, pp. 459–60.

34. Edwin DeLeon, "The New South," *Harper's New Monthly Magazine*, XLVIII (1874), 270–80; 406–22; XLIX (1874), 555–68. Edwin DeLeon, "Ruin and Reconstruction of the Southern States," *The Southern Magazine*, XIV (1874), 17–41, 287–309, 453–82, 561–90; Edwin DeLeon, "The Southern States Since the War," *Fraser's Magazine*, XC (1874), 153–63, 346–66, 620–37.

35. B. H. Hill, Jr., *Senator Benjamin H. Hill*, pp. 335–7.

36. On Hill's life see Haywood Pearce, Jr., *Benjamin H. Hill: Secession and Reconstruction* (Chicago, 1928).

37. Nixon, *Grady*, p. 245 *n*.

38. B. H. Hill, Jr., *Senator Benjamin H. Hill*, p. 342.

39. *Ibid.*, pp. 342–3.

40. William D. Trammell, Review of "*Address Delivered Before the Alumni Society of the University of Georgia*. By Benjamin H. Hill," *The Southern Magazine*, X (June 1872), 751–61. William D. Trammell, *Ça Ira, A Novel* (New York, 1874).

41. Trammell, *Ça Ira*, p. 41.

42. Another novelist who turned to the emerging New South point of view as a field for fiction was John Esten Cooke. One of his characters states that "the old Virginia system resulted in immense comfort, but it did not result in profit, which is a good thing, however it may be denounced by some. Profit means prosperity, and prosperity means churches, lyceums, academies, schools, railroads, material advancement and happiness." *The Heir of Gaymount* (New York, 1870), p. 56.

43. Margaret J. Preston, "Gospel of Labor," *The Southern Magazine*, IX (December 1871), 733–4.

44. Harris, ed., *Grady*, p. 6.

45. Nixon, *Grady*, p. 136.

46. Quoted in S. Frank Logan, "Francis W. Dawson, 1840–1889: South Carolina Editor" (unpublished master's thesis, Duke University, 1947), p. 74.

47. *Ibid.*, pp. 67, 214.

48. " 'The Great South' Series of Papers," *Scribner's Monthly*, IX (December 1874), 248.

49. Albion W. Tourgee, *A Fool's Errand, By One of the Fools: The Famous Romance of American History* (New York, 1879), p. 292.

50. *Ibid.*, p. 345.

51. Raleigh *News and Observer*, November 29, 1880, quoted in Broadus Mitchell, *The Rise of the Cotton Mills in the South* (Baltimore, 1921), pp. 89–90.

52. Atlanta *Constitution*, November 7, 1880.

2   The Opulent South

1. Atlanta *Constitution*, August 20, 1884.

2. *Manufacturers' Record*, August 20, 1887. See also William D. Kelley, *The Old South and the New* (New York, 1888), pp. 161–2.

3. *Manufacturers' Record*, June 1, 1889.

4. Charles R. Anderson, ed., *Sidney Lanier*, 10 vols. (Baltimore, 1945), IX, 230.

5. David M. Potter, *People of Plenty: Economic Abundance and the American Character* (Chicago, 1954).

6. C. Vann Woodward, *The Burden of Southern History* (Baton Rouge, 1960), p. 17.

7. Douglas C. North, *The Economic Growth of the United States, 1790–1860* (Englewood Cliffs, N.J., 1961), p. 122.

8. Eugene D. Genovese, *The Political Economy of Slavery: Studies in the Economy and Society of the Slave South* (New York, 1965), pp. 124–53.

9. Thomas Prentice Kettell, *Southern Wealth and Northern Profits, As Exhibited in Statistical Facts and Official Figures: Showing the Necessity of Union to the Future Prosperity and Welfare of the Republic* (New York, 1860).

10. Eric F. Goldman, *Rendezvous With Destiny: A History of Modern American Reform* (New York, 1952), p. 3.

11. The generalization holds true for lesser New South spokesmen as well. Nearly all of them were young men in the 'eighties. The years in which they matured had a sobering effect on them but, unlike the older generation—veterans

of secession and defeat—they were full of youthful optimism about the future.

12. Raymond B. Nixon, *Henry W. Grady: Spokesman of the New South* (New York, 1943), chaps. 2–3.

13. *Ibid.*, chaps. 3–9.

14. Joel Chandler Harris, ed., *Life of Henry W. Grady, Including His Writings and Speeches* (New York, 1890), p. 449.

15. Howard Bunyan Clay, "Daniel Augustus Tompkins: An American Bourbon" (unpublished doctoral dissertation, University of North Carolina, 1950), pp. 1–4.

16. *Ibid.* See also George Tayloe Winston, *A Builder of the New South, Being the Story of the Life Work of Daniel Augustus Tompkins* (Garden City, 1920). "The only thing I wanted the paper for," Tompkins declared, "was to preach the doctrine of industrial development and the reasons for it"; Clay, "Tompkins," p. 60.

17. Yoshimitsu Ide, "The Significance of Richard Hathaway Edmonds and His *Manufacturers' Record* in the New South" (unpublished doctoral dissertation, University of Florida, 1959), p. 34.

18. *Ibid.*, pp. 34–5.

19. *Ibid.*, pp. 43–5, 53–4.

20. Burton J. Hendrick, *The Training of an American: The Earlier Life and Letters of Walter H. Page, 1855–1913* (Boston, 1928), pp. 1–41.

21. *Ibid.*, pp. 42–108.

22. Joseph Frazier Wall, *Henry Watterson: Reconstructed Rebel* (New York, 1956), pp. 3–33.

23. *Ibid.*, pp. 34–50.

24. [E. L. Godkin], "The White Side of the Southern Question," *The Nation*, XXXI (August 19, 1880), 126.

25. Daniel A. Tompkins, *Fourth of July Address at Gastonia, N.C.* (n.p., 1902), p. 10.

26. Ide, "Edmonds," p. 25.

27. Kelley, *Old South and New*, pp. 2, 121.

28. *Ibid.*, pp. 121, 159.

29. Daniel A. Tompkins, *Manufactures* (Charlotte, 1900), p. 5.

30. Harris, ed., *Grady*, pp. 90–1; Atlanta *Constitution*, February 20, 1881.

31. John W. Johnston, "The Emancipation of the Southern Whites," *Manufacturers' Record*, July 9, 1887.

32. Kelley, *Old South and New*, dedication page.

33. Tompkins, *Manufactures*, pp. 4–5.

34. Ide, "Edmonds," pp. 85–6; R. H. Edmonds, *The Old South and the New* (n.p., 1903), pp. 3–5.

35. D. A. Tompkins, "Southern Prosperity," *Manufacturers' Record*, June 4, 1887.

36. W. H. Page, "Study of an Old Southern Borough," *Atlantic Monthly*, XLVII (May 1881), 648–58.

37. Hendrick, *Page, Earlier Life*, p. 161.

38. *Ibid.*, p. 168.

39. Nicholas Worth [pseud., Walter Hines Page], *The Southerner* (New York, 1909), p. 316.

40. Josephus Daniels, *Tar Heel Editor* (Chapel Hill, 1939), p. 256.

41. Hendrick, *Page, Earlier Life*, pp. 176–81.

42. W. H. Page, "The Rebuilding of Old Commonwealths," *Atlantic Monthly*, LXXXIX (May 1902), 654.

43. Atlanta *Constitution*, June 4, 1885.

44. Ide, "Edmonds," pp. 109–17.

45. Anderson, *Lanier*, V, 334–58.

46. *Ibid.*, I, 34–9. Lanier's role as a New South man is an interesting one, deserving a study in its own right. His "New South" essay and his sympathy for the farmer, expressed in such poems as "Corn," have led some students to see him as a forerunner of the Southern Agrarians of the 1930's, certainly no admirers of the New South movement. This view is re-enforced by his poem, "The Symphony," a poetic diatribe against the materialism engendered by the industrial movement (see Anderson, *Lanier*, I, 46–56). The Agrarians, however, were highly critical of Lanier, partly because they scorned his literary talents but also because they felt he had sold his soul by writing promotional literature for Florida and because they regarded him, in essence, as a New South publicist. Edwin Mims, *Sidney Lanier* (Boston, 1905), offered an interpretation of Lanier that pictures him as a New South man. Aubrey Starke's *Sidney Lanier, A Biographical and Critical Study* (Chapel Hill, 1933), appearing at the height of the Agrarian movement, aroused considerable controversy by depicting Lanier as a forerunner of the Agrarians. Robert Penn Warren, one of the Agrarians, attacked this interpretation in a scorching essay in *The American Review*, II (November 1933), 27–45.

47. *Manufacturers' Record*, December 11, 1886; Atlanta *Constitution*, January 11, 1882.

48. Atlanta *Constitution*, August 10, 1884.

49. *Ibid.*

50. *Ibid.*, December 13, 1882. For other editorials on crop diversification, see issues of January 11, 1882, March 4, 1882, September 30, 1882, October 14, 1883, August 10, 1884, and January 19, 1886.

51. *Ibid.*, February 24, 1883.

52. *Ibid.*; Kelley, *Old South and New*, p. 121.

53. Genovese, *Political Economy of Slavery*, pp. 180–220.

54. *Manufacturers' Record*, December 11, 1886.

55. Atlanta *Constitution*, January 19, 1886.

56. *Ibid.*, November 29, 1886.

57. William Peterfield Trent, "Dominant Forces in Southern Life," *Atlantic Monthly*, LXXIX (January 1897), 50.

58. *Manufacturers' Record*, March 9, 1889.

59. Harris, ed., *Grady*, pp. 113–14.

60. *Manufacturers' Record*, February 11, 1888.

61. Kelley, *Old South and New*, p. 75.

62. Richard H. Edmonds, *Tasks of Young Men of the South* (n.p., 1903), p. 9; *Manufacturers' Record*, March 9, 1889.

63. John C. Calhoun Newton, *The New South and the Methodist Episcopal Church, South* (Baltimore, 1887), pp. 9–27.

64. Kelley, *Old South and New*, pp. 12–13.

65. Harris, ed., *Grady*, pp. 204–5. In an editorial column, Grady fairly boiled with indignation because no native Georgia materials were selected in the construction of the Georgia capitol; Atlanta *Constitution*, September 27, 1884. The funeral oration was immensely popular with the New South spokesmen. Tompkins, for example, repeated it from memory on at least one occasion; Tompkins, *Manufactures*, p. 3. Edmonds made the same point, in a rhetorically less effective manner, when he wrote: "We use Northern stoves to cook our food; Northern tableware, from knives and forks to coffee and tea pots; we cover our table with Northern cloth and sit in Northern-made chairs; we furnish our homes with Northern-made carpets and furniture; we lie down at night on Northern-made beds, and cover ourselves with Northern-made blankets; we wash in Northern-made basins, dry our faces on Northern-made towels, brush our teeth with Northern-made brushes, comb our hair with Northern-

made combs, put on clothes made from Northern goods; we ride in Northern-made wagons and carriages drawn by Northern-made harness, travel in Northern-made cars running on Northern-made rails and drawn by Northern-made locomotives. We do all this in spite of the fact that the South is the best country in the world for manufactures. Not only ought we to manufacture all these things for home consumption, but we ought to be pushing out and supplying the wants of other sections." Ide, "Edmonds," pp. 82–3.

66. Quoted in Nixon, *Grady*, p. 182.

67. Atlanta *Constitution*, October 20, 1883, May 15, 1884, April 23, 1885, and December 5, 1889.

68. *Manufacturers' Record*, September 4, 1886, and April 20, 1889.

69. Edmonds, *The South's Redemption: From Poverty to Prosperity* (Baltimore, 1890), p. 5.

70. *Manufacturers' Record*, November 6, 1886; Ide, "Edmonds," pp. 195–207.

71. Sample works include William H. Harrison, Jr., *How to Get Rich in the South. Telling What to Do, How to Do It, and the Profits to be Realized* (Chicago, 1888), and Eugene C. Robertson, *Road to Wealth Leads Through the South* (Cincinnati, 1894). Evidence of the extensiveness of the promotional campaign is abundant, but for a particularly impressive source see the seventy volumes of pamphlets in the Francis W. Dawson collection at the University of North Carolina. Scarcely a volume of the collection is without several examples of promotional literature.

72. *Manufacturers' Record*, March 19, 1887. Grady was also enthusiastic about Hillyard's volume and Edmonds's scheme for promoting it. He believed that the book would "give outsiders a better idea of the material greatness of the new south than anything that has yet appeared in print." It was a happy omen, and "the signs of the times are all that we could desire." Atlanta *Constitution*, March 20, 1887.

73. Ide, "Edmonds," pp. 89–91. Annistonians followed up Kelley's article with a eulogy to "the great Pennsylvania statesman," and a paid advertisement seconding Kelley's designation of their community as "The Model City of the South"; *Manufacturers' Record*, February 25, 1888. Edmonds joined the chorus the next month, citing Anniston

as a wonderful example of the South's progress—progress
that had "already astonished the world"; *ibid.*, March 10,
1888.

74. Atlanta *Constitution*, November 16, 1881.

75. Eugene V. Smalley, "The New Orleans Exposition," *Century Magazine*, XXX (May 1885), 4.

76. Atlanta *Constitution*, October 12, 1887.

77. "Studies in the South," *Atlantic Monthly*, LI (January 1883), 95.

78. Rowland T. Berthoff, "Southern Attitudes Toward Immigration, 1865–1914," *Journal of Southern History*, XVII (August 1951), 328–60; C. Vann Woodward, *Origins of the New South, 1877–1913* (Baton Rouge, 1951), pp. 297–9.

79. *Manufacturers' Record*, February 11, 1888.

80. Atlanta *Constitution*, February 17, 1888.

81. W. N. Reeves, "The Unemployed—Send Them South," *Outlook*, XLIX (February 10, 1894), 286.

82. Atlanta *Constitution*, March 30, 1881.

83. *Ibid.*, April 11, 1885.

84. *Manufacturers' Record*, May 19, 1888.

85. Atlanta *Constitution*, March 20, 1885.

86. Robert L. Brandfon, *Cotton Kingdom of the New South: A History of the Yazoo Mississippi Delta From Reconstruction to the Twentieth Century* (Cambridge, Mass., 1967), p. 141.

87. Atlanta *Constitution*, April 23, 1886.

88. *Ibid.*, August 27, 1889.

89. Wilbur Fisk Tillett, "The White Man of the New South," *Century Magazine*, XXIII (March 1887), 776.

90. *Manufacturers' Record*, September 6, 1890.

91. *Ibid.*, July 2, 1887.

92. Harris, ed., *Grady*, p. 109.

93. Kelley, *Old South and New*, pp. 161–2.

94. Edmonds, *South's Redemption*, p. 3.

3   The Triumphant South

1. Henry Watterson, *The Compromises of Life* (New York, 1903), p. 289.

2. Quoted in William Malone Baskervill, *Southern Writers: Biographical and Critical Studies* (Nashville, 1907), p. 134.

3. Richard H. Edmonds, *Tasks of Young Men of the South* (n.p., 1903), p. 9.

4. Amory Dwight Mayo, "Is There a New South?" *Social Economist*, V (October 1893), 208.

5. Paul H. Buck, *The Road to Reunion, 1865–1900* (Boston, 1937), p. 22.

6. Henry Steele Commager, *The American Mind: An Interpretation of American Thought and Character Since the 1880's* (New Haven, 1950), p. 5.

7. C. Vann Woodward, *The Burden of Southern History* (Baton Rouge, 1960), pp. 18–19.

8. Edward Atkinson, *Address Given in Atlanta . . . for the Promotion of an International Cotton Exhibition* (Boston, 1881), p. 8.

9. Benjamin H. Hill, Jr., *Senator Benjamin H. Hill of Georgia: His Life, Speeches and Writings* (Atlanta, 1891), p. 460.

10. Edward Mayes, *Lucius Q. C. Lamar: His Life, Times and Speeches, 1825–1893* (Nashville, 1896), p. 187.

11. Quoted in Raymond B. Nixon, *Henry W. Grady: Spokesman of the New South* (New York, 1943), p. 253.

12. *Harper's Weekly*, XXI (July 7, 1877), 519.

13. Nixon, *Grady*, p. 110.

14. Atlanta *Constitution*, January 4, 1880.

15. *Ibid.*, September 20, 1881.

16. *Ibid.*, November 4, 1881.

17. *Ibid.*, May 18, 1884.

18. Nixon, *Grady*, pp. 238–9.

19. *Ibid.*, pp. 243–4.

20. Joel Chandler Harris, ed., *Life of Henry W. Grady, Including His Writings and Speeches* (New York, 1890), p. 83. Grady took considerable license in his opening paragraph. There is no record of a speech by Hill at Tammany Hall in 1866. Hill did address the Young Men's Democratic Union in New York City on October 6, 1868, but that speech does not contain the language attributed to Hill by Grady. The reconciliation theme is dominant, but Hill's tone was considerably more belligerent than Grady's as he scolded the North for unreasonable Reconstruction policies and urged the defeat of Grant in the November elections. The text of the speech appears in B. H. Hill, Jr., *Senator*

Benjamin H. Hill, pp. 320–31. The phrase closest to that used by Grady appears toward the end of the speech: "The South yields secession, and yields slavery, and *yields them for equal reunion*" (p. 330).

21. Harris, ed., *Grady*, pp. 85–6.
22. *Ibid.*, p. 87.
23. *Ibid.*, pp. 87–8.
24. *Ibid.*, pp. 88–93.
25. Nixon, *Grady*, p. 253.
26. Harris, ed., *Grady*, p. 200.
27. *Ibid.*, dedication page.
28. Robert Bingham, *The New South: An Address . . . in the Interest of National Aid to Education* (n.p., 1884), p. 4.
29. Charles Dudley Warner, "Impressions of the South," *Harper's New Monthly Magazine*, LXXI (September 1885), 548.
30. Charles Dudley Warner, "The South Revisited," *Harper's New Monthly Magazine*, LXXIV (March 1887), 640.
31. "Topics of the Times," *Century Magazine*, XXX (October 1885), 964.
32. Atticus G. Haygood, *Our Brother in Black: His Freedom and His Future* (New York, 1881), p. 27.
33. Harold F. Williamson, *Edward Atkinson: The Biography of an American Liberal* (Boston, 1934), p. 176.
34. Arthur S. Link, ed., *The Papers of Woodrow Wilson* (Princeton, 1966–   ), I, 618.
35. Arthur Krock, ed., *Editorials of Henry Watterson* (New York, 1923), p. 41.
36. Burton J. Hendrick, *The Training of an American: The Earlier Life and Lettters of Walter H. Page, 1855–1913* (Boston, 1928), p. 34.
37. Arlin Turner, *George W. Cable: A Biography* (Durham, 1956), pp. 247–8.
38. Harris, ed., *Grady*, pp. 180–98.
39. Isaac F. Marcosson, *"Marse Henry": A Biography of Henry Watterson* (New York, 1951), pp. 83–4.
40. Watterson, *Compromises of Life*, pp. 289–93.
41. Henry Watterson, "Oddities of Southern Life," *Century Magazine*, XXIII (April 1882), 885.
42. Richard H. Edmonds, *Unparalleled Industrial Progress* (n.p., n.d.), p. 673.

43. Yoshimitsu Ide, "The Significance of Richard Hathaway Edmonds and His *Manufacturers' Record* in the New South" (unpublished doctoral dissertation, University of Florida, 1959), pp. 54–5.

44. Buck, *Road to Reunion*, pp. 186–7.

45. [E. L. Godkin], "The White Side of the Southern Question," *The Nation*, XXXI (August 19, 1880), 126.

46. Atlanta *Constitution*, January 15, 1887.

47. Daniel A. Tompkins, *Fourth of July Address at Gastonia, N.C.* (n.p., 1902), pp. 2–5.

48. Walter Hines Page, "The Rebuilding of Old Commonwealths," *Atlantic Monthly*, LXXXIX (May 1902), 651–2.

49. Samuel C. Mitchell, "The Nationalization of Southern Sentiment," *South Atlantic Quarterly*, VII (April 1908), 110–12.

50. Atlanta *Constitution*, June 19, 1887.

51. Richard H. Edmonds, *Facts About the South* (Baltimore, 1907), p. 43.

52. Harris, ed., *Grady*, p. 88.

53. James Phelan, *The New South: The Democratic Position on the Tariff; Speech . . . Delivered at Covington, Tenn.* (Memphis, 1886), p. 2.

54. *Ibid.*, pp. 1–6.

55. David A. Robertson, "Amory Dwight Mayo," *Dictionary of American Biography*, XII, 461–2.

56. Mayo, "New South?", pp. 200–8.

57. Judson C. Ward, ed., *The New South: Thanksgiving Sermon, 1880, by Atticus G. Haygood*, in *Emory University Publications, Sources and Reprints*, Series VI (1950), No. 3, pp. v–xi. The best biography of Haygood is Harold W. Mann, *Atticus Greene Haygood: Methodist Bishop, Editor, and Educator* (Athens, Ga., 1965).

58. Ward, ed., *Haygood Thanksgiving Sermon*, p. vii.

59. *Ibid.*, p. viii.

60. *Ibid.*, pp. 1–12.

61. The most recent biography of Curry is Jessie Pearl Rice, *J. L. M. Curry: Southerner, Statesman and Educator* (New York, 1959), but Edwin Anderson Alderman and Armistead Churchill Gordon, *J. L. M. Curry, A Biography* (New York, 1911) remains useful and is particularly valuable for the number of contemporary documents reproduced in it.

62. J. L. M. Curry, *Address Delivered Before the Association*

of *Confederate Veterans, Richmond, Virginia, July 1, 1896*
(Richmond, 1896), pp. 26–7.

63. J. L. M. Curry, "Citizenship and Education," *Education*,
V (September 1884), 86.

64. J. L. M. Curry, "Annual Report . . . 1881," in *Proceedings
of the Trustees of the Peabody Education Fund, 1881–
1887* (Cambridge, Mass., 1888), III, 9; J. L. M. Curry,
"Address in Response to an Invitation from the Senate and
House of Representatives of Alabama, February 6th, 1885,"
ibid., III, 266.

65. "From the Address of Dr. Curry to the Legislature of
Alabama, 1 February, 1889," in *Proceedings of the Trustees
of the Peabody Education Fund, 1887–1892* (Cambridge,
Mass., 1893), IV, 152.

66. Atlanta *Constitution*, November 17, 1882.

67. *Manufacturers' Record*, January 4, 1900.

68. Bingham, *New South*, p. 22.

69. Burton J. Hendrick, *The Life and Letters of Walter H.
Page*, 3 vols. (New York, 1922–5), I, 74–9.

70. *Ibid.*, I, 79; Charles Grier Sellers, Jr., "Walter Hines Page
and the Spirit of the New South," *North Carolina Historical
Review*, XXIX (October 1952), 494.

71. Mark Twain, *Life on the Mississippi* (Boston, 1883), p.
412.

72. *Manufacturers' Record*, November 3, 1888.

73. *Ibid.*, August 14, 1886.

74. William D. Kelley, *The Old South and the New* (New
York, 1888), p. 95.

75. W. H. Wallace, *Three Essentials to Success: Money, Reputation, Character* (Newberry, S.C., 1887), p. 3.

76. *Manufacturers' Record*, June 23, 1888.

77. Watterson, "Oddities of Southern Life," p. 885.

78. Atlanta *Constitution*, September 23, 1881; Chapel Hill
Ledger, September 27, 1879; Edmonds, *Tasks of Young
Men of the South*, p. 2.

79. Atkinson, *Address for Promotion of Cotton Exhibition*,
p. 13.

80. Quoted in Nixon, *Grady*, p. 183.

81. Atlanta *Constitution*, April 9, 1882; Harris, ed., *Grady*,
p. 88; Atlanta *Constitution*, May 25, 1887.

82. Quoted in Ide, "Edmonds," p. 302.

83. Atlanta *Constitution*, August 15, 1880.

84. Wallace, *Three Essentials to Success*, pp. 4–5.

85. *Ibid.*, p. 4.

86. William S. Speer, *The Law of Success* (Nashville, 1885), p. 20.

87. Atlanta *Constitution*, July 23, 1881.

88. *Manufacturers' Record*, October 22, 1887.

89. Richard Hofstadter, *Social Darwinism in American Thought*, rev. ed. (Boston, 1955).

90. Quoted in C. Vann Woodward, *Origins of the New South, 1877–1913* (Baton Rouge, 1951), p. 148.

91. Howard Bunyan Clay, "Daniel Augustus Tompkins: An American Bourbon" (unpublished doctoral dissertation, University of North Carolina, 1950), pp. i, 318.

92. John C. Calhoun Newton, *The New South and the Methodist Episcopal Church, South* (Baltimore, 1887), p. 27.

93. Sellers, "Page and the Spirit of the New South," 497–8.

94. Nixon, *Grady*, p. 310.

95. Edmonds, *Tasks of Young Men of the South*, p. 3.

96. Mayo, "New South?", 204.

97. Edmonds, *Facts About the South*, p. 61; Richard H. Edmonds, *The Old South and the New* (n.p., 1903), p. 1.

98. Holland Thompson, *The New South* (New Haven, 1919), p. 7.

99. Henry W. Grady, *The New South*, ed. Oliver Dyer (New York, 1890), p. 166.

100. Edmonds, *Facts About the South*, p. 3.

101. Harris, ed., *Grady*, p. 119.

102. Ide, "Edmonds," p. 24.

103. Joseph G. Brown, *The New South* (Raleigh, 1902), p. 4.

104. Kelley, *Old South and New*, pp. 157–8.

105. Newton, *New South*, p. vi.

106. Broadus Mitchell, *The Rise of the Cotton Mills in the South* (Baltimore, 1921), p. 77.

107. Edmonds, *Tasks of Young Men of the South*, p. 9.

4   The Innocent South

1. *Manufacturers' Record*, March 14, 1891.

2. Joel Chandler Harris, ed., *Life of Henry W. Grady, Including His Writings and Speeches* (New York, 1890), p. 307.

3. *Ibid.*, p. 100.
4. Thomas U. Dudley, "How Shall We Help the Negro?" *Century Magazine*, XXX (June 1885), 277.
5. Frederick Jackson Turner, *The Frontier in American History* (New York, 1920), pp. 281–2.
6. Reinhold Niebuhr, *The Irony of American History* (New York, 1952), p. 24.
7. C. Vann Woodward, *The Burden of Southern History* (Baton Rouge, 1960), pp. 19–20.
8. For a good collection of foreign commentaries, see Henry Steele Commager, *America in Perspective: The United States Through Foreign Eyes* (New York, 1947).
9. Gunnar Myrdal, *An American Dilemma: The Negro Problem and Modern Democracy*, 2 vols. (New York, 1944), I, 1–13.
10. Works on the anti-slavery views of the Jeffersonian era are numerous. For a convenient summary, see William S. Jenkins, *Pro-Slavery Thought in the Old South* (Chapel Hill, 1935), chap. 1; Jefferson's thought is discussed in Dumas Malone, *Jefferson the Virginian* (Boston, 1948), chaps. 18–20. Robert McColley, *Slavery and Jeffersonian Virginia* (Urbana, 1964) minimizes the importance of anti-slavery thought of the period. The most recent study is Winthrop D. Jordan, *White Over Black: American Attitudes Toward the Negro, 1550–1812* (Chapel Hill, 1968).
11. The standard monograph on the pro-slavery ideology is Jenkins, *Pro-Slavery Thought*. A convenient collection of pro-slavery writings appears in Eric L. McKitrick, ed., *Slavery Defended: The Views of the Old South* (Englewood Cliffs, N.J., 1963).
12. The theory of retrogression is discussed in Guion Griffis Johnson's perceptive essay, "The Ideology of White Supremacy, 1876–1910," in Fletcher Melvin Green, ed., *Essays in Southern History* (Chapel Hill, 1949), pp. 139–43. White attitudes toward the Negro, with emphasis on the South in the post-Reconstruction period, are the subject of Claude H. Nolen, *The Negro's Image in the South: The Anatomy of White Supremacy* (Lexington, Ky., 1967).
13. Philip Alexander Bruce, *The Plantation Negro as a Freeman: Observations on His Character, Condition, and Prospects in Virginia* (New York, 1889), pp. 245–6, 259.
14. Charles Colcock Jones, Jr., *Georgians During the War*

Between the States: An Address Delivered Before the Confederate Survivors' Association (Augusta, Ga., 1889), pp. 29–31.

15. Thomas Nelson Page, "A Southerner on the Negro Question," *North American Review*, CLIV (April 1892), 403, 413.

16. Thomas Nelson Page, *The Negro: The Southerner's Problem* (New York, 1904), p. 253.

17. John C. Calhoun Newton, *The New South and the Methodist Episcopal Church, South* (Baltimore, 1887), pp. 31–40.

18. Atticus G. Haygood, *Our Brother in Black: His Freedom and His Future* (New York, 1881), pp. 128–30.

19. Henry W. Grady, *The New South*, ed. Oliver Dyer (New York, 1890), p. 232.

20. Atlanta *Constitution*, May 18, 1883.

21. Harris, ed., *Grady*, p. 95.

22. Arthur Krock, ed., *The Editorials of Henry Watterson* (New York, 1923), p. 313; William D. Kelley, *The Old South and the New* (New York, 1888), p. 111.

23. *Manufacturers' Record*, May 14, 1887.

24. *Ibid.*, August 16, 1890.

25. George W. Cable, "The Freedman Case in Equity," *Century Magazine*, XXIX (January 1885), 409–18. On Cable's life see Arlin Turner, *George W. Cable, A Biography* (Durham, 1956).

26. Henry W. Grady, "In Plain Black and White: A Reply to Mr. Cable," *Century Magazine*, XXIX (April 1885), 909–17.

27. Harris, ed., *Grady*, pp. 91–2.

28. Haygood, *Our Brother in Black*, pp. 43–4.

29. Henry Watterson, *"Marse Henry": An Autobiography*, 2 vols. (New York, 1919), I, 143–4.

30. Haygood, *Our Brother in Black*, pp. 73–81.

31. James G. Blaine *et al.*, "Ought the Negro to be Disfranchised? Ought He to have been Enfranchised?" *North American Review*, CXXVIII (March 1879), 231.

32. *Ibid.*, p. 241.

33. *Ibid.*, pp. 241–2, 231.

34. Atlanta *Constitution*, January 16, 1880.

35. Grady, "In Plain Black and White," 909–17.

36. Walter B. Hill, "Uncle Tom Without a Cabin," *Century Magazine*, XXVII (April 1884), 864.

37. Haygood, *Our Brother in Black*, pp. 74–5. Page spoke of the "wretched mess" that Reconstruction had made "of the principle of a fair ballot" in his introduction to Booker T. Washington, *Up From Slavery* (Garden City, 1924), p. xv; and in a private letter discussing the Fifteenth Amendment, he wrote: "I have no hesitation in saying that I regard its adoption, when it was adopted, as a grave mistake, but I should consider it a much graver mistake to repeal it now, even if it were possible to repeal it." Page to Edgar Gardner Murphy, April 15, 1900, Southern Education Papers, Dabney Series, University of North Carolina Library.

38. Harris, ed., *Grady*, p. 194.

39. *Ibid.*, p. 184.

40. Grady, *New South*, ed. Dyer, p. 232.

41. Page, "Introduction," in Washington, *Up From Slavery*, pp. x–xxii.

42. This brief summary of the political and economic role of the Redeemers is based on the analysis in C. Vann Woodward, *Origins of the New South, 1877–1913* (Baton Rouge, 1951). Earlier interpretations of the period are discussed in Paul M. Gaston, "The 'New South,'" in Arthur S. Link and Rembert W. Patrick, eds., *Writing Southern History: Essays in Historiography in Honor of Fletcher M. Green* (Baton Rouge, 1965), pp. 316–29.

43. Henry Watterson, "The Solid South," *North American Review*, CXXVIII (January 1879), 53–4.

44. Harris, ed., *Grady*, p. 90. For local consumption Grady expressed the same idea more bluntly: "Remove the outside pressure; eliminate the idea that the north, taking advantage of its power and influence, is bent on placing the negro in positions he is not yet able to fill; leave the south to deal with the situation as it exists, and there will be no limit to the kindness and friendliness with which the negro will be treated and advanced." Atlanta *Constitution*, January 3, 1889.

45. Harris, ed., *Grady*, p. 90; Atlanta *Constitution*, November 8, 1884.

46. Grady, *New South*, ed. Dyer, pp. 239–44.

47. Harris, ed., *Grady*, p. 100.

48. Arlin Turner, ed., *The Negro Question: A Selection of Writings on Civil Rights in the South by George W. Cable* (Garden City, 1958), p. 110.

49. Johnson, "Ideology of White Supremacy," pp. 143–6.
50. Robert Bingham, *The New South: An Address in the Interest of National Aid to Education* (n.p., 1884), p. 13.
51. Turner, ed., *The Negro Question*, p. 130.
52. Turner, *Cable*, pp. 259–60.
53. Turner, ed., *The Negro Question*, pp. 60–4.
54. Harris, ed., *Grady*, pp. 100–1.
55. *Ibid.*, p. 103.
56. Raymond B. Nixon, *Henry W. Grady: Spokesman of the New South* (New York, 1943), p. 289.
57. Harris, ed., *Grady*, pp. 101–2.
58. Daniel A. Tompkins, *Manufactures* (Charlotte, 1900), p. 22.
59. Bingham, *New South*, p. 13.
60. Yoshimitsu Ide, "The Significance of Richard Hathaway Edmonds and his *Manufacturers' Record* in the New South" (unpublished doctoral dissertation, University of Florida, 1959), p. 142.
61. Haygood, *Our Brother in Black*, p. 232.
62. Atlanta *Constitution*, January 12, 1885.
63. *Ibid.*, June 16, 1887.
64. Harris, ed., *Grady*, pp. 291–2.
65. Atlanta *Constitution*, January 1, 1885.
66. Harris, ed., *Grady*, p. 289.
67. J. C. Price, "Does the Negro Seek Social Equality?", *The Forum*, X (January 1891), 558–62.
68. Turner, ed., *The Negro Question*, pp. 78–9.
69. *Ibid.*, p. 124.
70. *Ibid.*, p. 109.
71. Lewis H. Blair, *The Prosperity of the South Dependent upon the Elevation of the Negro* (Richmond, 1889), p. iv.
72. Amory Dwight Mayo, "The Progress of the Negro," *The Forum*, X (November 1890), 338–9.
73. Turner, ed., *The Negro Question*, p. 69.
74. Quoted in Johnson, "Ideology of White Supremacy," p. 155.
75. Turner, ed., *The Negro Question*, p. 88.
76. Burton J. Hendrick, *The Training of an American: The Earlier Life and Letters of Walter H. Page, 1855–1913* (Boston, 1928), p. 172.
77. Haygood, *Our Brother in Black*, p. 133.
78. Atticus G. Haygood, *Pleas for Progress* (Nashville, 1889), p. 17.

79. Haygood, *Our Brother in Black*, pp. 184–92.

80. Turner, ed., *The Negro Question*, pp. 81–2.

81. *Ibid.*, p. 95.

82. Haygood, *Our Brother in Black*, pp. 144–5.

83. Page, "Introduction," in Washington, *Up From Slavery*, pp. xvi–xvii.

84. Henry Watterson, *The Compromises of Life* (New York, 1903), pp. 289–90.

85. *Manufacturers' Record*, December 25, 1886, and October 25, 1890.

86. Atlanta *Constitution*, December 31, 1888.

87. Grady, *New South*, ed. Dyer, p. 251; Harris, ed., *Grady*, p. 300.

88. Atlanta *Constitution*, October 21, 1883.

89. *Ibid.*, January 1, 1885.

90. Grady, *New South*, ed. Dyer, p. 245.

91. Atlanta *Constitution*, October 16, 1883.

92. Grady, *New South*, ed. Dyer, pp. 245–50.

93. Harris, ed., *Grady*, pp. 294–9.

94. *Ibid.*, pp. 104–5.

5   The Vital Nexus

1. The lines are from "The Conquered Banner," the complete text of which may be found in Abram J. Ryan, *Poems: Patriotic, Religious, Miscellaneous* (Baltimore, 1881), pp. 185–7.

2. John C. Calhoun Newton, *The New South and the Methodist Episcopal Church, South* (Baltimore, 1887), pp. vi–vii.

3. James Branch Cabell, *Let Me Lie, Being in the Main an Ethnological Account of the Remarkable Commonwealth of Virginia, and the Making of its History* (New York, 1947), p. 74.

4. Robert Penn Warren, *The Legacy of the Civil War: Meditations on the Centennial* (New York, 1961), p. 15.

5. Nicholas Worth [pseud., Walter Hines Page], *The Southerner* (New York, 1909), p. 86.

6. John Randolph Tucker, *The Old South and the New South* (Columbia, S.C., 1887), p. 1.

7. Charles Colcock Jones, Jr., *Georgians During the War Between the States* (Augusta, Ga., 1889), p. 24.

8. Charles Colcock Jones, Jr., *Sons of Confederate Veterans* (Augusta, Ga., 1891), p. 8.

9. Charles Colcock Jones, Jr., *The Old South* (Augusta, Ga., 1887), p. 17.

10. Edward A. Pollard, *The Lost Cause: A New Southern History of the War of the Confederates* (New York, 1866), p. 751.

11. *Ibid.*

12. *Ibid.*, pp. 750–2.

13. Bledsoe founded the *Southern Review* in 1867 and edited it in Baltimore until his death in 1877.

14. Albert Taylor Bledsoe, "Chivalrous Southrons," *Southern Review*, VI (July 1869), 109; and "The Present Crisis," *Southern Review*, XIII (January 1873), 4. Scarcely an issue of the journal is without an attack by Bledsoe on the materialism of his age made in the name of the principles of the Old South, but see particularly "North and South," II (July 1867), 122–46; "Causes of Sectional Discontent," II (July 1867), 200–30; and "Public School Education at the North," IV (July 1868), 1–36.

15. Robert L. Dabney, "The New South," in C. R. Vaughan, ed., *Discussions by Robert L. Dabney*, 4 vols. (Mexico, Mo., 1897), IV, 1–24.

16. Randall Stewart et al., *The Literature of the South* (Chicago, 1952), p. 438.

17. Benjamin B. Kendrick and Alex M. Arnett, *The South Looks at Its Past* (Chapel Hill, 1935), p. 105.

18. Frank L. Owsley, "A Key to Southern Liberalism," *Southern Review*, III (Summer 1937), 37.

19. Herman C. Nixon in Twelve Southerners, *I'll Take My Stand: The South and the Agrarian Tradition* (New York, 1930), p. 193.

20. Robert S. Cotterill, "The Old South to the New," *Journal of Southern History*, XV (February 1949), 3.

21. William B. Hesseltine, *Confederate Leaders in the New South* (Baton Rouge, 1950), p. 35. See also the same author's *The South in American History* (New York, 1943), pp. 539–42.

22. C. Vann Woodward has challenged the conventional view, sketched above, but his initial modification has not been worked out in detail by other historians. His discussion is concerned with the way in which the New South spokesmen contributed to the mythical image of the Old South but

does not address itself to the second facet of the New South attitude; that is, the interpretation of antebellum history in a way that makes the New South school out to be the keepers of the authentic Southern tradition. Consult C. Vann Woodward, *Origins of the New South, 1877–1913* (Baton Rouge, 1951), pp. 154–8.

23. William D. Kelley, *The Old South and the New* (New York, 1888), pp. 2, 121, 158–9.

24. Howard Bunyan Clay, "Daniel Augustus Tompkins: An American Bourbon" (unpublished doctoral dissertation, University of North Carolina, 1950), pp. 1–4, 60.

25. Alexander K. McClure, *The South: Its Industrial, Financial, and Political Condition* (Philadelphia, 1886), p. 31.

26. Atticus G. Haygood, *Our Brother in Black: His Freedom and His Future* (New York, 1881), pp. 41–2.

27. Newton, *New South*, p. vi.

28. Daniel A. Tompkins, *Manufactures* (Charlotte, 1900), p. 4.

29. Daniel A. Tompkins, "The Manufacture of Cotton in the South," *Manufacturers' Record*, March 24, 1884.

30. Daniel A. Tompkins, *Fourth of July Address at Gastonia, N.C.* (n.p., 1902), p. 1 and *passim*.

31. Richard H. Edmonds, *The Old South and the New* (n.p., 1903), p. 12.

32. *Ibid.*, pp. 3–5.

33. Richard H. Edmonds, *Tasks of Young Men of the South* (n.p., 1903), p. 4.

34. Richard H. Edmonds, *Facts About the South* (Baltimore, 1907), p. 43.

35. Edmonds, *Tasks of Young Men of the South*, p. 1.

36. Edmonds, *Facts About the South*, p. 43.

37. Yoshimitsu Ide, "The Significance of Richard Hathaway Edmonds and his *Manufacturers' Record* in the New South" (unpublished doctoral dissertation, University of Florida, 1959), pp. 56–7.

38. Edmonds, *Facts About the South*, p. 60.

39. Henry W. Grady, *The New South*, ed. Oliver Dyer (New York, 1890), p. 146.

40. Amory Dwight Mayo, "Is There a New South?" *Social Economist*, V (October 1893), 207; Joseph G. Brown, *The New South* (Raleigh, 1902), p. 13.

41. Page, *The Southerner*, especially pp. 46–7. The "Mummy Letters" are discussed above, pp. 61–2.

42. Burton J. Hendrick, *The Training of an American: The*

Earlier Life and Letters of Walter H. Page, 1855–1913 (Boston, 1928), p. 116.

43. Walter Hines Page, "Study of an Old Southern Borough," *Atlantic Monthly*, XLVII (May 1881), 658.

44. Woodward, *Origins of the New South*, p. 158.

45. Joel Chandler Harris, *Uncle Remus: His Songs and His Sayings* (New York, 1881 [i.e., 1880]); Thomas Nelson Page, "Marse Chan," *Century Magazine*, XXVII (April 1884), 932–42.

46. William R. Taylor, *Cavalier and Yankee: The Old South and American National Character* (New York, 1961), p. 82.

47. *Ibid.*, p. 92.

48. Thomas Roderick Dew, *Review of the Debate in the Virginia Legislature of 1831 and 1832* (Richmond, 1832); George Fitzhugh, *Sociology for the South; or, the Failure of Free Society* (Richmond, 1854); George Fitzhugh, *Cannibals All! or, Slaves Without Masters* (Richmond, 1857). The standard monograph on the pro-slavery philosophy is William S. Jenkins, *Pro-Slavery Thought in the Old South* (Chapel Hill, 1935).

49. John Pendleton Kennedy, *Swallow Barn; or, a Sojourn in the Old Dominion* (Philadelphia, 1832).

50. Francis Pendleton Gaines, *The Southern Plantation: A Study in the Development and the Accuracy of a Tradition* (New York, 1924), p. 23.

51. *Ibid.*, p. 30.

52. Julia Collier Harris, ed., *Joel Chandler Harris, Editor and Essayist: Miscellaneous Literary, Political, and Social Writings* (Chapel Hill, 1931), pp. 116–17.

53. Edmund Wilson, *Patriotic Gore: Studies in the Literature of the American Civil War* (New York, 1962), p. 438.

54. Joyce Appleby, "Reconciliation and the Northern Novelist, 1865–1880," *Civil War History*, X (June 1964), 117–29. See also Robert A. Lively, *Fiction Fights the Civil War: An Unfinished Chapter in the Literary History of the American People* (Chapel Hill, 1957).

55. The articles appeared in book form shortly after they were published in the magazine: Edward King, *The Great South: A Record of Journeys* (Hartford, Conn., 1875).

56. "Southern Literature," *Scribner's Monthly*, XXII (September 1881), 785–6. See also Herbert F. Smith, "Joel Chandler Harris's Contributions to Scribner's Monthly and Cen-

tury Magazine, 1880–1887," *Georgia Historical Quarterly*, XLVII (June 1963), 169–79; and Charles W. Coleman, Jr., "The Recent Movement in Southern Literature," *Harper's New Monthly Magazine*, LXXIV (May 1887), 837–55.

57. R. W. Gilder to Joel Chandler Harris, March 5, 1891, Harris Papers, Emory University.

58. Albion W. Tourgee, "The South as a Field for Fiction," *The Forum*, VI (December 1888), 404–7.

59. Gaines, *The Southern Plantation*, p. 82.

60. Ethel Moore, "Reunion of Tennesseans: Address of Welcome by Miss Ethel Moore," *Confederate Veteran*, VI (October 1898), 482.

61. Gaines, *The Southern Plantation*, pp. 63–6.

62. Thomas Nelson Page, *Red Rock: A Chronicle of Reconstruction* (New York, 1898), p. viii.

63. Joel Chandler Harris, ed., *Life of Henry W. Grady, Including His Writings and Speeches* (New York, 1890), p. 88.

64. Grady, *New South*, ed. Dyer, pp. 148–60, 260.

65. Harris, ed., *Grady*, p. 195.

66. Edmonds, *Old South and New*, p. 11.

67. Edmonds, *Tasks of Young Men of the South*, p. 12.

68. Brown, *The New South*, p. 3.

69. Booker T. Washington, *Up From Slavery* (Garden City, 1901), pp. 1–12.

70. *Ibid.*, pp. 12–14.

71. Irwin Russell, *Christmas Night in the Quarters and Other Poems* (New York, 1917), p. 67.

72. Washington, *Up From Slavery*, pp. 80–7.

73. Taylor, *Cavalier and Yankee*, p. 18

74. C. Vann Woodward, "A Southern Critique for the Gilded Age," in *The Burden of Southern History* (Baton Rouge, 1960), pp. 109–40. The three works discussed by Woodward are Melville's poem, *Clarel* (1876); Adams's novel *Democracy* (1880); and James's novel *The Bostonians* (1886).

75. Gaines, *The Southern Plantation*, pp. 2–3.

76. Gunnar Myrdal, *An American Dilemma: The Negro and Modern Democracy*, 2 vols. (New York, 1944), II, 1375.

77. The text is available in Robert Lemuel Wiggins, *The Life of Joel Chandler Harris: From Obscurity in Boyhood to Fame in Early Manhood, with Short Stories and Other*

Early Literary Work not Heretofore Published in Book Form (Nashville, 1918), pp. 263–8.

78. Harris, *Uncle Remus: His Songs and His Sayings*, pp. 175–85.

79. *Ibid.*, p. 184; Wiggins, *Harris*, p. 267.

80. John Stafford, "Patterns of Meaning in *Nights With Uncle Remus*," *American Literature*, XVIII (May 1946), 94–5.

81. Joel Chandler Harris, *Free Joe and Other Georgian Sketches* (New York, 1887), pp. 72–98.

82. See Stafford, "Patterns of Meaning," p. 97; Paul H. Buck, *The Road to Reunion, 1865–1900* (Boston, 1937), chap. 8; and John Donald Wade, "Profits and Losses in the Life of Joel Chandler Harris," *American Review*, I (April 1933), 28–9.

83. Sterling A. Brown, "Negro Character as Seen by White Authors," *Journal of Negro Education*, II (April 1933), 188.

84. Stafford, "Patterns of Meaning," 98–103, 108.

85. The lines are from Irwin Russell's "Christmas Night in the Quarters," the text of which may be found in his *Christmas Night in the Quarters*, pp. 3–24.

86. Virginia Frazer Boyle, "A Kingdom for Micajah," *Harper's New Monthly Magazine*, C (March 1900), 35.

87. Tourgee, "South as a Field for Fiction," 409.

88. Thomas Nelson Page, *In Ole Virginia; or, Marse Chan and Other Stories* (New York, 1887), pp. 1–38, 39–77.

89. Harry Stillwell Edwards, " 'Ole Miss' and Sweetheart," *Harper's New Monthly Magazine*, LXXVII (July 1888), 288–96.

90. Page, *In Ole Virginia*, p. 10.

91. Francis Hopkinson Smith, *Colonel Carter of Cartersville* (Boston, 1891), p. 61.

92. Howard Weeden, *Bandanna Ballads* (New York, 1899), p. 10.

93. Tourgee, "South as a Field for Fiction," 409.

94. John M. Webb, "Militant Majorities and Racial Minorities," *Sewanee Review*, LXV (Spring 1957), 335.

95. Tompkins, *Manufactures*, p. 22.

96. Smith, *Colonel Carter*, p. 99.

97. See, for example, *Confederate Veteran*, VI (October 1898), 493–8.

98. Woodward, *Origins of the New South*, p. 158.

99. Quoted in *ibid.*, p. 157.

100. Grady, *New South*, ed. Dyer, p. 147.

101. Cabell, *Let Me Lie*, p. 74.

6   The Emperor's New Clothes

1. Henry W. Grady, *The New South*, ed. Oliver Dyer (New York, 1890), pp. 267–8.

2. Lewis H. Blair, *The Prosperity of the South Dependent upon the Elevation of the Negro* (Richmond, 1889), p. 1.

3. Hans Christian Andersen, "The Emperor's New Clothes," in *Andersen's Fairy Tales*, trans. Mrs. E. V. Lucas and Mrs. H. B. Pauli (New York, 1945), pp. 267–8.

4. Judson C. Ward, ed., *The New South: Thanksgiving Sermon, 1880, by Atticus G. Haygood*, in *Emory University Publications, Sources and Reprints*, Series VI (1950), No. 3, p. 12.

5. Joel Chandler Harris, ed., *Life of Henry W. Grady, Including His Writings and Speeches* (New York, 1890), p. 88.

6. Wilbur Fisk Tillett, "The White Man of the New South," *Century Magazine*, XXXIII (March 1887), 769–70.

7. Charles Dudley Warner, "Society in the New South," *New Princeton Review*, I (January 1886), 1.

8. Charles Dudley Warner, "The South Revisited," *Harper's New Monthly Magazine*, LXXIV (March 1887), 638.

9. Quoted in William D. Kelley, *The Old South and the New* (New York, 1888), p. 91.

10. Marion J. Verdery, " 'The New South'—Financially Reviewed," *North American Review*, CXLIV (February 1887), 161–2.

11. Atlanta *Constitution*, July 7, 1881; August 30, 1882; and September 13, 1883.

12. *Ibid.*, December 6, 1884; July 17, 1885; July 12, 1886; and December 14, 1886.

13. Harris, ed., *Grady*, p. 182.

14. *Ibid.*, pp. 204–5.

15. Grady, *New South*, ed. Dyer, p. 268.

16. The first quote is from Richard H. Edmonds, *Facts About the South* (Baltimore, 1907), pp. 60–1, a short book that brought together many previously published pieces. The second quote is from Richard H. Edmonds, *The South's*

Redemption: From Poverty to Prosperity (Baltimore, 1890), p. 5.

17. *Manufacturers' Record*, December 18, 1886; February 11, 1888; March 3, 1888; June 30, 1888; and June 28, 1890.

18. Henry Watterson, *The Compromises of Life* (New York, 1903), p. 289; Daniel A. Tompkins, *The Unification and Enlargement of American Interests* (Charlotte, N.C., 1900), pp. 2–3.

19. Harris, ed., *Grady*, p. 87.

20. Paul H. Buck, *The Road to Reunion, 1865–1900* (Boston, 1937), is the best study of the reconciliation of North and South. While parts of Buck's interpretation have been challenged, his discussion of the common ground occupied by the New South spokesmen and their industrialist friends in the North is excellent.

21. Warner, "Society in the New South," p. 12.

22. Harris, ed., *Grady*, p. 88.

23. Grady, *New South*, ed. Dyer, pp. 181–4.

24. Kelley, *Old South and New*, p. 4.

25. Joseph G. Brown, *The New South; Address Delivered at the Convention of the American Bankers' Association at New Orleans, November 11, 1902* (Raleigh, 1902), p. 13; Charles Morris, *The Old South and the New . . . from the Earliest Times to the Jamestown Exposition* (n.p., 1907), dedication page.

26. Nicholas Worth [pseud., Walter Hines Page], *The Southerner* (New York, 1909), p. 17.

27. In a letter of advice on how to write about the civilization of the South, Page said that "the New-South point of view and the old-South point of view both have great perils. Couldn't you plunge in, in the middle?" W. H. Page to William P. Trent, September 5, 1896, Page Papers, Houghton Library, Harvard University.

28. Edmonds, with 432 shares, was the largest stockholder in 1895; Page held 360 shares. List of stockholders of *Manufacturers' Record*, May 23, 1895. Page Papers, Houghton Library, Harvard University.

29. Burton J. Hendrick, *The Training of an American: The Earlier Life and Letters of Walter H. Page, 1855–1913* (Boston, 1928), pp. 392–3.

30. For an interesting and perceptive account of Blair's activities, see Charles E. Wynes, "Lewis Harvie Blair, Virginia

Reformer: The Uplift of the Negro and Southern Prosperity," *Virginia Magazine of History and Biography*, LXXII (January 1964), 3–18. Blair's book has been recently reissued with a revised title: *A Southern Prophecy: The Prosperity of the South Dependent upon the Elevation of the Negro*, ed. C. Vann Woodward (Boston, 1964).

31. Blair, *Prosperity of the South*, p. 3.
32. *Ibid.*, pp. 3–4.
33. *Ibid.*, p. 4.
34. *Manufacturers' Record*, January 29, 1887.
35. *Ibid.*, March 24, 1888.
36. Quoted in Yoshimitsu Ide, "The Significance of Richard Hathaway Edmonds and His *Manufacturers' Record* in the New South" (unpublished doctoral dissertation, University of Florida, 1959), pp. 325–6.
37. Blair, *Prosperity of the South*, p. 7.
38. *Ibid.*, p. v.
39. *Ibid.*, pp. 14–15. Recent estimates of per capita income in the late nineteenth century help Blair's case. In 1880 Georgia's estimated per capita income was $86; in 1900 it was precisely the same: $86. See below, footnote 41.
40. C. Vann Woodward, *Origins of the New South, 1877–1913* (Baton Rouge, 1951), pp. 111, 318.
41. Everett S. Lee et al., *Population Redistribution and Economic Growth, United States, 1870–1950* (Philadelphia, 1957), pp. 349, 753. Changes in estimated per capita income in each of the Southern states were as follows:

| | Per Capita Income | | |
State	1880	1900	Increase
Alabama	$82	$ 88	7.3%
Arkansas	79	89	12.5
Florida	79	112	41.8
Georgia	86	86	—
Kentucky	107	120	12.1
Louisiana	138	128	−7.2
Mississippi	82	84	2.4
North Carolina	64	72	12.5
South Carolina	72	74	2.8
Tennessee	81	101	24.7
Texas	98	138	40.8
Virginia	85	110	29.4
West Virginia	89	117	31.5

42. H. H. Winsborough, "The Changing Regional Character of the South," in John C. McKinney and Edgar T. Thompson, eds., *The South in Continuity and Change* (Durham, 1965), p. 38.

43. Woodward, *Origins of the New South*, p. 311.

44. William H. Nicholls, *Southern Tradition and Regional Progress* (Chapel Hill, 1960), p. 24.

45. Woodward, *Origins of the New South*, chap. 11.

46. *Ibid.*, p. 304.

47. David M. Potter, *People of Plenty: Economic Abundance and the American Character* (Chicago, 1954), p. 84.

48. *Ibid.*, pp. 85–9.

49. Nicholls, *Southern Tradition and Regional Progress*, p. 27.

50. Harris, ed., *Grady*, p. 303.

51. Quoted in Booker T. Washington, *Up From Slavery* (Garden City, 1900), p. 238.

52. Robert Spencer, *Booker T. Washington and the Negro's Place in American Life* (Boston, 1955), p. 116.

53. Washington, *Up From Slavery*, p. 235.

54. This and subsequent quotations from Washington's address are taken from the text as printed in E. David Washington, ed., *Selected Speeches of Booker T. Washington* (Garden City, 1932), pp. 31–6.

55. Rayford Logan's careful study of press reaction to Washington's address concludes that its enthusiastic reception is an "excellent yardstick" for measuring the "victory of 'The New South,'" since he [Washington] accepted a subordinate place for Negroes in American life"; Rayford W. Logan, *The Negro in American Life and Thought: The Nadir, 1877–1901* (New York, 1954), p. 276. Most Negroes, Logan points out, were critical of the address.

56. "The Atlanta Exposition," *Outlook*, LIII (January 11, 1896), 52.

57. "The Jubilee of the New South," *Century Magazine*, LI (January 1896), 470.

58. Quoted in Washington, *Up From Slavery*, p. 226.

59. Woodward, *Origins of the New South*, pp. 205–6. For a brief account of the rise of the Jim Crow system, and an introduction to the literature, consult C. Vann Woodward, *The Strange Career of Jim Crow*, 2nd rev. ed. (New York, 1966).

60. Washington, *Up From Slavery*, p. 318. Page, who admired

Washington, rejected the picture of the happy Negro in the New South and was puzzled by Washington's optimistic utterances. Writing from Charleston, South Carolina, he said that "so far as the negro is concerned, I'd rather be an imp in hades than a darkey in S.C. One decided advantage that the imp has is—personal safety." In the same letter he wrote that "I can't find white men here whose view of the negro has essentially changed since slavery. Booker Washington told me last week that the result of his work of which he is proudest is the fast-changing attitude of the white man—the Southern white man. But he hasn't changed here—not a whit." W. H. Page to H. E. Scudder, March 18, 1899, Page Papers, Houghton Library, Harvard University.

61. Spencer, *Booker T. Washington*, p. 199.

EPILOGUE: The Enduring Myth

1. Walter Prescott Webb, "The South's Future Prospect," in Frank E. Vandiver, ed., *The Idea of the South: Pursuit of a Central Theme* (Chicago, 1964), p. 74.

2. Walter Prescott Webb, "The South's Call to Greatness: Challenge to All Southerners," *The Graduate Journal* (University of Texas), III (Supplement, 1960), 299.

3. New York *Times*, February 19, 1969, pp. 1, 28; Charlottesville, Va., *Daily Progress*, February 19, 1969, p. 1.

4. Joseph J. Spengler, "Southern Economic Trends and Prospects," in John C. McKinney and Edgar T. Thompson, eds., *The South in Continuity and Change* (Durham, 1965), pp. 109–11.

5. National Emergency Council, *Report on Economic Conditions in the South* (Washington, 1938), p. 1.

6. *Ibid.*, p. 8.

7. George B. Tindall, *The Emergence of the New South, 1913–1945* (Baton Rouge, 1967), p. 599.

8. Quoted in Wilma Dykeman and James Stokely, *Seeds of Southern Change: The Life of Will Alexander* (Chicago, 1962), p. 111.

9. C. Vann Woodward, *The Burden of Southern History* (Baton Rouge, 1960), p. 28.

10. Ellen Glasgow, *A Certain Measure: An Interpretation of Prose Fiction* (New York, 1943), pp. 28, 135–6.

11. V. O. Key, Jr., *Southern Politics in State and Nation* (New York, 1949), p. 4.

12. Webb, "South's Call to Greatness," pp. 299, 303.

13. Will W. Alexander, "Our Conflicting Racial Policies," *Harper's Magazine*, CXC (January 1945), 172–9.

14. Quoted in C. Vann Woodward, *The Strange Career of Jim Crow*, 2nd rev. ed. (New York, 1966), p. 145.

15. Jenkins Lloyd Jones, "The New South on the Move," Richmond, Va., *Times-Dispatch*, August 7, 1966.

16. Otto Kerner et al., *Report of the National Advisory Commission on Civil Disorders* (New York, 1968), p. 1.

Selective Bibliography

The best general history of the era in which the New South movement flourished is C. Vann Woodward, *Origins of the New South, 1877–1913* (Baton Rouge: Louisiana State University Press; 1951), a work at once original and yet reflective of two decades of revisionist scholarship. Holland Thompson, *The New South* (New Haven: Yale University Press; 1919), a brief volume generally sympathetic to the New South movement, successfully evokes the optimistic mood of the New South spokesmen. Philip Alexander Bruce, *The Rise of the New South* (Philadelphia: George Barrie & Sons; 1905), is long and tedious and written from the viewpoint of a New South spokesman, but is rich in detail. The literature of the period and changing interpretations of it are discussed in two historiographical essays: Jacob E. Cooke, "The New South," in Donald Sheehan and Harold C. Syrett, eds., *Essays in American Historiography: Papers Presented in Honor of Allan Nevins* (New York: Columbia University Press; 1960), pp. 50–80, and Paul M. Gaston, "The 'New South,'" in Arthur S. Link and Rembert W. Patrick, eds., *Writing Southern History: Essays in Historiography in Honor of Fletcher M. Green* (Baton Rouge: Louisiana State University Press; 1965), pp. 316–36. There are no published books on the intellectual history of the New South movement, but Robert Darden Little, "The Ideology of the New South: A Study in the Development of Ideas, 1865–1910" (unpublished doctoral dissertation, University of Chicago, 1950), should be consulted. Dr. Little's approach is quite different from my own, but I found his study interesting and helpful.

In the classified, selective bibliography that follows I have listed the works which I found most useful, but I include here a word about the sources. As the footnotes indicate, I have relied heavily on the two major journals of the New South movement, the Atlanta *Constitution* and the *Manufacturers' Record*, in which the ideas of Henry W. Grady and Richard H. Edmonds, respectively, are fully set forth. Because I was concerned primarily with the history of a public idea I used manuscript sources only sparingly. The Walter Hines Page Papers at the Houghton Library of Harvard University turned up a few useful items, but the Henry W. Grady Papers and the Joel Chandler Harris Papers, both at Emory University, were of little value. The public discussion of the meaning of the New South movement was carried on in all types of publications. The periodical literature of the period is particularly rewarding, and I examined the files of two dozen magazines, the most useful of which were: *DeBow's Review*, for the genesis of the New South creed; and *The Century Magazine* (published as *Scribner's Monthly* before 1881), *The Atlantic Monthly*, and *Harper's New Monthly Magazine*, for the 'eighties and 'nineties. The bibliography lists the individual articles which I found to be most significant.

A bibliography for the Epilogue, in which I set forth my interpretation of the significance of the myth of the New South in the twentieth century, would run to unmanageable proportions. George B. Tindall, *The Emergence of the New South*, *1913–1945* (Baton Rouge: Louisiana State University Press; 1967), is a comprehensive study that teems with bibliographical information. In Link and Patrick's *Writing Southern History* the historiographical essays by Tindall, on race relations, and by Dewey W. Grantham, Jr., on the twentieth century, are excellent guides.

A. *Memoirs, Works, Autobiographies, Biographies*
   (arranged by subject)

EDWARD ATKINSON

Williamson, Harold Francis: *Edward Atkinson: The Biography of an American Liberal, 1827–1905.* Boston: Old Corner Book Store, Inc.; 1934.

CHARLES BRANTLEY AYCOCK

Orr, Oliver H., Jr.: *Charles Brantley Aycock.* Chapel Hill: University of North Carolina Press; 1961.

GEORGE WASHINGTON CABLE

Turner, Arlin: *George W. Cable, A Biography.* Durham: Duke University Press; 1956.
————, ed.: *The Negro Question: A Selection of Writings on Civil Rights in the South by George W. Cable.* Garden City: Doubleday & Company, Inc.; 1958.

J. L. M. CURRY

Alderman, Edwin Anderson, and Armistead Churchill Gordon: *J. L. M. Curry, A Biography.* New York: Macmillan Company; 1911.
Rice, Jessie Pearl: *J. L. M. Curry: Southerner, Statesman and Educator.* New York: King's Crown Press; 1949.

ROBERT L. DABNEY

Vaughan, C. R., ed.: *Discussions by Robert L. Dabney,* 4 vols. Mexico, Mo.: Crescent Book House; 1897.

JOSEPHUS DANIELS

Daniels, Josephus: *Editor in Politics.* Chapel Hill: University of North Carolina Press; 1941.
————: *Tar Heel Editor.* Chapel Hill: University of North Carolina Press; 1939.

FRANCIS W. DAWSON

Logan, S. Frank: "Francis W. Dawson, 1840–1889: South Carolina Editor." Unpublished master's thesis, Duke University, 1947.

HENRY W. GRADY

Grady, Henry Woodfin: *The New South,* ed. Oliver Dyer. New York: Robert Bonner's Sons; 1890.

————: *The New South and Other Addresses with Biography, Critical Opinions, and Explanatory Note*, ed. Edna Lee Turpin. New York: Maynard, Merrill & Co.; 1904.

Harris, Joel Chandler, ed.: *Life of Henry W. Grady, Including his Writings and Speeches*. New York: Cassell Publishing Company; 1890.

Nixon, Raymond B.: *Henry W. Grady: Spokesman of the New South*. New York: Alfred A. Knopf; 1943.

JOEL CHANDLER HARRIS

Harris, Julia Collier, ed.: *Joel Chandler Harris, Editor and Essayist: Miscellaneous Literary, Political, and Social Writings*. Chapel Hill: University of North Carolina Press; 1931.

————: *The Life and Letters of Joel Chandler Harris*. Boston: Houghton Mifflin Company; 1918.

Wiggins, Robert Lemuel: *The Life of Joel Chandler Harris: From Obscurity in Boyhood to Fame in Early Manhood with Short Stories and other Early Literary Work not heretofore Published in Book Form*. Nashville: Publishing House Methodist Episcopal Church, South; 1918.

ATTICUS GREENE HAYGOOD

Dempsey, Elam Franklin: *Atticus Greene Haygood*. Nashville: Parthenon Press, Methodist Publishing House; 1940.

Mann, Harold W.: *Atticus Greene Haygood: Methodist Bishop, Editor, and Educator*. Athens: University of Georgia Press; 1965.

Ward, Judson C., ed.: *The New South: Thanksgiving Sermon, 1880, by Atticus G. Haygood*, in *Emory University Publications, Sources and Reprints*, Series VI, Number 3. Atlanta, 1950.

BENJAMIN H. HILL

Hill, Benjamin Harvey, Jr.: *Senator Benjamin H. Hill, His Life, Speeches and Writings*. Atlanta: H. C. Hudgins & Co.; 1891.

Pearce, Haywood, Jr.: *Benjamin H. Hill: Secession and Reconstruction*. Chicago: University of Chicago Press; 1928.

WILLIAM DARRAH KELLEY

Kelley, William Darrah: *Speeches, Addresses and Letters*. Philadelphia: Henry Carey Baird; 1872.

LUCIUS Q. C. LAMAR

Cate, Wirt A.: *Lucius Q. C. Lamar*. Chapel Hill: University of North Carolina Press; 1935.

Mayes, Edward: *Lucius Q. C. Lamar: His Life, Times, and Speeches, 1825–1893*. Nashville: Publishing House of the Methodist Episcopal Church, South; 1896.

SIDNEY LANIER

Anderson, Charles R. et al., eds.: *The Centennial Edition of the Works of Sidney Lanier*, 10 vols. Baltimore: Johns Hopkins Press; 1945.

Mims, Edwin: *Sidney Lanier*. Boston: Houghton Mifflin Company; 1905.

Starke, Aubrey: *Sidney Lanier: A Biographical and Critical Study*. Chapel Hill: University of North Carolina Press; 1933.

WALTER HINES PAGE

Hendrick, Burton J.: *The Life and Letters of Walter H. Page*, 3 vols. New York: Doubleday, Page & Company; 1922–5.

———: *The Training of an American: The Earlier Life and Letters of Walter H. Page, 1855–1913*. Boston: Houghton Mifflin Company; 1928.

DANIEL AUGUSTUS TOMPKINS

Clay, Howard Bunyan: "Daniel Augustus Tompkins: An American Bourbon." Unpublished doctoral dissertation, University of North Carolina, 1950.

Winston, George Tayloe: *A Builder of the New South, Being the Life Work of Daniel Augustus Tompkins*. Garden City: Doubleday, Page & Company; 1920.

HOKE SMITH

Grantham, Dewey W., Jr.: *Hoke Smith and the Politics of the New South*. Baton Rouge: Louisiana State University Press; 1958.

ALBION WINEGAR TOURGEE

Olsen, Otto H.: *Carpetbagger's Crusade: The Life of Albion Winegar Tourgee*. Baltimore: Johns Hopkins Press; 1965.

BOOKER T. WASHINGTON

Mathews, Basil: *Booker T. Washington: Educator and Interracial Interpreter*. Cambridge: Harvard University Press; 1948.

Spencer, Robert: *Booker T. Washington and the Negro's Place in American Life*. Boston: Little, Brown and Company; 1955.

Washington, Booker T.: *Up From Slavery*. Garden City: Doubleday, Page & Company; 1900.

Washington, E. David, ed.: *Selected Speeches of Booker T. Washington*. Garden City: Doubleday, Doran & Company, Inc.; 1932.

TOM WATSON

Woodward, C. Vann: *Tom Watson: Agrarian Rebel*. New York: Macmillan Company; 1938.

HENRY WATTERSON

Krock, Arthur, ed.: *The Editorials of Henry Watterson*. New York: George H. Doran Company; 1923.

Marcosson, Isaac: *"Marse Henry": A Biography of Henry Watterson*. New York: Dodd, Mead & Company; 1951.

Wall, Joseph Frazier: *Henry Watterson: Reconstructed Rebel*. New York: Oxford University Press; 1956.

Watterson, Henry: *The Compromises of Life*. New York: Fox, Duffield & Company; 1903.

———: *"Marse Henry": An Autobiography*, 2 vols. New York: George H. Doran Company; 1919.

HOWARD WEEDEN

Roberts, Frances C., and Sarah Huff Fisk: *Shadows on the Wall: The Life and Works of Howard Weeden*. Northport, Ala.: Colonial Press; 1962.

B.   *Contemporary Books and Pamphlets*

Atkinson, Edward: *Address Given in Atlanta . . . for the Promotion of International Cotton Exhibition*. Boston: A. Williams and Company; 1881.

Bingham, Robert: *The New South: An Address . . . in the Interest of National Aid to Education*. N.p.; 1884.

Blair, Lewis H.: *The Prosperity of the South Dependent upon the Elevation of the Negro*. Richmond: Everett Waddey; 1889.

Brown, Joseph G.: *The New South—Address Delivered at the Convention of the American Bankers' Association at New Orleans, November 11, 1902*. Raleigh: Edwards & Broughton Printers and Binders; 1902.

Bruce, Philip Alexander: *The Plantation Negro as a Freeman:*

Observations on his Character, Condition, and Prospects in Virginia. New York: G. P. Putnam's Sons; 1889.

Cooke, John Esten: *The Heir of Gaymount, A Novel.* New York: Van Evrie, Horton & Co.; 1870.

Curry, J. L. M.: *Address Delivered Before the Association of Confederate Veterans, Richmond, Virginia, July 1, 1896.* Richmond: B. F. Johnson; 1896.

Edmonds, Richard Hathaway: *Facts About the South.* Baltimore: Manufacturers' Record Publishing Co.; 1907.

————: *The Old South and the New.* N.p.; 1903.

————: *The South's Redemption: From Poverty to Prosperity.* Baltimore: Manufacturers' Record Publishing Company; 1890.

————: *Tasks of Young Men of the South.* N.p.; 1903.

————: *Unparalleled Industrial Progress.* Np., n.d.

Harris, Joel Chandler: *Daddy Jake the Runaway and Short Stories Told After Dark.* New York: Century Co.; 1889.

————: *Free Joe and Other Georgian Sketches.* New York: Charles Scribner's Sons; 1887.

————: *Nights With Uncle Remus: Myths and Legends of the Old Plantation.* Boston: Houghton, Mifflin and Company; 1883.

————: *Uncle Remus: His Songs and His Sayings.* New York: D. Appleton and Company, 1881 [i.e., 1880].

Haygood, Atticus Greene: *Our Brother in Black: His Freedom and His Future.* New York: Phillips & Hunt; 1881.

————: *Pleas for Progress.* Nashville: Methodist Episcopal Church, South; 1889.

Hillyard, M. B.: *The New South.* Baltimore: Manufacturers' Record Co.; 1887.

Johnston, William Preston: *Problems of Southern Civilization: An Address Delivered Before the Polytechnic Institute of Alabama.* N.p., n.d.

Jones, Charles Colcock, Jr.: *The Battle of Honey Hill: An Address Delivered Before the Confederate Survivors' Association.* Augusta, Ga.: Chronicle Printing Establishment; 1885.

————: *Brigadier General Robert Toombs: An Address Delivered Before the Confederate Survivors' Association.* Augusta, Ga.: Chronicle Office; 1886.

————: *The Evacuation of Battery Wagner and the Battle of Ocean Pond: An Address Before the Confederate Survivors' Association.* Augusta, Ga.: Chronicle Publishing Company; 1888.

————: *Funeral Oration Pronounced in the Opera House in Augusta Georgia . . . upon the Occasion of the Memorial Services in Honor of Jefferson Davis.* Augusta, Ga.: Chronicle Printing Establishment; 1889.

————: *Georgians During the War Between the States: An Address Delivered Before the Confederate Survivors' Association.* Augusta, Ga.: Chronicle Publishing Company; 1889.

————: *The Old South: Address Delivered Before the Confederate Survivors' Association.* Augusta, Ga.: Chronicle Publishing Co.; 1887.

————: *The Siege and Evacuation of Savannah, Georgia in December 1864: An Address Delivered Before the Confederate Survivors' Association.* Augusta, Ga.: Chronicle Publishing Company; 1890.

————: *Sons of Confederate Veterans: An Address Delivered Before the Confederate Survivors' Association.* Augusta, Ga.: Chronicle Publishing Company; 1891.

Kelley, William Darrah: *The Old South and the New.* New York: G. P. Putnam's Sons; 1888.

King, Edward: *The Great South, A Record of Journeys . . .* Hartford: American Publishing Company; 1875.

McClure, Alexander Kelly: *The South: Its Industrial, Financial, and Political Condition.* Philadelphia: J. B. Lippincott Company; 1886.

Morris, Charles: *The Old South and the New . . . from the Earliest Times to the Jamestown Exposition.* N.p.; 1907.

Newton, John C. Calhoun: *The New South and the Methodist Episcopal Church, South.* Baltimore: King Brothers; 1887.

Page, Thomas Nelson: *The Negro: The Southerner's Problem.* New York: C. Scribner's Sons; 1904.

————: *In Ole Virginia; or Marse Chan and Other Stories.* New York: Charles Scribner's Sons; 1887.

————: *Red Rock: A Chronicle of Reconstruction.* New York: Charles Scribner's Sons; 1898.

Phelan, James: *The New South. The Democratic Position on the Tariff: Speech Delivered at Covington, Tenn.* Memphis: S. C. Toof & Co.; 1886.

Pollard, Edward A: *The Lost Cause: A New Southern History of the War of the Confederates.* New York: E. B. Treat & Co., Publishers, 1866.

Russell, Irwin: *Christmas-Night in the Quarters and Other Poems.* New York: Century Co.; 1917.

Ryan, Abram J.: *Poems: Patriotic, Religious, Miscellaneous*. Baltimore: John B. Piet; 1881.

Smith, Francis Hopkinson: *Colonel Carter of Cartersville*. Boston: Houghton Mifflin Company; 1891.

Speer, William S.: *The Law of Success*. Nashville: Southern Methodist Publishing House; 1885.

Switzler, Col. William F.: *The Old South and the New: Speech Delivered in Charleston . . . at the Opening of the Industrial Exhibition*. Columbia, Mo.: Statesman Office Book and Job Print; 1885.

Tompkins, Daniel Augustus: *Fourth of July Address at Gastonia, N. C.* N.p.; 1902.

———: *Manufactures: An Address Made at the First Annual Dinner of the Progressive Association of Edgecombe County*. Charlotte: Observer Printing and Publishing House; 1900.

———: *The Tariff: An Address Made Before the Annual Convention of the American Manufacturers Association*. Richmond, 1909.

———: *The Unification and Enlargement of American Interests*. Charlotte, 1900.

Tourgee, Albion Winegar: *A Fool's Errand, By One of the Fools: The Famous Romance of American History*. New York: Fords, Howard & Hulbert; 1879.

Trammell, William Dugas: *Ça Ira, A Novel*. New York: United States Publishing Co.; 1874.

Trenholm, William Lee: *The South: An Address on the Third Anniversary of the Charleston Board of Trade*. Charleston: Walker, Evans & Cogswell; 1869.

Tucker, John Randolph: *The Old South and the New South: Baccalaureate Address Before the South Carolina College*. Columbia: Presbyterian Publishing House; 1887.

Twain, Mark: *Life on the Mississippi*. Boston: J. R. Osgood and Company; 1883.

Wallace, W. H.: *Three Essentials to Success: Money, Reputation, Character; Annual Address Before the Eutonian Literary Society of Clinton Academy, S. C.* Newberry, S.C.: Wallace & Kinard Printers; 1887.

Weeden, Howard: *Bandanna Ballads*. New York: Doubleday & McClure Company; 1899.

———: *Songs of the Old South*. New York: Doubleday, Page & Company; 1900.

Worth, Nicholas (pseud., Walter Hines Page): *The Southerner*. New York: Doubleday, Page & Company; 1909.

C. *Contemporary Periodical Articles*

Allston, Col. Ben: "Address by Col. Ben Allston. Delivered Before the Winyah Indigo Society, South Carolina, at its One Hundred and Fourteenth Anniversary, May 7, 1869," *DeBow's Review*, VI (August 1869), 669–71.

Atkinson, Edward: "Significant Aspects of the Atlanta Cotton Exposition," *Century Magazine*, XXIII (February 1882), 563–74.

———: "The Solid South?" *International Review*, X (March 1881), 197–209.

Atkinson, W. Y.: "The Atlanta Exposition," *North American Review*, CLXI (October 1895), 385–93.

"The Atlanta Exposition," *Outlook*, LIII (January 11, 1896), 52.

Blaine, James G., L. Q. C. Lamar, Wade Hampton, James A. Garfield, Alexander H. Stephens, Wendell Phillips, Montgomery T. Blair, and Thomas A. Hendricks: "Ought the Negro to be Disfranchised? Ought He to have been Enfranchised?" *North American Review*, CXXVIII (March 1879), 225–83.

Bledsoe, Albert Taylor: "Causes of Sectional Discontent," *Southern Review*, II (July 1867), 200–30.

———: "Chivalrous Southrons," *Southern Review*, VI (July 1869), 96–128.

———: "North and South," *Southern Review*, II (July 1867), 122–46.

———: "The Present Crisis," *Southern Review*, XIII (January 1873), 1–40.

———: "Public School Education at the North," *Southern Review*, IV (July 1868), 1–36.

Boyle, Virginia Frazer: "A Kingdom for Micajah," *Harper's New Monthly Magazine*, C (March 1900), 527–35.

Bruce, Philip Alexander: "Social and Economic Revolution in the Southern States," *Contemporary Review*, LXXVIII (July 1900), 58–73.

Burwell, W. M.: "The Book of Numbers," *DeBow's Review*, VII (October 1870), 800–10.

———: "To the Patrons of DeBow's Review," *DeBow's Review*, V (March 1868), 332–3.

Cabell, E. C.: "White Emigration to the South," *DeBow's Review*, I (January 1866), 91–4.

Cable, George W.: "The Freedman's Case in Equity," *Century Magazine*, XXIX (January 1885), 409–18.

————: "The Silent South," *Century Magazine*, XXX (September 1885), 674–91.

Coleman, Charles W., Jr.: "The Recent Movement in Southern Literature," *Harper's New Monthly Magazine*, LXXIV (May 1887), 837–55.

Curry, J. L. M.: "Citizenship and Education," *Education*, V (September 1884), 78–90.

————: "The South: Her Condition and Needs," *Galaxy*, XXIII (April 1877), 544–53.

DeBow, J. D. B.: "The Future of the South," *DeBow's Review*, I (January 1866), 6–14.

————: "Manufactures, The South's True Remedy," *DeBow's Review*, III (February 1867), 172–8.

————: "The Future of South Carolina—Her Inviting Resources," *DeBow's Review*, II (July 1866), 38–49.

Delavique, John C.: "Cotton," *DeBow's Review*, IV (December 1867), 562–71.

DeLeon, Edwin: "The New South," *Harper's New Monthly Magazine*, XLVIII (1874), 270–80, 406–22; XLIX (1874), 555–68.

————: "The New South: What it is Doing, and What it Wants," *Putnam's Magazine*, XV (April 1870), 458–64.

————: "Ruin and Reconstruction of the Southern States," *Southern Magazine*, XIV (1874), 17–41, 287–309, 453–82, 561–90.

————: "The Southern States Since the War," *Fraser's Magazine*, XC (1874), 153–63, 346–66, 620–37.

Dudley, Thomas U.: "How Shall We Help the Negro?" *Century Magazine*, XXX (June 1885), 273–80.

Edwards, Harry Stillwell: "De Valley An' De Shadder," *Century Magazine*, XXXV (January 1888), 468–77.

————: " 'Ole Miss' and Sweetheart," *Harper's New Monthly Magazine*, LXXVII (July 1888), 288–96.

"Exodus," *DeBow's Review*, V (November 1868), 979–83.

Gilman, S. H.: "Cotton Manufacturing in or Near the Cotton Fields of Texas Compared with the Same at Any Point Distant Therefrom," *DeBows Review*, V (September 1868), 837–40.

Godkin, E. L.: "The Political Outlook," *Scribner's Monthly*, XIX (February 1880), 613–20.

————: "The White Side of the Southern Question," *The Nation*, XXXI (August 19, 1880), 126–7.

"Governor Hampton at Auburn," *Harper's Weekly*, XXI (July 7, 1877), 519.

Grady, Henry W.: "In Plain Black and White: A Reply to Mr. Cable," *Century Magazine*, XXIX (April 1885), 909–17.

" 'The Great South' Series of Papers," *Scribner's Monthly*, IX (December 1874), 248–9.

Gunton, Matthew: "Is There a New South? Reply to Mr. Mayo," *Social Economist*, V (December 1893), 358–65.

Hill, Daniel Harvey: "Education," *The Land We Love*, I (May and June 1866), 1–11 and 83–91.

———: "Industrial Combinations," *The Land We Love*, V (May 1868), 25–34.

———: "The Old South," *Southern Historical Society Papers*, XVI (1888), 423–43.

Hill, Walter B.: "Uncle Tom Without a Cabin," *Century Magazine*, XXVII (April 1884), 859–64.

"The Industrial Policy of the South," *DeBow's Review*, VI (November 1869), 928–9.

James, Charles J.: "Cotton Manufactures—Great Field for the South," *DeBow's Review*, I (May 1866), 504–15.

Johnston, John W.: "The Emancipation of the Southern Whites," *Manufacturers' Record*, July 9, 1887.

"The Jubilee of the New South," *Century Magazine*, LI (January 1896), 470.

Lanier, Henry W.: "The New South's Industrial Future," *Outlook*, LIX (June 25, 1898), 477–9.

Lanier, Sidney: "The New South," *Scribner's Monthly*, XX (October 1880), 840–51.

Logan, T. M.: "The Southern Industrial Prospect," *Harper's New Monthly Magazine*, LII (March 1876), 589–93.

Maury, Matthew Fontaine: "The American Colony in Mexico," *DeBow's Review*, I (June 1866), 623–30.

Mayo, Amory Dwight: "Is There a New South?" *Social Economist*, V (October 1893), 200–8.

———: "The Progress of the Negro," *Forum*, X (November 1890), 335–45.

Merrill, A. P.: "Southern Labor," *DeBow's Review*, VI (July 1869), 586–92.

Mitchell, Samuel C.: "The Nationalization of Southern Sentiment," *South Atlantic Quarterly*, VII (April 1908), 107–13.

Moore, Ethel: "Reunion of Tennesseans: Address of Welcome by Miss Ethel Moore," *Confederate Veteran*, VI (October 1898), 482.

Moore, H. T.: "The Industrial Interests of the South," *DeBow's Review*, V (February 1868), 147–55.

"North and South," *Century Magazine*, XXX (October 1885), 964.

Oswald, Felix L.: "The New South," *Chautauquan*, XV (August 1892), 541–53.

Page, Thomas Nelson: "A Southerner on the Negro Question," *North American Review*, CLIV (April 1892), 401–13.

Page, Walter Hines: "The Rebuilding of Old Commonwealths," *Atlantic Monthly*, LXXXIX (May 1902), 651–61.

———: "Study of an Old Southern Borough," *Atlantic Monthly*, XLVII (May 1881), 648–58.

Patton, Robert M.: "The New Era of Southern Manufactures," *DeBow's Review*, III (January 1867), 56–69.

Pollard, Edward A.: "The Real Condition of the South," *Lippincott's Magazine*, VI (December 1870), 612–20.

Preston, Margaret J.: "The Gospel of Labor (What the South Says to Her Children)," *Southern Magazine*, IX (December 1871), 733–4.

Price, J. C.: "Does the Negro Seek Social Equality?" *Forum*, X (January 1891), 558–64.

Reeves, W. N.: "The Unemployed—Send Them South," *Outlook*, IL (February 10, 1894), 286.

Shaler, N. S.: "The Economic Future of the New South," *Arena*, II (August 1890), 257–68.

Smalley, Eugene V.: "The New Orleans Exposition," *Century Magazine*, XXX (May and June 1885), 3–14 and 185–99.

Smith, Hoke: "The Resources and Development of the South," *North American Review*, CLIX (August 1894), 129–36.

"Southern Literature," *Scribner's Monthly*, XXII (September 1881), 785–6.

"Studies in the South," *Atlantic Monthly*, LI (January 1883), 87–99.

Tillett, Wilbur Fisk: "The White Man of the New South," *Century Magazine*, XXXIII (March 1887), 769–76.

Tompkins, Daniel Augustus: "Southern Prosperity," *Manufacturers' Record*, June 4, 1887.

Tourgee, Albion Winegar: "The South as a Field for Fiction," *Forum*, VI (December 1888), 404–13.

Trammell, William Dugas: Review of "*Address Delivered Before the Alumni Society of the University of Georgia* by Benjamin H. Hill," *Southern Magazine*, X (June 1872), 751–61.

Trent, William Peterfield: "Dominant Forces in Southern Life," *Atlantic Monthly*, LXXIX (January 1897), 42–53.

Verdery, Marion J.: " 'The New South'—Financially Reviewed," *North American Review*, CXLIV (February 1887), 161–8.

Wagener, John A.: "European Immigration," *DeBow's Review*, IV (July and August 1867), 94–105.

Warner, Charles Dudley: "Impressions of the South," *Harper's New Monthly Magazine*, LXXI (September 1885), 546–51.

———: "Society in the New South," *New Princeton Review*, I (January 1886), 1–14.

———: "The South Revisited," *Harper's New Monthly Magazine*, LXXIV (March 1887), 634–40.

Washington, Booker T.: "The Case of the Negro," *Atlantic Monthly*, LXXXIV (November 1899), 577–87.

———: "Signs of Progress Among the Negroes," *Century Magazine*, LIX (January 1900), 472–8.

Watterson, Henry: "Oddities of Southern Life," *Century Magazine*, XXIII (April 1882), 884–95.

———: "The Reunited Union," *North American Review*, CXL (January 1885), 22–9.

———: "The Solid South," *North American Review*, CXXVIII (January 1879), 47–58.

Yerger, E. N.: "The True Strength of the Southern States," *Southern Magazine*, XI (May 1875), 520–5.

D.   *Secondary Works: Books*

Brandfon, Robert L.: *Cotton Kingdom of the New South: A History of the Yazoo Mississippi Delta from Reconstruction to the Twentieth Century.* Cambridge: Harvard University Press; 1967.

Brookes, Stella Brewer: *Joel Chandler Harris—Folklorist.* Athens: University of Georgia Press; 1950.

Brown, Sterling: *The Negro in American Fiction.* Washington: Association in Negro Folk Education; 1937.

Buck, Paul Herman: *The Road to Reunion, 1865–1900.* Boston: Little, Brown and Company; 1937.

Cash, W. J.: *The Mind of the South.* New York: Alfred A. Knopf, Inc.; 1941.

Clark, Thomas D.: *The Emerging South.* New York: Oxford University Press; 1961.

Clark, Victor S.: *History of Manufactures in the United States, 1860–1914.* Washington: Carnegie Institution of Washington; 1928.

Commager, Henry Steele: *The American Mind: An Interpretation of American Thought and Character Since the 1880's.* New Haven: Yale University Press; 1950.

Cooper, William J., Jr.: *The Conservative Regime: South Carolina, 1877–1890.* Baltimore: Johns Hopkins Press; 1968.

Gaines, Francis Pendleton: *The Southern Plantation: A Study in the Development and the Accuracy of a Tradition.* New York: Columbia University Press; 1924.

Going, Allen Johnston: *Bourbon Democracy in Alabama, 1874–1890.* University: University of Alabama Press; 1951.

Goldman, Eric F.: *Rendezvous With Destiny: A History of Modern American Reform.* New York: Alfred A. Knopf; 1952.

Gossett, Thomas T.: *Race: The History of an Idea in America.* Dallas: Southern Methodist University Press; 1963.

Green, Fletcher Melvin, ed.: *Essays in Southern History.* Chapel Hill: University of North Carolina Press; 1949.

Greenhut, Melvin L., and W. Tate Whitman, eds.: *Essays in Southern Economic Development.* Chapel Hill: University of North Carolina Press; 1964.

Hesseltine, William Best: *Confederate Leaders in the New South.* Baton Rouge: Louisiana State University Press; 1950.

Hofstadter, Richard: *Social Darwinism in American Thought,* rev. edn. Boston: Beacon Press; 1955.

Ide, Yoshimitsu: "The Significance of Richard Hathaway Edmonds and His *Manufacturers' Record* in the New South." Unpublished doctoral dissertation, University of Florida, 1959.

Kendrick, Benjamin Burke, and Alex Mathews Arnett: *The South Looks at Its Past.* Chapel Hill: University of North Carolina Press; 1935.

Kirwan, Albert D.: *Revolt of the Rednecks: Mississippi Politics, 1876–1925.* Lexington: University of Kentucky Press; 1951.

Lee, Everett S., et al.: *Population Redistribution and Economic Growth, United States, 1870–1950.* Philadelphia: American Philosophical Society; 1957.

Lewinson, Paul: *Race, Class, and Party: A History of Negro Suffrage and White Politics in the South.* New York: Oxford University Press; 1932.

Lively, Robert A.: *Fiction Fights the Civil War: An Unfinished Chapter in the Literary History of the American People.* Chapel Hill: University of North Carolina Press; 1957.

Logan, Frenise A.: *The Negro in North Carolina, 1876–1894.* Chapel Hill: University of North Carolina Press; 1964.

Logan, Rayford W.: *The Negro in American Life and Thought: The Nadir, 1877–1901.* New York: Dial Press, Inc.; 1954.

McKinney, John C., and Edgar T. Thompson, eds.: *The South in Continuity and Change.* Durham: Duke University Press; 1965.

Meier, August: *Negro Thought in America, 1880–1915: Racial Ideologies in the Age of Booker T. Washington.* Ann Arbor: University of Michigan Press; 1963.

Mitchell, Broadus: *The Rise of the Cotton Mills in the South.* Baltimore: Johns Hopkins Press; 1921.

———, and George Sinclair Mitchell: *The Industrial Revolution in the South.* Baltimore: Johns Hopkins Press; 1930.

Moger, Allen Wesley: *The Rebuilding of the Old Dominion: A Study in Economic, Social, and Political Transition from 1880 to 1902.* Ann Arbor, Mich.: Edwards Brothers, Inc.; 1940.

Murray, Henry A., ed.: *Myth and Mythmaking.* New York: George Braziller; 1960.

Myrdal, Gunnar: *An American Dilemma: The Negro Problem and Modern Democracy,* 2 vols. New York: Harper & Brothers; 1944.

National Emergency Council: *Report on Economic Conditions of the South.* Washington: Government Printing Office; 1938.

Nicholls, William H.: *Southern Tradition and Regional Progress.* Chapel Hill: University of North Carolina Press; 1960.

Nolen, Claude H.: *The Negro's Image in the South: The Anatomy of White Supremacy.* Lexington: University of Kentucky Press; 1967.

North, Douglas C.: *The Economic Growth of the United States, 1790–1860.* Englewood Cliffs, N.J.: Prentice-Hall, Inc.; 1961.

Odum, Howard W., et al.: *Southern Pioneers in Social Interpretation.* Chapel Hill: University of North Carolina Press; 1925.

Perloff, Harvey S., et al.: *Regions, Resources, and Economic Growth.* Baltimore: Johns Hopkins Press; 1960.

Potter, David: *People of Plenty: Economic Abundance and the American Character.* Chicago: University of Chicago Press; 1954.

Rose, Willie Lee: *Rehearsal for Reconstruction: The Port Royal Experiment.* Indianapolis: Bobbs-Merrill Co.; 1964.

Shugg, Roger: *Origins of the Class Struggle in Louisiana:*

A Social History of White Farmers and Laborers During Slavery and After, 1840–1875. Baton Rouge: Louisiana State University Press; 1939.

Simkins, Francis Butler: *The Everlasting South.* Baton Rouge: Louisiana State University Press; 1963.

Sitterson, J. Carlyle, ed.: *Studies in Southern History.* Chapel Hill: University of North Carolina Press; 1957.

Stewart, Randall, et al.: *The Literature of the South.* Chicago: Scott, Foresman and Company; 1952.

Stover, John F.: *The Railroads of the South, 1865–1900.* Chapel Hill: University of North Carolina Press; 1955.

Taylor, William R.: *Cavalier and Yankee: The Old South and American National Character.* New York: George Braziller; 1961.

Tindall, George Brown: *South Carolina Negroes, 1877–1900.* Columbia: University of South Carolina Press; 1952.

Turner, Frederick Jackson: *The Frontier in American History.* New York: Henry Holt; 1920.

Twelve Southerners: *I'll Take My Stand: The South and the Agrarian Tradition.* New York: Harper & Brothers Publishers; 1930.

Vandiver, Frank E., ed.: *The Idea of the South: Pursuit of a Central Theme.* Chicago: University of Chicago Press; 1964.

Wharton, Vernon Lane: *The Negro in Mississippi, 1865–1890.* Chapel Hill: University of North Carolina Press; 1947.

Wilson, Edmund: *Patriotic Gore: Studies in the Literature of the American Civil War.* New York: Oxford University Press; 1962.

Woodward, C. Vann: *The Burden of Southern History.* Baton Rouge: Louisiana State University Press; 1960.

———: *Reunion and Reaction: The Compromise of 1877 and the End of Reconstruction.* Boston: Little, Brown and Company; 1951.

———: *The Strange Career of Jim Crow,* 2nd rev. edn. New York: Oxford University Press; 1966.

Wyllie, Irving G.: *The Self-Made Man in America: The Myth of Rage to Riches.* New Brunswick, N.J.: Rutgers University Press; 1954.

Wynes, Charles E.: *Race Relations in Virginia, 1870–1902.* Charlottesville: University of Virginia Press; 1961.

E.   *Secondary Works: Articles*

Appleby, Joyce: "Reconciliation and the Northern Novelist, 1865–1880," *Civil War History*, X (June 1964), 117–29.

Atchison, Ray M.: *"The Land We Love:* A Southern Post-Bellum Magazine of Agriculture, Literature, and Military History," *North Carolina Historical Review*, XXXVII (October 1960), 506–15.

Baskette, Floyd K.: "Atticus G. Haygood's Thanksgiving Sermon," *Emory University Quarterly*, II (March 1946), 21–9.

Belissary, Constantine G.: "The Rise of Industry and the Industrial Spirit in Tennessee, 1865–1885," *Journal of Southern History*, XIX (May 1953), 193–215.

Berthoff, Rowland T.: "Southern Attitudes Toward Immigration, 1865–1914," *Journal of Southern History*, XVII (August 1951), 328–60.

Brown, Sterling A.: "Negro Character as Seen by White Authors," *Journal of Negro Education*, II (April 1933), 179–203.

Cotterill, Robert Spencer: "The Old South to the New," *Journal of Southern History*, XV (February 1949), 3–8.

Daumer, Louise: "Myth and Humor in the Uncle Remus Fables," *American Literature*, XX (May 1948), 129–43.

English, Thomas H.: "The Twice-Told Tale and Uncle Remus," *Georgia Review*, II (Winter 1948), 447–60.

Flory, Claude R.: "Paul Hamilton Hayne and the New South," *Georgia Historical Quarterly*, XLVI (December 1962), 388–94.

Johnson, Charles S.: "The Social Philosophy of Booker T. Washington," *Opportunity*, VI (April 1928), 102–5, 115.

Johnson, Guy B.: "Negro Racial Movements and Leadership in the United States," *American Journal of Sociology*, XLII (July 1937), 57–71.

Link, Arthur S.: "The Progressive Movement in the South, 1870–1914," *North Carolina Historical Review*, XXIII (April 1946), 172–95.

Owsley, Frank L.: "A Key to Southern Liberalism," *Southern Review*, III (Summer 1937), 28–38.

———: "The Old South and the New," *American Review*, VI (February 1936), 475–85.

Phillips, Ulrich B.: "The Central Theme of Southern History," *American Historical Review*, XXXIV (October 1928), 30–43.

Potter, David M.: "An Appraisal of Fifteen Years of the *Journal of Southern History*, 1935–1949," *Journal of Southern History*, XVI (February 1950), 25–32.

———: "The Enigma of the South," *Yale Review*, LI (Autumn 1961), 142–51.

———: "On Understanding the South: A Review Article," *Journal of Southern History*, XXX (November 1964), 451–62.

Rutman, Darrett B.: "Philip Alexander Bruce: A Divided Mind of the South," *Virginia Magazine of History and Biography*, LXVIII (October 1960), 387–407.

Sellers, Charles Grier, Jr.: "Walter Hines Page and the Spirit of the New South," *North Carolina Historical Review*, XXIX (October 1952), 481–99.

Smith, Herbert F.: "Joel Chandler Harris's Contributions to Scribner's Monthly and Century Magazine, 1880–1887," *Georgia Historical Quarterly*, XLVII (June 1963), 169–79.

Stafford, John: "Patterns of Meaning in *Nights With Uncle Remus*," *American Literature*, XVIII (May 1946), 89–108.

Stover, John F.: "Northern Financial Interests in Southern Railroads, 1865–1900," *Georgia Historical Quarterly*, XXXIX (September 1955), 205–20.

Tindall, George B., et al.: "The Status and Future of Regionalism—A Symposium," *Journal of Southern History*, XXVI (February 1960), 22–56.

Wade, John Donald: "Henry W. Grady," *Southern Review*, III (Winter 1938), 479–509.

———: "Profits and Losses in the Life of Joel Chandler Harris," *American Review*, I (April 1933), 17–35.

———: "What the South Figured, 1865–1914," *Southern Review*, III (Autumn 1937), 360–7.

Ward, Judson C., Jr.: "The New Departure Democrats of Georgia: An Interpretation," *Georgia Historical Quarterly*, XLI (September 1957), 227–36.

Webb, John M.: "Militant Majorities and Racial Minorities," *Sewanee Review*, LXV (Spring 1957), 332–47.

Webb, Walter Prescott: "The South's Call to Greatness: Challenge to All Southerners," *The Graduate Journal* (University of Texas), III (Supplement, 1960), 299–309.

Westbrook, John T.: "Twilight of Southern Regionalism," *Southwest Review*, XLII (Summer 1957), 231–4.

Whaley, W. Gordon: "The South Will Likely Fail," *The Gradu-*

ate Journal (University of Texas), III (Supplement, 1960), 311–21.

Woodward, C. Vann: "Hillbilly Realism," *Southern Review*, IV (Spring 1939), 676–81.

Wynes, Charles E.: "Lewis Harvie Blair, Virginia Reformer: The Uplift of the Negro and Southern Prosperity," *Virginia Magazine of History and Biography*, LXXII (January 1964), 3–18.

Index

Paul M. Gaston is Associate Professor and Director of Graduate Studies in History at the University of Virginia. Born in Fairhope, Alabama, in 1928, he received his B.A. at Swarthmore, where he was elected to Phi Beta Kappa, and his M.A. and Ph.D. at the University of North Carolina. He was a Fulbright Fellow at the University of Copenhagen in 1952-3, and a visiting lecturer at the Johns Hopkins University in 1963-4. Mr. Gaston is married, and he and his wife and three children live in Charlottesville, Virginia.

VERDAD Y MENTIRAS EN EL SEXO

VERDAD Y MENTIRAS EN EL SEXO

Lo que siempre quisiste saber, sin necesidad de preguntar

Eva Roy

EDICIONES B
GRUPO ZETA

Barcelona • Bogotá • Buenos Aires • Caracas • Madrid • México D.F. • Montevideo • Quito • Santiago de Chile

1.ª edición: mayo 2008

© Eva Roy, 2008
© de las ilustraciones: sus autores
© Ediciones B, S. A., 2008
  Bailén, 84 - 08009 Barcelona (España)
  www.edicionesb.com

Printed in Spain
ISBN: 978-84-666-3836-4
Depósito legal: B. 11.965-2008

Impreso por LITOGRAFÍA S.I.A.G.S.A.

A Paúl.
A Gamal.
Gracias por acompañarme en el viaje.

ÍNDICE

Introducción

Aunque este libro va mucho de eso, de «introducir», parece que en los prólogos han de darse varias explicaciones, generalmente de otro tipo. Una, impepinable, acerca del título. Podría decir la verdad, que es que los de Ediciones B ya lo tenían pensado cuando aquella tarde de julio de 2007 me recibieron en Barcelona para «hablar de mi libro» (de *otro* de mis libros). También puedo contar la versión de que una mañana, mientras trabajaba sobre estas páginas, leyendo una entrevista a un famoso diseñador de camisetas, encontré una frase: «las grandes verdades no están escritas». No sé si me tomé su afirmación como un reto, como un guantazo en la cara o como motivo de inspiración. Sea como fuere, me hizo mover el culo y esforzarme por explicar algunas grandes verdades y tremendas mentiras sobre sexo.

Hoy día se habla, se escribe, se emiten programas y se publican artículos sobre este tema a tal velocidad que, desde luego, se diría que no se piensa en nada más... Sin embargo, esa obsesión va acompañada de un montón de datos que pululan sin ser contrastados, y de tabúes, mitos, frases hechas y deshechas que, en realidad, por mi trabajo, barajo constantemente. «No te cuesta nada, llevas años hablando de esto», pensé al principio. Con los meses, me di cuenta de cuánto me equivocaba y me sumergí yo solita en una depresión motivada, entre otras razones, por aquello que León Tolstói decía: «Es más fácil escribir diez volúmenes de principios filosóficos que poner en práctica uno solo de sus principios.» Mucho me temo que la idea que se nos transmite es que el sexo es coito, puro mete-saca, que esto va de «correrse». Todos buscamos más y mejores orgasmos. Pero

¿dónde encajan ahí la emoción, la eyaculación precoz, las caricias, etc.? Y ¿qué pasa con el clítoris? Incluso yo misma arrastraba cantidad de prejuicios pegados. Estudiando manuales y consultando a expertos, he podido asimilar muchos conceptos que deberían enseñarse ya desde la escuela. No todos terminamos poniendo ladrillos, operando hernias, pilotando aviones, maquillando profesionalmente o vendiendo fruta. Personalmente, no he vuelto a utilizar un logaritmo neperiano para nada, y así de paso ahorro, por respeto, el millón de inutilidades que he memorizado con éxito de cara a los exámenes. Sin embargo, salvo celibatos cada vez menos frecuentes, o abstinencias elegidas y pactadas, todos los seres humanos contamos con nuestros órganos sexuales y los utilizamos, aunque, todo sea dicho, cada vez más desvinculados de la teleológica reproducción. Además, tenemos la innata necesidad de relacionarnos. Ahí está: el sexo, la sexualidad, la sensualidad y el erotismo van a formar parte de la vida de todos. Sepamos de qué van y disfrutemos.

Llevo tiempo escribiendo *Eva al desnudo*, el blog de sexo en *elpais.com*, convirtiéndome a lo tonto en la *blogger* más leída de España. Allí, he escuchado y resuelto cientos de consultas y curiosidades de lectores y amigos sobre relaciones y sexualidad. Asimismo, durante años he venido publicando artículos y entrevistas sobre la gente del porno e incluso un libro sobre la industria del cine X, y nótese, por favor, que diferencio ambas temáticas: sexo y porno. Aun así, no oculto que me sorprende y me enerva que desde los medios de comunicación se fomente una visión del sexo vinculada más bien a «la gimnasia», en detrimento de la pasión y del diálogo. Y esto no quiero que se lea como un puritano regreso al «sexo sólo con amor» o al «sexo conyugal» que, en realidad y en general, tanto daño han causado sobre la sexualidad femenina. No, nada de eso. Soy partidaria de buscar el placer y la felicidad y de disfrutar del sexo, del buen sexo, vaya o no vinculado a responsabilidades o emociones «más profundas» y siempre que no se haga daño a nadie ni se conculque la legalidad. Creo en la libertad sexual, pero mi experiencia me demuestra que su ejercicio se convierte en algo bastante más complejo que esa caricatura que de ello se nos pinta en la tele y en el propio porno. Después de tantos años de experiencia teniendo el sexo como tema de base y, según analizo y comprendo la sexualidad de las personas, y la mía propia, cada vez estoy más convencida de que pocos conceptos van tan unidos y al tiempo se separan tanto: sexo y porno, serían tan similares y tan distintos como dos gotas de agua. Pero ante la falta de referentes y de formación, es entendible que la gente eche la vista al X... Que no se me malinterprete, que esto lo digo también para que los hombres se relajen un poco. No es justo para ellos (y, de rebote, tampoco para nosotras) que se pretenda reproducir en la cama lo que se muestra en las escenas porno grabadas por actores. Lo cierto es que, como apuntaba antes, pocas cosas me parecen tan incompatibles como intimidad y pornografía. En este libro hablo de disfrutar, no de montar un *show*. Hablo de una experiencia enriquecedora, no de esfuerzos físicos hechos sobre un colchón por no hacerlos en el gimnasio. Hablo de que las personas, en el fondo, perseguimos sentirnos bien, no sólo lograr un orgasmo, y que en cualquier caso eso mismo se puede hacer tirando de manubrio. El porno es una ayuda, un recurso que puede provocar la excitación por vía ocular pero, una vez en el dormitorio, ha de quedarse fuera. Emular las prácticas y conductas de los actores es, además de casi imposible para la mayoría, innecesario y contraproducente. En el mejor de los casos, de realizar la proeza con éxito, si el señor no abandona el rol de «chuloputas» consustancial a casi todos los papeles masculinos en el cine X, la chica se va a sentir tan mal... Ver una peli porno y notar que la humillación sistemática y el trato violento —cuando no degradante— respecto de la actriz no van demasiado contigo, no es tan crudo como sentirte maltratada en carne y hueso por un gañán que no disimula que le importas cero. Tampoco todas hacemos todo lo que las actrices llevan a cabo en las escenas. No pasa nada por no practicar sexo anal, por preferir que no te arrastren de los pelos o por negarte a recibir la eyaculación en la cara o a tragarte el semen...

Cuando escribía mi primer libro ambicionaba, como lejano objetivo en el horizonte y, a la vez, tan al alcance de mi mano, destripar muchos de los secretos de la industria del porno. Con *Mi lado más hardcore*, conseguí demostrar que existen libros «porno» para «leer», ya que además de fotografías e ilustraciones, reuní, en aquellas 30 entrevistas sin censura que hice una por una a los grandes del sector, muchísima información y anécdotas. Y lo más jugoso de sus páginas ha pasado a las de este libro, en un capítulo especial.

Ahora, en *Verdad y mentiras en el sexo*, deseo divulgar un mensaje de normalización respecto del asunto. La clave del éxito de una relación es la complicidad y, sin duda, para lograrla, se precisa una buena comunicación entre los miembros de la pareja (aunque sea esporádica). Lo mismo que a cada uno de tus invitados le preguntas si la carne le gusta muy hecha, al punto o casi cruda, ¿por qué no ibas a interesarte por darle gusto a tu pareja en la felación o en la masturbación? Lo malo es que aún sobreviven muchos miedos y vergüenzas, e impera la presión de «no saberlo todo»... A ver: ¡pero si eso es imposible!

Como decía, no es que se precise mayor información —estamos totalmente saturados de ella—, sólo que servida en el «plato adecuado» y con un lenguaje que abandone la culpabilidad, huyendo de aburridísimos tecnicismos y que el mensaje se haga ameno y creíble... Será que personalmente huyo del postulado de quienes comulgan con Kierkegaard y su píldora de cilicio intelectual: «la tarea debe hacerse difícil, pues sólo la dificultad inspira a los nobles de corazón». Yo aspiro a que me lean y a que me entiendan y si además con mis palabras alguien aprende algo o se divierte, habré cumplido. Renuncio conscientemente al placer de que desencripten mis textos, y quizá con ello a una butaca en la Real Academia. El sexo, igual que otras facetas, es un conocimiento que se puede adquirir (practicando, hablando, leyendo, etc.), y lo bueno es que en este particular tema, a casi todos nos encanta hacer los deberes... Es cierto: en el arte amatorio un poquito de conocimiento cunde mucho, se trata de una disciplina muy agradecida y en la que siempre queda algo por decir: ahora, por ejemplo, caigo en la cuenta de que olvidé explicar en el capítulo sobre masturbación, el impactante truco de usar un collar de cuentas, enrollándolo desde la base del pene y echando un poco de lubricante...

Practicar sexo no consiste en sudar acompañado. Exento de emociones, medie o no amor, «lo otro» es hacer gimnasia, sólo que intercambiando fluidos de distinta naturaleza. Que una relación sexual sea buena, o continúe siéndolo, depende de que ambas partes se empeñen en ello: da lo mismo si se desarrolla sobre un lecho conyugal, dentro de un geriátrico o con la urgencia del apretón en un baño de una discoteca. Abordaré el fantasma de la rutina, el peor enemigo de la pasión, junto con la enfermedad, el cansancio físico, la falta de tiempo y el distinto grado de predisposición erótica, porque, por desgracia, no todos nacemos con la misma libido.

He querido indagar en el morbo femenino: ¿qué nos pone de verdad a las mujeres? Y de la psique masculina: ¿de veras son tan simples?, ¿se reduce todo a satisfacer unos impulsos desatados automáticamente por estímulos visuales?

Hemos de partir de una nueva situación: toca revisar los roles tradicionales, porque ya no se sostienen. La mujer demanda sexo (y del bueno). Veo muchas Caperucitas gritando: «¿dónde coño se han metido los lobos?», porque ahora son ellos los que comienzan a sentirse «acosados» y «presionados». ¡El mundo al revés! Pues parece que sí... La jaqueca y otras excusas se invocan por ambos; ya no somos nosotras las únicas que nos inventamos pretextos para no follar. Ahora, ellos están agotados, estresados, etc., y también nos rechazan.

Otra de las conclusiones a las que he podido llegar es que no hay reglas. En esto, verdaderamente, somos individuos y lo mejor es la buena voluntad: que alguien puede ser un gran amante si es generoso y se deja llevar y que, si bien la experiencia es muy útil, hemos de conocer ciertos mínimos, no todos los promiscuos se lo montan bien; que lo que a uno le gusta a otro le espanta, pese a que se ejecute con perfecto dominio de las posturitas. Aunque sobre técnica, y los masajes, y los afrodisíacos... he llenado folios y folios. Y hago hincapié en que la mujer no suele alcanzar el orgasmo simplemente con la penetración, y requiere de estimulación adicional del clítoris porque hay ahí un pequeño lío anatómico... Recordemos que Dios creó el mundo en sólo siete días y, claro, tanta prisa, al final se nota... Se debió de olvidar del clítoris y lo dejó bien lejos de la vagina, con lo que ni el pene más intrépido y robusto, lo alcanza. Bromas aparte, sí que recojo tanto pormenores físicos, como soluciones de maestro para remediar este «imprevisto» de la naturaleza.

Reflexionando un poco, opino que es un craso error simplificar la trascendencia del acto sexual. Si bien el ser humano está dotado del sistema respiratorio, excretor, nervioso, circulatorio... y cada uno de ellos se asocia a una serie de actos, de órganos y de funciones, ninguno de ellos alcanza, ni de lejos, las implicaciones del reproductor, donde se supera la estricta biología. Como acto que genera la vida —consideración que podría llevarnos al terreno poético y elevarlo a la categoría de milagro—, no deberíamos obviar, sin embargo, que la sexualidad hoy se ejercita utilizando medios anticonceptivos, amén de los profilácticos. Practicamos sexo como expresión de emociones, de búsqueda de contacto humano y fuente de placer físico; muchos, sólo somos «nosotros mismos», prescindiendo de caretas, en ese ratito que permanecemos con los ojos cerrados, abandonados a las sensaciones, sin necesidad de responder a expectativas ajenas... Y tampoco sería sensato ignorar que las consecuencias de estos actos adquieren tal envergadura que condicionan muchas de nuestras decisiones. Lo que complica el sexo es que su esencia no es tan simple como alcanzar un orgasmo (aunque esto pueda resultar toda una «misión imposible» en según qué casos) y que tampoco termina ahí... Si la práctica más buscada fuera el onanismo, no hablaríamos de «relación» sexual; si no involucrase a dos personas (o a más), la gente no sufriría tanto, no se enamoraría, no se formarían hogares y familias...

Hay una tendencia a difundir un mensaje de modernidad exacerbada que pretende instaurar un patrón de conducta más cercano al de los animales que al de los seres racionales. A día de hoy, se cae en los mismos errores que han venido denunciado los más rancios pensadores, filósofos y Papas, in sécula seculórum: «se ha producido una cosificación del ser humano». Dile tú esa frase a una que sale llorando de un *afterhours*, lamentándose de «ahora que hemos *follao*, el cabrón no me coge el móvil». Si hombres y mujeres fuéramos de verdad iguales, y nos tomáramos realmente el sexo del mismo modo, no habría ciertos dramas y drásticas evidencias de falta de sintonía. Que tengamos derechos y que a todos nos ampare el mismo ordenamiento jurídico en un plano de igualdad no significa, en absoluto, identidad entre los sexos. Por lo general, la mujer interioriza mucho más el sexo que el hombre (algo que quizá se explica por razones fisiológicas, por la localización de los genitales). En ella, mente y cuerpo van mucho más vinculados que en el hombre —por favor, no se utilice como motivo de debate sobre el feminismo-machismo—; simplemente, sucede que hombres y mujeres somos iguales, sí, pero dentro de la diferencia. ¿Y esto cómo se entiende? Pues con muchas matizaciones pero, básicamente, como que, si bien es imprescindible propiciar un marco legal que garantice nuestra igualdad de derechos, deberes y oportunidades, no es menos necesario disponer de información acerca de las sustanciales diferencias que son inherentes a cada sexo (además de las físicas, tienen mucho peso específico las emocionales), y que se manifiestan de modo espectacular en la vida privada y en la esfera de lo íntimo. Asumir esto genera tremendos conflictos y dudas, porque cierta «caballerosidad» puede malinterpretarse como señal de proteccionismo machista o de «estar *pillao*» o, desde el lado femenino, se sufre a menudo el castigo de ser insultada si decides ejercer tu libertad sexual en los mismos términos que hacen los tíos...

Me indigna que persistan tópicos machistas en el propio lenguaje, que una cosa sea «la polla» o «cojonuda» si es buena, que la vida sea «perra» o «una putada» en caso contrario. Y también dentro del propio pensamiento femenino: esto sucede cada vez que nosotras mismas nos reprimimos o posicionamos como «pasivas», cada vez que damos por hecho que es cierto que nos interesa menos el sexo que a ellos, cada vez que descartamos la sexualidad si no va asociada a la reproducción (menopausia, durante la menstruación, etc.). También me descompone que se nos haya privado, a todos, a varias generaciones en general, de la fase intermedia que debería haber existido entre la censura radical y el oscurantismo más infame y el actual circo mediático y el exhibicionismo descarnado y soez. Se han saltado la etapa de divulgación, de despenalización moral y de normalización del sexo dentro de la cultura. Detesto que se dé por hecho que «del sexo se sabe todo», porque en teoría, viviendo en un entorno donde parece tan fácil el acceso a la información y los contenidos pornográficos se difunden con total permisividad, debería ser así.

En este libro pasaré por encima de curiosidades clandestinas, de muchos miedos enquistados, y de problemas que no por frecuentes encaramos con mayor solvencia... Quizá pueda parecer que los ventilo con cierta frivolidad pero, si lo hago así es porque mi experiencia revela que rico o pobre, joven o maduro, intelectual o analfabeto, cuando el ser humano se enfrenta a una violación, a un gatillazo o, simplemente, se enamora, siente y padece exactamente lo mismo y que las crisis se plantean de idéntico modo en la esfera de lo privado, ya sea sobre una sábana de seda, en un descampado o en el maletero de una furgoneta.

Matizo que en determinadas prácticas mi opinión no irá refrendada por mi propia vivencia sexual, y espero que se entienda que no necesariamente has de practicar la zoofilia para escribir sobre ella con propiedad. En cualquier caso, las cuestiones que se abordarán a lo largo de estas páginas me son familiares y cuanto se diga en este texto está avalado por datos y experiencias. He recurrido a testimonios de lectores y amigos, de prostitutas, *escorts* y actores X, me he sepultado literalmente con libros especializados (por cierto: es posible odiar algo y sin querer, sin darte ni cuenta, convertirte en ello. Me explico: encerrada durante semanas, meses, rodeada de montones de fotocopias y de torres de manuales subrayados, anotados y coloreados, con mis gafas de culo de vaso y un lápiz clavado en el moño: he llegado a parecerme a Harry Potter en su biblioteca); he llenado la casa de DVD's de cine convencional y de cine X —¡que por primera vez he visionado a cámara lenta!— y, por supuesto, apelo a mis recuerdos y a mi propia vida. Obviamente no vendo el personaje de «he sido puta de lujo, cómprate mi libro», ni tampoco voy a promocionar una virginidad falsa, como hiciera

Britney Spears para alimentar el morbo de sus primeros discos... Y habrá parafilias y actividades que detallo y que, a según quién, le resultarán repulsivas. Esto es como lo de comer sushi. Hay quienes pagan una elevada cuenta y lo consideran un manjar, mientras que otros vomitan sólo de imaginarse masticando pescado crudo.

Mientras escribía los distintos capítulos, me daba cuenta de que me perseguían constantemente un par de ideas: Una, que las palabras «braguitas» y «hacer el amor» no sólo no están en mi vocabulario sino que me provocan alergia; y dos, que cada ser humano es distinto, y que hay que particularizar siempre. El mismísimo Kamasutra apuntaba esta idea de singularidad: «en cada clase de unión, los hombres deben emplear los medios que juzguen convenientes para cada ocasión determinada». Añadiría algo que yo misma he experimentado respecto del sexo y las técnicas y que se resume en «cuanto más sé, menos sé». (Idea compatible con el «¡cuánto se liga si se enteran que escribes sobre sexo!».) Usa la sabiduría amatoria, pero asimílala y, luego, déjala fuera de la alcoba. De verdad. No hay peor cosa que verse condicionado por todo lo que se ha escuchado, leído, visto, hecho con otros o a otros... Cada persona es diferente y merece ser especial.

Esto me lleva a hablar de las imágenes que contiene y que enriquecen este libro hasta cotas increíbles y para cuya descripción, por una vez, me quedo sin palabras. Contar con el trabajo de estos artistas en estas páginas no es sólo un regalo sino todo un lujo, un privilegio. Un gesto desinteresado y tan valioso como el amor. Sus preciosas obras de arte convierten este libro en todo un «manual de sexo ilustrado». Varios de los mejores ilustradores del momento tanto nacionales como extranjeros han dado a través de sus creaciones su particular versión y visión del sexo, del erotismo, de los juegos íntimos... Ya apuntaba antes que cada uno vivimos y sentimos el sexo de un modo distinto, como distintas son las manifestaciones de cada uno de estos artistas gráficos. Todo un buqué de percepciones. Gracias a Berto Martínez, a Carmen García Huerta, a Lau, a Nani Serrano, a Damián Pissara y a Ray Caesar, a Arturo Elena y a Kaik.

Si hay un asunto que oculta y se conecta con grandes miedos y tabúes, ése es, por excelencia, el sexo. No se te amenaza sólo con arder en el infierno si tu debilidad te empuja al pecado carnal, sino que cometer un simple error en la práctica de lo que más placer te puede proporcionar te hace pagar un precio carísimo: desde embarazos no deseados a las ETS, sida y VIH, pasando por el dolor de las rupturas y la sensación de fracaso, o ese infierno que soportas si te aferras a alguien inconveniente por el terror irracional a la soledad y el inconsciente rechazo a los cambios.

A lo largo de estos años he llegado a bastantes conclusiones, la fundamental es que en casi nada que tenga que ver con sexo cabe hacer predicciones, ni fijar normas que no estés dispuesto a llenar de excepciones: tantas como seres humanos existen —y en esto debo incluir a quienes, motu proprio, deciden sublimar el sexo y ejercitar su sexualidad desde el intelecto o lo emotivo, sin bajar nunca al terreno de la carne y de los que, bien por seguir un tratamiento de fertilidad, bien para innovar o dotar a su vida de pareja de alicientes, deciden darse períodos de descanso o abstinencia—. Sin embargo, tanto reflexionar, investigar y documentarme sobre sexo me permite corroborar ciertas aseveraciones populares, negar otras e incluso, esbozar mis propias teorías, algunas de las cuales explico aquí.

En definitiva, mi ambición se resumiría en que mi trabajo al menos sirviera para explicar conceptos sobre sexo y sexualidad que con frecuencia se tergiversan; querría volcar en palabras ciertos trucos y técnicas sexuales, muchas de las cuales se desconocen o aún se difunden en forma de susurros y que, admitámoslo, no vendría nada mal que se compartieran... Recuerda que nada inspira tanto al ser humano como las novedades. En la cama siempre resulta bastante motivador tratar de emular a aquellos que se consideran grandes amantes... pero ojalá, leyendo estas páginas, se comprenda que para dejar huella no hay necesidad de acrobacias, que no se basa sólo en la técnica sino en las ganas, porque te puedes comer a alguien por los pies y con los ojos, y que son fundamentales las conversaciones íntimas sobre sexo y dedicarle cierto tiempo a la tarea de comprendernos a nosotros mismos y a familiarizarnos con nuestra propia respuesta sexual. Hemos de conocer nuestra propia esencia, gustos, preferencias y necesidades, sin complejos y desde la honestidad. Ya se sabe: el Cielo es el límite y el sexo, en ocasiones, nos permite tocarlo.

MI PERFIL

Entre otros títulos, tengo uno que afirma que soy abogada. Conseguirlo me domesticó el cerebro, me llevó a buscar la excepción en toda regla y me inculcó la manía de leer toda la letra pequeña, lo que, con el tiempo, me ha convertido en alguien que repasa hasta las etiquetas del champú. Como me pierden la mitomanía, la fantasía y la belleza me gano la vida escribiendo, y quiero creer que a estas alturas mis entrevistas tienen cierto nivel. Sospecho que optimizo en solitario. Intuyo que me ocupo más de alimentar la mente que de limpiar el pis de mis gatos, lo que no quita para que sean los animales más queridos y cuidados de este mundo. Mi mesa de trabajo es sagrada. También es mi universo, mi refugio y un perfecto caos. Soy maniática de la higiene personal. Nunca me despierto de mala leche. Si tengo pasta, no sé decirme que no. Por las nimiedades no discuto. Ante la duda, en vez de los pasajes bíblicos sobre la abstinencia —genérica, no sólo sexual—, recuerdo el consejo que Al Pacino daba a su gato en *Esencia de mujer*: «ante la duda, folla». Por norma, rechazo a priori cualquier ayuda profesional, de esas que yo misma recomiendo a todo el mundo. A veces pienso que si Woody Allen fuera mujer me parecería a él: en las gafas y en la neurosis. Ah, una cosa más: odio despedirme y, como todo lo que odio, procuro que sólo me suceda una vez.

PRIMERA PARTE

CONOZCÁMONOS

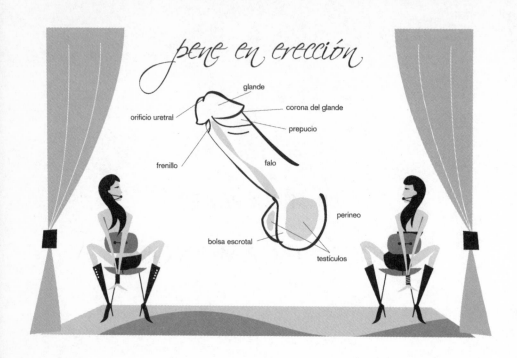

pene en erección

- glande
- corona del glande
- orificio uretral
- prepucio
- frenillo
- falo
- perineo
- bolsa escrotal
- testículos

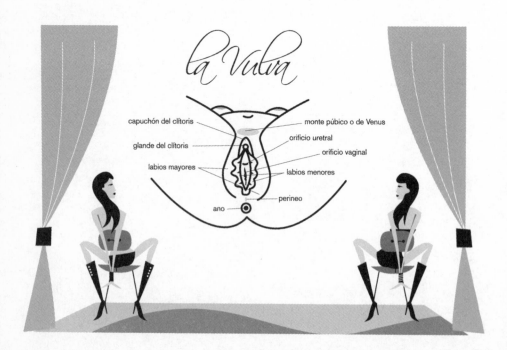

la Vulva

- capuchón del clítoris
- monte púbico o de Venus
- glande del clítoris
- orificio uretral
- orificio vaginal
- labios mayores
- labios menores
- perineo
- ano

1

Anatomía básica

GENITALES MASCULINOS

Las partes principales del pene son cinco. La cabeza o **glande,** en la punta; en erección, es esa terminación redondeada, de piel suave, algo más gruesa que el tronco. La **uretra,** el orificio que hay en el extremo del pene desde el que se expulsa el semen y por el que sale la orina. El **eje** o **tronco,** cuya parte dorsal está formada por dos cuerpos cavernosos, de tejido esponjoso; a causa de la excitación sexual, reciben irrigación de sangre y la retienen, van «llenándose», produciéndose la erección. Para hacer a un hombre volverse loco, hay que tener bien localizado el **frenillo,** ese trocito de piel que une el glande con el eje. Hay hombres que presentan un frenillo corto, es decir, cuando el pene está en erección, tira. Si se desgarra solo o si durante la penetración se actúa bruscamente, provoca un buen susto y una hemorragia —debe curarlo el médico—. En realidad, se debe resolver con una *elongación,* una intervención en la que simplemente se corta el frenillo, lo que alivia la tirantez. El **prepucio** es una especie de exceso de piel que recubre el glande y que se elimina con la circuncisión. El prepucio, cuando lo hay, no impide que el glande y el frenillo reciban la estimulación durante el coito, porque se echa hacia atrás de modo natural. Si esto no es posible, y representa un problema —de higiene, porque se acumula el esmegma, o sexual, porque duele la penetración o incluso, si es severa, dificulta la erección—, se debe realizar una operación que resuelve la *fimosis,* que es como se llama al estrechamiento de la piel del prepucio que impide su retracción.

Conviene lubricar bien antes de desplazar el prepucio y hacerlo con cuidado, si no, resulta muy doloroso. Como regla: la parte menos sensible del pene es la base —otra cosa es que sea la que antes se ponga erecta y, por alcanzar mayor grosor, a muchas mujeres les excite y focalicen ahí las caricias: ¡error!—, y la más sensible, la punta, el glande, donde se concentran muchísimas terminaciones nerviosas, y aún más, el frenillo.

El **escroto** es la «bolsa» de piel ubicada en la base del pene y que sostiene los **testículos**. En ellos se forman las hormonas masculinas y los espermatozoides. El **perineo** va desde el ano hasta el escroto y constituye una zona de extremada sensibilidad, con lo que también será muy receptiva a caricias manuales o con la lengua o vibradores. El punto G masculino, o **punto P** (por próstata) se halla dentro del ano, próximo a la uretra, a unos dos centímetros, en la pared frontal. Para estimularlo correctamente (dado que hay quien puede rechazarlo) siempre ha de haberse «consensuado» y ni hablar de ir directamente a meter por ahí nada, sin que haya lubricante y estimulación externa previa. Al tacto, es una glándula del tamaño de una nuez. También se puede abordar desde fuera, se puede presionar, masajeando con el pulgar en la zona del perineo, justo cuando se produce el orgasmo, para provocarlo o para potenciar su intensidad.

Genitales femeninos

Los genitales femeninos son algo más complejos que los masculinos. A simple vista, los externos se denominan con el genérico término «vulva», que debe ser estimulada «en general» y por partes. En ella se distingue el **monte de Venus** o **pubis**, que es esa especie de montículo cubierto de vello formando una V (algo que puede desaparecer o variar su diseño por arte de la depilación). Hay además dos pares de labios (sí, en total, nosotras tenemos tres pares: uno justo debajo de la nariz). En cada mujer la forma, tamaño y color de los labios es diferente.

Los **labios mayores** son dos capas de piel que rodean la vulva, también con vello, y que ocultan los labios menores. En los **menores** se hallan algunas glándulas sebáceas que segregan un fluido que lubrica la vagina. Cuando se produce la excitación, los labios aumentan de tamaño y se endurecen porque se concentra sangre en toda la zona, y se vuelven más rojos (aunque todo esto pueda ser tan discreto y pasar tan desapercibido que nadie lo note). La denominación labios «mayores» y «menores» puede no corresponder a la realidad, metro en mano —el tamaño varía mucho, y cabe que los labios mayores sean más cortos que los menores, de modo que éstos sean prominentes y sobresalgan—.[1] Algunas mujeres vírgenes presentan una membrana, el **himen**[2], que cubre la entrada de la vagina. Puede estar intacta —sólo con ciertos orificios que permiten la salida de la sangre menstrual—, rasgada o haber desaparecido del todo, debido a la práctica de ciertos deportes como montar a caballo o la gimnasia, o al uso de tampones.

Igual que en el hombre, existe una zona desde el orificio de la vagina hasta el ano, denominada **perineo**, y también en la mujer es muy sensible a la estimulación sexual —a algunas les excita que durante el coito o la masturbación, les introduzcan un dedo (¡lubricado!) pero, igual que ocurría con ellos, es algo muy personal, hay que preguntar antes porque muchas lo odian—. Justo encima de la entrada de la vagina se encuentra la **uretra**, un pequeño orificio por donde se orina.

En la parte superior de la vagina se halla el **clítoris**, la parte más sensible, el único órgano del cuerpo que no posee otra finalidad más que la de proporcionar placer. Su forma es la de un guisante, pero engaña: sólo vemos una pequeña fracción, el resto, de la misma composición que el glande, se encuentra oculto —terminaciones nerviosas—. Como el pene, el clítoris tiene un **glande**, que es justo «el botón» —aunque los hay de hasta 6 cm—, lo más sensible. El resto de piel que hay alrededor es el **capuchón**, que se puede desplazar hacia atrás manualmente para dejar el glande al descubierto y proceder con la boca o los dedos. Por debajo de la piel, el clítoris se extiende unos 8 centímetros a ambos lados de la vagina, con **dos ramas (crura)**, que van por debajo de los labios formando una V. Justo donde estas ramas y el cuerpo clitorídeo se unen por debajo de los labios, se denomina **bulbos vestibulares**, unos nódu-

---

1. Ver el capítulo de «Cirugía íntima».
2. Ver el concepto en la tercera parte del libro.

los eréctiles cuando se llenan por la afluencia de sangre con la excitación sexual, como pasa con el tejido cavernoso del pene.

La **vagina** no se ve desde fuera. Tiene un orificio, o entrada, por donde se expulsan la sangre menstrual y el flujo y por donde sale el bebé en el parto natural. La vagina en sí es un tubo de paredes musculares, elásticas, que cuando se estimula, se expanden, permitiendo alojar penes de casi cualquier tamaño con facilidad (recuerda que el feto la atraviesa y, por bien dotado que se esté, difícilmente tendrá ningún pene semejante diámetro). En un primer momento de la penetración los músculos de la vagina se contraen y agarran el pene, luego, mientras prosigue, se dilatan y relajan, perdiendo tensión —lo que explica que las primeras embestidas sean las más placenteras—. La vagina se estrecha[3] de nuevo con el orgasmo, mediante una serie de fuertes contracciones rítmicas que desencadenan un placer intenso.

El **punto G** es una zona esponjosa que se halla a pocos centímetros dentro de la vagina, en la pared frontal. Se localiza insertando los dedos índice y medio arqueados y su estimulación desencadenaría una sensación particularmente voluptuosa e intensos orgasmos, así como una eyaculación. Ver en el capítulo «El orgasmo», la eyaculación femenina.

El **punto A**, el punto erógeno del fornex anterior, ubicado en la pared frontal de la vagina. Para detectarlo has de introducir en la vagina dos dedos arqueados (y lubricados). La primera zona esponjosa que vas a encontrar es el punto G. Continúa hacia dentro, hacia el cérvix. A mitad de camino entre uno y otro, notarás una zona muy suave. Se estimula describiendo semicírculos de derecha a izquierda. Las posiciones de penetración que mejor acceso tienen a este punto son desde atrás (a cuatro patas o *doggie*) y ella sentada al borde de la cama y él de rodillas, ambos mirándose de frente.

Aunque parezca increíble todavía tenemos más puntitos. En 1998 la doctora Barbara Keesling encontró el prácticamente inac-

---

3. Existen técnicas quirúrgicas específicas para los genitales; constituyen la última moda en cirugía estética. Desde el estrechamiento vaginal, recorte y relleno de labios, o la reconstrucción del himen, al alargamiento del pene o el *lifting* que descubre el clítoris. Éstas y otras intervenciones se explican en el capítulo de «Cirugía íntima».

cesible **punto K**, casi al final de la vagina, llegando al cuello del útero. La propia descubridora lo llama «pasaje misterioso». Se trata de una zona erógena, que es necesario ejercitar, y donde se pueden desencadenar orgasmos muy intensos.

Cuello del útero o **cérvix**: el extremo inferior del útero, estrecho —de 1 cm aproximadamente—, con enorme capacidad de dilatación. Por él pasan los espermatozoides para fecundar el óvulo —que se encuentra (o no) dentro del útero—. La penetración profunda estimula este punto y en algunas mujeres desencadena orgasmos.

Las **glándulas vestibulares mayores** o **de Bartolino**, ubicadas justo a la entrada de la vagina, se ocupan de proporcionar lubricación durante la excitación. Este líquido viscoso se segrega desde los labios menores. Ver su epígrafe, así como el de **Trompas de Falopio, Útero, Ovarios** y **Musculatura pubococcígea.**

Zonas erógenas

Las zonas erógenas se denominan así porque al ser estimuladas provocan una respuesta muy concreta: activan el deseo sexual. Ello se debe a que poseen una gran cantidad de terminaciones nerviosas que reaccionan cuando son besadas, lamidas, mordisqueadas, azotadas, arañadas, acariciadas o se sopla sobre ellas...

Se pueden diferenciar las zonas erógenas genitales «principales» —las más famosas— de «las otras» que, sin calificarse como tales específicamente, pueden llevar también a una persona al orgasmo. Por otro lado, lo cierto es que la mente humana, el cerebro, es el órgano sexual más potente y puede ser erotizado a través de la contemplación de imágenes, o con ciertos sonidos o palabras, o con el olor... además de cierta concentración.

El cuerpo entero se puede lamer, acariciar o mordisquear, salvo el globo ocular y el párpado móvil. El resto, todo; eso sí, con sentido común, procurando dos cosas: no dejar marcas y no babear. Sólo los quinceañeros alardean de chupetones o lucen sus moratones en forma de dentadura. No significa que no se puedan dejar «señales de guerra», que constituyen recuerdos muy evocadores cuando con posterioridad se detectan en el espejo... —¿quién no se sonríe viendo la señal de una noche loca y rememorándola?—, pero pregunta antes y hazlas sólo si

al otro no le incomoda y siempre en sitios que la ropa pueda cubrir. Y por otro lado, mientras utilizas tu lengua como herramienta para estimular a la otra persona, vete secando con la mano, traga saliva o absórbela con disimulo porque los excesos, lo que no sirve estrictamente para lubricar, pueden dar un asco tremendo. Los soplidos han de ser de aire caliente y dirigidos. No estás ante tu tarta de cumpleaños... Si andas en la parte del cuello, los lóbulos de la orejas, el vientre o la cara interna de los muslos —esto se aplica a hombre y mujer—, trata de que tu nariz participe de la fiesta expirando con mayor intención: expulsa el aire caliente justo donde estás, por donde has pasado o vas a pasar la punta de la lengua o donde estés besando o acariciando.

En el cuello se localizan varias zonas muy receptivas. Hay mujeres que pueden llegar al orgasmo cuando les estimulan la zona que coincide con la yugular. Por favor, que eso no convierta a nadie en Drácula —y cuidadito con lo que hablamos de dejar moratones y chupetones—, y tampoco os obsesionéis: no a todas les pasa, pero sí que les dará placer.

Otra parte muy sensible es la nuca. Aquí, un consejo. Si vas a acariciar a una chica bajo la melena, date cuenta de cómo va peinada. Me refiero a que por buenas intenciones que tengas, y a que sepas cómo tocarla, debes preocuparte de no destrozarle el peinado —obviamente esto ya en privado y entrados en materia, no se aplica—. Por frívolo que suene, más de una esquivará la caricia, no porque no le guste o no la desee, sino porque le arruinas el *look*. Ve poco a poco. Evoluciona de la simple pasada con la mano abierta, a juguetear con mechones, a levantarle toda la melena y acariciar desde los hombros, o a darle pequeños tirones (siempre de la zona de la nuca y flojito). Cuidado que esto, en hombres con alopecia, puede provocar la misma reacción (desde un rechazo disimulado a reacciones muy irascibles). Tenlo en cuenta. Por otro lado, cuando él se afeita la cabeza o está calvo, sepas que es el masaje del cuero cabelludo lo verdaderamente excitante, el pelo en sí resulta secundario.

Para que realmente disfrute, necesitas que se relaje. Puedes ganar comodidad procurando que la cabeza repose sobre un cojín o que la apoye sobre ti, sobre tu pecho o en tus piernas, de modo que tengas acceso a toda la cabeza, al rostro y al cabello.

A estas alturas, ya has podido captar un detalle clave: en esto de acariciar (como en otras habilidades amatorias) siempre es preferible ir de menos a más. Sigue una gradación ascendente en cuanto a intensidad, velocidad, presión, profundidad, etc., porque siempre podrás ir aumentando. Sin embargo, si se comienza bruscamente, la otra persona puede molestarse, bien porque se la lastime o se la «espante». Mide el entusiasmo y dosifícalo. Cuando utilices las manos para acariciar, recuerda que no se trata de una mascota, nada de palmaditas..., y tampoco pases las manos como si estuvieras allanando una cordillera. Al revés: detente en cada forma, rodéala, ve poco a poco, genera expectativa... En cuanto a qué emplear: pues... sigue tu instinto, pero, salvo que se trate del típico polvo/meneo desatado —de esos de película, en los que cierto grado de dolor va en el contexto—, las uñas déjalas para momentos ulteriores. Comienza con las yemas de los dedos, altérnalas con el dorso de la mano, para ir apretando cada vez más, intensificando los pellizquitos, amasando más fuerte, pasando las uñas en trayectorias lineales o circulares, «rascando» hasta clavarlas —ojo, a ver dónde se las clavas—. Las marcas de arañazos son como los chupetones: no a todo el mundo le apetece que se los hagan. Es preferible para muchos notar cómo se hunden en la carne las yemas o las caricias a contrapelo con un ligero contacto.

Para documental el potencial erótico de la piel basta con aportar unos datos. En cada centímetro concentramos 3,65 m de nervios, 1 m de vasos sanguíneos, 10 folículos pilosos y 100 glándulas sudoríparas. Y en el espacio de una pulgada (2,5 cm) que concentran entre 14.000 y 18.000 receptores nerviosos. ¿Se comprende que el masaje sea tan apreciado?

La reacción física suele ser de estremecimiento, escalofrío, piel de gallina, alteración del ritmo cardíaco y de la respiración, erección y secreción de flujo vaginal. No a todos nos gusta todo o lo mismo. Si bien hay quienes ante determinado gesto tienen un orgasmo, otros no lo soportarán, o sólo disfrutarán de él a partir de cierto nivel de excitación o durante breves instantes (la intensidad del placer puede ser tal que se convierte en insoportable, o que se siente como las cosquillas...).

En él

Las zonas erógenas masculinas son el pene, el escroto, los testículos, el perineo y el ano (genitales) y también: pezones, orejas, cabello, labios, muslos. Sin embargo, un buen masaje en la espalda o en los pies, o una insinuante pasada de uñas por las pantorrillas arrancando desde los tobillos, pueden obrar milagros.

La punta del pene es la más sensible. Si se aborda, lo más natural es que se produzca una erección y que si no se interrumpe la estimulación, él eyacule. Conviene repartir la atención a todo su cuerpo: los testículos, los brazos, el cuello, los glúteos... Evita excitar el pene —el glande en concreto— durante mucho tiempo si pretendes que «dure» mínimamente en la penetración. Si te dedicas a otros puntos —el área de la base del pene, entre el escroto y el ano—, mantendrá la erección, pero no le llevarás al punto de «no retorno» a partir del cual se desencadena la eyaculación sí o sí. Como experiencia para un día o como técnica habitual, aplica un poco de lubricante en toda la zona y acaricia el pene o mastúrbalo. Las sensaciones serán mucho más intensas debido a la cantidad de terminaciones nerviosas que concentra... Viene detallado en «Masturbación masculina» y en «Sexo oral». La estimulación del ano se trata en profundidad en el apartado sobre «Sexo anal». Intensificar las caricias en el perineo, momentos antes de llegar al orgasmo, a muchos hombres les proporciona una mayor dosis de placer. En lo que respecta a las nalgas, si bien en la fase de calentamiento se aprisiona el centro del glúteo con las palmas de las manos y se rodea con los dedos, conforme la cosa se calienta, se agradecen otras cosas: cachetadas, largos lametazos o estrujar los glúteos con cierta fuerza.

Las axilas y el torso masculino frecuente, injusta y equivocadamente quedan abandonados como tierra de nadie. Los pezones de ambos sexos son muy sensibles y, lo mismo que hay mujeres que notan que nada más excitarse se les ponen erectos (se endurecen, se contraen), en ellos sucede también. Puede que, igual que a algunas, no les guste que se los toquen, o sólo de determinada forma, a veces muy sutil —pregunta, prueba, empieza despacito ante la duda—. Suele funcionar ir abordando la zona desde fuera yendo hacia la areola, dejándola para el final. Se puede chupar, succionar, acariciar con la mano, masajear todo el pecho, rozarlo con los dedos, tomar con el pulgar y el índice el pezón y girarlo un poco, pellizcarlo... En medio de los dos pechos existe un punto energético principal, uno de los siete chakras, el del corazón. Si dibujas con las yemas de los dedos espirales que se abren o estrellas que se extienden hacia fuera, estarás abriendo su corazón, esparciendo su energía de dar y recibir amor, estarás creando un mayor abandono y confianza, una inercia de cariño que optimiza la relación, la erotiza, la baña de sensualidad.

Las manos también se consideran zonas excepcionalmente erógenas. En sus palmas se localizan todos y cada uno de los órganos del cuerpo, pudiendo tratarlos desde ellas, sin necesidad de abordarlos directamente. En acupuntura se utiliza un punto concreto para activar la energía. Cualquier terapeuta (shiatsu, reiki, chi kung, etc.) conoce que las palmas son centros dadores de energía y a través de las yemas de los dedos se transmite energía positiva. No en vano, la sensación de contacto de una palma con otra, transcurridos unos segundos, nos permite notar cómo se restablece la armonía o la confianza, y cómo fluye de una persona a otra esa energía. Las manos se pueden acariciar de un modo «incidental», como cuando alguien te agarra para cruzar una calle o para no separaros entre la multitud. Ese casto «hacer manitas» ya logra excitarnos. Más allá, cuando besamos una mano, sea el dorso o la palma, estamos iniciando una vía a la sensualidad. Introducir el dedo de un hombre en la boca, acariciarlo con la lengua, hacerlo rodar, le procura un placer inmenso. Si haces eso, en realidad estás simulando la penetración o la felación, pero la sensación del placebo generalmente replica con enorme viveza a los «originales».

En ella

Debes saber que la mujer tiene muchas más partes erógenas además de sus pechos, sus nalgas y su vagina.[4] Algunos citan hasta diez zonas erógenas femeninas: pies, tobillos, detrás de las rodillas, muslos, abdomen, espalda, manos, muñecas, cuello, cabeza. Yo, presidiendo la enumeración, mencionaría los labios que, más allá de besarlos, admiten ciertas caricias. Ya no hay excusa para no triunfar como masajista particular con las maravillas que hay en el mercado en cuanto a aceites y cremas de masaje o incluso, ciertos utensilios, como rodillos de madera o metacrilato, elementos de raso y seda, plumas, borlas...

Los pechos. Si se les dedica cierto tiempo, se descubren sensaciones muy intensas (incluso orgásmicas para muchas). Se debe recordar la delicadeza de esta zona: no te cuelgues de ellos, no los aplastes, no los muerdas, no hagas gestos bruscos... (imagina que son tus testículos y obra en consecuencia). Conforme una chica se excita, mientras la besas, puedes ir acercándote a su pecho. El cómo llegues a ellos a veces es casi una odisea, sortearás varias prendas, luego el sujetador... No la arañes, no desgarres la ropa —salvo que forme parte del juego, claro—, no la pellizques y no vayas al pezón como si fueras un lactante hambriento. Ya estás destetado, compórtate como tal. Cuando te demoras en la base del cuello, o dando rodeos por todo el pecho —aunque esté casi plana, se puede recorrer toda la zona—, ella va «despertándose» y esa ansiedad de estar esperando que llegue «lo bueno» acentúa y potencia las sensaciones. Compagina manos y labios. No falla.

Si tu pareja tiene cosquillas y vas a dedicarte a sus pies, procura que el tacto sea firme, o de lo contrario, no lo soportará. Considerad que la higiene es crucial especialmente en lo que a olores y ca-

---

4. Para leer sobre la estimulación de la zona de la vagina vete a los apartados de «Sexo oral» y de «Masturbación femenina».

llosidades respecta. Se puede hasta comer en un suelo bien fregado, pues esto es lo mismo: recién lavados y con una pedicura decente, los pies —masculinos y femeninos— se pueden introducir en la boca incluso. Juega con ella, introduciendo el dedo gordo o los pequeños, o recorre el espacio entre los dedos con la lengua ayudada de tus dedos. Usa el pulgar para buscar el centro de la planta y masajearlo. Posiblemente, a priori, estas ideas a muchos les suenen extravagantes, sin embargo, las reacciones son de enorme excitación. Igual que las palmas de las manos, las plantas de los pies centralizan todos los órganos (con reflexología podal se tratan muchas enfermedades y dolencias). La digitopresión puede llevar a tu pareja al séptimo cielo, relajarla, excitarla, dormirla, conseguir el clima sensual que buscas o simplemente, recompensarla tras un día infernal en el trabajo, especialmente entre las féminas, un masaje dado en los pies, puede acercarlas al éxtasis.

El masaje de los tobillos se puede entender como una insinuación, e ir ascendiendo hacia la rodilla, si te los colocas sobre los hombros y vas avanzando, con movimientos circulares de los dedos o con los labios... También sirve de remedio terapéutico, ayudando al drenaje, sobre todo si están hinchados.

La parte posterior de las rodillas responde mejor a toques suaves, a caricias leves, igual que la espalda, donde se puede ir desde la nuca hacia abajo, insinuando, recorriendo cada centímetro.

El masaje

No toques a nadie si tienes las manos heladas.

Durante el masaje, no pierdas el contacto físico con su cuerpo. Si te vas a girar, a cambiar de posición o a echar más crema, mantén una mano sobre la otra persona (evita que se sobresalte cuando «regresas», mantiene la conexión energética; si no comprendes bien de qué va esto, haz un acto de fe).

Utiliza aceites o cremas. Si eliges bien, el propio olor te ayudará a crear sensualidad. El aroma de jazmín, rosa, madera o sándalo van bien para la zona del torso. En general, el de vainilla, o alguno con canela, o el de almendras dulces. Más en el capítulo sobre «Juguetes eróticos».

Adiestra tus dedos. No se trata de sobar a alguien, ni de amasar, ni de martirizar... Desarrolla tu sensibilidad y aprende a transmitir: deseo, cariño, tranquilidad, etc. Puedes hablar con ellas.

Hay otra máxima: las caricias que damos y cómo las damos, en el fondo, son las que nos gustaría recibir. Así que, cuando te toque dar el masaje, recuerda y repite lo que te hacía.

Las cosquillitas y los lamidos a presión por la zona de la cara interna del muslo y por el abdomen, junto con el aire caliente que podemos hacer que llegue hasta la vagina (ni se te ocurra soplar dentro), crean una tremenda tensión sexual. Nuevamente, funciona eso de detenerse y proseguir, ir ganando terreno muy poco a poco, pero manteniendo la vagina al margen, ignorándola. Es cuestión de expectativas, de que la mantengas con la incertidumbre de qué le vas a hacer y cuándo... Que vayas poco a poco jugando con el ombligo, avanzando entre sus piernas o deslizándote hacia su pubis, será motivo de que ella se predisponga a «recibir» más, querrá más.

La parte de las muñecas también suele ignorarse. Si agarras la mano de alguien, sujetándola, y la apoyas contra tu cara, mientras utilizas los labios y la lengua para lamerla y/o mordisquearla, recorriendo la base o yendo hacia el antebrazo, puede ser muy erótico.

Las orejas hay quien no soporta ni que se las rocen... Lo que tiene el pabellón auditivo es, precisamente, que centraliza el sentido del oído, lo que permite que te puedas abrir paso con palabras, rompiendo el hielo con una frase que impacte, susurrada entre el barullo de la multitud o a solas, creando una intimidad nueva e intensa: «esta noche es tu noche» o cosas así. Acertar con el grado de sutileza o pornografía del mensaje es todo un arte también. Puedes respirar cerca del oído, o pasar la lengua por los lóbulos, bajando después por el cuello. A ellos también les gusta mucho.

EL TAMAÑO

En el Kamasutra se clasifican los hombres y las mujeres en función del tamaño de sus genitales. Al pene se le denomina Lingam, y su tamaño determina hombres liebre, toro y caballo. La vagina se llama yoni (sí, con minúscula) y, según su profundidad y

su amplitud, clasifica a las mujeres en cierva, yegua o elefante hembra. (Por cierto: seguimos con el Kamasutra, no hemos saltado al pasaje bíblico del Arca de Noé.) El texto hindú afirma que se dan tres tipos de uniones iguales entre personas de sexo opuesto (liebre-cierva; toro-yegua; caballo-elefante), y seis uniones desiguales, cuando las dimensiones no se corresponden en absoluto. A las uniones entre mujer elefante y hombre toro, la mujer yegua y hombre liebre, la mujer elefante y hombre liebre, las etiqueta el texto como «unión muy baja, exageradamente baja, muchísimo más baja o del todo incompatible», respectivamente, y las define como «deficientes, las que no se desean, las que no deben efectuarse, y en fin, son las peores» y sigue: «para el hombre le resulta siempre más fácil. Al efectuar el acto sexual, el coito, no dañar a la mujer, mientras que en las segundas —habla de la uniones bajas— es difícil, problemático, que la mujer quede satisfecha»...

Clítoris. Se baraja el 30 % como cifra de mujeres que alcanza el orgasmo por medio de la penetración sin necesidad de añadir estimulación adicional a su clítoris.[5] Aquí, el tamaño del clítoris sí importa. A aquellas que cuentan con uno mayor les resulta más sencillo que exista una fricción con el pene durante el coito.

Vagina estrecha. Otro asunto viene determinado por la ley de la impenetrabilidad de la materia: si la vagina es demasiado estrecha, que también las hay, el coito resulta dificultoso y hasta doloroso. Muchas mujeres, tras dar a luz, sufren cambios en la apariencia y también en la elasticidad de sus vaginas. Considerando que no todas desean traer hijos al mundo —o lo harán, pero en un futuro—, se debe recurrir a medidas tan sencillas como efectivas. Tú y tu pareja debéis utilizar lubricante y ser conscientes de que la mejor forma de llevar a cabo la penetración es yendo muy poco a poco, y de que precisas muchos preliminares que garanticen una alta excitación para que haya lubricación y que se expandan las paredes de la vagina. Las mejores posiciones serán las que impliquen una separación de los muslos, pero, en cualquier caso, las que permiten que ella se relaje, y con ella, sus paredes internas.

Vagina grande. Caso contrario: cuando la vagina es demasiado grande, lo cual provoca que durante la penetración el pene quede «suelto», ya que los músculos que deberían estrecharlo no lo hacen y, consiguientemente, no resulta placentero para ninguno de los dos. Que no exista la suficiente tensión muscular tiene remedio, pero no se consigue en dos horas. Por una parte, de estar indicada la intervención, puede recurrirse a la cirugía.

La solución no quirúrgica implica hacer ejercicios que fortalezcan y confieran tono a la musculatura pubococcígea (PC). Se trata de los famosos ejercicios de Kegel. Ver su epígrafe en la tercera parte del libro y el apartado «Masturbación femenina».

5. Bakos, p. 114.

En él

El tamaño del pene. Adelanto que yo soy de las que opina que el tamaño del pene importa, y mucho, tanto por exceso como por defecto. También creo que se ha desviado dolosamente la atención hacia argumentos que sólo venían a encubrir esta realidad, hasta casi lograr que, cuando se formula esta pregunta, se conteste casi automáticamente eso de «lo que importa es cómo se use». Sí, en efecto, saber usarla es crucial pero ése es un debate distinto. Eso contesta a «¿sabes utilizar tu pene?» y no a «¿importa el tamaño del pene?». Por desgracia los hay que no saben usarla, ni pequeña ni grande, y para mejorar (o intentarlo) estamos aquí.

Vivimos en una sociedad que sufre una educación falocrática, por lo que a todos (y a todas) nos resulta importante —con excepción, probablemente, de las lesbianas— la penetración, y la sombra del sacralizado pene se cierne sobre cada relación sexual como si fuera un tótem. ¡Casi pertenece a la cultura popular la imagen de los niños y adolescentes dedicándose a comparar sus penes, su capacidad para la erección y midiendo el alcance de sus eyaculaciones! Por eso, cuando ya siendo adultos, algunos balbucean con (mal) fingido desinterés eso de «nunca me la he medido», a mí me da la risa... ¡Antes me creería que desconocen su fecha de nacimiento! Mienten. Lo saben al centímetro, claro que, es posible que el dato sea suficientemente humillante como para intentar olvidarlo.

Pequeño gran pene

Tanto si lo tienes tan grande que, a priori, ni cabe, como si casi no tienes pene, casi todo lo que voy a contar sirve. Ahora bien, cada caso requiere una serie de medidas distintas, las posturas, por ejemplo.

Cada uno ha de conocer sus puntos fuertes y los que no lo son tanto. Siempre comento que hay «guapos», hombres o mujeres con un físico espectacular, que en la cama no se lo *curran* nada o no transmiten demasiado, que se comportan como si estuvieran haciendo un favor al otro; les falta decir: «bastante es que he venido». Habría que preguntarles: «¿qué esperas, que la gente se corra sólo con verte?». Bueno, si esto resulta entre gracioso y evidente con tipos que están como para parar el tráfico —y que como mínimo ya estimulan la retina—, ¿no es incluso más obvio cuando nos codeamos con simples mortales, significativamente peor dotados genéticamente? Entre la tacañería emocional y la pereza física más despreciables y ser un esclavo rendido a la voluntad del otro, se extiende un amplio abanico de caricias, besos, posturas y mil recursos que ambos pueden disfrutar, tanto en el lado pasivo como en el activo, y tanto si se dispone de una herramienta monumental como si no.

En caso de los micropenes la solución para ambas partes nunca es fingir que las cosas son de «otro» modo (o tamaño). Si cuando él te penetra ni te enteras, no parece de recibo que sueltes alaridos, ¿no? El caso es que cuando hay química con alguien y apetece mayor cercanía e intimidad sexual, se pueden (y deben) intentar muchas cosas. A lo largo de este libro se dicen verdades como puños:

- La piel es el órgano más extenso del cuerpo y las zonas erógenas son todas, sólo es cuestión de estimularlas. La prisa es enemiga de lo bueno.
- Escucha: presta atención a lo que te dice con sus palabras y con su cuerpo, que muchas veces indica lo que necesita (y «métemela» no suele ser la canción más pedida).
- El cerebro debe ser tu meta: seduce su mente y el cuerpo irá detrás. Para ello necesitas un poco de empatía, adáptate al estado de ánimo que traiga ese día, que hay momentos para todo: dulzura, pasión, violencia...
- Sexo oral y masturbación. Se verán con detenimiento más tarde. No obstante, ahora que tratamos del tamaño, procede apuntar lo básico que resulta a la hora de que una mujer disfrute y se excite. Mientras realizas un cunnilingus puedes introducir dos dedos (o tres) en su vagina e ir estimulándola, metiendo y sacándolos o moviéndolos hacia los laterales para estimular esas paredes «olvidadas», o incluso, si a ella le gusta, entrar por su puerta trasera —despacio, con lubricación y,

fundamentalmente, con su permiso—... Cuando el pene es enorme, el sexo oral puede llevar a la chica al primer orgasmo, lo que determina que lubrique y la vagina se dilate. Cuando el pene sea pequeño, conviene desviar el protagonismo del coito a un plano secundario. Podéis intentar la penetración —siempre tratando que sea en posiciones de máxima profundidad—, por el placer físico y psíquico que produce, por la conexión emocional que permite. A la mujer le gusta sentir a su pareja dentro, pero sus orgasmos, en la inmensa mayoría de los casos, se producen por vía clitoriana, así que no debe causar frustración, ni preocupación, que el orgasmo no venga durante el coito: en serio, lo raro sería que así fuese. La relación sexual se puede basar en sexo oral recíproco, junto con otras caricias. Otro inconveniente de los penes pequeños es que suelen ir acompañados de eyaculaciones más rápidas, cuando no precoces, dada la concentración de terminaciones nerviosas —las mismas en todos, es algo común en la especie— en un área más limitada.

¿Ellas las prefieren gordas?

El grosor se puede también considerar una variable «de peso». Se oye mucho que «más vale que tape a que pinche». Cuando el pene es demasiado fino, ella debe permanecer en posturas donde sus muslos estén lo más juntos posible. Que uno más corto pero grueso sea preferible se explica por una cuestión de «geografía»: las zonas más sensibles del pene y de la vagina coinciden, se sitúan respectivamente en la parte del tercio superior (zona del glande, frenillo y superior del tronco del pene) y en ella, en los accesos de la vagina y los primeros centímetros del canal vaginal, donde se hallan el punto G y el punto A. Las penetraciones poco profundas y realizadas en el ángulo que permite estimular el punto G serán las que más gusten a los dos, y ello no exige una supertranca. Que un pene sea XXL permitirá penetraciones profundas y que pueda tocar el cérvix y el punto K, que también son extremadamente sensibles pero, para que este tipo de «prospecciones» tenga éxito es necesario invitar a la fiesta al resto (suelen precisar estimulación del clítoris).

Por otro lado, no supone ningún problema, más allá de si resulta llamativo a la vista, si un pene se arquea[6] o se orienta hacia derecha o izquierda de modo natural, puede deberse a la costumbre de colocarlo hacia uno u otro lado en el calzoncillo. Sería «parte de su personalidad».

A gran escala

Se podría adivinar, sin necesidad de compartir vestuarios, quién está dotado con un Ferrari. Los hombres viven pendientes de su pene, ese apéndice con personalidad propia que les domina y que influye hasta en su carácter. Sentirte el rey del mambo con los colegas es una cosa; saber hacer algo productivo con tu tercera pierna en la cama, otra. Principalmente porque para eso tienes que conseguir meterla. Ánimo. Piensa que en realidad, el canal de la vagina es capaz de conducir a un bebé hasta este mundo y, por grande que la tengas, siempre será menor que el diámetro de su cráneo. Un XXL debe armarse de paciencia y ser muy buen amante si no quiere que su pareja se largue dolorida y horrorizada. Puede ser el polvo de su vida o una tarde con el Empalador, de ti depende.

Aplícate lo explicado para los casos de vagina estrecha, dado que para ti, todas seremos así, será tu forma de vida. Lubricación, muchísima excitación, preámbulos, besos y sexo oral —más que otros que son talla «normal» o «mini»—. Además, ayuda mucho que vayas con calma: introduce sólo una tercera parte, despacio; deja que ella se acostumbre, que sea quien te pida más. Si tu pareja sabe de qué va el tema, hará su parte: realizará con los músculos va-

6. Cuando es tan marcada que resulta «extraño», acude al médico. Quizá se trata de la disfunción denominada Curvatura de pene o enfermedad de Peyronie, muy infrecuente (afecta a un 1 % de los varones, normalmente de entre 40 y 60 años, aunque se presenta cada vez más en hombres de menor edad). Consiste en la curvatura exagerada del pene —se queda en forma de jota— durante la erección, y está causada por la formación de tejido cicatricial, benigno, bajo la piel del pene, en su cara superior o inferior. No suele doler pero la deformidad del pene erecto puede dificultar o imposibilitar la penetración. Su tratamiento farmacológico implica, como efecto secundario indeseado, la disfunción eréctil; en otros pacientes se plantea la necesidad de cirugía.
Fuente: *http://www.medicina21.com*

ginales el gesto de expulsarte, lo cual provoca que entres mejor. Parece un poco contradictorio, pero no.

Los excesos no son tampoco buenos. Cuando se trata de penes descomunales hay mujeres que incluso se niegan a intentarlo. Sus dueños suelen ser conscientes de que gusta más mirarlos que arriesgarse a un desgarro, por lo que, en general, se trata de muy buenos amantes que saben cómo excitar a su pareja (les consta que si lo hacen bien, que sea enorme no supone un problema). Cuando la longitud es tal que duele, como truco se suele recurrir a enrollar una toalla en la base del pene, que actúa de tope y resta unos cuantos centímetros. Lo más cómodo es que ella se coloque encima —con él sentado y ella de rodillas, por ejemplo; o que él, desde detrás, despacio, la penetre, en lo que se denomina «cucharas»—, así puede controlar la profundidad de la penetración (por dar una imagen muy gráfica: de otro modo, ella se puede quedar ensartada y verse el glande entre los ojos...).

Pequeño (pero matón)

Antes de comenzar: nada de lo que se lea en este fragmento debe tomarse como un ataque personal. Frente a las diez líneas del XXL, aquí podría extenderse el asunto folios y folios. De los correos que recibo a diario como *spam*, cerca de veinte —no exagero— contienen mensajes ofreciendo alargadores o engrosadores de pene, así como productos contra la impotencia y la eyaculación precoz.

Como punto de partida, se dispone de lo que la naturaleza, vía dotación genética, coloca en la entrepierna (y aun así, después veremos algún truquillo o remedio para alterar ese desiderátum). Hubo uno que me dijo, literalmente: «yo a una mujer le hago el amor con la barbilla, con el codo, con todo lo que haga falta. Quiero que grite que no puede más, que toque el cielo cuando esté conmigo». Sólo de escucharlo me enamoré, y no tenía ni idea —y sigo sin tenerla, conste— de cómo la tiene de grande. Muerta de envidia, odié profundamente a su novia...

Somos muy dados a hacer todo tipo de chistes sobre micropenes pero, a diferencia del que estafa, del vago o del mentiroso compulsivo, deberíamos saber que el tamaño del pene es hereditario. No podemos pedirle a nadie cuentas por ello. La genética es como una lotería y, como otras cuestiones de la vida, tremendamente injusta. Hay hombres que serían «10», de no ser por la miseria de pilila que la madre naturaleza les adjudicó... ¿O son así de «10» porque lo saben y hacen todo lo preciso para compensar?

Otra verdad: se puede disfrutar muchísimo sin orgasmos y también correrse un montón de veces en una sesión de sexo, con independencia de que intervenga un miembro más o menos grande. Eso quede bien claro y presida nuestra lista de objetivos: disfrutar juntos del placer que el sexo proporciona, alcanzar con esa persona un estado de total intimidad y comunicación a nivel físico —y si es de mayor calado, tanto mejor—. Sea cual sea el tamaño del pene en erección, la realidad es que cuando una mujer se va a la cama con un hombre —peculiaridades y casos de laboratorio aparte—, valora un conjunto de cosas y baraja una lista de elementos tan extensa (y a menudo tan inverosímil) que, saber en realidad por qué está ahí en ese instante, sería más complejo que resolver muchos enigmas de la humanidad, por lo que no conviene obsesionarse ni autolimitarse por lo que esconda la bragueta. Porque si existen buenos y malos amantes, con independencia del calibre de su verga, sólo puede deberse a una cosa: su actitud durante la relación. El cómo venimos servidos condiciona, pero el resto, depende de cada cual.

Qué dicen ellas

Hace ya unos años que muchas mujeres «se atreven» a equipararse en sus testimonios públicos a los hombres. Ya caducó esa moralina que nos prohibía quejarnos o nos impedía sincerarnos a través de evaluaciones certeras de la anatomía masculina —con independencia del buen gusto o precaria gracia de susodichos comentarios—. Ellos, durante siglos, han podido manifestar abiertamente su pasión por un culo respingón o por un buen par de tetas, mientras que nuestra educación nos llevaba a dar respuestas del tipo: «me fijo, lo primero, en sus manos», «a mí me gusta que tenga una bonita mirada». Muchas mujeres me han referido su opinión (la de verdad, no la que se ven obligadas a compartir con sus amantes) sobre cómo valoran ellas el asunto.

Las hay que directamente rechazan los extremos: tanto el micropene como el XXL, aunque el primero suele llevar las de perder: todas se decantan por el grande, ante la necesidad de elegir. Preguntando a las interesadas, he llegado a escuchar: «si la tiene pequeña le dejo hacerlo por detrás».

La generalidad encuentra más apetecible un pene grande —domina claramente la falofilia—. Les gusta más, las excita más tocarlo, chuparlo, acariciarlo, notar cómo pasa del estado de reposo a la erección. Dicho lo cual, esa misma generalidad formula claras salvedades: para tener orgasmos, lo mejor es un pene «normal». El grande gusta para verlo, para «intentar metértelo», «para jugar con él», pero exige una mayor preparación (lubricación y estimulación extra) y estar en manos de un experto, para que no duela cuando te penetra y que durante el acto no se produzcan desgarros e irritación.

Ese plus de estimulación también se requiere cuando el pene es de un tamaño pequeño.

Tenemos su talla

La industria profiláctica se está haciendo cargo de que el estándar no es tan estándar, y lo mismo que introduce vanguardistas sabores, texturas y productos de «apoyo», desde anillos vibradores a lubricantes, se ha puesto las pilas y ha comprobado que el pene no es «talla única», por lo que ha ido incorporando modelos de preservativos XXL y, ya más recientemente incluso, los mini (otro tema es que al usuario que los necesite le haga más o menos gracia pedir el tamaño que le queda bien). Más que motivo de burla, el asunto de que un condón no ajuste se traduce en que no vale de nada ponérselo. Tras un par de embestidas, se cae, se sale y, o te dedicas a hacer vainica el resto de la noche o lo haces a pelo, lo cual, en estos tiempos, equivale a jugar a la ruleta rusa o a ser muy imbécil. No hay más opciones para cuando, aun estando erecto, el preservativo resulta demasiado grande. Un poquito de humildad y de realismo, pediría yo, a los señores de pequeño calibre. Entre este colectivo se manejan mucho las excusas de «no llevo condones», «no tengo nada, no hace falta», con tal de no tener que ponérselo y comprobar que les queda grande... Respuestas semejantes demuestran que lo único que tiene ese señor pequeño no es el miembro,

sino la sesera. Quede clarito que una picha corta puede dejar embarazada a una mujer lo mismo que una de 24 cm, y que su dueño es
igualmente candidato a pillar y contagiar todas las venéreas, ETS, y
a portar el VIH, que un gemelo de Nacho Vidal.

La «normalidad» en materia del pene viene dada en centímetros
(mal que les pese a algunos). Para esto, ni cuentan las buenas intenciones, ni beber hasta ver doble, ni hay valoraciones subjetivas. La
trascendencia del asunto puede soslayarse, incluso superarse, pero
no negarse. Así, el tamaño medio es de 13,5 cm, con un diámetro que
varía entre los 3 y los 4,2 cm. El 3 % de la población masculina tiene
un «pene pequeño», es decir: menos de 12 cm en erección. Se considera «pene medio» el que mide entre 12 y 17 cm en erección, y se lo
puede atribuir el 79 % de los hombres. «Pene grande» sería el que
supera los 17 cm en erección, y lo tiene el 18 % de los hombres.

2

Al alcance de la mano

MASTURBACIÓN MASCULINA

Me resulta interesante comprobar cómo los interdictos más antiguos afectan, uno, a la muerte, el famoso «no matarás», y casi todos los otros a la sexualidad: no fornicarás, no desearás a la mujer de tu prójimo, no yacerás con tus consanguíneos y, el que más procede recordar ahora: no derramarás la simiente. Ya decía Bataille que «el interdicto está allí para ser violado: el tabú nos incita a su violación. La trasgresión no niega el interdicto sino que dialécticamente lo completa y lo supera; jamás la prohibición aparece sin la revelación del placer». A mí todo esto me da que pensar...

Desde aquel «te saldrán granos», a los contundentes y terribles «te quedarás ciego y estéril» y el manido «te volverás loco», la historia lastra la libertad sexual del varón con inquietantes (y absurdos) maleficios que caerían irremisiblemente sobre quienes practicasen el onanismo. Para un chico es imposible no tener muy presente su pene: desde que nace está en permanente contacto visual con él, lo ve y lo toca para orinar, para vestirse... No tarda en descubrir lo placentero que resulta acariciarlo. Accede al autoerotismo de un modo natural. A los 18 años, más de un 90 % de los chicos conoce la masturbación, que llega a sus vidas en calidad de «compensación»: hasta que no disfrutan de relaciones sexuales plenas, se dedican a masturbarse.

A partir de los 12 a 15 años y hasta el final de su vida adulta, el esperma se segrega de forma continua y se deposita en los testículos provocando el deseo del organismo de liberarlo. Se trata de un proceso natural. Cuando no se eyacula durante el día, mediante una relación sexual, la naturaleza provoca los «sueños húmedos», las poluciones nocturnas para expulsar el semen y que se siga produciendo, y que se equilibren los niveles hormonales. Antes incluso de que los testículos generen esperma, es posible que el chico tenga orgasmos mediante la masturbación, aunque no eyacule. Frecuentemente los adolescentes se entusiasman con su sexualidad recién estrenada y dedican durante la etapa de los 14 o 15 años bastante tiempo y energía a ello (a esa edad el deseo les desborda). No es raro que algunos se planteen, con cierta preocupación, «si se están pasando», cuando «se matan a pajas». Mitos y rumores aparte, por masturbarse y eyacular varias veces al día, no hay riesgo para la salud: no condicionará su capacidad reproductiva, ni de erección y tampoco afectará al tamaño de su pene adulto; otra cuestión es, si semejante derroche de tiempo y energía no podría aprovecharse de otro modo «más productivo», pero dado que en nuestra sociedad las formas de entretenerse son incluso más insulsas —léase pasar horas matando «bichos» con la videoconsola, o tragarse sesenta horas de televisión a la semana—, sólo resta decir que esa afición-obsesión con la masturbación suele desaparecer con el paso de los años, conforme la vida sexual se haga más rica y las nuevas experiencias capten su atención. Hablo naturalmente de la generalidad, puesto que adicciones las hay a casi todo, siendo su tratamiento, en este caso, territorio de psicólogos, sexólogos y demás. En cualquier caso, manejándonos dentro de la «normalidad» —léase sexualidad sana—, masturbarse es señal de que existe apetito, impulso y deseo. Y la frecuencia depende de la energía que se tenga. Alguien desganado, deprimido o agotado, probablemente no se consagrará al onanismo desenfrenado. Las opiniones de los sexólogos determinan que lo negativo sería masturbarse sin placer o como sustitutivo de otras actividades, pero si se realiza como complemento o como parte de la vida sexual, sólo es indicativo de salud sexual. Además, que los adolescentes vayan aprendiendo a conocer las zonas que les proporcionan sensaciones agradables, a controlar su erección y su eyaculación, les servirá para sus futuras relaciones con una pareja.

La masturbación, junto con técnicas tántricas y de otros tipos, se puede utilizar como terapia de reeducación sexual, para combatir la eyaculación precoz. El hombre interrumpe o suaviza el movimiento y, controlando su erección, manteniéndola, evita eyacular. Reinicia el movimiento, evitando la parte superior del pene, y se detiene justo antes de la eyaculación. Practicando esta técnica, se puede manejar a voluntad el momento de eyacular.

Otra de las verdades que entiendo que debería mencionar es que —excepciones aparte, como las de los religiosos— todos practican la masturbación, eso sí: el cómo se estimula cada uno su pene y la frecuencia o regularidad con que se haga sí son asuntos muy personales que varían en cada hombre.

¿En qué estarán pensando?

Hay de todo, lo único que realmente suelen exigir unánimemente es un poco de intimidad. Sí, lo hacen en privado, excepto a determinadas edades, en las que las carreras y competiciones que organizan para descubrir quién se corre antes o eyacula más lejos, exigen presencia de amigotes o compañeros de colegio.

Muchos lo hacen en el sofá, mientras ven cualquier cosa —o porno— en la tele; otros se encierran con revistas más o menos eróticas en el baño y se sientan en la taza o se contemplan frente al espejo —la práctica parafílica de la espectrofilia consiste en esto mismo, en excitarse mirando la imagen propia en el espejo—; o en su cuarto, mientras fingen que estudian; o en la ducha, lo cual es mucho más práctico y limpio. La mayoría de los hombres se masturban directamente en una toalla o descargan sobre su propia mano o sobre su cuerpo y lo limpian con papel higiénico o con toallitas.

La excitación manual del pene generalmente requiere de una lubricación extra. Muchos se bastan con la propia saliva, pero cuando ésta no es suficiente, se recurre a líquidos y cosméticos que se tienen al alcance: desde gel de ducha a jabón, cremas hidratantes corporales o de manos, acondicionador de cabello, aceite de cocina o de cuerpo, mantequilla y derivados, vaselina... Se ayudan de casi cualquier fluido, lo cual, cuando no es una barbaridad o un riesgo para la salud (cabe que se introduzca por el orificio de la orina, el meato uretral, y provoque infecciones; también ciertos detergentes causan sequedad, grietas o irritaciones), es engorroso de limpiar o un verdadero asco en general... Diría que lo ideal es disponer de productos específicos, lubricantes con base de agua, que proporcionan la sensación resbaladiza adecuada y no suponen un atentado contra la propia integridad física, precisamente en el momento en que más se quiere uno a sí mismo...

Y su mente, mientras, fantasea. Los pensamientos que erotizan a un hombre van desde la chica Playboy a su vecina o la tendera del hipermercado, la novia, la esposa (propias o ajenas), la señora mayor, la niñita con el uniforme del colegio...

Como lo más habitual es emplear el puño, con la palma rodeando el pene y el pulgar arriba, sobre el glande, un truco que utilizan es sentarse sobre la mano que van a utilizar para que se quede dormida y de ese modo esa falta de sensibilidad crea la fantasía de que es la mano de otra persona la que está manipulando ahí abajo.

Las zonas en que se concentra cada uno también cambian: muchos se quedan un buen rato en la base y el tronco, con movimientos ascendentes y descendentes en vertical; otros se olvidan de todo lo que no sea su glande... El ritmo es lo crucial: mantener un ritmo y velocidad constantes es lo que les lleva a la erección y, más adelante, al orgasmo.

Masturbar a un hombre

Vivimos en la sociedad de la información. El saber es poder y el saber no ocupa lugar. Traigo a colación estos axiomas como preámbulo de una idea que muchas madres desearían que sus hijas no leyeran, aun a sabiendas de que tengo más razón que un santo. Ahí va: hoy día es más importante follar bien que guisar bien. En la cama sí que se «atrapa» a un hombre, objetivo que —al margen de mi opinión personal— mueve a muchas personas en su día a día, se convierte en su *leitmotiv*, tan respetable o cuestionable como cualquier otro.

Las empuñaduras, la posición o eje respecto del cuerpo, la zona del pene que se estimula y la velocidad en que cada uno disfruta durante la masturbación varían mucho y eso sí, todas se encaminan a un mismo objetivo: la eyaculación. Fisiológicamente, cuando se produce la excitación, el hombre siente una especie de picor —se trata del instante en que el líquido seminal comienza a avanzar por el conducto uretral, y recuerda al acto de orinar, sin serlo— acompañado de cierto subidón de calor en la zona pélvica y de una sensación de intenso placer. Detenerse en ese momento puede ser terrible... Se debe continuar con el movimiento, reduciendo o aumentando la presión y/o el vigor de acuerdo con la tolerancia y las preferencias de cada uno. Cuando el orgasmo se acerca, ellos normalmente aumentan el ritmo, suben y bajan a toda la velocidad de que son capaces. Trata de hacer tú lo mismo, pero ponte cómoda —te darás cuenta de que puedes tardar más de lo previsto y de que es más duro de lo que parece—. Si él es de los que tarda o si le has pillado completamente fláccido puede que se te duerma el brazo o necesitarás cambiar varias veces de posición. Ten en cuenta apoyarte sobre un codo para que tu propio peso no te complique la tarea y apartarte, para que el resto de tu cuerpo no interfiera tus movimientos: te puedes tumbar paralela a él, lo que permite que os beséis, te pueda acariciar y abrazar —y así, le ves la cara—. Si no tienes ni idea de cómo le gusta, pídele que lo haga, fíjate bien —toma notas mentalmente— y después trata de imitarle. Una ayuda inestimable es utilizar lubricante —cambia por completo la sensación, magnificándola... Le encantará, pero tú tampoco te quites méritos...

Quejas frecuentes

Ya, ya, encima de que... pues sí, se quejan. ¿Y de qué?

La más frecuente es sobre la intensidad: o demasiado suave o demasiado brusco. Si imperceptible ni lo notan —no es como nuestro clítoris, salvo la parte del glande, el pene no es tan delicado—, pero tampoco hay que amarrarlo como si fuera un picaporte. Lo mejor es usar lubricante porque la textura del gel permite nuevas sensaciones, mejor movilidad, emula la sensación de coito, ayuda a mantener el ritmo... Pero si no os gusta/no tenéis, lo mejor es echar saliva y mantener una sujeción firme moviendo la mano arriba y abajo en la zona central del mástil.

Parar antes de tiempo o demasiado tarde. ¿Cuándo debes detenerte? He ahí la cuestión. Los hay que prefieren que nada cambie hasta que terminan de eyacular la última gota; a otros, les va mejor que bajes un poco el ritmo cuando notan el orgasmo; también los hay que prefieren que te apartes y terminar ellos mismos...

Hacerlo realmente bien sin tener un pene propio requiere cierto arte y más paciencia aún. Haced que os cuente cómo le gusta y, si le da corte hablar de eso, proponle que lo haga y observa.

Técnicas de masturbación

La excitación del pene por vía manual la puede realizar el propio interesado, con o sin público, y su pareja, asumiendo él un rol pasivo.

Nadie mejor que uno mismo para darse placer. De ahí, la importancia de familiarizarse con el propio cuerpo para descubrir cómo se alcanza el orgasmo. Difícilmente podremos transmitirle al otro lo que nos gusta si no lo sabemos. A muchas personas, ver excitarse a su pareja mientras se masturba, contemplar cómo disfruta y llega al clímax sin tomar parte en ello, simplemente estando ahí (quizá con contacto corporal, besándole, acariciándole), les gusta, les agrada y consiguen excitarse también. Pero es posible que esto en sí mismo, a muchos les parezca muy aburrido y prefieran continuar, pasado un rato, con prácticas más «participativas» o activas. Hay quienes, incluso, encuentran ofensivo que su pareja se masturbe en su presencia, porque ven en ello casi un desprecio o una prueba de «no estar haciéndolo bien». Ante esto, creo que se debería tener muy presente que el orgasmo se puede lograr de muchas formas, y que, habiendo tiempo, se puede disfrutar de varios, cada uno de un modo: masturbándose, con la penetración, con el sexo oral...

En ocasiones, la masturbación es el único acto sexual que se lleva a cabo, bien por falta de preservativo, bien porque la chica no desea la penetración (cuando se trata de una virgen que desea seguir siéndolo, por ejemplo), bien porque damos con alguien que le saca partido a las sesiones de *petting* o, incluso, hay parejas en que dado que él se excita o se estresa demasiado con la penetración (algo de lo que muchos hombres se quejan: la presión de no defraudar), prefieren la masturbación porque les permite relajarse y simplemente, dedicarse a disfrutar del orgasmo...

Que una persona utilice las manos para llevar al hombre hasta el orgasmo establece un juego de poderes muy excitante también para el que proporciona las caricias. Internet está plagado de páginas que explican hasta el detalle técnicas, trucos, sensaciones, etc., del arte de la masturbación masculina, enfocados tanto a la práctica individual como en pareja. A modo de premisa, debemos diferenciar si estamos ante una relación estable o si se trata de un «polvo de una noche» donde, por desgracia, no disponemos de suficiente tiempo como para adquirir esa confianza y ese conocimiento del otro que nos permita saber cómo le gusta... y poder ir a tiro hecho. La comunicación será, en este asunto, crucial, así como la práctica. Cuando se disfruta de cierta intimidad, no es aconsejable romper la química y la magia del momento con un cuestionario teórico-práctico sobre ningún tema, algo que nos puede desviar del objetivo y terminar charlando sobre política agraria, pero sí que se debe establecer un diálogo (verbal o gestual) que nos facilite pautas para saber qué y cómo le gusta. La experiencia es un grado, eso parece innegable, pero como los gustos de cada uno varían, no cabe fijar una regla general que funcione a la perfección para todos.

Antes de proseguir, un apunte: el pene es lo principal, y siempre acapara la atención, pero ojo, que estaremos muy equivocados si ignoramos los testículos, la zona del perineo y la misma base y tronco del pene. Hay que saber que acariciar la bolsa del escroto con suavidad produce mucha excitación y, si ya vamos a más —y hay confianza—, introducir un dedo por el ano (bien lubricado, por favor) y alcanzar el punto P, que se halla justo ahí en el hombre, suele ser muy agradecido... (o razón de cabreo, pregunta antes). Tres notas: el propio líquido preseminal o la saliva suelen bastar para lubricar la zona, si no, se puede emplear gel específico, pero no se debe «trabajar» la zona en seco; tiene mucho éxito colocar el dedo pulgar, ejerciendo de tope y acariciar con movimientos circulares la zona del prepucio mientras se realiza el movimiento basculante con el resto de los dedos... Por último, hay que respetar el ángulo y la inclinación del pene. Se puede modificar un poco, juguetear, pero no «tronchárselo», teniendo presente que no se manipula la palanca de cambios del coche...

Durante la masturbación se deberían sentir bien ambas partes. Sin embargo, como en casi todas las relaciones humanas, a veces, se practica «por darle gusto al otro», es una concesión. Cuando la eyaculación tarda en producirse es fácil que caigamos en la desesperación («¿lo haré mal?», «¿le estaré haciendo daño?», «seguro que no siente nada», etc.), en el agotamiento (mantener el mismo movimiento y velocidad en según qué postura puede cansar mucho), o incluso, en el más profundo aburrimiento, como apuntaba antes. Con naturalidad, con simpatía, se puede pedir «ayuda». Seguro que él en poco tiempo es capaz de «acabar» lo que tú has iniciado (eso sí: no te vayas a la nevera y le dejes ahí tirado, estate cerca y que note tu excitación, aunque sea un poco fingida...).

Es normal que un hombre se masturbe en solitario, aun teniendo una vida sexual con su pareja, y ello no implicará que no quiera o no desee a esa persona ni mucho menos que con ella no disfrute. El onanismo ofrece un tipo de placer distinto y compatible con una vida sexual plena. También se explica que haya personas con un impulso sexual alto, o muy activas, y que deseen eyacular más a menudo que otras.

A veces, mis lectores me han planteado la cuestión de si es «normal» (siempre nos preocupa salirnos de la norma...) que mientras uno se masturba «se le vaya la cabeza» y fantasee con la vecina, la compañera de oficina, con Brad Pitt, con el fontanero, la prima, etc., por resumir: digamos que la única en la que no se piensa es la novia o la esposa. Deseo y fantasía caminan de la mano y no se sueltan ni cuando amenaza el monstruo de la infidelidad. Este matiz, lo de si es o no constitutivo de cuernos imaginarse haciéndolo con otra, lo dejaremos para el capítulo adecuado, y también su variante de disfrutar pensando que la pareja propia se lo monta con un tercero (el voyeurismo pone mucho...). Sí, en efecto: la mente es muy poderosa y son sus estímulos los que crean el impulso sexual. En esto, hombres y mujeres se asemejan. Y ambos pueden excitarse a base de fantasear. Todos podemos alcanzar el orgasmo con la sola proyección mental de imaginarnos en compañía de personas atractivas —con independencia de que, a lo mejor si la situación se presentase de verdad, la rechazaríamos—. Está demostrado que recurrir a la visualización de una imagen guardada en la retina produce el mismo efecto de excitación que tener ese mismo objeto delante. También fotografías o vídeos tienen poder para excitarnos. En cualquier caso, la fantasía es libre y es absurdo tratar de ponerle censuras y cortapisas.

Cubana o paja cubana

Se trata de masturbar el pene con los pechos, apoyándolo en el canalillo, él se mueve para estimularlo. Matices: cuando el tamaño de los genitales —bien de su pene o de los pechos—, no es demasiado grande, podemos ayudar juntándolos con las manos, sujetando el pene en el centro para incrementar así la fricción —e impedir que pueda sacarte un ojo en un descuido—. Para que «salga bien» hace falta práctica. En cualquier caso, son generalmente *ellos* los que más disfrutan de la cubana: el paisaje le encantará (la excitación visual), por no insistir en el hecho de que es *su* pene el centro de atención. La eyaculación será sobre el escote o donde se pacte.

¿Y cómo se lo hacen ellos?

Entre las mil y una maneras, se repiten tres como las más habituales:

Primera: Con la palma de la mano rodeando el pene se recrea una vagina y, con movimientos de sube y baja, se imita el acto de penetración. Cabe utilizar ambas manos, entrelazando los dedos, simulando una vagina, donde los pulgares acarician la cabeza del pene.

Segunda: Colocado boca abajo, se utiliza un objeto blando, una almohada, una camiseta, etc., y se frota el pene contra él. Algunos se masturban sin tocarse específicamente sino que, a través de la ropa, friccionan con la palma de la mano la zona del pene y los testículos.

Tercera: Se emplean chorros de agua para estimular la zona, bien en la ducha, bien en una bañera de burbujas.

Sin ánimo ni remoto de ser exhaustiva, porque los modos y maneras de cada uno en esta materia alcanzan hasta lo sorprendente, y la casuística es bien rica, cito algunas de las técnicas masturbatorias de los señores en la intimidad. El método más normal es el de utilizar la mano y mover con ella el pene de arriba abajo, ejerciendo la presión, los giros y la velocidad que a cada cual le guste más. Los hay que no bajan del glande —error— y quienes dedican atención a toda la zona: estimulan los testículos, el escroto, el piso pélvico —que alcanza indirectamente el punto P— e incluso, introducen varios centímetros un dedo —lubricado— por el ano. Hay quienes prueban a vendarse los ojos, a tocarse con la «otra» mano, a colocarse guantes de texturas distintas... Si se practica la masturbación colocando un condón, servirá para ensayar tanto la técnica como la sensibilidad que se tiene, y no ir de nuevas con una pareja real. A muchos les encanta darse cachetadas, golpecitos, o agarrársela y estamparla contra las piernas o el abdomen —es un truquillo muy de actor porno que a casi todos les pone—. Otros recurren al universo de los accesorios (calcetines, condones XXL rellenos de lubricante, un guante con forro de satén, collares con cuentas redondas), juguetes específicos: existen vaginas y bocas masturbadoras, aparatos con apariencia extraña pero textura humana donde se introduce el pene; moldes de las actrices porno, muñecas hinchables, las *real dolls* (ver «Juguetes eróticos»). Sólo un inciso: ni se os ocurra meterla en ninguna parte donde se pueda quedar apresada. Si se aprisiona, se hincha, lo que produce dolor y pánico —y a veces, terminar en Urgencias—. Otro detalle: los electrodomésticos deben quedarse fuera de ese «universo» de aparatos. Más de uno se ha dado cuenta ya de que las aspiradoras no saben chuparla.

Cuando el pene es muy sensible, se utilizan exclusivamente el pulgar y el índice para la zona superior, sujetando la base con la otra mano. Hay una variante que implica colocar las manos en posición que recuerda a una seta, rodeando el pene con una (el tallo) y poniendo la palma de la otra sobre el glande (la capucha), frotándola con movimientos circulares. Los hay que se ponen el pene entre las dos manos, frotándolo hacia delante y atrás, como si hicieran fuego con un palo. Muchos prueban a variar la posición de la mano, colocando el puño mirando hacia el cuerpo, en la base del pene, que aunque al principio pueda resultar raro, facilita el acceso a zonas generalmente «olvidadas». Al hilo de esto, los dildos ofrecen una posibilidad de explorar la zona de dentro del ano; hay juguetes con forma de herradura, y disponibles con y sin vibración, que alcanzan la zona del escroto, el perineo y el punto P. Existe la forma —nada fácil— de recrear una felación, empleando los dedos medio e índice, para simular los labios y empujando el pene con la otra mano.

Masturbación zen

O tántrica o ascética. Si quieres iniciarte en la práctica de ese sexo tan aplaudido y que consiste en que, misteriosamente, hay un orgasmo pero tú no eyaculas, puedes empezar a solas, a ver qué pasa. Hay técnicas pensadas para la contención de la eyaculación —pero sólo de eso, de la descarga—, y que permiten que tengas un orgasmo (al principio, por lo visto, más soso que después). Sin moverte, agarra el pene con la mano, colocando el dedo pulgar sobre el prepucio y moviéndolo en círculos. Lento y firme. Disfruta e interioriza la tensión sexual. Nada de prisas ni de manita arriba-abajo. En el momento de sentir que llega el orgasmo, detente. No muevas un solo músculo. Relájate. Si tienes una sensación orgásmica sin haber echado una sola gota, ésa era la idea. Tu pene sigue erecto y puedes retomar e ir hacia la segunda meta volante. Sería como cuando muchos, a punto de correrse, utilizan el truco de pensar en su tía la del pueblo para controlar; es ese cosquilleo que se produjo durante unos instantes, tras el cual, pudieron continuar la faena. Dicho esto en tono de broma, sí que hay técnicas que llegan a dominarse incluso sin emplear las manos. Los ejercicios de Kegel para hombre ayudan tremendamente a ejercitar la musculatura que controla la erección y aporta una total sensibilidad y plena conciencia de la respuesta sexual. Ver el capítulo «Sexo y espiritualidad».

Ventajas de la masturbación

Aunque no haga falta convencer a nadie (distinto de lo que les pasa a las chicas que pueden tener un sentimiento de culpa), hay varias razones (además del placer) por las que conviene practicar de vez en cuando a solas.

Son cuatro. Una: vaciar la bolsa seminal ayuda a renovar el esperma, que estará «fresco» y en mejores condiciones de fecundación. Dos: ejercita la próstata, evita su obstrucción y ayuda a prevenir posibles infecciones. Tres: cuanto más se practica y se ejercita, más en forma está. Cuatro y la más importante: la masturbación es un buen método para aprender a controlar la eyaculación y evitar la eyaculación precoz tras los períodos de estar a palo seco, cuando surge un encuentro y ese plus de ansiedad desencadena fiascos...

Un detalle que nadie debe obviar: los excesos no son buenos. La hipermasturbación puede reducir el recuento de esperma (si se mide en el momento en que se ha eyaculado recientemente). También puede desembocar en eyaculación retardada y producir irritación en las susodichas partes involucradas.

La eyaculación

Los efectos físicos de la eyaculación son bien visibles. Para empezar, se produce la descarga seminal. El resto del cuerpo también se ve inmerso en una especie de sacudida de energía: el placer provoca cosquilleo en cada músculo, que se tensará, y también los de la cara y el cuello, la respiración se hará más fuerte y entrecortada, y pueden producirse temblores. Tras la eyaculación llega una sensación de relax, que es precisamente el objetivo de quienes se masturban para combatir el estrés y los problemas de insomnio. Utilizan el onanismo en vez de un somnífero, ya que en efecto, la descarga seminal va seguida de una apacible relajación. Además, sucede que el pene se torna más blando progresivamente y suele preferirse que se interrumpa el contacto, y como está muy sensible, que no se toque durante un ratito. En unos instantes la sensación de «calentón» desaparece si nada lo impide... (es decir, si no se continúa con la excitación, y se reanuda la actividad sexual, bien a solas, bien con la pareja. El tiempo de recuperación para poder alcanzar la siguiente erección también depende de cada uno).

A la mayoría de los hombres les apetece disfrutar del momento tranquilos —otra cuestión es que, si tienen modales, no lo demuestren demasiado o lo disimulen con más o menos arte, caso de haber compañía—. Estaríamos en lo de «echar un cigarrito», darse la vuelta y quedarse sobados...; es decir: lo contrario que a las mujeres, que cuando alcanzan un orgasmo, si siguen siendo estimuladas, pueden tener más sin necesidad de parar, y que, en cualquier caso, es el momento en que más cariño demandan —cosa distinta es que se lo proporcionen o no, o que el contexto en que se mantiene la relación sea estrictamente sexual, desprovisto de implicaciones sentimentales—. Mi opinión al respecto, quizá no compartida por la generalidad, es que hasta al sexo esporádico se le puede incorporar, a ratitos o puntualmente, alguna pincelada de ternura. Que no pretendas comprarte un piso con el otro no le desposee de la condición humana y, por tanto, los afectos que nos son inherentes no deberían «prohibirse» automáticamente, como si de untarse vitriolo se tratara. Pienso que un abrazo, un beso apasionado o simplemente mantener el contacto físico con el cuerpo del otro, tras llegar al clímax, potencia el sexo y mejora el recuerdo que conservamos de la experiencia.

Generalmente el varón necesita su espacio, un *break*, pero el modo de disfrutarlo puede ser insultante para su pareja: es duro lo de contemplar una espalda ante tus narices o verle escapar a toda velocidad, subiéndose la bragueta ya en el descansillo una vez que ha descargado... Por su parte, muchas mujeres confirman que justo después de tener su orgasmo es cuando mayor placer sienten, de continuar con el coito o con otras prácticas. Su excitación es enorme, diríamos que se hallan en lo alto de una meseta que toma como base el placer del orgasmo y, si continúan excitándose, culmine o no en un nuevo orgasmo, esa actividad sexual es en sí misma muy satisfactoria.

En este punto, me parece procedente hacer un inciso. La tradicional forma de concebir el sexo y los roles convencionales que el hombre y la mujer han asumido me parecen un error e implican cierta injusticia, y cierto desprecio del derecho de la mujer a disfrutar de su cuerpo con su pareja. Me explico. La rancia concepción de las relaciones sexuales entre heteros determina que ella espere y afronte cual damisela en peligro el ataque, que sea más pasiva, se someta más o menos voluntariamente al juego erótico que él plantea; y que él sea el conquistador, lleve la iniciativa, luzca una potente erección; además, vivimos aún con la herencia de la tradición religiosa que impone que el sexo tenga una finalidad reproductiva. De ahí que la cópula sea lo primordial, hasta el punto de que muchos aún hoy consideran que, se haga lo que se haga con alguien en la cama, si no media penetración vaginal, es casi como si no hubiera pasado «nada». Que el sexo se realice con preponderancia del acto de penetración, siendo secundario o superfluo lo demás, los preámbulos, las caricias pre y poscoitales, etc., lleva a que en realidad, la mujer vea frustrada su satisfacción cuando él desconecta una vez que ha eyaculado: «*game over*. Me quedé sin juguete». De modo casi mecánico, con el clímax de él, se da por concluida la relación, algo muy frustrante para la mujer que, probablemente, querría proseguir. Deberíamos anular esta rutina que sacraliza el coito. La venimos arrastrando desde el pasado pero ya no representa la sexualidad tal y como hoy día se vive: casi todas las relaciones sexuales se practican por razones de placer y de afectividad, de comunicación y de diversión, quedando muy abajo en la lista el fin reproductivo y considerando que empleamos profilácticos en nuestras relaciones. La eyaculación del hombre se debe buscar, claro, pero tanto como el orgasmo femenino. Hay, por tanto, que conocer el cuerpo de ambos, su psique, y ajustar los tempos, de manera que la satisfacción sea mutua. La mujer, cuando su pareja eyacula, no siente deseos de multiplicarse por cero, y quizá lo que querría es continuar —bajando el ritmo, claro, y prescindiendo de la penetración por un rato—, con los juegos y caricias orales y manuales, con los besos... y considere este momento sólo un hito más dentro de los muchos que se pueden atravesar en una sesión de cama. Recurriendo un poco a la metáfora: ellas leen este instante como un punto y seguido. Ellos como un punto y final, ¿qué hacemos? Dicho esto, me veo en el deber de advertir a las mujeres que muchos tipos consideran que la «mujer 10» es aquella que recoge del suelo sus bragas y desaparece sin mendigar —ni exigir— otra cita ni una llamada, mientras ellos aún se están corriendo. Sonará a barbaridad, pero ya me gustaría a mí estar equivocada... Un «¡*Bye*, tigre! Ha sido excepcional», exclamado desde el ascensor, capta muy bien esta escena. Por supuesto no todos son así, pero cuando muchos de ellos se sinceran, eso es lo que quieren: que la tía salga por la puerta gritando que es un supermachoman, mientras ellos se están aún convulsionando en medio de un gran orgasmo. Éste es uno de los instantes en que la sexualidad femenina y la masculina se apartan más diametralmente (obviamente, esto no rige para las parejas enamoradísimas).

El semen

Al concluir el coito o la masturbación, el hombre eyacula, expulsando un líquido viscoso: el semen o esperma, que avanza por el canal seminal desde los testículos, que lo producen, hasta que alcanza el exterior. Normalmente, eyaculación y orgasmo masculino coinciden, pero cabe que haya eyaculación sin orgasmo, y orgasmo sin eyaculación. Existe además la eyaculación retrógrada, que se produce hacia dentro, por el conducto de la vejiga de la orina.

Dependiendo de diversos factores (la edad, la dieta, el tiempo de abstinencia transcurrido desde la última eyaculación, la excitación alcanzada, etc.), varía la abundancia, el olor, la consistencia de este tibio líquido blancuzco y la cantidad de él que se expulsa (de 3 a 5 ml, hasta 15 ml), así como el número de chorros (de 3 a 8) y la distancia a que éste puede ser propulsado (o que simplemente gotee). Los espermatozoides «nadan» en este líquido seminal pero no representan nada más que un 10 % del mismo. Que la composición del esperma sea fundamentalmente proteínas, minerales, fructosa, etc., no implica que se imponga su uso alimenticio... Muchos utilizan este argumento para persuadir a la pareja de que se lo trague. Ver el apartado de «Sexo oral». Otro tema, relacionado con el esperma y su ingestión: es uno de los fluidos corporales que mejor conduce los virus. Beberse el semen de alguien implica el riesgo de contagio de todo tipo de enfermedades, incluido el VIH, causante del sida. Por ello, en las relaciones esporádicas y cuando se vive una sexualidad promiscua, son imprescindibles los métodos profilácticos de barrera (los condones).

El líquido preseminal, el que se segrega antes de la eyaculación, es portador de espermatozoides (en menor concentración) y también de los virus. Ambas cuestiones deben tenerse en cuenta: los embarazos se producen y las enfermedades se transmiten igual que con el esperma de la eyaculación, por lo que hay que evitar el contacto directo del pene con la vagina y con la zona de la vulva.

La resistencia de los espermatozoides dentro del útero puede prolongarse mucho tiempo. Cabe, por tanto, que se mantenga vivo y fecunde un óvulo hasta tres o cuatro días después del encuentro. Por el contrario, si se halla fuera de su medio, húmedo y oscuro, y a temperatura ambiente, es muy frágil y perece.

Al igual que muchas mujeres encuentran la eyaculación muy excitante y demandan que la descarga vaya a parar a la cara, la boca, el escote, etc., se lo extienden por el cuerpo o lo tragan, no es infrecuente que muchas otras sientan un rechazo total por este líquido y deseen evitar cualquier contacto con él. Sugiero que se tenga en cuenta que lo que muestran las películas porno, en cuanto a las emisiones de esperma, por lo general, obedece más al dictado de la fantasía masculina que al deseo femenino.

Masturbación femenina

(Por favor, antes de nada, echa un vistazo al capítulo de «Anatomía básica». Lo digo por si acaso...)

Se puede definir la masturbación como la estimulación de las zonas erógenas con la intención de proporcionar placer sexual. Si bien la historia ha demostrado que nadie se muere por no tener un orgasmo, también hay evidencias de que el sexo —con o sin amor— es una fuente de placer y una vía de comunicación y de expresión de emociones y sentimientos... Por no hablar de los beneficios físicos que provoca la masturbación: aumenta la autoestima y anula el riesgo de que nos contagien ETS, se trata de sexo completamente seguro; nivela nuestros niveles hormonales, descargamos tensiones, nos relaja y ayuda a conciliar el sueño; quemamos calorías (pocas, tampoco vamos a exagerar); nos alivia el dolor menstrual; es placentero en sí mismo: nadie como tú sabe qué te gusta y qué necesitas en cada momento, con qué intensidad, presión y dónde... Sólo tú: sonará egoísta, pero lo bueno de estar sola es que puedes dedicarte a ti, sin estar pendiente de nadie más ni de que disfrute. Y, por si fuera poco, no hay nada mejor para la piel que una vida sexual feliz y satisfactoria (los que se lucran inyectando botox quizá me odien por lo que estoy a punto de escribir pero me río yo del elixir sagrado de la toxina botulínica que se pincha la gente: nada relaja el rictus y proporciona brillo a la piel como una buena sesión erótica enriquecida con orgasmos). Además, que una mujer conozca su cuerpo resulta crucial no sólo para su satisfacción íntima, a solas, sino para que sepa cómo guiar a su pareja y para que su cuerpo esté mejor preparado para recibir caricias ajenas (es decir: nos hace mejores amantes). Y ahí va otra de las verdades de este libro: las mujeres no sólo no somos frígidas, ni existe una tendencia «natural» a ello —como se nos «insulta»—, sino que en realidad somos multiorgásmicas, y muchas de nosotras lo descubrimos por medio de la masturbación, llegando una, y dos, y tres, y ocho veces en una sesión sin problema (dicho lo cual, también añado que no es prudente prescindir de los especialistas —psicólogos, sexólogos, ginecólogos— cuando se detecta una situación de anorgasmia). Cuantos más orgasmos alcances tú solita, más sencillo será que los tengas con tu pareja.

Sobre el autoerotismo femenino revolotean varios fantasmas. Algunos se conectan con los complejos, otros con el sentimiento de culpa. El asunto de la masturbación femenina, le pese a quien le pese, no es ninguna tontería y tampoco es algo sucio. Desde siempre se ha condenado el hecho de que una mujer demande placer (y que lo busque directamente aún era peor). Nos remontamos a la mentalidad que escindía a las féminas en torno a dos clases bien diferenciadas: las «decentes», que ni en sueños se permitían manifestar deseos sexuales, y las «prostitutas», quienes, en efecto, no sólo tenían fantasías sino también una vida sexual por la que se las estigmatizaba socialmente. Aprovecho para recordar que en la Grecia clásica, la prostitución no sólo era legal, sino que estaba regulada y que hubo prostíbulos públicos, a precios asequibles. Los atenienses consideraban la prostitución como un componente de la democracia y, algunas de las prostitutas, las independientes, las que captaban en la calle y las hetaeras (equivalentes a las geishas japonesas) eran, pese a todo, las únicas mujeres «libres», en el sentido de capaces de elegir con quién se acostaban, y las que hicieron fortuna, tuvieron acceso al lujo y al estatus de propietarias, algo que estaba vedado a las demás (esposas o concubinas), que tenían que vivir en la parte posterior de las casas, en los gineceos, junto con los esclavos, donde estaban destinadas a la reproducción. Las prostitutas que no eran esclavas —y por lo tanto una posesión más en manos de los «ciudadanos», de la que sacar rentabilidad— sólo se movían por interés económico y eran las únicas mujeres que manejaban dinero (algo muy criticado y que irritaba a los señores). En cualquier caso, con el devenir de los siglos, la moral durante la Edad Media se hizo represora del sexo y de cualquier manifestación de erotismo, tanto en público como en privado. La razón «oficial» era cumplir con el supuesto mandato divino —los libros sagrados de las religiones monoteístas fueron interpretados por los representantes de Dios en el mundo—, aunque probablemente se debía a que en épocas de malas cosechas o de epidemias, resultaba muy peligrosa la superpoblación y para bajar la tasa de natalidad optaron por arremeter contra la sexualidad «condenándola» y definiéndola como pecado. Del mismo modo, cuando lo que primaba era mantener las ciudades habitadas y los ejércitos nutridos de guerreros, se condenaba tanto la masturbación como la homosexualidad porque, lógicamente, tales prácticas no fomentaban los nacimientos.

En cualquier caso, para la mujer, sexo y honra desarrollan la pugna del caballo blanco-caballo negro. La prueba es que aún hoy, cuando se quiere hacer daño a una chica, nada hay más efectivo que cuestionar su virtud. Ahora, la realidad es que todo el mundo se masturba, pero pocos lo admiten y, sólo raras excepciones se atreven a hablar sobre ello abiertamente. Muchas mujeres creen que han de dejar de hacerlo una vez que tienen pareja estable, como si por masturbarse su relación sexual fuera insatisfactoria. El auto-placer proporciona diferentes sensaciones a las del sexo comparti-do, pero no es peor, ni «menos».

El mayor experto en sexo, el doctor Kinsey, afirmaba que cuan-do una mujer se masturba durante su vida, es más fácil que alcance orgasmos con sus parejas y, frecuentemente, enfrentan menos pro-blemas sexuales que las que no lo hacen.

Trabajos manuales

Muchas mujeres disfrutan de orgasmos casi espontáneos, pero otras, la mayoría, requieren de estimulación. Para que sus compa-ñeros se sientan un poquito más «ilustrados» y vayan tirando, pa-rece útil apuntar ciertas ideas y sugerencias.

La primera, y clave, sería que no todas las mujeres alcanzan el orgasmo de la misma forma, ni estimulando las mismas zonas. Di-cho de modo tan genérico e impreciso, entiendo que el mensaje alarmará a quien pretenda aprender algo concreto que le ayude a conseguir que su chica disfrute; por eso, se debe añadir algo: todas coincidimos en que la estimulación del clítoris es crucial, ya sea de forma oral o manual —y aquí ojito con un par de detalles: hay que lubricar los dedos antes de introducirlos, o con saliva (que será es-casa si hemos estado tomando copas, por lo que es recomendable tener agua cerca: dejar un vaso o una botella junto a la cama será la salvación cuando el alcohol nos deshidrate) o con productos es-pecíficos, que «haberlos haylos»: geles y lubricantes neutros o de sabores muy logrados—; además, se trata de acariciar, con las ye-mas, no con las uñas, de modo acompasado y sin detenerse: ésa es la segunda clave. Muchos, para cambiar de postura, o por cansan-cio, se paran y eso provoca que la mujer pierda la excitación. Cada vez que se interrumpe la secuencia, nosotras bajamos a cero: triste pero cierto... y requerimos que se nos preste atención como si aca-báramos de empezar: besos, abrazos, caricias y juegos de todo tipo, desde el principio. Es en serio: muchos no se dan cuenta o no saben que nosotras necesitamos estimulación continua y sin cambios de ritmo ni de intensidad (algo que en el hombre no sucede). Aquí el Cielo es para los que perseveran... Por eso, antes de empezar, haz que ella se ponga cómoda —tumbada boca arriba, con las piernas entreabiertas y las rodillas flexionadas— y busca tú una posición en la que te puedas pasar, tranquilamente, sin contracturas musculares ni que se te duerman las piernas, unos quince minutos (quién sabe, ¡lo mismo son sólo tres!).

Debo precisar algo, basado en los datos de investigaciones de Kinsey y en las del ginecólogo William Masters y la trabajadora social Virginia Johnson (que firman Masters y Johnson), acerca de cuánto tardamos, respectivamente, hombres y mujeres en alcanzar el orgasmo con la autoestimulación: el tiempo medio que precisa el hombre y la mujer para alcanzar el orgasmo es muy similar. Ellos de dos a tres minutos. Nosotras, cuatro —lo que derribaría ese terrorífico mito—. Seguro que alguno se sorprende, pero es cierto. No se trata por tanto de que él deba estar «ahí» eternamente, sino que por un lado tú te relajes, te toques tú misma y le dejes imitarte o le indiques cómo necesitas que te lo haga —o sea, tal y como tú te lo haces en privado, y que has comprobado que «funciona»— y le dejes hacer. De verdad: bastan cuatro minutos, eso sí, con la estimulación adecuada. Un truco que vale para todo: comienza siempre suave y lubricado, ya tendrás tiempo de aumentar la intensidad, la presión y la velocidad.

La comunicación no es la misma que en una reunión o que en la barra de un bar. Tú tienes la boca llena y ella, por lo general, prefiere abandonarse o se cohíbe. Has de entender su lenguaje corporal, observa sus reacciones para saber lo que le gusta o si lo haces bien. Ten bien presente que la anatomía femenina es más delicada, permite caricias menos fuertes y todas las zonas a tocar han de estar siempre lubricadas; el tronco del pene, por ejemplo, es mucho menos sensible.

Por otro lado, a muchas mujeres les preocupa «algo», no se abandonan, ¿por qué? Pues a veces se debe a que son conscientes de que a su pareja le molesta tener que dedicarle cierto tiempo, se sienten culpables por buscar ese placer —esto es psicológico, en efecto, pero la cabeza también la llevamos puesta en la cama, qué se le va a hacer—; saben que ellas no alcanzan el orgasmo sin determinada estimulación o hasta pasado un ratito, y en su mente resuena el «en cualquier momento se va a cansar y me dejará a medias», algo que en sí mismo dificulta que se relajen y disfruten del momento. Lo ideal sería, no sólo saber cómo y dónde tocarlas, sino ejercer cierta psicología, transmitirle que puede estar segura de que «vas a estar ahí hasta el final», que para ti «no supone ningún castigo» y que «quieres que ella lo pase bien» y más aún: asegúrate de que mentalmente ella «se permite» a sí misma disfrutar. En esto, como en tantas cuestiones vitales, la prisa es enemiga de lo bueno. Si ella está pendiente de «terminar pronto» o capta que a su pareja se le pone cara de mala leche, es improbable que termine con un orgasmo (terminará, claro, pero sacando tu mano o tu cara de ahí, cambiando de postura y renunciando).

Algo a tener en cuenta también son las habilidades manuales de cada uno. Hay hombres que parecen Eduardo Manostijeras, y que, por buena voluntad que le pongan, pues... mejor que se dediquen a otros menesteres. No pasa nada, no se puede ser bueno en todo. Mientras aprendes, recuerda que hay otras formas y partes del cuerpo para acariciarla. Además, con lo sensible que es la zona de la vagina y del clítoris, si se irrita y se causa dolor ya desde el comienzo, se dificultará enormemente que ella consiga tener un orgasmo. Por ejemplo: un dedo que se queda casi pegado por haberlo puesto sin lubricar produce una sensación de hipersensibilidad, de daño más o menos intenso, que ella arrastrará durante toda la relación sexual, lo confiese o no, puesto que si está muy excitada querrá continuar, eso sí, sin «premio», con el asunto del disfrute bastante mermado... Ciertamente, la barrera entre placer y dolor se desdibuja muchas veces, pero si nos referimos a un arañazo o a un mordisco fuerte en semejante parte, justo cuando ella espera «poder relajarse» y en el instante en que se abandona y «confía más en ti», será mejor que busques un buen DVD u otras alternativas de ocio para concluir la sesión...

Recuerda...

Recapitulo los imprescindibles de cara a la masturbación manual femenina. Previo a cualquier truco, debes saber que la zona púbica debe ser despertada. Se coloca la mano ahí, y se deja unos minutos, como toma de contacto. Leerás varias veces en este libro que no se debe ir directamente al clítoris (destino final) pero, cuanto más dure el viaje, mayor tensión, mayor deseo y mayor excitación, ¿estamos? Con la palma de la mano apoyada sobre el monte de Venus, muévela en círculos, balanceando un poco, frotando con la muñeca mientras con los dedos alcanzas el pubis (quizás ella esté vestida todavía). Se puede echar la parte del capuchón del clítoris hacia atrás, para descubrirlo. A muchas les gusta que jueguen en la zona del perineo según se van calentando. Atrévete a experimentar con un cambio de textura, probando con un guante de látex.

Los imprescindibles

Lubricar siempre antes de tocar. En esta zona no se debe utilizar nada más que lubricación natural, fluidos y saliva, o geles a base de agua y sin glicerina. Nada de lubricantes caseros (mantequilla y derivados, aceite...). Nada de sustancias dulces dentro de la vagina (ni helado, ni chocolate líquido, etc.).

Constancia en el ritmo. Cuando a una mujer le gusta así, mantenlo. No le va a gustar más porque se lo hagas más fuerte ni más deprisa. Sólo mantente ahí.

Una buena manicura. No tiene que ver con lucir unas uñas postizas kilométricas rematadas en esmalte de oro e incrustaciones de cristales de Swarowsky, no; basta que las uñas estén perfectamente limpias y limadas. No creo que sea mucho pedir.

Que pases al coito o al sexo oral no implica que ya no puedas volver a trabajar con las manos. Retoma el asunto cuando quieras. Recuerda que por su longitud y movilidad, el dedo corazón es el más indicado para alcanzar el punto G.

La parte más sensible es la de fuera y el tercio externo de la vagina. Si penetras con los dedos, no hace ninguna falta que intentes llegar al cuello del útero salvo que te lo pida ella. Durante estas incursiones, procura dejar el pulgar apoyado sobre el clítoris.

Casi me olvido de un pequeño detalle que para nosotras resulta crucial también: los besos. Si te pones a acariciarla, y te tumbas paralelo a ella, no debes dejar de besarla (en la boca, en el cuello, por todas partes a las que alcances, pero no se te ocurra interrumpir lo que estás haciendo ahí abajo ni cambiar el ritmo... La práctica es un grado, sí). Se puede, momentáneamente, mantener el contacto exclusivamente de la vagina sin más, pero casi todas preferimos ser besadas, abrazadas y acariciadas a la vez.

Parar o seguir durante el orgasmo

¿Paro o sigo cuando ella se corre? Igual que en el caso de ellos, con nosotras también «depende». Muchas quieren que nada cambie hasta que termina la última de las contracciones; otras, que justo tras el primer orgasmo, sigas estimulando para «llegar» otra vez; las hay que necesitan que bajes el ritmo un poco o que te detengas, pero manteniendo el contacto con tu mano inmóvil. Hay para todos los gustos.

Gimnasia pubococcígea

Trabajos vaginales: kegels o ejercicios de Kegel

A veces, a los grandes descubrimientos llegamos por error, o por casualidad. De este modo se inventaron los post-it. Y los kegels, pues más o menos... Allá por los años cuarenta o cincuenta, el doctor Arnold Kegel, un prestigioso ginecólogo americano, de quien toman su denominación, reparó en el positivo efecto de ciertos ejercicios de la musculatura pélvica que prescribía a sus pacientes. En un principio, la finalidad que se perseguía con ellos era terapéutica: la de mejorar la calidad de vida de las enfermas de incontinencia urinaria. Sin embargo, además de esto, las pacientes que los practicaban referían otros resultados beneficiosos, como una mayor lubricación vaginal; un parto más fácil —esto léase como «relativamente» más fácil; porque de eso se ocupa, lo sabe todo el mundo, la epidural—; mejora el prolapso uterino (descolgamiento del útero, hereditario o tras varios partos); mejor recuperación del perineo tras dar a luz; mayor sensibilidad —especialmente del punto G— y más placer durante las relaciones sexuales; así como la prevención de la incontinencia urinaria en mujeres sanas.

Los ejercicios de Kegel, ejercitan la musculatura pubococcígea

(PC). Para ubicar estos músculos, la próxima vez que vayas al baño a hacer pis trata de interrumpir y de reanudar la expulsión de la orina. Son los que se ocupan de esa acción en concreto, pero de mucho más, claro, y también son recomendables para los hombres. Lo cierto es que tonificar los músculos PC son todo ventajas.

Cómo se hacen

Consiste, básicamente, en contraer y relajar la musculatura PC, que es la que interviene en la micción. Dependiendo de quién escriba sobre ello, insistirán en una tanda de repeticiones más o menos larga. Puedes probar a contraer los músculos durante 3 segundos y relajar, haciendo una serie de 10. Otro: contrae y relaja, todo lo rápido que puedas, hasta 25 veces. Una variante del primero es contraer los músculos vaginales durante 3 segundos, como si estuvieras sujetando algo dentro. En muchos *sex shops* se vende una pesa específica para fortalecer la musculatura vaginal y que, gracias a su forma, se introduce y debe hacerse el esfuerzo —contrayendo los músculos de la vagina— de mantenerla sin que se salga. Lo ideal es practicarlos diariamente, el dónde y cuándo, depende de tu rutina. Puedes aprovechar mientras vas en el transporte público a trabajar, o el tiempo de ver la televisión o, ya en la cama, antes de dormirte. A muchas este ejercicio les provoca excitación sexual, tenlo en cuenta... como también has de saber que un exceso de entusiasmo al principio te provocará una sensación rara (agujetas), y que, como en toda disciplina, no se logra dominar en un par de días. Los resultados tardan meses en notarse. Ojo: para saber que los estás haciendo correctamente lo único que has de mover son los músculos vaginales —introduce un dedo para comprobar que queda aprisionado—, ni los hombros, ni los glúteos, ni los abdominales, ni las orejas (es un decir) tienen por qué moverse. Las series de contracciones-relajaciones puedes hacerlas coincidir con tu respiración: inspira al contraer, espira al relajar (aquí también trata de no agobiarte, ve poco a poco hasta que te salga y no te hiperventiles).

Los efectos de los kegels sobre la vida sexual

Se trata de gimnasia sexual, que da tonicidad a la vagina y hace que el útero se eleve. Además, permite conseguir un clímax que recorre toda la vagina, desde el principio hasta el final, en un increíble superorgasmo. La estrella de este intenso placer es el músculo pubococcígeo. Va, en triángulo, desde el pubis hasta el coxis. Este orgasmo increíble se consigue cerrando y abriendo el PC y presionando los músculos vaginales durante la penetración. Habilidad que es necesario desarrollar, pues no se trata de un reflejo espontáneo —que la domines será cuestión de ejercitarla; que puedas ponerla en práctica, dependerá del diámetro de lo que te introduzcas: si el pene o dildo es tan grueso que casi te revienta, te costará mucho más el gesto de aprisionar; eso sí, sólo el intento de hacerlo, facilitará el acoplamiento del pene en tu vagina. Con penes medios o pequeños, los kegels provocarán contracciones internas de tus paredes vaginales, serán como un masaje secreto.

Cuando notes que te excitas con la penetración, trata de hacer ese mismo ejercicio de contracción, verás cómo se incrementa el placer —y también el de él, ya que notará cómo las paredes de tu vagina le sujetan—. Además, suele ser un «truco» para acelerar la llegada del orgasmo; muchas veces sabemos que «andamos lejos» y que él está a punto de «llegar». Con los kegels adelantas tres o cuatro pueblos...

Ayudas

En el apartado de «Juguetes eróticos» encontrarás los mejores para ejercitar los músculos PC: desde las bolas a una barra de ejercicios (la pesa vaginal que mencioné antes).

Carrete birmano, siamés, afgano o filipino

Al hilo de las ventajas de ejercitar la musculatura vulvar y perineal, debemos recordar que muchas de las grandes amantes a lo largo de la historia (sí, esas que en su día fueron tachadas de «cortesanas» pero que seguramente supieron sacarle el jugo a la vida y, por descontado, a su sexualidad), en realidad, una de las disciplinas que dominaban era precisamente el movimiento del interior de su vagina. Como no quiero querellas, evito dar nombres de algunas contemporáneas quienes en la intimidad, además de una copita de *brandy*, seguro que ofrecen el carrete birmano[7] (este talento oculto explicaría que hayan atrapado a según qué magnates).

Como curiosidad, en Francia, por ejemplo, se denomina «carrete tailandés» a la práctica de introducir un collar de cuentas por el ano de un señor, e ir sacándolo a medida que se acerca su clímax, de modo que se potencia el placer. Es en Tailandia, precisamente, donde existe una especie de ignominioso show-tradición, que consiste en que las niñas adiestradas para ello lancen pelotas con la vagina. Esta habilidad ha sido incluso parodiada por los dibujos animados de *Beavis and Butthead*, en un capítulo en que pudimos ver a Winona Ryder, de espaldas, espatarrada y lanzando naranjas desde el escenario y, recientemente, en la película *Vaya par de productoreX*, con la *playmate* y ex vigilante de la playa Carmen Electra.

Fisting vaginal
(Mira la definición de *fisting* en la tercera parte del libro y vuelve.)

Cuando se está realizando la masturbación manual de una mujer, si se hace bien, cabe que se dé la siguiente coincidencia: que él quiera explorar y que ella sienta que necesita más. Que la mano quepa no tiene demasiado que ver con que ella posea una vagina descomunal —aunque aquí, efectivamente, el tamaño de la mano

7. El carrete birmano, o siamés, o afgano, o filipino (no hay unanimidad sobre la denominación de origen), consiste en constreñir el pene dentro de la vagina y, con los intensos movimientos de los músculos de ésta, masturbarlo como con la mano. El orgasmo de él sencillamente es espectacular, glorioso... Si dominas esta técnica, él se rendirá ante ti *forever and ever*. Para aprender a contraer con fuerza las paredes de la vagina, no hay nada mejor que entrenar: hazte con bolas de los *sex shops* —ésas plateadas que llevan otras bolitas dentro y cuya finalidad, más que relajante, es esta que apunto—, introduce una y prueba a que no se te salga mientras caminas por la casa o, si te atreves, por la oficina. Toda higiene es poca, y has de desecharlas cada mes.

también importa—. La clave, además de la enorme excitación necesaria, está en el control de los músculos PC, es decir: de ser capaz de relajarlos del todo. ¡Otra aplicación de los kegels!

Hay que respirar hondo, acompasando la inhalación y la exhalación con los movimientos de entrada y salida de la mano —que ya no debe estar en forma de puño, sino con los dedos juntos y extendidos—. Si «empujáis» con la vagina ayudaréis a la entrada del puño. Se trata de una jugada maestra, así que mejor irla comentando y al mínimo signo de dolor o incomodidad, parad. Una vez dentro, dejad que pasen unos instantes para acostumbrar a la vagina (y a la mente de cada uno ante lo que acabáis de hacer).

Como decía antes, a pesar de que lo explicado aludía a la mujer, la gimnasia pubococcígea en los varones también mejora las relaciones sexuales. Cuando, a base de práctica, consiguen mover el pene a voluntad (aquí viene el truco de la toalla, o de la bandera como hacen los *strippers* profesionales, que son capaces de ondear la tela con el balanceo de su miembro) resulta muy placentero notarlo durante la penetración. Y en ellos, los beneficios incluyen: erecciones más potentes, mayor sensibilidad, mayor control eyaculatorio, por no abundar en el asunto del incremento de la sensibilidad. Lamentablemente, el tamaño del pene no va a aumentar por muchos kegels que practiquen.

El punto G

Abordaré un asunto que resulta además de inquietante, polémico. A lo largo de los últimos años se ha establecido un duro debate teórico acerca de si existe o no el dichoso punto G, como si se tratara del Triángulo de las Bermudas...

Unos pretenden que se trata de un apéndice, como un botón, del tamaño de un guisante, que se situaría en la pared frontal de la vagina. Afirman que se puede tocar introduciendo los dedos hacia arriba y que, cuando la mujer se excita, su consistencia aumenta, endureciéndose. Entonces resulta más fácil localizarlo.

Otros, incluida la famosísima sexóloga Shere Hite, afirman que no existe el punto G y que, de haber algo, se trata de una zona esponjosa donde se centralizan las terminaciones nerviosas internas del clítoris. La doctora Hite ha dedicado mucho esfuerzo a cambiar la mentalidad sexual tradicional en pos de una mayor libertad, información y cultura sexual incluso, y ha reivindicado el derecho de la mujer a disfrutar de su cuerpo, desacralizando la penetración, más bien derrocándola, con su estudio que revela que, para masturbarse, las mujeres, en un porcentaje enorme, prescinden de introducirse nada en la vagina. Si a la mujer le basta para alcanzar el orgasmo con la estimulación manual u oral del clítoris, ¿dónde queda pues esa cultura falocrática que impone, además, la penetración reproductiva como centro del meollo de la sexualidad? Su objetivo parece contraatacar a quienes, so pretexto del descubrimiento de un punto G insisten en mantener el enfoque tradicional, y siguen obsesionados con la penetración, con el rendimiento del hombre, con que tenga que conseguir erecciones potentes y duraderas —aunque para ello haya de luchar contra Cielo y Tierra—, dado que es así como (siempre según esta rancia teoría, que se ha demostrado incorrecta) se logrará el orgasmo femenino.

Me arriesgaré a pronunciarme: yo creo que sí hay punto G como tal. No soy ginecóloga, pero me consta que por ahí anda. He tocado un apéndice pequeño, una zona esponjosa pegada a la pared del cuello del útero, situado a escasos centímetros de la entrada de la vagina. Otro tema es que no sea tan fácil para algunas su localización...

Algo de verdad debe de haber cuando gracias a los últimos avances de medicina estética se puede pedir (y conseguir, previo pago) una inyección de colágeno en el mismísimo punto G (el denominado *G-Shot*), que disparará el placer del coito, hasta que se reabsorba de forma natural pasados unos meses.

Respecto de su estimulación, la idea no es machacarlo, ni apretarlo, sino acompañar las caricias por toda la vulva, recorriendo el interior de los labios menores y terminar sobre él, con movimientos lineales o circulares. Por otro lado, la estimulación del punto G produce orgasmos más intensos en muchas mujeres e, incluso, eyaculación femenina.

Encuentro, sin embargo, que los estudios de la doctora Hite son correctos en cuanto al logro del orgasmo femenino mediante estimulación del clítoris, relegando la penetración a una de las posibles prácticas, pero no la que otorga más placer a la mujer. El sexo se ha de disfrutar en toda su riqueza y con toda la creatividad de que seamos capaces, practicando o no la penetración.

Por otro lado, y aludiendo a los datos de la doctora Hite referidos a los porcentajes menos apabullantes, otras muchas mujeres alcanzan el orgasmo sin que nadie tenga que «matarse» en la estimulación del clítoris: les basta una penetración vaginal —estimulando el clítoris o el punto G—, y varios embistes. Y en otros muchos casos, el clímax llega con una penetración profunda. Eso, obviamente, requiere ciertas premisas: que exista algo (pene u objeto) con lo que acceder, y no vamos a negarlo, aquí el tamaño resulta importante (se trata de alcanzar la zona del *cul-de-sac*, o cérvix, el fondo o saco de la vagina, que también puede desencadenar orgasmos).

Un poco de historia y de biología. La complejidad de los órganos sexuales femeninos ha inducido diversos estudios. Sólo las hembras de los bonobos y las mujeres tenemos el clítoris fuera de la vagina, lo que dificulta alcanzar el orgasmo con la penetración. Fue el investigador alemán Ernst Gräffenberg, al principio de los años cincuenta, quien descubrió el punto G, al que se accede a través de la pared frontal de la vagina. Se localiza tras el hueso púbico, es una zona rugosa, parte de la uretra esponjosa, donde se encuentran las glándulas de Skene o parauretrales, responsables de la secreción del fluido que constituye la denominada eyaculación femenina. Cuando se estimula aumenta de tamaño y suele despertar la sensación de que necesitas hacer pis —sólo es eso: no es que te lo hagas—, por ello, no te detengas. Enseguida comenzará el placer.

Las posiciones más adecuadas para estimular el punto G en pareja

Él estirado y tú encima, sentada a horcajadas e inclinada hacia atrás.

Tú debes estar tumbada, con las piernas dobladas y levantadas mientras que él, de rodillas se coloca entre tus piernas.

Tu debes tumbarte de lado y él en la misma postura, te penetra desde atrás.

Muchas mujeres, debido a la educación represora recibida, no se exploran ni se acarician jamás. De su vagina no conocen ni el aspecto porque, como para verla hay que maniobrar y colocar un espejo, y resulta que eso es pecado, inmoral y sucio, pues se pasan la vida ignorándola. Cantidad de chicas alcanzan los primeros orgasmos jugueteando. Se rozan con un bulto de ropa o se frotan contra la almohada. Otras se tocan tumbadas boca arriba con las rodillas más o menos flexionadas y emplean los dedos. Las hay que se sirven de objetos para penetrarse, desde vibradores a hortalizas, dependiendo de los recursos. En este asunto de los vibradores, hay que puntualizar dos aspectos. Uno es que pueden generar adicción y dependencia, dificultando alcanzar el clímax con un ser humano que, huelga decirlo, no es incansable y carece de siete velocidades de vibración. Otra es que emplear un cacharrito es la mejor forma de autosatisfacerse cuando, por ejemplo, tienes prisa y sólo dispones de cinco minutos.

En una ocasión una chica me contó que su primer orgasmo lo tuvo haciendo abdominales, en 7.º de E.G.B. y que se quedó alucinada. No supo que se trataba de un orgasmo hasta años después, pero en esa época le pilló tanta afición que desarrolló una «tabla de lavar» en la tripa que ni las gimnastas olímpicas (juro que es una anécdota verídica). Otra lectora me explicaba que ella lo hacía con un doble cruce de piernas, preferiblemente llevando pantalones, presionando y mediante el roce de las costuras que incrementaba el placer... Muchísimas, mientras se duchan, utilizan los chorros de agua como estimuladores y también los orificios por donde sale el agua y las burbujas con relativa fuerza en los *jacuzzis* o en los *spa* (lo del agua es para erotizarnos, el orgasmo lo buscamos un poco después generalmente).

La doctora Shere Hite clasificaba, en *El informe Hite*, en cinco grandes grupos las formas de masturbarse según los testimonios obtenidos entre 1972 y 1976, en su encuesta a 3.000 mujeres.

Tipo 1: Estimulación clitoridiana/vulvar indirecta y directa, boca arriba o boca abajo, con o sin penetración vaginal y/o anal: 78,5 %.

Tipo 2: Empujando una almohada u otro objeto blando, con o sin penetración vaginal y/o anal: 4 %.

Tipo 3: Cruzando las piernas y apretando los muslos y los músculos pélvicos: 3 %.

Tipo 4: Masaje de agua sobre la zona de la vulva y el clítoris: 2 %.

Tipo 5: Sólo inserción vaginal de objeto, dedos o dildo: 1,5 %.

Respecto del 11 % restante compaginan varias de las técnicas según el momento.

Seguramente los resultados de esta investigación sigan siendo válidas, en cuanto a la extrema diversidad de técnicas, aunque es probable que hoy, con las novedades en cuanto a ayudas sexuales y juguetes y el cambio de mentalidad de la mujer hacia sí misma, su cuerpo y su sexualidad, habría otras conclusiones que extraer.

La intensidad, la cantidad de dedos que emplean o el ángulo con que se los introducen, la zona que estimulan y demás detalles, como decía antes, va en función del momento del día, de la vida, del estado anímico, de la prisa y de las ganas... La mujer encuentra placer de varios modos simultáneos o sucesivos. Que ella misma se conozca no sólo le reportará placer en privado, sino que servirá para que sus relaciones sean más satisfactorias ya que, dé o no con una pareja experta, como cada una somos un mundo, será bastante más sencillo (y placentero para ambas partes, insisto) si es capaz de proporcionarle ciertas orientaciones. El sexo es una forma de comunicar, y podemos utilizar el lenguaje corporal para ir descubriendo al otro. Debería resultar «normal» preguntar/ofrecer información, ya que cada mujer es única, distinta; por eso, incluso las lesbianas, que poseen la anatomía femenina y mayor facilidad por tanto para saber qué y cómo tocan a otra mujer, se aclaran la una a la otra (o deberían) qué le gusta a cada una.

Vía masturbación, la mujer descubre su cuerpo y es capaz de ir desarrollando su sexualidad. Antes mencionaba la importancia de conocer la anatomía. A diferencia del hombre, la genitalidad femenina no es evidente ni se aprecia a simple vista. Ellos tienen su gónadas en el exterior, nosotras, salvo los pechos, que crecen a partir de cierta edad, tenemos la vagina oculta, y la autoexploración requiere de un «esfuerzo». De ahí que casi se exija una excusa para tomarse la molestia... Y yo pregunto, ¿es que el placer propio no es razón más que suficiente?

Los órganos erógenos femeninos trascienden del estricto clítoris. Cuando se pretende estimular a una mujer, no deberían olvidarse los pechos, la zona del vientre y del monte de Venus, la cara interna del muslo, el resto de la vulva (los pliegues interiores, denominados labios mayores y menores), la nuca, la parte posterior de las rodillas... pero también el rostro, el cuero cabelludo, el arco de las cejas, los pies...

Es además de extrema relevancia la posición de las rodillas. Hay quienes, a fin de acumular toda la presión posible en la zona, las juntan y elevan, cerrando los muslos (lo que no hace sino complicar la práctica del cunnilingus y de la masturbación manual ajena), mientras que a otras lo que les pide el cuerpo para alcanzar el orgasmo es separar las piernas dejándolas estiradas. Este detalle, que muchas veces la propia mujer ignora porque lo hace de modo inconsciente, condiciona el éxito de los intentos por obtener el máximo placer, y el hecho de juntar o separar las piernas (táchese en cada mujer lo que no proceda), conlleva que ya te puedes pasar horas masajeando y chupando, que ella disfrutará mucho, sí, pero correrse, no se correrá.

Conviene acariciar la zona empezando con suavidad —siempre se está a tiempo de incrementar fuerza, velocidad y presión—. Si lo haces accediendo desde abajo, casi en el orificio de la vagina, no desde el clítoris directamente, podrás aprovechar su propia lubricación (ya he comentado que hay que tener presente el detalle de que es imprescindible humedecer los dedos o lubricar el objeto con el que se vaya a acariciar cualquier mucosa, y no será la última vez que lo mencione en este libro). Presionar en círculos sobre el clítoris con el dedo medio y recorrer el tramo desde el orificio de la vagina, entrando en ella y haciendo contacto con el punto G, y regresar hasta el clítoris, si se hace medio bien, triunfa como la fórmula de la Coca-Cola. Espera a que esté muy excitada antes de introducir primero un dedo y después, dos o más. Puedes utilizar el índice y el corazón, pero es mejor si metes el corazón y el anular, y también valerte del pulgar para acariciar el clítoris. Imagina que eres Spiderman lanzando tela de araña... y si además consigues hacer presión sobre el monte de Venus con la palma de la mano que te queda libre...

Hay quienes se ponen a cien viéndose a sí mismas tocándose, y se tumban frente al espejo, desnudas; aunque esto mismo, para otras, lejos de ser una práctica para desinhibirse, les resulta desde ridículo a soez... Mientras algunas necesitan acariciarse enteras, otras se ciñen al clítoris. Algunas separan los labios con el índice y corazón de una mano, dejando el clítoris muy expuesto para ser acariciado por la otra mano y otras, por el contrario, lo hacen presionando toda la zona con una toalla enrollada, o a través de la ropa, o frotándolo contra una almohada y moviendo sólo las caderas y la pelvis... Unas boca arriba y otras boca abajo. Hay quien utiliza un solo dedo, y otras se tocan con toda la palma de la mano o incluso, el antebrazo; muchas refieren que les gusta el movimiento circular, cuando otras describen una trayectoria de línea recta, entrando y saliendo, o sólo sobre la zona externa de la vulva; el monte de Venus puede quedar desierto e inexplorado o bien, ser la base sobre la que se ejerce una gran presión que acumula el estímulo del clítoris; Algunas se dan golpecitos directos sobre el archicitado apéndice y otras apo-

yan la palma de la mano sobre él y se introducen uno o varios dedos en la vagina. O quizás hallan placer con la doble penetración: buscan un juguete sexual o un objeto similar al pene y se lo introducen por el ano y/o por a vagina, mientras que con los dedos ocupan el otro orificio (para esto es recomendable utilizar preservativo y que el instrumento sea lavable). Sin embargo, para muchas, sólo mencionar el acceso anal es motivo de «corto y cambio». Hay chicas que se quitan toda la ropa y otras, vestidas, simplemente apartan la braga hacia un lado. Las hay que gimen, que gritan, que maldicen, que rugen, que jadean y otras que parecen muertas de lo silenciosas que son. Las hay que terminan enseguida y las que tardan un buen rato. Las que saben a ciencia cierta dónde se encuentra su punto G, y las que llevan años intentando encontrarlo. Y las que, para motivarse, entran en una especie de meditación asceta frente a las que ojean revistas porno o leen libros de relatos eróticos... Variedad, infinita variedad. Imaginación al poder.

Personalmente, discrepo de los artículos de las revistas femeninas que recomiendan crear ese típico ambiente romántico, invariablemente descrito con «baño de espuma, velitas, música chill out...». No es así, o no para todas. Hasta donde yo sé, una mujer requiere privacidad y comodidad, y ambas cuestiones pueden conseguirse sin transformar la casa en un santuario zen ni aislarse en una cámara antigravedad como si las lanzaran al espacio. Tampoco comulgo con la sensación que transmiten, que parece que para masturbarte debas dedicar una jornada entera o entrar en trance. No es cierto. Igual que en el sexo, las ocasiones de placer individual comprenden desde el orgasmo que te provocas en quince segundos, sin acariciar más que la zona que ya sabes tú que funciona, a esa siesta de tres horas en la que tienes orgasmos de todas las clases y te corres veinte veces y pensando hasta en aquel compañero de pupitre...

La diversidad de métodos masturbatorios sólo puede significar algo ya apuntado antes: que nadie debe considerarse «rara» por estimularse de un modo u otro, ya que lo importante es que disfrute. La naturaleza del orgasmo sólo es una, da igual cómo lo logres. La sexualidad es personal y, por añadidura, tiene vida propia, evoluciona y varía por motivos diversos.

Como en otras facetas del sexo, en el que se practica en solitario, nada como experimentar. No debería suponer un problema sentir y seguir nuestra curiosidad e investigar acerca del propio placer. Sorprendentemente, muy pocas personas se toman tiempo para analizar sus propias respuestas sexuales a la excitación. Las técnicas propias siempre pueden verse mejoradas y complementadas por las de otras.

En la web *comomasturbarse.com* encuentro una impagable enumeración de formas de masturbarse una mujer, si bien afirma que hay más... Leer sobre la manera en que otras encuentran placer resulta, además de curioso —o excitante, incluso—, muy educativo e inspirador. Más de una coincidirá en que antes la muerte que hacerle, ni a tu amiga más íntima, la pregunta: «oye, ¿cómo se hace?». Por echar un vistazo, ¿qué pierdes? Apunto tres ejemplos:

> Ponte de espaldas con las piernas muy juntas. Usa la mano izquierda para tirar la parte de arriba de tus genitales y usar tu mano derecha para tocar el clítoris. Usa un movimiento circular comenzando despacio con una ligera presión, y después aumenta la presión hasta que comienza a llegar el orgasmo. Entonces desacelera acorde con la sensación que deseas hasta que se completa el orgasmo. Si quieres otro, comienza nuevamente.

> Mastúrbate boca abajo y usa la mano derecha para estimular el clítoris con un fuerte movimiento arriba-abajo, usando los dedos medio, índice y anular. La mano izquierda puede acariciar los senos. Muévete mucho en movimientos circulares y arriba y abajo. Mantén las piernas abiertas al comienzo y al sentir llegar un orgasmo cierra las piernas y levanta tu cuerpo.

> Saca la alcachofa de tu ducha para dejar salir un chorro de agua estable. Abre los labios de la vagina exponiendo el clítoris. El agua puede estar ligeramente caliente para mayor estimulación, y las caderas pueden moverse ligeramente para prolongar el placer.

«Cuanto más sé, menos sé», puede que estés pensando, me refiero a la enorme cantidad de posibilidades. En el caso de la masturbación femenina, no puntúa que ella note lo bien que sabes localizar sus puntos y zonas erógenas. En cada encuentro, utilizar una, o dos como mucho, de la infinidad de técnicas que conoces, a la velocidad y con la presión adecuada, es lo correcto. Un pene —salvo el glande y el frenillo— es menos delicado que la vagina y su estimulación no se resiente por parones, cambios de ritmo, acelerones y el empleo de una menor delicadeza. Una vagina no, y cambiar el ritmo, el tipo de caricia y la presión conlleva que nosotras perdamos la excitación, la zona se irrite o duela. Un amigo me contaba, con remordimientos, un fatídico encuentro: «Me aturullé. Quise hacerle en una sola sesión todo lo que sé que a otras les gusta... y la cagué. "¿Estás loco, qué haces?", me dijo textualmente. Y todo por impresionarla...»

En todo caso, respecto a la masturbación, aparte de las ventajas ya mencionadas, debemos considerar que es una de las formas más efectivas de madurar emocionalmente. La masturbación nos ayuda a diferenciar y separar sexo y amor, placer de sentimientos, «rollos» de «relaciones». Se tenga o no pareja o actividad sexual con otra persona, tened presente esta gran verdad: «Los amantes vienen y van pero tú puedes mantener un constante idilio contigo misma», Betty Dodson (terapeuta sexual).

3

A pedir de boca

Sexo oral

Sexo oral no es lo mismo que sexo «verbal», por mucho morbo que suscite hablar de sexo con alguien que te atrae o que en principio te da igual, pero que tras esa conversación, quizá te interese... Infinidad de relaciones surgen por haber compartido secretos de alcoba, fantasías o deseos. La razón es que participamos en una sobredosis de insinuación, de descripciones tórridas —empleando un lenguaje más o menos erótico o sucio—, en una charla donde nos permitimos desvelar nuestros sueños húmedos y que sean conocidos por alguien que sólo escucha, que no está ahí para vivirlos con nosotros... No resulta nada infrecuente que nos excitemos hablando de sexo, de cómo lo hacemos, de lo que nos gusta que nos hagan... y terminemos haciéndolo con esa persona que, en principio, sólo era un «amigo». De hecho, la narratofilia describe la fijación por la que una persona sólo se excita al escuchar historias eróticas.

Cuando estas confidencias o lecturas eróticas se dirigen a la pareja como destinatario único y especial, son, probablemente, lo más enriquecedor y lo más positivo para la relación.

¿Se debería incluir el beso dentro del sexo oral?

Yo abogo por hacerlo. Los labios constituyen una zona erógena de primer orden y absolutamente todas las mujeres valoramos un beso sensual, sugerente, apasionado. Sabemos que de un buen beso podemos pasar a sensaciones de muy alto voltaje. Que un tío sepa besarte es algo fundamental, puedes excitarte y sentir algo tan intenso que te lleva a querer más... También los hay que decepcionan, por torpes, babosos e insulsos, e incluso que producen náuseas, como cuando besas a un fumador que no se molesta en masticar un chicle ni en lavarse antes los dientes, y te parece que estás chupando un cenicero, o a alguien que comparte contigo no sólo la saliva, sino el regusto de su primer, segundo, tercer plato y del postre, si cabe.

Para hombres y mujeres, pues, tenemos dos enemigos naturales a la hora de dar o de recibir un beso en condiciones, y son: la falta de higiene y el mal aliento (por caries, ingesta de cebolla, ajo, etc.). Trucos: utilizar colutorios, remedio sumamente eficaz, pero cuyo efecto dura un rato nada más; aunque sea muy de macarras, y también una guarrería, llevar un chicle de menta en la boca mejora milagrosamente casi cualquier halitosis (lo malo es que cuesta mucho hacer según qué peripecias con la lengua, y requiere habilidad mantenerlo ahí sin tragártelo, pero vale la pena).

EL BESO

Se discute si su origen es una variación, una evolución, del gesto de succión del bebé, o si obedece a un vestigio de la costumbre caníbal de olfatear y morder a la presa humana. En cualquier caso, prohibido en público en determinadas épocas o censurado en el cine, recreado en obras de arte o grabado a fuego en los anales de la historia, como el de Judas. El beso, aparte de una demostración de afecto instintiva, constituye una práctica sensual y sexual.

Con un beso se inicia, se mantiene viva una pasión o se reaviva, sirve para establecer o recuperar el contacto emocional con el otro, acerca a las personas, transmite las sensaciones de una a otra... Son todo beneficios, puesto que a nivel físico, con el beso se ejercitan hasta treinta músculos, se intercambian colonias enteras de bacterias y se desatan las hormonas. Además, cuando se besa a la otra persona, se estimula la parte del cerebro que libera oxitocina en el torrente sanguíneo, provocando sensación de placer y deseo de abrazar. Con besos de cierta intensidad, también segregamos adrenalina, que acelera las pulsaciones y el ritmo cardíaco, sube la tensión arterial y el nivel de glucosa en sangre. Se ha estudiado que, a mayor pasión, mayores son los beneficios para la salud que reportan los besos. Muy probablemente las parejas duran juntas en función del grado de compatibilidad de sus respectivos estilos besando.

Tipos

El Kamasutra describía tres clases de besos: el nominal, en el que los labios apenas se tocan; el palpitante, en el que se mueve el labio inferior, pero no el superior; y el beso de tocamiento, en el que participan labios y lengua.

En realidad, hay formas infinitas de besar: desde un beso breve, seco y rápido, el típico «piquito»; el dado suavemente en las comisuras para despertarle; un beso profundo, mojado, con lengua, o «beso francés»; el frote de nariz, que se llama «beso esquimal»; el de película de los años cincuenta, haciendo que ella se incline un poco hacia atrás...

Órganos y elementos implicados

Para besar hacen falta instinto, ocasión y ganas, pero para que alguien nos quiera besar y que sea inolvidable (y no por repugnante), no va mal tener una boca sana, con buen aliento.

Los labios se consideran una zona erógena debido a que la piel que los recubre es una de las más sensibles del cuerpo. Habrás notado que cualquier herida o llaga en ellos tarda generalmente más tiempo en curarse y cicatrizar que en otros sitios. La mujer suele pintarse los labios, o echarse brillo, y *gloss*, y aunque se afirme con vehemencia que ya hemos superado la etapa de los metrosexuales, no voy a ahorrarme dar el consejo: hay que tener los labios hidratados, suaves, sin pellejos ni heridas, es fundamental. Hay cacaos, vaselinas y pomadas de todo tipo, olor, sabor, con y sin color, de precios inverosímilmente caros o asequibles para cualquiera. Compradlos y utilizadlos. En dos días se nota el cambio y, me atrevo a afirmar que se convierten en imprescindibles por méritos propios.

Una boca bonita incita al pecado, constituye un verdadero don. Bien perfilada y con labios gruesos, invita a besarla... Mientras que unos labios finos «como una puñalada», desdibujados o desiguales, harán menos sensual este rasgo. Se puede corregir con inyecciones de la propia grasa corporal (que se extrae y trata en determinadas clínicas) o colágeno (que se reabsorbe de modo natural pasados unos meses) o de artecol (u otras sustancias que se consideran permanentes porque a su alrededor el organismo genera una fibrosis. No aumenta el labio por el líquido que se infiltra, sino por la reacción de aislar ese cuerpo extraño). Suele quedar bien si se hace en clínicas de estética oficiales y si se realiza muy poco a poco (si no, se forman granulomas, esas bolas tan feas, etc., o si te pasas, terminas pareciendo una caricatura).

Personalidad y fisonomía

La forma de los labios puede definir el carácter de alguien. Se dice que una boca grande denota sensualidad, carácter aventurero, sincero, vital.

Los de boca pequeña se reputan frívolos y delicados, determinados en sus propósitos. Los labios delgados son indicio de dureza, frivolidad y perfeccionismo en todos los sentidos.

Los labios gruesos apuntan a personas que aman el placer y la comodidad, optimistas y que saben disfrutar.

Los dientes constituyen una de las piezas más claves del atractivo de una persona. Tenerlos todos, bien formados, alineados y colocados en su sitio, blancos —no amarillos, ni marrones— y limpios se considera una señal de juventud y de salud. De ahí que los dentistas sean millonarios, a base de realizar tratamientos de estética dental.

Los besos que se dan las personas establecen públicamente la pauta de su relación: fraterna, de amistad, de amor... Besar en la boca se considera mayoritariamente como lo más íntimo dentro de todas las prácticas sexuales. Por algo será... Eso implica que saber hacerlo bien es fundamental. Hay besos exigentes y muy sensuales que despiertan la libido de los muertos. Aprende a darlos. Ni reseco como un cardo, ni húmedo como una babosa. Si quieres imprimir pasión, transmitir firmeza y deseo, no se te ocurra emplear la fuerza bruta, sujetar la cabeza o el pelo inmovilizando al otro, o hacerlo chocando los dientes, o impidiendo que te devuelva el beso libremente... Dentro de los tipos de beso, cuando sea con lengua, cuidado con la forma de introducirla en la boca del otro (ni le asfixies, ni te instales ahí dentro y te quedes inerte, o por el contrario, no la muevas como si fuera una batidora), y antes de darlo, traga saliva, porque una cosa es «húmedo» y otra, que puede resultar muy desagradable, beberse las babas de otro. ¡Ah!, y evita sacarle un ojo con la montura de tus (o sus o vuestras) gafas.

Leí una vez que para llegar a dar a alguien el mejor beso de su vida debías tratar de imitar el beso que esa persona te está dando (deja que te bese e intenta «anularte», frenar tu inercia de besarla según acostumbras —imagina por un instante que quizás el tuyo no sea el mejor del mundo para ella...— y sólo devolverle lo que te da: en cuanto a intensidad, movimientos, giros de cabeza... Sé su espejo. Ése será el «beso perfecto» que, lamentablemente, es incompatible con tener mal aliento (esto ya es de mi cosecha). Retomando lo de la higiene, cuando por la situación no cabe cepillarse los dientes, recurre a caramelos, chicles, enjuagues... La boca es ese agujero que hay justo bajo los orificios nasales, ¿recuerdas?, así que todo, en serio, todo vale, menos acercarte a su nariz apestando a alcohol, ajo, cebolla, tabaco, etc., que son enemigos de un buen beso. Parece el momento de recordar que la mesilla de noche, además de albergar un ejemplar de la Biblia, puede servir para dejar un tubo de pasta de dientes, o caramelos de cualquier sabor que nos libren del mal aliento —sí, eso que a ti también te sucede cuando amaneces—. Para evitar que prescindan de tu beso de buenos días o no quieres que las arcadas abran tu jornada, es la solución.

Seguimos con el beso y algunas técnicas. Intercalar los labios con algún dedo, de manera que no sepa si el contacto proviene de lo uno o de lo otro, multiplica las sensaciones —las manos limpias porque, si huelen mal, la nariz lo detectará—; también se puede introducir un poco un dedo mientras continúas besándole y jugando con la lengua. Aunque tengas la sensación más estupenda, cabe que si no varías los movimientos durante mucho rato, para el otro resulte aburrido o pesado: alterna la duración y el ritmo de los besos, intercala cortos y largos, suaves con intensos, superficiales y profundos, de caricia con los que succionan...

A las mujeres generalmente les gusta sentir la pasión que despiertan en su pareja. Y la captan, precisamente, a través de los besos. Recibir besos y darlos es clave para excitarse y querer ir a más. A los hombres, los besos les hacen «arrancar motores». Besar inicia las fantasías eróticas de ambos, la mente comienza a imaginar qué vendrá después, tratando de anticipar cómo irá reaccionando el otro... A menudo los labios hablan sin hablar, indicándonos si procede avanzar (en cuanto a las manos, si ya se pueden subir o deslizarlas bajo la ropa), cómo ha de ir el resto del cuerpo, si has de abrazar con mayor fuerza, etc. A muchos les urge tanto penetrar a la chica, que olvidan algo clave: tomarse un ratito. Date (y dale) tiempo: si dedicas un plazo «razonable» dándole besos apasionados, seguramente sea ella quien, a medida que su deseo se despierta y gana seguridad y afianza su atracción hacia ti, te vaya pidiendo más con palabras o mediante gestos, mediante el acercamiento de su cuerpo, con gemidos, etc. Si se piensa fríamente, ¿qué suponen quince o veinte minutos comparados con horas de desenfreno?

Mala fama: la enfermedad del beso

Poco romántica esta alusión al virus Epstein-Barr... Se contagia por la saliva y en realidad, este patógeno ha infectado y permanece en más del 90 % de la población, de forma que la mayoría de los adultos son seropositivos para el VEB, sin notarlo ni llegar a enfermar. El período de incubación es de mes o mes y medio. Este virus infecta las glándulas salivares (la parte externa, el epitelio) y es capaz de atacar a los linfocitos, los glóbulos blancos. Causa una inflamación en los glanglios linfáticos junto con síntomas de fiebre, agotamiento, etc. Si se complica puede degenerar en mononucleosis y hasta en cáncer (carcinoma nasofaríngeo, entre otros). Afecta más fácilmente a personas inmunodeficientes.

La felación

El francés

Y no hablo de los habitantes del país vecino. Como en cada parcela de la sexualidad, aquí hay para todos los gustos. Desde mujeres adictas a chupar a detractoras de semejante asquerosidad; las hay que tragan y que escupen y quienes esquivan el esperma como si se tratara de ácido sulfúrico... Hay quienes consideran un reto lograr que un tipo se empalme gracias a su lengua y otras que son reacias a introducírsela en la boca hasta que no adquiere cierta textura y firmeza (porque para comer queso de Burgos...).

Debería evitar esta barbaridad, pero como ya he dejado caer otras en este texto, no voy a autocensurarme ahora. Dicen que lo único peor que una mala mamada es tener que hacerla, pero bueno, en esto de las felaciones todo es empezar y cogerle gusto. Aquí sí que la práctica es un grado (lo que no excluye felatrices vocacionales, artistas del karaoke con un incuestionable talento innato, que haberlas haylas). Además, otra gran verdad: es muy psicológico. En esto de hacerle sexo oral a un hombre, el vínculo emocional es determinante: si una chica siente «algo» por el dueño del pene que se mete en la boca, las cosas cambian. No sólo por el tiempo que va a emplear, sino por el entusiasmo y la dedicación con que acometerá la tarea. Cuenta mucho también el aspecto del pene. Hay penes que te gustan más que otros, siendo esto muy personal también: más o menos largo, fino o grueso, inclinado o recto, depilado o asilvestrado...

Dos premisas

La primera es que debes entender que no es una obligación, sino un privilegio hacerlo. Además, por pura ley de probabilidad y de justicia cósmica: para recibir nada como dar, ¿no?

Otra básica, independientemente de las características genéticas de cada uno, lo que de todo punto resulta inadmisible es ser un guarro o una guarra. Los bajos han de estar impolutos. Aunque te quedes helada al comprobar que su gayumbo huele a colonia —o sea, preveía que ibas a «bajar»... (tranquila, agradece mentalmente el detalle y sigue con lo que ibas a hacer)—, es preferible eso a que el pestuzo tire para atrás. El olor del esperma, de los fluidos vaginales y el corporal de cada persona son distintos pero, siempre que haya higiene, resultan atractivos para tu pareja, pudiendo ser muy excitantes en sí mismos, sin necesidad de utilizar disfraces, desodorantes, ni perfumes, si no te gustan. Depende mucho de la dieta que el sabor y el olor sea más o menos agradable. Tanto el semen como el fluido vaginal será mejor si las últimas comidas han incluido frutas o zumos (piña, melón, fresa, etc.), o verduras (salvo el brócoli y los espárragos). Son fatales: el café, el alcohol, el tabaco, algunas drogas, los lácteos, carnes y pescados.

Además...

Pues qué menos que lavarte las manos (¿vas a meter ahí —boca, vagina, etc.— los dedos después de llevarte todos los virus del pasamanos del Metro?), cepillarte los dientes (todo sobre ello en el apartado «El beso»), y prestarle un poco de atención a tu vello corporal. En nosotras la palabra no es «depilar» sino «aniquilar» cualquier resto de pilosidad que asome un poco (lástima que no todos se merecen el suplicio de pasar por las ingles brasileñas...). Las uñas, como ya se explica en varios puntos, deben estar bien recortadas y limadas y, si eres de los que se las muerde, cuida de no tener padrastros, ni picos que arañen.

Y respecto de ellos, no hablaré de depilación (un hábito del que, como se deducirá de estas páginas, soy defensora a ultranza, por motivos varios), sino de recortar el vello de zonas genitales y de las axilas también —huelen menos—, o por lo menos peinarlo —sí, así los pelos que se hayan arrancado se quedan en el peine y no entre los dientes de nadie—. Quizás odies la idea de afeitarte algo que no sea el rostro. No es amor lo que sientes por tu vello corporal, desengáñate. Además, lo siento, pero yo no te amo incondicionalmente como tu abuela, y te digo, bueno, te dirijo, palabras sinceras, quizá dolorosas: fuera pelos de la espalda, los hombros y la zona lumbar. Sepas que, salvo al grupo gay que se denomina «osos» y a ciertos parafílicos del vello (eso se llama hirsutofilia), a la mayoría de las mujeres no nos gusta, es decir, sí o no, pero siempre dentro de unos límites. Prueba con las cremas depilatorias si la cuchilla te da grima. Una opción estupenda es pasarte la máquina que no afeita del todo, sino que rebaja el cabello: úsala para el cuerpo al 2 o al 3. Pues si con esto no te he convencido, lee además lo apuntado en «Cirugía íntima masculina» —que recortar el vello de la base y alrededores crea la sensación de un pene más grande—. Y además, la depilación de una zona hace que cada lengüetazo o caricia vaya a la piel; los pelos son menos agradecidos, créeme.

¿Que por qué hago apología de la depilación? Pues porque es más higiénico en el sentido de la profilaxis también. Parecerá una simpleza pero, la depilación de la zona genital —femenina y masculina—, es de las medidas que mejor ayudan a la detección de las ETS. Como sabrás, las verrugas genitales y otras enfermedades e infecciones se manifiestan con simples puntitos, manchas y bultitos enanos y, encima, las hay que no presentan dolor ni escozor (asintomáticas)... ¿Cómo vas a notarlas, si se esconden bajo la maleza? Por ello, mejor tener la zona despejada, para que un vistazo pueda darnos la señal de alerta.

Esmegma

Fonéticamente, resulta casi indiscutible lo fascinante del término. Repetido «esmegma, esmegma», suena a contraseña secreta... «Esmegma, esmegma», evoca los nombres de lejanas princesas de Asia, o de las esencias florales... pero no. De pronto, al tomar tierra, las imágenes asociadas a este vocablo nos traen a la mente (a la de casi todos) sensaciones desagradables. A mí se me arruga el morro y pongo cara de morder limones. Mucho asco. Y «esmegma» pasa a ser la imprecación, lo indeseable... Ya se sabe que todo lo que sube baja: de la fascinación al repudio, del amor al odio, del éxtasis al sueño... Como la vida misma.

A todo esto, entiendo que procede aclarar qué es la susodicha: se trata de la secreción de las glándulas sebáceas de la mucosa del prepucio y de los labios menores, cerca del clítoris. Una poco empleada palabreja... y es porque hay cosas que no nos metemos en la boca ni para pronunciarlas... Afortunadamente, hay asuntos que pese a ser repugnantes (y preocupantes), se solucionan sin quirófanos, ni lágrimas, ni burofaxes y sin kilos de potingues y cosméticos.

Como introducción, apuntaría que además de las glándulas endocrinas que segregan el sudor, tanto hombres como mujeres tenemos las glándulas apocrinas en ciertas partes del cuerpo, que producen otros fluidos con un olor distintivo (no necesariamente desagradable); estas secreciones desempeñan un papel muy importante en la atracción sexual (de ahí que esté tan de moda hablar de colonias a base de feromonas).

Las glándulas apocrinas femeninas, más abundantes que las masculinas, se localizan en torno a los pezones, en el ombligo, bajo los brazos y, dentro de la zona genital, en los labios menores. El esmegma (detritus celular) es una secreción blancuzca, untuosa y de olor característico que puede resultar desagradable para algunas personas. Se cree que su función es proteger y lubricar el espacio prepucial. En la mujer se forma en la zona entre los labios mayores y menores y alrededor del clítoris. Las secreciones de la vagina son perfectamente normales, saludables y no necesitan ser eliminadas, además debido a la sensibilidad de estos tejidos los desodorantes pueden resultar perjudiciales.

De igual modo, el pene genera esmegma procedente del recambio celular del glande y la porción interna del prepucio junto con el sebo proveniente de las glándulas de Tyson.

Dado que es una secreción orgánica, su mal olor se debe a su descomposición: si se acumula y permanece en los genitales, apesta. Como se trata de un fluido que el cuerpo segrega de modo constante, no existe «nada» (ni jabón, ni pastillas, etc.) que lo erradique: se debe mantener una higiene continua.

El esmegma se produce en el glande y en el clítoris, por tanto, se trata de un fluido común a ambos sexos. Para todo el mundo las visitas continuas al bidé —ese casi olvidado aparato sanitario— son la mejor recomendación. En los casos de penes no circuncidados, el exceso de piel causa que se acumule y retenga el esmegma. Hay que, con la mano, desplazar el prepucio hacia la base del pene, descubriendo el glande, y lavarlo y secarlo. Muchos reclamos publicitarios repiten «sentirse fresco todo el día» como mantra; pues bien: con agüita y jabón se soluciona el tema. La clave radica en la higiene diaria, en lavarse y secarse antes y después de orinar y de tener relaciones sexuales.

Como curiosidad, y no sin náuseas, cuento lo que ponía una página de Internet. Por lo visto, en los países hispanohablantes, España incluida, denominan popularmente «requesón» al esmegma, dada su similitud con un derivado lácteo. En Cuba se denomina «fana». Actualmente, ciertos perfumes que pretenden ser afrodisíacos contienen esmegma de res, aunque los entendidos apuestan por la de ballena porque tiene el característico olor y sabor a queso y es además muy salada, lo que permite la rápida absorción del perfume.

Cuestiones de protocolo

Siempre es bienvenido el sexo oral, pero ojo, no en cualquier sitio, momento o circunstancia. Me refiero a que se debe saber que, si bien a la mujer le gusta el sexo oral tanto como al hombre, para nosotras el acto de dar o recibir sexo oral simboliza y alcanza a mucho más (en general). Las mujeres lo vivimos como un instante muy íntimo. Todo lugar es susceptible de convertirse en un rincón para el amor... para los hombres. Ya dice la frase: «ellas necesitan un motivo para el sexo. Ellos sólo un lugar». Por excitante que te parezca un callejón, un ascensor, un aparcamiento, etc., no siempre ella está dispuesta a seguirte... Procurad que no sea el clásico sitio donde os puedan pillar.

Otro detalle, cuando «bajes», por ridículo o absurdo que suene, ella necesita un chute de confianza extra. Concretando un poco: si eres capaz de decirle algo bonito acerca de su cuerpo, de lo guapa que te parece, de lo mucho que te apetece hacérselo, de lo bien que sabe o que huele, o de cómo te excita verla así... Es mano de santo. Esto se debería recordar siempre: la mujer y el oído, el hombre y la vista. Ellos se estimulan con la contemplación de una imagen; nosotras, podemos registrar una frase «erótica» o incitante y derretirnos al recordarla. No hay que complicarse en exceso: puedes decir palabras sueltas, pero constructivas, amables. Si entre ambos el código normal de comunicación incluye intercambiar insultos y palabras obscenas, di ésas; pero si no es así, quizá cuando estés con tu cabeza entre sus piernas, o con su boca rodeando tu glande, no sea el mejor momento para llamarla «zorra», «guarra» o «puta»...

Estar en boca de todos

Si hay una palabra que describe lo que ellos tienen en mente el 99 % de las veces cuando se trata de sexo, ésa es, indiscutiblemente, «mamada». El sexo oral es, para la mayoría, el mejor regalo que pueden recibir. El pene puede representar desde la masculinidad más atractiva al origen de la vida, la fuerza, el vigor... Contemplarlo en erección suscita deseo y respeto, atracción y excitación. No te dejes llevar por lo que has visto en algunas escenas de porno. Ellas lo hacen por dinero y fingen en el 90 % de las ocasiones. Con tu compañero —ocasional o estable—, sigue tus impulsos. Y recuerda siempre: delicadeza y atención.

Cuando el pene no está aún erecto, obviamente vas a acelerar el tema si te ayudas de las manos (a casi todas las mujeres les atrae contribuir activamente a la erección). Agárralo un par de centímetros por debajo del glande, rodeándolo, y mueve la mano de arriba abajo. Comienza con suavidad y ve progresivamente haciéndolo más deprisa, conforme notes que se endurece. Haz subir y bajar el prepucio cogiéndolo en tu puño. Compagina esto con miradas insinuantes, saca la lengua pero no le toques con ella, juega a acercarla y retírala sin abandonar lo que estás haciendo con la mano. Recorre la vena vertical de su pene con el pulgar, masajea con distinta presión y, desde la base hasta el glande, intenta incorporar leves giros de muñeca —ojito con entusiasmarte, no olvides que puedes hacerle daño: no lo estrujes ni se lo retuerzas—. Con la otra mano, dedícate a los testículos, al perineo, o fija tus dedos pulgar e índice en la base del pene formando un anillo y dale un masaje, o repite el movimiento ascendente y descendente. Tu boca debe estar cerca. Puedes, primero, lamer el glande, como si fuera un helado, o recorrer pequeños tramos con la punta de la lengua. Abre la boca como si fueras a engullirla (seguro que él se muere por que lo hagas), pero retírate y acomete la zona del tronco, asciende desde la base, rodea la corona, vuelve a bajar. Haz que se desespere. En determinado momento, puedes introducirte la parte superior del pene, siempre sin que tus dientes le toquen. Juega con tu lengua: súbela, pegándola al paladar, haz que su reverso toque la superficie del frenillo, gírala. Succiona, lame, acaricia y besa (si te parece insípido, echa lubricante de sabores o esconde un chicle en tu boca). Déjate llevar por lo que te apetezca, por tu instinto. Ten en cuenta que la piel que cubre el glande es de las más sensibles del cuerpo, junto con la de los párpados, y resulta muy agradable de besar y de chupar. Muchos terminan agarrándote de la cabeza, del pelo o convirtiendo tus orejas en un par de asas para conseguir que te metas el pene hasta dentro... Hay quien lo encuentra insoportable. Si no quieres que te ahogue metiéndotela hasta más atrás de la campanilla, es mejor que apoyes una de tus manos en la base del pene, así tendrás control en todo momento sobre la profundidad. Si relajas el cuello, lograrás introducirla en su totalidad (excepto algunos XXL, con quienes puedes recrear la sensación utilizando tu mano para cubrir la zona de abajo, donde tu boca ya no alcanza). Una vez así, mantenla un ratito, roza con la punta de tu lengua en la base, o mueve tu cabeza (guiada por tu mano si es preciso) dentro y fuera.

¿Qué más?

Acompaña con movimientos de tu mano la trayectoria que describas con tu cabeza, sube y baja, formando una O con los dedos para intensificar la fricción. En lugar de ir desde arriba, comienza en la base y ve subiendo con la lengua. Traza semicírculos con la piel que rodea la corona del glande. Si te concentras en el tercio superior, moviendo tu puño cerrado, coloca el pulgar como tope, de modo que incrementes la sensación de «penetración». Lleva su pene hacia el fondo de tu paladar, haciendo que sienta el recorrido. Simula la acción de mamar, tomando el pene desde la base con la mano y poniendo la boca en el extremo y también puedes hacer movimientos de succión. No implica hacer trampas eso de ayudarte con la mano. Además, ten en cuenta que desde los dientes hasta la campanilla hay entre 5 y 8 cm, y que la medida de su pene con casi total seguridad será mayor... Prueba a invertir la dirección de tu mano, colocando el anillo que forman el pulgar y el índice hacia abajo, justo en la base del pene, donde puedes aplicar mayor fuerza que en la punta. La velocidad puede variar pero, si te aceleras mucho, se correrá antes. Hablando de esto: la estimulación del punto P[8] provoca que se desencadene el orgasmo (si lo haces mal o a quien no debes, lo que conseguirás es que se moleste, se ofenda, piense que te has vuelto loca o incluso, que se marche). Y lo mismo con nosotras: puede que a ella le encante que acaricies el perineo y el ano, o que introduzcas un dedo, o que sólo con acercarte a esa zona se cierre en banda.

Notarás que no te quita la vista de encima, no es que «desconfíe» o que te vigile, es que le pone mucho verte en acción: supone presenciar una peli porno de la que es protagonista. Por tu parte, estate atenta a sus reacciones: así sabrás si le gusta o no, o si le estás excitando tanto que irremisiblemente va a eyacular (algo que quizá quieras posponer, en cuyo caso, debes aminorar). Disfrutará mucho si llevas la voz cantante —perdón por la referencia—. Logra que se excite y entonces desvía la atención hacia otras zonas: su cuello, sus pezones, etc., no tengas piedad: a ellos no les pasa como a nosotras que sí nos perjudican los parones y los cambios. Con ello, incrementarás el placer que sienta cuando de verdad «termine».

Si te da reparo comerle la polla a un extraño estás en tu derecho de colocarle un preservativo; más que eso: tienes que hacerlo, porque arriesgas tu salud. Hay infinidad de clases de condones pero, para el sexo oral, ya que el sabor del látex no es agradable, opta mejor por los de sabores o pon un poco de lubricante de fresa o de cereza, sobre un preservativo común. Como la sensibilidad no es la misma, puedes hacerlo sin preservativo, siempre que evites todo contacto con líquido preseminal y, por supuesto, con el esperma: mantén controlado el glande, chupa el tronco, los testículos, escupe saliva constantemente de modo disimulado, lo que proporcionará lubricación extra a tus dedos, y deja que sean ellos los que aborden la «zona de riesgo». De todos modos, no es seguro hacerlo sin profilaxis, ya que puedes contraer alguna ETS a través de la boca, especialmente si tienes llagas, cortes o heridas.

Ten en cuenta que ellos también necesitan preliminares (no te ti-

8. Sobre el punto P puedes leer más en «Sexo anal», en «Masturbación masculina» y en la tercera parte del libro.

res de cabeza a su falo como un caníbal); ellos también son «tímidos» y «aficionados»: les cuesta, como a nosotras, explicar qué les gusta y probablemente desconozcan los términos correctos para designar algunas partes de su propio cuerpo, los nombres técnicos de las caricias que quieren pedirte o de las posturas que desean hacer contigo; ellos también necesitan cumplidos o palabras que les tranquilicen (si no te ves gritando «métemela toda» o el tan comprometedor «¡eres el mejor!» —¿ah, sí? ¿El mejor de entre cuántos o comparado con quién?—, quizá puedas hacerle saber que todo va bien con un gemido de placer o un «me encanta»); ellos también disfrutan viéndote en acción: sé espontánea, déjate llevar y pásalo bien.

Si se olvida de avisarte de que está a punto de correrse, tú misma podrás darte cuenta, por sus movimientos de caderas, porque se pone rojo, se le acelera la respiración..., aunque igual eso te queda lejos del alcance de la vista... Pues bien: el pene se hincha, los testículos se pegan al cuerpo, y se le tensarán las manos (con las que te aferra la cabeza o del pelo). Tras el orgasmo, suelen preferir que te quedes quietecita, no todos valoran los mimos «post».

CUNNILINGUS

Habida cuenta que sabemos encontrar el clítoris, ahora viene donde la matan: ¿qué hacer con él y cómo?

Comienza por el perímetro externo, ve de fuera hacia dentro. Puedes avanzar desde arriba, habiendo dedicado cierta atención a su cuello y sus pechos y continuado por el estómago. También puedes ir desde los pies, recorrer los tobillos, las pantorrillas, rodear las rodillas, separarlas... Invierte unos minutos besando y pasando la lengua por el interior de los muslos, por el bajo vientre (haz como si tuvieras todo el día). Luego, mordisquea la zona del monte de Venus, dejando que note tu espiración: echa aire caliente, soplando poco a poco, nunca dentro de la vagina, porque puede causar una embolia. Aborda la zona de los labios mayores, puedes aprisionarlos y frotarlos con cierta controlada intensidad. Introduce la punta de la lengua, sepáralos sin prisa, juega con ellos, descubre los internos. Pasa la punta de la lengua desde el orificio de su vagina hacia arriba, pero no llegues aún al clítoris, deja que nazca en ella el deseo de que lo hagas, hazla esperar. Pasa un rato estimulando toda la zona con la boca (la cuestión es no morder. Para evitarlo, puedes rodear los dientes con los labios, pero parecerás una abuela sin la dentadura postiza. Basta con que formes una O con los labios). Para lograr más presión e intensidad, el truco está en succionar con los labios, tienes que optimizar tus recursos: la boca y las manos, que bien puedes dedicar a ayudarte con caricias o a seguir excitando sus pechos. ¿Qué más? Pues arrímate. No saques la lengua como si fuera la espada de Dart Wader. Los actores porno tienen que enseñársela a la cámara —que es la que importa—, pero si tienes a tu chica espatarrada y no te nota cerca... Otro detalle: la nariz y la barbilla. Una vez la zona está lubricada, si llevas ya un buen rato y notas que se te cansa el lengua, puedes echarle imaginación: usa la nariz —sí, el hueso, de forma que el frontal se apoye en el clítoris y el eje en la vagina, y presiona un poco—, o la barbilla (la barba puede ser como una lija, comprueba que no rascas, porque puedes dejarla en carne viva...).

Esta boca es mía

Cuando una mujer, estando tú ahí abajo, entre sus piernas, te agarra la cabeza y te acerca, es que necesita más presión. Si con su cadera esquiva tu boca, es que la zona a la que te diriges no es la que ella necesita que estimules, saca la lengua y sigue buscando. Si estás siendo demasiado suave, tanto que no está segura de si sigues en la habitación, ella casi no se moverá, le da vergüenza pedírtelo, pero se muere por que «hagas algo». ¡Pero tú ya lo estás haciendo! Exacto: dale un poco más de caña, prueba con tu lengua un poco más «dura» o cambia los toques: si estabas haciendo toquecitos tan sutiles como el aleteo de una mariposa o lamías como un gatito tímido, quizá sea hora de que tu lengua haga barridos verticales u horizontales cargados de intención. Si, por el contrario, se arquea y te ofrece el clítoris es que ya es hora de que te dediques a él —en principio, éste será tu último punto—, pero recuerda que no puedes hacerlo con demasiada fuerza, que no te confundan sus reacciones (resoplidos, convulsiones, temblores en los muslos, verla aferrarse a la sábana, mover la cabeza, morderse los labios). Búscalo y atrápalo con tus labios, si no sobresale, toma en la boca toda la piel que lo recubre, chupa fuerte y presiona. Suavemente, separa los labios descubriendo el clítoris y acarícialo con tu lengua rápidamente; en una mujer esto puede causar que se estremezca. Hazlo un rato, mantente pasando tu lengua en círculos o trazando líneas (hay quien afirma que escribe el abecedario completo, letra a letra). Cuando notes que está alcanzando el orgasmo pon tus labios en forma de O y toma el clítoris con tu boca. Empieza a chupar suavemente y observa su reacción. Si puede soportarlo, empieza a chupar más fuerte y, si le gusta, succiona con mayor intensidad aún. Si levanta la pelvis muévete con ella, no te separes ni te detengas —eso será lo que mentalmente, o a voces, está diciendo ella: «más», «sigue, sigue», «no pares»—. Pero no cambies el ritmo, no quieras «darle más» porque eso provocará que pierda el orgasmo o, si ya lo está teniendo, que sea de «peor calidad», menos intenso... y se decepcione. En el instante en que detectas que está muy excitada puedes utilizar dos dedos (uno es demasiado estrecho y con tres el grosor podría ser excesivo), siempre lubricados, y comenzar a penetrarla —sin dejar de ocuparte del clítoris con la boca—, primero con suavidad, luego con el ritmo que ella misma te demande con su reacción.

¿Qué más?

Cuando una mujer alcanza el orgasmo se mantiene excitada durante una hora, así que si perseveras, es sencillo que vuelva a correrse más veces. Si estabas haciendo sexo oral, mantén la posición, deja que su clítoris «descanse» y céntrate momentáneamente en la entrada de su vagina; si se los habías introducido, relaja un poco la presión que le hacías con los dedos, pero sigue acariciando con el movimiento de penetración menos intenso. No rompas el contacto, deja tu mano sobre el pubis, quizás apoyando el pulgar sobre el clítoris, pero sin moverlo y pasa tu lengua, lamiendo despacito por toda la hendidura vaginal.

Puedes «bajar» después de que ella haya tenido un orgasmo con penetración. Si lo haces, si te dedicas a sus pechos, a su cuerpo y terminas por hacerle un cunnilingus justo en ese momento —en vez de darte media vuelta y quedarte frito, por poner un ejemplo—, será tu esclava por los siglos de los siglos.

Si es una pareja esporádica, deberías tener la precaución de utilizar un preservativo femenino o cuadrante de látex, un trozo de film de cocina o en caso de emergencia, un preservativo o un guante de látex cortados.

Don de lenguas

Tu lengua, has de saberlo, es el músculo más fuerte que tienes. Son todo ventajas: siempre está lubricada —si tienes la boca seca, es tan sencillo como beber un refresco, algo dulce, mejor que agua—, y caliente —se ha demostrado que las zonas erógenas se excitan más a temperaturas elevadas—; no araña —algo que muchos no tienen en cuenta en la masturbación manual: imperdonable que te lastimen en medio de una caricia profunda...—. Además, la lengua es incansable —a diferencia de tu pelvis, tus abdominales o tus brazos, no se te va a entumecer, ni vas a romper a sudar aunque te pases moviéndola una hora—. Es flexible, moldeable —puedes «afilarla», o pasarla extendida, pinchar o lamer—, te sirve para empujar, para toquetear y para penetrar y, aunque se choque o se tuerza, no te duele —no se «troncha»—: recorre los pliegues de los labios, sigue su anatomía. Tienes mucho mejor dominio sobre ella que sobre tu pene e, incluso, que sobre tus dedos y (esto no es ironía) bien manejada, una mujer puede quedarse «colgada» por alguien que le proporciona buen sexo oral, antes que por otro que se lo hace mal o no se lo hace, por virguerías que haga cuando la penetra. Aprovecha que a muchos el sexo oral les da pereza/asco (algo absurdo si ella acaba de lavarse) y haz que tus sesiones amatorias rebosen de sexo oral, antes, durante y después de la penetración, y del orgasmo, sé generoso con esa boquita que tienes. Si ya lo haces, es que sabes de lo que hablas. Piénsalo: si a ti siempre te apetece recibir una sesión de sexo oral, a nosotras también.

Lo antedicho podemos utilizarlo con las consiguientes adaptaciones también nosotras. Más trucos: el calor natural de la lengua favorece la estimulación; puedes, también, alterarlo y «sorprenderle» añadiendo la variación de la temperatura: mantén un cubito de hielo en la boca hasta que se enfríe, o bebe algo caliente, para que suba unos grados. Y reanuda lo que estabas haciendo. Notará la diferencia, no lo dudes... Y también con caramelos mentolados, o con bebidas con gas. Si eres capaz de mantenerlas en la boca junto con su pene, también le proporcionará sensaciones distintas.

Hacer la boca agua

Muchas veces se oye la expresión «te voy a hacer un bikini de saliva», «verás el pijama de saliva que te pongo luego»... Se trata, una vez más, de dejar de centrarse en los diez centímetros de zona pélvica y disfrutar de todo el resto del cuerpo, a base de estimular su sensibilidad a través de la piel. Por favor, ve despacio. Recuerda que la sensualidad se puede despertar poco a poco para que el desenlace sea más intenso y placentero. Dando pequeños besos y toquecitos con la punta de la lengua —sin dejar babas, pero pudiendo soplar en la zona humedecida para que con el cambio de temperatura se acreciente la sensación— ve recorriendo a tu pareja. Da igual por dónde comiences: cómetela de pies a cabeza o dale un *tour* desde la nuca deteniéndote donde normalmente nadie lo hace. Esquiva los genitales —esto incrementa la tensión: ambos sabéis cómo termina la cosa, pero haz que dure, prolonga el momento—. Como «coser» podemos hacerlo todos, esto de confeccionar pijamas va también por vosotras.

ESAS IMPERDONABLES CAGADAS REALIZANDO SEXO ORAL...

Muchos alegan desde mal olor a miedo a asfixiarse... Si no quieres hacerlo no lo hagas pero, ¿has analizado por qué no te gusta?

En efecto, la falta de higiene es el n.º 1 de la lista en ambos sexos. Ante ello, puedes poner una espléndida sonrisa y llevar a tu pareja de la mano hasta el baño, jugar con sus genitales y un chorro de jabón que hará de lubricante —no es el más adecuado, pero...— y resolverlo por ti mismo/a.

A muchas les entra paranoia imaginando que se van a ahogar. Nada más fácil que meterla ladeada, en vez de recta hasta la garganta. Hay que evitar que nos dé contra la campanilla, porque provocaría arcadas y a él le parecerá que vomitas por el hecho de chupársela, lo que afectará mucho a vuestra química, y no para bien... Además, si cierras la boca involuntariamente, puedes ser la Lorena Bobitt de tu edificio; para evitar actos reflejos con posible resultado dramático, introduce el pene poco a poco, con movimientos lentos, permite a tu boca y garganta familiarizarse con la forma de él.

Otros errores: el empleo de dientes —aunque sea por accidente—, como acabo de apuntar; los arañazos de uñas mal cortadas o astilladas, padrastros, etc.; las raspaduras de barba incipiente nos destrozan los labios (los de la cara también).

Y ahora, vamos con «las demás cagadas».

Para él

Decir que huele mal. Habida cuenta que ella se ha lavado y que no tenga ninguna enfermedad o infección, el flujo vaginal no sólo no huele mal, sino que a la mayoría de los hombres les agrada y les resulta verdaderamente afrodisíaco. Si no quieres hacerlo, no pasa nada, pero no te extrañes de que te sustituya por otro amante en cuanto pueda.

No hacerlo durante el tiempo suficiente. Ya se ha hecho referencia a la enorme diferencia entre los tiempos de estimulación necesarios para que el hombre y la mujer se exciten. Si te pones a ello, cuenta con que quizá te lleve un rato, colócate lo más cómodo que puedas —entre sus piernas, tumbado boca abajo; o arrodillado en el suelo cuando ella se queda justo al borde de la cama— y, del modo que prefieras —con una frase más o menos tranquilizadora o amable—, hazle saber que a ti también te gusta, que la encuentras muy hermosa, lo que sea... Y haz que note que puede tomarse todo el tiempo que necesite. Parecerá una tontería pero basta escuchar algo así, para que tardemos menos.

Detenerse justo en el momento crucial. Cuando una mujer tiene un orgasmo mediante el cunnilingus no debes detenerte hasta que ella te lo diga, y estate seguro de que lo hará, porque en ese instante el clítoris se vuelve tan sensible que ella sentirá un «no puedo más» —generalmente después de la última contracción—, y se cubrirá con la mano, o te retirará la cara.

Falta de puntería. Parece un chiste pero, en efecto, en determinadas posiciones la visibilidad no es la mejor, además puedes estar maniobrando en la oscuridad y probablemente tu chica no te diga nada de nada, hasta que de pronto, te percatas de que te estás comiendo la colcha. Asúmelo, en esto, estás solo, es un hecho. Pues aun así, date cuenta de qué es lo que te estás metiendo en la boca y por dónde mueves la lengua... Además de reconocer y localizar dónde está cada «cosa» (clítoris, clítoris, clítoris), puedes ayudarte con las yemas de los dedos, ir situándote poco a poco —orificio de entrada a la vagina abajo (a las seis *o'clock*), labios menores alrededor, clítoris arriba, a las doce en punto, etc.—, pero, por favor, ¡no te tires tres cuartos de hora chupando lo que no es!

Ser demasiado brusco. La lengua puede aplicarse con mayor o menor fuerza. Si comienzas a chupar y lamer como un salvaje, o se te ocurre dejar que tus dientes entren en juego, por mucho que la intención sea buena y que la pasión te invada, en ocasiones puedes hacerle daño. Vete de menos a más —siento repetirlo tantas veces—, pero cuidado no sea que esos gemidos que oyes, sean de puro dolor.

Cambiar de ritmo o de movimiento. La perseverancia es la clave. Puede que elijas un tipo de caricia que no sea su favorito ni el *top ten* de los «sexpertos», pero si lo mantienes durante unos minutos —misma presión y velocidad constante—, terminará corriéndose. ¿Qué sientes si, mientras escalas, casi a punto de culminar la cima de la montaña, te cortan la cuerda? Pues que te caes al suelo, ¿no? Esto es lo mismo, no hay peor faena. Tiempo es el mejor regalo que puedes hacerle a una mujer.

Imponer la felación. Si ella es reacia a la felación, a veces, todo radica en ganar confianza —puede que en la siguiente ocasión que estéis juntos quiera hacerlo— y, para disfrutarlo, esto sí que es cuestión de práctica. Como decía antes, no debes agarrarla de la cabeza y conducirla por la fuerza o si ya está ahí, clavársela. Sí es cierto que hay un matiz que diferencia entre «comerse una polla» y «follarse una boca», y si a ella le va, pues adelante. Aquí sólo una precaución: si el movimiento de mete-saca en la boca se descontrola, puede cortarte con los dientes en tu miembro más preciado. Se dice que hay mujeres que incluso alcanzan el orgasmo haciéndolo... aunque no he tenido el gusto de conocer a ninguna.

Para ella

No querer hacerlo o actuar como si fuera un gran favor. Recuerda, querida: esto es sexo, no caridad. Por embobado que esté un tipo o por egoísta que sea, no hay mayor bajón para él que darse cuenta de que se lo hacen sin ganas o por cumplir. Además, salvo que seas una profesional —y esta parte del libro no va de eso—, lo que transmite alguien desde el rechazo resulta tan negativo que es antierótico. No vayas de víctima porque seguro que cosas peores te habrás metido en la boca. Leí en un libro de sexualidad —en general fantástico— algo que me pareció sin duda su peor frase. Proponía a las chicas que no sabían hacer una mamada que probaran con calabacines «o con un chico que no os guste demasiado». Jamás diré algo parecido, no soy tan moderna, ni tan imbécil (creo). No puedes ir por ahí comiéndote pollas al tuntún. Tienes derecho a ser escrupulosa —eso sí: no esperes que a ti sí te lo hagan si tú no bajas del cuello—. Y si el motivo por el que lo rechazas obedece a tu falta de experiencia, es preferible que admitas que no sabes cómo hacerlo. Probablemente le dará hasta morbo enseñarte y, si lo piensas, antes has hecho y aprendido cosas muchísimo más difíciles.

Morder o ser demasiado brusca. Ídem que ellos. No se trata de chupar una piruleta ni tampoco de intentar absorberle el alma a través de la uretra. A ellos les encanta el sexo oral. Verte ahí, con tu cara cerca de su pene y con la intención de lamerlo o metértelo en la boca, basta para ponerles a mil; con eso ya tienes mucho ganado. Si encima te lo curras un poco... No debes echar la piel del prepucio hacia atrás con tirones ni apretar demasiado fuerte, por mucho que te excite ver cómo ha aumentado de tamaño y lo dura que se ha puesto, recuerda que es parte de un cuerpo, y si la agarras como si fuera el mango de una sartén, puedes lastimarle de verdad.

Tragar o no tragar, he ahí la cuestión

Que la composición del esperma sea fundamentalmente proteínas, enzimas, ácido cítrico, ácido ascórbico, sustancias alcalinas y minerales (zinc, hierro), fructosa, etc., no implica que se imponga su uso alimenticio... Muchos utilizan este argumento para persuadir a la pareja a que se lo trague. Cuando esto se plantea, y el tipo insiste, el mejor argumento es proponerle que se coma él su propio esperma, mojando galletas o untándolo en una rebanada de pan, a ver qué cara pone. Si estuviera tan rico lo añadirían en los alimentos envasados con la advertencia de: «con el 20 % de la dosis diaria de esperma recomendada por Sanidad» o lo venderían en botellas, ¿no? Sentir repugnancia es lo más frecuente y deberían respetarlo: a ellos, en su placer, en su orgasmo, no les afecta en absoluto que tú tragues, escupas o te retires.

Aquí, además, cabe hacer varias consideraciones: la primera es que el asunto de que «es muy nutritivo» no es aceptable. Si alguien nota que su pareja está medio desnutrida, debería ofrecerle un filete, pero no agarrarla por las orejas y obligarla a algo que, si bien para muchas puede ser excitante, para tantas otras es repulsivo; se trata de algo muy subjetivo y con una elevada carga emocional.

Y dicho todo esto, lo que se debe tener es un poco de sentido común y, fundamentalmente, respeto. Una sexualidad bien canalizada implica respetar al otro tanto como a ti. El semen —aunque no te guste—, tendrá un sabor u otro según lo que él haya comido ese día o durante las horas previas. Si él no tiene una ITS o una ETS, no es venenoso, ni explosivo, ni corrosivo, así que no procede poner cara de asco, y además, normalmente, en el sexo se intercambian fluidos: ¿te pones como una histérica si empieza a sudar? O ¿cómo te sentirías tú si él se limpiara tu saliva o tu flujo con un algodón mojado en alcohol? Puedes permitir que eyacule sobre ti, en el escote, sobre el vientre (las descargas faciales, tan de peli porno, a nosotras nos espantan porque estropean el maquillaje, y además se pueden meter en el ojo, irritándolo). Lo ideal sería comportarse con naturalidad, porque eyacular lo es. Cuando lo haga, utilizad pañuelos de papel o toallitas higiénicas y a otra cosa. Si tragas, recuerda que te la juegas: el semen es uno de los mejores vehículos para la transmisión de sida y contagio de ETS.

4

El orgasmo: clases, fases y demás

CLASES

En el hombre se da un único tipo de orgasmo que suele ir acompañado de la eyaculación, aunque mediante técnicas de control se puede disociar y que el orgasmo se produzca sin expulsión de líquido seminal. Tanto en el hombre como en la mujer se producen en la zona sacra de la médula espinal. Kinsey y Miriam Stoppard,[9] ambos sexólogos de renombre, mantienen que en el hombre la eyaculación y el orgasmo son procesos independientes y separados, que pueden suceder uno sin la otra y viceversa.

Por otro lado, dado que en el hombre, durante una misma sesión amatoria, se pueden dar una segunda, tercera y ulteriores eyaculaciones —respetando siempre el período refractario o de «recuperación»—, es posible que la cantidad de semen expulsada en cada una sea progresivamente más escasa o incluso nula, sin que ello afecte ni al placer ni al orgasmo.

Acerca de las clases de orgasmo femenino se encuentran diversas opiniones y teorías. El otro día leía que hay orgasmos de tres clases: clitoridianos, vaginales (con punto G o de fondo de la vagina) y vulvares (que, entre otras cosas, explican que muchas refieran orgasmos con estimulación del monte de Venus, o del perineo y la penetración anal).

Otra clasificación aludía a otra clase, la del orgasmo mixto: mezcla del clitoridiano y del vaginal.

9. *The Magic of Sex*, Miriam Stoppard, Allen & Unwin, 1991.

Una mujer puede tener de los tres tipos, de dos o de uno en cada encuentro, según la pareja, según el día o según su etapa de maduración sexual, y evolucionar de ser vaginal a clitoridiana o viceversa, a lo largo de los meses o años e incluso, durante un mismo día. Quizá resulta incorrecto afirmar que la mujer tiene, o puede tener, varios tipos de orgasmo (dos o tres, según las distintas teorías). Tras las investigaciones de Masters y su compañera Johnson, parece más exacto afirmar que orgasmos sólo hay de un tipo, con independencia de qué órgano se estimula para que se desencadene (clítoris, vagina, cérvix), y que quizás el número de contracciones que se experimenta varíe: tres fuertes en caso de un orgasmo alcanzado con sexo oral, diez o doce menos intensas si se trata de masturbación por sí misma.

FASES

Masters y Johnson, de la Universidad de San Luis, diferenciaron 4 fases en el orgasmo: la de deseo y excitación, meseta, orgasmo y resolución, con las que arrojan conclusiones acerca de las reacciones físicas del cuerpo humano durante la relación sexual.

Deseo y excitación

Todo comienza (y termina) con ella. Las personas nos excitamos por cualquiera de los cinco sentidos (y por el sexto, la mayoría de las veces, también). Radica en el hipotálamo, órgano que centraliza la búsqueda de satisfacción del apetito sexual, así como también nos lleva a alimentarnos, a movernos y a sobrevivir por encima del otro (competitividad).

La lista de motivos inspiradores de algo tan etéreo podría ser interminable. Los estímulos son desde sutiles como una mirada o un perfume, a tan burdos como un plano de coprofilia. Todos indefectiblemente abocados a perder su efectividad: con el tiempo, eso que tanto nos ponía ya no lo hace. De ahí que la vida de muchos se convierta en una especie de comecocos, en una partida en la que persiguen incansables las frutas para engullirlas y puntuar, y pasar corriendo a la siguiente.

Hasta lo más *sexy* tiene fecha de caducidad: incluso esas chicas Playboy, esas conejitas todo *glamour* y exuberancia terminan cansando a quien, en su día, no podía creer que se estuviera tirando a semejante diosa, a la del póster, a la rubia de 115 de contorno de pecho, que le ponía a cien con sólo pensar en ella... Y lo propio para nosotras, tanto si estábamos con un Brad Pitt como si era un «normalito, pero muy gracioso»: o cambia el repertorio de chistes o... Y con los tigres en la cama ídem: da igual que la relación sexual no pueda ser mejor que, pasados unos meses —en torno al año como mucho—, ya habréis hecho todo, o probado todo —dentro de los límites de cada uno—; la cosa se agota. Ahí, ya se sabe: o existe algo más que una a esas personas o...

Si bien los efectos físicos de la excitación tanto en el hombre (el pene se va endureciendo, aumenta de tamaño hasta alcanzar la erección) como en la mujer (que comienza a lubricar y la vagina se hincha) se conocen, cuando nos movemos hacia el terreno de las causas, la ciencia no ha logrado sentar cátedra acerca de qué o con qué se excita más cada uno de los géneros. En general, se afirma que ellos se excitan a través de la visión de imágenes, algo que se ve respaldado por la más esplendorosa expansión de la industria de contenidos para adultos: la contemplación de revistas y películas eróticas y pornográficas suele ser una de las formas habituales de «ponerse a tono». De la mujer se dice que se excita por los demás sentidos, en especial, el del oído, por ello, muchos señores no especialmente agraciados, optan a mujeres espectaculares, porque les hacen reír, porque saben comprenderlas, etc., (oído); o porque son amantes estupendos, dan unos masajes increíbles... (tacto).

No me atrevo a generalizar porque me consta que hay personas que reúnen quizá lo peor de cada sexo, y a quienes las grandes pasiones se las trae la visión de una buena tableta de chocolate sobre la zona abdominal, unos labios carnosos, un par de pectorales partidos y las hendiduras de desafiantes oblicuos —algo visual, como se generaliza acerca de la excitación masculina—. Una amiga mía que trabaja en el mundo de la moda me comentaba que admitía que si no fuera porque ha madurado seguiría en ese plan. Me decía recientemente: «debo de haberme hecho mayor porque ahora llego a un *set* y a quien me quiero tirar ya no es al modelo, sino al fotógrafo, lo que no implica, en absoluto, que me haya quedado ciega de la noche a la mañana... Lo digo en serio, no hace tanto que yo durante una sesión ni habría detectado al fotógrafo... Él habría quedado eclipsado por los destellos de los dientes perfectos del modelo... Y repito que nadie sabe cómo me gustan a mí unos buenos brazos y ¡la de tonterías que habré escuchado a verdaderos idiotas, eso sí, dueños de una carrocería que..!». Y su confesión continuaba en la dirección de que quizás el sentido común nos va agudizando el oído y nos permite valorar las ideas interesantes y mantener conversaciones apasionantes con alguien que para subsistir utiliza más el cerebro que los bíceps. Lo malo es que, en realidad, lejos de ser una evolución, o un paso hacia la sensatez «yo creo que desde que dejas de ser literalmente incapaz de enamorarte de alguien estrictamente por su gran físico, lo que sucede es que sufres por partida doble: te encuentras intentando encajar las particularidades de los que ejercen de "guapos" y bregando con las de los "normales pero interesantes"..., que se las traen también». Algo de razón sí que tiene.

Estábamos con el asunto de lo que nos excita. Entrando en materia, cuando alguien nos gusta hay mil cosas que nos encienden: desde encontrarnos una mirada cargada de cierta intención, a asomar la vista por un canalillo o recibir una sonrisa... Y, por supuesto, besar, acariciar, escuchar algo al oído, que nos toquen por la espalda o nos enganchen de la cintura, que nos desvistan, que nos den un masaje, que nos aprisionen «sin escapatoria» en un ascensor o en la penumbra de un estrecho pasillo...

Ahora, en cuanto a los tiempos. Aquí sí que se produce divergencia. No sé dónde leí que una mujer precisa casi todo un día para alcanzar la misma excitación que un hombre en unos catorce segundos... No es un chiste. Nuestros cuerpos son distintos y por tanto, también sus reacciones. Me explico: si eres un chico y lo que te apetece es que cuando entres por la puerta de casa ella te devore vivo sin mediar palabra, entonces, querido, has de hacer los deberes. La tecnología nos permite estar conectados (mándale un sms fuertecito, llámala desde el cuarto de baño de la oficina y explícale con pelos y señales lo que planeas hacerle o escríbele un e-mail con lo que le espera por la noche). Mira bien que no estoy hablando de enviarle flores ni bombones, ni de llevarla a cenar a sitios caros... Basta de tópicos. Pasad página, que nosotras ya lo hemos hecho (ojo, que todo lo enumerado es estupendo, pero la pasión también se puede provocar...). Sabed que la mente femenina es muy sensible a ciertas insinuaciones (y si ya no son insinuaciones, sino un relato erótico del que encima te hacen protagonista...). Ya os adelantaba lo del oído. Si un tío te cuenta por teléfono, con ciertos detalles calentorros, lo que te quiere hacer o que le hagas tú, ya tienes cuerda para fantasear el resto del día (quiero creer que la cara de boba que tiene más de una en las reuniones se debe a que ocupa su mente en prepararse para la noche). Las hay que son muy educadas, de verdad, de esas mujeres incapaces de blasfemar o de hablar de sexo... bueno, pues hasta con ellas, si lo haces como juego privado, funciona. Pide por esa boquita: ¿que quieres que te espere ya desnuda sobre la cama?, pues dilo, y sé coherente cuando aparezcas, no vayas a dejártela allí, olvidada, porque el partido de fútbol acaba de empezar... Dudo que te perdone. O si no es el fútbol, pues no descuides ciertos detalles que son condición sine qua non: aséate. No sé si habrá una regla que sintetice lo crucial que es la higiene para el sexo. Cuando a las tías nos quieren martirizar con lo de adelgazar, respecto de los bombones nos recuerdan: cinco segundos en tu boca y cinco años en tus caderas, o una gilipollez por el estilo. Pues aquí, dadle la vuelta: cinco minutos de agua y jabón y una hora entera en la boca. No doy más pistas innecesarias, que este libro es para gente adulta. Igual en este tema peco de pesada, pero es que mil veces que lo escribiera serían pocas. El olor y el sabor de tu pareja son lo que más nos puede poner, pero los «atrasos» sólo los agradecen los agentes del CSI... No hay peor sensación que acercarse al sexo de alguien y que apeste a pis, a esmegma o a cosas peores.

Continuando con los tempos, ahora de la relación, las velocidades de unas y otros siguen siendo inversas. Apunta el Kamasutra: «Cuando se produce una primera relación entre un hombre y una mujer, la pasión de éste será intensa, desbordada y, por tanto, corto, muy corto, el tiempo que emplea; pero en las uniones subsiguientes del mismo día, ocurre de modo diferente, ocurre, sencillamente, lo contrario. También ocurre lo contrario en la mujer, ya que, la primera vez su pasión es débil y el tiempo empleado es largo, quizá muy largo; pero en las repeticiones del mismo día, su pasión se vuelve intensa y el tiempo corto, hasta que quede plenamente satisfecha.»

¿Y si eso de «estimularte» no resulta tan fácil? La mayoría de las personas atravesamos fases de mucho apetito sexual seguidas de otras en que nos cuesta más ponernos. El sexo es de esas cosas que cuanto más se ejercitan más fácilmente fluyen y también rige eso de «deja el sexo tres meses que él te dejará tres años». Considéralo como un juego y pon en práctica estas sugerencias. Alguna se adaptará a tu necesidad puntual, otras ni se te ocurriría... El sexo tampoco ha de ser dramático ni tan trascendental... Erotizarnos consiste en permitir que sucedan situaciones (aunque muchas sean secretas o no salgan de dentro de tu cerebro). No te cohíbas cuando, por ejemplo, te pongas a imaginar cómo se lo montará Fulano, ese de la oficina que te pone a mil con sólo cruzarte con él ante la fotocopiadora. No te quedes en el traje o en las «zapas», arriesga un poco, ve más lejos y crea la situación con él: fantasea, invéntate la película a tu gusto. Desde cómo te va a llevar a su casa y cómo la tiene decorada, a cómo crees que te quitará el sujetador, o si será de los que grita cuando se corre. A muchas mujeres nos cuesta «soltar» la imaginación. Tranquilidad: nadie puede leer la mente, y encima, soñar es gratis.

Cuando te asalta esa especie de etapa muermo teniendo una pareja, no permitas que la situación se prolongue. Más vale echar leña de más que encontrarte con que vuestro fuego se ha apagado. Esfuérzate un poco, hay un abanico enorme de medidas preventivas y hasta cautelares. Desde disfraces a juegos donde representáis cada uno un papel, a dejarle sin habla con tu nuevo corsé de cuero, o buscar localizaciones nuevas (valen la casa de amigos que estén de viaje, sitios públicos, hoteles, rincones de la casa aún sin explorar...). Buscar las novedades y documentación sobre juguetitos para adultos me llevó a visitar personalmente bastantes *sex shops*. Comprobar que muchos dan hasta asco y saber que a día de hoy muchas provincias carecen de este tipo de establecimientos, me llevó a montar en mi página web una *boutique* erótica. Por más que te digan que «está de moda llevar un vibrador en el bolso» no es cierto. A muchísimas personas aún les da reparo o no tienen tiempo para «ir de *sex shops*». Quien se anime a experimentar, que sepa que puede comprar de todo por Internet: desde lubricantes —si nunca los has utilizado, verás qué cambio con sólo echarte unas gotas y masturbarte/le como siempre... Sólo es un ejemplo—, o aceites que desprenden unos olores que te transportan (a nadie le desagrada que le reciban y le dediquen ciertas caricias y masajes con productos que huelen de maravilla, y que además, algunos son comestibles...), puedes probar qué tal se integra en la pareja un dildo, con o sin vibración —los hay para vagina, para ano y especiales para ellos: los que estimulan la zona de la próstata—. La lista de opciones se extiende mucho.

En tus ratos libres puedes dedicarte a ti, a tu cuerpo, a irlo despertando. Cuídate un poco: depílate, date algún masaje o tratamiento de belleza, cómprate lencería provocativa que te permita sentirte femenina y sexy también por dentro...

Por si alguien se siente molesto ante el recordatorio de ponerse «guapa», por aquello de que una mujer es más que su imagen, puntualizaré varios detalles. Que el mensaje feminista no se pierde por lucir unas piernas depiladas y tampoco llevar pelambreras de gorila en las axilas ha ayudado a que los derechos de la mujer se consigan más fácilmente. Hace años que, con los manifiestos y protestas políticos acerca de la libertad y la igualdad, se quemaron sujetadores y se reivindicó la «naturalidad» de la mujer. Hoy, aquellas mujeres que tanto lograron, que abrieron una puerta a nuestro estatus, comprenderían que en estos tiempos un poco de maquillaje o unos cuidados —aparte de la fundamental higiene— no implican renuncia a los derechos sino que denotan abandono y demuestran pereza y dejadez. Depilarse o no hoy carece de trasfondo político.

Y respecto de la mente, para mantener la conciencia erótica se recomienda activar tu parte creativa. No necesitas pretensiones de exponer en una galería, ni de que te publiquen en revistas o ser la autora de un *best seller* para volcar tus fantasías eróticas en dibujos, fotografías (tú misma puedes ser la modelo) o escribir las fantasías eróticas que querrías ver cumplidas en un cuaderno o en un blog (puedes utilizar un seudónimo). Si le involucras a él, podéis desde ver películas eróticas o porno, a grabaros a vosotros mismos en la intimidad. Sobre esta «moda» de grabarse y los riesgos que conlleva que la peripecia «aparezca» en Internet, publiqué un texto al que muchos lectores añadieron su experiencia y opiniones.

La excitación produce distintos efectos físicos dependiendo del sexo. Como dije antes, en la mujer, la vagina comienza a lubricarse y a hincharse. Ello se explica porque la sangre empieza a dirigirse hacia la zona pélvica, a la vulva. En el hombre, la respuesta física más evidente se produce en el pene, que va aumentando de tamaño, endureciéndose, hasta alcanzar una erección, que ulteriormente será imprescindible para acometer la penetración. Como curiosidad, el grado de erección del pene determina la clasificación de los contenidos para adultos: si en la imagen —foto, película, etc.— está erecto se denominará «pornográfico» o *hard*, si no, quedará como *soft* o erótico. A lo largo del pene hay dos cuerpos cavernosos o cámaras, compuestas de tejido esponjoso que ayuda a atrapar la sangre, reteniéndola y sosteniendo la erección.

Resultado de la secreción de oxitocina, del frío o de la excitación sexual los pezones, en ambos, se ponen erectos. Se produce por la contracción de músculos, no porque sea tejido eréctil.

Meseta

Puede que suene a lección de geografía y, realmente, si te acuerdas de lo que era la meseta, será muy gráfico. Es una altiplanicie (o sea, una vez que has despegado del nivel del mar, te estabilizas) en la curva descrita por la evolución de la respuesta sexual.

En la mujer la fase de meseta se prolonga más, acercándose al orgasmo de forma más lenta y paulatina que el varón. En este punto conviene recordar que para que se alcance el orgasmo, en esta fase no debe interrumpirse la estimulación del clítoris ni variar el ritmo que se estuviera empleando. Físicamente, la lubricación, que se inicia en la primera fase, al medio minuto aproximadamente de recibirse los primeros estímulos, continúa; los labios mayores se separan, los menores y el clítoris se hinchan, aumentando de tamaño, las paredes de la vagina se dilatan —ello, junto a la lubricación, facilitará la penetración—, la excitación irá en aumento.

La respuesta del hombre en la fase de meseta sigue siendo la erección. Durante la fase de excitación se cierra la salida venosa del pene; y ahora continúa cerrada manteniendo la sangre retenida posibilitando su crecimiento y endurecimiento progresivo. Puede que se acompañe de cierta segregación de un líquido claro preeyaculatorio proveniente de las glándulas de Cowper, susceptible de causar un embarazo porque contiene espermatozoides aunque en un porcentaje muy bajo.

Tanto en hombres como en mujeres suele producirse también aceleración del ritmo cardíaco, respiración entrecortada, aumento de la tensión muscular y ascenso de la temperatura corporal (lo de «estoy muy caliente» o «qué caliente me pones» va al hilo de esto). En la mujer, los pechos crecen, las areolas se contraen, el clítoris se «esconde» quedando recubierto por el capuchón o membrana que lo recubre, la vagina se dilata y se potencian los efectos de la fase de excitación: separación de labios mayores, aumento de los menores por la acumulación de sangre —congestión—. Otra reacción típica se denomina «rubor sexual», que se manifiesta con un enrojecimiento de la cara y del pecho y escote, que denota la mayor intensidad de la circulación sanguínea.

Si se prosigue con la estimulación se desembocaría en la siguiente fase, la del orgasmo. Sin embargo, de verse interrumpida sucede el famoso «dolor de huevos» masculino que equivale a la no tan reivindicada sensación de congestión de la zona genital y ansiedad femeninas (sería un «dolor de labios»). Y como ha salido el tema del dolor de huevos, diré que, en efecto, sí duelen. Se debe a que con la excitación el esperma ha salido de los mismísimos y se halla en mitad de ninguna parte, dado que el final feliz no se ha producido y no ha salido del pene. Esta congestión se une a la que ya había sufrido el pene, por la afluencia de sangre que hizo que se pusiera en erección y que, como no recibe la señal del cerebro de retirarse (recuerda: no ha habido eyaculación), pues se queda ahí durante más tiempo de lo deseable. Y por eso duele. Remite al rato, cuando la sangre se evacúa. Alivia que te frotes un poco los testículos. Ah, y a nosotras, cuando nos dejan a medias, pues o terminar solas o pedir una pizza, a ver si el que la trae sabe lo que se hace.

La meseta es una etapa durante la que se experimentan sensaciones eróticas muy placenteras y satisfactorias. Es cuando se practican los besos más profundos, el sexo oral, las caricias masturbatorias...

Orgasmo

En esta fase lo que sucede es que todo lo anteriormente señalado se precipita: las pulsaciones no pueden subir más, la respiración tampoco puede ser más intensa, ni más frecuente, y aparece la sensación de «no puedo más».

Si la trayectoria de la excitación es ascendente culmina en el orgasmo, con la descarga repentina de una enorme tensión muscular y contracciones en la zona ano-genital. Alcanzado determinado nivel de estimulación en el varón se produce la «fase de no retorno», donde la eyaculación se producirá de modo inminente, sí o sí, aunque cesara el estímulo (en esto somos diferentes. Si en una mujer desaparece la estimulación o se interrumpe, ella, aunque continúe excitada, perderá la respuesta orgásmica). De no ser así, igualmente alcanzará el orgasmo que en ocasiones —cuando el punto G se ve involucrado—, puede ir acompañado de una eyaculación, asemejándose al del hombre.[10]

Esta sobredosis de placer provoca reacciones distintas en cada persona, tanto a nivel físico como emocional. Aunque en la relación esté presente otra persona, u otras, en realidad el orgasmo es un momento que disfrutamos en solitario. Durante esos instantes nos olvidamos del otro, cabría traer a colación la palabra «egoísmo» —que nada tiene que ver con que no queramos a la pareja—. Es así: dejamos de preocuparnos por el otro —si es que lo hacíamos— y por todo lo que no sea dejarse llevar y que el placer nos inunde, para centrarnos en esas sensaciones y reacciones que tienen lugar en nuestro cuerpo, para pasar a no controlar ni siquiera eso. Lo mundano, lo divino, lo racional, todo, queda muy lejos en ese instante. Para alcanzar el clímax se requiere cortar cualquier conexión con el planeta Tierra. ¿Cuántas veces se escucha eso de «tienes que desconectar» o «relájate»? Más importante que dominar las posiciones del Kamasutra y que conocer las reacciones físicas de la pareja, es «estar en lo que se está»: sin interferencias, olvidando por un rato las preocupaciones, los problemas, y también al otro, sí, dejando de controlar si está bien o mal, si le gusta o no... Cuando el

10. La eyaculación femenina es un asunto que se aborda en el apartado de la «Masturbación femenina».

orgasmo está por desencadenarse, has de ir a lo tuyo, sin cohibirte por lo que demuestres (gritos, jadeos, caras de gozo...) y permitiéndote ese viaje destino al placer.

Pero, ¿qué les gusta a ellos y qué a ellas durante el orgasmo? La tendencia natural de casi todos es creer que justo cuando se tiene el orgasmo hay que dar más caña. Si estás haciéndolo con la mano, a muchas nos da por intensificar el ritmo olvidando que se trata de un pene, no de la palanca de cambio de marcha del coche, o a ellos, por apretar más, como si agarrasen una pelota de la bolera; y con la boca, pues ídem: la que no se retira a veces devora a su compañero o ellos, emocionados, van y le pegan un mordisco ahí mismo... No, no y no. Cada persona es distinta y debes saber lo que al otro le gusta, porque sus necesidades no necesariamente coinciden con las de tu última pareja ni con las tuyas. Pregunta, pídele que te lo cuente; muchas personas ni siquiera sabrán qué contestar. Eso es lo normal, que no hayamos dedicado tiempo a analizar este tipo de detalles: «¿Que si mientras me corro prefiero que te quedes quieto o que me abraces?» Hay mujeres que durante el orgasmo se callan, se quedan como muertas, se aíslan y no precisan del otro. A otras, justo en el momento de las contracciones lo que les pide el cuerpo es que las penetren con más fuerza o que las abracen con pasión, pero que su pareja se quede muy quieto mientras siguen besándolas. Otras gritan y quieren que las sigan moviendo, agarrándolas de las caderas...

Y ellos igual. Cuando veas que se congestionan, que las venas del cuello y de la cara se han hinchado, que se enrojecen, que casi no respiran, que literalmente parece que van a explotar, es que están «llegando». A cada uno le gusta una cosa, aunque la mayoría suele preferir que, en el último instante, tú no hagas «nada»: deja que se muevan ellos, o si se trata de una masturbación manual, es mejor que te ahorres este «toque final» que les molesta más que agrada. No acaricies el glande inmediatamente después de que eyaculen, se encuentra hipersensible. Notarás que el pene empieza a deshincharse, que va perdiendo la erección, ablandándose. Si sientes que te apetece tocarle, juega con los alrededores, pero suavemente. Él puede seguir, sí, pero dale un respiro.

Fase de resolución

Por ello, al terminar la respuesta orgásmica, cada cual precisa retornar al mundo de los vivos a su ritmo. Hay a quienes les da por reírse, o por saltar a la ducha con urgencia, o por quedarse dormidos o sumidos en un mutismo entre trascendental y filosófico. Otros necesitan ternura y requieren volver a conectar con la pareja y restablecen el vínculo afectivo mediante besos, abrazos y caricias. Mientras se descansa pueden regalarse maravillosos momentos de sensualidad. Pese a que las mujeres hoy día se acuestan con quien les da la gana simplemente por pasarlo bien, por morbo o para desahogarse, no deja de ser cierto que a muchas chicas les resulta vital que en ese instante pospolvo, les demuestren que todos los actos previos a la penetración obedecían a algo más que una estrategia para follárselas. Saber estar y demostrar ciertos modales no implica declarar amor, ni propósito de engendrar hijos ni de montar una vida en común. Como ejemplos de «urbanidad» sexual (léase, protocolo muy apreciado) se encuentra enviar al ratito o al día siguiente un sms, tan socorrido y tan interesante recurso para quienes no osan dar la cara o no están interesados en «nada más», o bajar hasta la calle a pedirle un taxi (si llevarla a casa resulta una gesta de todo punto inviable) o, al menos levantarse de la cama y acompañarla hasta la puerta y despedirte de un modo afectuoso. No te creas que ella te ama porque se haya corrido entre tus brazos. No, querido, esto no va así. Puede que ambos estéis de acuerdo en volver a veros pronto, o en no repetirlo nunca jamás, pero tratar al otro como a un ser humano y no como a un desecho tampoco es tan complicado.

En este momento del posorgasmo, según estén los ánimos, y considerando que ni todos los días apetece lo mismo ni necesariamente a las dos personas les pedirá el cuerpo dormir, cabe que siga la fiesta. En realidad el sexo provoca tensión, nos activa, pese a que momentáneamente colisione con ese abandono temporal que sobreviene tras el clímax. Tanto el hombre como la mujer pueden alcanzar más de un orgasmo, por lo que es posible reanudar la excitación. Basta, como ya se ha comentado, aguardar un tiempo para que él tenga otra erección; el período refractario, variable en cada hombre en función de su edad, estado de salud y excitación que le provoque la pareja o la situación, puede tardar cinco minutos o varias horas. La mujer, por su parte, es muy posible que desee continuar, aunque haya tenido un orgasmo, y si no, con mayor motivo. Para ella la eyaculación del hombre, si se traduce como *GAME OVER* de la relación —que, insisto, va más allá del coito— es posible que le repatee si la deja a medias y, de no ser así, quizás algo contrariada o frustrada pensando «¡lástima que se acabe, ahora que esto se animaba!».

No es broma, el «después» en una relación es lo que puntúa. Un buen amante no te deja tirada una vez se corre. A otro nivel, el «post» resulta el gran momento de intimidad, pero también sucede que si lo único que existía era una atracción exclusivamente física, ese vacío se evidencia justo entonces.

Qué bien, ya se ha corrido él (o en el mejor de los casos, los dos), y ahora, ¿qué? ¿Quizá te apetece tomarte una copa con esa persona y charlar o te inventas una excusa y te largas; la abrazas y te duermes pegado a ella o, según acabas, te encierras en el despacho para seguir con lo «importante» o te das la vuelta y roncas antes de decir «hasta mañana»; o tal vez preferirías echar una cabezadita y jugar un segundo asalto o te quieres morir por lo que acabas de hacer, pero te esfuerzas por soltar un par de comentarios amables mientras recopilas tu ropa y te vistes para irte?... Por la mente de unas y otros se suceden miles de pensamientos de todo tipo. Parece paradójico pero, cinco minutos después de haber desarrollado una intimidad tan enorme como haberte metido los genitales de otro ser humano en tu boca sin ningún tipo de escrúpulo, se puede sentir una vaharada de asco y de rechazo hacia esa persona. No todas las relaciones son así, pero tampoco todas se producen en el seno de maravillosas parejas estables exultantes de amor, ternura, comprensión y adorables rutinas consensuadas. Sucede que tras una relación, te quedas frente a frente con un perfecto extraño. Ese abismo tan incómodo al percibir que se está en pelota picada con un desconocido, ese no encontrar tema de conversación que interese a ambos, esa barrera que de pronto se eleva demostrando que, a menudo, la química —en el sentido de descargas de hormonas sexuales— va por su cuenta y nos emborracha, decide por nosotros y nos lleva la mano (y todo lo demás). Por ello decía que la talla de un hombre y lo que busca y ve en ti se manifiesta en ese lapso de tiempo. Sin embargo, no pasemos por alto que, por bien que haya ido la cita, por cuarenta orgasmos simultáneos que hayamos disfrutado, por amena que sea la charla e innegable la atracción, no siempre podemos/queremos/procede quedarse a desayunar...

En el Kamasutra se hace patente la diferencia en las reacciones: «en el coito, en la unión sexual, los hombres se detienen por sí mismos después de la emisión, y quedan satisfechos, pero no ocurre así con las mujeres, que se sienten, por el contrario, insatisfechas, y esperan algo más del varón que naturalmente no se produce nunca o casi nunca». Vaya, que no es que lo diga yo...

Un par de consejillos más. A ellas: evitad comparaciones acerca de otros amantes. Comentarios tipo «él sí que se lo montaba bien» huelgan. Tampoco hagáis bromas acerca de su pene (tamaño, dureza, destreza...). Recordemos que para la mayoría su pene es ni más ni menos que su agente en la Tierra, una especie de mascota sofisticada, un ente con la personalidad de un niño tirano que piensa y decide en nombre del resto del cuerpo, le representa, le hace salir por la puerta grande o en camilla... Y a ellos pues, ídem: por supuesto, las ex también están muy bien donde están (es decir, lejos, en el vasto océano del anonimato). Por tendencia innata demostramos cierto grado de tendencia cotilla y también masoquismos: en serio, aunque insistamos y juremos que nos da lo mismo, estamos mejor desconociendo la talla de sujetador de otras, o si ciertas cosas las hacía o no, mejor o peor.

Otra cosa: aunque es de bien nacido ser agradecido, no hace falta que verbalices nada como «gracias por la mamada». Este tipo de reconocimiento no nos enorgullece escuchado de viva voz... Basta que mientras te la hace seas lo bastante elocuente con gestos o palabras que evidencian que te agrada —o que correspondas con lo propio en cuanto tengas un minuto— y que tu respeto por ella incluya avisarla del momento en que vas a eyacular para que decida libremente (y a tiempo) si se retira o no. Tampoco nos sube especialmente la moral que nos informen de detalles tipo «te cabe entera», puesto que, primero: estaba ahí presente para notarlo, ¿recuerdas?, y segundo: ¿es que a las demás no?[11]

Ni la duración del acto, ni la de la penetración —si es que se practica—, ni el número de orgasmos conseguidos, determinan si una relación ha sido de calidad. Será la actitud de las personas que participan en ella, cómo se demuestran con los cuerpos lo que necesitan transmitirse, lo que de veras se vuelve determinante. Como en casi todo: calidad —respeto, cariño, detalles, empatía, sentido del humor, higiene, generosidad— es mejor que cantidad —expresada en centímetros, en número de amantes, de polvos, de coitos, de reglas trasgredidas sin permiso, de muescas en la culata por corazones destrozados, de puntos finales escritos unilateralmente.

Creo haber mantenido mi propósito de no teñir este libro de cursilería ni de lenguaje que contaminara la esencia de la realidad en la que vivimos. Pocas alusiones hago a la compleja maraña de emociones y de sentimientos que se entreteje bajo las sábanas y, sin embargo, planeo sobre ellas y las detecto, como un halcón a sus presas. Me parecía justo y ecuánime hablar de sexo en general, aunque no fuera acompañado de amor, por eso he evitado, hasta ahora, la paráfrasis fatídica: «hacer el amor». Pues sí, ése es el truco para ser un buen amante (¿cómo se define un amante sino como aquel que ama?). Hacer el amor es tomarte el sexo como algo espiritual, especial, mágico... Hacer algo es crear, es construir... Tanto da que sea un castillo de arena que se lleva la primera ola... Te has dejado el alma durante ese rato, has disfrutado, te has reído, has compartido con los demás tu arquitectura efímera. Pues con el sexo debería ser

11. Muchas mujeres interpretarían este comentario, lo de que le entra sin problema, como que das por hecho que es promiscua o que en el fondo estás pensando que «te la han metido tantos que se ha dado de sí», lo cual resulta más que ofensivo. Tras esta «fácil» penetración, las posibilidades son varias: que él la tenga pequeña, con lo que la vagina se encuentra rodeando un apéndice que a lo mejor podría ser dos o tres veces más largo y más grueso (apuesto que querrías morirte si en ese instante ella te contestara: «llevas razón, es que estoy muy mal acostumbrada, cielo, perdona, es que como a mi ex le medía 27 cm...»; es posible también que ella esté superexcitada, y que sus paredes vaginales estén dilatadas y además, la lubricación sea abundante y facilite que el acceso sea sencillo; además, puede darse el caso de que ella tenga una vagina de esas holgadas, igual que las hay estrechas. Actualmente se practican intervenciones quirúrgicas para reducir el canal de la vagina. Se explica en el apartado sobre «Cirugía íntima femenina».

así. Muchas de las muestras de arte de la India y de China, pese a su antigüedad, merecen ser reivindicadas por su mensaje acerca de que el amor canaliza la energía, es una expresión divina y artística. Por ello, el propio lenguaje marca la distinción: tener sexo o mantener relaciones suenan a poseer algo o a alguien, van cargadas de cosificación, de egoísmo; mientras que hacer el amor se mantiene ajeno a esa connotación, y resulta mucho más hermoso (por ñoño que me suene a mí).

Multiorgasmia

El concepto de multiorgasmia no se interpreta de modo unívoco. Para unos consiste en obtener varios orgasmos dentro de una misma sesión. Otros, entienden que se trata de extender y prolongar la excitación y el placer de un orgasmo hasta que se desencadene el siguiente. Es imprescindible saber que las reacciones físicas del organismo del hombre y de la mujer justo tras un orgasmo son distintas. A ellos, el relax les invade de inmediato. La descarga física y de energía que acompaña a la eyaculación es tal que sienten sueño a los pocos minutos. A nosotras, el primer orgasmo nos cuesta más tiempo (la excitación hasta la meseta tarda más en producirse para la mujer, pero una vez allí, instaladas en ese maravilloso nivel de excitación, duramos más en él). Desencadenado el orgasmo femenino —fase de resolución— nuestras hormonas del sueño llegan a la media hora y, estando en ese altísimo nivel de excitación, si la estimulación se reanuda, no es nada complicado tener un segundo orgasmo, o más. ¿Cómo lo hace él? Si bien es improbable que pueda volver a eyacular de inmediato —el organismo necesita un período de recuperación para producir esperma—, sí es posible disociar la eyaculación del orgasmo masculino, son cosas distintas, aunque por los siglos de los siglos, todos creamos que son inseparables. Él también puede ser multiorgásmico: disfrutará, se excitará y tendrá un orgasmo «mental» —en el sentido de placentero—, pero tan físico como el primero —sólo que sin líquido—. Una técnica que evita la eyaculación pero no interfiere ni al orgasmo ni a su erección es la de presionar con la mano en la base del pene, sobre el perineo, justo cuando vaya a eyacular. Ello permite que prosiga con el coito y mantenga el mismo nivel de placer, pudiendo llegar a la fase reeyaculatoria cuantas veces quiera y reservando la descarga para el momento en que así lo desee. Este truco no sale a la primera, así que cuidadito.

Las enseñanzas tántricas plantean que él no eyacule. Proponen la unión de los cuerpos en sesiones amatorias que excluyen la pérdida de energía que conlleva la eyaculación. Ver el capítulo sobre «Sexo y espiritualidad».

Sinceramente, creo que soy más defensora de que la multiorgasmia es lo normal, lo natural en la mujer, más que de la anorgasmia (excepciones y patologías aparte), otra cosa es que no con todas las parejas se alcance el nivel de compenetración que la multiorgasmia requiere, eso que mencionaba de la química, de la confianza, de saber qué y cómo le gusta. Últimamente entiendo que el sexo es como un baile: el objetivo es que ambos bailen lo mismo cada vez, sea ballet o samba (parecería absurda la simple imagen de una bailarina esbelta vestida con tutú clásico y unas puntas de raso compartiendo el mismo escenario que alguien con un traje carioca de lentejuelas, tanga y bamboleo de glúteos).

Todas las mujeres son multiorgásmicas o podrían serlo. Que lo descubran o no es otro tema. A veces, semejante «regalo» se recibe de tu pareja —de alguna de ellas—; en otras está al alcance de tu mano —nunca mejor dicho—, y nos los proporcionamos masturbándonos.

Ten orgasmos tú sola

Cuando experimentas, compruebas que la sola estimulación del clítoris te lleva al orgasmo sin que haga falta penetración de ninguna clase —ni dedos, ni objetos, ni pene—. Si no llegas, no te obsesiones, date tiempo. Encuentra qué necesitas tú. Intenta distintas posturas: boca arriba, tumbada; de rodillas, inclinada hacia delante; con la mano, con almohada, con dildos; con piernas juntas o separadas; con mayor o menor presión sobre el monte de Venus; con el clítoris muy expuesto, sujetando con los dedos, hacia atrás, todo el capuchón; recorriendo la zona de la entrada de la vagina con movimientos lineales o en círculos sobre el clítoris; juntando fuertemente las piernas y friccionando... Llegarás. Primer orgasmo. Luego, ya excitada, puedes dejarte un breve descanso (período refractario, que en nosotras es de entre 30 segundos y unos minutos; más no, o perdemos la excitación), y abordar el punto G. Los orgasmos que se alcanzan son los más intensos, las contracciones de la vagina las más fuertes. Van dos y no nos hemos metido nada (bueno, los dedos o un juguete pero sólo unos centímetros, el punto G está en el tercio externo de la vagina: haciendo el gesto de llamar a alguien con los dedos índice y medio, lo tocas). Vamos por el tercero: con penetración (pene o juguete) hasta el fondo de la vagina. En este caso, suele ser necesario que, con la otra mano, estimules el clítoris.

Conste que casi es más complicado describirlo que hacerlo, y muchísimo menos placentero. Dicho así, parece que necesitas un siglo. No, no necesariamente. Hay días en que tú, chica lista, decides quererte un poco y puedes dedicarte un buen rato, ten en cuenta que tu vida sexual es tuya, pertenece a tu intimidad. Masturbarte, leer, irte de compras... hay momentos para todo. También puedes pasar de un orgasmo a otro a la velocidad que las cajeras del Día te gruñen si no metes todo en la bolsa en cero coma tres décimas de segundo..., o plantarte si con el primero te quedas a gusto. Estimularte y «correrte» rápido puede acostumbrar (educar) a tu cuerpo a reaccionar y adaptarse a los diferentes tempos de tu pareja sexual de carne y hueso.

Fingir o no fingir, he ahí la cuestión

Sobre el concreto asunto «¿fingen las mujeres sus orgasmos?» Una revista americana publicaba que, preguntados los hombres, un 40 % afirmaba que, en efecto, las mujeres habían fingido un orgasmo estando con ellos; otro 40 % decía no estar seguros; el 20 % juraba que jamás les había sucedido. La respuesta a la misma pregunta, formulada a las mujeres fue: el 92 % de las mujeres admitía haber fingido alguna vez en su vida un orgasmo.

Una vez leí: «Si empiezas a fingir que te diviertes, quizá lo consigas incidentalmente», y me inspiró bastantes pensamientos. Conste que, para variar, no estoy frivolizando ni utilizando la ironía... Se trata de una frase extraída de una película (es literal; quien quiera puede intentar adivinar quién la dijo y dónde) y me he dado cuenta de que, aplicada al campo de la sexualidad, podría funcionar, pese a que vaya frontalmente en contra de todos los argumentos publicados y defendidos (incluso por mí misma) en pro de la comunicación fluida y honesta en la pareja, de la importancia de explicar lo que te gusta de forma clara, etc. Hay ocasiones en que basta poner buena voluntad, predisponerte a disfrutar y a divertirte, incluso fingiendo un poquito, y en determinado momento, cuando te dejas llevar y desconectas de tensiones y de otras historias, te percatas de que hace rato que lo estás haciendo...

También leí que una eminente sexóloga, la doctora Janet Hall, animaba a las mujeres a fingir: *«fake it until you make it»* (finge hasta que lo consigas), basado en lo mismo: si finges algo que quieres que ocurra, quizás acabará sucediendo. En este asunto, Hall pretende que si una mujer lleva a cabo, de modo fingido, las reacciones físicas de acelerar su respiración, gemir, arquearse, etc., y se dispone en el mismo umbral que cuando el orgasmo sobreviene, lo alcanzará. Yo aquí, como decía más arriba, disiento —y en esto, me apoyan muchos terapeutas sexuales—. A ver, ¿quién no se ha excitado escuchando[12] sus propios gemidos (incluso sabiendo que el primero quizá fue un pelín exagerado...)? Cierto, pero si con la misma pareja que te lo hace tan mal que no logras «correrte», finges una y otra vez que la cosa marcha, jamás cambiará de técnica. Será más y más decepción e insatisfacción.

Distinto es que si una vez, o de modo aislado, él no te satisface, cuando normalmente sí, casi por educación, no conviene someterle a una crítica despiadada. Es como si tu madre siempre hace un cocido para chuparse los dedos y, por una vez, le queda salado, tampoco hay que organizar una escena y romperle el corazón... Igual eres tú la que está rarita ese día.

También las mujeres fingimos cuando estamos cansadas, el preservativo nos está abrasando —eso pasa por no utilizar lubrican-

---

12. La acustofilia consiste precisamente en eso: en excitarte mediante sonidos, bien sean palabras de amor o vulgares que te dicen durante la relación, tacos, amenazas, gritos, o sentir la respiración de tu pareja justo en el oído. Se tiene como una práctica parafílica. Se reseña en su epígrafe correspondiente.

te— y queremos acabar. Si le hacemos ver que por su parte «ya ha cumplido», que puede relajarse porque tú «ya estás servida», lo habitual es que eyacule de inmediato y así terminéis.

¿Fingen ellos?

Siempre se dice que somos nosotras las que podemos hacer una verdadera *performance*. Desde que Meg Ryan en *Cuando Harry encontró a Sally* se puso a invocar a Dios en ese restaurante sin siquiera mediar contacto físico, muchos creen que todas fingimos o temen que lo hagamos. Pero ¿pueden ellos fingir los orgasmos? En principio «parece» más complejo, pero como en todo, sólo es ponerse. Por una parte, a veces, tras la primera y ulteriores eyaculaciones, cabe que la cantidad de esperma sea muy pequeña o nula, y sí haya orgasmo (o no, he ahí un momento en que pueden fingir). Otras veces, ellos se agobian de ver que van a tardar aún un siglo y están agotados, con lo que pueden hacer ver que alcanzan el clímax y, al quitarse el preservativo, disimular, tirarlo deprisa y limpiarse y todo como si hubiera «ocurrido» o, si coincide con la regla, hacer ver que no todo era sangre menstrual —nosotras tampoco estamos ahí, controlando...—. Otros hombres fingen porque han perdido la erección: están en medio de la penetración y algo les distrae y se les baja. Para muchos, es muy incómodo dar este tipo de explicaciones. En vez de comentarlo, dan un par de embestidas, resoplan, y se salen, haciéndote creer que «ya está».

Stairway to Heaven: *el camino hasta y desde el orgasmo*

Desde la infancia, las personas se masturban sin siquiera saber a nivel técnico o biológico en qué consiste lo que hacen. Descubrimos el autoerotismo simplemente disfrutando de la sensación que nos proporciona el contacto con nuestros genitales. Podemos graduar esa satisfacción física que nos autoadministramos en la intimidad, y a veces sí a veces no, probando posturas y tocándonos de uno u otro modo, llegamos a las cotas máximas de placer. Y por lo general, un buen día, las compartimos con otro, las alcanzamos también en compañía. En ese proceso, además de mejorar las técnicas, vamos descubriendo los efectos y las bondades del orgasmo: su capacidad para proporcionarnos una sensación no comparable a ninguna otra... Ah, y además, no hay ningún remedio natural más efectivo contra el insomnio.[13]

En realidad, a lo largo de la historia las mayores locuras, conspiraciones, crímenes y tragedias... las ha inspirado la adicción a tener orgasmos con alguien en concreto (algunos lo llaman «amor»).

Pero, ¿en qué consiste eso de «tener un orgasmo»? Tanto en el hombre como en la mujer, el orgasmo es la descarga de la tensión o acumulación sanguínea en los genitales que se alcanza durante la excitación y la meseta. Se manifiesta mediante una serie de contracciones más o menos regulares. En realidad es una respuesta involuntaria del sistema nervioso que se desencadena en la médula espinal —en la zona sacra— y alcanza la zona pélvica y perianal. Todos buscamos más y mejores orgasmos. Para ello, mente y cuerpo han de estar predispuestos. Implica deseo, pero también conocer —el propio cuerpo o el de la pareja—, y que anatómicamente, a un nivel físico, el organismo pueda responder (sistema nervioso, hormonas, tonificación de la zona pélvica, etc.).

13. El poder relajante del orgasmo lo vimos cuando en este mismo capítulo analizamos las cuatro fases de la respuesta sexual, y precisamente ésta, que sería la 4.ª, previa a la de «¿Te llamo un taxi?» —perdón por la broma—, la que sigue al clímax, tiene un poderoso efecto sedante. Detalle enemigo del romanticismo, que revela nuestro lado más animal...

5

Vamos a organizarnos: penetración y posiciones

Penetración

La penetración requiere que la entrada de la vagina y el pubis estén lubricados; a veces, ella está muy excitada pero no ha comenzado a segregar flujo vaginal o éste se encuentra dentro y no ha impregnado aún la zona externa de la vulva, por lo que se hace dificultosa la entrada del pene. En cualquier caso, para el acceso (para atinar, vamos) se pueden utilizar las manos como ayuda. La secreción vaginal —que haya o que no y en qué abundancia— depende de cada mujer, de su grado de deseo, de su ciclo, de haberse lavado justo antes y que no haya transcurrido suficiente rato para segregar flujo y de cuánto tiempo haya transcurrido desde su última relación (si hace mucho, la cantidad será menor).

El momento ideal para iniciar la penetración sería cuando el pene se encuentra en erección (o semi, y con los movimientos termina de estarlo) y ella está lo bastante excitada como para pedirle que lo haga, o se lo deje tan claro, mediante gestos, que no quepa duda. El deseo de la penetración suele ser consecuencia de una estimulación gradual y total de su cuerpo (ver «Zonas erógenas»), cuando ella nota que «no puede esperar más» y quiere sentirle dentro.

Salvo los vírgenes, que no deberían opinar sobre lo desconocido, todo el mundo ha experimentado el mayor placer justo en las tres o cuatro primeras embestidas. Ello se debe a que los músculos de la vagina al principio ejercen «resistencia», y conforme se «acostumbran» se van dilatando para albergar al pene, hasta terminar rodeándolo sin oponer resistencia —ello explicaría, en parte, la manía persecutoria masculina por el esfínter anal, que mantiene la opresión constante—. De hecho, el término «vagina», etimológicamente, significa «funda».

Trucos cuando hay poca confianza

Si es la primera vez que estás con esa persona, él puede sentir cierta ansiedad, porque la penetración de cada mujer es distinta. En ese momento, la tendencia masculina suele ser la de realizar embestidas fuertes, *«¡que no se diga!»*. Error. Lo más placentero no es meterla hasta dentro a lo bestia. Así, una y otro pueden hacerse daño. Como esto es cosa de dos, lo que mejor resulta es que ella eche una mano —nunca mejor dicho—. Puede guiar el pene —apunto que no tiene ojos, por si no se ha leído aún el capítulo «Anatomía básica»...—, colocar la punta justo en el orificio de la vagina, o jugar con él. No es mala idea sostener el tronco del pene y conducirlo con movimientos lineales desde el clítoris hasta la entrada de la vagina, recorriendo los labios menores (sería utilizarlo como un pintalabios). Tomarse su tiempo en esto optimiza todas las sensaciones, despierta cada zona al nuevo contacto: puede que ambos hayan dado y recibido estimulación oral o manual, pero el pene y la vagina están siendo «presentados» ahora. El acceso debería hacerse poco a poco, profundizando paulatinamente, centímetro a centímetro si se es capaz; para él suele ser más difícil no dejarse llevar, así que será la mujer la que se pueda ocupar de dosificar, ralentizar y procurar que suceda de modo gradual. Ella está al mando de esta «técnica de movimientos restringidos». De nuevo, lo ya explicado: crear expectativa con movimientos suaves pero precisos. Además, esto aumenta la lubricación.

Una vez dentro, los movimientos de acoplamiento los podéis hacer los dos. Ella colocando la pelvis de modo que él pueda alcanzar el fondo de la vagina y el cuello del útero o para que presione sus puntos mágicos (G, K, A...). Él tratando de estimular las paredes laterales de la vagina, realizando penetraciones laterales (ojito con troncharte el pene).

Se han descrito infinidad de posiciones en que se puede llevar a cabo la penetración. Una regla: situarte encima te hace con el poder, con el control. Pero es como lo de invitar a cenar: paga el que propone, así que el esfuerzo físico, como la factura, caerá sobre quien domina. Si ella está encima, tanto de rodillas, sentada a horcajadas como a pulso, en cuclillas sobre él, de frente o de espaldas —cuidado con no rebasar el eje y doblar el pene, alejándolo demasiado de su vientre—, dispone de la capacidad de gestión del coito: elegirá la inclinación de la vagina, la fricción del clítoris, la profundidad de la penetración, que se dosifica según el peso que dejas caer sobre él y consiguientemente, la presión que efectúa.

Más trucos. Almohadas y cojines colocados bajo la pelvis de ella ayudan a lograr ángulos más cómodos y a que se dé la fricción necesaria con su clítoris. Las hay que gustan de dejar la cabeza colgando fuera de la cama, lo que provoca cierto subidón: la sangre se baja a la cabeza y hace el orgasmo femenino mucho más potente.

Dicho lo cual, es evidente que, con o sin confianza, si nos dejamos llevar por la pasión y la excitación del momento, también podemos optar por la penetración rápida, sin miramientos y directa al fondo, que resulta de lo más placentera —si no hay falta de lubricación, ya que de lo contrario, puede ser dolorosa—. Otros movimientos son: el de avance de él en zigzag, conforme se introduce; ella complementando con movimientos circulares o desplazamientos laterales de la pelvis que contribuyen a intensificar el contacto y el acoplamiento; colocada sobre él, ella puede realizar movimientos de mete-saca muy rápidos y de escaso recorrido, sobre el glande nada más; retroceder y avanzar; realizar ella la introducción del pene y conducirlo en un único movimiento hasta dentro, dejando sus dedos en la base del mismo para aumentar la fricción, o bien, utilizar su mano para acariciarse el clítoris y al tiempo, estimular el pene.

Sobre la «actitud femenina» me permito reivindicar en su nombre que pocos quieren asumir toda la actividad (es decir, responsabilidad) durante el coito. Que una mujer demuestre imaginación y ganas suele entusiasmarles. Además, como para propiciar el orgasmo femenino resulta necesario apoyar la penetración con la estimulación del clítoris mediante caricias y movimientos, nadie mejor que ella para «echar(se) una mano». Igual que realizar contracciones vaginales durante la penetración (ejercicios de Kegel), que acelera e intensifica toda la sensación. Por el bien de ambos, repartir esfuerzos o alternarse tomando la iniciativa, convierte las experiencias buenas en inolvidables.

Posiciones

La tarea de enumerar las posiciones de la cópula me resulta imposible (por tediosa). Sólo en el Kamasutra se documentan 74, y no son todas: hay listados que nombran hasta seiscientas.

En realidad, las parejas suelen alternar la del misionero —con sus variantes de colocación de él más adelantado, TAC, o de situar los pies de ella por encima de los hombros de él, etc.—; la de Andrómana o ella encima, de rodillas sobre él; la del perrito o *doggie*, estando ella a cuatro patas y él penetrando desde atrás; la penetración de pie y la lateral. Variantes de estas cinco hay cientos. Me centraré en estas «básicas» y que cada cual cambie mentalmente el decorado —yo a lo mejor menciono «colchón» o «cabecero de la cama», pero se puede aplicar al interior de un coche, un cuarto de baño, un aula universitaria o una oficina...— o decida si sube una rodilla o baja la manita izquierda... Estas formas de penetración representan las mayoritariamente practicadas —sabiendo cómo se entra, lo demás es mete-saca, con distinto ritmo, ángulo, profundidad y fuerza—. Follar es como bailar: con saber las bases, el resto es pura inspiración e intuición.

Como sucede con casi todo lo que respecta al sexo, sería absurdo realizar generalizaciones vehementes a favor o en contra de cualquier posición. Las variables a manejar incluyen el físico de los amantes: diferencia de altura, peso y volumen corporal y de los respectivos genitales,[14] su agilidad, su salud, si ella está o no embarazada e incluso, de lo cansados que estén uno, otra o ambos. Influyen, por supuesto, las propias preferencias: hay personas que sienten más placer en determinada postura, y es ésa la que procuran o viceversa, sabiendo lo que «no gusta», lo evitan sistemáticamente. Dicho lo cual, que no cunda el pánico si las posiciones favoritas de ambos no coinciden. Como en el colegio: por turnos (con la precaución de recordar que quizá sea mejor que él «se corra» el último).

14. Ya el Kamasutra distinguía los tipos de hombre y de mujer en función del tamaño de su pene y de su vagina y proponía trucos para salvar las distancias. Desde las técnicas ancestrales hindúes de rodear el pene con brazaletes de madera o de metal para agrandarlo, a la quirúrgica de estrechamiento de la vagina... Toda la eternidad para aportar soluciones al mismo problema de siempre... Se explica mejor en «El tamaño».

El toque que debe acompañar el coito es, sin duda, la pasión. Se convierte en el hilo conductor, en la salsa sobre el guiso —si no estuviera, sería un trozo de carne casi absurdo—. Por seguir con esta idea, es el momento en que te comerías a la otra persona, que desearías que fuera posible que tu cuerpo se fundiera con el suyo. No escatimes en besos, abrazos, caricias... Deja que tus brazos, tus manos y tu boca atrapen, recorran y mordisqueen todo lo que esté a tu alcance. Un buen amante —aplicable a ellas, por supuesto— no tiene nunca una mano libre y mucho menos la boca...

Misionero

Se trata de un clásico, no sólo por ser la posición tradicionalmente «no censurada» por la religión sino porque, si no es como «principal», es una posición muy utilizada «de tránsito» o comodín. Sin embargo, pese a ser la más frecuente, tiene fama de aburrida —lo es, si se entiende el coito como un *show* circense—, pero sus «valores» son innegables. Permite besar a tu pareja, mirarla a los ojos, ver cómo se excita o las caras que pone según lo que estés haciendo... Lo recuerdo vagamente, de mis clases de Literatura, pero en *La casa de Bernarda Alba*, en determinado fragmento, se alude a que no hay nada como sentir el peso de un hombre, y lo mucho que se llega a echar de menos. Que nadie dude de que la mayoría de las mujeres lo suscribimos.

Por si alguien no lo recuerda, esta postura se hace con ella echada sobre su espalda, con las piernas abiertas y rodillas flexionadas. Hay variantes:[15] piernas extendidas, o con los pies apoyados en la cama o agarrándolos por los tobillos, o con los tobillos en los hombros de él..., y él estirado encima, lo que le permite controlar.

Es una forma de penetración en la que el ángulo de la vagina propicia la entrada del pene. Eso sí, él debe tener en cuenta que si deja caer todo su peso, la puede asfixiar y aplastar y no hay peor cosa que temer por tu vida mientras echas un polvo... Lo suyo es que clave los codos a los lados de la cabeza de ella, y cargue todo el peso sobre los antebrazos y las rodillas. Cuando él se coloca de ro-

15. Ver *Alineación coital, técnica de* en la tercera parte del libro.

dillas para penetrar, además de liberarse de parte de su peso, dispone de las manos para abrazar, acariciar y mover a su pareja.

Si eres mujer. No te gustará que te aplasten, que te impidan moverte. Tampoco será la mejor postura para que alcances el orgasmo, dado que cuando «alguien» inventó el cuerpo femenino, colocó el clítoris bastante lejos de la entrada de la vagina, con lo que la penetración sólo te llevará a orgasmos cuando lo alcances a través de la estimulación del cérvix. Acceder al punto G queda complicado en esta postura.

Sin embargo, te encantará cuando estés cansada y quieras que te lo den (casi) todo hecho. Además, por razones estéticas es la más favorecedora. Habida cuenta que la desnudez no se vive por todo el mundo con la misma naturalidad y que un elevado porcentaje de mujeres confiesa no estar contenta con su cuerpo, esta posición es la mejor. Por un lado, como él se echa encima, tú no estás tan «expuesta», te tapa. Además, acostada, la tripa se mete y los pechos quedan exentos de la fuerza de la gravedad. La cara, lo mismo: tumbada boca arriba, el rostro se tersa y entre el rubor de la excitación y la desaparición de pliegues, resultas más guapa que nunca.

Si no estás muy perezosa, es la ocasión para demostrar tus habilidades y que controlas tus músculos vaginales: trata de apretarlos, de «abrazar» el pene con las paredes de la vagina, así aumentarás la fricción y desencadenarás tu orgasmo mucho antes.

Agárrale con fuerza y atráelo hacia ti si necesitas más fricción o más profundidad. Oponte a sus movimientos para contrarrestar su empuje si es lo que te apetece o para fomentar el roce con tu clítoris. Gira las caderas como si bailaras lambada (no hace falta que lo sepas hacer en la pista de baile, la cama, para esto, es menos exigente).

Supongo que sonará contradictorio pero, si buscas tu propio placer, será lo mejor para ambos. Hace mucho que ellos saben de la existencia de las muñecas hinchables. Tú no lo eres, así que compórtate y estate a lo que estás. Participa.

Para él. Como tienes que cargar tu peso, sudarás como un esclavo egipcio enseguida, pero si no lo haces, esta postura será un fracaso porque la matarás a ella por aplastamiento. Lo bueno es que tienes todo el control sobre el acto: presión, velocidad, ángulo, ritmo...

algo que, para eyaculadores precoces es crucial, ya que podrán moverse o cesar las embestidas caso de notar que se «van». Muchas mujeres dan unos masajes y hacen unas caricias increíbles, con las uñas incluso, recorriendo la espalda, las nalgas... y siguen estimulándote con la mano —como buenamente pueden, habida cuenta la limitación de movimientos en que se hallan— el pene, los testículos y el perineo, mientras son penetradas. A nivel psicológico es incuestionable que al hombre le encanta dominar. Estar al mando. Ser él quien lleva la voz cantante y ser consciente de que con su miembro erecto entra en tu cuerpo. Si es así, y lo hacen bien, perfecto, que se quede encima un buen rato —siempre sin eyacular hasta que ella esté satisfecha—, pero si no, o si ella precisa estar encima, debe permitírselo, turnarse. El misionero mejora con la TAC. El hombre debe saber que aunque para ella alcanzar el orgasmo en esta posición resulta bastante difícil, ello no implica que no disfrute sintiéndose penetrada y bajo el peso de un hombre —cuidadito con la interpretación «peso»—. No cabe generalizar: las hay también que odian la penetración y que jamás sentirán placer con ella ni lo que conlleva. Lo malo de estar encima, es que no disfruta viendo el cuerpo de la mujer, ya que el contacto visual se restringe a la cara y al cabecero de la cama —sustitúyase por el decorado que proceda—. Una variante más: él de rodillas en el suelo, ella echada boca arriba al borde de la cama (postura conocida como la Cortesana).

Ella encima o postura de Andrómana

Depende del carácter de la mujer, pero, en general, a todas nos gusta estar encima, aunque sea un ratito. Es cuando mayor placer sentimos y, por una vez, no se trata de mandar, insisto: el clítoris obtiene la fricción y presión que necesitamos. Además, no te despeinas.

Lo malo: que te toca esforzarte. Que te tiene a la vista, con lo que ello implica... Quizás estés en un momento pletórico o ni te plantees cosas como las que voy a enumerar. Si es así, sáltate esto y lee desde el final de este párrafo. Cuando tu autoestima tenga anemia o no esté tan robusta como tu cuerpo, esta posición resulta incómoda. Sí, en casos de sobrepeso de ella, si no se encuentra cómoda con la forma o tamaño de sus pechos, o con el contorno de su cintura, o se hace con la luz apagada o ella, en vez de disfrutar, pasará bochorno. Cabe también que sea tímida, y que saber que él la mira acentúe esta inseguridad. Un truco: si te da corte que te vea poner esas caras, o el bamboleo de tus pechos, y tienes el pelo largo, hazte la leona y échatelo hacia delante. Queda un toque como muy salvaje y te oculta el rostro. Para lo de tapar las tetas caídas o intentar disimularlas, mejor ponte boca arriba, pero si te has encaramado, puedes adelantar tus dos brazos, apoyando las palmas en su pecho, de modo que te quedes tranquila habiendo escondido los pechos y te sigas moviendo a tu aire. Puedes también echarte toda tú hacia delante —cambia el ángulo de penetración—. Desde ahí, dejando todo tu peso sobre los antebrazos, puedes intentar lo que se ve en muchas pelis porno: ella hace un movimiento en vertical de metesaca rapidísimo y no demasiado profundo. A ellos les encanta pero a ti, si no estás en forma, te costará durar. Así comprendemos y valoramos su esfuerzo físico.

Lo básico es que su pene esté completamente duro, ya que en esta postura es muy fácil doblárselo y hacerle daño (léase: no te vuelvas loca y te vayas a echar para atrás y a troncharle).

Para él es justo lo contrario: es cómodo y muy excitante. El que tú decidas cómo quieres moverte les permite desvincularse de ese «deber», de la presión de preguntarse si lo están haciendo bien o si no te estará gustando. Y por si a alguien le cabe la menor duda, paradójicamente, lo que a nosotras nos da corte, por lo general a ellos es lo que más les pone. Tú, «¡qué horror que las tetas suban y bajen!» en su mente equivale a «¡guau, qué bien!». Por otro lado, el *show*, a veces, les abstrae tanto que les cuesta recordar que pueden acariciarte (tienen las manos libres, pueden ocuparse de pechos y clítoris e incluso, apoyar tus movimientos agarrándote por las caderas...). Desde ahí abajo le encantará contemplar cómo le provocas, que juegues con su pene, que hagas que entre y salga sólo un poco y lo alternes con recorridos más largos o que con la mano lo lleves por toda la vagina, recorriendo los pliegues de labios mayores y menores, o que tú misma te acaricies para él. El exhibicionismo en esto ayuda mucho. Has de ir soltándote —aunque hay muchas muy sueltas ya por naturaleza—; afortunadamente, este detalle, es algo que también se aprende con la práctica.

Como variantes de la postura de Andrómana, se puede realizar un giro de manera que en vez de estar mirándole a la cara, le cabalgues dándole la espalda. También puede utilizarse como base de operaciones una silla o un sillón, o el borde de la cama, de modo que él esté «sentado» y tú, sobre él (de cara o de espaldas). Otra modalidad es, estando él completamente tumbado boca arriba, que te estires sobre su cuerpo, manteniendo la penetración, y dejes tus piernas dentro de las de él, o rodeándolas. En esa posición, prueba a juntar las piernas, a apretar su pene con los abductores y a moverte desde ahí.

A cuatro patas o doggie

Ella de rodillas, echada hacia delante, con las manos apoyadas en la cama —a cuatro patas—, y él penetra desde detrás. Se trata de la postura del *doggie* o perrito, que se ve facilitada por los movimientos que ella puede hacer, como adelantar la pelvis para acercarse, o elevarla para mejorar el ángulo de acceso. Él disfruta del espectáculo y vuelve a tener las manos libres para agarrarla, moverla o acariciarla. Dado que apela a nuestros instintos más animales, resulta la posición preferida de la mayoría (también de ellas, lleguen o no al orgasmo). La mejor parte —para los dos— es que exige escaso esfuerzo físico porque no hay que soportar peso, podemos sencillamente bascular adelante y atrás. En contra: que no es posible mirarse a la cara, salvo que te retuerzas —algo que, para según quién es una ventaja, ya que nadie ve sus gestos y se desinhiben—. A él le permite fantasear con que eres otra —así colocada, salvo que tu corte o color de pelo te hagan única, ciertamente, podrías ser cualquiera—[16] y le excita el poder que esta posición le confiere, por no hablar de que, como ya se ha repetido, le coloca en un ángulo de visión privilegiado: lo primero es que a todos les encanta contemplar tu trasero —y ellos, no como nosotras, no están torturándose con la celulitis o la «piel de naranja»—; además, puede verse a sí mismo entrando y saliendo, manejando el cuerpo de una mujer desde detrás, moviéndola por las caderas o por

16. Alorgasmia: es una parafilia que consiste en excitarse fantaseando durante el acto sexual con otra persona que no sea la pareja.

la cintura, o incluso, echándose hacia delante y acariciando sus pechos —disfruta más de la vista que de la sensación, sin duda—. Lo malo de tanto entusiasmo es que les conduce al orgasmo en tiempo récord (recuérdese hacer esta postura si él, por más que lo intenta, parece que no consigue eyacular). Como nuevamente el clítoris queda olvidado, podría ser buena idea que tanto ella como él, se ocupen de acariciarlo con alguna mano que quede libre. Desde ese ángulo, si la penetración es corta o media, se alcanza de lleno el punto G, ése es el secreto de que nos guste tanto.

¿Y a nosotras?, pues, a muchas, también nos encanta ser dominadas y sometidas, hay quienes encuentran muy excitante asumir ese rol, aunque sólo sea en la cama. Repito lo que les contaba a ellos: si alterna penetraciones profundas con medias o cortas, el glande toca el punto G, ubicado en la pared frontal de la vagina, lo que explica por qué sientes ese viaje astral en esta postura. Puedes dejarte hacer o cooperar, realizando movimientos basculantes con los brazos, y cambiando la posición de tu cadera —así evitarás penetraciones excesivamente profundas, o esquivarás el pene cuando, por ejemplo, tengas un ovario inflamado y notes dolor con el impacto—. Lo mismo que él, ella puede imaginar que se lo está montando con cualquier otro. Posibles variantes: que ella se agache, bajando el tronco hasta que la cara se apoye en el colchón, o que baje todo el cuerpo, acercando la pelvis a la horizontal, mientras él continúa detrás. También cabe que la mujer se incorpore, que se quede arrodillada delante de él, lo que permite un abrazo muy sensual y besos en el cuello y también en la boca y, para mayor comodidad y que no falle el equilibrio ante los movimientos, ella puede apoyarse contra la pared o agarrarse al cabecero.

De pie

La penetración de pie, en vertical, no es precisamente la más sencilla, generalmente debido a la diferencia de estatura. Nada es imposible y se puede realizar, estando, por ejemplo, ella de pie, frente a él, con las piernas separadas o sujetando una de sus piernas en el hombro de él; o bien, ella separando las piernas, apoyando las manos sobre algo —un respaldo, una cisterna— y subiéndose a algo —una torre de guías de teléfonos, que para eso están—, arqueando la pelvis hacia atrás y él, colocado a su espalda, penetrando desde ahí. Esta postura se puede hacer también estando él detrás, inclinándose ella según le apetezca, ya sea un poquito o casi flexionada en ángulo recto, mientras él puede utilizar sus manos para acariciarla o para, agarrándola de la cintura, controlar los embistes o incluso, estrangularla un poco.

Lateral

Ella de costado y él, detrás de ella, la penetra. Sería el perfecto polvo de recién levantados, lento y dulce antes de decir siquiera «buenos días» —básicamente porque evita el mal aliento matinal—. Se puede hacer cara a cara, abrazados. Lo malo es que el movimiento de penetración resulta harto complicado, y el recorrido del pene suele ser limitado. Se considera una de las posiciones más adecuadas cuando él es XXL, hay mucha diferencia de estatura o, por cualquier razón —como un dolor de ovarios o llevar seis horas follando y necesitar un descanso—, conviene una penetración poco profunda.

SEXO ANAL

A lo largo de toda la historia, en la pintura, la escultura, la literatura y demás manifestaciones culturales, se aportan referencias a la penetración anal, si bien esta práctica no es de las que gozan de mejor «reputación», debido fundamentalmente a dos razones: que se aparta de la finalidad reproductiva atribuida a la sexualidad por la religión, y que se practicó por herejes maniqueos en la Edad Media. Los romanos incluyeron la pedicación con sus esclavos en su día a día, y miles de mujeres a lo largo de los siglos han evitado embarazos y conservado su himen intacto manteniendo relaciones por vía anal. A nivel lingüístico, existen infinidad de términos y expresiones, más o menos científicas o vulgares —pero con un tinte de tabú predominante— para referirse al acceso del pene por el ano y recto, desde «entrar por detrás», a «dar por el culo», «encular», «pedicar», «sodomizar», «coito anal», «abrir el cacas»...

Se considera sexo anal también cuando el sujeto activo es una mujer, que introduce por el ano de su pareja —femenina o masculina— un dedo, varios o incluso la mano *(fisting)*. Si mete un juguete o una prótesis, un dildo, bien sujetándolo manualmente, bien amarrado a un arnés, esta especialidad se denomina *pegging*. La palabra «sodomía» se deriva de Sodoma, ciudad que, al igual que Gomorra según la Biblia, recibió el castigo de Jehová por sus desenfrenos sexuales... que no fueron específicamente homosexuales, pero así quedó para el recuerdo.

Cuanto contienen estas páginas que siguen debería leerse con un «habida cuenta que no todo el mundo está dispuesto a practicarlo», por el motivo que sea (higiénico, estético, cultural, religioso...), puesto que, si bien se trata de uno de los orificios de la anatomía humana, común a ambos géneros, muchos no conciben que se involucre en la relación dado que lo circunscriben estrictamente a su «fin natural de ser un esfínter por el que defecar» y lo rechazan. Si bien este dato es innegable, para gustos, los colores y, obviamente, también hay personas para las que es una práctica esporádica y puntual y estrechamente condicionada y vinculada a la higiene, a la confianza en el otro y a la educación, mientras que para otros constituye un acto perfectamente normal y frecuente. Ante todo, se trata de encarar desde el respeto este tema como lo que es: una práctica sexual susceptible de generar filias y fobias, con adeptos y detractores. En general se detecta una timidez generalizada entre los señores heterosexuales a la hora de demandar que se les practique una estimulación anal, por temor a que se dude de su masculinidad (más bien de su heterosexualidad), lo cual es un error: el ano, por sus terminaciones nerviosas, es una zona erógena y su estimulación provoca placer, incluso orgasmos, tanto a mujeres como a hombres, con independencia de su opción sexual.

En cualquier caso, que la mayoría de los tipos estén casi obsesionados y lleguen a ponerse muy pesados a la hora de querer practicarlo (siendo ellos, casualmente, la parte activa) no implica que se haya de aceptar sin más. Los hay que lanzan chantajes emocionales del tipo de «si me quisieras lo harías» y similares, o que te retan, o los que hacen campaña política para convencerte de que son «muy buenos haciéndolo». Ni caso. Si no quieres, no lo hagas. Si alguien te quiere de verdad, ha de aceptar tus gustos y respetar tus límites. Por otro lado, una vez se siente el deseo de hacerlo, siempre viene bien tener un par de cosas claras.

Desde la retaguardia

Para muchas personas el coito anal produce un placer —si se sabe cómo hacerlo y con las debidas prevenciones— quizá más intenso en la mujer, que el vaginal, dado que se estimula el útero y que la zona ano-rectal cuenta con más terminaciones nerviosas que la vaginal, donde sólo el clítoris resulta receptivo a la estimulación, junto con el controvertido punto G; en el hombre, ahí se localiza el punto P y la próstata, a la que se accede a través del ano y constituye su punto máximo de sensibilidad —esto es un hecho, como lo es que casi ningún hetero afirmará en público cuánto le gusta recibir este tipo de estimulación—. Se puede acariciar también desde el exterior, localizándolo con el pulgar en el hueco que hay justo en la base del pene, tras la bolsa del escroto, cuando se recorre la zona del perineo, antes del ano. Cuando un señor es penetrado por detrás y se masturba a la vez hasta eyacular, su orgasmo se ve multiplicado porque las contracciones anales se producen «estrujando» algo. Otro modo de practicarlo sería que, mientras están disfrutando de una felación, o durante el coito, al acercarse su orgasmo, su pareja les introduzca «algo».

Se manejan estadísticas que revelan que el 40 % de las parejas heterosexuales ha intentado alguna vez el sexo anal —siendo él el activo—, pero, precisamente en este tema se da la tendencia al secretismo y no abundan los que airean que les encanta hacerlo, ¡y en el caso de ser ellos los pasivos, no digamos!

Si nos ceñimos a la fisiología, se debería tener bien presente que la naturaleza del ano es distinta a la de la vagina en varios aspectos. El ano no está diseñado para el coito, tiende a oponer resistencia, a contraerse. Este detalle es clave, hay que «dar de sí» este orificio y conseguir que el cuerpo se relaje (tener un orgasmo antes ayuda). Otra diferencia es que no se autolubrica como una vagina o como la boca, por ejemplo. Para ello se debe proceder a la lubricación natural —con saliva, fluidos vaginales o líquido preseminal— o artificial —con lubricantes compatibles con el material del preservativo, normalmente con base acuosa—, y a su estimulación, bien sea manual, a base de caricias externas o introduciendo un dedo —lubricado—, o varios, progresivamente; oral, mediante lametazos, besos; o mecánica, con la introducción de dildos específicos, en forma de cono.

Además de no trabajar en seco, se debería recordar otra exigencia: despacito. Poco a poco. Se trata de un esfínter que trabaja para impedir la salida de las deposiciones y que se abre puntualmente. La tendencia del ano es a cerrarse herméticamente. Debe recordarse que conviene ir introduciendo dedos u objetos[17] de modo gradual, de menor a mayor, para lograr que se «acostumbre», que se vaya expandiendo, primero el ano y después, si la cosa va bien, continuar por el recto. Ha de prestarse atención, por descontado, al lenguaje verbal: un «no» es «no». Pero hay además un más sutil lenguaje corporal. Cualquier gesto de retirarse debe respetarse. Es cosa de dos aprender a comunicarse, sea en relaciones largas, sea en los «aquí te pillo...». Si alguien no se encuentra a gusto, hay que parar. Si por el contrario, notas que se frota contra tu mano, que se aproxima y se ofrece, o que su respiración muestra excitación, adelante.

Volviendo sobre asuntos biológicos, señalar que el recto es especialmente apto para la absorción (de ahí que algunos medicamentos se prescriban por vía rectal, en formato supositorio o irrigación). Pero igual de bien que absorbe principios activos, lo hace con virus (VIH, VPH, etc.) y bacterias (gonorrea, clamidia, etc.), que se transmiten con independencia de que haya o no eyaculación. El tejido de la mucosa rectal es delicado: cualquier raspadura, un arañazo con

---

17. Los *sex shops* ofrecen un amplio catálogo de dildos: distintos tamaños, colores, materiales y configuración en función de qué zona han de estimular/penetrar. Hay tiras de bolas anales de diámetro progresivamente mayor; dildos «de iniciación» con puntas realmente finas que van ensanchándose, etc... Los específicos para la penetración anal tienen una punta redondeada que aumenta de tamaño y después vuelve a reducirse, formando una especie de huevito o huso, y con un tope junto a la embocadura que permite su manejo e impide que sea absorbido y quede dentro y protagonicemos una leyenda urbana de las de «se metió no sé qué por el culo y hubo que ir a Urgencias a que se lo sacaran». Cuidadito con meterse, por ejemplo, botellas: las de cristal pueden romperse, y en general, pueden hacer el vacío y al extraerlas, llevarse detrás tus entrañas. ¿Poco romántico? Tampoco lo pretendía...

una uña, una arista en el objeto que se introduce, o simplemente el desgarro causado por el grosor de lo que se esté metiendo, producen fácilmente heridas, úlceras, fisuras... De ahí que, como cuarto *must* o imprescindible, se insista en poner un preservativo tanto al pene como al objeto que se introduzca (léase guante de látex si lo que introduces son los dedos). Además, obviamente, para el que penetra también hay riesgo de contagios y de hacerse daño, por lo que el preservativo protege a ambas partes.

Para un recto proceder...

Por finiquitar los «considerandos», añado que el orden conveniente de las penetraciones, por evitar riesgos para la salud y facilitar la lubricación natural ha de ser: primero oral (felación/cunnilingus) luego vaginal y por último, anal. Si se decide alterar esta sucesión, tras el coito anal, ha de cambiarse el preservativo, por pura higiene y para no introducir en la vagina o en la boca las bacterias que se hallan en el recto. Que en las películas porno se hagan otras cosas no es óbice...

Otro truco que también ayuda a la distensión del ano es que la persona que es penetrada haga el gesto de empujar como si defecara —suena raro y además, sólo pensarlo incita a temer que salga de ahí alguna sustancia no deseada..., tranquilidad, que no ocurre—, provocando que el orificio se acople al pene/objeto y permita su aceptación.

En el pasivo (sea hombre o mujer) el orgasmo se intensifica si se masturba simultáneamente. Las contracciones que se producen en el ano sirven también como estímulo, muy intenso, que acusa el pene y que facilita el orgasmo de la persona activa.

Como en otras parcelas de la vida, aquí también aparece la sombra de la relación entre placer y dolor. No hay escena cinematográfica que soslaye el hecho de que la pedicación duele. Entre películas convencionales que plasman el coito anal se pueden citar *Infiel*, *Querelle*, *La buena estrella*, etc., o la mítica primera ocasión en la historia donde se mostró esta práctica, *El silencio*, dirigida por Igmar Bergman y también *120 días en Sodoma*, de Pier Paolo Pasolini y, por supuesto, lo vemos en cualquier cinta X. Se encuentran menciones literarias, además de en las obras del Marqués de Sade, en las de muchos autores como Boccaccio, Chaucer, Petronio o Rabelais, que han descrito este tipo de experiencia.

En general, los testimonios de celebridades y de particulares que lo practican coinciden en constatar, más o menos sutilmente, el daño que produce cuando se hace de modo brusco. La penetración anal requiere cierta preparación, tanto a nivel físico, donde parece oportuno englobar la higiene, la lubricación y la dilatación, como psicológico: ya no se considera ni antinatural ni pecaminosa, sino una variante sexual más; de hecho, este coito se asocia a la trasgresión, suele ser «la última barrera» dentro de la relación y para su práctica se requiere cierta liberación de prejuicios y superación de tabúes. Ah, sepa todo el mundo que lo de «¡uy, lo siento, creí que era por aquí!» es de tercera regional B. Este tan extendido falso «error» provoca desde un tortazo de revés, a un «vete de aquí», pasando por el generalizado corte de rollo y el «menudo gilipollas» en todas las mentes femeninas (aunque no lo digamos para poder seguir con lo que estábamos hasta la profanación).

Cuanto más se estimule sexualmente a la persona que va a ser penetrada, más le pedirá el cuerpo hacerlo y menos dolerá. Entrando en materia, cabe, por ejemplo, adoptar la postura del coito desde detrás que, salvo por el ángulo, será la misma, e ir recreando las sensaciones que se podrían alcanzar. También, para estimular el ano, se puede utilizar un cuadrante de látex si se hace con la boca, o un guante y, con lubricante, ir acariciando la parte externa e introduciendo poco a poco un dedo. Aquí, de nuevo, paciencia, sin prisas...

No es de recibo, ni honesto, saltarse la parte más escatológica, esa que revolotea en la mente de todos cuando se habla de sexo anal y que se refiere a los restos fecales que se encuentran después en el pene/dedo/objeto con el que se penetra. Hay medidas como los enemas y lavativas (a esto me refería con la «preparación» y con la «premeditación» que requiere «hacerlo bien»), además, los profilácticos evitan el contacto directo con las heces. El asunto de la limpieza parece de Perogrullo, pero por si acaso, mejor pecar por exceso de información... Que no falten agua y jabón neutro (hay además desodorantes específicos), y toallitas higiénicas, y una buena depilación (si no se es partidario del láser o del afeitado total, sí se debería barajar un «rasuradito» o un recorte del vello de la zona púbica y anal). Si afirmo esto no es por influencia de modas excéntricas ni de la pornografía, se trata exclusivamente de razones higiénicas: no es igual pasar la lengua con total facilidad por la piel, que encontrarse con una mata de rizos ensortijados entre los dientes; esto, por no mencionar que el olor de la zona es más intenso cuando hay vello, o que a los señores la medida de la depilación les hace el favor de que su pene gana un centímetro o centímetro y medio, por un efecto óptico.

Estas «recomendaciones» casi alcanzan el grado de «exigencia» cuando se aborda el beso negro o analingus, que consiste en lamer, chupar, pasar la lengua acariciando con ella el ano del otro hasta introducirla (tarea no especialmente sencilla, por la oposición del propio ano). Se trata de una de las prácticas que mayor placer proporciona a quien lo recibe, pero que, dicho sea de paso, no todo el mundo está por la labor de realizar. Retomando el asunto de los detalles sobre el olor y demás, para este instante en concreto, entiendo que todo cuidado es poco... Que cada cual haga lo que considere, pero, estando como están las cosas, aquí me permito desaconsejar que se realice este tipo de incursión con extraños. Incluso cuando se haga con la pareja estable, y medie promesa de fidelidad y demás, yo recomiendo medidas profilácticas.

Apunto un recurso que, si bien suena muy casero, es efectivo y económico, cuando no se dispone de los preservativos femeninos o cuadrantes de látex. El ingenio se despierta en este tipo de situaciones. Hablo del típico rollo de film transparente, el que se utiliza en la cocina para envolver los alimentos; se corta un trozo suficientemente grande y se coloca sobre la zona. Se pierde algo de sensibilidad, como es lógico, pero viene muy bien, siempre que no se desplace, se rompa —ojo con esos *piercings* y con las uñas—, y no se despiste nadie y le dé la vuelta sin querer y chupe justo el lado que estuvo en contacto con el ano... Cuando se haya terminado, quien haya sido la parte activa ha de lavarse a conciencia la boca, por dentro y por los alrededores y abstenerse de dar besos a su pareja hasta haberlo hecho. Así se evita que las numerosas bacterias que habitan en el ano y en el recto pasen a la saliva y entren en el organismo. Sigo con el bricolage: se puede utilizar también un condón —se corta la punta y se abre en canal, queda un rectángulo—, y también, con tijeras, abrir un guante de látex. Hacen las mismas funciones.

¿Y qué más?

Para realizar un coito anal y no estar pendiente de detalles engorrosos, ahí va una serie de recomendaciones —algunas que sólo abundan en las ya explicadas— y que cada cual, según lo escrupuloso o aprensivo que sea, emplee la que quiera.

Cruza tu puerta trasera. Si vas a dejar que otro entre ahí, deberías saber qué se cuece allá dentro. En la ducha, con calma, y con mucho cuidadito, ve probando a introducir un dedo. El jabón no debe acceder al recto, usa sólo agua, saliva o lubricante. Familiarízate con la sensación y recorre los distintos tramos que hay, porque después del ano, el esfínter externo cuya musculatura es como la de un anillo, que se contrae con fuerza y de modo voluntario desde el sistema nervioso central, la cosa sigue. Si avanzas un par de centímetros, notarás un segundo esfínter, interior, claro, gestionado sin que tú tengas nada que ver desde el sistema nervioso autónomo. En ese punto comienza el recto, dos curvas que dibujan una S de unos 10 a 15 centímetros. En su primer tramo está el músculo puborrectal, que controlamos a voluntad —apretándolo, impedimos «marrones» auténticos: accidentes y fugas—. El otro tramo es el canal rectal, una zona de tránsito. El colon es donde se depositan las heces y se ubica, tras el recto, a unos 20 o 25 centímetros del ano, en general, muy lejos de casi cualquier glande que visite la zona.

Dieta. Parecerá un anuncio pero es que la dieta rica en fibra va muy bien para casi todo y, en lo que nos (pro)ocupa, para evitar estreñimiento, es decir, hará que los esfuerzos de ir al trono sean los mínimos, que no te salgan dolorosas hemorroides y que tu ano, desde fuera, tenga su mejor vista, sin almorranas ni desgarros. ¿Suficientemente gráfico? Esto es lo que nunca dicen en los anuncios, pero es lo que todos entendemos. Las veinticuatro horas antes conviene ayunar, o comer ligero, en lo posible. Pero sí puedes tomar cualquier cosa antes de tu cita —como los alimentos tardan en procesarse casi un día, no llegarán a la zona de peligro— pero, por lo que más quieras, evita la fabada, la coliflor y manjares flatulentos.

Limpia tu interior, y no hablo de tu conciencia. A ver, según quién, se limita a la cara externa de la maldad... y se lava la zona con agua y jabón o pasa toallitas húmedas. Profundiza más, por aquello de ir sobre seguro. En caso de no disponer de nada de nada, hay quien se encañona la manguera de la ducha —sin el teléfono, por favor—. Otros recurren a esas «cosas» en forma de pera que venden en las farmacias y en *sex shops*, que se llenan de agua tibia y que se introducen —con lubricante— e irrigan la zona. Una vez has apretado la parte del depósito notarás que, con urgencia, necesitas echarlo todo: agua, heces, gases... Repite la operación hasta que no quede huella de que en definitiva sólo eres un ser humano. Hay lavativas y enemas de farmacia que llevan productos químicos, pero —como no estoy en plan sofisticada— diré de ellos que no se debe abusar puesto que crean adicción o pereza a tu sistema excretor, y puedes acabar dependiendo de ellos para evacuar. Por supuesto, recorta o afeita los pelos de la zona.

Aparejos e higiene. Lubricante por litros, sábanas y toallas de colores oscuros, toallitas higiénicas, guantes de látex, condones como para una orgía —por si se rompen o quieres cambiarlos con frecuencia—. Lee con calma el capítulo de «Menstruación», donde se explica cómo manejar situaciones con sustancias engorrosas. Un detalle: el dedo/dedos o juguetes o pene enfundado que se introducen en el ano no deben pasar a la vagina. Usa la otra mano o espera a lavarte bien o a quitarte el guante/cambiarte el condón. Puede que no salga nada de nada, pero puede que sí. Tras la sesión, hay que limpiar todo para evitar que se instalen las bacterias fecales en alfombras, sábanas, etc.

Mucho ojo

Merece la pena detenerse sobre el aspecto estrictamente psicológico. Los roles que cada uno asume en su vida profesional y social bien pueden ser asfixiantes o un puro disfraz del verdadero yo. Será durante el sexo cuando desarrollemos parcelas inexploradas, secretas o castradas. Algunos disfrutan siendo dominados o dominando, puesto que precisamente en su cotidianeidad les toca hacer lo opuesto. En esta práctica se manifiesta el juego de poderes, esa inquietante lucha soterrada que se mantiene sobre las sábanas, se conecta con el significado de «ser el otro» por un momento y con esa capacidad de asumir un papel distinto, con ese placer intrínseco de la ruptura de las normas. La actitud correcta irá hacia «ofrecer lo mismo que se pide»... y a ver qué pasa. Siempre, de menos a más: si es la primera vez que alguien se va a meter algo por ahí, no suele ser lo más adecuado empezar con un ariete de 30 cm ni con el pene directamente: el dedo, dildos especiales (dilatadores chiquititos, tira de bolas...). Para el receptor: si empujas como si quisieras gritar —sin sonido—, harás más fácil la entrada y la estancia.

Respecto de la diversidad de actitudes ante el sexo anal, si se va a hacer, hazlo, pero no te estreses, con mucha calma y mucha pasión a la vez. Y si no, no aconsejo que se apueste por la paciencia, en el sentido de «con el tiempo, la convenceré y lo hará», puesto que habrá casos en que ese «no» sea inamovible, por muchos años que transcurran. En el otro extremo, se dan infinidad de relaciones esporádicas con penetración anal, precisamente, porque hacerlo con un perfecto extraño, con alguien a quien no se volverá a ver, del que no se sabe ni el nombre, permite desinhibirse y aparcar los tabúes y limitaciones éticas que pesan sobre muchos, aprovechando el momento de calentón para cumplir fantasías y derribar barreras psicológicas.

Después de haber leído este capítulo cabe que alguien se plantee que la espontaneidad en este coito no tiene cabida... Sí, la tiene, pero con dolor y efectos secundarios. A veces, dejarse llevar por el calentón merecerá la pena, otras no.

6

Anticonceptivos

Los anticonceptivos se clasifican según distintos criterios. Uno habla de métodos reversibles: la píldora, el preservativo, el DIU, el diafragma, etc., e irreversibles: ligadura de trompas, vasectomía. Pero hay otros: naturales, químicos y quirúrgicos; femeninos y masculinos, en función de quién deba utilizarlos; si requieren prescripción médica o no: la píldora anticonceptiva, los implantes, las inyecciones, el dispositivo intrauterino (DIU), el diafragma y el protector cervical requieren receta médica; los condones, los espermicidas y las esponjas, no.

Se puede utilizar más de un método anticonceptivo cada vez, considerando que las relaciones sexuales además de un embarazo no deseado pueden ocasionar contagios de ETS. Aunque la mujer puede, unilateralmente, anular su fertilidad, si se tiene pareja, entre los dos deberían decidir el que se aplica. Sólo los directamente implicados pueden valorar el grado de confianza —y de fidelidad— como para eliminar el preservativo; sopesar quién asume el «sacrificio» que supone, por ejemplo, la responsabilidad de acordarse de tomar la píldora todos los días; o el trago de colocarse el dispositivo intrauterino; o de someterse a la intervención, éste, con el añadido de que se trata de un método irreversible, etc. Ventilados en la intimidad los aspectos que acabo de apuntar, debe ser un médico quien, evaluando la salud de los interesados y su proyecto de vida en común, les recomiende el más adecuado. Me parece una temeridad, desde aquí, abogar por uno en detrimento de otro o recomendar de modo generalizado otro que no sea el preservativo.

Mecánicos o de barrera

Preservativo masculino o condón

Si hay un artículo sexual que en los tiempos que corren se hace imprescindible es el preservativo. Aunque tiene un peso específico sobre la vida y la muerte —ojo, que ahora no bromeo—, no bebe de la esencia divina y, por lo tanto, no basta con «invocarlo» —hablar de él o discutir sobre sexo seguro está bien para debates televisivos o para reportajes sexológicos, pero para estos fines que tratamos, no sirve— y con «tenerlo» —¡qué bien!, llevas dos en la cartera/en el bolso, pues ponlos cerquita de la cama o del sofá, para que no dé pereza en plena faena levantarse a rebuscar—. Insisto: por desgracia, para que el preservativo haga efecto, hay que ponérselo a él en el pene. Lo de usar condón, a día de hoy, no es negociable, se debe dar por hecho. Si topas con alguien que no quiere usarlo, recoge tus bártulos y lárgate.

Saber cómo y cuándo se coloca un condón es imprescindible —esto no es como un masajeador, que uno puede dejarse llevar por la imaginación o como la cantidad de aceite de vainilla, que podemos echarlo a ojo sobre la espalda sin que pase nada si sobra o falta—. Aquí sí que es clave tener en cuenta cada detalle para asegurar la protección, tanto de embarazos no deseados como de ETS y sida.

Lo primero: comprueba la fecha de caducidad y que estén homologados por la Dirección General de Farmacia (debe llevar una numeración seguida de las letras CC).

Alguno pensará que le tomo por idiota, pero abrir el condón es algo más delicado que quitar la tapa de un yogur. Si lo rompes o lo pinchas sin darte cuenta, no cumplirá su misión. Cuidado con uñas, anillos, pulseras y cualquier objeto metálico, punzante o estriado. Por eso mismo, tampoco debes emplear los dientes para sacarlo del envoltorio, podrías rasgarlo sin querer.

Sobra, supongo, comentar que son de un solo uso. A diferencia de los juguetes sexuales, los condones son de un solo uso y no se lavan (lo que no impide echar un polvo en el mar, en la piscina o en la bañera, para lo que se debe colocar en tierra firme).

No lo coloques antes de que el pene esté totalmente erecto.

No apures el preservativo: cuando lo pongas, has de dejar una especie de bolsa en el extremo, que hará de depósito para el semen. Para que no quede llena de aire, mantén los dedos presionados sobre la punta del condón mientras lo pones (lo apoyas en la punta del glande y lo vas desenrollando hasta llegar a la base). Ahí sí se ha de apurar: que cubra todo el pene y que la goma que sobre, permanezca enrollada abajo de todo, en la base —así a ella no le machacará la vagina cuando se produzca el movimiento mete-saca, ni a él le estrangulará como cuando se le queda en mitad del pene—. Si detectas alguna burbuja de aire, quítala pasando los dedos con un movimiento hacia la base.

Ponlo siempre antes de que entre en contacto con la vagina. Ni se te ocurra proponer/ceder a chorradas tipo «sólo la puntita». Si lo haces, y lo colocas después de haber estado jugando, penetrando un poco e intercambiando fluidos, habrás abierto la posibilidad al contagio y quién sabe si al embarazo.

Conviene añadir un poco de lubricante. Ahora, con el pene enfundado, éste no contribuye a la lubricación con el líquido preseminal, con lo que si el flujo de ella no es abundante, al rato, la vagina será víctima de esa horrible quemazón que ha sido la causa de la mala fama de los preservativos.

Cuando se haya producido la eyaculación, saca el pene. No se debe esperar a que se ablande. Se hace sujetando el condón por la base, con firmeza. El asunto de que se saque de inmediato es para evitar que el condón pueda quedarse dentro de la vagina —cuando el pene pierde la erección disminuye de tamaño, es como si un calcetín te queda grande—, y existe el riesgo de que el semen se derrame dentro. Con el pene apuntando hacia abajo, se enrolla el condón y se tira. Como el váter no se los lleva, y de cara a la responsabilidad de todos para con nuestro planeta, mejor hacer un nudo y echarlo a una papelera o a la basura. Él debe lavarse el pene y las manos si va a continuar la sesión o a empezar una nueva. (No sólo para quitar cualquier resto de esperma, sino para, y esto ya va por los dos, eliminar el asqueroso sabor a goma, que será percibido de inmediato en cuanto él pretenda hacer un cunnilingus o ella se acerque el pene o la mano a la boca. La solidaridad debe demostrarse con hechos.)

El condón puede colocarse con la boca —muchas prostitutas lo hacen sin que el cliente se entere siquiera—. Nadie nace enseñado y éste, como todo arte, conlleva su práctica. Si te interesa, puedes ensayar con plátanos: prueba si eres capaz de desenrollarlo y de ajustarlo sólo con la lengua y los labios, con los dedos te puedes ayudar un poco, pero sólo a fijarlo en el glande. Por supuesto, será preferible elegir algún sabor, cualquiera es más agradable que el látex. Ver más en «Juguetes eróticos».

Preservativo femenino

Un método más comentado por «curioso» que por ser efectivamente empleado. Se trata de una especie de rectángulo de poliuretano con dos anillas blandas, una en cada extremo. Se debe agarrar entre los dedos la anilla que se encuentra en el extremo cerrado e introducirla en la vagina, todo lo profundamente que se pueda y hacia arriba, hasta detrás del hueso del pubis, lo que describirá una especie de saco donde se introduce el pene. Tras la eyaculación, se debe oprimir y girar el anillo que ha quedado fuera y que ha servido para proteger los labios de todo contacto, y tirar suavemente hacia fuera hasta extraer el preservativo, con el semen dentro, y echarlo a la basura. No es lavable ni reutilizable. Va bien en caso de alergia al látex y porque se coloca antes de iniciar el coito, con lo que no hay «interrupciones», pero los hay que se quejan porque da la sensación de hacerlo con una bolsa de plástico. Comparado con los condones pierden por goleada: resultan más caros y, habiendo visto el aspecto de la vulva con él colocado —queda recubierta por el poliuretano y con la anilla ahí en medio—... Y lo peor es que la sensibilidad del pene dentro de él es mucho menor, porque no permite que se capte ni el calor de la vagina, ni se tiene el mismo contacto con las paredes internas que el preservativo facilita.

Diafragma

Se trata de una especie de membrana circular de látex en cuyo borde se encuentra un aro de metal flexible. Los hay de varias medidas; el ginecólogo determina la «talla» de cada mujer en cada momento, ya que puede variar por partos, aumento o pérdida de peso... Será también el médico quien enseñe cómo se usa, porque para muchas no resulta tan fácil, hasta que se les coge el truquillo. Además, se debe practicar en privado antes, para familiarizarse con la colocación y la extracción. El diafragma se pone antes del coito dentro de la vagina untado con espermicida, que ayuda a su inserción y potencia su efecto anticonceptivo. No hace falta que se haga justo en el momento de la relación, sino que puede hacerse con más anticipación, eso sí, añadiendo más espermicida si han pasado más de dos horas desde que se puso. Algo que ha de tenerse en cuenta es que no se debe retirar hasta que transcurran al menos seis o siete horas desde el coito —desde el último de ellos, si es que hay más de uno— para asegurarse de que la crema espermicida acaba con los espermatozoides. Una vez que se saca, ha de lavarse con agua y jabón y secarlo bien, antes de meterlo en su cajita.

Dispositivo intrauterino (DIU)

Se recomienda para mujeres que ya han tenido al menos un hijo. Consiste en un pequeño dispositivo metálico o de plástico que es colocado por el ginecólogo dentro del útero a través del cuello uterino y que impide la gestación. Normalmente se coloca durante la regla, para garantizar que no existe un embarazo.[18] Este método en realidad no evita el embarazo sino la implantación del cigoto en el útero. Tienen un índice de seguridad del 97 %. Los hay de varios tipos y su eficacia dura entre 2 y 4 años, pudiendo sustituirse por uno nuevo. El DIU hormonal contiene levonorgestrel, una hormona que se libera de modo constante. El de cobre, que se encuentra en diversas formas, de «T» o espiral, provoca mayor sangrado y dolor menstrual. El DIU sirve para estimular la capacidad de ciertas células de la mucosa uterina para aniquilar los espermatozoides. Puede suceder que el DIU sea rechazado por el organismo y haya que retirarlo, y también que se expulse o se desplace por

18. Precisamente porque cuando sospechan que puede haberse producido un embarazo no deseado, algunas mujeres recurren a la colocación de un DIU como método no ya anticonceptivo, sino potencialmente abortivo. Será en cada caso el ginecólogo quien valore, respecto de cada paciente, si está indicada esta solución de emergencia.

accidente —esto, por ejemplo, se capta con una ecografía, por eso es fundamental realizar revisiones—. Además, el DIU no previene de embarazos ectópicos (fuera del cuerpo uterino). Si se produce una enfermedad o infección vaginal, los hilos del DIU que quedan en la vagina pueden alcanzar las trompas y producir inflamación e infección de las mismas (EIP o enfermedad inflamatoria pélvica). Estos hilos pueden quedar demasiado largos y molestar al practicar penetraciones profundas.

QUÍMICOS Y HORMONALES

Píldora anticonceptiva, «la píldora»[19]

Desde que se comenzase a comercializar en Europa la primera versión, en 1961, ha habido una significativa mejora de la píldora anticonceptiva en cuanto a sus posibles efectos secundarios (engordar y provocar sofocos, mareos, vómitos, dolor de cabeza y tensión en los pechos). Debe recetarla un ginecólogo. Este anticonceptivo oral a base de hormonas no se indica para menores de 16 años, para que las chicas terminen de madurar sexualmente de modo natural, y tampoco a mayores de 45, por posibles interacciones cardíacas y circulatorias. Se recomienda no fumar si se toma la píldora. Ventajas: Muchas. Hay que saber que se prescribe a veces para estabilizar el ciclo menstrual de mujeres muy irregulares (vendrá la regla siempre cada 28 días), así como para casos de menstruaciones excesivas que provocan anemia, o muy dolorosas, ya que reduce o elimina el dolor de la regla «natural». Además, previene la enfermedad inflamatoria pélvica, una ETS; reduce la frecuencia de quistes ováricos y protege frente a determinados tipos de cáncer (de ovario y de endometrio, que afecta a parte del útero). Incluso se usa como tratamiento de ciertos tipos de acné...

Información básica: la píldora se presenta en tabletas de 21 pastillitas. La primera se toma el primer día de sangrado de la regla y las demás, una al día, procurando dos cosas: tomarla a la misma hora y que no se olvide, en cuyo caso hay que procurar tomarla

19. Datos de Schering España, S.A.

dentro de las siguientes 12 horas, si no, omitirla y tomar la siguiente a la hora acostumbrada. Si sucede esto o si, por ejemplo, vomitas dentro de las 3 o 4 horas siguientes a haberla tomado, o si tuvieras una diarrea muy fuerte, se recomienda utilizar otro método anticonceptivo para asegurar. Pasados los 21 días, terminada la caja, se interrumpe la toma diaria durante 7 días; es la semana de descanso, durante la cual se producirá el sangrado menstrual. Pasados estos 7 días, digamos que el 8.º día, se comienza otra vez: 21 días/21 pastillas, semana de descanso/regla. La píldora es eficaz desde el primer día, pero si empiezas con este método hormonal después de haber utilizado otros (de barrera, como el preservativo) es recomendable que sigas utilizándolo durante el primer mes que la tomas.

Inyección hormonal

Previene embarazos durante 3 meses, precisa por lo tanto, 4 al año. Su eficacia como anticonceptivo es elevada y su administración, relativamente cómoda.

Implante hormonal subdérmico

Es una especie de tubo de plástico muy fino que, mediante una incisión realizada con anestesia local, se coloca bajo la piel del brazo. La protección puede prolongarse hasta 5 años, pudiendo implantarse unos nuevos o retirarse a voluntad —es decir, mediante el mismo procedimiento quirúrgico...—. Se detecta al tacto pero no se nota a simple vista. Lo peor de este método es que si ha de suspenderse por rechazo, reacción adversa o «cambio de idea», requiere intervención quirúrgica —por mínima que sea— para su extracción, que siempre es menos sencilla que su implantación.

Las píldoras, las inyecciones y los implantes hormonales son muy efectivos porque evitan la ovulación, imposibilitando el embarazo porque no hay un óvulo que fecundar. Además, causan otros cambios en la mucosa cervical y en el útero que ayudan a impedir el embarazo. Lo malo es que no ofrecen protección contra las enfermedades de transmisión sexual y provocan, en ocasiones, períodos irregulares.

Espermicidas

Sustancias químicas que matan o alteran la movilidad de los espermatozoides para evitar que alcancen el óvulo. Se presentan en gel, líquido, espuma o crema, lo que hace que sirvan además como lubricante, aunque su sabor es desagradable para el sexo oral. Se emplean, generalmente, asociados a los métodos anticonceptivos de barrera (condón, diafragma) para potenciar su efecto anticonceptivo. Los óvulos vaginales se utilizan solos; hay que introducirlos hasta el cuello del útero y esperar unos 20 minutos para que se disuelvan. En general, los espermicidas no previenen contra ETS y las abrasiones que producen en las mucosas incrementan el riesgo de contraer sida. Además, puede resultar peligroso si se es alérgico a cualquiera de sus componentes o a su principio activo, el nonoxynol-9. Tras la relación sexual ha de mantenerse en la vagina unas siete horas; los enjuagues y lavados vaginales debilitan su eficacia.

QUIRÚRGICOS

Ligadura de trompas

Se trata de un método definitivo. La fecundación se imposibilita porque se cortan y ligan (se cierran) las trompas de Falopio, que son los conductos por los que descienden los óvulos desde el ovario y por los que ascienden los espermatozoides desde el cuello del útero. Es imprescindible que antes de someterse a la operación, la mujer cuente con asesoramiento médico para que efectivamente sea consciente de que es irreversible. Debe tener bien presente que su capacidad reproductiva desaparecerá y que, aunque sus circunstancias cambien, no podrá ser madre de modo biológico; es decir, si una mujer joven o relativamente joven se esteriliza, cabe que se arrepienta si, por ejemplo, cambia de pareja y juntos desean tener hijos. La operación requiere quirófano, anestesia, varios días de recuperación y tomar analgésicos para el dolor. Pueden presentarse complicaciones, como en toda cirugía: desde infecciones a hemorragias, y existe riesgo de embarazos ectópicos, etc. En cifras globales, la ligadura de trompas es el método más utilizado en el mundo. Cabe intentar una cirugía para revertir la ligadura, pero es complicada y el éxito de poder embarazarse de nuevo no está garantizado.

Vasectomía

Se trata de la operación quirúrgica que liga los conductos deferentes —los que conducen el semen desde los testículos hasta la vesícula seminal— y cuyo objetivo es la esterilización masculina. La incisión se practica en el escroto, se extraen los conductos deferentes, se cortan y se sellan —se cauterizan—. La intervención, practicada con anestesia local, dura unos 10 minutos. No produce dolor, ni la inyección, ni el posoperatorio. En una semana se pueden reanudar las relaciones sexuales. Para asegurar que no queden espermatozoides, hay que «vaciar» los testículos. Se calcula que éstos se expulsan en unas 15 eyaculaciones. Por falta de información, muchos temen que su virilidad (capacidad de erección, potencia, control eyaculatorio) se vea mermada. No es cierto, la operación no la afecta, lo único que hace es que la eyaculación no contiene espermatozoides, pero incluso el aspecto del líquido expulsado será el mismo. Los espermatozoides, como quedan en el interior del organismo, son reabsorbidos de modo natural. A diferencia de la ligadura de trompas, esta intervención sí es reversible, con lo que si la vida y las circunstancias cambian, se puede intervenir de nuevo para recuperar la fertilidad. Suele resultar sencillo, salvo que, por el tipo de vasectomía realizada, se dificulte, o por haber transcurrido más de diez años desde que se practicó.

MÉTODOS NATURALES POCO FIABLES

Método de Ogino-Knaus o del calendario

Ideado por el ginecólogo japonés Ogino, en 1924, emplea la abstinencia de relaciones sexuales con penetración durante la ovulación para evitar embarazos. Se basa en contar los días, evitando las relaciones cuando la mujer es potencialmente fértil. Una profe-

sora me dijo una vez: «hay toda una generación de hijos de Ogino», y me temo que se refería a la cantidad de fallos, no a los acier-
tos en el uso del método en cuestión... Para su eficacia, además de
mucha disciplina, exige una enorme regularidad en los ciclos. Se
cuenta el primer día del ciclo como el primer día de la menstruación y el último día del ciclo es el día anterior al inicio de la regla
siguiente. Se aplica la siguiente fórmula: se restan dieciocho días al
ciclo más corto y once días al ciclo más largo. Suponiendo que los
ciclos son de veinticinco y de treinta días, el período de abstención
de las relaciones coitales será el comprendido entre los días siete y
diecinueve.

Temperatura corporal

Consiste en estudiar la temperatura del organismo de la mujer
para conocer el momento de la ovulación. Todos los días, en estado
de reposo, al despertarse, se ha de tomar la temperatura bajo la lengua durante 5 minutos. Durante la ovulación se producirá un aumento de casi un grado, rebasará los 37 °C, lo que nos indica que el
riesgo de embarazo es mayor.

Método moco cervical o Billings

Estudia el aspecto y textura del moco cervical, que va cambiando
a lo largo del ciclo. Cuando aparece amarillento, opaco y más espeso
o denso, se trata de la etapa infértil. Los días en que adquiere humedad, transparencia y flexibilidad, serán los de fertilidad.
Teniendo en cuenta que el óvulo vive 24 horas y los espermatozoides de 48 a 96 horas, hemos de calcular un período de fertilidad
de 3 a 5 días. Y éstos son los días en los que habría que evitar mantener relaciones sexuales si no se desea un embarazo.

Como métodos anticonceptivos se consideran poco fiables
puesto que tanto la ovulación puede adelantarse o retrasarse, el
moco cervical sufrir alteraciones —causas hormonales, psicológi-

cas, de infecciones o enfermedad física o estrés—, y la temperatura basal también varía por circunstancias del día a día. Además, ninguno protege de las ETS o de contraer el sida.

Lactancia prolongada

Junto con los lavados vaginales, el coito interrumpido y mantener relaciones sexuales durante la menstruación, existe la creencia errónea de que la lactancia prolongada es un método anticonceptivo.

Este método basa su eficacia en que la hormona de la prolactina está en una tasa alta, y ello impide la ovulación; sin embargo, ésta puede ocurrir aun antes del restablecimiento de las menstruaciones y por tanto producirse el embarazo.

Lavados vaginales

Consiste en limpiar la vulva y la vagina con agua después del coito para eliminar el semen que se deposita en ellas tras la eyaculación. Al igual que los inductores menstruales, no se considera un método anticonceptivo porque, por rápido que se haga, la potencia de los disparos eyaculatorios hará que los espermatozoides lleven una gran ventaja al agua en el ascenso por el cuello del útero. De hecho, podría ser contraproducente: podrías ayudar con la irrigación a que los «rezagados» alcancen la «meta». Se desaconsejan también porque cambian el pH de la vagina y eso la hace más débil ante las infecciones y la irritación. En otro orden, el mal olor obedece a una causa mucho más severa que la simple falta de higiene.[20] Suele responder a una ETS, a una infección o a motivos hormonales casi siempre, con lo que un simple lavado no bastará. Las prostitutas francesas usaban, ya en el s. XVII, jeringas para irrigar la vagina después del coito, pero su escasa utilidad es la ya descrita.

---

20. Ver la acepción *esmegma* en la tercera parte del libro y el apartado de «Sexo oral».

Coito interrumpido

Viene de la acepción del latín *coitus interruptus* y vulgarmente se denomina «marcha atrás». Para usar correctamente este método, el hombre debe sacar el pene de la vagina antes de la eyaculación. Esto requiere gran disciplina y mantener cierta conciencia durante el coito. Se debe retirar el pene cuando la excitación sexual está llegando al punto álgido, cerca ya del orgasmo, y alejarlo para que no salpique a la vagina ni los genitales externos. El contacto con las secreciones cervicales puede transportar los espermatozoides al interior del aparato genital.

Los expertos calculan que el método del coito interrumpido registra una tasa de embarazo típica del 19 %, pero reconocen que este cálculo se basa en investigaciones limitadas. Las encuestas nacionales indican que este método es el que más se usa en Rumania (35 %), en Turquía (27 %) y en la República Checa (24 %). Entre los países donde también se utiliza mucho figuran Mauricio (16 %), Sri Lanka (8 %) y el 5 % en Brasil, Colombia, las Filipinas, Trinidad y Tobago, y Zimbabue.[21]

No es recomendable porque implica un elevado riesgo, y por partida doble. Respecto del embarazo: cabe que el hombre no tenga control de su momento de eyaculación. Además, hay espermatozoides en el líquido preseminal que pueden quedarse en la vagina y pese a que el pene sea retirado a tiempo, provocar un embarazo. Obviamente, el otro riesgo atañe a la ausencia de profilaxis. Si no se dispone de otro método, es mejor que no utilizar ninguno, pero no debería ser «el método». Como efectos secundarios a medio y largo plazo, puede afectar psicológicamente al varón y alterar su capacidad de control de la eyaculación. Muchos países lo emplean debido a la falta de recursos económicos o la dificultad de acceder a los métodos anticonceptivos.

21. Información extraída de Family Health International (FHI), 2007.

Nuevas fórmulas contraceptivas

Parches anticonceptivos

Se trata de un adhesivo que contiene principios activos —hormonas— que se liberan directamente en el torrente sanguíneo y evitan la ovulación. La mujer se coloca uno cada siete días, durante tres semanas. Durante la cuarta «se descansa» y se producirá el período. Ha de cambiarse el parche siempre el mismo día de la semana, ya que su eficacia se prevé exactamente para 7 días. Va a gustos, pero se recomienda colocarlo en zonas no visibles, que no rocen con la ropa y que no se desprendan si se lleva alguna prenda muy ceñida (en muslo, culo, hombro, etc., pero nunca sobre el pecho). Se debe fijar sobre la piel limpia, seca y sin vello. Ventajas: su eficacia anticonceptiva es muy alta. Indoloro y fácil de colocar, es como ponerse una tirita.

Anillo vaginal

Fabricado en poliuretano (de plástico), es muy flexible y tiene un diámetro de 5 cm y 5 mm de grosor. Se introduce en la vagina y se deja dentro 3 semanas, durante las que libera una dosis de hormonas muy baja y constante, que evita la ovulación. Transcurrida la tercera semana se extrae y durante la cuarta semana, vendrá la regla. Después, computando el fin de la cuarta semana, se coloca un anillo nuevo, y así sucesivamente. Precisa receta médica. Su colocación no exige demasiado, sólo que permanezca dentro de la vagina; si lo sacas durante esas 3 semanas, no debe pasar fuera más de 3 horas, o perderá eficacia. Se mete con los dedos y da igual la posición que adopte —no es un método de barrera—, procurando, por supuesto, que no moleste. El anillo y el parche suponen calidad de vida porque no se notan durnte la penetración, no duele llevarlos ni colocarlos. Además, la mujer no depende de terceros ni para ponérselos ni para quitárselos. Los dos riesgos de su uso son que se caiga/despegue sin que ella se dé cuenta y que no protegen de contagios genitales ni de contraer sida.

Minipíldora

A diferencia de los otros anovulatorios orales, sólo contiene gestágeno (progesterona), a fin de eliminar los efectos secundarios que producen las otras hormonas. Es adecuada para mujeres que no toleran los estrógenos y se indica también como anticonceptivo durante la lactancia. En España actualmente se comercializa Cerazet, que contiene 0.075 mg de desogestrel. Funciona inhibiendo la ovulación. También hace el moco cervical más espeso e impermeable a los espermatozoides y causa cierta involución en el endometrio para que rehúse la recepción del óvulo fecundado. Se toma de forma continuada, no se deja período de descanso. Cada envase tiene 28 pastillas. Exige mucha regularidad en las tomas —fundamental que sea a la misma hora—. Si hay un retraso de más de tres horas respecto de la habitual, se debe utilizar un método anticonceptivo adicional durante las 48 horas subsiguientes. Requiere prescripción médica. Es efectiva desde el séptimo día de tratamiento.

ANTICONCEPTIVO DE URGENCIA

Píldora del día después o pastilla poscoital[22]

Se trata de un método anticonceptivo oral para casos de emergencia y siempre sujeto a un plazo: ha de tomarse dentro de las 72 horas que siguen al coito de riesgo. Cuanto más tiempo transcurre, menor será su eficacia de haberse producido el embarazo.

Método de emergencia. Lo de «emergencia» significa: cuando ha fallado o no se ha empleado el método habitual (léase preservativo que se rompe o se sale, violación, fallo en el diafragma, olvido en la toma de la píldora, etc...). El fármaco, Postinor, a base de levonorgestrel, es una pastilla blanca que se da gratuitamente en los Centros de Planificación Familiar (por lo menos, en Madrid), después de una consulta en la que el médico realiza un informe, tras conocer los antecedentes de la paciente (en lo que respecta a riesgos coronarios, antecedentes oncológicos, alergias, intervenciones quirúrgicas, gesta-

22. Datos de Schering España, S.A.

ciones o abortos previos, etc.). Durante la consulta informa a la mujer de riesgos, eficacia, etc. No es exagerado calificarla de «bomba hormonal». Quede claro que no es un anticonceptivo que pueda utilizarse regularmente. ¿Se entiende el significado de la palabra «excepcional» como opuesto a «habitual»?

Particularidades y similitud con la píldora. Como la píldora, protege de embarazos no deseados pero no del posible contagio de ETS o sida. Cuando la píldora poscoital falla, existe riesgo —bajo— de embarazo ectópico: el óvulo fecundado se implanta fuera del útero. Al igual que la píldora, no se debe administrar a menores de 16 años, ni a embarazadas, debiendo evitarse en la etapa de lactancia porque el principio activo pasa al bebé por la leche. Se aconseja tomarla dentro de las primeras 12 horas, pero no después de las 72, ni si se ha producido ya un retraso en la regla. Caso de vomitar dentro de las 3 o 4 horas después de tomarla, se debe contactar con el médico para que prescriba otra, ya que, tal y como sucede con la píldora, la expulsión o la mala absorción determinan riesgo de ineficacia. La regla debería venir en las fechas previstas, aunque cabe cierto adelanto o retraso (se recomienda el test de embarazo).

7

Cuando no funciona

Eyaculación precoz o retardada

«Si el hombre prolonga el acto durante largo rato, la mujer ama más, se siente mejor, más llena, más satisfecha en suma, y si lo hace demasiado deprisa, ella queda, por supuesto, descontenta de él, se siente desgraciada, se pregunta si no sirve o si no se la ama lo suficiente», dice uno de los pasajes del Kamasutra.

«¿Ya está? ¿Cómo que ya está?»

¿Precoz? ¿Y cuánto es eso? Como Einstein no colabora conmigo, ya le cito yo: el tiempo es relativo, en esto también. El adjetivo «precoz» suele aplicarse a la eyaculación que se produce antes de haber mediado siquiera contacto (sin que se haya podido iniciar la penetración o justo al intentarla), y también si lo ha habido pero la eyaculación se desencadena sin poderse evitar. No hay una marca oficial en segundos, minutos u horas del coito perfecto, como tampoco sirve determinar que alguien es eyaculador precoz basándose en el número de movimientos pélvicos que realiza...

Se entenderá en cualquier caso por eyaculación precoz cuando no existe control sobre ella, cuando es «demasiado pronto» para él o su pareja. En los años cuarenta y cincuenta, Kinsey[23] publicaba

---

23. *The Kinsey Institute New Report on Sex.* St's Martin's Press, Nueva York, 1990.

que el 75 % de los hombres eyacula en dos minutos desde que se produce la penetración. Hoy esa duración media se ha incrementado en torno a un minuto, o sea, unos tres aproximadamente. Esta disfunción fue abordada de modo clínico por primera vez por Masters y Johnson, en sus estudios sobre sexualidad.

Las eyaculaciones precoces esporádicas encuentran como causas más habituales la abstinencia prolongada (lleva fuera de mercado un siglo y tiene hambre atrasada); la hiperexcitación (cuando le has puesto como una moto o acaba de ver realizado su sueño erótico más preciado); separación de la pareja (el deseado reencuentro juega malas pasadas)... No hay mujer que no sepa justificar estas situaciones (o no debería). Sin embargo, aunque quizá tú no te des cuenta, estate seguro de que ella sí y si cada vez que mantienes una relación el coito termina antes de tiempo, quizá no pase nada la primera vez, ni la segunda, pero tres y sucesivas se traducen como «mi vida sexual es una porquería» o un «y María se moja las ganas, en el café», como cantaba Mecano.

El resultado de ese «¿ya está?», verbalizado con inocencia o con mala leche, o no mencionado siquiera —pero pensado—, es la insatisfacción sexual de ella. Esa frustración arruina la vida de pareja cada vez más a corto plazo. La gente hoy día no está por la labor de privarse de nada: «los jóvenes no aguantáis nada», decía mi pobre abuela (claro que no es lo mismo solicitar el divorcio porque recibes malos tratos que porque te molesta el modo en que sacude las alfombras o el desorden de sus cajones), pero llevaba parte de razón: ciertas generaciones tenemos el virus de la prisa inoculado, sabemos que el tiempo vuela y que prácticamente todo es sustituible. Lo mismo que aparcas las sandalias que te hacen rozaduras, o que cambias de lavadora antes que arreglarla, ocurre con los amantes.

Deprisa, deprisa

Ciertas «explicaciones» de la eyaculación precoz son vox pópuli, pero no por ello ciertas ni aceptables. Unos recuerdan que las primeras masturbaciones se realizaban a contrarreloj para no ser pillados con las manos «ocupadas»; otros aluden a que muchos señores se inician en el sexo con «chicas de pago», que van con prisas para acabar cuanto antes y aceleran premeditadamente el coito (teoría muy pasada de moda); otros apuntan a unos escarceos homosexuales adolescentes —de los que, por supuesto, sólo se habla de oídas— y que se realizaban a toda prisa también; muchos se refieren a las competiciones de chavales que se empeñaban en que el primero que «terminaba» era el más machote...

Si bien es cierto que la prisa, la clandestinidad o el miedo a ser descubierto masturbándose o practicando sexo han acompañado la vida sexual de muchos varones, como no a todos les causa eyaculación precoz, no cabría generalizar; además, tampoco es de aplicación puesto que cuando se masturban en privado, pueden durar más, controlan la descarga de modo voluntario. Por otro lado tampoco se cumple si se extrapolase a la mujer, que en la adolescencia igualmente se tiene que esconder y apresurarse para masturbarse. Que yo sepa, no por haberlo hecho en esas idénticas circunstancias la mujer tiene orgasmos «precoces» con la pareja, por haberse acostumbrado a una masturbación apresurada y prohibida.

El problema de la eyaculación precoz reside y está causado, fundamentalmente, por la ansiedad y la angustia que el hombre siente. El varón en la cama asume la responsabilidad por los dos: ha de conseguir el placer propio y el ajeno. Sobre él, es decir, sobre su pene, se cierne la presión del éxito o fracaso del encuentro. Debe cumplir. Debe lograr satisfacerse a sí mismo, a veces luchando contra su propio impulso, ralentizando lo que siente. Debe proporcionarle placer a ella, para lo que además de saber qué hacer —tremenda la injusticia que les exija ciencia infusa—, debe prolongar su erección retardando su eyaculación para adaptarse al tempo de su pareja... Además, otras causas pueden ser el estrés, los nervios, una crisis de autoestima y... sentimiento de culpa (a veces, ponerle los cuernos a tu pareja tiene castigos inesperados).

Hay hombres que sólo sufren eyaculación precoz con determinadas parejas, con las que por un motivo u otro necesitan quedar bien o a las que pretenden impresionar o que les producen tal excitación que la cosa se desborda, literalmente. Justo esa exigencia aumenta los neurotransmisores en su cerebro y provoca que se les dispare el control eyaculatorio. Si cualquier estímulo provoca su eyaculación, podéis optar por reducir el ritmo. Hay expertos que recomiendan evitar todo contacto físico previo, es decir: penetración sin casi roce corporal y que dure todo lo posible. Resumido sería que la meta y se mueva hasta que aguante. A mí, personalmente, me da hasta miedo que esta sugerencia se malinterprete y que derive en una relación sin besos, sin caricias, sin nada... sólo para que podamos decir que la penetración ocurrió (supongo que a muchas les pasará lo mismo: si como terapia esto de ir al grano funciona, no descuidéis el resto del cuerpo de cada uno tras el coito). No es eso. El objetivo está en identificar el «punto de no retorno» y cesar los estímulos cuando se alcanza (para eso, nadie mejor que él); detenerse y relajarse hasta que, pasado el momento crítico, se pueda volver a comenzar. Se debe realizar a solas, luego con la pareja, incluso pidiéndole que intervenga (que agarre el pene, que vaya masturbándolo hasta que la avise), después intentarlo con el coito. Normalmente lleva mucho tiempo y práctica y requiere paciencia, mucha paciencia. Nadie dijo que fuera fácil.

Trucos y remedios

Descargar antes. Muchos aconsejan tener una eyaculación poco antes de iniciar el acto. No ha de ser necesariamente él en privado, antes de la cita, puede realizarse una masturbación con la pareja, como parte de los juegos sexuales. Que haya eyaculado previamente convierte la excitación durante el coito en más controlable y se retarda la ulterior descarga.

Fármacos. Hay medicinas que actúan directamente sobre el sistema nervioso adrenérgico que controla la eyaculación, pero el problema es que, a veces, provocan que desaparezca la erección (anulan el deseo y provocan disfunción eréctil, siendo peor el remedio que la enfermedad).

Reaprendizaje. Consiste en practicar una técnica de «parada y arranque»: cuando nota que va a eyacular, se detiene durante el tiempo suficiente para evitar que se produzca y pasado «el peligro» reanuda el coito o la masturbación, así unas tres o cuatro veces, hasta que finalmente sí se permite la eyaculación. Se trata de «reaprender» la conducta que se ha seguido quizá durante años en cada eyaculación y controlar esa urgencia eyaculatoria. Se realiza con la mano, rodeando con los dedos la parte superior del pene (glande), presionando con el pulgar sobre el frenillo, hasta que se reduzca la excitación y se pueda reiniciar (técnica de Semans). Para paliar la eyaculación precoz no basta con hacer esto una vez, sino que en distintos encuentros se excluirá el coito y se tratará de ir avanzando en el control eyaculatorio (se debería tomar como «hacer los deberes», o en plan juego «vale todo menos penetración»...).

Ocupar la mente en «nada». También ayuda a reducir la excitación centrar los pensamientos en absurdas cuentas atrás (de 500 a 0), o pensar en cualquier cosa que no resulte erótica.

Abordar el asunto en pareja. Resulta crucial y requiere mucha comunicación puesto que mientras ella acaricia y maneja el pene, él ha de dirigirla, darle instrucciones, advertirle que se detenga o prosiga. Con esta terapia se pretende solucionar un problema que afecta a ambos, pero no convirtáis la cama en una «consulta» porque pronto el sexo parecerá muy aburrido —o un patíbulo— y puede degenerar en una verdadera obsesión. Si bien os vais a dedicar al pene, no conviene descuidarla a ella, que también quiere pasarlo bien... Si no, será frustrante y dejará de interesarle tener sexo contigo.

Las técnicas de parada y la de «frenar» manualmente la eyaculación se pueden practicar en solitario pero, una vez se mejora a solas, se alcanzan mejores resultados realizadas en pareja, puesto que la ansiedad la provoca, precisamente, un exceso de deseo, la exigencia de tener que cumplir y la presión psicológica que al hombre le causa llegar a satisfacerla a ella. Cuanto más se masturbe él en privado, buscando controlar la excitación, conociendo sus respuestas eróticas, mejor.

Evitar el contacto. Muchos eyaculadores precoces optan por evitar la estimulación genital directa de ella durante un buen rato intentando que no resulte muy artificial, y que a ella no le parezca raro ni sospechoso. Como los tempos de una y otro son ciertamente dispares, el objetivo es «darle ventaja» a ella: podéis realizar un montón de juegos eróticos —caricias, besos, masajes— procurando excitarla. Lo suyo es continuar hasta lograr que «se corra», bien acariciándola o chupándola, o procurando que se masturbe —si le apetece—. Sólo cuando sabes que ella está satisfecha, permite que te toque. Id despacio, recula si ves que la cosa se acelera y se te va de las manos. Ayuda a retrasar la excitación que él no se baje los pantalones, ni acepte que ella le meta mano durante un rato. Parecerá una tontería, pero no lo es: el efecto psicológico de saber que ella ya ha disfrutado, que está satisfecha, hará que la presión de él se esfume y pueda pasarlo bien, eyaculando cuando su cuerpo se lo pida. Y ella, por su parte, si se percata de que existe una elevada posibilidad de que él termine antes de tiempo, debería dosificarse, adoptar una postura pasiva —que en otro caso no es admisible—. Mi consejo para ella: cuidado con las caricias demasiado intensas —el sexo oral sería una de ellas—, nada de clavarle las uñas apasionadamente, refrena los gestos de excitación (recuerda que a ellos les pone cachondos verte y oírte gozar), a su pene ni te acerques... En fin, déjale hacer y estate calladita y tumbadita. Pese a que sea aburrido, considéralo una inversión. Se supone que es una etapa, hasta que la situación quede bajo control.

Un momento, por favor

Muchos hombres son eyaculadores precoces de modo puntual o habitual y las chicas con las que mantienen relaciones esporádicas ni siquiera se dan cuenta y encima les recuerdan como amantes maravillosos. Todo es cuestión de actitud, como señalo en otro capítulo.

Si notas que te corres inevitablemente y que, pese a que dediques tu mente a acordarte de que tienes que pagar una multa o a reparar una gotera, la cosa es imparable, salte. Sácalo, evita todo contacto directo con el pene. Olvídate de él y ponte en una postura en la que ella no logre alcanzarlo y hazle de todo lo que se te ocurra: sexo oral, acaricia su cuerpo, bésala, lame sus pechos, ponla boca abajo y comienza un masaje desde la nuca sin dejar de estimular su clítoris. Si te detienes o interrumpes este contacto, será un error fatal.

La posición del misionero se considera adecuada para casos de eyaculación precoz. Estando él en posición dominante, puede dosificarse: controla el ritmo, la velocidad, la profundidad y el ángulo de la penetración conforme evoluciona su excitación. Estar encima le permite parar o salirse si nota que va a eyacular.

También puedes dejarte ir, eyacular cuando así lo sientes, pero no «terminar». Cuantas más veces eyacules, mejores serán los sucesivos coitos. Aprovecha que, tras una eyaculación, la siguiente tarda más en producirse. Que tú te corras en veinte segundos —por decir algo— y te des media vuelta para dormir implica que ella se queda a dos velas, comiéndose las uñas.[24] Bien, pues pasado tu momentazo, lo limpias todo con un pañuelo de papel y sigues con ella, no importa. No sé de ningún hombre al que le moleste que su chica se corra cinco veces. Normalmente, a todos les vuelve locos notar que ella está disfrutando, y cuanto más, mejor. Pues a nosotras tampoco nos molesta ni nos ofende que os corráis... Un gran amante no es necesariamente el que te conduce diez veces al clímax sin despeinarse, o sin tener él uno siquiera; es quien hace que los tengas y los vive contigo (sea antes que tú, después, o logrando el tan mitificado y ansiado orgasmo simultáneo).

En realidad, el auténtico objetivo es lograr que el nivel de angustia de él se reduzca, que el acto sexual sea más un acto erótico y sensual en el que se involucran cuerpo (todo él) y mente; un momento íntimo para disfrutar juntos, los dos, no durante el que él ha de someterse a un examen.

¿Y si es justo lo contrario? Cuando, estando muy excitado, no eyacula

Al contrario que la «precoz», se denomina «retardada» o «aneyaculación» a la situación en la que él puede estar erecto durante horas sin conseguir eyacular. En un hombre «normal» puede suceder puntualmente cuando se ha bebido mucho, se han tomado drogas, etc. Sin embargo, a veces, apunta a un trauma infantil o un problema psicológico (hay quienes han sufrido por haber dejado a una novia em-

---

24. Se habla de que los hombres sufren «dolor de huevos» después del calentón que no culmina en eyaculación, debido a que tarda un par de horas que la sangre que se ha ido acumulando en el pene sea drenada, algo que si se da la eyaculación, se realiza fácilmente. Pues a las mujeres les sucede algo similar. Las que reciben cierta estimulación que se interrumpe y no logran tener un orgasmo sienten la misma molestia, debida a la congestión que causa la concentración de sangre en la zona de la vulva. A nivel emocional, también se da cierta reacción de angustia e irritabilidad. Cuando esto sucede a menudo, la frustración causa desinterés por el sexo. Y las multiorgásmicas, con el primero abren boca, es el aperitivo... Si él no sigue, sienten que se quedan a medias. La consecución del primer orgasmo sitúa a la mujer en un estado de mayor receptividad, su umbral del placer sube y, casi inmediatamente, a los breves segundos, pueden perfectamente ir a por el siguiente.

barazada sin buscarlo y su mente reacciona bloqueando la eyaculación); será psicológico —estrés, ansiedad, presión o pudor— si puede masturbarse y eyacular, o si tiene poluciones nocturnas y, sin embargo, con una persona en concreto, con su pareja, no eyacula. Tipos: parcial o total, dependiendo de si se da o no en todos los momentos de excitación, sea por masturbación o por relaciones con una pareja.

Otro caso distinto es la «eyaculación retrógrada», que consiste en que en vez de expulsarse el semen por la uretra, ésta se cierra, se contrae, y el líquido se redirecciona hacia la vejiga y no sale del organismo hasta la siguiente micción. Se trata de una «complicación», no de una enfermedad, en la que interviene la próstata o el sistema nervioso central.

En todos estos casos, se debería acudir a un especialista.

IMPOTENCIA O GATILLAZO

«Si yo soy un monstruo, pero en el momento clave,
me vengo abajo...»

Que el pene del hombre a veces va por libre no es sólo una frase hecha. En esa relación amor-odio que dura toda la vida entre mente y pene, no siempre se impone la primera. Bien sabido es que se levanta cuando quiere y que erecta cuando no procede —por ejemplo, cuando mamá recibe en casa a sus amigas, o en la oficina, en una playa llena de niños, u otro sitio público donde no viene muy a cuento— y que, justo en el instante en que, precisamente, se espera que aquello se endurezca y aumente de tamaño —él está excitado, le apetece—, su miembro se encuentra «apagado o fuera de cobertura». Existen estudios[25] que revelan que el 35 % de los varones españoles entre los 60 y los 70 años y el 7 % de los hombres entre 50 y 60 años padece disfunción eréctil.

Coloquialmente, a la impotencia se la denomina como «tener un gatillazo», que describe cuando no hay erección concurriendo las circunstancias que inducen a esperarla (excitación, deseo, intimidad y erotismo...).

25. International Journal of Impotence Research.

Y ante todo...

Ante esa situación, se equiparan pene grande y pequeño y la actitud de la mujer resulta determinante. Las hay que reaccionan agarrando el bolso y largándose o tomándoselo como si nada. Depende de ella... pero también, y mucho, de él. Antes de seguir, advierto que el término «gatillazo» mejor ni nombrarlo... Lo mismo que aludir a la palabra «impotencia». Tampoco hace falta herirle y, encima, sólo su mención genera una enorme ansiedad. La propia mente masculina —también aquí por el peso de la sociedad y de la cultura machista y falocrática— determina que algunos se vean a sí mismos sólo como un rabo. Craso error, porque si un rabo es todo lo que eres y puedes ofrecer, el día que «pinchas», entonces no te queda nada. En el sexo juega tanto el cuerpo como el cerebro. Y tanto el primero como el segundo —aunque en determinados casos cueste creerlo—, dan para mucho más. Las frases que se manejan de un lado y de otro son: «No pasa nada», cuando ambos sabemos

que sí que pasa, y «no me había pasado nunca» o «es la primera vez que me sucede», «¿ah, sí? No me digas...», pensamos casi todas.

Las sensaciones que se adueñan de cada uno son también diversas. Él está sufriendo, eso es seguro. Muchos se quieren morir literalmente cuando su maldita polla no se pone dura o no sube. Además de perderse «lo mejor», su autoestima y su «necesidad de demostrar lo hombre que es» pesan muchísimo. Evidentemente, resulta muy injusto que sobre ellos descanse toda la responsabilidad y contribuye que intentes hacérselo saber. Escuchar que «no pasa nada» no tranquiliza demasiado, se precisa algo más... Es posible que él, en efecto, atraviese por este episodio por primera vez o que sea una persona con disfunción eréctil habitual (¿he mencionado antes que ellos mienten tanto como nosotras?).

Y la otra, por su parte, puede frustrarse por el hecho de no poder practicar el coito, o decepcionarse cuando se encuentra con un «algo» pequeñito y blandengue en lugar de un lustroso pene erecto... Poner cara de desilusión, reírse de él o enfadarse son erróneas pero posibles actitudes femeninas. Sin embargo también cabe que la mujer se plantee si será culpa de ella y se hunda en la miseria atribuyendo esa ausencia de erección a que no le gusta lo bastante o creyendo que él no se empalma porque ella «no sabe hacerle bien» eso que le excita... Se desata su inseguridad y se autoinculpa.

Estas reacciones que he descrito aparecen con frecuencia, se dan en casi todos los casos. El objetivo, lo que debemos tratar de conseguir, es que duren sólo unos instantes y, si ninguno se bloquea y se va, seguir adelante. En cualquier caso, ante la imposibilidad de erectar, ambos debéis plantearos varias posibles razones: ¿habéis bebido alcohol o tomado drogas, él lleva dos días sin dormir y se encuentra agotado, está medicándose, es diabético o hipertenso, se siente culpable por estar siendo infiel, etc.? «Hay muchas otras cosas que podemos hacer» sería una de las frases que salvarían el momento, y podemos articularla cualquiera de los dos, ¿verdad?

¿Y qué más puedes decirle? (Yo, decir, diría lo justo, y con mucho tacto, puesto que ser crítica precisamente en la cama es uno de los motivos de gatillazo más frecuentes.) En realidad, si nos paramos a pensarlo, nosotras, nuestro cuerpo, a veces, tampoco «está a la altura» de las circunstancias: nos pasa que, por muy a gusto que estemos, no lubricamos o aquello se queda seco sin venir a cuento... Bien es verdad que con saliva o gel se puede suplir ipso facto nuestra ausencia de flujo pero, si «comparamos», estamos ante el mismo caso: inadecuación de la respuesta física al estímulo sexual. En el caso de que el pene no logre la erección, optar por un juguete, un dildo o vibrador, salvo que sea algo ya hablado entre los dos o que a ambos les resulte familiar la incorporación de alicientes de este tipo (que en la circunstancia se calificarían de «ayuda» y no al ego de todo el mundo le entusiasma admitirlo), a mí no me parece buena idea. Él se verá comparado, medido, «sustituido», y no se trata de eso.

... *mucha calma*

En serio: sobran la mala leche, convertir el momento en una especie de tratado sobre el gran reparto de culpas, el agobiarse o sentir ridículo... Fuera todo eso. Facilita que ella en vez de adoptar un rol pasivo —no es que todas lo sean, pero en este tipo de situación conviene llevar un poquito la iniciativa—, le demuestre con hechos que eso es cosa de dos y que, si bien su pene le encanta, dado que se va a dejar de lado la penetración, tiene otras partes de su cuerpo que le interesan tanto o más...

Reitero lo que apuntaba antes: él no es sólo un rabo. Pues imaginación y a dejarse llevar: sexo oral, caricias...

Quizá «consuele» a alguien saber que cada vez se impone más que la relación sexual principal se base en el sexo oral, sucesivo o simultáneo. Ella puede lograr que él llegue al orgasmo aunque no alcance la erección, así que manos (y boca, y todo tu cuerpo) a la obra. Hay varios mandamientos. El primero: no te detengas. No olvides que, como en ti, sus zonas erógenas se distribuyen por todas partes. No fuerces la situación; a veces, ante el mínimo indicio de erección cantamos el ¡Aleluya! y nos precipitamos reintentando el coito, e intimidando a nuestra amiguita, que vuelve a minimizarse. Puedes masturbarte tú y que él te mire, o masturbarle a él. Sé creativa: colócate sobre él y frota tu clítoris sobre su pene, que tu vulva sea lo que le acaricie y, si alcanza algún tipo de erección, sigue hasta que eyacule (es posible que ambos tengáis así un orgasmo; eso sí, ten en cuenta que esta práctica es de riesgo si se realiza sin preservativo, por lo que no debes llevarla a cabo con un extraño o hazla, pero vestidos, impidiendo el contacto piel con piel y de los fluidos). Ayúdate de manos y boca, usa lubricante, masajea toda la zona, recuerda que el glande es lo más sensible junto con el frenillo, pero ahora conviene crear cierta expectativa —que a ellos les gusta igual que a nosotras—. No vayas directa a la cabeza del pene. Baja hasta su base, acaríciale y aborda con las manos en una intensidad creciente el escroto, testículos y perineo, y con la lengua, dedícate a sus pezones, cuello, cuero cabelludo; no dejes marcas ni chupetones, no le muerdas salvo que te lo pida: sólo chupa y mueve la lengua, succiona con los labios en forma de O, envolviendo con ellos los dientes. Por cierto, deja que te vea: ellos se encienden con la contemplación de imágenes eróticas, y cuando encima las protagonizan, la cosa suele ir rápida... Permítele contemplarte mientras haces todo eso (si te da corte, no le mires a los ojos, pero no pierdas su pene de vista).

Si en vez de hacer de ello un drama, comentas que «sí, yo también creo que he bebido mucho», o dices algo como que te alegras de que «al fin vas a tenerle entero ocupándose y preocupándose sólo de ti», puede que le quites hierro al momento. A veces, el Cielo es para los que perseveran: introduciendo el pene fláccido —con ayuda imprescindible manual, suya o tuya—, sólo gracias al contacto con la vagina, el «notarse dentro», acompañando de ciertos movimientos pélvicos, se produce la erección.

Meter o no meter

Como decía antes, otro asunto que tranquilizará a más de uno, y que en general conviene saber, es que la penetración se ha posicionado como uno de los actos que podemos (o no) practicar. El coito como «plato principal» ha quedado desbancado. En una relación puede no practicarse, no es imprescindible, dado que la mujer alcanza el orgasmo con la estimulación del clítoris y que, de suceder durante el coito suele ser porque está colocada en una posición tal —generalmente ella encima, cabalgándole—, que la fricción de la vulva y la presión sobre el clítoris permite que «parezca» que el clímax se logra por la penetración. Antes, el sexo oral se consideraba parte de los absurdamente llamados «preliminares». Ya comento este tema en otros lugares del libro: ¿preliminares? ¿Saben los hombres que regalarle a su chica una buena sesión de sexo oral la hará adicta a su compañía? ¿Alguna les ha confesado que lo que más le puede gustar es que durante la misma penetración se salga y «baje»? Hay pocas sorpresas tan gratas para una mujer como que, mientras se coloca en la posición de *doggie* (el perrito), de vez en cuando, en vez de recibir la embestida del pene, lo que se note sea su lengua recorriendo desde el clítoris a la entrada de la vagina o incluso, llegando al ano. Esto ya vale el precio del libro. No es cuestión de prescindir del sexo, sólo de hacerlo dejando de lado la penetración.

¿Qué se puede hacer?

Para empezar dejar de beber, seguir una dieta baja en grasas, controlar la tensión arterial y el colesterol y hacer ejercicio. Dejar de fumar (¿sabías que el tabaco, a la larga, puede obstruir de modo irreversible los vasos sanguíneos del pene? Por eso en las cajetillas, que pone lo de que «puede matar», debería poner «puede matarte en vida»).

También hay múltiples tratamientos. A continuación, enumero los más eficaces.

Autoinyección en pene. Este tratamiento consiste en inyectarse con una aguja muy fina un medicamento en la parte lateral del pene. La respuesta (la erección) se produce en pocos segundos y se mantiene aproximadamente durante treinta minutos.

Esta técnica requiere práctica, pero tiene la ventaja de ser un método seguro y con muy pocos efectos secundarios y de tipo local (algún tipo de molestias en el pene).

Un famoso actor porno me contaba que cuando actúa en salas haciendo sexo en vivo ante miles de personas, no quiere arriesgarse a no tener una erección y se pincha él mismo en el pene. Es infalible, eso sí: el truco está en pinchar dos veces, una cada lado, para evitar que el pene quede torcido una vez que se pone erecto...

Sildenafilo (Viagra®). La viagra® es un medicamento relativamente nuevo sobre el que existen pocos estudios pero son lo suficientemente seguros como para recomendar su uso en determinados pacientes. Hay que recordar que requiere prescripción médica. El tratamiento consiste en la toma de un comprimido aproximadamente una hora antes del coito. Para que pueda actuar el medicamento adecuadamente es necesario tener un deseo y estimulación sexual. No debe tomarse más de un comprimido al día.

En el estudio más importante realizado con este medicamento se consiguieron erecciones suficientes y mantenidas en más de la mitad de los casos. La principal ventaja de este tratamiento es que los posibles efectos secundarios son poco frecuentes, leves y transitorios, siendo los más habituales el dolor de cabeza (12 %), enrojecimiento facial (10 %), ardor de estómago (5 %).

Si alguien tiene problemas de corazón, probablemente no podrá tomarla, sobre todo combinada con ciertos medicamentos, en estos casos deberá consultar a su médico.

Clorhidrato de apomorfina (UPRIMA). Un medicamento destinado a tratar la disfunción eréctil, un compuesto a base de clorhidrato de apomorfina que actúa sobre el sistema nervioso central. Se trata de un comprimido que se coloca debajo de la lengua y se disuelve enseguida. En aproximadamente 20 minutos tiene lugar la erección. Para que la apomorfina sea efectiva es necesaria la estimulación sexual. No está indicado en mujeres. Precisa prescripción médica.

Sistema de vacío. El propio paciente coloca en su pene un aparato que mediante un sencillo dispositivo mecánico crea un vacío que da lugar a la erección. Ésta se mantiene mediante un anillo de goma que se coloca en la base del pene, estrangulándolo. No conviene prolongar su uso, ya que en realidad, se trata de cortar la circulación y retener la sangre en el pene. Este método requiere un pequeño adiestramiento y sus mayores inconvenientes pueden ser molestias en el pene y la falta de espontaneidad; si se tolera, es un método muy seguro y eficaz.

Prótesis de pene. Mediante una intervención quirúrgica se coloca una prótesis en el pene. Debe ser indicada y realizada por un urólogo. Este tratamiento se recomienda como último método a intentar por los riesgos inherentes a toda operación. Existen dos tipos de prótesis: maleables e inflables. Las maleables consiguen una erección permanente que se disimula durante la actividad normal gracias a que se puede colocar el pene hacia arriba o hacia abajo. Las inflables no tienen este inconveniente puesto que la erección se consigue en el momento deseado mediante tocamientos en la zona donde ha sido implantado el mecanismo de inflado. Estas últimas parecen más naturales pero su riesgo de fallo es mayor que en las maleables.

Cosas que conviene tener en cuenta

La tercera parte de los casos de impotencia son causados por problemas físicos. Quizá sea necesario visitar a un urólogo o, de detectarse que el motivo tiene que ver más con tu forma de vida (problemas laborales, adicciones, etc.) visitar a un psicólogo.

Si la cuestión es que sólo se produce impotencia con una persona en concreto, cabe recurrir a terapeutas sexuales (o analizar si, por ejemplo, en realidad ella no te pone, porque la ves en el fondo como a una hermana; o que te excite tanto y te obsesione tanto «dar la talla» que eso sea lo que te inhiba el impulso eréctil).

Lo principal es que lo puedas hablar con tu pareja. Muchos hombres refieren que tras haber compartido su miedo, tras haber charlado con ella sobre la posibilidad de que «no se levante» no ha habido gatillazo, así que relájate. Es importante que ambos desdramaticen (porque, ocasionalmente, él no tenga una erección, no hace falta llamar a Urgencias), pero fingir que ha sido genial o disimular lo que sucede tampoco ayuda. Un enfrentamiento del problema conjuntamente, buscar el placer y lograr orgasmos por otros medios pueden probar que no es el fin del mundo, aunque dentro de la mente masculina, llegue a parecerlo.

Hoy no toca

La libido es algo personal y fluctuante, y podemos (o no) tener la suerte de dar con una pareja con el mismo nivel de apetito sexual. Según nosotras vamos adquiriendo naturalidad e iniciativa a la hora de disfrutar de nuestra sexualidad, parece que el consagrado rol de «macho-man-siempre-dispuesto» empieza a flaquear, seguramente, porque era tan falso como que nosotras no tuviéramos impulsos sexuales. Ni nosotras somos de piedra ni ellos son máquinas de follar. Los clásicos «me duele la cabeza» o «tengo la regla» eran pretextos típicamente femeninos.

Con el manual de excusas para rechazar el sexo se vende un CD con el *hit* del verano: «Estoy agotado», que choca con la idea preconcebida de insaciabilidad y voracidad masculina —sí, *ladies and gentlemen*, es posible que un señor diga «no me apetece» sin que ello implique nada grave—. Antes de someterle a un tercer grado con escenita en la que se le acusa de tirarse a otra incluida, o de aferrarte a su braguera con los dientes habiéndote disfrazado de doncella francesa (quizá su fantasía sexual, pero nunca la satisfará si es a punta de pistola; aguarda al momento ideal), piensa que su «hoy, no» en los tiempos que corren obedece generalmente a cansancio físico —sí, los hay que se matan en el gimnasio y no dejan ni una gota de energía para la cama o que llegan a casa a punto del coma, en cuyo caso, confórmate con ratitos de sexo y no te frustres si la sesión amatoria no dura hasta el alba—, o mental, o al estrés o a conflictos emocionales —sí, ellos también los tienen—, o al más terrible aburrimiento —sí, ellos también se hartan de repetir el mismo tipo de aproximación, de follar en la misma postura y siempre el mismo día de la semana, así que, dedicad más tiempo a excitaros, a juguetear e inventar opciones para cada encuentro, en vez de ir directamente a la posición que funciona y a la penetración—, o incluso, muchos sufren verdadero miedo a la expectativa que se cierne sobre ellos —sí, ellos son humanos y cumplir en la cama, con tanto como se airean los récords de algunos superhombres, no parece asequible si has tenido un día duro en la oficina.

Quizá la solución pase por tomarse unos días libres, despejar un poco la agenda... suena triste, pero a muchos les pasa que están tan liados que necesitan hacer un hueco y anotarse que a tal y tal hora van a irse a casa para echar un polvo, lo cual acaba fulminando las ganas de cualquiera.

PT141 e Intrisa

Como colofón, por abordar el asunto del «gatillazo» también desde el lado femenino, debo informar acerca de **PT141** y de **Intrisa**. Recientemente, leía con consternación algo que ya venía yo intuyendo: que las personas no somos libres de sentir deseo, sólo de seguirlo o no. Es cierto que lo que nos une a lo animal, esa pulsión, ese desatarse de las hormonas, no es controlable. El deseo nace o no, pero poco podemos hacer para forzarlo. Lo que está en nuestra mano elegir y hacer de modo consciente se limita a, o bien abortarlo, a frenarlo (de ahí todos los estudios del mismísimo Freud, entre otros, acerca de la represión) o a dejarnos llevar, satisfaciéndolo.

Manejando diversos manuales, he averiguado que la principal causa de que los estudios sobre la sexualidad femenina vayan por detrás de los de la masculina —en unos quince o veinte años ni más ni menos—, es que para la supervivencia de la especie, el placer femenino no era imprescindible. Triste pero cierto: tengamos o no un orgasmo, podemos traer hijos a este mundo. Los tiempos han cambiado y, si desde los años 90, la Viagra está siendo el top en la lista de ventas de Pfizer, la gallina de los huevos de oro de Eli Lilly se llama Cialis y la cuenta de Levitra mantiene a GlaxoSmithKline con una enorme sonrisa, con la consiguiente revolución entre los señores, que el PT141 vea próximamente la luz y que Intrisa ya se recete, puede alcanzar incluso más repercusión y provocar que se reescriban muchas teorías sobre sexualidad. Estos fármacos, seguramente, supondrán todo un fenómeno social como en su día lo fue la píldora.

¿PT141? A priori puede sonar al nombre de alguno de los robots que no promocionaron en la Guerra de las Galaxias, o a un pesticida para clonar hortalizas... Pues no. Lo novedoso del PT141 (aún en fase experimental) sería que afecta al deseo: es un chute —se inhala— que va directo a la sangre y que activa la libido. Aunque se lo denomina «la Viagra femenina», no es del todo exacto. La Viagra, aparte de sus contraindicaciones de índole cardiovascular, tiene efectos secundarios e interacciones con medicación concurrente, y sufre limitaciones: sin una previa excitación no vale para nada; además sólo se prescribe para hombres (en mujeres no funciona) y sus efectos tardan cerca de una hora en empezar a notarse y dura lo que dura (depende del día y del señor).

Bien, pues por lo visto, el PT141 va más allá, y no interactúa con otros medicamentos, ni con tabaco, ni alcohol, y sirve para hombres tanto como para mujeres. Aseguran que no provoca efectos secundarios —en nosotras serían síntomas suaves, como náuseas, dolor de cabeza y congestión nasal—. Al actuar directamente sobre el cerebro erradica el riesgo cardiovascular y, también por ello se nota el efecto en el deseo, porque no implica que se desvíe sangre hacia los genitales, sino que libera en la mente las ganas de sexo, con erecciones espontáneas y, en la mujer, que goce de un despertar de la libido. La erección y el rendimiento sexual durante la penetración mejoran y hace efecto de inmediato. «Tras la aplicación los resultados mostraron la eficacia del producto, las ratas se mostraban superestimuladas sexualmente y buscaban a sus compañeros masculinos para copular», tal cual lo leía, no sabría si considerarlo un fármaco liberador para la mujer o un nuevo modo de ser utilizadas por ellos... Según Jim Pfaus, jefe de la investigación realizada por la Universidad de Concordia, «la falta de apetito sexual en algunas mujeres puede ser debida a una "mala conexión" en la zona cerebral que regula el apetito sexual —esto ya suena mejor—. La composición del PT141 está basada en sustancias hormonales humanas y si las pruebas en seres humanos resultan satisfactorias podría comenzar a ser comercializado dentro de unos 3 años.» A seguir soñando, pues.

Respecto de Intrisa, también se considera como la «Viagra femenina», sólo que se trata de un parche, del parche fantástico. De comercialización relativamente reciente, Intrisa se fija del mismo modo que una tirita y funciona liberando de modo continuo cantidades pequeñas de testosterona (hormona responsable de la libido) en la sangre a través de la piel. Por lo tanto, la finalidad fundamental de este fármaco se orienta a superar la disfunción sexual femenina y a recuperar el deseo sexual. Otro efecto de este medicamento es que facilita el orgasmo. En principio, se receta a mujeres menores de 60 años que presentan problemas de déficit de deseo sexual, denominado Desorden del Deseo Sexual Hipoactivo (HSDD), y a las que han sido intervenidas para la extirpación de ambos ovarios o del útero —una menopausia prematura que determina una caída de hasta el 50 % en los niveles de testosterona— y en pacientes que ya reciben tratamiento hormonal para los problemas de la libido. Normalmente el efecto se nota en unas 4 semanas. Los parches se colocan en la parte baja del abdomen, fijándolos cada vez en zonas de piel distintas. Cada parche se mantiene 3-4 días, no son reutilizables. Permiten realizar vida normal, ducharse o bañarse, nadar, etc., ya que pueden mojarse, sin embargo, no conviene que el sol dé sobre la zona del parche, que ha de cubrirse. No todas las mujeres pueden utilizarlos. Requiere prescripción médica.

ANORGASMIA Y FRIGIDEZ FEMENINA

Más de una vez hemos oído eso de «frígida» en tono más que peyorativo, referido tanto a la falta de excitación como a cierta (o

total) inhibición de respuesta orgásmica. Aunque el insulto se aplique indistintamente, el problema radica en dos cuestiones independientes.

La anorgasmia designa la ausencia de orgasmo o de respuesta a la estimulación erótica de modo reiterado. Se presentan diversos tipos. Se habla de *anorgasmia primaria* si la disfunción se da desde siempre: es la de quienes nunca han tenido un orgasmo, ni masturbándose, ni con juguetes, ni con penetración, ni con estimulación manual u oral de otra persona. La *anorgasmia secundaria* se detecta desde un momento o situación concreta, es decir, tras haber tenido orgasmos con normalidad, ciertas mujeres dejan de tenerlos. Se habla de *anorgasmia total* si a la mujer le resulta imposible alcanzar el orgasmo, bien por medio del coito o de la estimulación del clítoris o de otra zona de la vagina. Un cuarto tipo sería la *anorgasmia situacional*, cuando no se alcanza el orgasmo en determinadas circunstancias específicas, o con determinadas personas.

Causas

Desde las fisiológicas naturales: agotamiento, embarazo, climaterio, vejez, etc., o accidentales: mutilación genital por accidente, operaciones o ablación —que alude a una mutilación, y tiene origen delictivo—, a las de origen patológico y por influencia de fármacos: enfermedades y medicamentos que afectan a la respuesta sexual; Arnold Kegel apuntaba también una causa física: la falta de tono en la musculatura PC o la fibrosis en los músculos de la vagina, que determinan la incapacidad para desencadenar el orgasmo.

A otro nivel, intervienen factores educativos, culturales y psicológicos: la falta o negativa educación sexual, vergüenza, culpa, pecado, fobias, neurosis, psicosis, mala relación de pareja actual o pasada, ambiente familiar alterado, exceso de estrés, sentimientos negativos hacia el propio cuerpo, problemas de autoestima, etc.

El desinterés sexual puede producirse tanto en hombres como en mujeres, dependiendo de factores tan diversos como la ignorancia (en el sentido de no saber cómo acariciar, penetrar, etc.) propia o de la pareja, problemas físicos, depresión, el estrés laboral o la preocupación. Determinados conflictos producen cambios endocrinos y el descenso del nivel de andrógenos, responsables de la apetencia sexual. Paralelamente, algunos fármacos también actúan sobre el cerebro en este sentido, inhibiendo la respuesta a los estímulos o anulando el apetito sexual.

Cabe señalar otro tipo de causas del desinterés, esta vez, estrictamente femenino. La propia educación que durante siglos ha recibido la mujer provoca que para salvaguardar la reputación de «casta y señorita», una chica aborte toda curiosidad. Esa incultura de la propia sexualidad explicaría en parte el fiasco, tanto la anorgasmia como la falta de deseo podría deberse a estar recibiendo una «estimulación errónea». Cuando una mujer desconoce qué es lo que a ella le da placer, salvo que se líe con un vidente o un gurú del sexo, resultará bien difícil satisfacerla. Además, no todos los hombres disponen de una «formación sexual», y a lo mejor su devoción por ella como pareja no alcanza como para «tomarse la molestia de averiguar» qué necesita. Está demostrado que el tiempo que un hombre precisa para llegar al orgasmo mediante la estimulación con su pareja ronda los tres minutos. Nosotras precisamos entre veinte y treinta. Eso explica que la mujer sea tan aficionada (es decir, necesite) a los juegos previos, los besos, los masajes... —me niego a llamarlos «preliminares»—, así como esa actitud suya tan reprochada de «hacerse la difícil» cuando se nos nota a la legua que estamos deseándolo: muchas veces sólo es algo que hacemos instintivamente para poder «calentar motores».

Falta de comunicación

Otro grave problema sería la falta de diálogo en la intimidad. La falta de comunicación, por puro pudor, es un lastre que también ellos arrastran. Cuando das con un amante maravilloso, no puedes dejar de pensar que, seguramente, hubo una mujer que le enseñó. Es así. Otra antes le explicó qué y cómo... y cumplió una misión para el bien común de la humanidad. Por lo general, salvo que se trate de un energúmeno, a todos les encanta notar que te excitas, quieren darte placer, pero nadie nace enseñado. El varón, in sécula seculórum, ha cargado con un tremendo peso: «has de ser un campeón», «sé un machote», les repiten desde pequeñitos en casa, en el colegio... Lo que se traduce en: ten un apetito insaciable, da igual con quién. Ten una erección instantánea, automática, que «suba» con la sola presencia de una hembra viva en el área de 2 km a la redonda y que sea muy potente, duradera. Satisface tu instinto a cualquier hora, etc. No todos logran salir de ese rol. A cualquier hombre normal, da igual que se trate de un marido o de un polvo de una noche, le pone mucho ver a su pareja disfrutar, así que espabila: conócete a ti misma y permite que te conozca (sexualmente). Dale pistas, evidencias de si va bien o si te está haciendo daño, por ejemplo.[26]

El lenguaje corporal o los cambios de respiración, a veces, resultan demasiado sutiles. Muchas nos morimos de vergüenza sólo de tenerle ahí abajo como para, encima, verbalizar algo tan explícito (de

---

26. Imagina la escena: la cara de él entre tus piernas, comienza a hacerte un cunnilingus. No os habéis acostado antes y tampoco habéis charlado sobre el asunto. Si tú jadeas, él probablemente no sepa, desde allí abajo, con las orejas tapadas por tus muslos, si te gusta o si necesitas que cambie de sitio, o quieres que lo haga más fuerte...

nuevo, la cultura represora: el no me lo merezco, el no debo disfrutar, el seguro que no le gusta, bla, bla, bla. ¡Ya es mayorcito! A él le apetece hacer lo que está haciendo. Relájate y goza). «Ni loca —pensamos— voy yo a pronunciar frases como "métemela ya" o "cómeme el coño"...» Lo malo es que un simple jadeo «hummm» no da para mucho, puedes moverte un poco, ofrécele la parte que quieres que chupe, exagera tu reacción (no es lo mismo que fingir) de modo que realmente «escuche» un gemido inequívoco de placer, o pídele cosas concretas: que te toque el clítoris, o que lo atrape con los labios y succione...; o si te da corte, llévale la mano o hazlo tú y que te imite él después. En este instante, es cuando instintivamente recurrimos a la geografía («más arriba», «abajo», «dentro»), a la religión («Ohhhh, dios, síiiiiii»)...

Chapuzas

Como estamos con los «problemas» a la hora de llegar al orgasmo, aludo a los egoístas que obvian dedicarle tiempo al placer de su pareja (algo que en las recientes generaciones se considera lo más normal). Es vox pópuli que durante siglos el hombre iba a lo suyo, se satisfacía con la prisa de un animal en celo y le daba lo mismo el orgasmo de su compañera o que su mujer, en el fondo, estuviera asqueada y deseando que él se corriera para terminar de una p... vez. Acabo de describir la vida sexual de miles de parejas. Cientos de historias de polvos a oscuras, rápidos, con el pijama puesto. Un mete-saca nauseabundo. ¿Resultado? Ella, cada vez menos interesada en algo que cuando no le duele, le da asco (o ambas cosas), y él, a su bola. ¿Por qué se habla del «débito conyugal»? ¡Tiene narices!, pues porque o se la obligaba (y por desgracia, en muchas casas aún hoy lo que se sigue produciendo son auténticas violaciones) o ¿cómo iba ninguna a desear algo así? La cosificación del cuerpo, la frustración acumulada, el no «llegar» nunca... han provocado en muchas mujeres una total falta de apetito sexual (¿a quién va a apetecerle que un cerdo sude sobre ti hasta correrse sin mirarte ni a la cara?) o la inhibición orgásmica (de ahí que, como sabemos, muchas madres de familia numerosa hayan dejado este mundo sin saber lo que es un orgasmo). ¿Nosotras frígidas? ¡Cuando a una mujer le gusta un hombre, y existe comunicación y reciprocidad, a quien hay que parar es a ella! Y así, regalando consejos como estoy, añado otro: que, a veces, lo más difícil de conseguir no es algo «físico», sino «mental»: que ella se relaje, que desconecte. Muchos se amargan porque «se lo curran a muerte» y, pese a todo, ella no alcanza el clímax. Dos cosas, una: que en nosotras, orgasmo y placer no son sinónimos, así que tranquilos, vuestro esfuerzo siempre se agradece; pese a no llegar al orgasmo, se puede gozar hasta perder el norte... Otra: que en determinados momentos, estáis follando con el cabrón de su jefe, con el niño enfermo de paperas, la declaración de la renta o con las goteras del salón... «No mandé mis naves a luchar contra los elementos», se quejaba uno, pues eso... Tenéis que conseguir que no se meta con los problemas en la cama.

Cuando a una mujer no le apetece, comienza a alegar excusas archiconocidas, se hace la dormida, etc. Ser mujer en esta época resulta agotador, de verdad. Cuando llegas a casa, lo último que te sientes es sexy. No te ves una chica, sino una superviviente: tu cabeza está agotada de la cantidad de cosas que has hecho o que habrás de solucionar al día siguiente; eso se suma a que comemos a toda prisa (y, frecuentemente, basura), no tenemos tiempo para ponernos guapas, así que la imagen que el espejo nos devuelve no tiene mucho que ver con la de las actrices americanas que lucen piel nacarada y canalillo hiperhidratado. Es la de una alimaña urbana deseosa de meterse en la piltra, para dormir. Quieres una caricia, la necesitas —si te levantan el pelo de la nuca y notas unos besitos o una respiración insinuante, te derrites; o si, mientras te peleas con las bolsas de la compra, te dan un abrazo por detrás, al tiempo que te meten mano un poco, con suavidad, la cena parecerá que se ha hecho sola—, pero no estás para un acercamiento con exigencias ni demasiado brusco.

Y cuanto más tiempo transcurra sin sexo más distancia mediará entre ambos. Como ante cualquier conflicto, lo ideal es hablarlo, pero sin presión, sin chantajes y sin que la hagas sentirse culpable. Cuando una mujer dice «no» no es «sí» —quede clara la diferencia entre un juego de seducción, un «te lo pongo difícil, juega conmigo» y la imposición porque él tiene más fuerza—. Una mujer puede estar harta del «más de lo mismo»; averigua si necesita más sexo oral, o que la beses durante más rato, que la ayudes a deshacerse de su pesadilla profesional mediante un masaje o que eche de menos cómo la abordabas, esa pasión que hubo allá en el principio de la relación. Esto se ve en profundidad en el apartado sobre «Fantasías sexuales y cómo reavivar la chispa».

Traumas

Mayor complejidad adquieren los traumas que muchas mujeres arrastran, bien por malas experiencias de relaciones anteriores (paciencia, cariño, reeducación, diálogo, y si no, terapia), o por abusos, violaciones y vejaciones que se asocian a la práctica sexual de modo casi reflejo e instintivo, dificultándola o imposibilitándola. Ciertos traumas, por desgracia, no se curan solos. Es cosa de dos (cuando lo es) o de ella recurrir a especialistas. Hay que pedir ayuda y aceptarla, porque por buena voluntad que tengan los amigos y la pareja, normalmente no basta, por la profundidad del daño y la complejidad del tema. Resulta necesario acudir a profesionales. Limítate a abrazarla, sin juzgarla ni comenzar a predicar consejos improvisados.

Cuando una mujer nunca ha sentido un orgasmo, ni siquiera masturbándose, cuando practica sexo por «obligación», puesto que en realidad no se excita ni disfruta, procede recurrir a un terapeuta. Puede obedecer a traumas no resueltos de la infancia; por desgracia, hay muchos casos de abusos. O deberse a recuerdos reprimidos, que la mujer evita revivir abortando cualquier sensación que otro tipo de relación le proporciona.

All We Need Is Love

Querría volver sobre el orgasmo femenino y su importancia. Decía antes que el placer de la mujer se ha despreciado desde antaño puesto que no es imprescindible para la supervivencia de la especie. Que la fémina no disfrute de orgasmos no obsta para que se pueda quedar embarazada. Esto explica, de paso, por qué desde siempre se ha menospreciado el erotismo femenino y que se le haya dedicado tan poquita atención y esfuerzo, también desde el punto de vista científico. El trato de la mujer en muchas culturas, en el fondo, simplemente refleja esta idea: se la considera en cuanto a hembra y en torno a su capacidad reproductiva, disociando y anulando sus otras facetas, de lo que también deriva esa obsesión por encuadrar a la mujer como madre y esa especie de estigma de «bicho raro» que se genera sobre las que, alcanzada cierta edad, libremente o por circunstancias, no procrean.

La lista de razones para que una mujer sienta que el sexo no va con ella y, por tanto, haga por evitarlo, es larga: los amantes monótonos, egoístas, que sólo van a buscar su orgasmo, la medicación —los antidepresivos anulan el deseo—, el estrés, la tristeza —ojito porque los problemas, ya lo he comentado, se acuestan con nosotras—, las enfermedades físicas —no sólo las sexuales—, así como haber recibido una educación restrictiva y culpabilizante respecto del propio cuerpo y del sexo, o haber sufrido agresiones sexuales.

En resumen, muchas de las disfunciones encuentran su causa, aparte de en las referidas (afectivas, educativas, de desarrollo, de salud general, de abuso de tóxicos, etc.), en conflictos de identidad sexual, homosexualidad latente, en casos fortuitos previos, elevadas exigencias de rendimiento sexual, comunicación poco afectiva de la pareja, falta de atracción física, conflictos de rol sexual o incluso, hostilidad y recelo hacia el otro.

Amar es cosa de dos

Masters y Johnson desarrollaron técnicas específicas para cada disfunción y trataron de entrenar las habilidades sexuales de la pareja. Para estos sexólogos cualquier disfunción atañe a ambos, convirtiéndose en un problema de comunicación. Por ello, la terapia se realiza por los dos persiguiendo mejorar la comunicación entre ellos a todos los niveles. Mejorar la información, desterrando ideas equivocadas y actitudes perjudiciales (afán de lucimiento, demostración de hombría, vergüenza al demostrar el orgasmo, etc.). Eliminar sentimientos de culpa, temor, frustración, resentimiento hacia el otro. Realizar un aprendizaje nuevo y adquirir habilidades sexuales, integrando el sexo como una faceta más de la relación. Reducir la ansiedad que provoca la idea de que el orgasmo es imprescindible, para lo que imponen que la pareja se dedique a los preliminares y juegos eróticos, prohibiéndoles la penetración durante varias sesiones.

8

Darle cuerda

Fantasías sexuales y cómo reavivar la chispa

En el texto el Ananga Ranga se alerta de que «la monotonía de la posesión a veces arroja al marido en brazos de mujeres extrañas y a la mujer en los de hombres extraños. [...] La razón principal por la que una pareja se separa, y la causa de que el marido caiga en brazos de otras mujeres y la esposa en los de otros hombres es la falta de placeres variados y la monotonía que indefectiblemente sigue a los días del ardor inicial». Y a continuación, sentencia: «La monotonía engendra la saciedad y la saciedad, el disgusto del coito.»

Cuando la rutina entra por la puerta, la pasión se tira por la ventana

Millones de personas contemplan con pena cómo la rutina se adueña de su vida sexual. Descubrimos que conforme el amor se consolida e incluso aumenta, la pasión se esfuma. Demasiada familiaridad, demasiada prisa, demasiada confianza, demasiada repetición (de situaciones, de posiciones), etc., nos aburre.

Conforme se asienta la relación, nos olvidamos de los detalles y perdemos lo esencial que había al principio: el deseo. La novedad deja de serlo. Lo que antes tenías que buscar, ahora está garantizado... Eso mata nuestro interés. El ser humano es cazador por naturaleza. Por otro lado, un día analizas que en el buzón sólo y siempre te esperan un montón de facturas y de panfletos publicitarios, y que ya ni se te ocurre imaginarte que tu pareja te vaya a enviar una carta llena de tórridas sugerencias; gruesos pijamas de franela holgados ocupan en tu armario el lugar donde colgaban antes los saltos de cama de raso; el olor de fritura en tu moño mal hecho anula el recuerdo de esa colonia que te hacía única; él ya no tiene pelo del que aferrarte durante las noches de pasión que ya no disfrutas; hace tiempo que la tabla de lavar ha quedado sepultada por lorzas; las llamadas «porque sí», que buscaban sólo escuchar tu voz, se convierten en el automatizado parte diario sobre qué hay de cena; ese hogar con que soñabas es una jungla con vida propia que cada día se descompone como por arte de magia; tu casa es tu cárcel, no sales porque no te llega sino para pagar los colegios de los niños y además, ¿con quién vas a dejarlos mientras?; sus besos, si es que te los da, no saben igual; acariciar su piel no te produce la sensación de antes, y hace años que no te toca más que en los sitios donde sabe que va a tiro hecho; las apasionadas maratones de sexo se acortan hasta el formato «polvo» y se repiten idénticos hasta hacerte imposible distinguir uno de otro, aunque para como son, mejor ni recordarlos. Pero os queréis.

Muerto el romanticismo, exprimido hasta el tedio el catálogo de posturas más habituales, las ganas de mantener relaciones con tu pareja se esfuman. El sexo se ha hecho tan insípido que da hasta pereza. Es hora de que resucitéis de entre los muertos.

Se ha demostrado que las personas con bajo deseo sexual lo incrementan y recuperan mediante la recreación de fantasías sexuales, que son representaciones mentales creadas por el inconsciente y que tienen como tema principal las relaciones sexuales.

Soñar despiertos

Suele pensarse que es el hombre el que mayormente fantasea. No es cierto: las mujeres lo hacen también, sólo que de distinta forma. Las fantasías pueden ser voluntarias (nos aplicamos a la tarea de recrearlas) o involuntarias (nuestra mente trabaja sola).

Fantasías las tiene todo el mundo, de hecho, su ausencia puede ser síntoma de deseo sexual hipoactivo, revelar un cuadro de estrés, estar provocado por baja autoestima o implicar un altísimo grado de represión sexual interior.

Son irreales, por eso se denominan fantasías, y a través de ellas, podemos hacer todo lo que nos gusta; no hay límites y la imaginación y la creatividad se desbordan. Es un terreno donde nada está prohibido y todo puede ser posible. Su efecto estimulante y erótico se perdería de bajar a la Tierra y tener que enfrentar la multitud de detalles que se barajan aquí. Son privadas y exclusivas —salvo que decidas compartirlas con la pareja o con un tercero— y se generan dentro de la mente y, salvo que se expliquen o se cumplan, no salen de ella; son personales, distintas en cada individuo, que puede fantasear con infinitas cosas: desde rememorar situaciones pasadas a recrear encuentros con desconocidos, con famosos o con personas inaccesibles, inventando lugares... Mandamos sobre ellas: en tu universo quimérico sólo decides tú, tanto su contenido como su evolución, o si lo aniquilas de golpe... y sin darle cuentas a nadie.

Efectos especiales

Las fantasías pueden potenciar la respuesta sexual, tanto a nivel fisiológico como psicológico, de muchas maneras: contrarrestando el aburrimiento y acercándonos a situaciones inalcanzables; focalizando los pensamientos y sentimientos, borrando distracciones o presiones; mejorando nuestra propia imagen; facilitando la respuesta previa a una relación sexual o intensificando el placer durante ella; si es muy intensa, conduciéndonos al orgasmo en ocasiones, etc. Se trata de pequeños viajes mentales en los que podemos imaginar cualquier cosa que nos excite, sin tener responsabilidad ninguna sobre ello y, tanto en soledad (se emplean habitualmente para «ocupar» la mente y «encenderla» con algo excitante para masturbarnos), como acompañados (seguro que has oído lo de «cierro los ojos y me imagino que es Angelina Jolie»).

Nuestra mente, apoyada por las imágenes o ideas ilusorias que en ella elucubramos, genera el deseo y notamos el impulso sexual (no son sinónimos: una fantasía es «irreal» y se produce en la imaginación, y «deseo» es anticipar algo que sucederá después en el mundo real). Muchas personas recurren siempre a la misma, no todos desarrollamos por igual la capacidad de imaginar, otros generan y fantasean con diversas escenas nuevas cada vez.

Algunas de las fantasías dan hasta miedo; otras, sabemos que son del todo imposibles o nunca nos atreveríamos a llevarlas a cabo, y otras, elegimos no realizarlas para que sigan siendo eso, fantasías. Lo bueno de que sean secretas es que, pese a que se vuelquen sobre un tercero o no nos las inspire precisamente nuestra pareja, no se consideran una infidelidad puesto que a nivel físico nunca sucede el encuentro. Y tampoco cabe predicar absolutamente nada acerca del carácter de una persona en el mundo real basándose en el tipo de fantasías que desarrolla.

Las fantasías no son lo mismo que los sueños eróticos (éstos se producen de modo inconsciente mientras dormimos, son involuntarios). La razón y la imaginación conscientes crean las ideas con las que fantaseamos mientras estamos despiertos.

Hit Parade

Hombres y mujeres tendemos a fantasear con encuentros y experiencias sexuales pasadas. Nos gusta rememorarlas, revivirlas y ello nos excita poderosamente. Sentirse observado por alguien mientras se está haciendo el amor también suele ser una fantasía recurrente.

Los hombres fantasean magnificando su potencia, su virilidad, se ven dominando situaciones eróticas que son verdaderas proezas. También les gusta verse con mujeres que no son su pareja, o practicando sexo en grupo (el trío es muy recurrente, pero también las orgías o haciéndolo con más de una mujer a la vez), recibiendo sexo oral y anal (algo que muchos heterosexuales ansían experimentar pero que no se atreven a intentar), ser espectador de otros mientras mantienen relaciones sin ser descubiertos, o ser observados mientras lo hacen, tomar a una mujer por la fuerza (nunca es una escena de violación, sino que en su sueño, ella cae rendida de placer ante su pericia y su miembro superdotado; no hay víctimas, todos felices, ella incluso más que él). Las prácticas que en su vida cotidiana no realizan (sexo anal, gay, posturas que aún no han intentado, y con enfermeras, doncellas, amas, niñas de uniforme...) y lugares inusuales (por bizarros, paradisíacos o irreales).

Respecto de la mujer, apuntar que el tiempo que duran sus fantasías suele ser mayor que en las del varón. En cuanto a los temas, se repiten: amantes anteriores, hombres distintos a su pareja, encuentros lésbicos —con o sin testigo masculino—, localizaciones y vestimentas inusuales (que nos permiten ser «otra» y hacer lo que nos apetece, sin obedecer a lo que esperan de la persona «de verdad»), tríos (de dos hombres y ella, por supuesto, que se ocupan de cada centímetro de tu piel, a veces, incluso al tiempo) y sexo en grupo que permita ser tocada y penetrada por varios hombres —o mujeres también— y dar placer del mismo modo... Como fantasías femeninas se pueden incorporar algunas específicas: la de ser violada —que el sexo se le imponga por la fuerza, contra su voluntad—, con violencia, sin capacidad para negarse ni rebelarse, bien con un único hombre o con más de uno. Y la contraria: encontrarse con un hombre rendido y sometido que cumple sus órdenes y satisface sus deseos, al que azotar, humillar y reducir. Resulta constante y específica de la fantasía femenina la de la incapacidad de ver la cara del amante. Muchas coinciden en que querrían tener un amo, unas para rendirse, obedeciendo y haciendo cosas que «por supuesto, ellas, tan decentes, nunca harían», y otras para plantar resistencia y ser obligadas a entrar en razón a base de ataduras, mordazas y penetraciones varias. Ser prostituta, bailarina de *striptease* o señorita de compañía, cobrar por sexo y erotismo, en definitiva (da igual que tu profesión sea harto más divertida, edificante y enriquecedora, por una noche apetece experimentar qué se siente cuando te dan un fajo de billetes para que te bajes las bragas). Sentirse «sucia», en una palabra, atreverse a ir más allá, con prácticas extremas (eyaculaciones en cualquier parte «no convencional», dobles penetraciones, penetraciones por sorpresa de desconocidos...), el placer de ser humillada, rebajada, anulada... A otras les pide el cuerpo vestirse de hombre y actuar como tal: con un rol de poder sobre su pareja, empleando un arnés con un dildo incluso, para poder recrear lo que se siente teniendo un pene.

Es perfectamente posible y saludable que no te identifiques con ninguna de las fantasías que he relacionado y que tengas las tuyas propias; se trataba sólo de recopilar algunas.

Haz realidad tus sueños

La fantasía, como vía de escape de la cotidianeidad, constituye un verdadero afrodisíaco y es el único antídoto efectivo para contrarrestar la rutina. Muchas parejas que entran en barrena logran reactivar su vida íntima mediante juegos sexuales que consisten en ir cumpliendo los anhelos de cada uno. Como en todo, utilizadas como incentivo sí son saludables, si se produce una obsesión, se cae en el campo de las parafilias o se puede condicionar la relación sexual, mediatizándola y limitándola de forma compulsiva o adictiva respecto de la práctica concreta, que desplaza el objetivo inicial de tener relaciones con tu pareja.

Más sugerencias para combatir el tedio

Como parte de las causas[27] de la pérdida de interés en mantener relaciones sexuales, además del aburrimiento sexual, se hace patente el afectivo, la distancia que se genera entre dos personas que organizan sus ratos de ocio para hacer cosas cada uno por su lado. Entre las horas de oficina y las obligaciones, y que cada uno va a su aire, no es extraño tampoco que esa falta de comunicación y de intereses que compartir —más allá de los que devenga el crédito que paga la hipoteca— se instale en la cama. En pareja, la práctica continuada del sexo genera más ganas, provoca casi una dependencia. Y cuando el organismo está habituado a las sensaciones orgásmicas no puede pasar sin ellas... No me lo invento, se trata de la Ley de Fisher: «cuanto más sexo practica una pareja más se incrementa su interés hacia él; mientras que si deja de practicarlo, o espacia las relaciones, las ganas disminuyen hasta desaparecer».

Recuperad el beso. Besad mucho, mucho, mucho y todo el rato. Siendo lo más básico —todas las relaciones han pasado por fases en las que lo principal o incluso lo único que se hacía era besarse—, parece mentira que con el paso del tiempo nos olvidemos de hacer-

---

27. La falta de interés sexual (manifestada por la impotencia de él y la falta de excitación de ella) puede deberse a depresiones, estrés, ausencia de fantasías sexuales, traumas afectivos y/o de la infancia.

lo, o demos besos cutres: cortos, sin ganas, sin pasión... He escuchado a mujeres de todos los perfiles imaginables decirme, casi con las mismas palabras, lo mucho que echan de menos los «besos de antes»: «ya no me besa igual», «sus besos ya no son los de entonces» y el «no me besa», tal cual. El beso es imprescindible para que una mujer se excite, y para ambos, es el modo de conectar, de teñir de sensualidad vuestra relación: ¿o es que sólo sois amigos? Ah, y jugad con su pelo, acariciad la nuca.

Meteros mano. Cuando era furtivo o «había que ganárselo», sólo meter la mano por debajo de la blusa daba un morbo tremendo; o esa época en que te aceleraba las pulsaciones notar que su paquete se hinchaba cuando ponías «accidentalmente» tu cadera encima. Hay que jugar con la ropa y ser más imprevisible (esto va también de probar zonas de su cuerpo que hace tiempo que no visitas). Cuando se ha experimentado, se valora suficientemente que te echen un polvo sin terminar de desnudarte, y sólo se extraña lo que una vez se tuvo, así que lo dicho: recuperadlo.

Buscad, dentro de lo posible, actividades que compartir, donde podáis recuperaros a vosotros mismos y reencontrar a la persona de la que en su día os sentisteis atraídos.

Balnearios y spas. Cada vez más de moda, algo tendrá el agua cuando la bendicen. Si te puedes permitir desconectar un par de semanas, dedicarte a la balneoterapia (chorros, baños termales, de lodo y sulfurosos, millones de burbujas, duchas), al descanso (lo que implica dormir bien y comer mejor), posiblemente recuperes también tu apetito sexual hacia tu pareja.

Unos días en la playa. Sol, calor, nada que hacer y cuerpos semidesnudos (o del todo) a tu alrededor. Quizás, al llegar al hotel/casa, la inspiración se persone...

Vete de compras. A muchas mujeres esto les sonará a pasaje al paraíso, pero para otras y para muchos de ellos, supone una pérdida de tiempo, un aburrimiento. No me refiero al hecho de comprar sino a renovar el vestuario, el íntimo en concreto. Ciertamente, la lencería y la ropa interior ha sido una de las parcelas que más se han desarrollado de la moda. Utiliza tu sentido común, aplica cierta dosis de autocrítica y de realismo. No todos somos *top models*, ni

atletas, pero cada uno podemos encontrar las prendas que, dentro de la comodidad, nos favorezcan más. Si bien nosotras podemos llevar un conjunto de medias y liguero negro durante una velada erótica o un corsé en raso y pedrería para una fiesta, quizá para el día a día encontremos tejidos, colores y diseños que nos permitan vivir y respirar sin que se nos claven las varillas. Y ellos... aparte de los metrosexuales, de los ubersexuales, y de los homosexuales, ¿saben los demás realmente la talla y el modelo que necesitan?

Lujo y glamour. Sí, las joyas íntimas no son prerrogativa de los faraones y los estilistas de *Playboy*. No hablo de los *piercings* y los anillados de todo tipo y ubicación —glande, frenillo, escroto, pezones, labios vaginales y faciales, etc.—. Hablo de lo último: joyería íntima. Date un gustazo y a él una sorpresa. A grandes males, grandes remedios: joyería íntima *prêt-à-porter* y lencería de lujo. Conviértete en eso que siempre has denostado: sé un objeto... de placer.

Compartid un baño caliente. Juguetea con la ducha tibia, disfruta de la textura de la espuma del jabón que más te gusta oler mientras acaricias cada milímetro de su piel. Hay quienes convierten el sexo en la bañera en una fijación; la parafilia que lo define es la alveofilia.

«Cada vez tardamos menos en hacerlo...» Y seguro que es cierto. Saber qué tocar y cómo es una ventaja, pero también nos empuja a ir tan al grano que optimizamos los procesos hasta batir récords... Si lo analizas: ¿qué tienes mejor que hacer luego? Vete sin prisa. Prueba nuevas posiciones —lo que no exige saltos, proezas y flexibilidad de acróbata—, intenta disfrutar del momento; si lo analizas, muchos caemos en el mismo error. Cuando queremos a alguien y convivimos con esa persona, damos por hecho que siempre va a estar ahí. Deberíamos valorarlo y disfrutarlo, pensando «aprovecha hoy, por si se acaba mañana».

Intentad hacer vida social juntos. Salid por ahí, a cenar o a tomar una copa, además del efecto desinhibidor del alcohol, resultará un regalo (especialmente para la vista) que él se afeite/perfume y que ella se peine/depile ex profeso. Si te cuidas para ir al trabajo, ¿por qué no hacerlo para tu pareja y que, por una velada, te disfrute sin el pijama de cuadros?

Pedid tiempo muerto. No llegues de una bronca con tu madre o de una presentación de producto a una empresa alemana, y pretendas echar un polvo. Desconecta antes. La mente ha de dejar de tener «ruido», tranquiliza tu cabeza, y tu cuerpo te seguirá. Date una ducha, tómate algo, lee un ratito o mira la tele un momento —con la programación que hay será difícil que te enriquezcas pero no que te abstraigas—. Espera una hora —es lo que tarda en hacer efecto la antirrábica— y entonces, busca a tu pareja y charla con ella. En un elevadísimo número de ocasiones, demostrar un poco de interés por el otro o mantener una conversación mínimamente interesante, termina en un revolcón.

Adéntrate en ese gran universo de los juguetes sexuales. Hay que perderle el miedo a los *sex shops* (o mantenlo si quieres, y recurre a las tiendas que venden *on-line* y sirven a domicilio, y te ahorras el paseo). Ahora hay *«boutiques* eróticas», que ya no dan asco, no dan miedo, no intimidan y no son ni pizca de sórdidas. Además, han ayudado bastante a normalizar y a acercar el sexo, los juegos eróticos y la sensualidad a la mujer. Y, una vez allí, lo mejor es que, si te apetece, puedes preguntar con toda tranquilidad, que te explican lo que haga falta. Confieso que, antes de montar mi *boutique* erótica y probarlos casi todos, me ocurría que, con los adelantos tecnológicos y algunos diseños, agarraba un cacharro y sinceramente, no sabía por dónde había que meterlo...

Hay quienes dan una vuelta de tuerca a su relación y la «abren». Los clubes de gente libre y de intercambio de pareja reciben matrimonios y parejas estables que deciden incorporar a un tercero, a otra pareja o hacer sexo en grupo. Salvo que la relación esté absolutamente consolidada y ambos acepten sin reservas a lo que van, participar de este tipo de juegos suele pasar una factura muy cara a la pareja. ¿Estás listo para ver a tu mujer correrse con otro o chuparle la polla a un extraño? ¿Aguantarás que tu chico le coma el coño a otra? Si no me equivoco, existe una parafilia concreta, la Candalagnia o candaulismo, sobre el placer que sienten quienes ven a su pareja copulando con otra persona. Esto, aparte de las quejas que algunos usuarios refieren, como que para poder entrar, muchos hombres llevan a prostitutas que suplantan a la «esposa», pues se exige acudir en pareja; o que las orgías que se montan ignoran las prácticas más básicas de sexo seguro (o no se pide analítica y, a veces, no se utiliza el condón); o que la idea de fiestas orgiásticas, esas bacanales exclusivas y secretas, pletóricas de sexo y *glamour* que recrea, por ejemplo, la escena de la película *Eyes Wide Shut* dista mucho, a todos los niveles —estético fundamentalmente— de la cruda realidad.

... Y una pequeña maldad

Sin llevarlo al extremo, y con todas las connotaciones negativas del mundo, el truquillo de provocar unos ligeros celos en tu pareja siempre ha funcionado. Eso sí: no te pases, y tampoco lo hagas por sistema o dejará de hacer efecto. Basta que notemos que peligra algo que es «nuestro» y «seguro» para que lo valoremos. Somos así de idiotas. Lo «seguro», como apunté más arriba, nos aburre, pero recibir la puñaladita que nos recuerda que en cualquier momento podemos perderlo nos devuelve los sentimientos de amor, de deseo y, en definitiva, de valoración hacia nuestra pareja. Y del otro lado, lo mismo: podemos ignorar a nuestro marido durante semanas, o meses, pero, basta que llegue una «lista» que se lo intente ligar (o que nos dé esa sensación) para que acudamos a besarlo, marcando el terreno como una gata en celo y, al llegar al dormitorio, le hagamos una demostración que le recuerde por qué está contigo y no con ninguna otra...

Afrodisíacos

Afrodisíaco/a (del lat. *aphrodisiăcus*, y este del gr. ...???, *venéreo*): Cualquier sustancia o actividad que estimule o aumente el deseo sexual. Su nombre es una referencia a Afrodita, la diosa griega del amor que simboliza la sensualidad, el placer y el erotismo. La mitología cuenta que surgió de la espuma del mar cuando el dios Cronos mató y castró a su padre, arrojando sus genitales al océano. Algunos alimentos se predican afrodisíacos, desde la canela a las ostras y el marisco crudo en general, o las especias, el ajo o el caviar, pero, por desgracia, tales efectos no se han demostrado y, en la mayoría de los casos, parece más significativo su poder psicológico que su efectividad. Algunos afrodisíacos actúan directamente sobre cualquiera de los sentidos (vista, tacto, olfato); mientras que otros son distintas sustancias presentes en alimentos, bebidas, remedios medicinales y «filtros» amorosos que, como se hace patente estudiando las diversas culturas antiguas, han recibido la reputación de poseer la capacidad de estimular el instinto sexual y de revigorizar. Su detección e identificación obedece a la eterna búsqueda humana de nuevos alicientes que alejen la rutina de la intimidad, combatan el desinterés femenino hacia el coito o la falta de potencia masculina. Muchos de estos secretos se han perdido pero otros, mediante el boca a boca, aún se preservan. Ya en el Kamasutra se apunta el poder de la leche y de la miel para activar el vigor sexual masculino, e incluye una receta afrodisíaca que consiste en mezclar cardamomo con jengibre y canela y extenderla sobre cebolla y guisantes; lo mismo que los huesos de tigre, el pene de foca o la raíz de ginseng en la medicina tradicional china —que trabaja básicamente con hierbas y plantas— y que consideraba además que propiciaba la longevidad. Los árabes utilizaban perfumes, esencias y aceites esenciales para incrementar el placer sexual. Los pueblos sajones asocian efectos afrodisíacos a hortalizas y verduras de forma fálica (zanahoria, espárrago). Hay quienes otorgan esta cualidad a las infusiones bien cargadas a base de romero, menta, salvia, orégano, enebro y nuez moscada. Para darle un buen masaje a un hombre, se utiliza aceite de almendras dulces con extracto de jengibre, y para masajes íntimos en general, recomiendan el aceite de hammamelis, de romero o de hinojo.

Es muy famoso el remedio que incluye *Spanish fly* o cantárida, fabricado a base de las alas pulverizadas de escarabajos (*Lytta vesicattora* o *Carotharia vesicatora*). Tradicionalmente se usa para abrir heridas que han curado en falso y para incitar a los animales domésticos al apareamiento. No conviene usarlo porque pese a que aparenta despertar la zona, eso sólo se debe a la irritación que provoca tanto en la vejiga como en la uretra (puede aparecer sangre en la orina y dolor al hacer pis). Se han dado casos de priapismo y de fiebre, de daños renales y genitales irreversibles e incluso, de muerte.

Con cierto rigor científico, sin embargo, podemos reconocer relativo poder a las *bebidas alcohólicas*, por su efecto desinhibidor. Según la cantidad que se tome y en función de la tolerancia personal, puede, en efecto, liberar el deseo sexual o bien bloquear los nervios que permiten desencadenar el orgasmo (la excitación se prolonga sin llegar a eyacular él ni alcanzar ella el clímax). Hay distintos tipos de bebida. La absenta, por ejemplo, más conocida por las referencia literarias que por pedirse en los bares de tapas, con su graduación alcohólica de libro Guinness (70 º), parece causar efectos sexuales inmediatos en dosis mínimas —mojarte los labios y punto—, en mayor cantidad tiene efecto narcótico; debido a uno de sus componentes (el ajenjo), beberla habitualmente causa daños diversos en el cerebro (locura) y destruye la potencia sexual. También se habla del *ajo* y los *picantes* (en Oriente se mezcla pimienta sezchuan, curry y jengibre a partes iguales), por su notable efecto calentador; del *apio* y la *trufa*, que contienen feromonas, las hormonas masculinas; del *tomate* se predica que aumenta la cantidad de semen que se eyacula; de la *jalea real*, que tiene poder reconstituyente, rejuvenece y tonifica. La *vitamina E* se conoce vulgarmente como la vitamina de la vitalidad, ya que activa la producción hormonal y logra efectos más que notables sobre la vida sexual. Se encuentra en los aceites vegetales, las semillas, los frutos secos, los cereales, los huevos, la lechuga y el brécol.

Aunque no afecta ni a la potencia ni a la libido, la *Vitamina B-1* es necesaria para la consecución del orgasmo, ya que facilita las contracciones musculares adecuadas. Está presente en los cereales, la levadura de cerveza y el germen de los cereales.

El *cobalto*, entre sus propiedades, cuenta la de evitar la angustia y la ansiedad. Por tanto, quizás ingerir alimentos ricos en él (ostras, riñones, cereales integrales, huevos, legumbres y pescado) ayude en casos de tensión ante una relación sexual nueva o inesperada. Colabora a evitar que se produzca una descarga de adrenalina que impida la erección.

El *cinc* es imprescindible dentro de todo el proceso de la sexualidad, puesto que interviene en la formación del esperma, del líquido prostático y de las hormonas gonadotropinas, y en la función testicular: mantiene a los espermatozoides con la adecuada movilidad, etc.... En los alimentos se concentra en la col, carne, champiñones, espinacas, marisco, melocotón, naranja, lechuga, remolacha, tomate, zanahoria, y la yema de huevo. Su carencia, en relación con la sexualidad, provoca, entre otras alteraciones y enfermedades, impotencia, hipogonadismo, hipertrofia de próstata, esterilidad, amenorrea.

Cuidemos el medio ambiente

Además de los alimentos y de las bebidas, siempre se ha conferido un enorme poder afrodisíaco al ambiente en que éstas se desarrollan porque favorece la estimulación y la sensualidad. No hay nada nuevo bajo el sol, sin duda, pero siempre se pueden incorporar alicientes a las relaciones. Cuidar los detalles es crucial. Haz que el sitio sea cómodo, cálido y esté limpio. Las recompensas son enormes a los pequeños esfuerzos, como disponer una mesa en condiciones; embellecer con flores naturales o plantas —su presencia en una casa da la sensación, además, de que eres capaz de responsabilizarte de otros seres vivos—; prender incienso o elegir un buen ambientador; buscar una iluminación de velas o luces indirectas; que suene una música envolvente —el heavy o el bakalao puedes escucharlos en otro momento, para éste, busca opciones como los recopilatorios de chill out—. Si está en tu mano, procura que se sienta como en casa —así no querrá irse—. Puedes ofrecerle ropa más cómoda o que se descalce —demostrarás sensibilidad, ya que pocos hombres conocen la tortura de los zapatos de tacón—. El desorden tiene su encanto, pero en las primeras impresiones no es la mejor imagen que puedes proporcionar. La temperatura ambiente es crucial. Un detalle: pon un radiador. Lo que un hombre percibe como «caldeado o normal» a una mujer la hará temblar de frío. Preferible que necesite quitarse ropa a que esté con los labios morados y tiritando, ideando la manera de largarse.

Por narices

El afrodisíaco más efectivo es inherente a cada uno de nosotros, es nuestro propio olor corporal, las feromonas humanas, que se emiten a través de la transpiración. Se producen en la zona ano-genital y en las axilas. De modo involuntario, todos impregnamos de nuestra esencia las prendas íntimas y para «el otro» ese olor causa cierta predisposición erótica, despierta nuestro instinto sexual; es bien común que los amantes inhalen las bragas usadas o las quieran conservar como fetiche, o que a nosotras nos encante dormir con la camiseta que él ha sudado durante el día.

En materia de afrodisíacos hay mayor sugestión que resultados «físicos» comprobables a nivel científico. La imaginación y dejarse llevar por el deseo alimentan constantemente el deseo. Por concluir: «La mente es el afrodisíaco más potente», por lo que el sentido del humor, el ingenio, la cultura, el talento... de las personas, nos pueden atraer con más fuerza que ninguna mariscada.

JUGUETES ERÓTICOS

Los juguetes sexuales o «para adultos» estimulan la imaginación, introducen el factor lúdico y experimental a la relación, la re-erotizan muchas veces, y cabe, además, vincular algunos de ellos con la salud. Enterarme de que muchos médicos prescriben artículos de *sex shop*, como las bolas chinas o la pesa vaginal, para ejercitar los músculos PC (ayudan a evitar la incontinencia urinaria, aceleran la recuperación tras el parto, etc.) fue otra de las razones por las que puse una *boutique* erótica en mi web. Ya he comentado que opino que debería perderse el miedo a los *sex shops*. Sin embargo, a muchos, hombres incluidos, aún les da reparo entrar en ellos. Saben que les encantaría tener un disfraz de enfermera y con gusto probarían el lubricante comestible de plátano, pero prefieren ahorrarse el trago de ir personalmente... Es normal. La población de a pie no está familiarizada con el uso de cacharritos, puesto que la simple adquisición de preservativos no se ha normalizado aún entre las féminas (apunto el anonimato y la comodidad como ventajas de comprar *on-line*...). Una vez prueban, casi todos los clientes repiten (enormes avances en diseño, sumergibles, textura real, sin ruido, versatilidad, variedad de modelos, ofertas...).

Cristóbal Icaza, director de *amantis.net*, uno de los *sex shops* más prestigiosos en España y pionero dentro del concepto «*boutique* erótica», revela ciertos datos:

- Hace dos décadas sólo existían juguetes con formas fálicas de calidad media. Actualmente se hace hincapié en materiales de mayor calidad como la silicona, han evolucionado especialmente en materiales y tecnología, desarrollando juguetes con menor ruido, control de velocidades y movimientos. Las formas y el diseño invitan al juego y la imaginación.
- Han dejado de ser un artículo clandestino o para pervertidos: según cifras del informe Durex sobre «Hábitos de consumo y Comportamiento sexual», el 23 % de los españoles declara haber usado juguetes para adultos.
- Es posible asociar los juguetes y la salud, como el clásico ejemplo de las bolas chinas para la recuperación posparto, o la pesa Energie para practicar los ejercicios de Kegel, que frenan o previenen la incontinencia urinaria. Esto ha permitido que muchas mujeres se acercaran a las tiendas eróticas en busca de un producto recomendado por el médico y terminaron como clientas frecuentes.

Dildos y vibradores

Además de llevarnos al clímax de un modo relativamente más sencillo, los vibradores pueden ayudarnos a dosificar el placer, a decidir cuándo queremos corrernos bajando la potencia de vibración o subiéndola; aplicarlo en una zona próxima a los genitales e ir acercándolo poco a poco, o abordar directamente el clítoris o la zona del perineo o de la base del pene, dependerá de los gustos de cada uno y de su sensibilidad.

Una de las razones por las que está tan de moda utilizar juguetes apunta a nuestra ya endémica falta de tiempo. Los vibradores, aplicados en la vulva (la zona externa, no como en las pelis porno que se los introducen hasta las amígdalas), estimulan de forma rápida y eficiente y nos llevan al orgasmo sin esfuerzo en cuestión de sesenta segundos a tres minutos (¿no te lo crees? Prueba...). Dicho lo cual, apunto que no conviene engancharse a ellos —no es un chiste—. Un pequeño guiño sobre este tema se ve en la serie *Sexo en Nueva York*, cuando Charlotte, la pija, en uno de los episodios, se compra un modelo de vibrador en rosa y plata, con unas pestañas en forma de conejito (especiales para estimular el clítoris; el juguetito se llama «Conejo rampante», no tiene desperdicio), varias velocidades y, tras empezar a utilizarlo, literalmente desaparece: es incapaz de salir de casa porque todo lo demás que el mundo pueda ofrecerle deja de interesarle... No es que sea la peor adicción que se puede tener, pero sí que posteriormente dificultará alcanzar orgasmos «naturales», con seres de carne y hueso, simples humanos desgraciadamente desprovistos del botón de selección de velocidades o de rotación del eje.

A muchas, los dildos les sirven para acompañar la masturbación manual, se lo introducen casi al final, cuando están a punto de llegar. Les proporciona la sensación de sentirse «llenas» cuando se desencadenan las contracciones vaginales que lo aprisionan. Los dildos se pueden emplear también para suplir la falta de manos: cuando estás masturbándote en solitario, puedes utilizarlos para la penetración de otro orificio: si estás estimulando con las manos la vagina, el dildo puede usarse en el ano; si colocas el vibrador sobre el clítoris, te queda libre la otra mano para acariciar los labios menores, el perineo y/o penetrar la vagina o el ano.

Y para ellos también se fabrican dildos que estimulan el punto P (el punto G masculino). Actúan sobre el perineo y el esfínter. Mejoran la erección y permiten conseguir potentes y continuados orgasmos no eyaculatorios.

Existen líneas de juguetes específicamente diseñadas para aprender a localizar con facilidad los dichosos puntos G (por ejemplo

Stubby o Rock Chic) y P (los modelos más vendidos son los estimuladores prostáticos Aneros y Rude boy). Estos artículos, al aplicar el estímulo necesario en cada persona y complementado con una respiración adecuada, ayudan a alcanzar un intenso orgasmo. Además de su uso para la autosatisfacción, pueden ser empleados con la pareja, añadiendo cierta complicidad y nuevas sensaciones.

Para el control eyaculatorio, una de las disfunciones más preocupantes, existen juguetes que facilitan las claves para descubrir el juego de músculos implicados, fundamentalmente los denominados Kegel masculinos, y así poder fortalecerlos. Al tomar conciencia de ellos, se podrá controlar la tensión y distensión, aprendiendo a adelantarse al punto de «no retorno» (en el que la eyaculación se presenta inminente e incontrolable) para poder cambiar el ritmo y/o ángulo de penetración a tiempo. A mayor tonificación y control de esta musculatura, mayor capacidad de manejo de la eyaculación hasta el punto de lograr inhibirla o sincronizarla con la pareja. Para este fin, o para la simple autosatisfacción masculina, existen juguetes que permiten ejecutar distintas tablas de control eyaculatorio, familiarizar la conciencia con las distintas fases que desencadenan la eyaculación y aprender los innumerables ritmos y preferencias de cada cual. Los más efectivos: Flesh-Light, SensoPocketPenis y All 4's LoveClone.

Otro dildo muy específico se llama plug anal. Tiene forma de huso y, además de como estimulador, actúa como dilatador. Consta de un tope —una base más grande que sirve para manejarlo— que impide que el objeto sea succionado y quede atrapado en el interior: lo que suele significar algo tan poco glamuroso como desplazarse al hospital para que lo encuentren y lo saquen.

Una de las variantes del uso de los dildos es fijarlos a un arnés —los hay de cuero muy espectaculares—, sujetarlo a la cintura y que simulen un pene. Cualquiera puede ponérselo, aunque lo más frecuente es que se lo coloque ella y se recree la fantasía del intercambio de roles.

Lubricantes y geles

Siempre escuchamos que la elección de los juguetes y potingues para la cama es muy personal. Sí. Personal por su intransferibilidad, por razones básicas de higiene; personal también por los gustos, aficiones y preferencias particulares de cada cual y, en especial, la elección del lubricante dependerá de la suerte que personalmente tenga cada uno. Sí, de su suerte: de si es o no alérgico y del dinero que quiera o pueda gastarse. Una prueba más de la desigualdad que gobierna el planeta.

Como su propio nombre indica, se emplean para suplir la lubricación natural o cuando ésta es deficiente pero, también, otra de sus posibilidades, sería la de alterar la percepción, tanto del tacto natural de la piel como de los juguetes, intensificándola. Sí, eso dicen todos los anuncios, pues esta vez, sin que sirva de precedente: créetelo... Ocurre que a muchos les da cierto apuro llevar encima el tubo o que lo descubra la última conquista en el cajón de la mesilla de noche. Dos cosas: el lubricante mejora tanto la práctica del sexo que quien lo utiliza una vez, continúa haciéndolo —y no sirve sólo para sexo anal—; además, sabed que se vende en sobrecitos que duran lo suficiente como para pasar un montón de horas en activo. Para ellas: si quieres evitarte dar explicaciones, y sabes que necesitas lubricación extra, vete al cuarto de baño, introduce un poco dentro de la vagina, lo más arriba que llegues, y con el calor del organismo y la lubricación natural, irá bajando.

Actualmente, además de infinidad de marcas, el mercado ofrece todo tipo de lubricantes —buscad siempre que sean compatibles con el uso de preservativos: los de base de agua—. Los venden de efecto frescor, efecto calor, natural y de sabores. Otro detalle: no manchan y todos se limpian fácilmente.

Hay también geles y *sprays* para aplicarlos sobre el pene o la zona vaginal, con efecto estimulante, vigorizante, relajante y dilatador o retardante de la eyaculación. Otros predican aumentar la consistencia y tamaño del pene o prometen «despertar» el clítoris e intensificar el orgasmo femenino. Para los pechos se puede utilizar un *spray* que asegura endurecerlos y tensarlos, y aplicar geles de sabores para que la tarea de su estimulación oral resulte más agradable y alimenticia (hay hasta un kit de pincel y crema de chocolate para el cuerpo, otro que lleva ginseng y vitaminas).

Anilla para el pene

Lejos de ser bisutería, pese a que se fabrica en diversos materiales como el acero y la silicona, su utilidad no es ornamental, sino la de ayudar a aumentar la erección y a mantenerla. Se coloca en la base del pene una vez que éste ha comenzado a aumentar de tamaño, y mantiene la sangre en la zona. Por ello, nunca debe de dejarse puesta más de media hora, es realmente peligroso excederse en el tiempo.

Bolas chinas

Se trata de un par de bolitas sujetas entre sí que se introducen por la vagina, dejando en el exterior la punta del cordel. Caminar con ellas puede resultar estimulante, pero su finalidad principal es ejercitar y fortalecer los músculos vaginales, pubococcígeos y el suelo pélvico (igual que los ejercicios de Kegel, que sirven para tratar y prevenir la incontinencia urinaria por estrés, mejoran el parto y la recuperación tras él, proporcionan mayor control y sensibilidad durante la penetración e intensifican y permiten encadenar los orgasmos). El uso de bolas exige una enorme higiene —son lavables— y cambiarlas cada poco tiempo, como máximo un par de meses (no hace falta llevar al extremo lo del reciclaje: se tiran, no querría descubrirlas colgadas del árbol la próxima Navidad). Para llamar a las bolas chinas por su nombre: busca *«balls»*. Hay de muchos tipos.

Huevo del amor

De reducido tamaño (5 × 3 cm), este juguetito se puede utilizar en pareja, tanto en casa como fuera, iniciando juegos de complicidad. Dispone de un control remoto que permite su manejo a distancia: encenderlo y apagarlo, aumentar o disminuir la velocidad y la vibración o activar la escalada.

Parches

Mediante la colocación en la muñeca de un parche, por lo visto, se aumenta el poder de atracción personal a través del olfato, que se estimula con su fragancia. Actúan durante 24 horas. Sin efectos secundarios —habría que experimentar los primarios—. Se comercializan en cajas de 30 parches.

Anillo vibrador

Desde los encartes de las revistas masculinas a las campañas de televisión se han ocupado de que este complemento, que nada tiene que ver con alta joyería, si no es por el nombre, se metiera en nuestra cultura sexual reciente y fulminantemente. Se coloca en la base del pene en erección y sirve para estimular tanto el clítoris como el propio pene. Como desventajas diría que cuesta concentrarse, hay que pararse a colocarlo y estar pendiente de que de veras toque el clítoris y, sumado al condón, aquello parece cualquier cosa, con tantas superposiciones... Son de un solo uso.

Disfraces y lencería

Te costará decidir si guardas tu lencería comestible en el cajón de las bragas o en la despensa. En los *sex shops* se encuentran miles de modelos de braguitas, tangas, medias y sujetadores de caramelo, junto a todo tipo de prendas íntimas —camisones, saltos de cama, corsés, ligueros, etc.— confeccionadas en red, lamé, raso, látex, cuero y plástico, de distintos colores, aunque en lo erótico predominan el negro, el rojo y los estampados de leopardo o cebra. Plumas de marabú, lentejuelas, encaje... estas prendas «aguantan» de todo. Otra opción son los disfraces de enfermera, estudiante y doncella —los tres más habituales—, junto con los de policía y animadora. Como accesorios: esposas, fustas, pañuelos para vendar los ojos y los imprescindibles tacones, sea en zapato de salón, sea en bota de caña alta. Los antifaces generan la sensación de mantener oculta la identidad, con la consiguiente liberación de muchos prejuicios y vergüenzas. Muy antiguos, pero rescatados con fuerza por los *sex shops* modernos, son los cubrepezones, unos adhesivos de distintos materiales y formas, y que sirven para «no estar desnuda, estándolo», lucir transparencias y escotes y añadir un toque erótico a la vista de la pareja.

Para masaje

Recurrimos a ellos para potenciar e incrementar el deseo sexual, para relajar tensiones y despertar pulsiones, para romper barreras y acortar distancias, para mimos y «torturas». Hay de todo: aceites, cremas, geles y polvos para espolvorear sobre el cuerpo con espectaculares plumas... Los sabores están muy logrados, son deliciosos, y los olores, te transportan.

Juegos

Basados en el arte del *striptease* o en el Kamasutra, casi todos los juegos eróticos que se han ideado se encaminan a que el perdedor se quite la ropa o «haga algo». Otros exigen superar pruebas más o menos divertidas o que exigen cierta audacia. En el fondo, el objetivo es incorporar el humor y el sentido lúdico que tanto favorece el contacto y la comunicación.

Preservativos

El preservativo tiene doble naturaleza: profiláctica y contraceptiva. No son ningún juguete, pero comparten la naturaleza de los enumerados en cuanto a objetos (invitados extraños) que se añaden a la relación. Disponibles en farmacias, máquinas expendedoras de bares, se compran también en gasolineras, *sex shops*, a través de Internet, etc., Aquí sí que hay variedad: en tamaños, sabores, colores, formas, propiedades y utilidades. Se fabrican en látex —que hay a quienes les produce alergia y que son incompatibles con algunos lubricantes con base de silicona— y poliuretano.

No son lavables ni reutilizables, a diferencia de dildos, anillas, vibradores, etc. que tienes que lavar con agua y jabón neutro antes y después de cada uso y secarlos bien antes de guardarlos (o esconderlos).

Cuadrante de látex

Se denomina «preservativo femenino», ideado para el cunnilingus y las relaciones lésbicas, pero sirve para la práctica segura del beso negro también. Se trata de unos rectángulos fabricados en látex de distintos sabores (desde cola a vainilla), que se colocan cubriendo la zona a estimular oralmente (vagina, ano) y que evita el contacto genital directo durante las relaciones sexuales chica-chica. Son perfectos si eres escrupuloso y además, si tienes la precaución de que no se desplace y de que no se dé la vuelta, te ahorrarás disgustos de ETS, tanto de origen bacteriano como vírico. Se encuentran en determinados *sex shops* y en algunas farmacias. Más caros que el condón convencional, su uso no está tan extendido.

Muñecas

Pediofilia: fijación sexual por las muñecas. De las grotescas hinchables a las de textura humana el recorrido es largo.

Pocas cosas al parecer más comunes que jugar a las muñecas. Por ejemplo, se dice que fue Hitler quien, como proyecto personal, encargó el desarrollo de éstas para evitar que sus soldados se relacionasen con mujeres que no fueran de raza aria, previniendo además cualquier contagio por vía de transmisión sexual. Las muñecas que el Führer solicitó al médico Olsen Nauseen, hará ya 65 años, encarnaban el prototipo de la estética germánica pura: atléticas, de 1,76 m, de pechos grandes, rubias, y «piel» blanca.

Asimismo, Andy, la *real doll* estrella del catálogo del californiano Matt McMullen cuesta 21.000 euros, y tiene esqueleto y textura similar a la humana, suda, posee lengua, dientes, punto G, pelo natural, y es virgen, pues de cuando en cuando le ponen un himen... artificial, por supuesto.

Si se tira del hilo en la evolución de las rudimentarias muñecas hinchables hitlerianas hasta llegar a las impactantes *real dolls*, parece ineludible hacer una paradita en el admirado y siempre paradójico País del Sol Naciente. Desde que el *boom* se divulgara en la prensa, hará ya un par de años, es perfectamente público y notorio que las muñecas para adultos se han instalado en la cultura japonesa y casi en su cesta de la compra, desbancando a las prostitutas de la calle y creando una especie de género sexual independiente que ha trascendido hasta la prensa (la revista *i-doloid* es sólo un ejemplo, con portadas y artículos sobre las muñecas más novedosas y acerca de cómo disfrutar de encuentros sexuales con ellas) y el cine X, siendo de látex y silicona (todo el cuerpo, no sólo las prótesis mamarias o de pómulos) las protagonistas de la cinta *Love Doll*, del director Baksheesh Yamamoto, estrenada en 2005.

Calificadlo de enfermizo, de *freak* o de perverso (seamos un poquito honestos y, antes de vomitar blasfemias sobre el vecino, recordemos que aún tararean por ahí el «pobre de mí»..., que los Sanfermines aún no se han prohibido...), pero esta obsesión nipona por las muñecas también puede obedecer al loable avance de la tecnología: ¿por qué contentarse con una PDA último modelo o la «cojolavadora» silenciosa, pudiendo tener a tu disposición una verdadera e incondicional esclava sexual, que permanece eternamente en la niñez, que jamás se queja, ni pide más, ni comete imprudencias criticando tu capacidad amatoria..?

Puntualicemos: ya no hablamos de las muñecas hinchables; ésas son ya una generación obsoleta, casi como flotadores chabacanos, con rostros y tacto tan horroroso que casi debía dar pavor pensar en tirárselas. Se trata de muñecas de textura humana, con tacto «piel». ¿Lo más sorprendente?, pues dependerá de lo viajados y leídos que seáis, pero quizá lo flipante de verdad sea la evolución del *business*. Como su precio resultaba ciertamente prohibitivo para que cualquiera pudiera comprarlas (más de 4.500 euros), algunos vislumbraron el negocio y organizaron un sistema de alquiler por horas o días. Su alquiler está sujeto a ciertas reglas de uso. No se puede: dañar a la muñeca con arañazos, mordiscos, navajazos o cortes de cualquier otro instrumento o con quemaduras; usar líquidos distintos de la loción; doblar en exceso las articulaciones de la muñeca; ensuciar o desgarrar la ropa; ensuciar el pelo o derramar semen fuera del «agujero especial», de modo que mejor... ¡asegúrate de utilizar un condón!

LAU*

El siguiente paso —quizás el más bizarro— fue la apertura de burdeles de muñecas, donde los clientes acuden para disfrutar de un ratito de intimidad con cualquiera de las nínfulas artificiales, y tocarlas, y ponerles trajecitos, y hasta hacerles fotos... Por supuesto, mientras tanto, los pudientes coleccionistas se las compran de diez en diez y hacen sus propias webs donde cuelgan las fotos de sus adoradas y sigilosas amantes.

Siguiendo los gustos mayoritarios, la imagen de estas compañeras de juegos lúbricos imita a la de adolescentes de 12 años y algunas recrean el aniñado aspecto de las protagonistas de los tebeos manga.

Entre los distintos modelos de muñeca disponibles las hay desde las más elaboradas, que cuestan entre 740 y 1.060 dólares, con una altura de 156 cm y medidas de 80-56-80 —eso sí, sólo pesan 4 kg—; a las de 120 o 100 cm de altura, con aspecto colegial, un poco más baratas. Con la compra de la muñeca, la peluca y las medias van incluidas, así como el minikit con lubricante básico, pero si quieres el set de cosméticos o que venga maquillada, o algún otro accesorio o vestidos, se paga extra. Para el caso de fallecimiento de los dueños de las muñecas, las empresas fabricantes ofrecen un servicio de ritual funerario budista, así como hacerse cargo de la recogida de la muñeca.

Pero lo más *fashion* son los juguetes «mutilados»: un tronco —con o sin cara— desprovisto de extremidades, un simple busto con 2 orificios (boca y vagina) de 90 cm de largo, o bien, otros fragmentos del cuerpo (culo, vagina, pechos...).

Por cierto, la industria juguetera no es exclusivamente para hombres, ya que se han fabricado modelos de muñeco con penes inmensos para mujeres y homosexuales.

Según los datos del informe anual de Durex sobre Hábitos de Consumo y Comportamiento Sexual, entre 2004 y 2006 se aprecia que se consolida la afición por la juguetería sexual (del 16 % al 22 % de los españoles encuestados la emplea). Los objetos más comprados son los de usar y tirar (condones y anillas con vibrador), por su precio (más baratos), higiene y promiscuidad (mejor estrenar uno con cada pareja, evitando ascos comprensibles y riesgos de contagios) y accesibilidad (farmacias e hipermercados).

TODO LO QUE SIEMPRE QUISISTE SABER... SIN NECESIDAD DE PREGUNTAR

1

Don de gentes

El mismísimo Kamasutra apunta que «hay personas que jamás consiguen el objeto de sus deseos, ni aun después de practicar todo lo enunciado en este libro, por lo que entonces deben tratar de conseguirlo por otros medios distintos»; maquillaje exterior, como se le podría denominar en Europa y América. Si no se tiene buena presencia, juventud, belleza, tanto en el hombre como en la mujer, si por una causa u otra no resultan agradables, es entonces cuando deben recurrir a estas otras artes, a los medios artificiales, al «maquillaje exterior» y, a renglón seguido, explica un montón de fórmulas afrodisíacas que se echan sobre el pene y demás, para que tu amante te pertenezca. No es el caso. De afrodisíacos ya se habla en otra parte. Ahora, vayamos a las pocas cosas imprescindibles que conviene saber.

Hagamos un ejercicio de autoanálisis honesto: tan malo es que permanezcamos horas contemplándonos ante un espejo, como hacía la bruja de la Bella Durmiente, como que nos descuidemos hasta el extremo de no darnos cuenta de que llevamos un lamparón en la camiseta. Ni Narciso en el estanque ni el vagabundo de la plaza, hay que encontrar, dentro de esa *aura mediocritas*, ese estilillo que nos favorece y que a esa persona le agrade (lo genial es que le parezcas «lo más», pero para poder empezar «algo», confórmate con no desagradarla).

La imagen (como conjunto de factores: ropa, olor, modales, tono de voz, etc.) es importante. Vivimos en una sociedad de consumo, donde la apariencia es crucial y en la que no se nos dan segundas oportunidades casi nunca.

Sé un hombre

Si no te importa, y con todo respeto al artículo 14 de la Constitución española, que proclama la igualdad de derechos y deberes entre hombres y mujeres, deja que te aclare que seguir siendo caballeroso no significa que renuncies a tu igualdad. Déjala pasar, ábrele la puerta del coche, cédele el asiento... Algunos lo hacen siempre, otros hasta que te han echado un polvo —como técnica de conquista para impresionarte a base de galantería—, y otros, lamentablemente, seguro que no saben de qué hablo.

Aromaterapia

Cuando te acercas a esa persona tanto como para besarla es el momento en que puede, además, olerte. No seré yo quien copie las frases de los anuncios de colonias, pero había una en concreto: «en las distancias cortas, una colonia de hombre (o de mujer) se la juega».

A dedo

De esas mismas manos que van a recorrer luego todo tu cuerpo, sudorosas, débiles, demasiado frías... Todas las sensaciones cuentan. Se van evaluando. Por ello la importancia de la higiene, de si te muerdes las uñas, o las llevas mugrientas, o largas, o eres devoto del cutrísimo hábito de dejar que la del meñique crezca, como los guitarristas, la otra persona lo detectará e inconscientemente se sentirá decepcionada y menos atraída por ti, se reducirán las probabilidades de llevártela a la cama. Cómo te colocas, cómo te sientas, qué partes del cuerpo te acaricias «por accidente»... son detalles que también puntúan.

Se dice «pechos»

Y sólo estás autorizado a llamarlas «tetas» si tienes un par propio. No se estrujan como si fueran bolas antiestrés. No se muerden. El sujetador no se rompe —salvo que traigas otro carísimo de repuesto para regalárselo antes de marcharte—. Suele ser el segundo paso a dar tras los besos, lo que no implica que sea correcto bajar de cabeza como un lactante desnutrido. Salvo que sean operados —o ella una bendecida por la naturaleza— no suelen ser idénticos (siempre hay uno más grande y más arriba) y el paso del tiempo, los embarazos, los cambios hormonales, etc., pasan factura. Son muy sensibles (algo que también puede variar en función del momento del ciclo en que esté). Las areolas y los pezones se contraen y son eréctiles (señal de excitación o de frío). Y nosotras: además de amarlas y de aceptarlas (u operarlas, va en gustos y presupuestos) hay que saber utilizarlas. Sirven para acurrucar, para dar masajes, para amamantar, para masturbar, para abrirte paso entre la multitud o que te dejen pasar a ciertos sitios (¿qué pasa, es que nunca lo habéis pensado siquiera?). Muchas ascienden gracias a ellas.

Una invitación

En principio, si seguimos con la democracia, lo de pagar debería hacerse a medias. No hay cosa más fría y menos romántica que estar dividiendo... En fin, a riesgo de que me caigan críticas de todo tipo, lo que parece adecuado es que él pague por lo menos las dos primeras veces. A partir de ese momento, en función de la capacidad de cada uno o de su nivel de ingresos, o por turnos, o paga el que propone el plan. He mantenido conversaciones con abogadas y cirujanas forradísimas, que no «necesitan» que las inviten, pero lo valoran, lo ven un gesto cortés. Y coinciden con las putas —sí, de distintos niveles de precios— a las que también he preguntado sobre el asunto, en la primera etapa, sólo que estas últimas no aceptan la siguiente fase: con ellas paga él siempre... Señoras y señores: vean pues que, lo de las mujeres «normales», no se trata de nada crematístico, sino del detalle.

Juguemos limpio

España no es precisamente de los países que peor se lleva con el sano hábito de la ducha diaria. Sin embargo, no viene mal tener en cuenta que salvo que seas un ángel, las horas del día pasan y tu frescura matutina decae. Para tu cita, aséate, échate colonia, maquíllate, aféitate, depílate, lávate los dientes, usa enjuagues, cremas hidratantes con buen olor... Saberte más atractivo aumenta la autoestima y te dará seguridad saber que ciertas cosas están bajo control —deja que sean otras circunstancias, las que no dependen de ti, las que te amarguen la vida—. Juguemos limpio y limpios. Limpieza de bajos (fundamental, si piensas que la cosa puede ir a mayores, además de por salud —evita ITS causadas por hongos y bacterias—, por respeto a las fosas nasales). Las manos son también una tarjeta de visita. Siempre: uñas limpias, limadas y bien recortadas, cálidas y secas —sin sudor—, suaves —sin callos— y sin anillos que arañen, por ideales que te creas que son.

Sé atento

Existe todo un juego de miradas y de sonrisas. Una mirada combinada con una amplia y cálida sonrisa se considera en todo el mundo como una demostración de interés sexual, que hincha el ego de cualquiera que la reciba y encima, sale gratis. Cabe que no te la devuelva, en cuyo caso, puedes seguir con lo que estuvieras haciendo (tomar una copa o charlando), pero si se da por aludida y te corresponde, es un eficaz modo de allanar el camino.

Si has quedado con alguien, qué menos que dedicarle al menos una parte de tu consciencia. Lo que quiero decir es que has de respetar su presencia (escribiría «honrar su presencia» pero temo que quede cursi y se malinterprete como «rancio»). Eso implica que valores que está ahí y que se lo hagas ver.

Sería estupendo para que se haga una idea de tu inmensa popularidad y de la suerte que tiene de que le dediques parte de tu tiempo que tu móvil sonara varias veces, tanto por llamadas, que, si has sido tan grosero/a de contestar, cortarás de inmediato —nada de salirte del bar, dejándole tirado/a, para pegarte una charla de diez minutos—, como sms. No puedes pasarte la cita escribiendo. Popularidad sí, mala educación, no. ¿Se capta el matiz? Te vendrá bien que compruebe que el mundo, tu mundo, no gira a su alrededor, pero de ningún modo debes ponerte a contestarlos. Mucho ojito con las conversaciones breves que pretenden sonar intrascendentes, pero que dejan entrever que se trata de alguien «con derechos» sobre nosotros. Este tipo de llamada, si pretendes ocultar que tienes una relación, mejor contéstala en privado.

¿De qué me hablas?

Todo el mundo sabe que en la conversación hay que evitar la religión y la política. Pero también aquellos temas en los que se es un verdadero experto, porque cabe que conviertas la conversación (recuerda que son dos los que participan) en una ponencia. Quizá tengas la suerte de que «tu» tema sea algo sobre lo que tu futura presa siente fascinación —o que se lo expliques todo con tal gracia y encanto que se quede impresionado, pero aun así, no sé si lo recomendaría...—. Es mejor que te reserves la especialidad para las siguientes veces que os veáis, para que te conozca mejor.

La primera cita debe fluir sin demasiadas profundizaciones, es una toma de contacto. Trata de sentirte a gusto. Si eres de los que hablan mucho, hazlo, pero no boicotees la cita, no invadas su espacio, deja que meta baza y demuestra interés por su vida y obra (y presta atención). Si muestras brotes sicóticos, vehemencia anormal (cuidado con el fútbol y aficiones similares, que a mucha gente se le hincha la vena del cuello defendiendo su «causa») o contradicciones, sin duda espantarás a esa persona y preferirá no verte más.

Recuerda también que discutir no apetece. Si notas que entras en colisión con alguna de sus opiniones, trata de no obstinarte. Puedes hablar, responder, preguntar (no interrogar), pero: respeta que cada cual opine lo que quiera (escucha y analiza si además de gustarte, te cae bien). Si percibes su entusiasmo hacia algo —se ríe, te hace comentarios sobre ello—, continúa por ahí. Y haz lo propio: si empieza a explicarte algo y notas que le resulta importante, demuestra no sólo que estás oyendo, sino que quieres saber más: haz alguna pregunta (a veces, resulta que no conoces ni una palabra del asunto. No pasa nada por que tus frases sean breves o incluso por que le pidas que te cuente más: se trata de que se cree un ambiente agradable, no de ultimar el desarrollo de una fórmula matemática).

Habla de lo que te dé seguridad, pero no seas pedante, no monopolices el tema y asegúrate de que no se aburre. El mejor conversador no es quien mejor habla, sino quien mejor escucha. Adáptate al tipo de persona que tienes delante. Si es de las trascendentales, sería muy grave por mi parte sugerirte que hables de trapos como si todas las tías fuéramos *shoppaholics* (aunque lo somos en casi un 90 %). El clima como recurso ya no se usa ni para dar palique en los ascensores. Evita topicazos y discursos de ligón de playa. No suele fallar algún referente que tenga dos o más puntos de vista: un escándalo de las noticias del corazón con implicaciones económicas o políticas. Esos temas suscitan charlas distendidas tanto entre ejecutivos que leen *The Financial Times*, como entre «marujas» que viven para despellejar y cotillear. Funciona también que hagas comentarios positivos y sobre generalidades (no necesariamente trivialidades, no insultes su inteligencia). Si el tema que sacas le interesa, ya podrás dejarla hablar, que es lo que a todas, en el fondo, nos encanta.

Bajo ningún concepto saques a relucir: ex novias o ex amantes, ni las nombres y, si lo haces, que sea con cierto respeto pero sin añoranza, y que no salgan por tu boca insultos ni frases machistas; ni una palabra sobre cómo eran en la cama, o pensará que eres el típico imbécil que va por ahí largando detalles íntimos. Los grandes dramas personales y problemones (económicos o de salud), por favor, evítalos, al menos por ser el primer día. Y si te cuesta mucho reprimirte y no exasperarte ante esas injusticias laborales de las que estás siendo víctima, desahógate, pero sepas que la conversación será un coñazo.

Y humor. Siempre con humor. Si no eres gracioso, no la cagues contando chistes malos. Sonríe (así te relajarás), pero no pretendas ser uno de esos que se creen el alma de la fiesta. Recuerda que si bien las cosas bellas atraen en un primer momento, a la larga interesa más que la persona irradie buena energía, alegría y naturalidad.

A todo trapo

Ten en cuenta que la primera impresión es la que queda y que la ropa nos define, derrocha connotaciones (tus gustos, tu adscripción a una tribu urbana u otra, tu capacidad adquisitiva, tu grado de pulcritud, tu talento como estilista, tu estado de ánimo, tu carácter...). A primera vista nosotras evaluamos también lo que un hombre esconde. No son ellos los únicos que investigan, elucubran y tratan de adivinar lo que hay bajo esos tejanos apretados o se escapa por ese escote de vértigo.

Lo mejor para que tu carrocería destaque es que la ropa sea de tu talla —no te ofendas si ya lo sabías—. Sí, parece una obviedad, pero muchas personas no se lucen por culpa de que llevan prendas que les quedan mal: o demasiado grandes, con cuyos volúmenes pierden esa definición lograda a base de matarse en el gimnasio, o demasiado pequeñas, que parece que se han propuesto reventar las costuras. Si tienes un físico estupendo haz que tu cita lo note pero nunca, bajo ningún concepto, centres el peso de la conversación en los aminoácidos que tomas, las repeticiones de sentadilla o las horas de aeróbicos que haces. Si lo que ocultas vale la pena, sírvete de ello, haz que juegue a tu favor (por favor, con sutileza. Cuidado con los gestos esos de «qué seguro que estoy de mí» o «no sabes la suerte que tienes de tenerme aquí delante» que hacen algunos, recostándose sobre la barra cargando todo el peso y apretando glúteo o agarrando el cubata como si pesara cien kilos, para que se les marque el bíceps...).

Si tus curvas están descontroladas porque tu único deporte es encender el DVD y la genética se ensañó contigo, no pasa nada. Si ha decidido verte ya tienes claro que te está brindando una oportunidad. No te pases las horas metiendo tripa. Cada cual se ha de conocer y poner énfasis en sus puntos fuertes. Eso sí, debes procurar sacarte el mejor partido. Si te encuentras bien, se te notará en la actitud, tendrás mayor seguridad en ti mismo. Eso es algo que se percibe a nivel instintivo: como el miedo, o la angustia... son cosas que se huelen. Si estás confiado, todo irá mejor. No es viable hacer un asesoramiento personalizado desde aquí pero, en titulares: cree lo que decía Tom Ford de «menos es más» e imítalo. Seas como seas, y vayas adonde vayas, ir de negro es la mejor opción. (Y recuerda que sea de tu talla.) Si lo que falla es la barriga, trata de ponerte algo que no la marque, algo por fuera, que disimule —huye de cinturones que te estrangulen como a un chorizo embutido—. Si tu espalda es estrecha, ponte alguna prenda que lleve algo de refuerzo en las hombreras —por favor, no desentierres a Locomía—. Si sigues el consejo de ir de negro, lo mejor es una americana —sin corbata si vas informal— o una chaqueta de cuero (esto va en estilos y modas). La idea es que te «arme» un poco, no sé si me explico...

Los hombres también tienen problemas de estatura. Si es el caso, lo ideal es permanecer sentado cuanto más tiempo mejor y elegir asientos que permitan hablar cara a cara. Hay truquillos, como las alzas, o elegir zapatos con una suela más gruesa, pero al final, uno es como es y, salvo que te pongas unos zancos de Drag Queen, no vas a arreglar demasiado.

Primer contacto

La educación nos marca ciertas pautas de distancia. No es educado ir tocando por ahí a la gente, pero claro, todo depende de quién se trate y, fundamentalmente, del contexto. Hacerte hueco en la cola del cine para sacar las entradas o dejarla pasar delante pueden ser la ocasión. Años después, se recuerdan las cosquillitas que producen esos primeros contactos. En este libro se explica cómo dilatar un ano para introducir un puño, pero no sé qué agita más el corazón, si eso o el primer achuchón con beso...

Si estás en un sitio con música y la gente baila (si no, ni se te ocurra ponerte tú ahí en medio a dar saltos porque parecerás un desequilibrado o que no toleras el alcohol), y tú sabes moverte aunque sea un poco, pregúntale si le apetece (insiste una vez, pero si dice «no», déjala sentadita). Si acepta o si es ella la que lleva la iniciativa, síguela a la pista. No te eches encima, por mucho que te ponga verla mover la cadera y te esté provocando con esa melena y tal... Acércate muy poco y, si la canción lo permite, ve ganando terreno (recuerda: no le estás metiendo mano en un parque, estás bailando con ella), agárrala, y eso romperá el hielo. En estos momentos, lo que hay que hacer es que sea ella la que se arrime o la que «marque» el grado de proximidad. Los hay muy guarros que te restriegan el paquete so pretexto de menearse a ritmo de lambada y que, por hacerlo tan a saco, se cargan el encanto.

Si la agarras de la mano y no la quita, ya está. Y para eso, pues no queda más remedio que probar...

Lo que con chicas «normales» definitivamente no funciona es que vayas a tocar su culo directamente, o cosas así.

¿Con premeditación y alevosía...?

En esto de conseguir citas cada persona es un mundo, y además cada individuo fluctúa socialmente como si fuera un activo bursátil (¿no parece que alguien, de pronto, una temporada está en alza y luego pasa tres meses desaparecido y anulado?). Mientras los hay que no logran interesar a nadie durante un siglo, determinadas personas que han nacido con estrella y son auténticos imanes carismáticos, tienen unas agendas con tantas anotaciones que parecen un diario. Por ello, hagamos como que conseguir esa primera cita es sencillo y que ya tenemos una.

A veces, si se dispone de demasiado tiempo para pensar, igual te obsesionas y premeditas excesivamente la situación, aniquilando la naturalidad (¿cómo explicarías que «surgió espontáneamente lo de atarle y rociarle con un gel comestible de chocolate picante»?, pero ¡si ya saliste de casa con todo un arsenal amatorio en el bolso!).

Siempre he pensado que una cita ideal no requiere seguir el típico protocolo de manual de Don Juan, pero hay errores que no deben cometerse, si es que pretendes volver a ver a esa persona. Parece complicado que «todo sea mágico y que encaje», pero ha de haber un estadio intermedio entre esta perfección maravillosa casi extraída de las páginas de Corín Tellado y lo que pueden llegar a depararte los hados...

Antes de cada cita conviene fijar objetivos e identificar el espíritu del contrato, como dirían los juristas: ¿qué nos trae aquí? Eso es el difícil arte de buscar (y encontrar) un término medio entre velas, *jacuzzi* y resolver el calentón en la parte de detrás de su coche, aparcados en un callejón oscuro...

Cuesta imaginar, a priori, con qué nos sorprenderá la noche, qué va a suceder entre el encuentro y ese saludo con dos besos y la visión que te asalta acto seguido, donde sacas del bolsillo del abrigo una garrafa de lubricante...

Aunque en derecho penal se trata de una circunstancia agravante, la premeditación en las relaciones puede jugar a nuestro favor. Desde haber pensado el nombre de un segundo sitio adonde ir a tomar copas para tenerlo en la recámara, pensado por si la opción inicial fracasa porque está cerrado, atestado de gente o no os gusta, a plantearte qué te vas a poner para triunfar.

Vale, pero, ¿quién lleva el condón?

Sinceramente, a estas alturas, por experiencia propia y (muchas) en cabezas ajenas, creo que esperar que un hombre en su casa tenga de todo es utópico, aunque también los hay, y te reciben con tantos detalles que te sientes en un hotel de lujo. Muchos, a veces, no tienen ni condones, como para encontrarte parafernalias y robots sexuales... Por este motivo, por favor, señoras y señores, lectores todos, los preservativos son imprescindibles y no es exclusiva obligación de ellos comprarlos... Los usamos ambos, ¿no? Y si no los hay, pues nos quedamos los dos con idéntico corte de rollo... No parece de este siglo tener que justificar mucho más: si llegado el instante en que procede colocarlo, él no se decide o no tiene y tú abres el bolso y sacas uno, sería motivo suficiente para dejarle ahí plantado que torciera el gesto o te insultara con comentarios al respecto de que «una chica lleve gomas».

Despedida

Que nadie pierda de vista un detalle: nos gusta sentirnos especiales. Ello implica muchas cosas como que, llegado el momento de finiquitar la velada, el que tenga coche se ofrezca para llevar al otro. Si es demasiado lejos, ya tiene manera de llegar, ha de pasarse por otro sitio antes, etc., te lo hará saber y declinará tu oferta, pero al menos, tú has quedado estupendamente. En serio: no se trata de otra cosa que demostrar modales. Más allá de si nos da miedo o no eso de volver a casa solas, es un hecho que quedarte tirada en mitad de ninguna parte no suele ser lo que nos induce a enloquecer por alguien...

Si la cosa ha ido bien, se nota. Pero, de todos modos, da como «vértigo» eso de lanzarse... Como mujer siempre me ha parecido más cómodo no tener que arriesgarme, que el otro dé el primer paso (ya daré yo el segundo, tercero y cuarto). Pero sí, el primero, cuesta. Hablando con muchas amigas y lectoras, creo que a la mayoría de las mujeres nos encantan los besos... pero ojo, que estamos hablando del primero. Por favor, que todo el mundo lea y memorice el apartado «El beso» que para eso me lo he currado.

¿Ya? Bien, pues situémonos en que estás a punto de decir eso de «nos vemos», «hablamos», «mándame un sms cuando hayas llegado», «no olvides pasarme eso por e-mail», o cualquier gilipollez que, en el fondo, sólo te sirve para alargar un minutillo porque no quieres dejar que se vaya. Trata de que parezca un «accidente» y termina con esas frases en alguna parte de la vía pública más tranquila o aparca (no frenes nada más, tómate la molestia de dejar el coche en un sitio del que no te echen con pitidos histéricos). Si no te atreves al beso directo en los labios, haz algo que produce cosquilleo y que luego recordamos todas. Agárrala de la cara, con suavidad, metiendo casi los dedos detrás de la nuca —odiamos que nos desmaquillen y también que nos despeinen—. Acércate a cámara lenta —tortúrala y, además, así te aseguras de no hacer el ridículo, de que no se va a apartar—, dale el primer beso en una mejilla y ahí has de decidirte: beso sí o beso no. Si ves que sí, aplica lo que has aprendido: poco a poco pero apasionadamente, demuéstrale cómo te apetece. Dedica unos minutos al típico besazo (sólo la boca, no muevas las manos salvo para acariciar la cara, un poco el cuello) que se quede muerta y mándala irse. Haz como que no quieres tirártela.

Si no hay opción a beso pues... dignamente pero sin soberbia ni cagadas de ego maltrecho, despídete. Puede que la cosa quede ahí o que haya otro mejor momento.

Llamar o no llamar

Hay ciertas «normas no escritas» (o sí, que hoy día en Internet...) acerca del protocolo o de lo que «se supone que» se debe hacer o cabe esperar.

Cuando conoces a alguien durante el fin de semana (en cualquier sitio, desde una discoteca a una reunión de negocios o en la típica barbacoa familiar con niños gritones) y te pide el teléfono, espera hasta el miércoles. Si no ha llamado para entonces, una de dos, o perdió el número o es que no piensa utilizarlo. Prueba una vez (deja que suene pero no grabes mensaje) pero si ves que en tu segundo intento, dejando ya mensaje, no hay respuesta, olvídate. No se te ocurra llenar un buzón de voz ni un contestador con tus «Hola, nos conocimos el sábado... ¿te acuerdas?». Si reivindicamos igualdad, pongámosla en práctica. Si él puede llamar, tú también —a veces, los teléfonos efectivamente se pierden—. Dicho esto, que conste que sería lo correcto, todos sabemos que si un tío ve que vas detrás, pierde todo su interés... Otra cosa es que domines el asunto: que llames siempre tú, que «decidas». Si no, en serio, déjate de igualdad... Puedes llamar tú, la primera vez, pero si él no aprovecha esa puerta que le abres, será señal de que «no».

Otra cosa. Si te has acostado con alguien, ¿quién llama? Por favor, lee todo lo que he investigado sobre la oxitocina. Vete a dos capítulos: «Enamoramiento» y «El orgasmo».

¿Ya? Vale. El caso es que él se va/tú te vas. «Te llamo luego» o «luego hablamos» o cosas más tiernas incluso. Vas viendo que las horas pasan... y no llama. Llega el día siguiente. Y tampoco llama. Esperas. (Ahora está muy de moda no llamar al día siguiente para dejar bien claro que sólo fue sexo, que no les importas como para llamar. La «llamada del día siguiente» en el código actual implica que te has quedado pillado/a, y por eso, todos tratamos de evitarla.) Tú te estás muriendo —si de verdad te has leído esos capítulos sabes por qué—. Aguanta, no le llames. Él no siente lo que tú a ningún nivel: ojo, que probablemente, lo que te pasa no sea nada de lo que «crees» que te pasa a juzgar por cómo te sientes. Si transcurren dos días desde que estuvisteis juntos y no te ha llamado, es que no va a hacerlo. Vale, dale una oportunidad (justifícate pensando lo de siempre: que se le ha extraviado tu número, o que estaba marcando tu número y dio a «borrar» por error o algo así...). Llámale tú, a ver cómo reacciona. No hay peor cosa que marcar y que tu llamada quede en «perdidas» y el muy gañán no la devuelva. No insistas. No hay feminismo que valga. Si en ellos que vayan detrás resulta hasta romántico —a ver, con su justo punto y cuando el interés es recíproco, si no, no...—, en nosotras resulta que «les agobiamos», que somos unas plastas, etc. Cuando te has acostado con alguien y no te llama de inmediato, o al día siguiente o, como máximo, en dos días, malo. No se te ocurra seguirle el juego si ves que te cuenta historias tipo enfermedades horribles, cambios de piso, viajes..., acontecimientos todos ellos sobrevenidos fatídicamente en las últimas 48 horas. Los hombres, siendo unos cabrones, son incapaces de asumir que lo son: te dirá cualquier cosa «para no hacerte daño», y así es como te lo harán de verdad: dejándote ahí, consumida.

Otro detalle: si no quieres volver a estar con una chica, estás en tu derecho, pero no necesitas ser una mala persona. Hay cosas que son de simple educación, de protocolo. Cuando alguien no te interesa (da igual que hayáis pasado la noche haciendo de todo) no te marches con una falsa promesa de «luego te llamo» o «después hablamos», si a ciencia cierta sabes que ni loco quieres volverla a ver... El mundo se está llenando peligrosamente de gañanes que son capaces de las mayores groserías. Eso de desaparecer o de no tener el detallito más mínimo (como puede ser, si no quieres «hablar», el de escribir cuarenta caracteres con una especie de «hasta la vista» respondiendo su llamada «perdida» en plan cordial), es de ser un maleducado, no es ser guay, ni un machote. El sexo, al fin y al cabo, es el acto que genera la vida, muestra un poco de respeto con todo lo que involucra. Hay fórmulas indoloras que además no son groseras. Por ejemplo: «ya nos veremos». Así ella no te estará esperando con cara de Bambi viendo cómo asesinan a su madre. Si alguien con quien has intercambiado fluidos no te merece el respeto suficiente como para enviar un sms «neutral», sin propuestas de ninguna clase ni compromiso de repetir, es que el que no se merecía echar un polvo eres tú.

2

Tópicos

La infidelidad femenina en cifras

«Según un estudio realizado por el equipo Kinsey, en 1953, el 26 % de las casadas cometió adulterio. En 1980, otra investigación apuntaba que el 40 % de las mujeres había tenido una aventura en torno a los 40 años. Una encuesta de la revista *Playgirl* a mediados de la década de 1980 afirmaba que una de cada dos esposas había echado una canita al aire. Según un informe de la edición norteamericana de la revista *Woman*, realizado en 1989, la mitad de las mujeres que habían tenido relaciones con compañeros de trabajo eran casadas. El 70 % de las casadas que contactan a través de Internet se acuesta con el ciberamante.»

A oscuras

Hacerlo con la luz apagada ahorra mucha energía eléctrica pero, indiscutiblemente, a él le priva de su principal fuente de excitación: la que le proporciona «mirar», por eso, no suele gustarles la idea de que cierres a cal y canto persianas y cortinas y apagues todas las luces. Además, una total oscuridad puede ser contraproducente si te desorientas y recibes un rodillazo o un codazo en mal sitio —aunque para esas cosas no se me ocurre ninguno bueno—. Sin embargo, puede utilizarse esporádicamente como forma de que los demás sentidos se espabilen, sería una experiencia similar a cuando te vendan los ojos durante un buen rato de la relación y las caricias las notas con más intensidad. A la mayoría, en algún momento, nos ha dado vergüenza o nos ha costado desinhibirnos para acometer ciertas posiciones o meternos ciertas cosas en la boca... Sin embargo, a menudo, cuando se exige el fundido en negro se debe a problemas de inseguridad (complejos derivados de que no nos gusta nuestro cuerpo, por razones varias: exceso o defecto de peso, celulitis, pechos caídos, michelines, etc.), a timidez (nos apetece tener una relación sexual, pero nos cuesta dejar que nadie nos vea desnudos o la cara que ponemos al excitarnos), etc. Soluciones: las luces indirectas —vale la rendija de luz que entra desde el pasillo—, las velas —al principio, hasta que se acostumbra la retina, cuesta ver algo, pero al instante alumbran lo justo y necesario—. Ante la posibilidad de elegir, mejor los tonos de bombilla rojo o anaranjado, por su calidez y porque favorecen. A medida que las inhibiciones se disipan, que nadie se engañe: a nosotras también nos encanta mirar...

¿«No» significa siempre «No»?

Hay un «no» rotundo, absoluto, diáfano e incuestionable. Todos lo entendemos meridianamente. No hablamos ahora de este tipo de «no» (se trata en el apartado sobre «Sexo anal» y en el de «Sexo oral»).

¿Por qué «ellas» dicen que «no» si luego resulta que «sí»? A ver... Unas veces será por aburrimiento. Sí, es cierto que en ocasiones el asedio termina dando fruto. Otras, por puro instinto: si os retiramos la mano o esquivamos caricias dirigidas a los genitales en un momento concreto y al cuarto de hora os damos acceso, se debe, generalmente, a que en ese segundo instante, ya estamos lo bastante excitadas como para desearlas y recibirlas. A lo largo del libro se hace referencia a la respuesta sexual humana, al abismo que suele haber entre los tempos de excitación de hombre y mujer. Si vas demasiado deprisa puedes encontrarte un «no» que esconde en la estructura profunda de la frase la palabra «todavía» y que viene a ser: «aún no, pero sigue».

¿Cuándo un «no» es «no» en los juegos sadomasoquistas y de rol? En este tipo de prácticas donde el dolor se involucra como un elemento crucial, debemos acordar una palabra clave que ambas partes respeten. Ello sirve para orientar a quien está siendo activo, que bien podría confundirse ya que los gemidos, alaridos, contracciones del cuerpo, etc., con los que reaccionamos al placer son idénticos a los que nos produce el martirio. Aquí, por descontado, además de cierto sentido común, se exige plena confianza en la pareja.

Otra manifestación del «no» es la que se produce cuando, entrados en materia, algo falla y uno de los dos decide que ya basta y que no desea seguir. Quede claro que el sexo es algo que se experimenta libremente y que una demostración de dicho albedrío es la de dejarlo en el instante que nos sintamos mal, contrariados, incómodos, aburridos, desesperados, decepcionados, con la libido por los suelos, con mareos, con remordimientos... No importa lo lejos que las cosas hayan ido (o estén yendo en ese mismísimo instante), que si ella o él han tenido suficiente, has de respetarlo. En el caso de que sea ella quien no quiere «más», lo razone o no, y causado por el motivo que sea, por el hecho de que tengas más fuerza —y muchas ganas— no debes imponer el coito. Insisto: aunque te esté devorando el pene en ese mismo momento, si te dice *en serio* que basta, debes parar.

El orgasmo está sobrevalorado

Tipos de orgasmo, orgasmo exprés, orgasmo femenino y orgasmo masculino, potenciadores del orgasmo, fármacos contra la anorgasmia, fármacos contra la disfunción eréctil, puntos orgásmicos, etc. Hay toda una industria orgásmica. Hasta ahí, normal, dado que vivimos en una sociedad de consumo. Pero la cosa empieza a ponerse fea cuando la cultura, el pensamiento de la gente, se tiñe de esta idea. La gente folla mucho, muchísimo... pero no lo hace necesariamente cada vez mejor. Nadie cuestiona que hacemos acrobacias, nos introducimos objetos indescriptibles por cualquier agujero y gastamos en tecnología sexual auténticas fortunas para tirarnos a muchísimas personas de las que no tenemos tiempo de aprendernos ni el nombre y, aun así, «no nos sentimos llenos» —de hecho, la sensación de insatisfacción se va agravando—. Es que resulta que hay un error de base: estamos obsesionados por conseguir orgasmos. Pero, por placenteros que sean, al final se desvanecen, duran lo que duran, unos segundos... y eso desgasta tremendamente. Porque la vida es otra cosa, y el sexo, también. Parte de la cagada se debe a menospreciar la trascendencia del acto sexual que, en definitiva, es el que origina ni más ni menos que el milagro de la vida. Quizá nos ahorraríamos muchos malos polvos si nos detuviéramos a pensar: «¿si el condón falla querría tener a esta persona cerca *forever and ever* como padre/madre de mis vástagos?», porque, paradójicamente, la única mujer que es para toda tu vida es precisamente «la ex», la madre de tus hijos, de quien te quisiste librar... (Sólo es una reflexión.)

Nos hemos excedido, hemos malinterpretado los conceptos de libertad y de modernidad. Bien está librarnos del oscurantismo; perfecto lo de desmitificar tabúes y desenmascarar falacias. Totalmente necesaria la información anticonceptiva y de prevención de ETS e ITS: conozcamos las reglas del juego; imprescindible lo de equiparar a la mujer y al hombre en deberes y placeres... Pero, de ahí a perderle el respeto, a trivializarlo, a infravalorarlo... Al final, como no somos animales —o no solamente—, nos sentimos tremendamente defraudados. La relación sexual supera al estricto orgasmo. El orgasmo es algo que si viene, bienvenido sea, pero no ha de ser la meta. La meta es disfrutar de un buen rato en compañía de alguien que nos gusta, que nos divierte, a quien admiramos, a quien respetamos e, incluso, queremos... Durante ese tiempo que compartimos podemos darnos el lujo de pasar la lengua por todo su cuerpo, de acariciarlo, de contarle nuestro pensamiento más profundo o delirante, podemos abandonarnos y que sus manos nos saquen de este mundo por un rato...

Me da pereza (e impotencia) tratar de sintetizar en una línea toda la sabiduría que durante milenios ciertas culturas han acumulado. El sexo es una fuente de placer. Podríamos entenderlo como si fuera viajar. Si eres aficionado a ello, embárcate con la idea de aprovechar cada instante, de empaparte de lo que ves, de lo que oyes, de lo que experimentas... Deja que te lleve, ya regresarás de allí dondequiera que aparezcas. Disfruta del viaje, sin obsesionarte por el destino. Como verás, aludo al viaje de placer, el de vacaciones, lo que para muchos es sinónimo de quitarse el reloj, apagar el móvil, repantingarse en un entorno cómodo y agradable... Prepárate para ser un turista modelo: aséate bien para no atufarles; ponte algo que te favorezca para salir ideal en las fotos; respeta a tus compañeros de viaje, hazles el trayecto ameno, compórtate como te gusta que ellos hagan contigo; ofréceles lo mejor que tienes —en realidad, se trata de un privilegio estar ahí, del merecido premio que te estás dando, ¿no? Pues alegra esa cara—. Acepta una parada fuera de itinerario, la visita de monumentos no anunciados en la guía, un retraso «por culpa» de alguien que tuvo un contratiempo; sé capaz de improvisar una ruta alternativa si algo obstaculiza la marcha prevista. En definitiva, sé abierto y generoso.

Sexo instantáneo

Si bien es real como la vida misma que muchas relaciones se establecen para la estricta satisfacción de un impulso sexual y, una vez logrado, nos dejan entre gastados o utilizados o con la convicción de haber perdido el tiempo, también lo es que los *quickies*, los *one night stand* o polvos esporádicos pueden ser increíbles.

Si queremos disfrutar también del «aquí te pillo, aquí te mato» no debemos caer en el simplismo. La química ha de crearse a base de cierta atracción física, por supuesto, pero para que esa chispa sea una hoguera, hemos de lograr complicidad y desarrollar comportamientos sensuales que transforman un polvo corriente o lamentable en un polvazo digno de ser recordado (o repetido).

Las caricias que extienden la excitación hacia otras partes del cuerpo despertarán cierta afectividad y harán del encuentro algo grato. Es clave conocer este matiz. Cuando no existe un vínculo emocional con el otro, tendemos a la urgente satisfacción del instinto, y ello se traduce en que nos ceñimos exclusivamente a los genitales, vamos muy «al grano». Muchos refieren incluso que cuando sólo es sexo, ni siquiera besan en la boca, o lo hacen muy «de pasada». (¿Recordáis *Pretty Woman*? Pues lo mismo que decía Julia Roberts en su papel de prostituta, lo de «no beso en la boca porque eso es muy íntimo», lo comentan muchas personas y, sin embargo, ello no obsta para que practiquen una felación, cunnilingus y/o penetraciones de todo tipo.)

No tiene mucho misterio el final del cortometraje si el argumento va de dos extraños que se miran y se esconden en un cuarto de baño de una discoteca o si estamos resolviendo una pelea que instantes atrás nos tuvo con la vena del cuello hinchada y desgañitándonos, pero sendas carreras hacia el orgasmo se pueden hacer de dos modos. O bien en solitario, con el apoyo presencial de un cuerpo en usufructo, o bien adueñándonos del pronombre «nosotros» por un rato, y darla juntos, para que no sea un acto insípido, decepcionante para ambos: tras eyacular él se encuentra con que no tiene nada que decirle y ella, aunque alcance un orgasmo, se siente con un vacío hasta doloroso. En relación al hombre, se necesita que en la fase de acercamiento —los preliminares, como se entienden normalmente— se desvíe la atención del pene y se tengan en cuenta todos sus demás puntos erógenos. Su erección será la misma pero, al encontrarse «mimado» en todo su ser, la reacción física se verá teñida de cierta afectividad, de una sensualidad que definitivamente satisface a ambos mucho más y que, por descontado, tiene dos efectos positivos: retrasa la eyaculación y potencia la sensación orgásmica. Por el lado de la mujer, si bien la tendencia es meter la mano y agarrar los pechos o bajarla y colarte entre sus bragas nada más empezar, será más interesante y logrará mayor placer si le haces sentir la pasión mediante largos morreos de película —no de las porno, por favor, sino, sin que sirva de precedente, de las de adolescentes americanos—, caricias paulatinamente más intensas y que avanzan por todos los rincones de su cuerpo. La clave será ir creando una expectativa, ganar terreno dando rodeos por las zonas próximas a sus puntos más erógenos (clítoris, pezones, entrada de la vagina...), haciéndola desear que avances hacia las zonas genitales. Ambos pueden satisfacer ese deseo de sexo sin amor por turnos, dándose tiempo para recibir y regalar apretones, lametazos, caricias y besos y siendo receptivos a las señales (jadeos, susurros, alteración de la respiración, movimientos de la pelvis, acercamiento/alejamiento del cuerpo, abrazo más intenso, rechazo, quejido, etc.) del otro.

Verdades sobre tu cuerpo

El cuerpo sigue a la mente. Si la activas, éste se pondrá alerta; si la relajas, él lo hará. Por lo mismo, si la erotizas, todo tu cuerpo se predispondrá. Has de entrar en situación.

La piel es nuestro órgano más extenso y todo el cuerpo es una zona erógena. Ante semejantes evidencias, parándonos a pensarlo, nos desbordamos: se nos acumula el trabajo. Que no cunda el pánico: las manos, los brazos, la lengua, la pelvis, las piernas... al cabo de un rato se agotan y se entumecen. Sin embargo, a la lengua no le pasa. Sé consciente de que es tu músculo más potente y úsala para algo que no sea hablar. Lo cual nos lleva a la siguiente gran verdad: ninguna mucosa debe acariciarse en seco y cualquier estimulación será más intensa si va lubricada.

2 + 2 no siempre es 4

Por desgracia (y por suerte) el sexo no es una ciencia exacta. Si escuchamos «tal cosa funciona» o «debes hacer tal postura porque les gusta» es porque existe cierta tendencia o porque la mayoría de los testimonios a los que hemos tenido acceso apuntan datos en un sentido u otro. Como base, no está de más conocer ciertos básicos —como que nuestro clítoris equivale al glande masculino—, pero la realidad es que cada persona es única y será en la faceta sexual donde se manifiesta toda la riqueza de la biodiversidad. Cada pareja sexual es un mundo. Le enseñarás cosas, las aprenderás, modificarás tus técnicas para sincronizaros, etc. Cada vagina es distinta, como lo es cada pene, así como los gustos y preferencias, filias y fobias de sus respectivos dueños. Solución: habla, pregunta, observa, imita...

El inevitable «Cuando tú vas, yo vengo...»

Que la excitación de él cada vez es menor y que la tuya aumenta según se asienta la relación es un hecho. Otro asunto será mantener esa pasión, pero lo cierto es que mientras que a ti te gusta más porque ganas en confianza, y cada ocasión te enriquece más porque te atreves a probar, a pedir, a relajarte, incluso te familiarizas con la multiorgasmia, a él, sin embargo, para estar tan excitado como las primeras veces, no le basta con mirarte. La familiaridad surte efectos opuestos sobre la pasión que experimenta cada sexo. Así de crudo es el tema. Recurriendo a los recursos literarios, novelando un poco, en eso del primer encuentro, el hombre bien podría representar al conde Drácula: para él, el primer encuentro sexual con una mujer parece el mejor o, por lo menos, el más excitante. Le permite desarrollar su faceta depredadora, pero es que además, hace suya a la víctima y le cambia la vida, ejerce de conquistador, y algo fundamental: saborea sangre nueva... Para nosotras, generalmente, el asunto es bien distinto. Es notorio que al hombre le pone la novedad mientras que el erotismo femenino parece potenciarse cuando alcanza un grado de complicidad mayor con su pareja. Por resumir: el primer polvo para él es el mejor, cuando para ella quizá lo sean los siguientes, a partir del segundo o del tercero... Téngase en cuenta.

Todas sois iguales

Sí, ya, pero algunas son más iguales que otras, decía no sé qué refrán... (o todos los tíos son iguales, que ahora no va de la guerra de siempre). «Los intocables» podría denominarse a ese colectivo de seres inconvenientes con los que nos acostamos, pero sin los que estaríamos bastante mejor.

Los hombres a evitar son: casados, gays, compañeros de trabajo, insultantemente jóvenes o peligrosamente viejos, delincuentes, marido de tu amiga, primo carnal, vagos, impotentes, narcisistas, donjuanes, psicópatas, Peterpanes...

De entre las mujeres a evitar, destacan: la de tu mejor amigo; las tías con alma de zorra (o sin alma); las que trabajan, sí, pero ascienden gracias a su coño; la Maruja disfrazada de *femme fatal* (hasta que se casa y se arranca la careta y los *stilettos* para siempre); la atrapamaridos, la que no quiere un marido pero se casa por quedar bien, la que sólo busca ser madre (con quien sea), a la que le encanta provocar situaciones y ver cómo te peleas...

¿Por qué resulta tan tentadora la sensación de «sólo la punta?»

Además de estar experimentando el placer de alto voltaje, lo que ocurre es que ese contacto afecta a las zonas más sensibles, porque acumulan mayor número de terminaciones nerviosas. En él se involucra al extremo del pene (que abarca el glande, el frenillo y el prepucio retirado). Para nosotras, toda la zona de la entrada de la vagina, y el canal vaginal, hasta adentrarse unos seis u ocho centímetros, el tramo más receptivo, que además es donde se halla el punto G. Como gusta tanto, es verdaderamente difícil que, llegados a este momento, nos conformemos con «sólo la puntita»... Por una vez, unos y otras coincidimos.

¡Caca!

Después de que las manos (dedos, puños), bocas (labios, lenguas), juguetes, penes, etc., entran en contacto con el ano o el recto, se ha de utilizar el jabón bacteriológico.

Para la zona genital mejor un jabón neutro, para no alterar su pH.

El enjuague dental no mata por sí solo los agentes patógenos que causan las ETS, lávatelos a conciencia con pasta dentífrica.

«Dejé bien alto el pabellón»... Pero ¿de qué me hablas?

Si al tener una relación la idea de él es eyacular lo antes posible sin tener en cuenta cómo va la chica... mal. Mal, mal, mal, da igual lo estupendamente bien dotado que ande, el dinero que tenga, o lo ocurrente que sea contando chistes. Si asociado al pensamiento «tener sexo» en la cabeza de un tío simplemente habita la idea de que la mujer es «algo», un cuerpo con sus constantes vitales normales, que viene bien tener cerca para correrse con más facilidad que solo, entonces no estamos hablando de lo mismo. Puede que esa persona sólo te interese para echar un polvo. Perfecto: sólo estáis utilizando mutuamente vuestros cuerpos y gastando juntos un poco de tiempo. Si el acuerdo es ése, adelante, pero hasta eso, el puro sexo, también se puede y se debe optimizar para ambas partes.

Muchas personas no son agraciadas o no disponen de cuerpazos privilegiados genéticamente o, digamos que podrían ser mucho más atractivas y, sin embargo, tienen una vida sexual envidiable. En este tema, la clave es: actitud es más que aptitud. Cuando una tía se engancha a ti porque la haces suplicar «más», eso sí es dejar el pabellón bien alto.

¡Qué pereza y qué lío de roles!

Resumiendo unos pocos milenios: señoras, ustedes están aquí para perpetuar la especie. Embarácense y callen. Sean dóciles, sumisas y pasivas. Señores, ustedes han de ser machos. Ni una lágrima ni media explicación a nadie por nada. A huevos, que nadie os gane. Sean dominantes y activos.

Divertidísimo este momento en que casi no quedan hembras procreadoras, ni conozco a una sola tía sumisa, y de ser pasivas, sólo en manos de un buen masajista; tampoco quedan machos, ni dominantes ni de otro tipo... ¡pero si las publicaciones gays sólo anuncian muchachotes «pasivos»!

La sexualidad femenina se acaba con la menopausia

No, en ese momento lo que se acaba es la regla, esa hemorragia que cada mes nos deja algo tocadas, con dolores, etc. No podemos tener hijos, pero sí amantes, y con la tranquilidad de que no habrá embarazos no deseados.

Ellas son menos fogosas

Que la capacidad y el deseo sexual de la mujer son menores que los del varón es una teoría, bueno, uno de los topicazos sobre sexualidad femenina favoritos del gran público y que no obedece a la realidad. Pensamos en sexo tanto o más que ellos y nos gusta el sexo tanto como a ellos —o más, pero claro, sólo si es bueno—. No tenemos distintas necesidades; ni apetito sexual diferente, vendrá determinado por las circunstancias de formación, cultura, creencias y experiencias personales, no de sexo; ni tampoco nuestra frecuencia es menor. Lo que sí se diferencian son las respuestas sexuales de hombres y mujeres ante la excitación.

Él necesita descargar o reventará

Falso. Los testículos van produciendo espermatozoides de modo constante. Si no se expulsan en eyaculaciones conscientes (léase en el coito o masturbándose), el esperma saldrá en forma de poluciones nocturnas (el que las tenga, que no todos las tienen), o bien será reabsorbido por el propio organismo de modo natural.

Pajearse es de viejos verdes y de fracasados

No señor. Todos y todas nos masturbamos, otro tema es que a ciertas edades o en períodos de la vida concretos, el único modo de obtener sexo sea la masturbación —léase pubertad y adolescencia, etapas de enfermedad que impiden el coito, etc.—. Se tenga o no pareja, y con independencia de lo feliz y plena que sea la vida sexual de ambos, los seres humanos, continúan masturbándose. El onanismo no equivale a sexo de segunda ni a sexo denigrante. Salvo casos patológicos y obsesivos, se trata de una forma más de ejercer la sexualidad sana.

No conviene bañarse estando con la regla

¡Lo que hay que oír! Precisamente es cuando más higiene hace falta. La vida se puede desarrollar con total normalidad, habrá meses peores o con mayores molestias, con mayor o menor apetito sexual... No mojarse, no hacer esfuerzos, no mantener relaciones sexuales... ¡Basta ya de tonterías! Cuando estás con la regla, pues te tienes que acordar de meter compresas o tampones en el bolso y punto. Ver «Menstruación».

¿Sexo o no sexo cuando estás con la regla?

El período de la mujer, la regla, viene cada ciertos días, en teoría es cada 28, pero varía según lo regulares que sean sus ciclos menstruales.

Para comprender a tu pareja (y para que ella misma lo haga) conviene conocer los síntomas, los efectos sobre la libido así como otras implicaciones, tales como si la regla impide o no los embarazos.

3

Menstruación

Acerca de menstruación y dolor

El sexo no es especialmente más doloroso por estar con la regla. Pese a que la mujer puede sentirse mal (la menstruación causa desde mareos a vómitos, hinchazón, retención de líquidos, hipersensibilidad en los pechos, pinchazos y dolor abdominal...), casi todas, una vez «en ello», sentimos muchísimas ganas de una buena sesión de cama. Ciertas posturas dolerán porque implican una profundidad de penetración mayor, y el choque o el golpear del pene las hará sentir incómodas. Probad la que mejor resulte.

El orgasmo —las contracciones que provoca— resta dolor a la menstruación.

Psicológicamente, para una mujer resulta un subidón que su pareja se muestre dispuesto y que no la trate como a una apestada por estar con la regla.

Obviamente, durante los días de menstruación, pueden aparecer problemas de todo tipo, salvo de lubricación.

Asco

La sangre resulta un engorro, no vamos a negarlo. A nosotras nos da pudor que nos vean con el dodotis o que detecten el cordoncito dichoso, y precisamos «preparación» en privado —o sea, como siempre, sólo que más, puesto que casi ninguna perseguimos dejar «ese tipo de huella» en nuestros amantes—, lo cual puede interrumpir la escena durante unos minutos, restándole la espontaneidad. Y ellos, ante la sangre menstrual, sienten desde total desconocimiento a indiferencia, o repugnancia y aprensión, pasando por pánico reverencial, o por una franca fascinación... en todo caso, conste que la sangre que se segrega durante la menstruación, es decir, durante todos los días de hemorragia, no supera la que cabe en dos cucharas soperas —vamos, que no es un tsunami—. Y sí, señores, se puede mantener una relación sexual plena (es decir, con penetración y también con sexo oral) y sin que las sábanas terminen como la matanza de Puertourraco. ¿Que cómo? Pues hay modos.

Seguro que alguna persona me tacha de cualquier cosa pero preguntando se llega a Roma y, lo mismo que las abuelas tienen sus trucos —como lavarse profundamente con agua fría para cortar la hemorragia, técnica que funciona, pero sólo un ratito—, las actri-

ces porno también, y quiénes mejor que ellas para saber que «esos días» también caen dentro del calendario laboral, lo mismo que cualquier otro, y que la cámara no debe captar ni rastro de sangre.

Tampón, esponjas y tampones esponjosos

Si llevas un tampón y te lo quitas justo en ese momento y te lavas, te quedas sin lubricación, pero bueno, todo llegará —o bien, recurre a la artificial—. Y lo de dejarse el tampón[28] puesto no es la panacea porque, si no te lo introduces tú misma para ocultarlo, con la penetración se meterá el cordón y, como encima el pene lo habrá empujado hasta arriba, sacarlo de ahí resulta la mar de complicado —aunque no es imposible—; eso sí, requiere no ser escrupulosa, tener mucha paciencia y la flexibilidad de un faquir. Ha habido casos de no poder extraerlo sola, y de necesitar ir a Urgencias... Menudo cuadro. Dicho lo cual, los tampones resultan ideales: si te lo colocas después de lavarte a conciencia, no se nota —él, si no se lo cuentas, no lo detectará—, absorbe toda la sangre que puedas generar en ese rato —ahí estás tú para visitar el cuarto de baño y lavarte y sustituirlo por uno nuevo—. Sin embargo, lo que las profesionales recomiendan son las esponjas de bañar a los bebés. Se compran en farmacia, se corta un trozo y se introduce. Absorbe, es blandita y tampoco se nota. Según el tamaño que pongas, dura más o menos y se extrae mejor o peor. La solución digna de una sociedad como la nuestra, de primer mundo, son los tampones esponjosos sin cordón, que se venden en los *sex shops*. En realidad, serían una mezcla implementada de todas las soluciones explicadas.

Como en tu intimidad haces y dispones libremente, esos días también puedes optar por colocar una toalla oscura sobre la sábana y aquí paz y después... Si eres de los que está al cabo de las novedades en útiles (nunca mejor dicho) para el sexo, cómprate una sábana bajera de plástico en un *sex shop* (las hay de color negro, que disimulan perfectamente colores tan de moda como el rojo y el marrón. Ya que

---

28. La hemotigolagnia es una parafilia que designa la atracción sexual por los tampones usados. Hay quien se excita contemplando a alguien colocarse un tampón, o sacárselo y juguetear con él, chuparlo y metérselo en la boca... una vez manchado...

te acercas, y para que no hagas tantos paseos: aprovisiónate de toallitas higiénicas, condones de colores oscuros... y lo más de lo más en profilaxis: protectores o cuadrantes de látex para el cunnilingus, se pueden utilizar siempre, pero con la regla, pues... Otra opción estupenda sería hacerlo en la ducha. O aprovechar para el sexo oral el instante en que justo ella sale del baño de haberse lavado.

El rechazo que los hombres sienten hacia la sangre menstrual podría equipararse al que algunas mujeres sienten por el esperma, y la reacción de unos y otras debería ser de tranquilidad, procurando desdramatizar. Puede que mientras estás con la regla él se niegue a practicar sexo oral, puede que no, los hay que lo ven tal cual es: algo natural y, con las oportunas medidas higiénicas, lo hacen como cualquier otro día. Depende de sus sentimientos por ti, de la confianza entre los dos y de la higiene que mantengáis durante el coito.

Riesgo de embarazo

Tratar este tema generalizando es bastante absurdo y arriesgado. Es cierto que será más difícil que se dé un embarazo justo esos días, pero cada mujer tiene un ciclo y además, en él se producen irregularidades constantemente. Datos más o menos orientadores: los espermatozoides pueden sobrevivir varios días —hasta 3 o 4— dentro del tracto reproductivo femenino, así que cuidadito con los cálculos, especialmente cuando los ciclos son cortos —cada 22 días o menos—. Otro dato: la ovulación suele producirse 14 días antes del primero de regla —y ha de contabilizarse así, no desde el último de sangrado—. La probabilidad de embarazo desciende si el coito sin protección se produce en torno al primer día de sangrado.

Riesgo de ETS

Existe mayor riesgo de contagio de una ETS o ITS que pueda estar padeciendo cualquiera de los dos. Para ella, la presencia de sangre ayuda a extender el patógeno que causa la enfermedad inflamatoria pélvica, entre otras.

Herencia cultural: dos matices

En ocasiones topamos con personas que vienen cargadas de pensamientos rancios, y el rechazo, entonces, no es hacia la sangre ni hacia la menstruación, sino hacia la ausencia de probabilidad reproductiva. Se desestima la relación sexual porque no «sirve para nada». Si se suma que el placer de la mujer no contaba con que no está bien tener relaciones cuya finalidad no esté encaminada a procrear, nos queda una actitud de «¿sexo durante la regla? ¡No, por Dios!».

La sangre menstrual se ha añadido como ingrediente secreto en filtros de amor, en amarres y en todo tipo de brebajes para inducir a un hombre a enamorarse perdidamente o para adueñarse de su raciocinio —cuando lo tenía, claro—. Brujas, hechiceros y celestinas han utilizado su poder a lo largo de la historia, y relatos de santeros y alquimistas refieren su poder entre mágico y sobrenatural. Si es cierto o no, me temo que, humildemente, confieso que no lo sé, pero tampoco he «visto» la alegría y la experimento muchas veces...

4

Sexo y embarazo

Recuerda: estás embarazada, no muerta

Salvo que el médico así lo desaconseje, puedes mantener relaciones durante la gestación. Recuerda: estás embarazada, no muerta.

Que las embarazadas no deben mantener relaciones sexuales constituye una de las grandes mentiras que se han instalado en la conciencia popular. La mentalidad de casi todos está más que empapada de pensamientos de todo tipo —excepto eróticos— cuando se baraja el concepto «futura mamá»: candor, dadora de vida, responsabilidad, dulzura, educadora, modelo a seguir... Bueno, pues las mamás también tienen relaciones. Salvo complicaciones —en los embarazos de alto riesgo las precauciones habrán de ser especiales, y el médico que siga la gestación las señalará y tendrá en cuenta—, las relaciones sexuales no dañan al bebé ni provocan abortos. Por otro lado —perdón si alguien encuentra que con esta puntualización insulto su inteligencia—, el feto, por supuesto, no «escucha». ¿Alguien recuerda cómo se lo montaban sus padres durante aquellos meses? Y acerca de si a la embarazada le hará daño o le causará molestias, pues parece que más bien es al revés...

Cierto es que muchas mujeres embarazadas pierden el interés de modo radical por el sexo: se debe al agotamiento permanente, a la sensación de tener sueño siempre; y también al rechazo de su nueva figura y a la vergüenza de mostrarse desnudas ante su pareja por los cambios que su cuerpo está experimentando: en semanas se despide de un vientre de aspecto «normal», delgado o incluso atlético, y contempla atónita que se le pone una barriga como la del Buda Feliz...

Sin que sea consuelo (para ellos), esta situación no se prolonga eternamente, sino sólo hasta unos meses después del parto.

¿Y las demás? Pues a las demás, todo lo contrario. Precisamente esos cambios (tener más pecho, verse más voluptuosas y aceptar que se trata de algo pasajero) las hace sentirse más *sexys* que nunca. Esto se suma a las descargas hormonales que se producen durante el embarazo. En algunas, desencadenan estados de desesperación y de tristeza por los que se deshacen en lágrimas, mientras que a otras, por eso mismo, la libido les estalla. Muchas (y sus parejas) disfrutan durante esos nueve meses —o alguno menos, descontemos los del malestar, vómitos, mareos y el posparto...— del mejor sexo de toda su relación. Eso sí, depende, más que de ella, de la actitud de él. Por la mente de una futura madre pueden atravesar —y de hecho lo hacen— pensamientos fugaces de toda índole: ascéticos («las madres no hacen estas cosas»), de preocupación («¿le hará daño al bebé?», insisto: cualquier manual sobre maternidad o el médico informarán de las posiciones y momentos arriesgados), negativos (como querer asesinar a todas las que pueden meterse en la talla 36, sentir mucha inseguridad ante su pareja y odiarse a sí misma por su nuevo aspecto), de pánico y ansiedad («esto es demasiada responsabilidad», «¿será feliz?», «¿nacerá sano?», «¿cómo me irá en el parto?»). En esos miles de momentos de flaqueza, es crucial cómo él la haga sentirse, y si logran, juntos, considerar que el hecho de traer un hijo al mundo sea una especie de «fenómeno global», con un montón de efectos maravillosos asociados —incluido el de su vientre redondeado—. De hecho, a muchos hombres les vuelven locos las embarazadas, no en vano hay todo un género pornográfico dedicado a este tipo de prácticas. El lado parafílico, denominado maieusiofilia describe una perversión sexual muy popular que consiste en excitarse viendo mujeres embarazadas, y se conecta con la lactafilia: excitación por los pechos en período de amamantamiento. Otra parafilia sería la cyesolagnia: la excitación sexual sólo con embarazadas.

La forma en que se desarrollan las relaciones sexuales durante la gestación puede también alterarse y no sólo por la falta de deseo o la insaciabilidad sobrevenidas. Hay además curiosos efectos «paranormales» que pueden ir asociados, como la secreción de leche por los pezones durante el orgasmo. Algunas posiciones resultan menos convenientes a la gestación, y los gustos y preferencias de la embarazada serán distintos. Me explico. Los sentidos del olfato y del gusto de la mujer embarazada se alteran, pudiendo volverse extremadamente agudos. Quizás en este período ciertos olores o sabores le resulten insoportables. Le ocurrirá con el cuerpo de su pareja y con los alimentos, los lugares, las colonias... No es personal, pero puede suceder que no soporte practicarte una felación, por ejemplo. Por otro lado, lo que va siendo cada vez más grande es su

vientre. Ella dejará poco a poco de dormir boca arriba, lo cual se explica para evitar que el peso del útero en crecimiento oprima vasos sanguíneos importantes, por lo tanto, la posición del misionero se desaconseja a partir del cuarto mes aproximadamente (es importante que él no cargue su peso sobre ella). Se pueden realizar las posiciones de lado —cucharas—, de ella encima y de él desde atrás. Otros cambios: es importante saber que los labios vulvares y la vagina están más voluminosos y las secreciones vaginales serán más abundantes, lo que incrementa la lubricación provocando sensaciones distintas.

Notas acerca del sexo durante el embarazo

Practicar relaciones con penetración vaginal ejercita y ayuda a mantener tonificados los músculos que intervendrán en el parto (entre otras cuestiones, por las contracciones que se producen durante el orgasmo). Sin embargo, lo mismo que hay que evitar los ejercicios violentos, de competición o que produzcan fatiga, habrá que realizar «concesiones», como prescindir de prácticas sexuales extremas (sadomasoquismo, por ejemplo) y suprimir las drogas, alcohol o estimulantes químicos, caso de que para el sexo recurras a ellos. Se aconseja evitar las relaciones sexuales durante el último mes antes del parto por el posible peligro de infección y rotura prematura de la bolsa de las aguas.

Cuando una pareja ha buscado el embarazo durante mucho tiempo, habrá atravesado por el calvario de hacerlo siempre en la fecha adecuada, midiendo la temperatura corporal adecuada, colocándose en la postura adecuada... Cuando se ha logrado, poder disfrutar de la relación de un modo espontáneo será un alivio.

El hecho de abordar juntos y voluntariamente un proyecto de vida como es traer un hijo al mundo acerca a muchas parejas. A los embarazos se les debe agradecer que muchos hombres presten a sus parejas otro tipo de atención, que se comporten de un modo más romántico, que descubran las caricias, que despierten la sensualidad, la ternura y hasta el amor —¡a estas alturas!—, muchas veces.

En esta fase, como en cada ocasión en que dos personas van a unir sus cuerpos, lo ideal es la comunicación honesta, con enormes dosis de humor y comprensión.

Aunque parece, de nuevo, un atentado contra el sentido común del lector, prefiero insistir en el asunto de la prevención de ETS. No todas las mujeres llevan a término su embarazo con una pareja estable y maravillosa con la que camina de la manita y que asiste feliz y dispuesto a las clases de preparación del parto (no es por desconfiar, ni por crear paranoia, pero ojito con las canas al aire de los

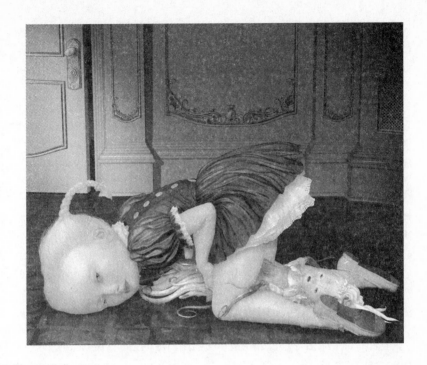

maridos). Dicho lo cual, recupero otra idea: evitar la promiscuidad es una de las mejores formas de prevención y, en cualquier caso, siempre que una embarazada mantenga relaciones con alguien «no-de-absoluta-confianza» debe utilizar preservativo.

Química natural para el embarazo

En el apartado de «Afrodisíacos», junto a otras vitaminas y alimentos con poder para inducir el deseo sexual o aumentar el vigor, se explica que la Vitamina E se conoce vulgarmente como la vitamina de la vitalidad, ya que activa la producción hormonal y logra efectos más que notables sobre la vida sexual. Se vincula estrechamente a la fecundidad, el embarazo y el desarrollo de los genitales externos. Se encuentra en los aceites vegetales, las semillas, los frutos secos, los cereales, los huevos, la lechuga y el brécol. En estados carenciales provoca gestación anormal, abortos espontáneos, atrofia testicular o descenso incompleto del escroto.

Otra vitamina, no estrictamente afrodisíaca, pero imprescindible para la salud sexual es la Vitamina A, necesaria para la producción de las hormonas sexuales, para el normal desarrollo de los testículos y la formación de la placenta durante el embarazo. A nivel sexual, es imprescindible para llevar un embarazo a feliz término y asegurar un buen parto; favorece la fertilidad, tanto del hombre como de la mujer. En estado carencial se produce vaginitis —que hace imposible la penetración— y en mujeres menopáusicas, sequedad en los labios internos y externos, lo que hará muy doloroso el coito; escasa resistencia a las infecciones; degeneración de los ovarios y disminución de la fertilidad de la mujer. Se encuentra en los lácteos, aceite de hígado de bacalao, zanahorias y frutas y verduras de color naranja y amarillo.

Vitamina D no es muy abundante en la naturaleza, la contiene el hígado y otras vísceras y, en pequeñas dosis, los lácteos. Su carencia no sólo afecta al parto, haciéndolo muy doloroso, sino que disminuye la fertilidad y provoca que se engendren niños raquíticos o prematuros.

La Vitamina B-2 la contienen la carne, la leche, el pescado, las espinacas y las alubias, interviene en la liberación de la energía y el buen funcionamiento vascular, entre otras cosas. Su carencia, además de dolores de cabeza y calambres, provoca reabsorción fetal, tendencia al aborto, y nacimientos prematuros. En la mujer, su deficiencia puede producir sequedad en la mucosa vaginal, úlceras vaginales internas y en el hombre, dolor y grietas en el prepucio.

5

Sexo y espiritualidad

Flujo de energía

He buscado algunos rasgos de ciertas filosofías que apoyen algunas de las alusiones que se realizan a lo largo de este libro, como las técnicas tántricas de economizar energía sexual, vinculadas a la no eyaculación. Entre las distintas disciplinas, el Reiki[29] puede contribuir al bienestar (desbloquear la sexualidad, asumir la opción sexual, darse el derecho de disfrutar, aceptarse...) o el Chi Kung, que comparte con el Yoga y el Tantra la postura que aboga por no desperdiciar el semen (la energía vital) si no es por fines reproductivos, algo que permite al hombre seguir siendo «potente» y fuerte hasta la vejez. Además, el Feng Shui aporta principios fundamentales acerca del flujo de energía erótica y de cómo potencia la comunicación y la sensualidad de la intimidad del dormitorio.

Antes de empezar, haré una matización: no es lo mismo un masaje relajante que uno erótico; no se toca de la misma forma. Como tampoco se parece en nada el que nos da un fisioterapeuta o un osteópata, que nos coloca los huesos o nos libra de contracturas, al tacto de un maestro espiritual, y ninguno de ellos será como el de un amante.

---

29. Personalmente practico Reiki desde hace años pero, de las demás disciplinas, sólo he recibido terapias puntuales o me he documentado a través de libros. Admito que me produce entre pudor y cargo de conciencia cometer la osadía de intentar resumir y sintetizar principios tan profundos y cuya asimilación exige tantos años en unas pocas páginas.

El Reiki

Reiki viene de «Rei», universal, y «ki», que es energía vital. Todos somos energía y formamos parte de una energía universal, y el Reiki la utiliza para la curación y para aumentar el bienestar. Con origen en Japón, esta técnica iniciada por Usui Reiki emplea las manos para trasmitir paz y equilibrio físico, mental y espiritual. Tocar al otro es una forma de comunicación, implica dar pero también recibir su energía. Los siete centros de energía del cuerpo humano se denominan «chakras». El Reiki trabaja cada centro de energía. El chakra sacro (*Svadhistana* o «dulzura» en sánscrito) se considera el segundo de los siete y se ubica justo en los genitales —tranquilidad: un terapeuta nunca pondrá las manos encima, ni demasiado cerca, las dejará a los costados—, se asocia con la vitalidad sexual y, en el cuerpo femenino, además, se conecta a los dolores y problemas menstruales y urinarios y con dar a luz. A veces, el Reiki se combina con aromaterapia, con aceites esenciales, para sanar de forma natural. «Ellos relacionan los cuatro niveles de los sentidos entre sí. El físico con el emocional, con el mental y con el espiritual. Justo por ese motivo, causan efecto más rápidamente. La clave está en que nos proporcionan lo que necesitamos en cada nivel...», explica Gamal Abdul el Sami Kaki, quizás el maestro Reiki más famoso a nivel mundial (aunque él huye de esta definición). Vive en El Cairo, a cinco minutos de Las Pirámides, y hace más de veinte años que realiza tareas de sanación. Grupos de todo el mundo acuden a recibir sus enseñanzas, píldoras de verdad, amor y sabiduría —casi nada...—. Lo cierto es que Gamal fue uno de los primeros investigadores de las recetas secretas de los aceites en los templos de Dendera y de Saqqarah: «Como ya sabemos, la gente crea en muchas ocasiones su propio dolor y su propia pena. En el fondo de su ser ellos saben de qué se lamentan y cuál es su verdadera causa pero, la mayoría de las veces, no son honestos consigo mismos y, en muchas ocasiones, tampoco lo son con sus sanadores. Este hecho es muy comprensible, es su secreto, su vida. Con los aceites es diferente. Cuando la gente sabe su función, se puede sanar ella misma, porque cuando se trata de sanarse a uno mismo, no se puede seguir mintiendo. Cuando la gente se permite realmente sanarse a sí misma, elige el aceite correcto, el que le sanará. Todo ello sin tener que desvelar su secreto. Los aceites nos acercan a nuestra verdad y nos permiten arreglarla. Nos ayudan a poder asumir de qué verdaderamente nos lamentamos, a qué tenemos miedo realmente, por qué estamos tristes, por qué nos castigamos, de dónde proviene realmente nuestro dolor y nuestra pena. Todos ellos son temas muy profundos y a pesar de ello funcionan, porque como ya hemos dicho anteriormente, los aceites trabajan a través de los sentidos, de nuestro sistema olfativo, y por ello nos hacen efecto tan pronto. Una de sus cualidades especiales es su aroma. Es algo maravilloso que muestra el amor, que es al final lo único que puede causar la sanación. La gente puede querer estos aceites porque los puedan encontrar agradables, porque no dañan o hieren a nadie. Es por esta razón que se les denomina aceites sagrados. Cuando trabajes con los aceites sobre ti y les permitas ayudarte, tu vida cambiará. Permitirás que otra energía natural te ayude y no sólo tu entendimiento. Porque la razón tiene límites. El cuerpo físico, el emocional y el mental tienen fronteras. El cuerpo espiritual es el único que carece de ellas.» Gamal explica sus usos, ahora bien distintos de los ritos funerarios de momificación y más cercanos a la purificación de actos cotidianos: «También son muy buenos para utilizar en quemadores (jazmín y Kashmir) o como aceites de baño (ámbar rojo, musk y sándalo) o como masaje (rosa y loto). También refuerzan el aura.»

Estás a solas con una persona: escucha las palabras y observa el cuerpo. Muchas veces mediante su postura, el propio cuerpo nos indica lo que le apetece o lo que necesita, y lo que no. Como apunta Gamal, frecuentemente somatizamos conflictos y traumas, convirtiendo situaciones hostiles o negativas en enfermedades, contracturas y dolores físicos. Como ejemplo: los miedos de las personas se acumulan en la parte superior de los hombros y en la parte delantera de los muslos; si trabajas esta zona antes de provocar la erotización, eliminarás una barrera y la sensualidad será después mucho más sencilla e intensa... Los problemas de autoestima e hipersensibilidad a las críticas, otro ejemplo, se centralizan en la zona de entre las costillas (corresponde al tercer chakra, plexo solar). Si sabes que tu pareja está triste o melancólica, aborda la zona del corazón —no es un masaje de reanimación por ahogamiento, recuérdalo— y, si el problema es un bloqueo creativo, será la garganta o el cuello donde se manifieste. Si abordas la parte del bajo vientre, entre el ombligo y los genitales, estarás sobre un punto de energía muy especial: el chakra sacro, asociado a las cosas que hacen la vida dulce: el placer, la sexualidad, la nutrición... Representa las pasiones y deseos sexuales, que sólo si son ignorados o reprimidos implican un peligro. Recuerda que ahí se pueden tratar problemas relacionados con la impotencia, la frigidez o la ninfomanía, enfermedades de vejiga y de próstata. El aceite esencial que se corresponde a este chakra es el almizcle.

Chi Kung

El Chi Kung basa su enseñanza en que la energía sexual del cuerpo se puede emplear para mejorar la salud y la creatividad. Dentro de cada persona existe una energía sexual que no sólo afecta a la reproducción, sino a la salud en general. Recibimos parte de la energía sexual por medio de la transferencia genética hereditaria, de nuestros padres; el resto está contenido en los riñones, y otra parte la adquirimos con los alimentos: chi heredado, chi de los riñones (los chinos se refieren a los testículos como los riñones externos) y chi adquirido. Toda esta fuerza la almacenamos en los órganos sexuales, pero si logramos expandirla por el resto del cuerpo, contribuirá a la salud y a la creatividad.

El Chi Kung no prejuzga el sexo, no lo define como bueno ni malo, correcto ni incorrecto, sino como una fuerza natural que discurre por cada uno de nosotros, tan poderosa que puede desbordarnos. Lo mismo que el deseo nos inspira obras de arte también, descontrolado, nos empuja a lo peor de lo peor... Por ello, defiende que ejercer un control sobre la energía sexual evitará que la vida esté dominada por el deseo. El Chi Kung diferencia la energía sexual fría (la que tenemos en estado de reposo) de la caliente (cuando estamos excitados, mucho más poderosa, causante de reacciones físicas en todo el organismo y, por descontado, mucho más difícil de controlar).

Los trabajos y ejercicios que podemos hacer para controlar la energía fría se concentran en la zona de la pelvis y en la respiración y, en realidad, son los ejercicios de Kegel, sólo que además de la musculatura PC involucran al ano —realizaremos contracciones del ano hacia arriba y hacia dentro— y al perineo.

Las técnicas de control de la energía sexual caliente se utilizan durante las relaciones sexuales y, aunque funcionan mejor si las practican ambos, también puede hacerlas sólo uno de los dos. En el caso de los hombres, lo primero es, conforme se siente esa energía, contraer los órganos sexuales, el perineo y el ano —sería más «cerrar» que «tirar hacia arriba»— y tratar de tirar de ella hacia arriba y hacia dentro, sincronizándola con la respiración y bombeando el chi (energía) hacia la columna y el interior de la cabeza. En teoría, esto se realiza a través de una técnica de meditación que nos permite visualizar la energía. Ese desplazamiento de la energía proporciona la sensación de vacío en los órganos sexuales y de tener la cabeza llena. Entonces, se ha de presionar la lengua contra el paladar, relajar la zona del vientre y dejar que esta energía se quede en el tan tien inferior —un centro energético situado en el abdomen—. A continuación, se puede volver a excitar la energía sexual y a repetir el ejercicio. Desde la perspectiva del Chi Kung, que un hombre permita que su energía sexual alcance su cota máxima y eyacule debería depender de su edad y de su salud, pero, en general, no considera beneficiosa ni recomienda la pérdida de su esencia.

Sexo tántrico

El sexo tántrico se ha puesto de moda a pesar de que casi nadie tenga ni idea de qué está diciendo. Se deriva del Tantra (literalmente: telar, hilo, tejido, ritual, doctrina), una filosofía hindú y tibetana y, originariamente, una práctica abierta a todos y basada en la libertad y el respeto incondicional por todas las personas, encaminada a alcanzar la trascendencia. Cuesta «entrar» en esto del Tantra porque se parte de concepciones radicalmente distintas. Lo primero que hay que tener claro es que el Tantra no enseña sexualidad, simplemente afirma que el sexo puede ser una fuente de felicidad y considera que el sexo sólo es el principio, no el fin.

Para empezar, no sirven los patrones ni los roles occidentales. En el Tantra existen deidades femeninas —no sólo masculinas— y a la mujer no se le presume ser origen del pecado, la tentación y semilla de la discordia, conforme llevamos oyendo de las tres religiones monoteístas más importantes, sino que es emisora de energía.

Por otra parte, la sexualidad tántrica no hace distinción entre lo puro y lo impuro, la belleza y la fealdad, el bien y el mal.

Otra de las pautas mentales a cambiar tiene que ver con la prisa y con las ansias europeas y americanas de correrse. Nada que ver. Para empezar, quítate el reloj porque en el sexo tántrico, todo se basa en encuentros largos —a lo mejor «no tienes tiempo», pero has de acometer el acto y sentirte como si tuvieras un siglo—; durante la relación se comienza con besos, que se alargan un buen rato, sin tocarse. Después, se va descubriendo poco a poco la piel del otro, mediante masajes de todo tipo. Además, frente a la intrascendencia de las emisiones de esperma en Occidente, el semen se considera la fuente y el elixir de vida. La aún vigente medicina ayurvédica, medicina tradicional de la India, calcula que hacen falta cuarenta gotas de sangre para fabricar una gota de semen, y que para prolongar la vida se debe evitar su emisión. El orgasmo en Occidente se une a la eyaculación. El sexo se compra y se vende, se usa como herramienta de poder, de dominación. En el Tantra no, porque considera que el sexo es nuestro origen y nuestro manantial. El Tantra dice: «aborda el acto sexual como si entrases en un templo sagrado»; para el Tantra todo es sagrado y sería un modo de que en la mente lo sagrado y lo humano queden unidos, sin conflicto, formando una unidad.

En general, el gran mensaje tántrico es la aceptación del sexo como algo natural. Osho comparte uno de los secretos del Tantra: «acepta el deseo, adéntrate en él pero con profunda sensibilidad, con consciencia, con amor». En el camino del Tantra no hay que luchar contra lo que sentimos o nos esclavizará, porque cada uno de nosotros forma parte de la realidad, de lo Supremo. El conflicto, la oposición a la naturaleza, no es necesario. Se debe ser indulgente, eso sí, con consciencia, a fin de ir más allá en aquello que seas o sientas. Respecto de la energía sexual, se considera neutral; si bien si la reprimes se crean bloqueos, si se utiliza correctamente, puede ser un escalón.

Otro asunto de vital trascendencia en el sexo tántrico será la respiración. Y un matiz más: la penetración. En el Tantra no se convierte en «el gran momento», sino que llega de modo natural, gradual y además, nada de mete-saca. Continúan los besos y el abrazo pero, una vez que el pene se introduce, lo único que se mueve serán los músculos de la vagina y los del propio pene. Es posible que se desencadenen los orgasmos. Él, si puede, lo evitará a través de la respiración y de los ejercicios de contracción de los músculos del ano y del perineo. El Tantra considera que sólo el amor y la muerte se dan en el ahora, y durante ambos, no hay pasado ni futuro. Por ello, durante el instante del amor, tocamos la eternidad —traducido a lenguaje de los centros comerciales: si se mantiene la posición durante media hora, seguramente el orgasmo sea de traca—. El orgasmo se vive en soledad, en ese instante no hay amante. Sólo estás tú y para tu amante tú no estás. Para interiorizar esta unidad que crea el orgasmo, estés masturbándote a solas o con la pareja, el Tantra recomienda hacerlo «como las mujeres», con los ojos cerrados.

Dentro de la filosofía hinduista, acerca del uso de la energía sexual hubo dos escuelas. Mientras que las dravídicas afirman encontrar la libertad a través del sexo, el Yoga con la influencia aria comenzó a evitar la eyaculación a través del celibato; el Yoga se opone al Tantra en la raíz. El Yoga propone el conflicto, la supresión con consciencia de tu yo real —y del deseo de sexo— y la dualidad. Hay dos: el ser Superior al que imitar y el ser humano, imperfecto y limitado, lleno de pecados y defectos que jamás alcanzará, o excepcionalmente, la perfección. El Tantra, no obstante, prefirió la relación en pareja y el intercambio de energías sutiles, es decir, durante la relación el hombre puede evitar la eyaculación sin dejar de experimentar su orgasmo. Es el llamado *coitus reservatus*, que equivale a las técnicas Vajroli Mudra y Mula Bandha. A nivel práctico, el Vajroli Mudra implica cerrar el esfínter uretral como cuando se corta la orina a la mitad de una micción. Permite separar conscientemente el uso de la musculatura del ano respecto de la musculatura urogenital. Para la mujer implica experimentar otros niveles en su sexualidad, casi insospechados. Mula Bandha (típica del Yoga) trabaja la musculatura, la respiración y la atención. Se empieza contrayendo desde el perineo, hacia delante, hacia los genitales, la pelvis y la parte baja del abdomen, una sensación similar a la de retener el paso de la orina o las heces.

El encuentro tántrico está deliciosamente explicado en el libro de Osho *Tantra, espiritualidad y sexo*, donde reflexiona acerca de la causa de la impotencia, de la actitud que haría que tuviéramos una sexualidad plena (satisfactoria de verdad, no en términos de contabilizar polvos), de la sensación de plenitud que el sexo nos puede regalar (eso que se dice de tocar el Cielo o de participar de la Eternidad).

El antiguo arte chino de la colocación, el Feng Shui, es una ciencia milenaria y podría pensarse en ella como acupuntura para los edificios; su finalidad es la de dirigir la energía de modo que resulte favorable y propicia a sus ocupantes. En Oriente, ya desde el instante del trazado de una torre cuentan con expertos en esta disciplina para que asesoren y den sus pautas, a fin de crear entornos que estén en equilibrio con el paisaje y con la naturaleza. *Feng Shui* significa en chino «viento y agua», las dos grandes fuerzas de la naturaleza que debemos respetar. Cualquier diseño Feng Shui las tendrá en cuenta para que vayan en armonía.

Hay diversas especializaciones de Feng Shui: para edificios, para la oficina, para el jardín, para la casa y, más concretamente, para el dormitorio. Detalles acerca de cómo están colocados los muebles, qué tipo de adornos incorpores y en qué número, etc., resultan «sin importancia» para los occidentales y, sin embargo, determinan el flujo de la energía, del chi. El chi es la fuerza de la vida, y está en el aire que fluye en todas las cosas. Somos energía y formamos parte de un todo que, a su vez, es energía. Con un Feng Shui adecuado podemos propiciar determinados aspectos de nuestra vida: el dinero, las relaciones personales, la creatividad... El Feng Shui potencia nuestros esfuerzos a cualquier nivel, personal o profesional. En el centro de la filosofía Feng Shui yacen los conceptos de «yin» (femenino) y «yang» (masculino), dos fuerzas que no han de entenderse como opuestas o contrarias, ni como «buena» y «mala», o viceversa. Son complementarias. De hecho, el yin y el yang juntos componen el Tao, «el camino» o «la vía», una filosofía que no juzga y que conduce a una visión del mundo en la que se vive y se deja vivir.

Dentro de los aspectos de la vida que rige en yin, el lado femenino, se encuentra el dormitorio. Para reforzar la unión de la pareja y para evitar el sentimiento de soledad de cualquiera de los dos, contribuye que los objetos de adorno vayan a pares: dos lámparas iguales, dos marcos de fotos, dos jarrones... Habida cuenta que es en la habitación donde principalmente se desarrolla la pasión, es ahí donde el elemento fuego ha de primar. Puedes potenciarlo con velas, lámparas indirectas, etc., y permitiendo que la luz del sol dé directamente sobre la cama en determinados momentos del día. Nada de agua (el agua apaga las llamas): ni peceras, ni imágenes de playas, ni marinas, etc., y tampoco plantas. Los grandes maestros de Feng Shui aconsejan que en el dormitorio no se coloque ningún aparato eléctrico (ni televisor, ni ordenador, etc.) cuyas vibraciones interfieren con el natural fluir del chi, generando energía yang, muy masculina. Para dotarlo de energía sexual positiva, se recomienda que no haya desorden. Conviene ventilar a diario la estancia. El chi puede fluir de modo positivo cuando recorre curvas. Las líneas rectas y las esquinas agudas hacen que se acelere creando efectos negativos —el mal chi se denomina «sha»—. También las obstrucciones físicas dan lugar a su estancamiento: los muebles que impiden su paso interrumpen el flujo de chi. Por eso, lo primero que se debe hacer para que un dormitorio resulte el entorno adecuado es despejarlo de trastos, de montones de ropa apilada y demás (estas cosas estancan el chi). Otro detalle: jamás coloques espejos en lugares donde quedes reflejado mientras duermes (a muchos ello les entusiasma, para verse haciendo posturitas): se trata de un gran enemigo del descanso. En su lugar, sí ayuda incorporar estatuillas eróticas o alguna foto de la pareja. El tipo de cama y dónde se coloque son determinantes. Lo primero: busca una pared sin ventanas para ubicar el cabecero y trata de que la puerta del dormitorio no quede ni enfrente ni por la espalda: lo ideal sería que quedara en diagonal. No se recomienda almacenar nada debajo de la cama, precisamente para permitir que la energía circule, y sobre ella, cuantas menos cosas mejor: no apiles muñecos y cojines. Los materiales de almohadas, cubrecama, sábanas, etc., han de ser naturales. ¿Qué más? Si hay un baño junto al dormitorio, la puerta de éste ha de permanecer cerrada para que no se escape el chi. Los colores que erotizan son los calientes: rojizos, granates y rosas, marrones, anaranjados... El amarillo favorece la comunicación, por lo que también sería favorable. Otros truquillos para que la libido se despierte: para él, poner algún objeto de cobre en su lado de la cama o en su mesilla potencia la virilidad; cubrir con un tapete o tela decorativa la mesilla de ella también repercutirá en su sensualidad (y si su cajoncito oculta aceites de masaje, juguetes, lubricantes y demás caprichos, tanto mejor).

6

Enamoramiento

¿Es grave?

Estar enamorado y amar a alguien pueden sonar a la misma cosa, pero no lo son. El enamoramiento es una atracción motivada principalmente por la apariencia y la personalidad del otro y su ajuste con la propia —obedezca a realidad o a pura proyección—. En el enamoramiento (eros, placer/pasión en estado puro) intervienen el cuerpo y la mente. El amor se relaciona con el ser del otro, su auténtico ser, con su interior, más allá de sus atributos físicos o de cómo manifieste externamente su personalidad. El amor conoce al otro y valora su esencia, se ve afectado por la decisión, por la preocupación activa acerca del otro y por el crecimiento y desarrollo de esa persona; el enamoramiento, generalmente, se desarrolla en la superficie y se mueve en el plano de las emociones.

La pasión es bien capaz de regir tus decisiones, condicionar tu vida y adueñarse de tus pensamientos, de tus actos, de tus días y de tus noches. Es, creo, una enfermedad tan maldita como maravillosa. Los síntomas de nerviosismo, taquicardia, sudoración, vértigo, miedo, subida de tensión y enrojecimiento en las mejillas, etc..., propios del enamoramiento, nos colocan bien cerquita de la locura o de la condición de superhéroes, que no notan ni el cansancio, ni el frío, ni el paso de las horas, ni el dolor... Son todo lo malos que pueden ser los causantes de la más intensa felicidad. Maldita paradoja. Porque aunque hasta ahora sonaba «como muy poético», me temo que detrás de esta parrafada sólo se esconde el juego de la Quimicefa. Tranquilidad, tengo la fórmula.

El origen de estas reacciones y conductas tan «peculiares» está en la secreción de un compuesto orgánico derivado de las anfetaminas: la feniletilamina (produce desasosiego), que encharca el cerebro. La reacción inmediata de éste es segregar dopamina (responsable de la sensación de deseo y placer) y oxitocina (un compuesto químico que transmite la necesidad de crear lazos y el deseo sexual, ver la tercera parte de este libro). Al «cóctel» debemos añadir además serotonina y melatonina (antidepresivos que provocan nerviosismo, alegría y felicidad e incrementan la actividad sexual, cardiovascular y digestiva). Y como último ingrediente, la imprescindible adrenalina (segregada por las glándulas suprarrenales).

Este subidón, estos sentimientos que escapan al control de la razón —porque sólo nos da con determinadas personas, mientras a otras ni las vemos y porque cuando notamos rechazo o se nos impone la distancia, desatan sufrimiento y ansiedad—, sólo nos posee durante x tiempo: lo que dura el flechazo, la chispa, la pasión... En efecto, este vértigo dura entre 18 y 30 meses, que es lo que tarda el organismo en hacerse inmune a la sobredosis de sustancias químicas, que si bien son naturales y propias, nunca se segregan en tasas tan elevadas ni interactuando conjuntamente.

El estado bioquímico de una persona enamorada se compara al de un yonqui... Por ello, es equiparable el dolor que se siente, casi insoportable, cuando se produce una ruptura o ese amor no es correspondido, con el síndrome de abstinencia. Hay dos remedios naturales y muy efectivos. Uno es matarse en el gimnasio. Hacer ejercicio intenso para regular la producción de adrenalina y serotonina. El otro es comer chocolate, que resulta un tratamiento de choque contra «el mono» y un antídoto estupendo ya que es rico en feniletilamina, que ayuda a suplir esa abstinencia.

Adicción

Química, química, química. Está demostrado que hay personas «enganchadas» a estar enamoradas. El trastorno se definió como disforia histeroide por los psiquiatras M. Leibowitz y D. Klein. Los adictos son incapaces de continuar una vez disminuyen las descargas de endorfinas (producen placer, se denominan opiáceos endógenos, con efectos muy similares al opio y a la morfina) y comienzan a «ver» al otro tal cual es.

En un primer momento, ante la novedad, algunos dicen que nos enamoramos al encontrar a la persona que llevamos «congelada» dentro, formada a base de referentes paternos, familiares, aspiracionales o sociales, biológicos (genética compatible) o por las feromonas que captamos... Con independencia de cuál sea la causa, el caso es que le miramos y sentimos esa punzada premonitoria: «es él/ella», automáticamente nuestro cuerpo segrega sustancias que hacen que nos sintamos felices, alegres, en las nubes... La percepción del tiempo se altera, y sólo por ver a esa persona somos capaces de todo. Podemos hacer de tripas corazón, olvidamos el cansancio y la pereza, pasamos por encima de la dificultad: todo se sobrelleva para estar con ese alguien. Para mí, lo que hace más especial este estado de ánimo es que escapa a la voluntad: es incontrolable. Nadie manda sobre él. Y tampoco se elige. Surge y muere espontáneamente. Miles de parejas se han casado y se casarán por conveniencia y puede que jamás, por veinte años que convivan y veinte hijos que engendren, sientan el uno por el otro nada parecido... ¡ya querrían poder experimentarlo estos condenados a la perpetua! Se trata de una de nuestras emociones más intensas y sobre las que, paradójicamente, menos dominio ejercemos. Por dinero puedes dar y recibir sexo, pero con billetes nadie te provoca (ni tú causarás) los síntomas que estamos analizando.

Trastornos en el apetito (desaparece la sensación de hambre), en el sueño y la vigilia, en la memoria y en el aprendizaje, etc., hay una serie de emociones conectadas al hipotálamo —no al amor, lo siento—, ya mencionado y que se responsabiliza de todas estas funciones. El buen humor es, junto a la desaparición de la agresividad —hacia esa persona, todo son frases amables y dulzura en el tono—, la ilusión por agradarle (que suplanta al egoísmo innato y que nos ocupa más tiempo que escucharle o conocerle de verdad...) y la deformación del mundo, alguno de los síntomas, como lo es la incapacidad de concentrarse y la idealización del otro (al que cargamos de virtudes y le eximimos de una mirada crítica, y encontramos que todo es perfecto en esa persona y sentimos que nos comprende, ¡no, mejor aún, que nos adivina sin hablar siquiera!)

En realidad, estar enamorado es un proceso bioquímico que

equivale a estar drogado (mismas causas, reacciones, adicción...). Lo malo es que a diferencia de cuando consumes, aquí la cosa va a su aire: surge y termina teniendo tú muy poco que decidir al respecto. Las ventajas de este «pedo» son varias: que es totalmente legal —ahora, para todos—, sin narcotraficantes ni camellos de por medio, ni farmacéutico sobornado; que es gratis y se origina de modo natural en nuestro propio cerebro y de ahí pasa al sistema endocrino, provocando respuestas fisiológicas naturales —como la secreción de fluidos, olores, dilatación y erección—, con lo que en principio, no castiga el organismo. Más difícil de dar y de entender resulta el paso del enamoramiento al amor, porque, precisamente, empezamos a amar cuando dejamos de estar enamorados.

Cuando cesan los efectos, parece que salimos de una hipnosis y, repentinamente, todo lo que considerábamos valores, los percibimos desde su aspecto negativo (de admirar su autocontrol a verle sumiso, etc.).

Para poder amar...

Para poder amar a otro debemos partir del principio de que nadie da lo que no tiene. Un ser sin autoestima o que no se quiere a sí mismo, difícilmente amará a nadie (no valorará lo que el otro es). Suele suceder que las personas enfermas —con perturbaciones— atraen a seres semejantes, buscará a otro que complemente sus neurosis. El enamoramiento se alimenta de la incertidumbre y de la inseguridad; fenece ante la rutina, la convivencia estrecha, que desenmascara el yo verdadero y mata la fascinación ante ese desconocido; cede ante la responsabilidad de la interdependencia que choca con lo lúdico. Dice Isabel Salama en su artículo «El arte de amar»: «Una relación de pareja perdura porque lo que unió al principio se fortalece. Se debilita o termina por lo contrario. Para que la relación permanezca se necesita, según opinión de Walter Riso que comparto, una combinación adecuada de eros, filia (amistad/camaradería) y ágape. Este último es el amor que no pide nada a cambio y que se manifiesta en respeto por los demás. Lo que diferencia a ágape de eros y filia es el desinterés, por ello nunca causa sufrimiento a otros. La clave de ágape es poderse desprender del ego, de las necesidades de la perso-

nalidad. Se puede amar sin estar enamorado. Cuando se está enamorado se cree amar, pero es muy posible que sólo se esté percibiendo
la apariencia de quien creemos amar. Se ve sólo lo positivo, lo que
integra, no lo que desune. [...] Una buena relación de pareja debe tener ambos componentes, amor y enamoramiento, pero debe predo-
minar en ella el amor expresado en filia y en ágape. [...] La vida de pareja perfecta es eros, filia y ágape en cantidades adecuadas, que se
adapten a las necesidades de cada uno. Hay parejas que son más eróticas, otras más fílicas o más agápicas, dependiendo de sus preferencias. Aun con amor, si no hay enamoramiento es poco probable que
pueda existir una excelente relación de pareja. Si no fuera así la mejor
pareja sería el mejor amigo/a.»

7

Adicción al sexo

Ninfómanas

La ninfomanía describe un trastorno exclusivamente femenino que consiste en un comportamiento sexual compulsivo que eclipsa las demás facetas. El equivalente de este trastorno en los hombres se denomina andromanía o satiriasis.

Etimológicamente viene de las «ninfas», criaturas que habitaban en los bosques, y de «manía», que implica obsesión. Se trata de una obsesión por practicar sexo. Y este apetito sexual voraz y desmesurado puede deberse a alteraciones bioquímicas del cerebro que provocan la hipersexualidad, o emocionales y psicológicas: cuando lo que se busca es afectividad y lo que se necesita es amor, y sin embargo sólo se da y recibe sexo, la sucesión de relaciones sexuales provoca aún más insatisfacción y el vacío se hace cada vez más doloroso.

Cabe que esta conducta se desarrolle hacia la pornografía, el sexo *on-line* o la masturbación. En casi cualquiera de sus vertientes, el impacto sobre la economía del adicto puede ser brutal (especialmente si la afición deriva en el consumo de prostitución y demás sexo de pago) y generalmente también daña su vida social y laboral. La adicción al sexo existe y, como cualquier otra, constituye una enfermedad a tratar por especialistas. En qué punto marcamos el límite entre «aficionado», «entusiasmado» y «enganchado» va en el sentido común, que ya sabemos que es el menos común de los sentidos, y aplicándolo al tema que nos ocupa, sin duda, el primero en anularse. Las personas adictas al sexo caen en una compulsión que las hace olvidarse hasta de las medidas profilácticas «básicas». Pier-

den el control —las adicciones se caracterizan, precisamente, por que obnubilan la razón, y la necesidad de satisfacerlas se antepone a lo demás—, se van con cualquiera porque lo suyo ya no va de placer, va de conseguir sexo... La sensación que sobreviene es de una enorme frustración y de culpa. Las personas que la padecen suelen mantenerla en secreto; en realidad, uno de sus efectos es que les conduce a aislarse. La adicción al sexo puede resolverse con terapia.

Enganchados

Las personas adictas al amor buscan de modo enfermizo las sensaciones que se desencadenan en cada relación afectiva: se entregan, gozan y sufren sin medida. Se dan cuenta de que han perdido el control pero no pueden dejarlo. Y tras cada ruptura se lanzan a la siguiente con las mismas ansias insanas. La fase de enamoramiento se define por muchos como una suerte de enajenación mental transitoria.

Determinadas personas desarrollan adicción a la sensación de estar enamorado, y se «enganchan» sucesivamente a quien sea, en realidad importa muy poco el objeto sobre el que se deja caer todo el deseo y el entusiasmo, porque lo que pesa es la química: las descargas que se producen. Cuando estar enamorado se convierte en adicción se torna nocivo. Como dice Isabel Salama: «Los adictos a estar enamorados son esposos o esposas, notoriamente malos. El enamoramiento es una poesía, corta, vibrante... el amor conyugal, una novela frecuentemente tediosa, de muchísimas páginas. Necesitan estar enamorados, muy enamorados, y la rutina y el exceso de seguridad del matrimonio debilitan y a veces matan el amor romántico pues éste se alimenta de incertidumbre.» El adicto al amor padece una fijación patológica, afectiva, de convertir la fase del enamoramiento en crónica —lo malo es que sólo dura aproximadamente un año...— y no soporta las relaciones cuando ese nivel de apasionamiento decrece. El psiquiatra Carlos Sirvent, director del programa de Formación en Adicciones y fundador del Instituto Spiral, explicaba los síntomas: «un estado de dependencia similar al de cualquier otro adicto (un deseo irresistible de estar con el otro); un síndrome de abstinencia en ausencia de la otra persona; un estado de subordinación con respecto a la pareja; el pensamiento obsesivo sobre el otro; la sensación de sentirse atrapado en una relación y no ser capaz de salir de ella; la búsqueda de sensaciones especiales con otra persona pero de forma patológica; la incapacidad para soportar la soledad. Son buscadores de sensaciones pero ya no disfrutan con ellas. Están como desgastados. Pasa de alguna manera lo que con los drogadictos: llega un momento en que la droga ya no les satisface del todo y sólo son conscientes de su dependencia. Respecto de la ruptura, es vivida de forma mucho más tormentosa. En general, no es aceptada. Una persona que no es adicta, cuando vive una ruptura pasa por varias etapas: incredulidad ante lo sucedido, búsqueda de culpas y duelo, que es la fase de aceptación. Los adictos no superan la fase de duelo, o la deforman y se eternizan en un debate interno de inculpación, nostalgia y obsesión. El adicto al amor adopta alternativas de huida hacia delante: sigue buscando pareja pero es curioso comprobar cómo le han marcado las relaciones anteriores y cómo las recuerda. Es la eterna insatisfacción. El "don Juan", en cambio, está satisfecho con todas las relaciones que ha tenido. Empieza y cierra las relaciones. Un adicto empieza las relaciones pero no las cierra nunca».

Dependencia del amante

¿Cómo explicar esa dependencia hacia la persona con la que tenemos orgasmos? ¿Por qué se da ese amarre, que va más allá de la pasión, que se genera aunque el sexo no sea «cinco estrellas»? De nuevo, la respuesta está en la química. Culpad de todo a la oxitocina, que se segrega después del parto y del orgasmo, y también cuando se succiona el pezón, se estimulan los genitales y hay distensión del cuello uterino. Este neuropéptido se libera desde la hipófisis, que es donde se almacena, hacia la corriente sanguínea. En el primer caso, tras el alumbramiento, es la causante de que, a pesar de todos los pesares (embarazo problemático, náuseas, mareos, episiotomía, dolores, etc.), la madre quiera a su criatura. Pero la oxitocina se llama la «hormona de la fidelidad», «molécula de la monogamia» o de «la confianza» porque además de servir para la circulación del esperma y para las contracciones orgásmicas, tras el clímax, provoca placer, impulso de tocar, de abrazar y la necesidad de que se creen vínculos afectivos. Es también responsable de desencadenar cambios en las conexiones nerviosas de los miles de millones de circuitos cerebrales, y esas alteraciones provocan nuevos patrones de interacción entre las células. O sea, que no se trata necesariamente de amor. Es química. No es una frase eso de que «hay química entre dos personas». Ese cuelgue, o afecto, o enganche, se explica por el efecto de hormonas sexuales (especialmente la testosterona, que marca la intensidad del deseo sexual, pero también los estrógenos, andrógenos y la progesterona) y por las sustancias que segregamos de modo involuntario al tener un orgasmo. Todas ellas nos hacen sentir esa «necesidad» del otro —con independencia de que el otro u otra, a nivel consciente, no nos interese en absoluto o resulte un amante venenoso—, o nos llevan a estupideces como decir «te quiero» a un tipo que hemos conocido dos horas antes...

8

Fijaciones sexuales o parafilias

Filias

Dentro de las distintas prácticas sexuales, aquellas cuya denominación termina en la desinencia «filia» implican especial predilección, amor, afición o simpatía hacia lo que designa. *Para*, en griego, significa «al lado» y *philéo*, «amar». Otras, mayoritariamente, terminan en «agnia» o en «astia» y se asocian a lo excéntrico.

En general, el término «parafílico» se emplea de modo despectivo, señalando a personas «raras», con preferencias «enfermizas» o «aberrantes», lo cual es injusto además de incorrecto. Deberíamos ser capaces de distinguir a un parafílico patológico de alguien con un gusto «especial» dentro del sexo, que introduce ciertas pinceladas, a modo de juego y siempre de acuerdo con su pareja: hablando y consensuando lo que le gustaría hacer. Lo patológico implicaría que el sujeto no sea capaz de disfrutar de sus relaciones sexuales sin que su parafilia o fijación intervenga, o cuando ésta ocupa su mente de tal modo que condiciona sus otras actividades y trastorna sus facetas cotidianas.

Fue Richard von Krafft-Ebing, autor de *Psichopathia Sexualis* (1886), un pionero en la sexología y la medicina forense, quien inventó los términos «sadismo» y «masoquismo», e ideó una clasificación de las fijaciones sexuales o parafilias. En la edición de *Psichopathia Sexualis* que he manejado se encuentran sólo 69 de los 238 casos originales estudiados, una recopilación de las muestras más representativas, y muchas ya obsoletas: masoquismo, homosexualidad, lesbianismo, fetichismo-canibalismo, bestialismo, coprolagnia, autobiografía de un transexual, etc. En el prólogo, Luis García Berlanga afirma: «El psiquiatra austrohúngaro estaba convencido de que la simple abstinencia bastaría para abolir el deseo, y de que el matrimonio heterosexual, unas cuantas sesiones de hidroterapia y una faradización general, versión temprana del electrochoque, harían desistir de sus tendencias al homosexual o al fetichista más avezado. Hoy sabemos que esto no es así y que no hay razón para abolir nada ni para perseguir con encono a un aficionado a las prendas femeninas...»

Anomalías sexuales

Como planteamiento, ya obsoleto, pero ilustrativo a modo de clasificación de las distintas clases de comportamiento sexual, Ganon y Simon, en 1967, defendían tres grupos de anomalías sexuales:

I) *Anomalías normales*: pese a que la sociedad las reprueba, se realizan con tal frecuencia y, a su vez, sin entrar en conflicto con el orden social, que se podría decir que son «moderadamente» anómalas. De un modo íntimo, todo el mundo participa de ellas, complementando su vida sexual. Estos autores citan como ejemplos la masturbación, las relaciones extra y prematrimoniales, la promiscuidad, el sexo oral entre heteros, los juegos anales, e incluso, el sexo en presencia de otros.

II) *Anomalías subculturales y socialmente estructuradas*: en este grupo incluían las reprobables conductas que atentaban contra el statu quo social y familiar, como la homosexualidad, el intercambio de pareja y el sexo grupal.

III) *Anomalías patológicas*: realizadas sin consentimiento del otro muchas de ellas, otras «condenadas» por la religión, etc., este epígrafe subsumía conductas tales como el incesto, el contacto sexual con niños, la coprofilia y la coprofagia, la urolagnia, el voyeurismo, el exhibicionismo, las injurias agresivas, el sadomasoquismo, el bestialismo, la transexualidad, el travestismo y la necrofilia.

Y es que, para el psicoanálisis ortodoxo, un acto sexual normal alude, invariablemente, a la sexualidad genital del adulto sano, orientada a la procreación y placentera, tal y como se plasmaba, allá por los años sesenta, la definición del diccionario de psicoanálisis de Laplanche y Pontalis: «Coito conducente a la obtención del orgasmo con penetración vaginal con una persona del sexo opuesto.» Este modelo de «normalidad» considera que serían «anormales» las actividades sexuales autoeróticas como la masturbación, las homosexuales, las realizadas con más de una persona, aquellas en las que no hay penetración o ésta es anal u oral o mediante estimulación diversa a la específica para alcanzar el clímax, etc.

Pansexualismo freudiano

Incorporado por Freud, el padre del psicoanálisis y responsable de frases tipo: «la sexualidad humana es perversa y polimorfa», su concepto de pansexualidad describe la atracción sexual hacia cualquier cosa. Esto implica que el objeto de deseo pueda ser también cualquier otra persona, independientemente de su sexo (trasciende, por tanto, el concepto «bisexual», porque lo supera). Es una orientación sexual caracterizada por la atracción hacia «la persona», en el más amplio sentido y abierto a todo tipo de prácticas sexuales, sin que ello se traduzca en que «les vale» cualquier cosa. No obstante su orientación sexual «sin distinciones» entre sexos, algunos pansexuales pueden sentir preferencias por determinadas personas.

Los pansexuales pueden sentirse atraídos por alguien en el plano estético, romántico o incluso sexual —lo que apuntaría más a lo metafísico—; sin embargo, en un nivel más terrenal, de lo puramente físico, pueden excitarse con diferentes actos sexuales —sin importarles que los compañeros de juegos sean de un sexo u otro—. Simplemente, son capaces de amar y desear a otro ser humano guiándose por un sentimiento que surge y se enfoca en detalles y valores que no se ciñen estrictamente a la genitalidad o al sexo.

En la ficción hay alusiones. En la serie de televisión *Will & Grace*, Karen Walker afirma que se considera pansexual, después de revelar que ha tenido relaciones sexuales con Will, Karen y Rosario. Y el personaje Jack Harness de la serie *Doctor Who*, desarrollada en el año 5000, es pansexual. Dice que no clasifica a las personas en función de su sexo, y que tiene una capacidad potencial de sentirse atraído por cualquier persona o incluso por seres de otros planetas.

Concepto de la sexualidad sana (OMS)

La sexualidad sana se configura como «la aptitud para disfrutar de la actividad sexual y reproductiva, amoldándose a criterios de ética social y personal. La ausencia de temores, de sentimientos de vergüenza, de culpabilidad, de creencias infundadas y de otros factores psicológicos que inhiban la reactividad sexual o perturben las relaciones sexuales». Esta definición de «salud sexual» de la OMS (Organización Mundial de la Salud, Ginebra, febrero de 1974) afirma que «Salud sexual es la integración de los elementos corporales, emocionales, intelectuales y sociales del ser sexual, por medios que sean positivamente enriquecedores y que potencien la personalidad, la comunicación y el amor».

Al disociar actividad sexual y reproductiva e incorporar todos los aspectos del ser humano: corporal, emocional, intelectual y social, podríamos deducir que en el sexo todo y nada es «normal». Los únicos límites han de ser, sólo y siempre, aquellas prácticas que atentan contra la integridad física y que hacen daño, las no consentidas y en las que intervienen menores, disminuidos psíquicos o personas que no pueden prestar su consentimiento.

Recapitulando

Como prácticas sexuales que cualquier adulto en su sano juicio realiza, las parafilias, para no considerarse una patología, deben cumplir determinados requisitos, algunos apuntados de modo recurrente en cada epígrafe concreto:

Que sean consentidas: que quien participe sea consciente y libremente decida. Ello excluye a menores, a incapaces, a personas que estén bajo los efectos de drogas (alcohol, psicofármacos, estupefacientes...).

Que se introduzcan como una pincelada, como un juego: se realizan para divertirse, para disfrutar, para excitarse. «Todo lo que se hace se puede hacer», eso sí, de un modo lúdico, sin imposiciones, ni arbitrariedad de una parte.

Que cesen en el momento en que así uno lo decide: tanto en las que consisten en que, por ejemplo, uno de los participantes del acto sexual interprete el papel de un animal (el más recurrido es el papel de perro; se trata del adiestramiento animal o AT, *animal training*), como si hablamos de caminar sobre una espalda desnuda con zapatos de aguja que se clavan, ha de haber una palabra clave que, pronunciada, permita dejarlo.

Que no sean exclusivas ni excluyentes del resto de las fantasías, y la sexualidad se viva y se disfrute igualmente sin ellas: no deben convertirse en una obsesión o en un fin. Se han de entender como un medio para el placer (excitarse o alcanzar el orgasmo ha de ser posible de otros modos).

Las prácticas sexuales que se escapan a lo «común» forman una divertida familia, la de las «parafilias», que engloba desde la agrexofilia, que consiste en excitarse ante la posibilidad de ser oído por otros mientras se practica el sexo, para lo cual se acude a lugares que lo posibilitan: hoteles, etc.; o la excitación sexual mediante la ingesta o manipulación de heces (coprofilia); tener sexo con animales (o zoofilia, también designada como bestialismo), etc. Habida cuenta que estas relaciones «especiales» conforman una larga lista, he seleccionado varias, las más frecuentes o anecdóticas, si se me permite. Otras aparecen a lo largo del libro y también en la tercera parte, pero hay más, muchas más...

Agorafilia: atracción por la actividad sexual o el exhibicionismo en lugares públicos.

Alopelia: experimentar un orgasmo sólo viendo a otros teniendo una relación sexual, o sea, el voyeurismo llevado a la enésima.

Anaclitismo: alcanzar la excitación sexual mediante actividades propias de los niños pequeños. Estas actividades pueden ser que te enseñen a hacer pipí en su sitio, que te coloquen unos patucos o que te pongan a jugar con muñecas. Las prostitutas ganan fortunas cambiando pañales...

Anisonogamia: atracción por una pareja sexual mucho más joven o mucho mayor.

Blastolagnia: atracción por mujeres muy jóvenes.

Consuerofilia: obtención de placer sexual al coserse zonas de la piel con aguja e hilo. Ya he dicho que hay gente para todo...

Crematistofilia: excitación producida al pagar por sexo.

Douching (viene del francés *douche*, «ducha»): esta práctica consiste en inyectar un líquido, por lo general agua, en la vagina, ya sea por higiene o para potenciar la excitación sexual.

Erotofonofilia: excitación al realizar llamadas telefónicas utilizando lenguaje erótico.

Fratrilagnia: atracción por las relaciones sexuales incestuosas (con hermanos/as).

Gerontofilia: atracción sexual de una persona joven por un hombre

de edad mucho mayor. La atracción de jóvenes por mujeres maduras se llama *graofilia* y la atracción tanto por ancianas como por ancianos se llama *cronofilia*.

Hirsutofilia: atracción por el vello.

Ipsofilia: excitación sólo por uno mismo. No es lo mismo que masturbación, donde el objeto sexual puede ser una persona presente, una fotografía o una fantasía.

Jactitafilia: excitación producida por el relato de las propias hazañas sexuales.

Microgenitalismo: excitación por los penes pequeños.

Nosolagnia: excitación proveniente de saber que la pareja tiene una enfermedad terminal. (Esto, y no la persecución ciega y codiciosa de una cuantiosa herencia, explicaría ciertos matrimonios.)

Picacismo: excitación sexual al introducir alimentos en alguna de las cavidades del cuerpo con el fin de que la pareja los recupere con la boca. Los dulces no deben penetrar en la vagina porque causan infecciones (hongos y demás).

Retifismo: se refiere al fetichismo que despiertan los zapatos.

Toucherismo (viene del inglés *touch*, «tocar»): pero la atracción sólo se produce al tocar personas desconocidas. Igual esto explica el éxito de los cuartos oscuros y de las multitudinarias fiestas *rave*.

Vincilagnia: excitación por hacerse atar.

Xenofilia: la excitación sólo se produce ante parejas de distintos países. Justo lo contrario de la xenofobia...

9

Sexo virtual

Cibersexo

¡Tanto por hacer y tan poco tiempo!, nos lamentamos a menudo. Para sobrevivir en nuestro entorno social se nos exige, casi, que desarrollemos superpoderes (otra cosa es que, dado que lo hacemos todos, nunca se nos reconozca tanto arte como llegamos a destilar). Realizamos un montón de tareas en diversos ámbitos y formamos parte de modo simultáneo de colectivos bien dispares y ello, por fuerza, exige que nos dosifiquemos, que nuestra agenda registre cada detalle ajustando hasta el minuto y que podamos dedicarle menos tiempo del que nos gustaría a cada una de las facetas imprescindibles o superfluas (comer, higiene personal, dormir, ir a trabajar, ir al gimnasio, de compras, amistades, ligar o pareja, hijos, *hobbies*, mascotas, etc.). Por largo que sea el día y rápido que hagamos todo, a veces, uno siente que no da para tanto... Ya dicen que «quien mucho abarca poco aprieta». La prisa nos empuja a la superficialidad, y no sólo en lo laboral... La proliferación de empresas de contactos, de servicios de encuentros, de citas y de reuniones que se organizan *on-line* o vía sms, no son sino la prueba de ello. Muy ocupados profesionalmente, pero, al final del día, muy solos. Por multitarea que seamos, no perdemos la humanidad, y el ser humano, del mismo modo que las plantas necesitan agua, precisa de la comunicación con sus semejantes. No podemos vivir sin amistad, sin amor, sin sexo... O sí, pero muy mal, y terminaremos tiñéndonos de color gris por dentro (y por fuera). Lo que se esconde detrás de estas citas para sexo exprés, además de mucho vicio —léase sin tono peyorativo—, que es el principal motor de la mayoría y especialmente de los que cuentan con pareja estable y aun así no se privan de engañarla echando un polvo sin explicaciones, es la conciencia de que quizá no sea la solución permanente, pero es la de hoy. Avanzamos matando indios de uno en uno, como podemos, y vamos tirando. Se trata de aguantar el tipo, de seguir hacia delante, siempre adelante... Quizá no podamos curar la herida, pero sí colocarle una tirita. Será pan para hoy y hambre para mañana, pero es lo que hay, como la vivienda de 25 metros cuadrados, aspiracional antesala de la mansión en El Viso...

Esa misma conciencia de prisa, de que estamos en este mundo muy poco y de prestado, nos conduce prácticamente a una revelación filosófica: «no estamos aquí para pasarlo mal» que, si se formula en positivo, se convierte en un «esto es una fiesta», y claro, se mueven los hilos que sean precisos para cumplir con ello... Preferimos sustituir lo que se estropea por algo nuevo, antes que perder el tiempo en arreglarlo. Eso ocurre con coches, ordenadores, móviles y relaciones. Vivimos con la conciencia de que no hay pero que valga, que todo es material fungible, que no hay que encariñarse con nada ni con nadie porque para lo que va a permanecer con nosotros... Hemos desarrollado una intolerancia al dolor que no nos permite sufrir, y que nos lleva a huir de todo lo que suponga un problema u obstáculo. Hay que llegar muy lejos, aunque no sepamos en qué dirección vamos corriendo.

Navegando en Internet (*adultfriendfinder.com*, *meetic.com*, *sexsearch.com*, *iwantu.com*, *badoo.com*, *match.com* y muchas más), en cuestión de media hora, y casi siempre de modo gratuito, se puede uno dar de alta y configurar un perfil, publicando fotografías e información personal (desde los intereses laborales, a la medida del pene; de *hobbies* y gastronomía, a preferencias en cuanto a depilación corporal, tatuajes y *piercings*), y comenzar a intercambiar mensajes con personas afines (o no tanto) y dispuestas a tener citas y sexo inmediato. El mundo se convierte en una gran pastelería donde cualquier goloso enloquece ante la gran variedad de tartas y pasteles... Queremos probarlo todo, hasta empacharnos o sin saber que nos mata la diabetes... En cualquier caso, bienvenidos a la era del «multiloving», del «cyberlove» o como quiera que lo denominen...

Es preciso reparar en un riesgo que conlleva Internet: la adicción al cibersexo. Ese estar pendiente de quién se conecta, de quién está *on-line*, de quién te mandó un mensaje o visitó tu perfil, amén de la «facilidad» de quedar con personas que quieren sexo sin preguntas —comparado con la tradicional forma de ligar—, o de alcanzar orgasmos sin moverte de la pantalla de tu ordenador, acceder con dos clics a esa riqueza de contenidos de todo tipo y para todos los gustos (en la red hay desde zoofilia, a páginas donde se organizan las quedadas para montar orgías o para avisar de una sesión de *dogging*; los adeptos del intercambio de parejas o «gente libre» se ponen en contacto a través de las páginas de los propios locales donde se realiza, etc.), esos romances sin responsabilidades, o esa maravillosa forma de poder dar rienda suelta a la fantasía, tiene su riesgo. En efecto, lo malo es que toda esta magia provoca que miles de personas vivan pegadas a la pantalla del ordenador, aban-

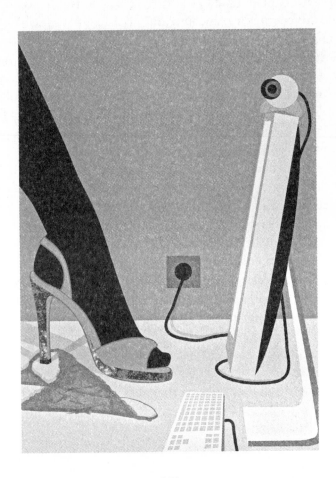

donando o perdiendo la referencia con sus familias, con sus amigos, sus empleos y parejas. Mientras el sexo cibernético no genere tal dependencia que sustituya a las relaciones «reales» (*vs* virtuales) o no cause trastornos compulsivos y adicción —hay personas que literalmente viven conectadas, que dedican a navegar por Internet las 24 horas del día—, supone una forma más de comunicarse y de relacionarse. Degenerada la afición hasta el grado de patología en su uso, ha de tratarse como cualquier trastorno psicológico.

Otra de las necesarias reflexiones acerca del «cyberlove» es si interfiere o no en la relación de pareja o si se puede catalogar como una infidelidad esa relación virtual. Cabría hacer algunas consideraciones sobre el controvertido asunto de la infidelidad, la exclusividad sexual y los cuernos, ese apéndice que no lucen sólo caracoles y herbívoros.

¿Cómo nos sentaría saber que nuestra pareja se está tocando cuando alguien le escribe un par de frases? ¿Nos importa que se corra viendo a otra a través de la *webcam*? ¿Realmente te planteas que está pendiente del reloj y lo supedita todo para coincidir *online* con su «amante» virtual? ¿Te das cuenta de que vive para el momento de conectarse y chatear con esa «persona», que necesita su dosis diaria de *sex-text* y que esas frases eróticas que «él» le dedica le importan más que respirar? ¿Es posible sentir celos cuando, en «realidad», no se produce ningún tipo de contacto físico? Internet facilita la liberación de un montón de fantasías. Nos despoja de «herramientas» y lastres que interfieren en las relaciones físicas, en las «reales», mantenidas vis a vis, y se tiende a ir al grano... Todo se magnifica y se acelera. Según una ciberencuesta,[30] el 70,9 % de las mujeres considera la infidelidad virtual como un engaño, frente al 57,7 % de los hombres.

Como experimento de campo, me di de alta en una web donde puedes hacer contactos, chatear, ligar y demás, con otros internautas. En cuestión de siete horas recibí cerca de trescientos mensajes de hombres diferentes. ¡Casi trescientos en unas horas! Ya formo parte de esa cuota del millón de españoles que mensualmente utili-

---

30. Datos de *http://erotizatumente.blogspot.com/*

za este tipo de páginas de contactos para obtener sexo esporádico, que han desbancado drásticamente a las de «contactos tradicionales» enfocadas a encontrar pareja estable, tipo *match.com* como fueron los comienzos de este modelo de relaciones. Aquí ya nadie le llama amor cuando quiere decir...

Mi página fue visitada en menos de tres días por más de quinientos usuarios, de los que casi todos me han mandado algún mensaje. Algunos son mayores, otros más jóvenes, muchos solteros, algunos reconocían tener pareja; me contactaron abogados, escayolistas, publicistas, escritores, electricistas, bomberos... Para mi alegría (y sorpresa también), he localizado a algunos de mis amigos «reales» —no «virtuales»— suscritos a este mismo *site*.

Tras una semana *on (hot) line*, puedo desvelar que existen ciertos patrones de conducta: lo habitual es que tras saludarte, te pidan una dirección de *messenger* para salir de la web oficial, y en cualquier caso, casi todos van muy al grano (demasiado para mi gusto): tras el «hola, qué guapa estás en las fotos», muchos pasan a informarte de que tardan mucho en correrse... Los más jóvenes son adictos a las abreviaturas, las palabras contraídas y la fonética transcrita; no median más de diez mensajes hasta que te preguntan si estás casada, tienes pareja o novio; en general, el trato es de lo más cordial, amable, distendido, siendo cierto en ocasiones que algunos sólo pretenden hacer amigos y conversar. Casi todo el mundo (hombres y mujeres y de cualquier edad) emplea fotos muy explícitas, mostrando carnaza desde el primer instante (se encuentra mucha variedad de género, desde solomillo a casquería putrefacta y, hasta dentro de éstos, tan orgullosos, detectas sin querer muchas herederas de esa moda a lo Paris Hilton, que posan en plan «mira qué guapa que soy y qué tipo tengo», con un sujetador y en bragas sacados de una tienda de chinos). Se huele a distancia ese «con lo bueno que estoy no necesito pagar»; guapos y guapas hay, pero sin ser jurado de belleza ni psicóloga, me atrevo a afirmar que predomina el narcisismo peor canalizado... Hay que tener en cuenta que las fotos pueden ser o no auténticas, así como la información que cada uno publica sobre sí: yo, sin ir más lejos, estoy henchida de orgullo al haber sido contactada por «los mismísimos» David Beckham, Nacho Vidal y George Clooney, entre otros astros... Lo de las fotos falsas no es el único truco o engaño. Comenzando por el nombre (*nick*) y continuando con los detalles acerca de tu personalidad, todo, absolutamente todo, puede ser inventado. Los hay que se hacen pasar por personas del sexo opuesto, bien por diversión, bien para contactar con quienes de otro modo, les rechazarían.

Además, por pura prudencia, se deberían tomar ciertas cautelas mínimas dado que, concertada una cita, no sabemos realmente con quién vamos a encontrarnos. Utilizar *webcam* te asegura que quien chatea contigo existe, y es quien la imagen de la pantalla —más o menos nítida— te ofrece. Otro asunto será quién acuda al encuentro o quién te abra la puerta, si es que decidís quedar en la casa de uno de los dos. Lo revolucionario de Internet es que permite un total anonimato si ése es tu deseo. Puedes chatear (mantener conversaciones *on-line*) con personas de cualquier lugar, en todos los idiomas que domines, acerca de todos los temas y aficiones que se te ocurran, ¡y sin salir de tu casa! Sorprende que, tan sólo tecleando, sin necesidad de más esfuerzo que mirar imágenes y de leer texto, muchas personas disfruten de orgasmos. En este terreno, casi todos los usuarios configuran un perfil ficticio con el que acceden a foros y chats donde se debate sobre cualquier asunto y que cuentan con privados, donde se establece ya una conversación entre dos que puede llegar todo lo lejos que se quiera.

Esto de los contactos sexuales por la web parece un ejemplo de negocio global, ya que estas páginas cuentan entre sus más de 25 millones de miembros en todo el mundo (lo de miembros no se trata de una metonimia) con personas pertenecientes a todas las edades, estratos sociales y culturales, eso sí, con un predominio de varones.

Internet, esa inagotable fuente de pajas gratuitas, ha irrumpido con fuerza demoledora suponiendo, quién sabe, el top manta del negocio de la prostitución... Si con conectarte diez minutos consigues que alguien venga y te haga lo que tú quieres, ¿por qué vas a pagar?

Por último, este eficaz sistema proporciona «novios instantáneos». Lo malo es que, igual que el zumo de naranja de polvos, nunca será igual que el recién exprimido, pero bueno, si tienes mucha sed y pocas ganas de currártelo...

10

Cine X

Todo el porno NO es igual

Con todo mi respeto, este comentario denota falta del susodicho y un elevado grado de incultura; es erróneo. Dentro del cine X hay distintos géneros (*mainstream*, gay, bisexual, transexual, interracial, grandes pechos, gordas, enanos, embarazadas, ancianas, coprofilia, etc.), y estilos (desde el porno chic más cuidado a los gonzos más salvajes, de producciones fetichistas «pura pose» a espectaculares alardes de diálogo). Cada director imprime su particular criterio estético y determina las prácticas sexuales y la historia que quiere plasmar en su trabajo. Muchos lo saben, aunque para no airear su afición al X, insisten en afirmar que tanto da una peli que otra.

Superman

Las expectativas que casi todas tenemos acerca del rendimiento sexual de estos tremendos sementales es que nos van a dejar extenuadas y sin poder juntar las piernas en una semana... Sin embargo, una cosa es la «interpretación» ante cámara (indiscutiblemente gimnástica) y otra, la vida privada. A lo largo del libro los actores me han contestado a la pregunta: *¿Los actores porno en la vida privada decepcionáis?* Aquí van algunas de las respuestas.

ANDREA MORANTY: Sí decepcionamos, te lo digo yo [risas]. [...] Si no podemos «mostrar», nos aburrimos. O tenemos una verdadera loca en la cama que nos llame la atención, o nos aburrimos.

Cuando llega una señora en plan normal y se nos abre de piernas, nos aburrimos, nos reímos... Queremos algo fuerte. Cuando quieres a alguien, si haces el amor con una persona, ya es diferente, pero para divertirnos, sí, la verdad es que sí, podemos llegar a ser muy decepcionantes.

SOPHIE EVANS: No decepcionan, no. Ser actor porno es diferente de cuando estás en la vida privada, donde no estás actuando. Pero no hay tanta diferencia entre lo que hacen en una escena y lo que hacen en la vida privada.

NACHO VIDAL: Te sientes muy presionado... Se piensan que les vas a hacer un doble tirabuzón en el aire con triple salto mortal y que no se van a correr ni una, ni dos, ni tres veces, sino que se van a estar corriendo toda la noche...

¿Y si no cumples?

NACHO: ¡Claro! ¡Yo también soy humano! Igual echo un polvo de 5 minutos y me corro... No soy Superman ni nada raro, soy un hombre de a pie, y cuando me gusta una tía y se la meto y la siento caliente, me corro como todos. Puedo tener algún truco más que otro, pero a veces los trucos fallan.

Porno y prostitución

Otra leyenda negra que quise enfrentar en *Mi lado más hardcore* es la que afirma que los actores y actrices porno ejercen la prostitución. Quizá no todos los lectores se crean las respuestas...

DORA VENTER: Con todo respeto, la prostitución supone una mierda de dinero comparada con las cifras del cine porno. Además, los trabajos no son ni parecidos... Yo hago un trabajo muy bonito y gano mucha pasta. Con mi carrera me he comprado una casa maravillosa en la que he puesto unos muebles alucinantes... Tengo una buena vida, viajo...

LUCÍA LAPIEDRA: ¿Molestarme que lo piensen?, a mí no me molesta casi nada. Pero están equivocados. Yo interpreto sexo, tal y como se hace en las películas convencionales. Me parece un papel o una situación a interpretar. Prostituirse no es lo mismo, aunque tampoco veo negativo que alguien libremente se prostituya.

¿Cómo que el tamaño no importa?

El cine X es uno de los sectores en los que la belleza no está precisamente en el interior. La cámara lo capta todo y es lo que se ve lo que puntúa. No se hace actor porno quien quiere, sino quien puede, y ello implica, como condición sine qua non, disponer de una buena herramienta y saberla manejar, tener un perfecto dominio sobre ella (es decir, controlar mentalmente la erección y la eyaculación). Los urólogos, sexólogos y psicólogos cobran por consolar a quienes sufren disfunciones o cuentan con un miembro pequeño. Hay novedades químicas, quirúrgicas y de aparatología a disposición de quien las precise, pero ojo, ¡que no hay por qué compararse con los actores porno! Sin embargo, en la cama hay que currarse muchas cosas, como las caricias (a muchos no les suena siquiera la palabra «preliminares»), innovar posturas (sin replicar el Kamasutra, resulta interesante y saludable probar nuevas posiciones hasta dar con lo que a ella le gusta), etc. Pero los propios actores confiesan que el principal truco es «tener ganas», y eso no le falta a casi nadie... A lo largo del libro les pregunté a directores, productores, actores y actrices X si el tamaño importa, y la respuesta fue casi unánime: SÍ importa.

ROCCO SIFFREDI: La importancia se la dan más los realizadores y los fotógrafos, que siempre dicen que las grandes dan mejor en cámara. Pero en el porno, por supuesto que si tu polla es grande es más creíble. Cuando te follas a una tía por el culo con una polla enorme, la gente dice «¡guau!», porque o le está gustando o le está doliendo, pero seguro que algo está ocurriendo. Si la polla es pequeña y oyes los aullidos de la chica, lo normal es pensar: «está fingiendo».

NACHO VIDAL: Yo cuando trabajo con alguien que la tiene más grande que yo le digo: «Tío, ¡tú no tienes una polla, tienes un problema!» De hecho, si cuando trabajas a veces te cuesta empalmar, si encima es muy grande... no hay sangre suficiente para bombear eso...

Porno para mujeres

Cuando veo porno me planteo un montón de cosas: ¿es que el *casting* sólo lo hacen ellas? Últimamente hay actores más jóvenes y guapetones, con buenos cuerpos, depilados, bronceados, pero, hasta hace nada (diría que la cosa empieza a cambiar con la llegada al X de Rocco Siffredi), los grandes del género, capitaneados por Roberto Malone o Ron Jeremy, eran de espanto... ¿A qué chica le puede apetecer tirarse a semejantes seres? De nuevo, el machismo se evidencia: respecto de los actores basta con que aguanten y empujen —da lo mismo si no se quitan las gafas de pasta ni los calcetines para follar, o si están fofos y sin depilar—, mientras que las actrices han de ser jóvenes, delgadas y guapas, lo cual, además, genera en la espectadora una sensación de complejo de inferioridad que los hombres se ahorran... Los productores justifican este tema con que se busca que el espectador (siempre varón) pueda identificarse con lo que ve y creérselo. Por lo visto, lo que «las espectadoras» piensen da igual... Otra cuestión que me indigna es el guión, la historia de las películas. El cine X generalmente adolece de buenas tramas, entendiendo siempre con esto «buenas excusas» para introducir sexo explícito, aunque tampoco nos engañemos: cuando pones una peli porno, no buscas grandes argumentos elípticos, tipo *Seven*. Para excitar a una mujer, sí hace falta un poco de imaginación... No basta oír el ding-dong de la puerta, que aparezca el fontanero y se abra la bragueta... Lo peor, sin duda, es que nadie se ocupa de poner un *coach* que sepa sacar registros e interpretaciones verosímiles de los actores.

Conrad Son inició en España la producción de películas eróticas para mujeres: «las mujeres no buscan la cantidad, ni grandes intervenciones de sexo gimnástico. Les interesa la calidad. La trama creíble y cotidiana...», pero la cosa, dentro de la industria, no parece ir a más. Porqué está de moda decir que se produce «cine X para mujeres», la realidad, viendo las producciones en cuestión, es que no es así. El *marketing* ha revelado oficialmente que el público femenino está muy olvidado y desatendido en esta parcela y, por ello, en aras de llenarse los bolsillos, promocionan cintas «porno para mujeres» que bien poquito se diferencian de las *mainstream*...

Así, así, cariño, me encanta...

Si el cine convencional tiene como objetivo proporcionar entretenimiento, el cine X persigue lograr la excitación y, habida cuenta que los espectadores son en un 90 % hombres, parece haber olvidado una verdad meridiana: muchas de las cosas que a un señor como hombre le encantan, a las mujeres nos asquean o nos cabrean casi siempre. Hablando con la directora X Sandra Uve, decía: «Hay que eliminar los roles baratos de "te gusta que te folle, puta". Eso no me gusta a mí, como tampoco me gusta que se me corran en la cara, por eso lo elimino de mis escenas, pero no por ello suprimo los anales...»

Antes de su retirada del porno, Celia Blanco opinaba: «Desecho las prácticas que estéticamente no me gusta ver, por ejemplo el anal. Lo he hecho, pero no lo pondría en una cinta mía, no porque no me guste practicarlo, sino porque visualmente no me gusta cómo queda.»

Cuando les preguntaba a las actrices qué les parecía ser tratadas de forma humillante, tener que soportar tanta sumisión, esos azotes, esos escupitajos, esos tirones de pelo, esas aberturas anales extremas... ellas lo justificaban alegando que es una fantasía de la mayoría de las mujeres ser tratada así. Otras, más profesionales que honestas en su respuesta, alegaban que se trata de exigencias del guión, y que la brutalidad (y asquerosidad) de las prácticas constituyen gajes del oficio. Sólo las más sinceras admitían que a ellas les horrorizan las descargas faciales —que, por añadidura, estropean el maquillaje—, o confiesan lo doloroso que resulta hacer una doble penetración (... y no digamos la triple), o lo que sintieron en su primer anal, o lo difícil que es no vomitar con las *deep throat*. Por algo dicen que el trabajo es algo tan malo que es por lo único que pagan...

Nadie ve porno

Ésa es otra. Por lo visto, nadie mira pelis porno. Sin embargo, las audiencias desvelan que lo que de veras nadie ve son los documentales sobre aves migratorias... ¡Ejem! Un nuevo ejemplo de doble moral. ¿Por qué casi nadie admite que consume pornografía?

Hace unos años, cuando cada lunes realizaba el volcado de datos para saber las cifras de películas X que se habían visto a lo largo de la semana en Quiero Tv, la plataforma de televisión donde trabajaba como gerente del cine de pago, comprobaba personalmente que el porno era lo más vendido: por encima de cualquier estreno de cine convencional y a veces incluso por delante de algún partido de fútbol. La aplicación informática no mentía y, por ejemplo, una vez, los abonados, a través de los descodificadores, habían comprado sólo en un fin de semana 7.589 veces *Marranas a cuatro patas*... ¡y puedo jurar que no fui yo desde el descodificador de mi casa!

El cine X mueve millones

La prensa, a veces, publica cifras y datos no contrastados, lo cual hincha desmesuradamente la supuesta rentabilidad de la pornografía. El error reside en confundir el negocio del sexo (que indudablemente sí genera ingentes beneficios, y donde podemos incluir desde la lencería a los preservativos, los fármacos y productos relacionados con disfunciones, profilaxis y ETS, los portales de sexo *on-line*, las revistas pornográficas, la prostitución, los contactos, etc.) y el cine X en sí mismo, que está atravesando la peor crisis de su historia, por culpa de Internet, fuente inagotable de contenido X gratuito, la era digital, que provoca el exceso de producto, y las televisiones locales que emiten porno en abierto. Ya están las productoras moviéndose para frenar esta debacle...

JUAN A. (Productor y distribuidor. Interselección): Mira, me parece que todo esto de los miles de millones que mueve el porno es simplemente que la prensa y la televisión se inventan unas cantidades que no tienen que ver con la realidad. ¿Cómo pueden publicar que el porno en España mueve 60.000 millones de pesetas? ¿Es que la gente es gilipollas? Si tiramos adelante es porque tocamos todos los mercados: vendemos a televisión, a kioscos, a *sex shops*... Y con todo y con eso, con dificultad llegamos a amortizar los derechos, el doblaje, la carátula... El conjunto de todo sí te permite ir para delante, pero con el negocio del porno en España nadie se ha hecho rico. Aquí, las cantidades son ridículas...

Porno gay

Cuando dirigí el primer canal de porno gay de pago en este país, el TripleXXX de Vía Digital, allá por 1999, se registraron récords de taquilla. Detectamos picos de consumo a media mañana, indicio claro de que entre las amas de casa el porno gay era algo muy bien recibido. Esto es comprensible, ya que, igual que a los chicos les excita mucho ver a dos o más mujeres montándoselo, (constituye una de las fantasías masculinas más recurrentes), a las mujeres, ¿por qué no?, también nos encanta ver juntos a dos o más maromos de gimnasio, musculosos, curtidos por el sol y rasurados. (¡Viva el porno gay americano!) Si se aplicara un criterio estricto, deberían incluirse en este género también las secuencias en las que se realizan dúos o tríos lésbicos. Sin embargo, por puro machismo, de modo habitual cada película porno incluye escenas de dos o tres chicas enrolladas y metiéndose enormes juguetes por cualquier parte, sin ninguna participación masculina... El cine X gay se considera un subgénero dentro del porno, lo que implica que los actores gays cobren más,[31] especialmente los Top Man... (no así las chicas, que cobran menos por las escenas lésbicas). Por cierto, Top Man es el actor principal, el centro de atención de la escena; él no chupa nada de nadie, ni tolera que le eyaculen encima, ni es penetrado. El Top Man, da, da, da (además de contar con un físico espectacular, secretamente informaré que suelen ser heterosexuales).

---

31. Esto era cierto hasta hace poco. Por no extenderme: ahora en el mercado pornográfico se ha devaluado todo tanto, que hay quienes participan en películas sin cobrar, totalmente gratis. Desde ciertas productoras se ha logrado manipular a la opinión pública, consiguiendo mentir a la sociedad entera, haciendo ver que «mola ser actor porno» porque, supuestamente, viven en la opulencia. Falso, falso, falso. En el porno sólo se forran cuatro y, encima, ahí están decenas de chicos que se mueren de hambre en sus países de origen, dispuestos a todo por cincuenta euros, metiéndose una polla ajena en la boca o por el culo, con la improbable meta del estrellato en el horizonte, eso sí, revalorizándose como gogós de discoteca, *strippers* y, especialmente, como chaperos, que de algo hay que comer. Lo dicho se aplica a infinidad de actrices X dentro del *mainstream*. Mis palabras están exentas de crítica moral, pero no de crítica...

¿Lo suyo es puro teatro?

En el porno, ¿todo es trabajo puro y duro? Si se piensa fríamente, se trata de actores pero, habida cuenta que el 90 % de su interpretación se basa en realizar actos sexuales que terminan en orgasmos grabados, cuesta encontrar «sólo» el matiz laboral... Sí, en efecto, hay ocasiones en que el placer y la atracción son reales entre los actores, pero no siempre. Ellos lo explican muy bien ante mi pregunta: *Oye, las chicas, las actrices, con tanto gemido y tanto alarido de mentira... ¿tú te acabas de creer los gritos que escuchas luego en tu vida privada?*

MAX CORTÉS: La que haga eso en su vida privada es que es imbécil, porque el tío se cree que lo está haciendo muy bien y así ella nunca va a disfrutar. Yo también finjo en las películas, pego unos gritos que no son, a veces no me gusta la chica pero hago ver que sí, [...] busco algo que me guste en ella [...]. He llegado a rodar una escena completa pensando en los pendientes que llevaba puestos. Te lo juro. Tengo la desgracia de que el dinero no me la pone dura. Pienso que un actor porno nunca podrá interpretar un papel tan bien como un actor convencional, porque no somos iguales, y probablemente Brad Pitt no podrá follar ocho horas encima de una palmera. No pasa nada.

LAYLA RIVIERA: Lo que más me gusta es que el tío esté cachondo. Si lo está, yo me excito mucho y entonces, me meto en la escena y no tengo que fingir. Si está bueno y tiene ganas, para mí es perfecto porque no tengo que actuar, me dejo llevar... Somos él y yo, y nada más, e incluso te diría algo más, y es que yo no suelo correrme, no, en serio, no me corro, pero en esos casos, sí que me corro.

Curro duro

Nadie es ajeno al hecho de que todos los trabajos tienen facetas ingratas. Aquí he recogido algunas de las confesiones de los protagonistas del *hard*, acerca de los sacrificios, el dolor o lo más escatológico, lo que no vemos de una peli porno.

SILVIA SAINT (actriz): En esta industria nada es fácil... Este trabajo no es fácil, especialmente si te metes en producciones de bajo presupuesto. Piensa que, además, siempre hay gente maleducada, incorrecta, que no es puntual... Desde fuera se ve el cine X como algo que va exclusivamente de «di esta frase» y de follar... No es así. Hay mucho más, mil aspectos más. No es fácil ser independiente, créeme.

Riesgo de sida y otras enfermedades

So pretexto de que sólo se filma si el reparto aporta una analítica reciente, en España no se utiliza preservativo a la hora de rodar las escenas de las películas X, a diferencia de Francia o de Estados Unidos donde sí es habitual e incluso obligatorio.

MAX CORTÉS (actor): El test de las enfermedades me parece fiable en la misma medida que cuando, al subir a un avión, te dan las instrucciones del chaleco salvavidas. En teoría estamos suficientemente cubiertos. Nosotros nos hacemos el test cada 15 días y, ahora, se ha generalizado lo que llamamos el *full test*: es VIH, hepatitis y clamidia, gonorrea y sífilis. Estas últimas, si las tienes, hoy día son 5 días lo que tardan en irse, hay medicamentos. Las otras, sí son graves: la hepatitis, por ejemplo, es algo a lo que los doctores tienen mucho miedo, más que al VIH.

Mamá: quiero ser... ¡estrella porno!

Durante este tiempo de mi vida he reflexionado acerca de detalles tan pintorescos como: «Mientras tú te debatías entre Letras o Ciencias mixtas, hay quienes optaban por meterse en el porno»... Convertirse en estrella del cine X no es algo que ninguno se planteara de pequeño, eso os lo garantizo. Al preguntarles *¿cómo llegas al porno?* Obtuve la misma respuesta en el 95 % de los casos: «Por casualidad.» Ya, ya, así es como te encuentras un billete por la calle... pero bueno. También caí en el topicazo de interesarme por *¿Y tu familia se tomó bien esta decisión?*

RAMÓN NOMAR: Ahora se lo toman bien, pero al principio... Fueron días duros, de los de pensarse si volver o no a casa. Mi familia sentía rechazo hacia un negocio que no conocía. Ahora lo llevan de otra forma, saben que hay pruebas de sida, que no hay tantas mafias como parece, que las drogas no me tienen por qué influir...

ANASTASIA MAYO: Mis padres son mi primer apoyo. Creo que sin ellos, hacer esto me resultaría muy difícil. También cuento con mis amigos y el resto de mi familia. Cuando me inicié en esto, tampoco se asombraron, ni mucho menos...

Ellas y el sexo

Una de las cuestiones que más morbo suscita es tratar de imaginar qué les gusta de verdad a estas musas del erotismo. Cuando, puntualmente, he logrado acceder a la intimidad de algunas de estas mujeres descubro la paradoja de que son idénticas a las demás, siendo a la vez diametralmente opuestas. Me explico. Casi todas buscan, o si no buscan —ya está bien que hasta yo me meto en la corriente de que «la tía persigue atrapar a un hombre»— sí que disfrutan de lo mismo que cualquier chica. A todas nos gusta que nos traten un poquito mal, en el sentido de que «el canalla» y «el duro» interesan más que «el babosito» y «el tímido», pero luego, pasado un primer instante (el de la conquista), queremos reírnos, tener algo de lo que hablar y disfrutar de buen sexo. Eso sí, ellas, a fuerza de práctica y por haber sufrido en sus propias carnes la decepción de enamorarse del actor con el que «sólo» estaba «trabajando», han aprendido a desconectar sexo y emociones. Dunia Montenegro me aconsejaba: «Lo mejor es disimular esa carita de boba que se nos queda a todas cuando nos acostamos con alguien que nos gusta y evitar decirle lo típico: "mañana nos vemos", "llámame luego"... Lo que funciona es hacer como si nada, aunque por dentro estés enamoradita perdida.»

Muchos se sorprenden cuando saben que tienen novios o maridos, relaciones más o menos estables... y es que son verdaderas expertas en separar sexo de amor o afecto, lo cual a la mayoría les deja perplejos, ya que ¡se comportan como los tíos!, y eso rompe esquemas. Pretender ligarse a una *pornstar* es tarea difícil, están hartas de que les entren y, ciertamente, las tácticas usuales parecen sacadas de un libro comprado en un Todo a cien, a base de patéticas frases hechas, que no las sorprenden y que denotan siempre desesperación y falta de imaginación (y frecuentemente, de tacto). Cuando me preguntan, amigos y conocidos que saben que en alguna ocasión he salido por ahí o he coincidido con ellas en fiestas, yo les digo: «Si te cruzas con una, adelante, inténtalo. Tienes un 350 % de posibilidades de estrellarte, pero también es difícil ganar en la lotería, y hay a quien le toca, ¿no?»

La química del amor

Los actores a veces deciden con quién trabajan, pero lo normal es que lleguen al set de rodaje y conozcan allí mismo a sus compañeras de escena... *¿Qué pasa si no se gustan, se detestan, o si tienen un día malo?*

RAMÓN NOMAR: Todos hemos tenido algún gatillazo. En el porno un gatillazo significa no cobrar. Conseguir una erección es muy importante para ganarse el dinero. Para tirar para delante se puede recurrir a medicamentos, Viagra, inyecciones y todo tipo de drogas. Hay trucos, cada uno utiliza el suyo. No todas las mujeres me gustan, evidentemente. Cuando veo que puedo tener un gatillazo, como sé las consecuencias que eso implica, que es no cobrar, pues recurro a medicamentos y me olvido de todo.

PEDRO MARTÍN MAZZA (uno de los actores porno gay españoles de mayor proyección mundial): Te juro que yo tampoco lo entiendo, porque incluso con la Viagra... Tú te tomas una Viagra y te ayuda, pero necesitas estar un poco motivado. Si no, tampoco te empalmas. Luego hay otras historias, como el Cavernjet, que yo lo uso para los *shows* en vivo, porque hay tanta gente delante que no te puedes concentrar... En las salas, en esos bolos con miles de personas delante, no te empalmas, y entonces me lo pongo, pero dura una hora u hora y media. Se inyecta la mitad en cada lado de la polla, si no, si sólo lo pones en un lado, se te queda torcida. Ya tengo práctica. Sólo lo hago para los *shows*, para las películas nunca me ha hecho falta. Cuando voy a hacer bolos me preguntan preocupados «¿y si te corres?», ¡pero no sé cómo me voy a correr yo ahí, con tres mil personas gritando! En un *show* o en un *striptease* estás pendiente de la coreografía, del foco, de no tropezar... Trabajo cada mes en París en una sesión gay y me preocupo del *show*, no de mi polla.

El caché

¿Cuánto cobran los actores porno? ¿Resulta rentable? Un matiz: los profesionales del porno obtienen ingresos por varias vías. Intervienen en películas X y en editoriales de fotos *hard* y *soft*, gestionan sus páginas web (muchas con contenidos de pago), actúan en salas, eventos y festivales con números eróticos y haciendo sexo en vivo, acuden como invitados a los programas de televisión, etc.

SALVADOR DIAGO (Productor. IFG): El caché va desde 500 a 2.000 euros, pero hay gente que no tiene precio. Si tú quieres trabajar con Rocco resulta que no lo vas a poder contratar, porque él sólo hace sus películas y, si acepta hacerla contigo, igual no te pide dinero, sino [...]. O Nacho, que no trabaja ya para nadie. Si trabaja para nosotros lo hace por amistad, y no cobra, porque si cobrara [...]. Un actor normal cobra desde 400 euros por escena.

MARTÍN MAZZA: Claro, es por dinero. Incluso en productoras fuertes como Belami, que saca siempre chicos muy guapitos, tipo modelo, siempre sonriendo y tal... Es una cosa muy rara. Los chicos del Este cobran muy poco, pero allí, en países como Hungría o Chequia es una fortuna. Los de las productoras los cogen y además les pagan los estudios, o la casa para su familia, por eso no salen del porno, siguen y siguen durante años, te hablo de tíos heteros que hacen porno gay sólo por la pasta. Por eso los chicos españoles nunca vamos allí, porque pagan poco.

Estigma

Como esto es algo que he vivido en primera persona, no necesito que nadie me cuente que, por tener relación, sea del tipo que sea, con la industria del porno, se sufre rechazo. Resulta que los mismos que exigían ver mis títulos universitarios y los certificados de los másters para hacerme el contrato, o mis propios compañeros, que conocían mi trabajo, luego me trataban como a una apestada por ser quien gestionaba los contenidos para adultos (eso sí: cada viernes, se acercaban por mi despacho, de uno en uno, para pedirme el mejor DVD porno para verlo en sus casas...). ¿En qué quedamos? Me planteo que, si a mí, que no hago porno y que mi opción sexual es hacerlo en privado y gratis, se me trata así, *¿cómo tratan a los actores?*

ROCCO (actor y director): Siempre pienso en una balanza, para cada decisión en mi vida. Sabía los riesgos: el sida, estar en el gueto, que la gente te mire como a un animal... pero mi caparazón era lo bastante duro como para estar en la industria, así que pensaba «¡que les den!», y busqué y encontré mi felicidad en ella.

SALVADOR DIAGO (Productor. IFG): Creo que es un problema de cultura y también de doble moral: aquí todo el mundo niega que ve porno, y todo el mundo va de que es perfecto. Por eso, cuando se enteran de que trabajas en el porno, ya eres un bicho raro. Es, primero, por desconocimiento, porque yo te aseguro que tengo amistades de todo tipo: políticos, médicos, empresarios... y porque no puedo hablar, que si yo te contase cosas que han pasado... Yo he visto cosas más fuertes, y mucho peores, fuera del mundo del porno, bastantes más. Hay mucho más desmadre y se explota mucho más a la gente en el mundo del cine convencional que en el del porno. Es la doble moral. Yo mismo, hasta que mis hijos no han sido mayores, no he sido capaz de decir que trabajaba en esto, porque ellos iban a un colegio privado, y así evitaba que les mirasen con mala cara... Y como ahí, en muchos sitios. Luego ya no, ahora son mayores y de hecho, uno de ellos trabaja conmigo y está orgulloso.

Cine amateur: sexo y cintas de vídeo

Varios elementos confluyen estos días: mucho sexo en todas partes, cuerpos desnudos en cine, publicidad, televisión...; mucho narcisismo, en una era donde el físico manda, registramos los mayores índices de exhibicionismo de la historia, carne y más carne por donde mires; ya no se reserva nada a la intimidad, ni el más mínimo pudor a la hora de ventilar asuntos delicados —en otro tiempo— como el duelo y la muerte, las rupturas sentimentales, las operaciones quirúrgicas... Hoy todo es «contenido» de televisión o de Internet. Hay más prisa que nunca por forrarse sea como sea y a costa de lo que haga falta. «Ser famoso», eso es lo que los niños de hoy responden al clásico: «Y tú, de mayor, ¿qué quieres ser?», pero saltándose el «¿y qué vas a hacer para merecerlo?». Charlas morales aparte, el caso es que la gente ahora lo cuelga absolutamente todo en Youtube y páginas parecidas. ¿Democracia en la creación y emisión de contenidos? Sí, y bienvenida sea, pero salta a la vista que algo falla cuando se quema a un mendigo con el único propósito de subir el vídeo... Y en esto, llegamos al fenómeno del cine X *amateur*. Una mezcla de tecnología básica y de erotismo a partes iguales. El voyeurismo, el exhibicionismo, la pasión, la afición por el porno, las vocaciones de actor/actriz frustradas, el sentido del humor y la ausencia del más mínimo pudor (o de las nociones básicas de ridículo), la curiosidad, las ganas de experimentar tanto sensaciones como técnicas, lleva a muchas parejas a grabar sus polvos. El destino de esas cintas, las pruebas del «delito», ha sido causa de más de un disgusto y quebradero de cabeza, porque, cuando la relación va viento en popa, nadie se acuerda de las películas caseras.

11

Cirugía íntima

Si desde sus comienzos la mayor parte de los arreglitos de cirugía estética se demandaban para eliminar complejos y deformidades visibles, un alto porcentaje de las más recientes intervenciones se encamina a la implementación del atractivo «íntimo»... Cirugía de aumento de pene, vaginoplastia, recorte de los labios mayores y/o menores de la vagina, implante de prótesis mamarias, etc., son el último grito (¿de dolor?) en esta especialidad, la Estética, en la que nuestro país ocupa el cuarto puesto, a nivel mundial, en cuanto a número de intervenciones anuales, precedido sólo de Estados Unidos, Brasil y Venezuela.

Cirugía íntima masculina

Aumento de pene

Se ha desarrollado una técnica con la que se logra un alargamiento de tres o cuatro centímetros, mediante el corte del ligamento suspensorio del pene. Se practica una incisión justo en la base del pene, se dan unos puntos y ya está. Esta operación no influye en la erección. El corte es en el ligamento, lo cual no tiene relación con ninguna otra funcionalidad. Está indicado para pacientes que tengan el pene pequeño o disminución de pene, ya que ganarán varios centímetros.

No está indicada una operación cuando el pene es «normal».

Técnicas quirúrgicas

A lo largo de estos meses, he leído que otro método para agrandar el pene consistiría en un aumento de la circunferencia a través de la inyección de las propias células grasas del paciente, extraídas por liposucción, dentro del espacio entre la piel del pene y el tejido eréctil a lo largo del tronco. Sin embargo, no he dado con ningún cirujano que apueste por este sistema. Afirman que es una práctica condenada al fracaso, en parte por la fragilidad de las células grasas (sólo aproximadamente un 10 % realmente sobrevive a la extracción). Por otro lado, aunque el sistema inmunológico del paciente no reaccionaría contra su propio tejido, la grasa que sobreviviría a la extracción y reinyección dentro del pene sería a menudo reabsorbida, resultando en una apariencia grumosa, distinta al tronco del pene. La mayoría de los pacientes sometidos a esta técnica manifiesta un alto nivel de descontento con la apariencia estética de sus penes posquirúrgicos; detestan la cicatriz, el ángulo de sus penes erectos, la apariencia desigual del tejido graso bajo la piel del pene, la suavidad del tejido graso comparado a la dureza subyacente del pene erecto, etc.

Describen en ciertas páginas web una técnica más moderna conocida como «injerto dérmico», que consiste en tomar tiras de tejido graso de la hendidura de la nalga en la parte de arriba de la pierna, y la inserción de este tejido bajo la piel del pene. Parece que este proceso da mejores resultados y mucho más estables en el tiempo. En cada caso, el cirujano decidirá si es posible y está indicado.

Remedios estéticos

Se trata de un recurso casero, un truco sencillo pero que funciona, es barato, eficaz y al alcance de cualquiera: recortar el vello púbico de toda la zona, incluidos los testículos, dejando la base del pene despejada. El efecto óptico es que el pene se ve más grande.

La bioquímica

Cuidadito con los productos que prometen aumentar el tamaño del pene y que actúan como vasodilatadores. Ninguno funciona y pueden ser tóxicos e irritantes. Los extractos de ginseng y de ginkgo biloba, considerados afrodisíacos, tienen poder energizante y vigorizante; en determinados casos «animan» la cosa, pero no producen crecimiento.

Aparatos

También se ha aplicado la física y sus leyes gravitatorias a este asunto. Cada año se comercializan aparatejos que prometen alargar, a base de permanecer con el pene introducido en ciertas boquillas o piezas de succión durante varias horas al día, a lo largo de meses... Otros han probado los masajes manuales eternos, que se dan a diario, o incluso se cuelgan un peso importante del pene a fin de lograr que se alargue, que se estire, con la intención de que ceda o dé de sí como hacen otros tejidos del cuerpo humano (los agujeros de las orejas de los africanos, o los labios en que se llega a meter un plato...). No ofrecen resultados perdurables aunque sirven en casos de disfunción eréctil para propiciar la irrigación y favorecer el endurecimiento del pene.

Lamentablemente estos procedimientos no funcionan, prometan lo que prometan sus prospectos... Aún no existe una técnica que consiga que el pene humano aumente su tamaño de modo permanente, salvo el procedimiento de faloplastia de aumento, intervención quirúrgica de cortar el ligamento suspensorio (que sólo logra aumentar, y no mucho, en estado de reposo, ¿y a quién le interesa eso?), y el «cosmético» de rasurar el vello. *Sorry, boys!*

Andropenis

El AndroPenis®[32] es un método mecánico, de tracción, para el alargamiento del pene. Asegura un aumento de 5 cm de largo y 1 cm

---

32. Clasificado como Aparato Médico de Tipo 1, ostenta la certificación sanitaria CE, en Europa.

de ancho, en un plazo relativamente breve (de 4 a 6 meses, eso sí, exige un uso constante).

Otros arreglos: ginecomastia

Cuando a los hombres se les desarrollan glándulas mamarias. Obviamente es un fenómeno anómalo y patológico y, aunque se considera «benigna» en la mayoría de los casos, tiene implicaciones físicas y psicológicas. Puede suceder durante la pubertad o como parte del envejecimiento. Cabe que se produzca la ginecomastia por cambios en el balance de dos hormonas: los estrógenos y la testosterona. En casos raros la ginecomastia es ocasionada por medicamentos (sean o no prescritos), por drogas, por tumores o por una enfermedad. Puede aparecer en un lado o en ambos y en algunos casos se observa galactorrea o salida de un flujo blanquecino por el pezón. Cuando el aumento se debe sólo al depósito de grasa subcutánea, se habla de *seudoginecomastia*. Si el problema no se soluciona dejando de tomar el medicamento o droga que está ocasionando la ginecomastia, o cuando está causada por una enfermedad o un tumor, procede el tratamiento y en ocasiones puede ser necesaria la cirugía para remover el exceso de tejido mamario. El tratamiento consiste en la extirpación de la glándula a través de un pequeño corte en la areola, cuando es una ginecomastia verdadera (con glándula mamaria), o bien eliminar la grasa con lipoescultura. Normalmente se realiza una combinación de ambas técnicas, con anestesia local y sedación y de forma ambulatoria, es decir, sin hospitalización. Cuesta entre 3.500 y 3.600 euros.

Mamoplastia masculina

Muchos hombres, especialmente preocupados por su aspecto y desarrollo muscular, acuden a esta técnica que consiste en la colocación de prótesis en la zona pectoral. El posoperatorio es bastante molesto y doloroso, pero se obtiene el resultado mucho más rápido que yendo al gimnasio a sudar... Suele realizarse con anestesia local y sedación, y no requiere ingreso hospitalario. Cuesta entre 4.500 y 5.000 euros.

Gluteoplastia

La búsqueda de la perfección no tiene límites... Hay quienes, literalmente, vienen sin culo de serie y los hay que, movidos por la envidia suscitada por traseros de iconos como Brad Pitt o Antonio Banderas, los exhibidos hasta la saciedad, llegan a las consultas de cirugía en pos de unas nalgas que revienten el vaquero. La operación se practica con anestesia local y sedación, mediante una incisión en la zona de entre los glúteos, formando un bolsillo hacia el lado donde se coloca cada prótesis y con una sutura que después no se ve. El paciente se va a casa al rato. El coste ronda los 8.000 euros.

CIRUGÍA ÍNTIMA FEMENINA

Labioplastia

En algunas ocasiones los labios mayores pierden la grasa y se ven muy plegados debido al envejecimiento u otros factores. Puede corregirse mediante un procedimiento de microcirugía de invasión mínima llamado lipoescultura, en el cual se puede tomar grasa de la parte interna de los muslos u otro sitio y ser trasplantada a los labios mayores para lograr una apariencia más natural y joven de éstos.

Perineoplastia láser

Consiste en restaurar el perineo rejuveneciéndolo o reparando los daños sufridos por partos o por el transcurrir del tiempo, lográndose una apariencia más joven y estética de la vulva. El 90 % de partos vaginales llevan aparejado un corte (episiotomía) que facilita la salida de la cabeza del bebé. Cuando ha habido más de un corte, la apariencia de la vulva, por más que el vello lo pueda disimular —caso de no preferir la depilación—, se ve bastante desmejorada.

Clítoris

En ocasiones es necesaria su reducción y remodelación. Cuando es excesivamente largo, mediante una serie de incisiones con el objeto de que se reubique hacia atrás, es decir, hacia el interior. También se realiza la exposición de clítoris oculto *(lifting)*, a través de la reducción de la piel del capuchón que envuelve el mismo. Ambas se realizan bajo anestesia local y sedación, la duración de la intervención es de una hora aproximadamente, sin hospitalización, logrando que muchas mujeres disfruten de mejores relaciones, así como de una mejor calidad de vida.

G-Shot

Una inyección de colágeno en el punto G que mejora la satisfacción y el placer de la mujer durante las relaciones sexuales. Efectos: cuatro meses, porque se reabsorbe.

Vaginoplastia

Técnica quirúrgica de rejuvenecimiento vaginal. Se emplea para corregir el ensanchamiento de la vagina, como consecuencia no deseada de los partos, del envejecimiento o del deterioro muscular. Es una intervención sencilla llevada a cabo a través de la vagina, estrechándose la misma sin repercusión muscular. Se realiza bajo anestesia epidural, la duración de la intervención es de una hora aproximadamente, no requiriendo hospitalización médica.

Himenoplastia

Es la cirugía que repara el himen y «revirginiza» a la mujer. Al someterse a esta intervención las mujeres intentan mejorar sus vidas sexuales. Suele combinarse con una reducción quirúrgica del canal vaginal. La Sociedad Estadounidense de Cirujanos Plásticos (ASPS, por sus siglas en inglés) afirma que se trata de una de las cirugías más demandadas en los últimos tiempos. La mayoría de las pacientes la solicita por motivos religiosos y culturales (deben ser vírgenes para poder casarse) y también se plantea en ciertos casos de abuso sexual. Se realiza con un pequeño colgajo de la mucosa vaginal bajo anestesia local y sedación; sólo requiere anestesia local y algunos puntos reabsorbibles. La duración de la intervención es de 45 minutos aproximadamente. Este tipo de cirugía no requiere hospitalización. La recuperación lleva unas seis semanas y el riesgo de fiebre o de infección es bajo. Sin embargo, hay que ser consciente de que cuando la membrana vuelva a romperse, causará una ligera hemorragia y cierto dolor e incomodidad durante las relaciones sexuales, que puede prolongarse durante semanas. La segunda inconveniencia es que ésta es una operación bastante costosa para que dure sólo una noche...

Mamoplastia de aumento y mastopexia

El aumento del pecho mediante colocación de implantes o la reparación de los senos son las intervenciones estéticas más solicitadas, ya que la feminidad se vincula desde siempre a las mamas. Se describen tres tipos de intervención: periareolar, submamaria y axilar.

Los formatos habituales de la telerrealidad más soez se ven desplazados por programas sobre cirugía, sean de producción americana o *made in Spain*. Ya no es ciencia ficción eso de jugar a Dios o a los médicos siendo bien mayores; hoy que podemos, previo pago, escoger nuestra apariencia ante los demás, tampoco extraña que alguien demande una liposucción del monte de Venus o el diseño personalizado de la estructura vulvar, como son los labios mayores, menores, perineo, introito e incluso, la recuperación del himen. Infinidad de mujeres recurren a la cirugía para «subsanar particularidades» de sus zonas ocultas con las que no se sienten bien o para paliar el paso del tiempo. Se trata de anomalías que producen una quiebra de la autoestima o que les impiden sentirse seguras de sí mismas.

TERCERA PARTE

EL SEXO, DE LA *A* A LA *Z*

A, el punto A: el punto erógeno del fornex anterior, ubicado en la pared frontal de la vagina, a un tercio de distancia desde el cérvix, próximo al punto G, es un punto extremadamente sensible, casi de «orgasmo instantáneo». Fue descubierto oficialmente en 1996 por el sexólogo Chua Chee Ann, investigando acerca de la sequedad vaginal, y por pura casualidad constataron que un 95 % de las mujeres se excitaba enormemente con la estimulación de ese punto y que lubricaban en menos de 10 minutos. Algunas participantes tuvieron su primera experiencia orgásmica durante el estudio científico. Ver el capítulo «Anatomía básica».

Ablación: significa amputar o extirpar. La mutilación genital femenina (MGF) comenzó a practicarse en África y Oriente Medio. Existen varios tipos de ablación: la *clitoridectomía*, que amputa el clítoris en su totalidad; la *circuncisión*, que retira la parte de alrededor o capuchón del clítoris; la *escisión* o *mutilación total*, que abarca el clítoris y labios menores, conservando los mayores; y la *infibulación* —la más cruenta—, mediante la que se extirpan el clítoris y labios mayores y menores, para proceder a coser la vulva a cada lado hasta que queda casi cerrada, dejando un orificio para que salgan la orina y la sangre menstrual.

La ablación aún se realiza en determinados países con el fin de iniciar a la niña en la pubertad y que llegue virgen al matrimonio. Aunque se buscan excusas religiosas, ni en el Corán ni en la Biblia se justifica; en realidad, persigue privar a la mujer de los órganos genitales externos, los que pueden darle placer sexual, puesto que el efecto que causa es la eliminación de la sensibilidad y un enorme dolor con la penetración. La precariedad del instrumental y la falta de cualificación de quienes la llevan a cabo (curanderas y mujeres mayores) causan numerosas muertes por desangramiento e infecciones gravísimas (gangrena, úlceras, septicemia y tétano). Para las mujeres que son víctimas de la ablación el coito siempre será doloroso —es un modo de impedir que ejerzan libremente su sexualidad, de convertirla en un infierno—; correrán riesgo de complicaciones a largo plazo —retención de flujo menstrual que causa infertilidad, obstrucciones que impiden la salida de la orina—; la tasa de muerte del bebé si la madre ha sido mutilada es hasta un 55 % más alta, y los traumas psicológicos permanecen de por vida. Leí que son 130 millones de mujeres y niñas las afectadas por esta mutilación, y que cada vez se realiza a edad más temprana, para impedir que la eviten o se revuelvan. Actualmente, ya no queda margen de duda entre la colisión de un derecho a las costumbres y a las raíces culturales y los derechos fundamentales a la vida, a la seguridad y a la libertad, la integridad física y la salud, por lo que casi todos los países tipifican las distintas clases de ablación. Sin embargo, y pese a la labor de UNICEF y de Naciones Unidas, aún se practica de modo clandestino y se sigue trasladando a niñas a sus países de origen para someterlas a MGF.

Aborto: interrupción voluntaria o involuntaria del embarazo. Se habla de aborto cuando la interrupción del embarazo se produce antes de la semana 21 de gestación (a partir de entonces se denomina *parto pretérmino*). Durante el primer trimestre de gestación las probabilidades de que se produzca un aborto espontáneo se elevan. Más de un 50 % de los abortos se produce por alteraciones genéticas en el embrión; además, se puede deber a malformaciones uterinas, miomas y otras patologías orgánicas en el útero, insuficiencia del cérvix uterino, insuficiencia hormonal, sobre todo de progesterona, y enfermedad materna sistémica grave, como la diabetes o enfermedad tiroidea.

A veces, el aborto viene provocado por causas extrínsecas como grandes dosis de radiación y ciertos fármacos. Sólo en un porcentaje muy reducido de los casos son desconocidas las causas del aborto. El aborto tardío o «bebé muerto» se produce por una dilatación prematura del cuello del útero o cérvix incompetente, que provoca la ruptura de la bolsa de líquido amniótico, y por problemas de la placenta.

Ante el sangrado o los dolores o cualquier signo o síntoma de amenaza de aborto, se debe buscar asistencia médica prenatal inmediatamente.

Se distingue pues el aborto incidental o espontáneo del provocado, que no es, en ningún caso, un método anticonceptivo... A continuación recojo la legislación española vigente. El aborto en principio está tipificado, tanto para la mujer como para quien se lo practica. Otra cosa es que se haya incorporado una lista de supuestos que establecen unas circunstancias (plazos, dictámenes médicos) que, de concurrir, lo despenalizan. Lo explico así porque casi todo el mundo cree que «el aborto es legal en España». No, no lo es; otro tema es que para determinados casos se pueda practicar sin sanción penal, y otra, comúnmente barajada en la calle, que con alegar en una clínica privada «sufrir depresión», previo pago, al final resulte relativamente sencillo abortar. Para la mujer las secuelas físicas de un aborto no suelen ser graves. Se recomienda esperar unos tres meses para intentar una nueva gestación. Otro asunto son las secuelas morales y psicológicas, que sí se dan. La pérdida de un bebé deseado causa desde depresión a crisis de pareja y, dentro del aborto provocado, hasta en los casos más claros (malformaciones del feto; grave riesgo para la vida de la madre) la mujer atraviesa estados de ánimo bajos, de depresión y de tristeza.

Sobre la colisión entre derecho a la vida y derecho a decidir sobre la capacidad reproductiva se podrían escribir cien libros, pero éste no es uno de ellos.

Artículo 145 del Código Civil.

1. El que produzca el aborto de una mujer, con su consentimiento, fuera de los casos permitidos por la Ley, será castigado con la pena de prisión de uno a tres años e inhabilitación especial para ejercer cualquier profesión sanitaria, o para prestar servicios de toda índole en clínicas, establecimientos o consultorios ginecológicos, públicos o privados, por tiempo de uno a seis años.

2. La mujer que produjere su aborto o consintiere que otra

persona se lo cause, fuera de los casos permitidos por la Ley, será castigada con la pena de prisión de seis meses a un año o multa de seis a veinticuatro meses.

El artículo 417 bis del Código Penal queda redactado de la siguiente manera:

1. No será punible el aborto practicado por un médico, o bajo su dirección, en centro o establecimiento sanitario, público o privado, acreditado y con consentimiento expreso de la mujer embarazada, cuando concurra alguna de las circunstancias siguientes:

1. Que sea necesario para evitar un grave peligro para la vida o la salud física o psíquica de la embarazada y así conste en un dictamen emitido con anterioridad a la intervención por un médico de la especialidad correspondiente, distinto de aquel por quien o bajo cuya dirección se practique el aborto.

En caso de urgencia por riesgo vital para la gestante, podrá prescindirse del dictamen y del consentimiento expreso.

2. Que el embarazo sea consecuencia de un hecho constitutivo de delito de violación del artículo 429, siempre que el aborto se practique dentro de las doce primeras semanas de gestación y que el mencionado hecho hubiese sido denunciado.

3. Que se presuma que el feto habrá de nacer con graves taras físicas o psíquicas, siempre que el aborto se practique dentro de las veintidós primeras semanas de gestación y que el dictamen, expresado con anterioridad a la práctica del aborto, sea emitido por dos especialistas de centro o establecimiento sanitario, público o privado, acreditado al efecto, y distintos de aquel o bajo cuya dirección se practique el aborto.

4. En los casos previstos en el número anterior, no será punible la conducta de la embarazada aun cuando la práctica del aborto no se realice en un centro o establecimiento público o privado acreditado o no se hayan emitido los dictámenes médicos exigidos.

Abstinencia: consiste en no realizar algo libremente o decidir no tomar partido. En el terreno sexual, según muchos, es la mejor manera para evitar el embarazo y para no contraer ETS, pero en estos momentos, habiendo y pudiendo emplear métodos anticonceptivos y profilácticos apropiados, no hay razón para ello. En sociedades menos desarrolladas o con menor acceso a la cultura, se trata de controlar a la población mediante la abstinencia, con la finalidad de frenar la propagación de sida —aunque esta pandemia sólo se frena con el uso de preservativos— y otras enfermedades o de controlar la superpoblación. Puede ser una opción personal o decidirse en pareja, bien referida a la totalidad de las prácticas o a algunas —por ejemplo, si se sigue una terapia, no practicar la penetración en las fases de reaprendizaje para frenar la eyaculación precoz; o no hacer sexo anal porque a ella le desagrada—. Otro motivo para optar por la abstinencia sería la prudencia: cuando se aguarda a conocer el resultado de análisis de enfermedades y por la concurrencia de síntomas, se teme estar infectado; o si se intenta recuperar el deseo sexual, la pareja puede decidir, por ejemplo, que sólo besarse está «permitido», creando un juego de excitación durante las fechas convenidas para acrecentar las ganas.

Adicción al sexo. Ver su capítulo específico.

Adulterio: consiste en mantener relaciones sexuales con alguien distinto del cónyuge. Equivale, por tanto, a la infidelidad matrimonial. Según la Iglesia, basta con mirar y desear a otra mujer, si eres un hombre, y viceversa; la posición religiosa, además de más estricta (incurres en él incluso sólo con el pensamiento) y vinculada al pecado y al fuego eterno, es estrictamente heterosexual. Así se pronuncian el Sexto mandamiento («No cometerás adulterio») y todo el Nuevo Testamento. De un modo civil y lingüístico, el adulterio se condena también. La misma expresión «cometer» adulterio ya lo connota. El adúltero es quien rompe su compromiso de fidelidad, atenta por tanto contra la institución del matrimonio, que no es sino un contrato donde pone bien clarito que la fidelidad es una de las obligaciones. Legalmente, en 1978 dejó de ser un delito privado —sólo perseguible por querella y donde cabía el «perdón» del marido agraviado— y que aparejaba la pena de prisión menor (de seis

meses y un día a seis años); se regulaba junto con el amancebamiento: tener una «querida» o amante, que por cierto, también castigaba al esposo culpable con misma pena de prisión menor, igual que a la amante... En la actualidad, la infidelidad ya no se sanciona con cárcel, y que se sea adúltero no condiciona la concesión de la guarda y custodia de los hijos, por ejemplo. Sin embargo, sí se aduce como causa para solicitar separaciones y divorcios y sí cabe desheredar a quien te ha puesto los cuernos (¡faltaría más!).

Afrodisíaco: cualquier sustancia o actividad que estimule o aumente el deseo sexual. Su nombre es una referencia a Afrodita, la diosa griega del amor que simboliza la sensualidad, el placer y el erotismo. Se maneja la palabra «anafrodisíaco» como término que designa justo lo contrario (lo que nos baja la libido, nos «corta el rollo» o nos da repugnancia en vez de excitación). Ver el apartado sobre «Afrodisíacos».

Algofilia: designa la excitación mediante el dolor y también a su búsqueda durante el orgasmo. Se considera una de las parafilias. La activación del mecanismo de estímulo-respuesta, en este caso, hace que intervenga primero la piel (un pellizco, un azote, etc.), desde donde la señal será llevada al cerebro. Una sensación de dolor prolongada desencadena como respuesta de autodefensa del cuerpo la secreción de endorfinas. Ésa es la razón por la que el dolor gusta, porque la sensación que prevalece —ojo, si a nadie se le va la mano, porque mantener el frágil equilibrio dolor-placer es todo un arte— sería la de este opiáceo endógeno que causa analgesia, además de un efecto sedante similar al que genera la morfina (las endorfinas se segregan por estrés y dolor continuado, acupuntura, relaciones sexuales, práctica de deporte —especialmente aeróbico—, lo que explica que los deportistas tengan mejor humor y su umbral de dolor sea considerablemente más alto). Suele suceder, como en todo proceso donde se descarga adrenalina, que cada vez se precise mayor dolor para lograr la misma excitación/placer. Ello sólo significa que el dolor puede ser adictivo —con el riesgo que implica no ser consciente de si llegamos demasiado lejos, o en determinados casos, ser incapaz de parar a tiempo—. Por ello, muchas personas que comienzan con un simple azote (ver *spanking*), continúan en una peregrinación de sensaciones que pueden tener parada en cera derretida (quema; esta afición se denomina *candling*), pinzas (pellizcan, afición denominada zlipsosis), pinchazos (pungofilia), electrodos (descargas, llamada electrocutofilia), dispositivos de succión (ventosas o mecánicos, se llama *cupping*), penetraciones de extrema dilatación *(fisting)* e introducción de objetos por la uretra (gradualmente más grandes, desde termómetros a bolígrafos; una práctica común entre los gays, que se llama *stuffing*), ataduras, mordiscos, sexo en lugares peligrosos...

Alineación coital, técnica de: creada por Edward Eichel, psicoterapeuta y una eminencia dentro del campo de la sexualidad, la TAC (Técnica de Alienación Coital) es una variación de la postura llamada «misionero», tan denostada actualmente, pese a sus incuestionables ventajas de proporcionar una enorme intimidad, por aquello de estar frente a frente y poder besarse y mirarse a los ojos; pero, vamos, que si ha dejado de estar de moda es por su enorme mérito de generar la insatisfacción generalizada de las féminas. La diferencia con la tradicional es que con la TAC sí se estimulan el punto G y el clítoris, propiciando la simultaneidad de orgasmos. Se deben seguir algunos pasos para su logro: después de la estupenda hartada de besos, caricias y de proporcionarse placer mutua y recíprocamente, la pareja comienza colocándose en la postura del «misionero». El hombre se pone encima de la mujer, echando su peso sobre los codos. Ella deja caer sus piernas alrededor de los muslos del hombre quien, adelantándose algunos centímetros, la penetra, de modo que la base del pene quede apoyada contra el clítoris. Lo fundamental de esta técnica es que implica un movimiento rítmico, ondulante de ambos —aquí, para que funcione, no cabe que ella sea como una muñeca hinchable que se deja hacer, ni que él se dedique a las perforaciones incontroladas...—. Ese juego de presión, ese movimiento suave de ir y venir más que la incursión profunda del pene, permite que algunas veces logremos el tan ansiado orgasmo simultáneo por penetración.

Ambiente liberal: ver *swingers/swinging*.

Amenorrea: ausencia permanente o temporal de menstruación («a» significa «sin»). La fisiológica (normal) se da, por ejemplo, desde que la chica nace hasta su primera regla —menarquia, que viene normalmente entre los diez y los quince años—. Tampoco hay regla durante los meses (normalmente nueve) de embarazo, durante el inicio de la lactancia y, por supuesto, con la menopausia. Otro momento de amenorrea sería el que transcurre de «retraso» cuando se han mantenido relaciones sexuales y la regla no se produce en la fecha prevista. En su vertiente patológica, es decir, indicativa de enfermedad, se puede presentar amenorrea por anorexia, excesivo estrés y tumoraciones en los ovarios, el útero, etc. Lo más conveniente es acudir al ginecólogo.

Amor: sentimiento intenso de atracción, apego y deseo hacia alguien o algo. Muchas veces se confunde con el enamoramiento y con la lujuria. El amor tiene tres elementos básicos: intimidad, compromiso y sexo.

Andrógenos: término que engloba todas las hormonas sexuales masculinas: la testosterona, la androsterona y la androstendiona. Las segregan fundamentalmente los testículos y las glándulas suprarrenales, pero también los ovarios en el caso de las mujeres (androstendiona). Su función es virilizante y anabolizante de las proteínas.

Andrómana, postura de: ella arriba, hombre abajo. Ella controla la situación, decide la profundidad, la presión y la velocidad. Inclinando sus caderas hacia delante, frota su clítoris contra el pubis de su compañero logrando una intensa estimulación que facilita el orgasmo femenino durante el coito.

Andromanía: el trastorno adictivo respecto del sexo. Es como la ninfomanía, pero para ellos. Se denomina también satiriasis. Ver capítulo sobre «Adicción al sexo».

Andropausia: lo que en la mujer se denomina menopausia encuentra en el hombre su equivalente, o casi. En el hombre se produce la andropausia que, además de efectos psicológicos de asumir el paso del tiempo, actúa sobre su virilidad (menor capacidad de erección, menor cantidad de semen en las eyaculaciones, mayor necesidad de estímulo y alargamiento del período refractario). Lo que no se ve mermada por el paso del tiempo quizá sea su capacidad reproductiva. Un hombre puede ser fértil hasta muy avanzada edad, ellos no tienen un reloj biológico. Resulta curioso, y extraordinariamente preciso, el «Siete yin y el Ocho yang», cifras que los antiguos chinos empleaban para explicar el desarrollo de la mujer y del hombre. El número 7 en Chi Kung representa el «yin espiritual», y describe los períodos de la vida de la mujer. A los 7 años sus dientes y cabello crecen. A los 14 empieza a menstruar y puede tener hijos. A los 21 ha completado su crecimiento y su condición física se encuentra en su mejor punto. A los 28 sus músculos son firmes y su cuerpo florece. A los 35 el rostro empieza a tener arrugas y el cabello a caer. A los 42 sus arterias empiezan a endurecerse y el cabello se vuelve blanco. A los 49 cesa la menstruación y ya no puede tener hijos.

El número 8 representa el «yang espiritual» y cumple el mismo papel en la vida del hombre. A la edad de 8 años, crece y empieza la segunda dentición. A los 16 empieza a secretar semen. A los 24 los testículos ya están formados y ha alcanzado su estatura máxima. A los 32 tiene los músculos firmes. A los 40 los testículos se empiezan a debilitar, empieza a perder pelo y los dientes inician su deterioro. A los 48 su vigor masculino está agotado, aparecen arrugas en su rostro y le salen canas. A los 56 sus secreciones disminuyen y los testículos se deterioran.

Aneyaculación: describe una disfunción sexual masculina que consiste en que, pese al deseo de eyacular, y tras un tiempo de estimulación, ésta no se produce. Es distinto del priapismo. Ver el apartado sobre «Eyaculación precoz o retardada».

Anorgasmia: disfunción sexual que implica la falta de orgasmos. Ver el capítulo «El orgasmo».

Anticonceptivo: cualquier método o procedimiento destinado a evitar o impedir el embarazo. Hay que saber que hasta el 50 % de los embarazos que se producen no son buscados. Los métodos anticonceptivos ayudan a que las personas puedan planificar su vida reproductiva (tanto en el número de hijos como en el tiempo que transcurre entre los nacimientos). Actualmente, existen muchos. El método ideal combinaría un 100 % de eficacia, con un 0 % de efectos secundarios, que impidiera todo tipo de contagio, tuviera bajo coste —o, ya puestos, que fuera gratuito—, que no interrumpiera la relación sexual y que fuera fácil de usar e indoloro. Aún no existe, lamentablemente. En el pasado, mujeres de todas las civilizaciones han empleado errónea y supersticiosamente desde brebajes, a saltos y posturas que ayudaban a expulsar el semen. El descubrimiento de las barreras aislantes se consideró lo más efectivo, ya que impedían que el semen llegara al óvulo. Se introducían en la vagina esponjas de mar envueltas en un trapo suave y empapadas de vinagre o de jugo de limón (considerados como espermicida). Las mujeres orientales recurrían a papel encerado y las europeas se introducían en la vagina cera de abejas. Una de las vitrinas del Museo Egipcio de El Cairo guarda una funda hecha con piel de cabra que, teóricamente, se empleó ya por los faraones como preservativo.

Los métodos anticonceptivos funcionan de diferentes maneras. Pueden:

- Evitar que el esperma llegue al óvulo.
- Matar los espermatozoides.
- Inhibir la ovulación mensual.
- Modificar la membrana mucosa que recubre el útero.
- Espesar la mucosa del cérvix para dificultar el acceso del esperma a través del mismo.

Ver el capítulo específico sobre «Anticonceptivos».

Areola: círculo entre rosáceo y marrón que rodea el pezón. Como los coches, los hay de muchos tamaños y colores. Ver el apartado de «Zonas erógenas».

Armarizado: viene de «estar en el armario», y se denomina así a la persona que aún no ha afirmado públicamente su homosexualidad.

Asfixia erótica: la respiración normal de las personas suele ser de 12 veces por minuto. Sin embargo, se puede variar el ritmo así como la profundidad de las inhalaciones para producir una leve alteración de la conciencia, breves desvanecimientos... La idea es provocar un desmayo mediante privación de oxígeno durante el orgasmo (bien apretando con la mano el cuello, bien metiendo la cabeza en una bolsa de plástico) y despertar al ratito con esa misma sensación (no se confunda con el momento en que con toda la pasión del momento, uno agarra firmemente, pero con cuidado, al otro del cuello). Las películas *El imperio de los sentidos* y *El sol naciente* refieren esta práctica. En la primera, se muestra cómo las prostitutas indochinas lo practicaban con sus clientes para potenciar el orgasmo; en la segunda, la modelo Tatiana Patitz, que encarna a una prostituta de lujo, muere durante el acto porque él se excede en el tiempo que mantiene la bolsa puesta y se asfixia.

La hiperventilación consiste en inhalar mucho más deprisa y superficialmente, exhalando demasiado dióxido de carbono, lo que causa mareos, hormigueo en determinadas zonas del cuerpo e incluso espasmos. Se pasa respirando dentro de una bolsa. El cerebro necesita oxígeno, y cuando le falta lo flipa. Se denomina anoxia a la falta de oxígeno en el cerebro (puede causar lesiones cerebrales irreversibles, coma y es potencialmente mortal). La hipoxia afecta a la capacidad para recordar, altera la percepción y ralentiza las respuestas físicas, produce somnolencia, mareo y euforia —causada por los mismos neurotransmisores que desencadenan la respuesta orgásmica, por ello, hay quien se desmaya durante el clímax—. Determinadas personas, por cuestiones obvias (edad avanzada, enfermedades cardiorrespiratorias, asma, hipertensión, etc.) no deben ni pensar en ellas. Por otro lado, no todo el mundo que ha oído hablar de estas prácticas de asfixia erótica domina la técnica (es muy fácil que te dejen en el sitio si no controlan de verdad y, aun así, siempre puede fallar algo y que tu organismo reaccione de un modo no esperado o que se produzca una situación que lamentar: ataque epiléptico, crisis cardíaca, daños irreversibles en laringe, tráquea y en la médula espinal). El término técnico es asfixiofilia. Algunas personas practican la asfixia autoerótica con la misma finalidad: intensificar los orgasmos —se estrangulan a sí mismas durante la masturbación, algo que, según datos de J. Money, causa entre 250 y 1.000 muertes anuales en Estados Unidos—. Como parafilia, la persona aficionada a la autoasfixiofilia halla el estímulo en ser asfixiada durante el acto sexual (a solas o con otro).

Autofelación: chicas, imposible. Tu gata puede, pero tú no. Sin embargo, ellos sí lo pueden lograr. Obviamente, si hay tráfico en las calles es porque ya han desistido de intentarlo —todos prueban alguna vez, por si sucede el milagro—. Supongo que la cuestión depende no sólo de que la tengan larguísima, sino de su flexibilidad. La posición más sencilla sería echar la barbilla hacia delante, inclinándose sobre el glande hasta atraparlo con la boca, pero como eso cuesta —y difícilmente se acercan a la meta—, algunos lo intentan colocándose en la cama, boca arriba, levantando los pies por encima de la cabeza hacia atrás. Así encontraron muerto a uno de los personajes de la inimitable película *Clerks* —la policía comentaba que el cadáver tenía los huevos en la boca, ¡así que lo logró!—. Ficción aparte, yo lo he visto hacer con mis propios ojos. Fue en la primera película porno que tuve que visionar, era porno gay y el tipo aquel tenía el típico cuerpo de maestro de yoga, nada que ver con los cachas de gimnasio americanos y un miembro que, por seguir con la referencia, parecía la serpiente kundalini recorriendo desde el chakra base al corona... muy larga, vaya.

Autosatisfación: otra forma de practicar la sexualidad sana. Ver *masturbación*.

Aversión: se trata de un desorden o disfunción sexual que indica rechazo hacia el sexo. Se puede dar el caso de rechazar toda conducta que implique juego o práctica sexual bien por causas hormonales o bien por haber sufrido episodios de violencia, agresión o abusos sexuales —violación, incesto, etc.—, o haberlos presenciado en su entorno cercano. Se trata en el capítulo «El orgasmo».

Azotes: ver *spaking*.

Balanitis: ETS que designa la inflamación del glande. El paciente con una balanitis se queja de hinchazón, punteado rojizo, secreción superficial (que no viene de la uretra) y picazón en el glande y prepucio. Raras veces se trata de una infección grave y, en la mayoría de los casos, es consecuencia de un contacto sexual con una persona que no muestra señales de infección pero que puede tener una candidiasis (hongo) o flujo vaginal patológico. El diagnóstico se hará tras un examen médico y estudio microbiológico. El tratamiento dependerá del germen que lo produzca.

Bareback: «a pelo». Sexo sin condón. Hacerlo sin protección no sólo implica riesgo de embarazo que, en general, es la gran amenaza bajo la que todos crecemos, sino que realmente implica jugarse la salud y, a veces, la vida por las ETS y el VIH. Lo peor es que se ha puesto de moda como una práctica «cotizada» en el ambiente gay especialmente, en la penetración anal, precisamente la que conlleva de por sí mayor peligro...

Bartolino, glándulas de: pertenecen al aparato reproductor femenino (en el hombre su equivalente son las glándulas de Cowper). Se trata de dos pequeñísimos apéndices ubicados a ambos lados del orificio vaginal. Su misión es la de segregar un fluido que contiene feromonas y que lubrica los labios vaginales y facilita, por tanto, la penetración. En principio, no son perceptibles a simple vista, salvo si se produce la bartolinitis, es decir, su inflamación por obstrucción o por una infección bacteriana y la subsiguiente acumulación de pus, que las hace además de bien visibles, muy doloro-sas. Se trata con antibióticos, antiinflamatorios y analgésicos, o bien, drenando la glándula mediante una incisión.

Beso negro: nada que ver con los inocentes «piquitos», ni con el apasionado «beso francés» (con lengua), que se dan en la boca, y mucho menos con los besos sociales que depositamos en las meji-llas de cualquiera. Tampoco marca tendencia en colores de pintala-bios. Por pérfido que sea el adjetivo «negro» colocado junto a casi cualquier sustantivo, en este caso, no es puro simbolismo... El *an-nalingus* consiste en la estimulación del ano de la pareja haciéndole caricias y succionando con la lengua y los labios. Con frecuencia, un *cunnilingus* deriva en ello, por pura proximidad geográfica. Es un error considerar o presumir que cuando lo recibe un varón se trata de un acto homosexual, puesto que el ano es una zona eró-gena —en todo el mundo: mujeres, hombres, heteros y gays—, concentra infinidad de terminaciones nerviosas y participa de las contracciones orgásmicas. Se explica en «Sexo anal», junto con los detalles a tener en consideración para hacerlo bien y de un modo seguro.

Bestialismo: esta práctica, que ninguno de los miembros de Green-peace alabaría, consiste en practicar sexo con animales. En porno-grafía, existe un género relacionado: la zoofilia. Considerada *extreme* o bizarra, las películas de esta disciplina muestran escenas con pene-traciones, cunnilingus y felaciones de mujeres con perros, cabras, ca-ballos, angulas, serpientes... Obviamente, también existen produc-ciones de *gays* abusando de sus animales. Ver *zoofilia*.

Bisexual: la persona que siente, indistintamente, atracción física por los de su mismo sexo y también por los del opuesto, y mantie-ne relaciones de tipo heterosexual y homosexual. Si bien cabe con-siderarlos como los «más confusos», también son los aventajados que tienen ante sí todo el Universo para elegir... lo que no implica ni indecisión ni promiscuidad (o no especialmente). Como opción sexual, se puede experimentar puntualmente, durante cierta etapa y condicionado por circunstancias que bien pueden permanecer o evolucionar a lo largo del tiempo. En el porno, las escenas de sexo entre chicas que después, o antes, han interactuado con hombres, no se catalogan como «bi». Por otro lado, existe una especie de ley no escrita en virtud de la cual, no se incluyen escenas homosexuales dentro del cine X *mainstream*. El género pornográfico «bi» se define por presencia de escenas homosexuales masculinas además de las de coitos heterosexuales. En ocasiones, la penetración del hombre se realiza mediante prótesis sujetas por un arnés a la cadera de la actriz. También suelen aparecer tríos formados por dos hombres y una chica donde, a diferencia del porno «convencional», sí interactúan los dos actores entre ellos.

Bondage: práctica que consiste en atar e inmovilizar al otro antes o durante la relación sexual, utilizando cuerdas especiales, mordazas o cadenas. Relacionado con el fetichismo, la estética erótica, los juegos de amo-esclavo y la dominación (SMBD, especialmente si emplean cadenas), en esta aparatosa pero inofensiva afición libidinosa, la persona que se encuerda puede estar vestida o desnuda. Durante determinadas épocas, el *bondage* se censuró y se prohibieron las ataduras en el cine X *mainstream*; en general, se considera un subgénero pornográfico, con escenas en las que prima la pura estética, con la excusa de la presencia de amas y esclavas con sus accesorios y decorados de mazmorras, cierto lenguaje de humillación, o *spanking*, pero sin argumento. Fue la archiconocida *pin-up* Betty Page quien, a mediados de los cincuenta, protagonizó para el director Irving Klau las primeras películas de *bondage*. Muchas actrices porno, antes de retirarse, adoptan el papel de dóminas o *mistress* en estas producciones, dado que dirigir un ritual de azotes no implica dolor físico ni esfuerzo y que, en la sumisión masculina, se incorpora la presencia de mujeres de cierta madurez en ese rol.

Bukkake: ésta es una práctica sexual que se engloba tanto dentro del «sexo en grupo» como de las denominadas «de sumisión». Consiste en que varios hombres, por turnos, eyaculen sobre una persona (hombre o mujer) quien, al acabar, se beberá ese esperma que se ha ido recogiendo en un vaso o en un recipiente. Existe cierta leyenda en torno a su origen. Por un lado, circula que era un castigo que se imponía en el Japón de la época feudal para humillar a las esposas infieles: se las ataba a un árbol en un lugar público y todos eyaculaban sobre ellas. La otra versión, no sé si más plausible o más basada en cifras de ventas y en la ley de la oferta y la demanda, señala que es la industria del porno nipona la que, debido a la rígida censura —en Japón no se puede mostrar ni vello púbico, ni planos frontales de los genitales—, y por esa guerra para «ir más lejos» y para ofrecer cada vez más morbo al espectador, les hace avanzar por terrenos de violencia, humillación y prácticas extremas: anoxia, escarificación, mutilaciones... Ver *pornografía o porno*.

Candidiasis: es una infección por hongos, organismos que, pese a su mala reputación y al miedo que inspiran, siempre están en nuestro organismo, sólo que controlados. Hay varios factores que provocan el desequilibrio y la proliferación de los hongos, causando la infección: desde los cambios hormonales (embarazo o los tratamientos de infertilidad), a enfermedades (un sistema inmunodeficiente, diabetes, obesidad, etc.), variaciones del pH (algunos detergentes y jabones), fármacos e incluso, anticonceptivos. Se transmite por la ropa, por objetos o por contacto sexual. Su período de incubación es de 8 a 15 días. Afecta normalmente a las zonas húmedas y cálidas de la piel y las mucosas, como las axilas, la boca, uñas, el glande y la vagina; de hecho, la candidiasis es la más frecuente causa de vaginitis. Se manifiesta con flujo blanquecino, edema de los labios menores que se puede extender hacia labios mayores, perineo, pliegues inguinales e interglúteo, acompañado de prurito y «quemazón». La misma sintomatología puede darse en los genitales externos masculinos.

Castración: operación que se encamina a la extirpación de las glándulas sexuales (los testículos o los ovarios o el útero). Puede ser necesaria en caso de enfermedades (tumores, cáncer...). Con la esterilización se impide la reproducción y conlleva que determinadas hormonas dejen de segregarse (testosterona) y que en la mujer se reduzca el efecto de los estrógenos. Históricamente, la castración se empleaba en las guerras como castigo a los vencidos, como humillación, como tortura y para mermarlos aún más. También era frecuente realizar ofrendas a los dioses con los órganos amputados. Se incorporó a los códigos legislativos y, previamente, se aplicaba por las normas consuetudinarias, como modo de sancionar a los delincuentes sexuales. Otra «utilidad» de la castración era proveer de esclavos «fiables» que custodiaran y convivieran con las concubinas y las mujeres (los eunucos). Los célebres *castrati* eran niños de voz prodigiosamente aguda a quienes se practicaba la mutilación genital para que no perdieran ese don con la pubertad.

Existe un tipo de castración, la castración química, que se emplea en determinados países, aunque no resulta un tema pacífico; como siempre que colisionan derechos fundamentales, la unanimidad deviene inalcanzable. La polémica afecta a determinados colectivos (enfermos mentales recluidos, pederastas, violadores y otros delincuentes sexuales en prisión) y a su peligrosidad en cuanto a que amenazan la vida y la libertad sexual de los demás. Los efectos de la castración química son varios: elimina el impulso sexual, desciende la frecuencia y la intensidad de los pensamientos eróticos; impide la erección, ya que frena la irrigación de sangre al pene, lo que hace imposible la obtención del orgasmo mediante la eyaculación. El estado de California, en 1996, fue pionero en establecerla de modo opcional para acceder a la libertad condicional o bien de modo obligatorio para casos de reincidentes. El tratamiento dura dos años y consiste en administrar fármacos que inhiben las hormonas sexuales masculinas. En ambos casos, los condenados pueden escoger entre la castración permanente (extirpación quirúrgica de los testículos) y la temporal (inyecciones semanales de Depo-Provera, que se emplea como método contraceptivo femenino que inhibe la ovulación durante 12 semanas; también se utiliza para tratar el cáncer de endometrio). La iniciativa fue seguida por Florida y otros estados. En 2004 Francia aprobó un programa piloto de castración química de violadores y pederastas encarcelados, a fin de desmasificar la población carcelaria.[33]

El complejo de castración refiere en el varón el miedo a la pérdida del falo (que significa no sólo perder el pene sino el poder, la fuerza y la superioridad inherentes).

Celibato: no se refiere específicamente a la vida religiosa, sino que describe el estado personal de quien no está casado ni emparejado y manifiesta voluntad de abstenerse de practicar sexo. Es una re-

33. Datos de *adeguello.net*

nuncia al ejercicio directo y propio de la sexualidad, en pro de un amor universal, de fomentar otros valores que, de crear una familia, se verían pospuestos. Los hay que encuentran más fácil escalar el Everest con zapatos de tacón de aguja... Ver *abstinencia*, no porque se identifique, sino para evitar la confusión conceptual.

Cérvix: extremo inferior, angosto, del cuello del útero que conecta con la vagina. Designa una pequeñísima parte del aparato genital femenino. Se trata del extremo inferior, estrecho —de 1 cm aproximadamente—. Sirve de puerta de acceso a los espermatozoides (de ahí que muchos anticonceptivos basen su eficacia en bloquear este orificio, aumentando la densidad del moco cervical) y, llegado el momento del parto, el feto lo atravesará, en su salida del útero; esto es posible gracias a su enorme capacidad de dilatación. Dependiendo de cada mujer, la estimulación directa de esta zona mediante penetración profunda puede desencadenar orgasmos o causar un intenso dolor si la embestida es violenta.

Chancro: es una infección sexual bacteriana. Se contagia de una persona a otra a través del contacto sexual, de una piel que tiene lesiones o úlceras a otra piel. Tras su incubación, que dura entre un día y dos semanas, surge en forma de un bulto pequeño que da paso a una herida dolorosa (de entre 3 y 5 mm) al día siguiente de su aparición. Zonas donde se produce el contagio son las perianales, en ambos sexos. Los síntomas habituales, además de la úlcera (que en el hombre será única y en la mujer varias), son: dolor al orinar y al mantener relaciones sexuales. Inflamación de los ganglios linfáticos inguinales (entre las piernas y la parte inferior del abdomen) que, si se desarrollan, terminan formando abscesos drenantes en la piel. Tras su detección, debe acudirse al médico inmediatamente para que ponga tratamiento con los antibióticos adecuados.

Chancro de la sífilis. Comienza de modo similar, una úlcera que aparece en los genitales, sólo que es más duro al tacto. Antes de que se desencadenen las fases secundaria o terciaria de la sífilis, hay que acudir al médico —si no, puede ser incluso mortal—. El chancro en los genitales masculinos usualmente se localiza en el glande, prepucio y en el frenillo. En la mujer puede localizarse en los labios, vagina, cérvix. Otros sitios son la mucosa oral, la faringe, el septo nasal, los dedos, el recto. Además de la vía sexual, pasa de la madre al feto. Su evolución conlleva desde dolor a síntomas y enfermedades por la afección de tejidos (sus manifestaciones son cutáneas, sífilis en el sistema óseo, cardiovascular o neurosífilis).

Ciclo menstrual: es el proceso de formación y maduración de los gametos femeninos; en teoría suele durar 28 días, pero muy pocas mujeres lo cumplen con exactitud. Hay cuatro fases en el ciclo, aunque según cada una, pueden acortarse o alargarse.

Primera. El ciclo se inicia, el día 1 se computa como el primer día de sangrado —no el último, ojo—. Si no estás embarazada, desde el útero se produce la expulsión del revestimiento y del óvulo no fecundado en forma de una hemorragia que dura entre 3 y 7 días. *Segunda*. La pituitaria —glándula ubicada en el cerebro— da instrucciones al útero para que engrose su revestimiento y permita la anidación del óvulo fecundado. *Tercera*. En esta fase, la pequeña burbuja situada en la superficie del ovario, que ha ido creciendo durante varios días, estalla y se desprende el óvulo. A esto se le llama ovulación. Entonces el óvulo comienza su camino hacia el útero, pasando a través de las trompas de Falopio. *Cuarta*. En esta fase, el recubrimiento del útero, al no ser necesario para nutrir al óvulo, comienza de nuevo el proceso de desprendimiento. Es la menstruación. El fin del ciclo es el día anterior al inicio de la siguiente menstruación. Si el espermatozoide ha fecundado el óvulo, el útero mantiene el revestimiento y tras la acción de las hormonas sobre él, lo hace más grueso para nutrir al cigoto y facilitar su anidación. La mujer no volverá a tener más períodos durante nueve meses, hasta que nazca el bebé.

Circuncisión: consiste en cortar una parte del prepucio, un procedimiento inducido por razones religiosas —judíos y musulmanes la practican— o higiénicas, mediante el cual se elimina el exceso de piel del pene. Hay dos técnicas, cortando y cosiendo la piel al glande o dejando que siga cubriendo el glande cuando no esté el pene en erección. El procedimiento en sí es sencillo —aunque ellos se desmayan—. Suele practicarse en casos de fimosis, que se podría evitar si desde bebé se enseñara a los niños a que se echen la piel del prepucio hacia atrás, hasta que sea flexible.

Cistitis: inflamación del interior de la vejiga normalmente causada por una infección. Cuando las paredes de la vejiga se irritan e inflaman puede ser inicialmente una infección localizada en la uretra, donde las bacterias (bacteria Escherichia Coli, es la causante habitual) se multiplican y ascienden a la vejiga —como en la mujer el camino es más corto, la cistitis se da con mayor frecuencia—. Los síntomas son dolor al orinar, hipersensibilidad en la zona y sensación constante de necesitar hacer pis —aunque no haya líquido que expulsar—. Las relaciones sexuales resultan dolorosas y además, la infección se agrava con la penetración. El tratamiento con fármacos (antibióticos) es rápido y eficaz, pero conviene abordarlo cuanto antes (para impedir que pueda complicar a los riñones). Trucos: al hacer pis, limpiarse desde delante hacia atrás: desde la parte de la vagina hacia el ano. Cuidar la higiene, beber mucho líquido. Orinar después del coito para expulsar posibles bacterias que hayan entrado por el tracto urinario.

Clímax: orgasmo, correrse, llegar. Determina el momento de mayor excitación en el sexo. El capítulo «El orgasmo» desarrolla el concepto y sus fases, anomalías, etc.

Clítoris: localizado en la parte superior de la vulva, fuera de la vagina y a una distancia variable de su entrada, lo que explica por qué el pene solito normalmente no logra que la mujer alcance el orgasmo con los movimientos de la penetración exclusivamente. Su parte visible se llama glande, igual que en el pene. Este apéndice eréctil tiene el tamaño de un guisante y sus terminaciones nerviosas (más de 8.000, el doble que en el pene) se extienden hasta dentro de la vagina. Su estimulación conduce al orgasmo a casi todas —por no decir a todas— las mujeres. Ver los capítulos de «Anatomía básica» y «El orgasmo».

Climaterio: fase de la vida femenina tras la retirada de la menstruación y, por tanto, de su capacidad reproductora. Aunque tradicionalmente se ha considerado la menopausia como un «fin», como el paso que resta hasta la vejez, la verdad es que con el cambio en las costumbres y la longevidad de los países desarrollados, esta etapa cada vez se vive con mayor alegría y casi con alivio: las mujeres se libran de la regla y pueden seguir ejerciendo su sexualidad sin preocuparse de evitar embarazos —habrán de recurrir, seguramente, a los lubricantes, al reducirse la secreción de flujo—. Sin embargo, sí que se ven afectadas por cambios hormonales durante varios años (pre y posmenopausia), con todo tipo de síntomas físicos y altibajos emocionales.

Cliptorquidia: una irregularidad en la ubicación de uno o los dos testículos debido a anomalías en el proceso de formación o descenso. Al examinar al niño no se hallan, y eso se debe a que no han descendido, la bolsa escrotal está vacía, o solamente se puede palpar uno de los testículos. Se recurre a la cirugía para, una vez localizados, fijar los testículos a la bolsa escrotal. Conviene practicar la operación en el niño antes de los seis años. Puede producir problemas de fertilidad —la finalidad del escroto, precisamente, es suspender los testículos fuera del organismo, para que el esperma esté a la temperatura adecuada—. Caso distinto es cuando, debido a la excitación, uno o los dos testículos, ascienden y quedan momentáneamente ocultos, recuperando su sitio de modo natural.

Coito: introducción por vía oral, vaginal o anal del pene (si se introduce un dedo, dildo u objeto, no se llama coito, sino simplemente penetración). Se habla también de cópula.

Coitus interruptus: ver el capítulo «Anticonceptivos».

Compatibilidad: en el terreno sexual equivale a disfrutar de los mismos gustos o intereses, tanto en lo que respecta a parafernalias (látex, disfraces, etc.) como en lo que a prácticas se refiere. También se refiere al tamaño de los genitales. Ver el apartado «El tamaño».

Condilomas o verrugas genitales: se manifiestan como protuberancias del color de la piel, con una superficie rugosa, en los genitales o alrededor del ano. En ocasiones se localizan dentro de la boca, como resultado de un contacto urogenital. Están producidas por el VPH (virus del papiloma humano), un virus que presenta distintas cepas y se transmiten pene-vagina, vagina-boca, pene-boca y con juguetes sexuales que hayan tocado las verrugas —que a veces están en sitios donde es imposible verlas—, por contacto directo de la piel con ellas, de ahí que el preservativo sea imprescindible. Algunas infecciones aparecen sin síntomas y tanto la mujer como el hombre pueden ser portadores y vehículos de las mismas. Esa infección, cuando aparece en el cuello del útero, puede malignizarse y producir cáncer del cuello del útero (dependerá del momento en que se detecte y la fase de la enfermedad: puede ser una displasia epitelial leve, CIN I; moderada CIN II, o grave, CIN III, es decir, cáncer). Es una de las infecciones de transmisión sexual más comunes en la actualidad. Aunque el diagnóstico de esta ETS es relativamente fácil cuando aparecen las lesiones, la posible presencia de infección por VPH hace necesario un exhaustivo estudio del cuello del útero, vagina, vulva, uretra, perineo y ano, siendo recomendable, cuando se detecta su presencia, el examen de la pareja o parejas sexuales por el especialista. Para la prevención del cáncer de cérvix, se está incorporando a los distintos planes autonómicos de vacunación el Gardasil, una vacuna, cuya comercialización se anunciaba el 20 de septiembre de 2007 en España, que previene con un 100 % de eficacia determinados tipos de cáncer de cuello de útero, una enfermedad que causa que cada día mueran 40 mujeres en Europa y el segundo tumor más mortal entre la población femenina. Se indica el tratamiento, que consiste en tres pinchazos, para niñas de entre 9 y 26 años, preferiblemente antes de que inicien su vida sexual. El precio de cada una de las inyecciones es aproximadamente 140 euros.

Condón: preservativo. Profiláctico de barrera que, a día de hoy, resulta no sólo un método anticonceptivo —para los heteros—, sino el pasaporte al sexo seguro —para todos y para todas las prácticas—. Se coloca forrando el juguete sexual o desenrollándolo a lo largo del pene en erección, antes de introducirlo (en vagina, boca o ano). Más información acerca del preservativo y sus indicaciones de uso en el capítulo «Anticonceptivos» y en el apartado de «Juguetes eróticos».

Contracepción: métodos, procedimientos quirúrgicos y sustancias encaminadas a evitar el embarazo. Existe una gran variedad, desde el método de Ogino (contar días) a la marcha atrás —ambos denominados «naturales», tan en desuso como arriesgados—, o las píldoras anticonceptivas (que no son lo mismo que la píldora abortiva o «del día después»), lociones y cremas espermicidas, preservativos, parches de hormonas, hasta la ligadura de trompas de Falopio y la vasectomía (estos últimos irreversibles). Ver capítulo de «Anticonceptivos», donde se explica cada uno.

Coprofilia: afición erótica por la defecación y la manipulación de excrementos humanos. La coprofagia da un «pasito» más, ya que consiste en ingerir las heces humanas. La estimulación sexual obtenida de este modo tan minoritario y casi clandestino ha convertido las producciones pornográficas escatológicas —que también dan cancha a esta fantasía— en un subgénero ilegal desde los años setenta en Estados Unidos, y cuentan con el rechazo casi unánime de la industria porno convencional. En las cintas de coprofilia el término «caviar» equivale a... (*Caviar eaters* se titula una). En Holanda y Alemania es donde se producen este tipo de «rarezas» marginales y, aunque lo habitual es que los participantes sean anónimos —y que también el equipo se esconda bajo seudónimos—, la excepción sería, por ejemplo, la película de Riccardo Schicchi, *Chocolate con bananas* (1986), donde Cicciolina —que ha toreado en todas las plazas, en la de zoofilia también— se caga encima de un político (y por una vez, no se trata de ningún eufemismo).

Corrida: vulgarismo que designa la eyaculación, la descarga de líquido seminal (en caso de eyaculación femenina, del fluido cuya naturaleza aún se discute...).

Cowper, glándulas de: ubicadas bajo la próstata, la misión de estas dos glándulas es la de secretar líquido preseminal, donde puede haber espermatozoides viables para fecundar. Esta sustancia tiene base alcalina y sirve para lubricar la uretra durante la penetración y antes de eyacular. Ver el capítulo de «Anticonceptivos».

Creampie: puede que recuerde a la peli *American Pie*, que suene a un festival de música de nombre semejante (con perdón para sus patrocinadores) o que un nivel de inglés macarrónico induzca a traducir literalmente *creampie* como «pastel de crema». Sí, pero no. Independiente como género dentro de la pornografía, el *creampie* alude a las escenas con eyaculación interna (es decir: dentro de la vagina, del ano o de la boca, contrariamente a la costumbre del cine X que exige que los actores eyaculen fuera, en sitios bien visibles —pecho, cara, etc.— para que la cámara capte la descarga) y a los planos donde se muestra el semen saliendo de nuevo. Como en el porno todo se mueve por modas, el *creampie* ha tenido cierto éxito últimamente porque se parece más al acto sexual tal y como lo realizamos los mortales en la intimidad (pese a que, como me han contado varios profesionales del gremio, actrices sobre todo, se considera una práctica de alto riesgo, a pesar de todo eso de que llevan los test y la analítica en regla...). Y ahora, para completar la información, el «creampie, 2.0», que se llama *feltching*, sólo espero y deseo que se lea en ayunas... Delego en la definición de Wikipedia, que lo explica fenomenal: «consiste en aquella práctica sexual en la cual una persona, usualmente es una mujer, lame el semen que sale de la vagina o ano de otra mujer. Otra variante de esta práctica consiste en succionar el semen directamente del interior de la vagina o ano, o ubicándose los participantes en la posición adecuada, esperar a que éste gotee en la boca del receptor». Amén. Ya en otro capítulo, hablamos de Góngora.

Cuello del útero: ver *cérvix*.

Cunnilingus: palabra «culta» —e intimidante por puro compleja— que designa hacerle sexo oral a una mujer. Tiene su equivalencia en expresiones coloquiales y vulgares como «comer el coño», «bajarse al pilón», que designan el acto de lamer y succionar la vulva (labios, entrada de la vagina y clítoris). El cunnilingus es uno de los momentos de máxima intimidad, para muchas mujeres incluso más que la penetración. Salvo que te muerda el clítoris —por decir algo—, jamás lo hace «mal»: lo hará genial, bien o regular pero sólo el gesto de que te lo haga, ya implica muchas cosas. Cuando él lleva ahí ya un rato, puedes corresponder con caricias en su pelo, o notar que necesitas cierto contacto físico con él: agárrale de la mano (si le queda alguna libre: los hay que pilotan de verdad e insertan algún dedo mientras «trabajan» con la boca y la lengua, o con un par de dedos abarcan la zona del clítoris y los labios. Si es así, es mejor que ocupen sus manos en dicha tarea... Tú, agárrate de la colcha). Cabe que pro-pongas un giro numérico: hacer un 69, para muchos, su postura favorita; otros se desconcentran y prefieren el sexo oral por turnos. Va a gustos. Ver el apartado de «Sexo oral».

Débito conyugal: la mentalidad más tradicional contempla que si la procreación es un fin del matrimonio, el débito conyugal está implícito en la relación matrimonial. Los canonistas y el Espasa definen «débito conyugal» «como la obligación que en el matrimonio tiene cada uno de los cónyuges de realizar la cópula con el otro cuando éste lo exija o pida. Es obligación jurídica; pero las leyes civiles positivas no la sancionan atendido a que no puede penetrarse en el sagrado de la familia y a que del empleo de la coacción pudieran derivarse mayores males. La obligación de prestar el débito es consecuencia de los fines del matrimonio y aparece terminantemente mandada por san Pablo: *Uxori vir débitum reddat, similiter autem et uxor viro* («Tribute el varón el débito a su mujer, y de igual modo la mujer al marido») (Corintios I,7), y añade: «Su negativa sin motivo grave produce pecado mortal. Son causas graves para negar el débito: el grave daño de la prole, el escándalo público, el pedirse en lugar sagrado y otros.»

Afortunadamente, está más que superada y se encuentra estéril y muy trasnochada la concepción del sexo forzado, ese que las mujeres del s. XIX mantenían —perdón, padecían— respecto del coito conyugal, que se sintetiza en la frase tan elocuente de «las manos sujetas a los barrotes de la cama y pensando en el Imperio» con que tenían que soportar una relación que detestaban para satisfacer el ansia primitiva de un señor que se firmaba como su esposo.

En efecto, como se señala en la *Revista de Derecho Privado* «el actual desarrollo de los derechos humanos no permite concebir un deber que vaya en contra del respeto a la intimidad e integridad del ser humano. Las personas no son el objeto para la consecución de un fin sino que son sujetos con dignidad y con derecho a ejercer su libertad de procrear».

Despertar o despegar: el conjunto de sensaciones físicas o mentales que se producen en el cuerpo cuando alguien que nos gusta nos toca en determinados puntos y que conducen a la excitación. Excitarse o calentarse, ponerse.

Dildo: Objeto utilizado para los juegos sexuales. Puede imitar o no al pene. Los hay de todos los tamaños, materiales, texturas, movimientos y aplicaciones, colores y con y sin vibración (de ahí el término «vibradores»), con y sin motor, a pilas o a la red eléctrica, algunos son específicos para la penetración vaginal, otros para la anal. A veces, si prescindimos de *sex shops*, podemos utilizar un dildo ecológico (la naturaleza nos brinda hortalizas con aspecto muy aparente...) o servirnos de otros utensilios a mano. Dos consideraciones: que todo lo que entre, salga igual que entró (que no sea fácil de romper, ni de astillarse, ni de quedar atrapado dentro del organismo, ni de hacer el vacío) y que esté muy limpio (tanto si te metes un plátano o una zanahoria como si tiras de mango de martillo, utilizar un preservativo es lo más recomendable). Me niego a denominarlos «consoladores». Ver *juguetes sexuales*.

Disfunción sexual: el prefijo «dis» implica negación, ausencia. En el sexo implica que algo va mal, no rinde, que hay un trastorno. Normalmente, se barajan como disfunciones sexuales la anorgasmia, las relacionadas con la eyaculación (precoz, falta de eyaculación, retardada, etc.), la disfunción eréctil o impotencia, el dolor durante la penetración (dispareunia), etc. Casi todas se abordan a lo largo del libro. Lo primero que hay que hacer es perder ese pudor que tenemos cuando se trata de cualquier enfermedad o problema sexual. Cada disfunción sexual se debe abordar de modo independiente, tendrá su causa (física, psicológica, emocional, laboral...) y su tratamiento, que sólo puede establecer un médico.

Dismenorrea: término para designar las menstruaciones dolorosas. Los síntomas: dolor abdominal bajo, tipo cólico, antes del comienzo del período menstrual y que dura de uno a dos días durante el período. Náuseas y vómitos. Diarrea o estreñimiento. Dolor de espalda. La sufren especialmente las adolescentes y no siempre se debe a una enfermedad (es la dismenorrea primaria), sino a la presencia de una sustancia, la prostaglandina, que hace que el útero se contraiga. La dismenorrea secundaria está causada por endometriosis y enfermedad inflamatoria pélvica. El médico realizará un estudio (si la chica es virgen, se practicará por el recto, no vía vaginal), para descartar enfermedad o malformaciones y prescribirá tratamiento que alivie el dolor (a base de analgésicos o incluso, de anticonceptivos orales). Si bien es cierto que la regla puede ser un infierno según para qué mujer, no está de más saber que la práctica de deporte ayuda enormemente a que el dolor desaparezca. Otro detalle importante: puede ser hereditario, las mujeres de la misma familia suelen ovular a la vez y no es raro que el grado de dolor o molestia menstrual que sienten sea parecido. Es fundamental educar a la niña acerca de la menstruación. Ha de saber que es «normal y natural», que esa hemorragia no es algo sucio, ni una maldición, ni señal de pecado y barbaridades como las que nuestras abuelas escuchaban. Como en todo, la mente influye poderosamente y si a una niña se le ofrecen referentes de mujeres que cada mes se meten en la cama «muertas» por estar con la regla, de modo inconsciente asumirá que lo normal es que el mundo deje de girar cuando ella tenga el período (lo que no ayuda a la integración femenina en el mundo laboral, por ejemplo).

Dispareunia: alude al coito doloroso. El dolor puede presentarse tanto en el hombre como en la mujer y en cualquier momento durante la relación sexual, por ejemplo, en el momento de la penetración, durante la erección o la eyaculación. Las causas pueden ser desde «una tontería» (cuando se va «con prisa» y no hay lubricación suficiente, el calentón nos lleva a un coito brusco que puede doler a una y otro), o presentarse una reacción alérgica al látex de un diafragma o un condón, o vincularse a asuntos más serios como operaciones o partos recientes, infecciones urinarias (de la uretra o de la vejiga), infecciones genitales (de la vagina, del glande, etc.), enfermedades o estados carenciales de hormonas, malformaciones (si el asunto no es puntual, si «siempre duele, en todas las posturas» quizá se deba a deformaciones en los ovarios, útero, vagina, etc., o de la próstata). También, cuando se mantiene una relación bajo demasiada «presión», lo natural es que los músculos involucrados no se relajen y ello causa que duela el coito. Cabe que el sexo en sí sea «la presión», en casos de personas que han sido víctimas de abusos y delitos sexuales. Si el dolor se prolonga, la persona puede perder interés en cualquier actividad sexual. A nadie le gusta sufrir y tendemos a evitarlo.

DIU: Ver el capítulo sobre «Anticonceptivos».

Doble penetración: una de las prácticas de «alto rendimiento». Consiste en acceder por el ano y la vagina simultáneamente, ¿con qué? Pues, en principio, con sendos penes, lo que requiere que al menos haya tres personas. Esta práctica, en la vida privada, admite muchas variaciones (no como en el porno, que la DP es un tipo de escena concreta que se ejecuta tal cual: dos hombres y una mujer. Tampoco «cuenta» como DP que a la actriz la penetre uno y ella, mientras, haga una mamada al otro). Como digo, en la vida real hay opciones: como la sustitución de uno de los penes por un dildo, o incluso la sustitución de los dos penes (cuando una mujer se masturba con manos y juguete, por ejemplo).

Dogging: se trata de un anglicismo relativamente reciente (que nadie se enfade: nada nuevo hay bajo el sol, dicen en Egipto... Pues eso, que me perdonen quienes lleven haciéndolo dos o tres décadas). Nota: *dogging* no es sacar al perro, ni ser un perro (de vago), ni una perra (de... perra). El *dogging* alude a tener o contemplar sexo al aire libre, en un lugar público. Es «irse a un oscuro» con el coche. En España se ha dado a conocer como «cancaneo». Se practica en parques, playas, aparcamientos... En la red se encuentran webs específicas que organizan «quedadas». Muy vinculado al voyeurismo, habitualmente los mirones participan de esta práctica sexual (y en ocasiones, también los curiosos que acechan a los que practican el sexo se unen al sarao, que termina en una orgía normalmente disuelta por la policía...). Lo malo de tanta espontaneidad es que frecuentemente se olvidan de utilizar preservativo. Por lo tanto, según las Autoridades Sanitarias, el *dogging* podría incluirse entre las prácticas no recomendables por el riesgo de transmisión de ETS, etc.

Ducha vaginal: mediante un irrigador que se introduce en la vagina, se expulsa agua u otro líquido para limpiar su interior. Aunque parezca un contrasentido, siendo imprescindible la higiene más escrupulosa en el exterior, en realidad, la ducha vaginal no sólo es innecesaria, pues la vagina se limpia constantemente a sí misma con sus propios flujos, sino que puede causar una alteración en el pH de la mucosa y hacerla más vulnerable a las infecciones de hongos, etc. Durante muchos cientos de años se creía, erróneamente, que este lavado urgente tenía capacidad para evitar un embarazo. No es así. Ver el capítulo sobre «Anticonceptivos».

Embarazo: consiste en la fecundación del óvulo por un espermatozoide. Desde ese instante, se desencadenan importantes cambios en la mujer, tanto a nivel físico (hormonales fundamentalmente) como emocionales y psicológicos. La gestación en los humanos dura, normalmente, 9 meses. El embarazo ectópico o extrauterino se produce cuando el cigoto (óvulo fecundado) anida fuera del útero (en una trompa de Falopio, por ejemplo) y requiere intervención quirúrgica que evite las complicaciones obvias que produce. Se repite en varios momentos del libro pero, procede insistir: toda penetración y muchas prácticas de contacto pene/vagina, realizadas sin protección, conllevan riesgo de embarazo, haya o no eyaculación, cualquier día del ciclo.

Endocrinas, glándulas: se ocupan de la producción y secreción de hormonas. Las sexuales son los ovarios y los testículos, que dependen de la hipófisis.

Enfermedad del beso: ver capítulo sobre «El beso».

Episiotomía: es el corte que se practica en el perineo durante la mayoría de los partos vaginales. Evita los desgarros y facilita la feliz salida del bebé (tal como se quejan muchas, se mete bisturí antes de terminar de dilatar, porque ahorra un tiempo precioso al personal sanitario, deseoso de irse a casa cuanto antes). Ver el apartado de «Cirugía íntima femenina». Los puntos y la herida exigen curas y una extremada higiene —habida cuenta que se halla justo donde hacemos pis y caca, el riesgo de infección es elevado—. Las relaciones sexuales se pueden y deben reiniciar cuanto antes, conforme el cuerpo lo pida, por la salud emocional de ambos (lo de que haya penetración es algo que tarda más: por eso se habla de la famosa «cuarentena». Ver *puerperio*). En esto el ginecólogo ha de dar su veredicto, pero se recomienda no reiniciarlas hasta seis semanas después del parto (hay inflamación y una sutura reciente que puede doler). Además, el riesgo de infección uterina es alto, puesto que el cérvix está abierto aún. Los ejercicios de Kegel son una técnica estupenda para recuperar el tono de los músculos vaginales. Ver *Kegel, ejercicios de.*

Erección: cuando se trata del pene, la respuesta física a la estimulación se denomina también «ponerse dura», «empalmarse»; también se produce ese endurecimiento y reacción en los pezones y, en la mujer, en el clítoris (aunque éstas son, digamos, bastante más «discretas»). Se explica por la irrigación o afluencia sanguínea a la zona, y esta concentración provoca su «crecimiento». Sobre la excitación, ver el capítulo «El orgasmo». Además de una «prueba» de excitación y de agradecimiento por el placer recibido, la erección del pene tiene un fin biológico: sirve para facilitar la penetración y, ulteriormente, la descarga seminal y la procreación. La erección describe cambios físicos sorprendentes: el pene aumenta su tamaño (depende de cada hombre, pero puede hacerse hasta tres veces más grande que en estado de reposo), asciende, se eleva (hasta describir un ángulo de entre 45 y 90 grados, es decir: puede subir tanto que se queda justo pegado a su vientre). El pene se mide en estado de erección —lo comento para que no cunda el pánico cuando se airean las medidas de veintipico centímetros...—, y será en ese momento cuando se aprecia su forma y orientación: si es recto, curvado, etc. Ver *peyronie*, una enfermedad en la curvatura.

Erógena, zona: determinadas partes del cuerpo muestran una específica y mayor respuesta a la estimulación sexual. Aunque varían mucho de una persona a otra, en general, además de los genitales, se considera que son zonas erógenas los labios, el cuello, los lóbulos de las orejas, la cara interna de los muslos, los pechos, los pezones, etc. Soy de las convencidas de que en este apartado hay que otorgar al cerebro una posición destacada, muy seguida de los tímpanos. Y mi experiencia me lleva a afirmar que, en realidad, no hay zona no-erógena, sino mal estimulada o ignorada. Ver el apartado «Zonas erógenas», dedicado a ellas.

Erótico: sería todo aquello encaminado a provocar una respuesta sexual, ya sea en una representación gráfica, plástica o artística (en fotos, películas, revistas, etc.) o en cualquier aspecto de la vida, realizado con «buen gusto», en contraposición a lo pornográfico (considerado como «obsceno», sórdido y todo eso).

Escroto: cavidad donde se alojan los testículos. Se trata de una «bolsa» que cuelga fuera del cuerpo para que su temperatura sea menor en dos o tres grados y el esperma se forme correctamente. La bolsa escrotal tiene siete capas; dos son musculares, que permiten el movimiento de elevación hacia el abdomen y que hacen que se contraiga o relaje según los estímulos, especialmente los cambios de frío a calor, y el resto de las capas están compuestas de piel. Está recubierto de vello desde la adolescencia (si no se tiene la costumbre de depilarse).

Esmegma: pensaba obviar este término. Normalmente evito hasta citarlo, porque hay cosas que no me meto en la boca ni para pronunciarlas... Se trata de la secreción de las glándulas sebáceas de la mucosa del prepucio y de los labios menores, cerca del clítoris. El esmegma (detritus celular) es una secreción blancuzca, untuosa y de olor característico que puede resultar desagradable a cualquier ser humano que no sea «especialito». Se cree que su función es proteger y lubricar el espacio prepucial; en la mujer se forma en la zona entre los labios mayores y menores y alrededor del clítoris. Esta secreción siempre tiene el papel de «malo» en la escena de sexo oral porque da asco, mucho asco en general. Hay mucha más información sobre el tema en el apartado de «Sexo oral».

Esperma: se trata del líquido blanquecino producido por los testículos que expulsa el hombre por el pene en el momento de la eyaculación (que suele ser cuando alcanza un orgasmo, vía coito, polución nocturna, masturbación...). El olor y sabor, así como la densidad y grado de transparencia del semen, dependen de la dieta, de la salud, del tiempo que haga que no eyacula, etc. Se compone de espermatozoides (cerca de un 10 %) y fluido seminal o semen (el resto), aunque varía en cada eyaculación y cada señor (un espermograma lo determinará). Se considera uno de los mejores transmisores de enfermedades sexuales, de ahí que se imponga el uso de preservativos y se deba evitar tragarlo o que penetre en el organismo (vía vaginal o anal) cuando no estemos seguros de la salud de su dueño. Los espermatozoides pueden sobrevivir hasta 72 horas dentro del cuerpo femenino, por lo que pueden fecundar el óvulo tras el encuentro sexual con eyaculación. Para que el semen sea apto para la fertilización su concentración ha de superar los 20 millones de espermatozoides por mililitro. Considera que factores tan kafkianos como aficionarse a llevar vaqueros muy ajustados, que pueden subir la temperatura de los testículos, o que el sillín de tu bici puede obstruir la arteria que recorre la zona y que controla el flujo de sangre al pene, pueden perjudicar la calidad del esperma y la potencia sexual. Ver *eyaculación* y el apartado sobre «Sexo oral».

Espermatozoides: son las células reproductoras masculinas. Se componen de una cabeza, la parte ancha redondeada; una parte central o «cuerpo», y la cola, mucho más larga, que les permite desplazarse. Se producen en los conductos seminíferos de los testículos, en cantidades elevadísimas, de millones. En la eyaculación salen propulsados a través de la uretra nadando en el semen, tras atravesar los conductos deferentes y las vesículas seminales, con una misión «casi» imposible: en su corta vida, han de fecundar el óvulo (pese a que un espermatozoide es unas 10.000 veces más pequeño que el óvulo) y, si lo logran, aportan la información genética. La prueba médica que mide la concentración y viabilidad del esperma se denomina espermiograma.

Espermicida: los productos espermicidas se aplican antes del coito en la vagina o sobre el diafragma o el preservativo para evitar embarazos. Son sustancias químicas cuyo efecto mata los espermatozoides. No previenen las ETS y pueden aumentar el riesgo de infección por VIH y causar alergia. No garantizan eficacia al 100 %, sino que deben utilizarse junto con otro medio de barrera. Ver el capítulo sobre «Anticonceptivos».

ETS o ITS: enfermedad o infección de transmisión sexual. La lista es tan larga como terrorífica: se contabilizan treinta tipos (enfermedad inflamatoria pélvica, gonorrea, herpes simple, infecciones por clamidia, sida, vaginitis, sífilis, uretritis inespecífica, tricomoniasis, verrugas genitales, virus del papiloma humano, etc.), y encima, cabe que se padezca más de una simultáneamente y que, una vez «curadas», algunas rebroten. Son las conocidas «venéreas», esas infecciones que se transmiten de una persona a otra por contacto sexual, ya sea epidérmico o por intercambio de fluidos por cualquier vía: vaginal, anal u oral, por lo que la garganta es igualmente una vía de contagio. Es triste pero, en los tiempos que corren, justo en el momento en que alguien te atrae más y más intimidad alcanzas (y mejor lo estás pasando), más miedo debe darte. Si se mantiene una relación sin protección, al menor síntoma de «alteración» en los fluidos o sensación de picor o de escozor, o aparición de úlceras dolorosas o indoloras, granos, ronchas en la región genital, verrugas abultadas, ampollas, ganglios en la ingle, molestias al orinar, secreción por el pene, dolor en el bajo vientre, etc., ha de acudirse a un especialista que determinará si es preciso realizar pruebas o prescribir medicamentos (ojo, algunas ETS pueden no presentar síntomas). Respecto de si las ETS se curan, depende, como en otras enfermedades, del momento en que se detecten y se empiecen a tratar. Cada ETS es distinta. Pueden curarse con pocas o ninguna consecuencia grave o permanente para la salud, salvo el sida —aunque con el tratamiento se puede retrasar la aparición de la enfermedad y mejorar la calidad de vida del paciente— o determinados casos, los más graves, del VPH. Las demás, casi todas se pueden tratar, pero, dependiendo de su origen (hongos, bacterias, virus o parásitos), las hay que no se curan del todo, como el herpes. Por muchas veces que se repita, nunca se insistirá lo suficiente, la mejor prevención: higiene, responsabilidad en la elección de parejas sexuales (en quién y en cuántas porque, en efecto, la promiscuidad multiplica los riesgos de contraerlas) y practicar sexo seguro (utilizar siempre condones y no hacer según qué cosas con gente cuya historia sexual no se conoce). El preservativo es el mejor método para evitar la mayoría de las ETS. Ante la sospecha de haber contraído una ETS, debes acudir a tu médico para que te diagnostique mediante análisis sanguíneos y de cultivo de líquidos corporales o del tejido donde se ha producido la infección. Mientras obtienes tus resultados, has de evitar tener más relaciones sexuales o donar sangre y, en caso de estar infectado, hasta terminar el tratamiento y que hayan remitido los síntomas. Es tu responsabilidad informar a tu/s pareja/s sexual/es de que estás enfermo, para que también acuda/n al médico. No debes automedicarte: no sirven los mismos medicamentos para curar distintas ETS (además puedes enmascararlas). Aunque nos podemos contagiar todos, suelen afectar más gravemente a la salud de las mujeres. La sífilis y el sida pueden transmitirse por vía sanguínea o de la madre embarazada al feto dentro del útero o al bebé durante el parto, pero el riesgo puede reducirse y hasta ser eliminado si la madre se diagnostica y se trata durante el embarazo.

Esterilización: son procedimientos cuyo objetivo es impedir la reproducción. Ver el capítulo de «Anticonceptivos», donde se explica la ligadura de trompas y la vasectomía. También hay información relacionada en *castración*.

Estrógenos: las hormonas sexuales femeninas. Se forman en los ovarios. Sus funciones son diversas, algunas conectadas con el sistema excretor (tracto urinario), pero también con el circulatorio y con los huesos, la piel y las uñas, el cabello, las mucosas, los músculos pélvicos y el cerebro; otras muchas funciones se relacionan con la regulación del ciclo menstrual (hacia el día 14 del ciclo es cuando más abundan, con la ovulación). Al llegar la pubertad se produce un aumento de estrógenos que fomenta que se desarrollen los caracteres sexuales secundarios, que determinan los rasgos «femeninos»: se ensanchan las caderas, aparece vello (en axilas y zona púbica), crecen los pechos, se desarrolla el pezón, se acumula tejido adiposo sobre el hueso púbico formando el monte de Venus...

Exhibicionista: normalmente se acusa de pervertidos a quienes imponen su disfrute de ser vistos desnudos por los demás. Suele ser un comportamiento tipificado y penado, especialmente si su público se compone de menores. Muchos se excitan sabiendo que son observados mientras practican sexo, y fomentan encuentros en lugares públicos, o privados pero en ubicaciones desde donde se les ve (delante de la ventana con la persiana abierta, o en el jardín a plena luz del día...). En el caso de los exhibicionistas se da una «inversión» en la emisión-recepción de los estímulos. Lo habitual es excitarse viendo a la persona que te gusta. Pues aquí es al revés: quien se excita es el exhibicionista y lo logra, mostrando sus partes a quien sea, porque lo que les pone es precisamente causar ese «susto», «enfado» o «sorpresa». La víctima poco o nada cuenta. Puede ser cualquiera que pase por la calle y que, sin mediar palabra, se encuentra con un tipo que se abre el abrigo y le enseña sus partes pudendas. Aparte de patéticos no suelen ser peligrosos, huyen si la persona acechada grita. Los exhibicionistas presentan una clara necesidad de terapia sexual, ya que suelen ser personas inseguras, incapaces de prácticas satisfactorias. Se considera una parafilia y, en relación con ella se pueden estudiar la llamada *ecdiosis* en la que la excitación sólo se produce al desnudarse ante desconocidos, y el *flashing*, que consiste en mostrar rápidamente los genitales a personas que se va uno encontrando en la calle.

Eyaculación: expulsión del semen acompañado de una serie de contracciones musculares muy placenteras. En cada eyaculación se expulsan entre doscientos y cuatrocientos millones de espermatozoides, lo que equivale a un 1 % del fluido total... El alcance de la eyaculación depende de la edad y de la apertura del orificio uretral (cuando se es más joven está más cerrado y eso hace que el líquido salga propulsado con más fuerza). Ver el capítulo sobre «El orgasmo», donde se trata ampliamente la diferencia eyaculación-orgasmo, junto con la eyaculación femenina, etc.

Eyaculación precoz: situación que da pie al ya conocido «nunca me había sucedido antes». Bromas aparte, no existe una «marca» o tiempo oficial que determine cuánto ha de durar alguien en erección y manteniendo contacto e interacción sexual. Sin embargo, sí suele considerarse tal cuando la excitación le impide controlar voluntariamente la eyaculación, y ésta se produce antes de o justo al intentar penetrar o transcurridas tres o cinco embestidas —el cómo se queda ella no es igual en ninguno de los tres casos—. En hombres menores de 35 años, suele deberse a nervios, ansiedad, sobreexcitación o sequía prolongada. Se trata de una disfunción que se resuelve entrenando y con el reaprendizaje (son muchos años yendo a toda prisa para acabar el primero o antes de que te pillen...). Además de los ejercicios de Kegel masculinos, existe una técnica denominada *Squeeze* o «de compresión» por Masters y Johnson, que consiste en estrangular la cabeza del pene en el momento en que él nota que va a eyacular para evitarlo, posponerlo y que el coito dure más (es una terapia que se practica a solas también y que sirve para curar la eyaculación precoz y ganar en control eyaculatorio). Este procedimiento debe efectuarse antes del «punto de no retorno», porque una vez rebasado será inevitable que descargue. Ver el apartado sobre «Eyaculación precoz o retardada».

Fantasía sexual: imaginar situaciones o actos sexuales con gente o circunstancias reales o inventadas. Por mencionar algunas, las más recurrentes: los tríos, la violación, el sexo con un extraño, con disfraces (doncella, enfermera, bombero, policía), empleando parafernalia fetichista (fusta, látigos, corsés, esposas, cuerdas), en determinados escenarios (una playa, en un avión, en un ascensor). Ver el apartado específico sobre «Fantasías sexuales», que además trata sobre la reactivación del deseo.

Fecundación: implica que uno de los espermatozoides ha cumplido su objetivo vital y ha alcanzado el óvulo. Conlleva, por tanto, la unión de los dos gametos (óvulo y espermatozoide) y desencadena de inmediato una serie de cambios y procesos. El cigoto, la nueva célula resultante de la unión de las otras dos, se desplaza hasta el útero y se implanta en el endometrio donde, si todo va bien y se lo permiten, pasará los siguientes 9 meses mutando y engordando tan a gusto.

Fellatio **o felación:** palabra técnica que designa el acto de estimular el pene con la boca (labios, lengua). Se habla de «hacerle una mamada», de «chupársela»... Ver el apartado sobre «Sexo oral».

Feromonas: etimológicamente, la palabra viene del griego y significa «llevo excitación». Son sustancias químicas incorpóreas secretadas con el fin de provocar un comportamiento determinado en otro individuo de la misma especie. Se trata de olores. Pese a ser tan sutiles, tienen un enorme alcance y, dentro de lo sensual, un poder incalculable de atracción. Son emitidas por las glándulas odoríferas que tenemos en los órganos genitales, las plantas de las manos y de los pies, y en las axilas. Ya en Egipto se fabricaba perfume dotado de poderes afrodisíacos empleando como base, junto con fragancias, el sudor de hombres sanos seleccionados. El protagonista del *El perfume*, de Patrick Süskind, afirmaba que el mejor perfume es el que desprende un individuo enamorado, porque es el olor natural del amor. Uno de los casos más estudiados y explicados es el de

sincronización del ciclo menstrual de mujeres que conviven en un mismo ambiente.

Fértil: designa la aptitud o capacidad de reproducirse (ella, de quedarse embarazada y él, de dejarla embarazada). Se califican como fértiles los días del ciclo menstrual durante los cuales el óvulo podría ser fecundado. La vida real del óvulo es de entre doce y veinticuatro horas. Si en ese momento es fecundado por algún espermatozoide viable (es decir, «fértil»), se producirá un embarazo. Contra esta palabra («embarazo») y lo que conlleva ver el capítulo sobre «Anticonceptivos». Lo contrario de fertilidad es la *infertilidad* o *esterilidad*, cada vez más frecuente, y que suele obedecer a razones médicas y a la forma de vida actual: sedentaria, con estrés y ansiedad, dieta nada saludable y mil vicios (de entre los legales: alcohol y tabaco). Si al cabo de un año de intentar un embarazo, una pareja no lo logra, debe acudir al ginecólogo/andrólogo, para que determine el motivo y en su caso —contando con que ella se hace las revisiones anuales— plantee tratamiento o realice las pruebas pertinentes y específicas, como la analítica del esperma.

Fetichismo: conducta sexual, considerada parafílica, que consiste en que, para alcanzar la excitación y la satisfacción, ha de intervenir o estar presente algún objeto, material o prenda; los más frecuentes son el fetichismo del pie, las medias de rejilla, el cuero negro, las máscaras o los tacones. Podría decirse que el fetiche es el detonante que activa el deseo sexual. Cada época desarrolla sus propios fetichismos, en función de los tejidos y de las prendas (botines de charol, guantes o corpiños de cuero, tangas de látex, ¿qué más da?), en realidad, los materiales suelen ser el objeto de deseo y devoción más que el cuerpo sobre el que se colocan. También se genera cierta fijación erótica sobre detalles concretos de la anatomía femenina (el empeine del pie, los orificios nasales, pequeñas cicatrices, marcas o lunares, que algunos consideran «parcialismo», no fetichismo), o de su vestuario (ligueros, camisones, bragas...). Muchos hombres roban ropa de mujer, la tocan, la huelen, se la ponen o la colocan componiendo una silueta femenina para excitarse, y se masturban. Para otros, los fetiches sexuales han de estar presentes, pero sobre la pareja, que ha de llevarlos puestos o jugar con ellos (al hilo de esto, se conoce como «Disciplina de las enaguas» cuando te obligan a ponerte ropa interior femenina como parte de un ritual de humillación o de excitación sexual). Según el grado de fetichismo, podrá existir desde una «cierta atracción» hacia el fetiche o que su presencia sea imprescindible para que se pueda alcanzar la erección o eyacular. Recientes teorías explican esta asociación de placer y un objeto determinado, vinculándola a una experiencia producida durante la infancia y que perdura ya en la etapa adulta con el mismo significado, sería una especie de aprendizaje.

Ilustra bien al respecto la obra *Psichopathia Sexualis* (1886), de Von Krafft-Ebing. Cito un fragmento del prólogo a una de las ediciones de la obra mencionada, escrito por D. Luis García Berlanga, cineasta y aficionado al fetichismo, donde se hace referencia a uno de los casos que se recogen en el libro, junto a la opinión del propio Berlanga: «"K., de cuarenta y cinco años, zapatero, al parecer sin antecedentes familiares hereditarios. [...] Se le confiscaron más de trescientos artículos de *couture* femenina, entre ellos, aparte de camisones y bragas, gorros nocturnos, ligueros y una muñeca. Desde los trece años vivía esclavizado por el impulso de robar prendas de mujeres. [...] De noche, al acostarse, se ponía la ropa interior robada y fantaseaba con hermosas mujeres, lo que le provocaba agradables sensaciones y la subsiguiente eyaculación. Éste era, aparentemente, el móvil de sus robos; nunca se desprendía de los artículos sino que los escondía aquí y allá. [...] Era incapaz de comprender la anormalidad de su condición y lo equivocado de sus actos." Este último comentario nos lleva al aspecto menos atractivo de Kafft-Ebing: su creencia de que las fijaciones sexuales reflejaban una condición moral degradada, y de que debían ser corregidas.»

Feto: designa al embrión humano durante el período de gestación.

Fidelidad: en lo sexual implica no tener relaciones con nadie que no sea la pareja (¿límite? Muy discutido...). Para muchos significa demostrar lealtad hacia alguien, respetándole.

Filias: dentro de las distintas prácticas sexuales, aquellas cuya denominación termina en la desinencia «filia» implican especial predilección, amor, afición o simpatía hacia lo que designan; *para*, en griego, significa «al lado» y *philéo*, «amar». Otras, mayoritariamente, terminan en «agnia» o en «astia» y se asocian a lo excéntrico. En general, el término «parafílico» se emplea de modo despectivo, señalando a personas «raras», con preferencias «enfermizas» o «aberrantes». Habida cuenta de la enorme evolución de la opinión pública y de la comunidad científica respecto de estas relaciones «especiales» y dado que conforman una larga lista, parece interesante dar un breve recorrido por algunas de ellas, ver el capítulo «Fijaciones sexuales o parafilias». De entre ellas, algunas, las más conocidas, aparecen puntualmente en el libro y también a lo largo de esta tercera parte.

Fimosis: que es como se llama al estrechamiento de la piel del prepucio que impide su retracción. Dependiendo de lo severa que sea, puede requerir intervención quirúrgica —muy sencilla—. Ver el capítulo sobre «Anatomía básica».

Fisting y **variantes**: con este anglicismo se denomina a una práctica sexual extrema y de alto riesgo que consiste en la introducción de la mano —y antebrazo a veces— por la vagina o por el ano durante la relación y cerrar el puño una vez allí. Sin duda, un momento de verdadera intimidad y de experimentar eso de «estar dentro de su piel»... Obviamente, el porno se hace amplio eco de esta especialidad y, aunque la legislación americana lo penaliza por obsceno, se encuentran numerosos casos de *fisting* (censurado o encubierto) dentro del cine convencional. Recordemos la película de Al Pacino, *Cruising*, que, allá por los años setenta, narraba la historia de un asesino en serie de homosexuales en Nueva York. Más manifestaciones del *fisting*: *Persiguiendo a Amy*, 1997, con una descripción de un *fisting* vaginal, o *Austin Powers: El espía que me amó*, donde la protagonista parece estar practicando un *fisting* a su *partenaire*, como parte de un gag... Hasta en *Calígula* hay una escena...

Para practicar el *fisting* la mano se introduce poco a poco y, una vez dentro, el movimiento de mete-saca se realiza, o bien con los dedos que continúan estirados, o bien éstos se cierran formando un puño. La penetración puede ser de poco más que los cuatro dedos (lo permitido por las leyes americanas), hasta casi del brazo, rebasando la muñeca. Además de toneladas de lubricante con base de agua o de silicona (no de látex ni de aceite), se aconseja una gran higiene, limado de uñas de quien lo realiza y el empleo de guantes (de látex o incluso de los largos que se utilizan para reconocer al ganado). Aunque incrementa el riesgo, no es extraño que se recurra a relajantes musculares y otras drogas *(poppers)* para lograr la relajación de la zona y facilitar la penetración. Hay además lubricantes con efecto anestésico y dilatador. A veces se recurre a los *slings* o hamacas suspendidas —valen las almohadas colocadas debajo de quien está siendo penetrado— para facilitar la postura de ambos.

Existe la práctica del *double fisting* realizada por quienes, con más experiencia, alcanzan una enorme capacidad de dilatación, y que consiste en la introducción de dos manos simultáneamente. Por lo referido, ahí el placer deriva más de la contracción del ano o de la vagina que del movimiento de mete-saca. Las contraindicaciones y riesgos de una práctica incorrecta del *fisting* ocuparían casi una página: desde esterilidad, infecciones de tracto urinario o inflamación pélvica, a desgarros musculares, incontinencia fecal, fístulas y laceraciones en las mucosas. Se han descrito casos de transmisión de hepatitis A y C asociados al *fisting* realizado sin guantes.

En la carrera hacia el «y esto no es todo, señores» que la industria del porno promueve y encabeza, he de decir que en realidad, si bien todo lo descrito más arriba sobre el *fistfucking* («follar con el puño», que es como se denomina en porno esta práctica) impresiona —y a ello yo puedo añadir detalles de haber contemplado bolas más grandes que las de billar siendo expulsadas del ano sin apenas esfuerzo, o la introducción de un dildo de más de un metro de alto y de un grosor digno de tronco de árbol—, la verdad es que, cuando presencias un *footfucking* la sensación que se te queda es de «¡vaya, pero si no había visto nada!». En efecto, hace años, visionando cintas de porno gay —era mi época en Quiero Tv—, dentro de una caja de muestras me llegó una cinta alemana donde había una escena que no voy a olvidar: durante una orgía dentro de una comisaría o algo parecido, a uno le metían un pie por el culo con la bota militar puesta. Ver para creer. En todo caso, por si alguien arruga el morro y piensa en «degenerados», se ha de saber que se editan libros de autoayuda sobre *fisting* anal, y que ninguna editorial publica nada que no se vaya a leer... Ver el apartado de «Sexo anal» para detalles imprescindibles.

Volviendo a la realidad, el *fisting* vaginal no es sinónimo de vaginas de dimensiones catedralicias ni de mentes pervertidas. Ver el apartado de «Masturbación femenina».

Flujo vaginal: se trata de una ITS femenina que se manifiesta con una anomalía en el flujo. Cuando hay una ITS es de color, olor y cantidad anormal. Puede estar producido, como la secreción uretral, por varios gérmenes: como el gonococo, las clamidias, las trichomonas, las cándidas (hongos) o la gardnerella vaginalis, entre otros. Todos estos gérmenes producen flujo, pero variarán sus características según sea uno u otro el causante de la infección. Los gonococos y las clamidias dan lugar a un flujo similar: amarillo o verdoso, con molestias al orinar. Aunque en ocasiones estas últimas pueden ser asintomáticas. Las trichomonas causan un flujo espumoso, amarillento y de mal olor que se acompaña de intenso picor. En las candidiasis (hongos) el flujo es blanco y espeso (leche cortada), también acompañado de intenso picor. La gardnerella produce un flujo gris acuoso y maloliente. Las candidiasis y las vaginosis por gardnerella, en la mayoría de los casos pueden producirse sin un contacto sexual previo.

En general la mujer con flujo causado por una ITS se quejará de manchas en su ropa interior, flujo, picazón, molestias al orinar, enrojecimiento o hinchazón de la vulva y dolor abdominal bajo. El diagnóstico debe hacerse con una toma y análisis del flujo para detectar qué germen lo está produciendo. El tratamiento, si se da un diagnóstico precoz y correcto, es sencillo y la curación no deja secuelas. Siempre deberá hacerse un control de curación analítico postratamiento.

Complicaciones. Cuando las infecciones por gonococos y clamidias se dejan evolucionar sin tratamiento pueden producir enfermedad inflamatoria pélvica, esterilidad, embarazos ectópicos (extrauterinos), infecciones en las trompas de Falopio, ovarios... etc. Los hijos recién nacidos de las mujeres infectadas, al pasar por el canal del parto, pueden infectarse y padecer una ceguera. En la actualidad se previene esta enfermedad administrando tratamiento a todos los recién nacidos. Un flujo de color, olor y cantidad anormal puede ser indicativo de Infección de Transmisión Sexual.

A veces, el primer síntoma de una ITS es la enfermedad inflamatoria pélvica, que se manifiesta con dolor abdominal bajo y que puede terminar en una peritonitis. El motivo de esto es que la infección, localizada en un principio en la vagina, puede extenderse por vía ascendente y afectar al cuello del útero, las trompas de Falopio y el peritoneo. La enfermedad inflamatoria pélvica deja como secuelas dolor pélvico crónico, esterilidad y un mayor riesgo de embarazos ectópicos (extrauterinos).

Frenillo: en general, sería cualquier pliegue de piel que impide que un órgano se desplace (el de debajo de la lengua, el del labio superior y el del inferior). Existe uno en el clítoris y otro que sostiene los labios menores. El que se encuentra en el pene une el prepucio —tejido que recubre el glande, limitando su movimiento— con la mucosa. El frenillo es extremadamente sensible a la estimulación manual u oral (él se excita mucho), y hay que tener cuidado de no desgarrarlo cuando el pene está en erección. Más en «Anatomía básica».

Frigidez: su correspondiente adjetivo, «frígida», cargado de mala leche, se empleaba en el antiguo régimen para describir (y reprochar) a una mujer que no tenía interés en el sexo o que no alcanzaba orgasmos (en contraposición a «calentorra» o «caliente», que era igual de malo, justo por lo contrario...). De aparecer en una conversación, se recomienda no hacer caso, hablar de la multiorgasmia femenina o aportar luz al asunto de la localización y correcta estimulación del clítoris, pudiendo amenizar con la falta de pericia y de sensibilidad masculinas. Ver «anorgasmia», «frigidez», y otros temas relacionados en el capítulo «El orgasmo».

Fuck: en la antigua Inglaterra la gente de a pie no podía practicar sexo sin contar con el consentimiento del rey (a menos que se tratara de un miembro de la familia real). Cuando cualquier persona deseaba tener un hijo debía solicitar un permiso especial al monarca, quien le entregaba una placa que debía colgar en la fachada mientras tenía relaciones. La placa decía: FORNICATION UNDER CONSENT OF THE KING (F.U.C.K.), origen de la popular palabra. Traducido, *fuck* significa «joder», como taco, y «joder», en el sentido de cópula.

G, punto: descubierto por el ginecólogo alemán Ernst Gräfenberg, se trata de un área ligeramente elevada, situada dentro de la vagina, en la pared frontal, detrás del hueso púbico. Su estimulación requiere un movimiento de la lengua o dedos, que se han de introducir entre 2,5 y 7,5 cm en la vagina, en dirección hacia arriba, imitando el gesto de llamar a alguien. Provoca la mayor intensidad en el orgasmo y produce la llamada «eyaculación femenina». Ver en el capítulo «El orgasmo» la eyaculación femenina, aunque se aborda en diversos momentos, como en «Anatomía básica», «Posiciones», etc.

Gang-Bang: dentro de las múltiples opciones que permite el sexo en grupo, se da esta variante de elementos tomados a partir de nueve. Para que constituya *gang-bang*, y no una orgía, por ejemplo, la relación ha de establecerse 8 a 1, es decir: al menos ocho hombres con una mujer. Se trata de un género pornográfico independiente que se pudo ver en el clásico *Tras la puerta verde* (1973), y que se traduce como «follada de pandilla». La industria del porno ha ido subiendo la cifra de participantes hasta establecer marcas que resultan inverosímiles: una americana, una tal Lisa Sparxxx ha fijado el récord en 919 hombres, lo que no se ha divulgado es en cuánto tiempo lo logró, cuántos descansos necesitó, ni en qué estado quedaron sus genitales (ni su cerebro). Si se trata de muchas mujeres y un hombre se denomina *gang-bang* inverso o *reverse gang-bang*. El primero, en 1994 lo protagonizó Rocco Siffredi, en *Rocco Unleashed*. Dentro de este género se ubica el *bukkake*.

Garganta profunda: consiste en introducirse el pene en la boca hasta el fondo, en plan tragadora de sable. El arte está en que su choque con la campanilla no nos provoque arcadas ni el cierre automático de la boca con él dentro... La verdadera experta en esta técnica fue la actriz porno norteamericana Linda Lovelace, que lograba engullir como nadie en la historia el miembro masculino hasta su embocadura, sin importar el tamaño, y acariciarlo y masturbarlo con la lengua y el fondo de su garganta. Ver el apartado sobre «Sexo oral».

Gatillazo: algo completamente distinto de la eyaculación precoz. Se llama gatillazo a una pérdida repentina de erección durante la relación sexual (se baja de pronto) o a la incapacidad para erectar a pesar de la estimulación. Véase el capítulo «Cuando no funciona».

Gay: homosexual. Suele emplearse para el colectivo de varones que se sienten atraídos y practican sexo con hombres. La palabra que prefieren las mujeres homosexuales es «lesbiana». En España, el año 2005 trajo la legalización del matrimonio gay. En detrimento de esta medida, se dijeron barbaridades, como eso de las peras y las manzanas, que me pareció el eufemismo más despreciable que había escuchado, porque bajo el cutre disfraz de pensamiento naíf inoculaba un mensaje humillante. El caso es que a día de hoy, y aunque quede pendiente una resolución del Tribunal Constitucional que dé firmeza a la disposición legal que aprueba el matrimonio homosexual, los gays y lesbianas pueden celebrar matrimonio en condiciones de igualdad, si así lo desean. La siguiente batalla se libra para equiparar el derecho de adopción. A ver si agilizan la cosa, que el asunto afecta por igual a familias monoparentales y a parejas heterosexuales que desean adoptar, tengan o no descendencia biológica. No parece de recibo que se exija el pago de semejantes cantidades de dinero o que se obligue a garantizar elevadas cifras de ingresos que, de no mediar adopción, no se exigen a nadie a la hora de parir (¿o acaso se ha de «sacar el carné de madre/padre»? Pues, bien pensado, no estaría de más: puestos a pedirlo para conducir o para tener armas, generar una vida no parece más trivial, ¿o sí?). Mientras miles de niños se mueren de hambre y de enfermedades que aquí ni recordamos ya, las personas que quieren adoptar esperan años hasta conseguirlo. ¿No falla algo? En países que sufren pandemias, donde «sobran niños» —es decir, donde se mueren sin remedio—, lo que hay que agilizar es que se «coloquen» para proporcionarles una subsistencia digna. A ver si las cabezas pensantes «se iluminan» y se dan cuenta de que penalizar el amor, por el hecho de que se manifieste de un modo distinto, es una indecencia y una barbaridad.

Géneros pornográficos: la lista de subdivisiones, categorías y clasificaciones sería interminable. En realidad, cada especialidad viene a aglutinar las cintas por la temática: es decir, por las «fantasías sexuales» que recrea. Desde las cuatro grandes divisiones (*mainstream*, gay, bi o transexual) a pormenorizadas tipologías *ad gustum*: grandes pechos, enanos, *freaks*, gordas, viejos, cuero, descargas faciales, *spanking* (azotes en el trasero), adolescentes, embarazadas, chic, lésbico o *G/G* (de girl/girl), *pets* (por mascotas, zoofilia), interracial, asiáticas, látex (subgénero del B/D), etc.

Genitales: los órganos sexuales externos, ubicados en la zona pélvica. En el hombre, los testículos y el pene. En la mujer: labios mayores y menores, clítoris y vagina.

Glory Hole: no es el último temazo de Madonna y no estamos invocando una plegaria... Con este (también) anglicismo nos adentramos en ese morbosísimo mundo de los cuartos de baño, y no para fregarlos precisamente. Cuando uno tiene un desconchón en casa, o se despega una baldosa, lo suyo es llamar corriendo a un «ñapas», pero si esto sucede en un baño público, en vídeo-cabinas o en una discoteca... la utilidad del boquete es otra. *Glory Hole* es ese orificio de la pared de baño por el que puede aparecer desde un dedo a un pene, mientras tú visitas el WC. Dicho así, podría parecer el Gran Hermano o un *poltergheist*... Sin embargo, en realidad el «agujero del amor» es uno de los planos y recursos más utilizados en porno (gay sobre todo) y casi un clásico de las noches urbanas. Cuando alguien mete su miembro por estos orificios espera una generosa *fellatio* o practicar sexo anónimamente, así que no le pidas el teléfono a la salida.

Ginecólogo/a: médico especializado en el aparato reproductor femenino y todo lo que conlleva: embarazos, enfermedades, etc. Después de ti, debería ser la primera persona en conocer y ayudarte ante cualquier «marrón». Por otro lado, igual que los coches pasan la ITV, cada mujer sexualmente activa debe hacerse una revisión ginecológica completa cada año (las hay *hiperactivas*, a las que convendría doble de lo dicho). Las pruebas consisten en: analítica de sangre, exploraciones manuales, con aparatos (ecógrafos), toma de muestras (citología y colposcopia). Ya, ya, yo también he estado más cómoda y mucho más «digna» que ahí, sin bragas, sobre una banqueta, encaramada con el culo pegado al borde, despatarrada literalmente, y con los tacones metidos por unos estribos de una especie de mesa-camilla-potro de tortura... Pero hay que ser práctica: son cinco minutos, no duele, y cualquier anomalía, tumor, infección, etc., detectado a tiempo, puede salvarte la vida. Si se trata en su fase inicial, casi todo puede quedarse en «un susto» y es probable que no ocasione complicaciones. Si tienes un seguro médico privado la mayor complicación consistirá en que pidas cita —no te vas a herniar...— y si dependes de la Seguridad Social, vete pidiendo cita para la del año siguiente según te den los resultados de la de éste. Mejor prevenir... Por cierto, el equivalente al ginecólogo pero para ellos se llama andrólogo —y lo visitan tan poco que casi ni se conoce el término—. Más vale hacerse revisiones periódicas para evitar ETS...

Glande: con un tejido suave y de los más sensibles de todo el organismo, es la parte superior del pene, la cabeza (si imaginamos que se parece a una seta, sería el sombrero). Suele ser más ancho que el tronco y si no está en erección el pene, el glande queda cubierto por el prepucio. Una vez a la vista, se puede apreciar un pequeño orificio en el centro: la uretra, por donde orina y también eyacula.

Gónada: son los órganos sexuales o reproductores, encargados de producir los gametos. Respectivamente, los ovarios y los testículos.

Gonorrea: enfermedad sexual de origen bacteriano que se localiza y afecta al cuello del útero y a la uretra (provoca uretritis y prostatitis). Otras señales de gonorrea son el dolor al hacer pis, acompañado de sensación de quemazón; cuando del pene sale una excreción uretral mucosa (blanquecina o transparente) o purulenta (espesa, con tono amarillento). Si él está infectado, puede contagiarla aunque no eyacule. En la mujer se presentan los síntomas de una infección bacteriana, con posible fiebre y dolor en el vientre, excreción vaginal, aumento de ganas de orinar y molestias al hacer pis. Puede desembocar en vaginitis y cervicitis, pero también en enfermedad inflamatoria pélvica aguda, esterilidad, etc. Además de por vía sexual, se transmite al bebé durante el parto si la madre está infectada y puede causar ceguera en el recién nacido. El uso de toallas, ropa interior, pastillas de jabón, etc., que hayan estado en contacto con la bacteria puede provocar la transmisión de la gonorrea. Suele desaparecer con antibióticos, por lo que si se diagnostica y se recibe la prescripción del adecuado —no conviene automedicarse ya que, como muchas otras bacterias, desarrollan inmunidad o se enmascaran, pudiendo, además, presentarse combinada con otra, como la clamidia—, no tiene por qué causar complicaciones.

Goma: condón, preservativo. Ver en apartado de «Juguetes eróticos».

Hacer el amor: construcción lingüística cuyo simple sonido, a muchos, nos causa estridencia en muchos sitios. Preferimos utilizar: tirarse a, hacerlo con, follar, acostarse con, tener relaciones, practicar sexo, montárselo, echar un polvo, estar con, liarse con, chingar, beneficiarse, cepillarse, echar un quiqui, enrollarse con, mojar, etc. Como prueba, baste que en este libro, creo que sólo utilizo hacer el amor en dos o tres ocasiones... Nuestro castizo «fornicar» (tener cópula carnal fuera del matrimonio) y el «joder» de cada día suenan menos explícitos cuando van encubiertos con ese amplio abanico de posibilidades que ese edulcorado y melifluo «hacer el amor», tan global y tan genérico, ofrece. Para algunos es la forma cursi de decirlo y, para otros, sirve para marcar diferencias: es un encuentro sexual donde median ciertos sentimientos y que no produce la necesidad de que el otro desaparezca a la mayor brevedad, etc. Muchas veces utilizamos eufemismos como «acostarse con» (éste, algo más preciso que «dormir» que es, precisamente, lo que menos hacemos esa noche).

Hentai: tebeos japoneses pornográficos. Es un tipo de manga para adultos donde conviven criaturas monstruosas con preciosas nínfulas de apariencia humana (jovencitas dotadas de hiperdesarrolladas y espectaculares gónadas) siempre dispuestas a correr aventuras y a introducirse por cualquier orificio, tentáculos inmensos, apéndices inverosímiles de todo tipo o penes de seres de distintas especies.

Herpes genital: hay dos tipos de herpes: el labial y el genital. La presencia de lesiones vesiculares, como bolsitas de agua que posteriormente se rompen dejando erosiones en la piel, indicará que se trata de un herpes genital. Sus síntomas generales son fiebre, malestar, dolor generalizado (mialgia) y disminución del apetito. Cuando el virus es transmitido por las secreciones de la mucosa oral o genital, la lesión inicial se localiza habitualmente sobre el glande y otras partes del pene y del escroto en hombres; vulva, vagina y cérvix, en mujeres. Y la boca, ano y cara interna de los muslos puede también ser un sitio de infección en ambos sexos. Las lesiones desaparecerán tras el tratamiento y podrán volver a aparecer sin necesidad de un nuevo contacto sexual. Se trata de una infección recidivante (que reaparece con la exposición al sol, en estados de debilidad, estrés, etc.).

Heterosexual: persona que siente atracción y practica sexo con personas del sexo opuesto.

Himen: pocas partes del cuerpo humano han suscitado tantos mitos y tragedias. Asociada a la virginidad y a la pureza femenina, se trata de una membrana situada en la vulva —forma parte de los genitales de la mujer—, en la entrada de la vagina (no dentro, como erróneamente se cree) y que se rompe con la primera penetración (si es que la hay y si es que se rompe). Esta membrana es el resto del tejido que recubre la vagina y que permanece tras formarse la abertura vaginal en el desarrollo del feto. Sin embargo, no todas las mujeres la tienen. Debido a determinadas actividades más o menos bruscas (desde la colocación de un tampón o masturbarse introduciendo objetos, a montar a caballo) el himen puede desgarrarse, frecuentemente sin sangrado ni dolor. Esta membrana es elástica en algunas mujeres, lo que plantea casos de penetración, e incluso gestación, conservando parte o todo el himen. Ver *virgen* y el capítulo de «Anatomía básica».

Una curiosidad, hablando del himen, esa membrana que puede (o no) estar en la entrada de la vagina de una mujer y cuya rotura se asocia con la práctica de penetración sexual, es de destacar el antiguo rito del *mizuage*, en Japón. Se trata de una ceremonia de «subasta» del himen de una *maiko* (la aprendiza de *geisha*) entre los hombres de negocios y potentados que estuvieran interesados en «estrenarla». Todo se llevaba a cabo con suma discreción, pero eligiendo siempre el mejor postor, el que más dinero ofreciera. Tras este rito, la *maiko* se convierte en *geisha*; puede por tanto vestir y trabajar como tal, lo que implica dar la vuelta al kimono, utilizar en sus maquillajes los colores y motivos que antes le estaban vetados, cambiar su peinado al *ofuku*, celebrar la ceremonia del té, tocar instrumentos, cantar y bailar para amenizar las reuniones en los salones de té, y empezar a pagar a su *okiya* (casa de *geishas*) la deuda de su período de aprendizaje. Un detalle: ser *geisha* no implicaba ser lo que entendemos normalmente. No eran prostitutas. Podían lograr la protección de señores con mucho dinero y poder y, en efecto, conseguir regalos y, a veces, también cobrar por sus favores sexuales, pero no eran necesariamente prostitutas. Muchos (incluso acompañados de sus esposas) solicitaban que una *geisha* les amenizara la velada y era eso lo que contrataban: su compañía, no sexo. La casa de té y la *geisha* se repartían el dinero calculado en base al número de inciensos consumidos. Las *geishas* desarrollaban muchas de las disciplinas más valoradas: cantaban, bailaban, sabían de arte… Sólo su presencia —frágiles, espectaculares— era como contemplar una mariposa.

Histerectomía: intervención quirúrgica por la que se extirpa todo o parte del útero, provocando la esterilidad. Suele necesitarse para frenar un cáncer o eliminar tumores malignos. Obviamente, a semejante trago se añade el sufrimiento de la pérdida de la capacidad reproductora —su frustración dependerá de la edad y de la planificación que haya hecho para sí y su pareja y del deseo de cada mujer de ser madre—. Es fundamental que reciba apoyo, tanto de su pareja, si la tiene, como de especialistas. No obstante, es necesario que se pierda ese atávico peso que llevan muchas sobre los hombros: una mujer lo es, plena y total, aunque no tenga hijos. Su vida sexual, pasada la operación, por supuesto, no se ve alterada en absoluto.

Homofobia: conducta más o menos agresiva de rechazo contra los homosexuales. Magnus Hirschfel encabezó los movimientos de liberación sexual en Alemania, solicitando al Reichstag que suprimiese las leyes contra los homosexuales. Autor de diversas obras, como *Patología Sexual*, donde clasifica todas las patologías sexuales, originando la *Sexología*. También escribió *Safo y Sócrates*, el primer tratado sobre homosexualidad humana de relevancia y fundamentado. Defendió a las personas que por sus tendencias eran víctimas de ataques moralistas y maltratadas. Debido a su condición de bisexual, la llegada de Hitler al poder le obligó a exiliarse y sus libros fueron quemados. Ver también *Money, John*.

Homosexuales: personas que sienten atracción y mantienen relaciones sexuales con personas de su mismo sexo. Ver *gay*. Se trata de una orientación sexual, no es una desviación ni una enfermedad. Ahora, pasadas las de Caín, resulta que casi se diría que ser gay está de moda. Pese a que el matrimonio civil homosexual es legal en muchos sitios, España incluida, la Iglesia católica condena la homosexualidad, la considera un pecado (por más que se descubra cada semana que tal sacerdote y el obispo cual practican sexo con hombres, o niños. Seguro que S.S. Ratzinger ve distintos canales de televisión...). No obstante, ser gay o lesbiana en determinadas zonas geográficas supone aún ser un delincuente, porque es una conducta tipificada como delito. La intimidad de las parejas gay no ha de ser especialmente «distinta» —salvo, como es lógico, que en las de dos hombres no se habla de clítoris, ni de vagina, ni de ciclos menstruales, y en la de dos mujeres, nadie necesita preocuparse de si «eso sube» o no o de cuánto dura en erección—. La sexualidad sana se entiende como una forma de expresión de la personalidad; mediante las relaciones sexuales nos comunicamos, damos cariño y lo recibimos, explotamos su faceta lúdica y es una hermosa manera de volcar nuestra ternura. Eso, que yo sepa, puede hacerse igual, y el cómo, pues mediante imaginación y ganas (que también son las mismas). Por cierto, hay homosexuales que no practican penetración anal.

Hormona: sustancia química presente en animales y vegetales segregada por las glándulas endocrinas y epiteliales. En función de su origen, las hay naturales y sintéticas. Intervienen y regulan procesos corporales tales como el crecimiento, el metabolismo, la reproducción. Las sexuales son producidas por los testículos (andrógenos, testosterona) y los ovarios (estrógenos, progesterona).

Impotencia: disfunción eréctil. Incapacidad de conseguir una erección. Ver el apartado específico.

Infección de transmisión sexual (ITS): el manual *Sexualidad y Juventud: Guía Educativa para un sexo más seguro* explica que hay ITS cuya transmisión se produce por contacto sexual con una persona infectada, como la gonorrea, herpes genital, clamidias, etc. Otras, como el VIH/sida y las hepatitis víricas, se transmiten a través de la sangre, el semen y el flujo vaginal. Además existen infecciones, como la sarna y la pediculosis del pubis (ladillas), que pueden ser adquiridas, además de por vía cutánea, por contacto con ropas u objetos contaminados.

¿Qué son? Son infecciones cuya transmisión se realiza, fundamentalmente, a través de las relaciones sexuales (orales, vaginales o anales) mantenidas con una persona infectada o enferma. Los gérmenes causantes de las ITS tienen muy poca resistencia al medio ambiente exterior, muriendo rápidamente en contacto con el mismo (con excepción de los ácaros de la sarna y las ladillas, que requieren champúes y planchado concienzudo de la ropa). La creencia de que este tipo de enfermedades se transmite por baños públicos, piscinas, etc., es errónea.

¿Son muy frecuentes? Las ITS han aumentado considerable-

mente. Las razones son, entre otras: un comienzo más precoz de las relaciones sexuales, el turismo y mayor movilidad geográfica, la escasa información y formación sexual, la carencia de centros especializados, etc. Sin embargo, no se conocen las cifras exactas ya que, por un lado no todos los casos se tratan (muchas personas se automedican sin acudir al médico, o siguen los consejos de un amigo, un farmacéutico o sanitarios no médicos) y, por otro, muchas de estas infecciones no son de declaración obligatoria, como las infecciones de origen vírico (verrugas genitales o herpes genital) que precisamente son las que más han aumentado en los últimos años. Algunos autores sugieren que las cifras oficiales de que disponemos sean multiplicadas, en algunos casos por 10 y en otros por 30, dependiendo del rigor de la declaración, para estimar el alcance de las ITS.

Complicaciones. Al principio estas infecciones, tratándolas de forma adecuada, se curan fácil y rápidamente. Sin embargo, si evolucionan sin control pueden producir consecuencias muy graves tales como esterilidad, cáncer, lesiones cardíacas, enfermedades del sistema nervioso, abortos, malformaciones fetales, etc.

Inmunidad. A diferencia de otras enfermedades infecciosas (como el sarampión, la rubeola, la varicela, etc., que se padecen una vez en la vida), la mayoría de las ITS se pueden adquirir tantas veces como se tenga contacto sexual con personas infectadas. El motivo es que estas enfermedades, en su gran mayoría, no crean defensas.

¿Cómo se manifiestan las ITS? Las manifestaciones clínicas de estas enfermedades son muy variables.

En general los signos de presentación más frecuentes son:
- Supuración uretral
- Flujo vaginal
- Úlceras genitales
- Condilomas o verrugas genitales
- Inflamación del glande (balanitis)

Otros síntomas. En ocasiones, pueden presentarse al principio otros síntomas, como manchas en la piel, molestias al orinar, dolores en las articulaciones o supuración por el recto.

Complicaciones. También es posible que se manifiesten directamente por sus complicaciones, como dolor abdominal bajo, dolores en los testículos, etc.

Sin sintomatología. Por último, pueden cursar sin sintomatología al principio de la infección o bien pasar desapercibidas, como en las hepatitis víricas o el VIH.

Juguetes sexuales: también llamados ayudas sexuales, probablemente sean, de todos los asuntos relacionados con el sexo, los que más han evolucionado, tanto a nivel tecnológico como en su consideración y percepción social. Baste decir que se han metido en la vida (y en la cama) de muchas mujeres que actualmente los compran sin ningún tipo de sensación de culpa ni de vergüenza. De colores, texturas, formas y aplicaciones casi infinitas, los juguetes para adultos se utilizan en solitario o con la pareja, en seco o en la ducha o bañera (los hay incluso con pilas sumergibles), para aumentar la excitación, aprender a alcanzarla, intensificar y acelerar el orgasmo. Ojo con aficionarse demasiado o con «engancharse» a ellos... No es que todo el mundo deba colocar una barra fija para hacer un *show* de *striptease* cada noche en el dormitorio, pero nada como unas bolas vaginales para fortalecer la musculatura PC (ver *Kegel, ejercicios de*) o un dildo estimulador del punto P para él, un aceite de masaje comestible para un masaje erótico en los pies, un gel estimulador-potenciador de sensaciones para aplicarlo sobre el clítoris, o recibir a tu *amore* vestida de enfermera, cualquier día, por variar un poco... Fíjate que se llaman juguetes, ¡pues juega! Ver el capítulo específico.

Kamasutra: se considera el primer tratado sobre la sexualidad humana. El texto hindú original estaba escrito en sánscrito. Fue Vatsyayana Mallanga quien, hacia el s. IV o V d. C., reunió, tradujo y adaptó a las costumbres occidentales los 1.000 capítulos de este legado universal de enseñanzas sobre relaciones amorosas y sexualidad. Infinidad de posiciones para hacer el amor, por supuesto, pero también: besos, alimentos que aumentan el vigor, actitudes frente a las conquistas, cómo crear un ambiente sensual, compatibilidad sexual de las personas, implementación de juegos eróticos... y todo aquello que excite o provoque reacciones placenteras a través de nuestros sentidos y sentimientos, que a lo largo de generaciones se habían transmitido. En la India el sexo es sagrado y forma parte de la vida, por lo que en Occidente nos puede sorprender la desinhibición del lenguaje empleado, así como la fusión de la espiritualidad con lo físico. Actualmente, se considera un clásico de la literatura y cuenta con adaptaciones y versiones (lésbico, gay, con ilustraciones y vídeos, etc., casi todas desnaturalizando el original, contaminándolo de pornografía y limitándolo a ser un catálogo de posturas para el sexo).

El otro libro de singular valor erótico, curioso e instructivo pese a su antigüedad, es el *Ananga Ranga*, de Kalyana Malla, que en su cubierta aclara: «Enciclopedia del amor sexual», escrito especialmente para instruir en los secretos amorosos a una joven perteneciente a la casta de los poderosos. Algunos de sus planteamientos tienen una actualidad sorprendente. Por ejemplo: «Los goces externos» son los procedimientos que han de anteceder siempre al «goce interior» o coito. En sus páginas se explica que antes de la penetración son necesarios «ciertos preliminares, numerosos y variados, tales como los diversos abrazos y besos. Estas clases de caricias despiertan los sentidos y ponen el ánimo propicio.» El texto aclara que se trata de «escaramuzas que preparan a los amantes a una grata diversión erótica».

Otras obras sobre sexualidad son los libros chinos de Almohada y los *shungas* de Japón. Por otro lado, la literatura erótica árabe apunta el efecto de los perfumes, fragancias y cosméticos para multiplicar el placer sexual. En el célebre libro *El jardín perfumado* (s. XVI), cuya primera traducción se atribuye al británico sir Richard Burton, su autor, Shaykh Umar ibn Muhammad al-Nefzawi, hace particular referencia a los efectos estimulantes de las especias picantes y otras sustancias sobre los órganos sexuales. Ver el apartado sobre «Afrodisíacos».

El libro del Tao, más antiguo que los ya citados, recopila la sabiduría china. Existe la moda de citar alguna frase o párrafo, a fin de impresionar, de enriquecer un discurso o un artículo. Las sencillas palabras del Tao ocultan un complicado tratado filosófico traducido con más o menos fiabilidad. A partir de las enseñanzas del Tao, que se apoyan en ocho disciplinas (filosofía, revitalización, dieta equilibrada, dieta de los alimentos olvidados, arte de curar, sabiduría sexual, poder y éxito) se ha desarrollado lo que se denomina Tao sexual, una técnica oriental como muchas otras, que parte del dominio de la mente sobre el cuerpo mediante métodos naturales. El punto neurálgico de esta filosofía es el orgasmo: su control, su contención. Algo de esto entronca con las técnicas tántricas, cuya práctica y dominio las convierte en las más eficaces contra la eyaculación precoz. Las enseñanzas acometen lo espiritual desde lo físico, se encaminan a prolongar la excitación, a extenderla por todo el cuerpo, a trascender el aquí y el ahora para alcanzar lo eterno... Cuando se decide uno a «hacer el amor» y a tratar al compañero en consecuencia, aunque técnicamente se esté «follando»; cuando el tiempo se detiene, a pesar de no disponer de mucho rato; cuando en vez de exhibir el tatuaje lo que se intenta es pintar sobre la piel de la pareja, tratándola como un lienzo y siendo tu lengua una especie de pincel; cuando cada centímetro de su cuerpo merece respeto y eliges abandonarte a mimarlo y despertarlo; cuando cierras los ojos e interiorizas el placer y la emoción; cuando disfrutas del viaje sin plantearte siquiera el destino... el sexo pasa a otra dimensión. Estaremos en el plano de los dioses, ese del que no queremos regresar. Y todos los trucos y conocimientos de este libro sirven para que pasees por el paraíso con frecuencia.

Kegel, ejercicios de: trabajan sobre la musculatura pubococcígea (PC), el suelo pélvico. Sirven para tonificar y fortalecer los músculos del amor, y la buena noticia es que no hace falta pisar un gimnasio para trabajarlos (lo único malo es que no vais a poder lucirlos en la playa). En ella, ejercitan los músculos de la vagina —los de la entrada pero también los de las paredes—, lo que favorece el orgasmo, incrementa la sensibilidad, previene y mejora los problemas de incontinencia urinaria, facilita el parto y la recuperación de la zona del perineo tras el corte de la episiotomía. En él, potencian el control sobre la erección, mejoran la sensibilidad, propician orgasmos más intensos y allanan la vía hacia el multiorgasmo... Se ven en detalle en el apartado de «Masturbación femenina», y en «Juguetes eróticos» hay ayudas para entrenarlos. Empieza ya a practicarlos...

Kinsey, Alfred: su obra *Conducta sexual del varón humano* (1948) reveló el dato de que sólo el 20 % de los varones humanos son homosexuales o heterosexuales exclusivamente; el resto, el 80 %, se mueve en un continuo homo-hetero, es decir, *sensu estricto*, son bisexuales. A este resultado le condujo su profunda investigación llevada a cabo a través de sus más de quince mil entrevistas a personas de toda condición, origen o estrato social. Años después, publicó estadísticas sobre la conducta sexual femenina, arrojando cierta leña al fuego. Afirmaba que el 13 % de las mujeres de 45 años había tenido contacto sexual y llegado al orgasmo con otras mujeres; un 7 % había mantenido relaciones físicas continuadas con otras mujeres, un 8 % reconocía haber tenido deseos o fantasías sexuales hacia las de su mismo sexo y un 38 % del total de sus entrevistadas admitía algún tipo de inclinación homosexual; entre el 3 y el 8 % de las solteras (de entre 20 y 35 años) afirmó su tendencia predominantemente homosexual, con poca o ninguna experiencia heterosexual. (Pese al rigor del estudio, el concepto actual de lesbiana es mucho más evolucionado.)

Labios: aparte de los faciales, en la vulva se encuentran dos pares de labios. Los labios mayores, que recubren la entrada de la vagina y el clítoris, pueden presentar mucho o escaso vello (hipertricosis o hirsutismo, en lenguaje científico). Los labios menores, que van desde el clítoris al orificio vaginal, alcanzado el desarrollo, frecuente y paradójicamente suelen ser más grandes que los otros.

Lesbiana: mujer homosexual. Fémina a quien le atraen sexualmente otras mujeres. Safo (630 a 560 a. C.), poetisa griega, de la isla de Lesbos, fundó una academia donde las chicas de la alta sociedad aprendían danza, poesía, música… y probablemente muchas más «artes». A lo largo de la historia, comparadas con los homosexuales, han sido bastante más ignoradas como colectivo. Como mujeres, se las ha sometido igual que a las demás. En épocas como la Grecia antigua debían engendrar para abastecer de soldados a las tropas, dando lo mismo que fuera sin placer —o sea, como todas—. En todas las culturas prácticamente, la mujer no ha tenido derechos y se la ha considerado propiedad de la familia donde nacía; el padre podía venderla —o pedir la dote— a quien considerase más conveniente... Jamás se planteaba si ella tenía otra opción o hubiera deseado elegir a alguien distinto. Se puede encontrar una explicación de trasfondo económico a toda la caza de brujas de la que durante siglos han sido víctimas los homosexuales: las tres religiones monoteístas más importantes (cristiana, judía y musulmana) han condenado, aplicando sus representantes en la Tierra de un modo más bien interpretativo sus respectivos textos sagrados, el desarrollo de prácticas sexuales que no fomentaran la natalidad. Ello engloba el onanismo, la eyaculación fuera de la vagina —el coito anal o el *coitus interruptus*—, etc. Si a la ausencia total de semen en la relación se suma la moral puritana y su virulenta condena de la homosexualidad y del lesbianismo, que se etiquetaban como «perversiones» y «aberraciones» y se clasificaban dentro de la lista de patologías sexuales, el peso de la legislación homofóbica y demás, añadiendo lo ya señalado: que el placer femenino no interfiere para la reproducción, tenemos el por qué a las lesbianas ni fu ni fa. No es por generación espontánea que actualmente pueda celebrarse una gran fiesta con motivo del Orgullo Gay en casi todas las grandes capitales del mundo. Para que hoy dos mujeres vayan de la mano o se besen sin que nadie las apedree, hay miles de personas que han luchado para reivindicar y consolidar sus derechos fundamentales.

Libido: apetito o impulso sexual. Deseo o ansia de tener sexo. En medicina y psicología significa deseo sexual, las ganas o urgencia de tener sexo. Cualquier estímulo externo puede desatarla, siendo éstos, por supuesto, tan variados como personales. Para Freud sería la energía dialéctica de las pulsiones sexuales. Ojo, no confundir con «lívido», que es estar pálido, quedarse blanco, que se pronuncia (esdrújula) y escribe distinto (con «v»). El apetito sexual puede perderse (causas físicas, psicológicas, ambientales, laborales) y recuperarse (ayudas externas: juguetes, terapia, afrodisíacos, cambio de pareja, etc.).

Líquido preseminal: fluido que segrega el pene previamente a la eyaculación, desde el momento en que comienza la excitación erótica. Sirve como lubricante natural. Conviene tener en cuenta que contiene espermatozoides, por lo que cabe el embarazo si hay penetración, aunque después se coloque un preservativo o eyacule fuera (son muchos los hijos fruto de la marcha atrás).

Lluvia dorada: práctica sexual que consiste en orinar sobre el otro o dejar que contemple la micción. Algunos van más lejos y se beben el pis, se restriegan con él... Se trata de una práctica escatológica cuyo nombre técnico es urolagnia. Hay países que prohíben la emisión de este tipo de secuencias e incluso la distribución de las cintas de pornografía sobre este género. Esta especialidad X recibe el nombre de *pissing*, y en las escenas específicas se muestra a varios hombres meándose sobre una actriz, a ella orinando sobre él...

Lubricación: las glándulas de Bartolino, ubicadas en la vagina, segregan el lubricante natural femenino. La lubricación depende de la excitación, suele ser la primera reacción ante el estímulo sexual. Varía en cada mujer la abundancia con que se segrega este líquido. Algunas, incluso, después del orgasmo lo expulsan junto con el líquido que se produce en las glándulas preuretrales (ver lo referente al *punto G*), produciéndose la «eyaculación femenina» que, en realidad, no es más que el reflejo de una gran excitación. En el mercado existen lubricantes (aceites, cremas, geles) que aportan hidratación a la zona genital —al reducir la fricción hacen que el sexo sea más cómodo y placentero—, y descubren nuevas sensaciones. Imprescindible utilizar lubricante en cualquier penetración anal.

Lucha femenina: además de la no televisada, de la cotidiana, la del día a día (con las amigas, suegra, vecinas, compañeras de trabajo, etc.), existe un subgénero de entretenimiento para adultos que se denomina *catfighting* (= lucha de gatas) que regala alguna escenita lésbica, además de mamporros simulados. En Estados Unidos el *wrestling* combina el deporte con el *show* televisivo de masas. La categoría femenina se desarrolla en un cuadrilátero. Cuenta con una variante, el *mud wrestling*, que constituye, después de un relojazo de oro, el regalo que todo hombre desearía recibir alguna vez por su cumpleaños: un par de rubias exuberantes en bikini dispuestas a revolcarse en una piscina llena de barro.

Lujuria: aparte del nombre de uno de los pecados capitales más divertidos, se trata de uno de los sentimientos más poderosos y que arrastran al ser humano hasta lo más alto (o bajo). Es el fuerte deseo de tener sexo con alguien. Ver los capítulos «Enamoramiento» y «El orgasmo», donde se analizan las fases de la respuesta sexual humana.

Mainstream: anglicismo que se ha adoptado para designar las producciones X «convencionales»: sexo entre heterosexuales, exento de parafilias o de especificidades que las destinarían a géneros concretos. Sería «el porno de hombre con mujer, sin más».

Mamada: término coloquial que designa la felación. Ver el apartado sobre «Sexo oral».

Marcha atrás: «método» anticonceptivo natural que consiste en que «él se sale justo antes». Cuando nota que la eyaculación es inminente saca el pene de la vagina y, mediante estímulo manual propio o de ella (masturbación), «termina». Dado que el líquido preseminal contiene espermatozoides y que a veces puede haber parte de semen que se escapa, no es fiable del todo a la hora de evitar embarazos. Obviamente, deja abierta la puerta a todo tipo de infecciones y al VIH. Ver *coitus interruptus* en el capítulo sobre «Anticonceptivos».

Masaje erótico: técnicas de masaje específicas para provocar la excitación y despertar o acrecentar la sensualidad. Pueden ser aplicados sobre los genitales o abordarlos conjuntamente con otras partes del cuerpo o, incluso, evitarlos a propósito.

Masoquista: la persona o práctica que encuentra el placer en el dolor. Ver *sadomasoquismo*.

Masters y Johnson: William Howell Masters y Virginia Eshelman Johnson se consideran los investigadores pioneros en el estudio de la conducta sexual humana. Trabajaron juntos en la Universidad de San Luis, especializándose en el área de la respuesta sexual humana. Llevaron a cabo un estudio en el que filmaron y observaron miles de actos sexuales en un grupo de 382 mujeres (de edades entre 18 y 70 años) y 312 hombres (de edades entre 21 y 89 años) durante la actividad sexual, con el fin de describir de forma científica y objetiva los cambios físicos que se producían durante la actividad sexual. En total se examinaron más de 10.000 secuencias de actos sexuales, tanto de parejas como individuales. Tras esa investigación publicaron en 1966 *Respuesta sexual humana*, donde describieron la famosa curva de la respuesta sexual humana. Lograron definir la reacción de la persona y la evolución que sigue: inicio, excitación, meseta, orgasmo y resolución. Se explica en el capítulo «El orgasmo». Ellos incorporaron el sentido más médico de la sexualidad, ya que identificaron disfunciones como la eyaculación precoz y la impotencia sexual. Elaboraron y desarrollaron su terapia llamada *dual-sex* o «equipo dual» del tratamiento para la disfunción sexual de hombre/mujer, donde los terapeutas tratan a la pareja en vez de a los individuos.

Masturbación: sexo en su variante de onanismo. Consiste en practicar el autoerotismo, en amarse a uno mismo. Búsqueda del placer (y del orgasmo especialmente) mediante la estimulación de los propios genitales. Cabe realizarla o recibirla de la pareja sexual. Se denomina paja, gayola, etc. ¿Lo hago bien? ¿Me masturbo demasiado? ¿Cómo se hace? ¿Soy rara? A estas y otras mil dudas intento dar respuesta en los apartados sobre «Masturbación femenina» y «Masturbación masculina».

Ménage à trois: expresión francesa que designa los tríos sexuales. Constituye una de las fantasías eróticas más comunes. Hasta ahora, debido a la cultura machista, lo habitual era un par de chicas y él; sin embargo, las modas cambian y el «que venga tu amigo del gimnasio» suena cada vez con mayor naturalidad.

Menarquía: nombre que recibe la primera menstruación. Suele tener lugar entre los 10 y los 14 años.

Menstruación o período: hemorragia que se produce cada vez que la mujer expulsa el óvulo maduro y no fecundado. La duración varía en cada mujer (entre 2 y 5 días), así como los síntomas. Respecto del dolor, las contracciones que provoca el orgasmo lo alivian bastante. Hay un epígrafe sobre el sexo durante la menstruación, ver capítulo de «Menstruación» y ciclo menstrual.

Misionero: es el clásico de los clásicos en lo que a posturas sexuales se refiere. Él se echa sobre ella. Muy denostada, quizá por reminiscencias de otros tiempos que sólo contemplaban esta «casta posición», garantiza sin embargo una enorme intimidad porque permite mirarse a los ojos, contemplar los gestos... Probablemente sea la «más humana» de las formas de practicar el coito. Más en el capítulo sobre «Posiciones».

Money, John: uno de los que más han contribuido a la liberación gay en Estados Unidos. Definió la identidad sexual y la distinguió de la identidad de género: la primera es biológica, basada en evidencias como la producción de óvulos o de esperma, o en la forma en que orinamos; la otra es social. Sus descubrimientos en el campo de las fijaciones sexuales explican que un objeto sea de un sexo y no de otro, se imprimen en el cerebro de manera inconsciente antes de los cuatro años constituyendo todas ellas lo que denominó mapa erótico cerebral, un mapa de cuyo trazado no podremos salirnos el resto de la vida. Fue el primero que propuso el tratamiento con hormonas para delincuentes sexuales, la terapia de reasignación sexual en el transexualismo y también se le debe a él la progresiva desaparición de leyes discriminatorias y que atentan contra la libertad sexual de los individuos, especialmente de los homosexuales.

Monogamia: opción de restringir las actividades sexuales a las que se practiquen con la pareja. Puede ser vitalicia o temporal/sucesiva. Existe un eterno debate acerca de si atenta contra la naturaleza humana, que según avalan cifras de cientos de civilizaciones polígamas.

Monte de Venus o monte púbico: situado en el bajo vientre femenino, es un tejido adiposo que presenta un vello ensortijado que comienza a crecer en la pubertad y que después —va en gustos— es susceptible de sufrir toda suerte de estilismos, depilaciones, decoloraciones, etc. Ver el capítulo «Anatomía básica».

Necrofilia: significa «amor por los muertos» pero, como tantas otras veces, lo que quieren decir es sexo. En efecto, la atracción por los muertos a veces desemboca en la afición de ciertos hombres por la práctica de sexo con el cadáver «relativamente fresco» de una mujer. Se considera una parafilia, una práctica tan extrema que excede el mal gusto personal de cualquiera. Ya dicen por ahí, como chiste: «Me gustan todas. A mí, mientras respire...»

Ninfómana: además de como insulto, sirve para describir un apetito sexual desmedido en la mujer. Esta hipersexualidad puede estar provocada por problemas orgánicos (lesiones en la zona límbica del encéfalo, tumores o accidentes angioencefálicos) o psicológicos (algunas esquizofrenias, estados psicóticos, la fase hipomaníaca de la psicosis maníaco-depresiva). Algunas drogas (anfetaminas, opiáceos y andrógenos) pueden desencadenar episodios de deseo compulsivo, de copular urgentemente. En el hombre, este apetito sexual desmedido se denomina satiriasis o andromanía. Ver el capítulo sobre «Adicción al sexo».

Normal: así suele definirse todo el mundo —parecen quedarse más tranquilos—, en contraposición a «raro», «excéntrico», «enfermo», «bizarro»... En realidad, resulta difícil encontrar personas verdaderamente normales, tanto en lo que respecta a psiquiatría como a sexualidad y, cuando aparecen, suelen ser bastante aburridas.

Oral, sexo: *cunnilingus, fellatio, annilingus.* Consiste en emplear la boca (lengua, labios, dientes) para acariciar, succionar, masturbar, etc., los genitales de alguien. Más en el apartado sobre «Sexo oral».

Orgasmo: ver *clímax.* Es la tercera de las fases de la actividad sexual, el pico de excitación, durante el que se desencadenan contracciones musculares muy placenteras. En el hombre, orgasmo y eyaculación no necesariamente suceden a la vez. «Orgasmo» es la sensación, mientras que «eyaculación» es el acto físico de expulsar esperma. Conforme él eyacula, la cantidad de esperma que sale en sucesivas eyaculaciones será menor, manteniéndose la intensidad del placer.

Orgía: sexo en grupo. Siguiendo las reglas de la pornografía, para que se considere tal han de participar más de cuatro personas. Tan de moda ahora en los *chill out* como en la antigua Roma, los excesos sexuales van muy de la mano de los etílicos y lisérgicos.

Ovarios: las dos glándulas sexuales femeninas responsables de la producción de óvulos. Situados uno a cada lado del útero. La ovulación o formación de un óvulo tiene lugar (teórica e idealmente) cada 28 días.

Oxitocina: es una hormona que interviene en algunas funciones básicas tales como el enamoramiento, orgasmo, parto y amamantamiento. De igual manera está relacionada con la afectividad, la ternura y el acto de tocar. Se segrega cuando besamos a otra persona, durante el orgasmo, al dar a luz, con la caricia de los pezones. Al mezclarse con el torrente sanguíneo produce sensación de felicidad. La mayoría de las sensaciones que provoca el sexo tienen que ver con lo físico (lubricación, orgasmo, etc.), sin embargo, la liberación de ciertas sustancias químicas, como la oxitocina, en la sangre provoca la «beatitud poscoital», responsable de que necesitemos «abrazar» al otro, o de que tras la masturbación nos sintamos algo decaídos. Ver más en el capítulo sobre «El orgasmo».

Paja: nombre coloquial o vulgar de masturbación, onanismo o autoplacer... Se maneja con perífrasis: «cascarse una paja», «hacerse una paja». Hay información específica en dos apartados: «Masturbación femenina» y «Masturbación masculina».

Paja cubana o cubana: se trata de masturbar el pene con los pechos: apoyándolo en el canalillo, él se mueve para estimularlo. Ver el apartado «Masturbación masculina».

Pap test (**examen de Papanicolau**): examen citológico (frotis vaginal) que permite detectar inflamación, infección, y células premalignas y/o cancerígenas en el cuello del útero. Si los resultados apuntan una anomalía significativa, se realiza una colposcopia para examinar la vagina y el cérvix (cuello uterino). Ulteriores pruebas serían el examen de Schiller, en el que se recubre el cérvix con una solución de yodo que colorea de marrón las células sanas, mientras que las células anormales mantienen su típico color blanco o amarillo, y la biopsia, la más eficaz en la detección de cáncer, que consiste en la extracción y análisis de una muestra de tejido. Se recomienda hacerse esta prueba cada tres años a toda mujer mayor de

16 años, cuya vida sexual activa sea de al menos tres años, tiempo que tarda en producirse la modificación de las células a causa del virus del papiloma humano (VPH). El Papanicolau permite detectar a tiempo, y con mayores probabilidades de éxito, este cáncer invasivo de cérvix —infrecuente en mujeres menores de 25 años—. En todo caso, las pruebas y su frecuencia han de ser prescritas y recomendadas por un ginecólogo.

Pasivo: en contraposición a «activo», implica asumir un rol de recepción de la acción o de no-acción. Suele referirse al sexo y, en concreto, a quien es penetrado (siendo «activo» quien penetra, sea con un pene o con un dildo), con independencia de la opción sexual de la pareja, puesto que entre los heteros también se practica la penetración anal y no siempre es la mujer la parte pasiva. Si las parejas homosexuales realizan penetración, pueden establecer roles de modo que uno sea pasivo y otro activo siempre, o bien, intercambiarlos, según el momento. Algunas lesbianas incorporan juguetes a sus relaciones, algunos son simples vibradores pequeños, otros sí imitan la forma de un pene; se podría decir que es activa cada vez quien lo sostiene y penetra a la otra. La acepción «pasivo» va más allá de la penetración, alude a la falta de iniciativa, a la pereza o a dejarse hacer en la cama.

Pediofilia: atracción sexual por las muñecas.

Pedofilia: término que se emplea lo mismo que paidofilia (en griego *páis-paidós*, significa «niño» o «muchacho»), y *filia*, «amistad», «gusto por», «amor»). En sentido estricto consiste en la atracción sexual primaria hacia un niño o niña, aunque no se lleve a cabo ningún acto sexual. Sin embargo, y pese a que «pedófilo» no es un término jurídico, el uso de esta palabra se ha generalizado y abarca desde personas que sienten el deseo sexual por un menor (puramente secreto y sin consecuencias), a casos de consumo y producción de pornografía infantil. Un matiz: en este caso será delito cuando se utilice a menores, pero en la industria X se trata de un género pornográfico como otro cualquiera cuya especialidad es que incluye a actrices adultas pero de aspecto aniñado —están planas, sin curvas, y aparentan ser menores— para disfrute de aficionados a esta estética;

las visten como colegialas, como animadoras, etc. Se denomina «lolicon» o «complejo de Lolita».

Cuando se trata de atracción por muchachos, por chicos adolescentes, se considera efebofilia, y el porno, por supuesto, también se hace eco en los mismos términos. Ambos conceptos se relacionan pero no son lo mismo que la pedofilia.

Existen casos de explotación sexual de menores (cuando se trafica con niños y niñas para prostituirlos) y de abuso sexual infantil (aprovechando una situación de proximidad, familiares, profesores, vecinos, etc., bien por la fuerza y bajo amenaza, bien manipulándoles o engañándoles, se imponen al niño actos de carácter sexual. Se conocen casos en que se involucra incluso a bebés).

La OMS no fija una edad: habla de adolescencia como el período comprendido entre los 10 y los 20 años. La legislación de cada país define concretamente la mayoría de edad y prevé incluso excepciones y casos especiales en que ésta se rebaja para determinados actos jurídicos. Las relaciones con menores de edad son ilegales por la sencilla razón de que participar en una relación sexual ha de ser una decisión libre y consciente, y para tomarla y dar un consentimiento válido, hay que tener capacidad. Un menor no tiene tal capacidad —y aunque lo aparente, siempre puede tratarse, como decía antes, de una manipulación, una amenaza, una coacción, una necesidad económica, etc.—. El perfil de un pedófilo se ve mucho en el cine: maniáticos, raros, pervertidos de baja autoestima, cargados de rabia e inadaptados. La clave para detectar este tipo de casos muchas veces reside en observar la conducta de los niños o incluso señales físicas en su cuerpo. Normalmente, los menores suelen ocultarlo, porque parte de la manipulación incluye que todo permanezca en secreto, o se les convence de que constituye un juego que nadie más puede saber... Los abusos sexuales de menores son una de las causas de infelicidad más frecuentes, aparte de provocar graves problemas sexuales en la edad adulta: rechazo, bloqueo, miedo, anorgasmia, vaginismo, etc. Las víctimas requieren terapia especializada para superarlo y para borrar esa errónea conciencia de culpabilidad que muchas sienten.

Parafilias: ver *filias*.

Pechos: se dice «pechos», y sólo si tienes un par propio estás autorizado a llamarlos «tetas», y tienen unas normas de uso. No se estrujan como si fueran bolas antiestrés. No se muerden. El sujetador no se rompe —salvo que traigas otro carísimo de repuesto para regalárselo antes de marcharte—. Suele ser el segundo paso a dar tras los besos, lo que no implica que sea correcto bajar de cabeza como un lactante desnutrido. Salvo que sean operados —o ella una bendecida por la naturaleza— no suelen ser idénticos, siempre hay uno más grande y más arriba, y el paso del tiempo, los embarazos, los cambios hormonales, etc., pasan factura: hacen que se vayan cayendo o se llenan de estrías. Son muy sensibles, algo que también puede variar en función del momento del ciclo menstrual en que esté. Las areolas y los pezones se contraen y son eréctiles (señal de excitación o de frío). Y nosotras, además de amarlas y de aceptarlas (u operarlas, va en gustos y presupuestos) debemos saber utilizarlas. Sirven para acurrucar, para dar masajes, para amamantar, para masturbar, para abrirte paso entre la multitud o que te dejen pasar a ciertos sitios (¿qué pasa, es que nunca lo habéis pensado siquiera?). Todos sabemos que muchas ascienden gracias a ellas...

Pegging: una de las variantes del sexo anal cuando el sujeto activo es una mujer que introduce un juguete, una prótesis, un dildo (bien sujetándolo manualmente, bien amarrado a un arnés) en su pareja, sea masculina o femenina. A nivel coloquial se recurre a la expresión *bend over boyfriend*. Probablemente, este término induzca a error puesto que, en otro contexto, *pegging* sólo lo mencionan los economistas (significa estabilizar el precio de una divisa o título valor mediante la intervención en el mercado). El cine X recurre a esta parafernalia en multitud de escenas fetichistas y, en especial, cuando se graban esos lésbicos que tanto fascinan a los hombres heteros. En la vida privada no es infrecuente que el sexo anal —sea proporcionado con la boca, con dedos o con dildos— resulte lo más placentero para algunos (otro asunto es que nunca se admita, debido a la asociación del mismo con la homosexualidad, considerada un delito aún en muchos países).

Pene: órgano sexual masculino. Eréctil, alargado, sensible. Para ellos su mejor amigo, su centro neurálgico, su motivo de orgullo o de obsesión. (A veces contiene su única neurona...) Su capacidad eréctil es la que permite la penetración, y ello, en definitiva, perpetúa la especie. Ver el capítulo «Anatomía básica» y los apartados «El tamaño», «Masturbación masculina», «Posiciones»... ¡Si casi es el protagonista del libro!

Penetración: suele estar referida a la inserción del pene en la vagina, la boca o el ano, aunque se aplica también a cualquier dildo u objeto que haga las veces. Se denomina de muy diversas formas: coito, cópula, follar, meterla... Más en los apartados sobre «Penetración» y «Posiciones».

Perineo: zona que va desde el ano a la vagina/escroto. Dotado de innumerables terminaciones nerviosas, en él se localiza uno de los centros de placer. Se menciona en distintos epígrafes.

Período refractario: espacio de tiempo que transcurre entre un orgasmo y otro —fácil, aquí, hacer el chiste...—. En la mujer es casi nulo, ya que de inmediato, si la estimulación continúa y es la adecuada, llegará al segundo orgasmo y a sucesivos. Pero en él es distinto. Su período refractario es el tiempo que necesita un señor para recuperarse desde que eyacula una vez hasta que puede volver a tener una erección. A los 16 o 17 años puede eyacular dos veces sin perder la erección, pero con el paso de un par de años se pierde esta capacidad y, conforme transcurre el tiempo, irremediablemente se hace cada vez más largo. Influye, por supuesto, el grado de motivación o interés (las ganas) y la salud.

Perversión, pervertido: como en casi todos los temas, la edad, moda, cultura, creencia religiosa, etc., determinarán la aplicación de esta palabra, que implica una calificación moral pues significa error, corrupción, maldad, vicio, perturbación, depravación. En general, se considera tal cualquier práctica sexual bizarra, inusual o extrema o a quien la lleve a cabo.

Petting: este anglicismo seguro que a alguno le puede parecer que va a versar sobre zoofilia (por aquello de que su conocimiento de la lengua de la Gran Bretaña les apuntará que *pet* significa «mascota»).

No. Normalmente empleado cuando se habla de las relaciones juveniles, el *petting* equivale, más o menos, a nuestro «enrollarse», y alude a cualquiera de las manifestaciones sexuales sin penetración, aquellas que practicamos durante la fase previa de las relaciones. Incluye los besos, las caricias, los abrazos, los mimos... El *petting* son los juegos afectivos-eróticos-sexuales, en los que intervienen manos, lengua, boca, pechos, pene... con la finalidad de estimular y disfrutar mutuamente pero siempre sin llegar a la penetración. Que no se produzca el coito (que sólo es una práctica sexual más, pese a que esté tan sacralizada) no excluye la presencia de orgasmos. Precisamente el *petting* lo que fomenta es la comunicación entre las dos personas que, a base de gestos o de palabras, pueden experimentar, ofrecer y demandar del otro qué les gusta y cómo, hasta llegar al clímax. Estudios sexológicos demuestran que la mayoría de las mujeres llega al orgasmo mediante estimulación del clítoris, y que la penetración requiere generalmente un «apoyo» extra —por ello se recurre al *petting*: sexo oral, dedos, juguetes sexuales...—. Por su parte, el hombre se excita y alcanza el orgasmo mediante la masturbación, el *petting* y el coito. Se recomiendan largas sesiones de esta práctica en los reaprendizajes necesarios para tratar disfunciones sexuales.

Peyronie: enfermedad muy poco frecuente del pene. Ver el apartado «El tamaño».

Pezón: la parte central del pecho o mama, de tonalidad rosácea o marrón, redondo, semejante a un botón, más o menos grande, con capacidad eréctil cuando se excita o hace mucho frío. En las mujeres, los pezones sirven para amamantar a sus bebés, ya que de ellos sale la leche producida por las glándulas mamarias. Son zonas erógenas (del hombre también) pero, la intensidad de su estimulación ha de adecuarse a los gustos de cada persona. Se pueden abordar con los dedos, pellizcarlos con más o menos fuerza, lamerlos, succionarlos... Hay quien no soporta que se los rocen siquiera y mujeres que tienen un orgasmo con su estimulación. Ver el apartado de «Zonas erógenas».

Píldora, «la píldora»: bien sabe más de una que después de la luz eléctrica es el invento que más agradece... Dentro de los métodos anticonceptivos reversibles, se considera el más efectivo, siempre que se tome correctamente. Ver capítulo de «Anticonceptivos».

Píldora del día después: erróneamente consumida como método anticonceptivo, esta pastilla incorpora una enorme dosis de estrógenos. Su efecto es evitar el embarazo no deseado. La eficacia de este fármaco (léase bomba hormonal) está condicionada a que se tome dentro de las 72 horas subsiguientes al coito de riesgo. La suministran en centros de planificación familiar, de modo gratuito. La píldora poscoital se prescribe en casos de «accidente»: rotura del preservativo, violación, etc., es decir, cuando existe un fallo/ausencia en la profilaxis que puede desencadenar un embarazo no buscado. Ver capítulo de «Anticonceptivos».

Platónico, amor: una relación entre dos personas que se desarrolla maravillosamente en el plano laboral, en el deportivo, en el intelectual, en el musical, en el literario... en cualquiera de los planos... menos en el físico (entiéndase sexual). Normalmente se disfraza de amistad, estando una de las partes absolutamente colada por la otra, que a veces, ni se entera o no se plantea siquiera que la otra persona, más que el amigo perfecto, en realidad está enamorado hasta las trancas. Se basa en la idealización del otro y su esencia radica más en la espiritualidad que en la sensualidad. En términos de andar por casa, suele denominarse amor platónico aquel que, por la razón que sea, es imposible. Coloca lejos al objeto de ese amor, en el plano de lo inalcanzable, más ubicado en el terreno de la imaginación y de la fantasía. Esto significa que en la actualidad, hemos desposeído de su significado a ese amor de Platón, que encontraba su origen en la búsqueda del conocimiento, la sabiduría y la belleza, al margen de todo impulso pasional. En la antigua Grecia surge el arte de la conversación y de ahí el concepto de amor platónico. Platón daba una primera aproximación a lo que es el amor en boca de Sócrates. Este personaje afirmaba «el amor es desear que la persona amada sea lo más feliz posible». En los *Diálogos* plasma otras ideas: «El amor es una forma de necesidad que tiene una meta y su relación con esta meta es de deseo, de exigencia. El amor anhela siempre lo bello y lo bueno y, por tanto, no es ninguno de éstos sino algo intermedio entre lo bello y lo bueno. El amor, dice, no puede ser considerado un dios, porque si fuera un dios no amaría, puesto que en un ser perfecto es imposible que haya anhelo, deseo o pasión. Por lo mismo, el amor es un ser entre mortal e inmortal, es decir, un espíritu.» «La meta real del amor es la belleza, la cual, según Platón, no es diferente del bien. Esto significa que el amor busca la felicidad, es decir, la posesión del bien, al cual tiende todo el género humano.» Según Platón existe una vía ascendente, un ascenso erótico, que atraviesa varios grados para conocer el verdadero amor:

1. El amor a la belleza corporal que posee dos momentos: el amor a un cuerpo bello determinado y el amor a la belleza corpórea en general.
2. El amor a la belleza de las almas, es decir, a la belleza moral que se manifiesta en los quehaceres y en las reglas de conducta de los hombres.
3. El amor a los conocimientos, el cual trasciende la servidumbre de los seres concretos.
4. El amor a lo bello en sí, el cual es el nivel supremo de amor y que se nos revela de súbito, cuando hemos recorrido correctamente los senderos anteriores en todas sus etapas.

Polución nocturna: la eyaculación masculina involuntaria que tiene lugar durante el sueño. Siendo algo normal, a veces se produce cuando no se ha eyaculado de modo voluntario durante algunos días, dado que el esperma se acumula y el cuerpo tiende a expulsarlo. Los «sueños húmedos» femeninos son de carácter erótico y provocan sensaciones orgásmicas o muy próximas (y pese a su nombre, no son comparables en «humedad» a las poluciones masculinas).

Polvo, echar un: significa realizar el acto sexual y sustituye y equivale a «hacer el amor» y a «follar» para denominar el coito de modo coloquial. «Polvo somos, del polvo venimos y en polvo nos convertiremos», viene a asociar el origen de la vida a la cópula. Una modalidad de polvo es «el rapidito» o *quickie* (del inglés) que supone una relación sexual muy breve, en la que lo que prima es realizar la penetración cuanto antes, pasando por alto todo tipo de preámbulos y consideraciones. Sería un «aquí te pillo, aquí te mato» para satisfacer el calentón, un ir al grano. Normalmente se suele utilizar para dejar claro que la cosa no va en serio, que sólo es sexo, respecto de otro tipo de vínculos afectivos más profundos o que impliquen compromiso (¿mande?).

Pornografía o porno: según la RAE se vincula al carácter obsceno de una manifestación artística u obra literaria y al tratado de la prostitución. Olvidando la definición, la sociedad emplea este término para designar contenidos para adultos que contienen sexo (bien plasmado en imágenes, como las revistas, las películas X, etc., bien en forma de relatos, de instalaciones, de objetos...). Dentro del porno hay dos niveles de intensidad, en función de lo explícito que sea el contenido sexual. El *hardcore*, o porno duro, incluye planos explícitos de penetraciones, de eyaculaciones, frontales del pene y de la vagina, incluso del ano dilatado, etc., recrean cada detalle sin censura (hay especialidades en función de la legislación vigente en cada país). El *softcore*, o porno blando, evita los planos que recogen la penetración, la descarga de semen, los genitales... Normalmente, para rentabilizar, durante la grabación de una misma escena se colocan varias cámaras para montar después dos versiones distintas, la *hard* y la *soft*, que se distribuirán por separado. Ver *géneros pornográficos* y el capítulo sobre «Cine X», con sus grandes verdades y sus aún mayores mentiras.

Habida cuenta que en determinados países no es legal la producción, la distribución ni la emisión de pornografía, lo que genera un mercado negro, y que determinadas opciones sexuales se consideran aún delito (hablo de la homosexualidad, por ejemplo), por lo que prácticas como el sexo anal, la sodomía, está penada, según dónde si te pillan grabando determinadas escenas, terminas en la cárcel, como me contaba un actor de porno gay que estuvo trabajando en Jordania.

Además, respecto del porno, la legislación de cada país, junto con la idiosincrasia de cada uno, su cultura estética y demás referentes y valores, condicionan la producción y la distribución de pornografía. Si bien unánimemente se prohíbe la participación de menores, respecto de otros asuntos concretos, las normas varían. El porno europeo admite, por ejemplo, un *fistfucking* de puño o de los cinco dedos, no así el americano, que sólo permite el de cuatro. Incluso dentro de Estados Unidos, como cada estado puede legislar en determinados asuntos de orden público y moralidad, podemos encontrarnos que lo que en California es legal, en Tejas, no. Otra diferencia sería que Estados Unidos rechaza las escenas donde aparezca comida (no dejan que nada que pueda echarse a la ensalada actúe como dildo).

El Alemania, Holanda y países nórdicos en general, los gustos van más hacia lo extremo: más parafernalia sado, más castigos y sumisión, menos rubitas de silicona y más fustas y alfileres... Y otra muestra de diversidad sería Japón. En el porno se evidencia, sin duda, el enorme abismo cultural entre Oriente y Occidente. Se pueden destacar varias llamativas diferencias entre las prácticas y normas de producción. Por ejemplo, la absoluta prohibición de mostrar el vello púbico. Los directores se las ingenian para colocar a los actores de espaldas o boca abajo o bien para interponer algún objeto oportunamente entre el objetivo y las partes pudendas y peludas, aunque lo que más «choca» es que sean capaces de pixelar partes de la imagen —ponen cuadraditos para distorsionarla y que no se vea, de tan borrosa como queda—. A los occidentales, además, nos deja pasmados el enorme nivel de violencia que incorporan las producciones porno japonesas. Si bien cumplen a rajatabla la censura del vello púbico, las licencias en cuanto a tortura, ahogamiento, empleo de utensilios cortantes, punzantes o abrasivos, es una constante. Sexo y violencia van muy unidos por lo general, nada que ver con Occidente, donde sí se producen cintas donde se simulan desde violaciones a secuestros, pero nada que ver... El pueblo del Sol Naciente ha convertido el sadomasoquismo y las ataduras en las herramientas básicas de su lenguaje audiovisual para adultos. Veremos vejaciones, palizas, violaciones colectivas, cuerdas, flagelaciones... Los japoneses, ese pueblo a la vanguardia de la tecnología que nos lega preciosismo, *ikebana* y *geishas*, es de lo más sórdido en lo suyo. Por su afición al frotismo o *frottage* —restregar los genitales contra quien o lo que sea—, se han visto obligados a crear vagones de metro sólo para mujeres.

Pinky violence es un subgénero de cine japonés que se posiciona entre lo erótico y lo violento. Una especie de serie B con marcado tinte sexual, que surge en los años setenta, donde las protagonistas son chicas guapísimas y malas, muy malas. Desde monjas pervertidas a ladronas sobre motos de potente cilindrada, internas de reformatorios y reclusas de prisiones, *yakuzas* maestras de la espada, policías infiltradas en bandas... todas dispuestas a ejecutar su misión, cueste lo que cueste. El sexo —siempre simulado— se integra en la acción: se presenta en momentos puntuales, siendo parte de la trama, no lo prioritario o lo único. Como ejemplos: *Terrifying Girl School: Lynch Law Classroom* (1973) o *Sex & Fury* (1973).

Preliminares: mal llamados así porque deberían estar presentes en el antes, en el durante y en el post de cada encuentro sexual. Conjunto de besos, caricias, cosquillas, masajes, juegos y demás, que se encaminan a excitar al otro y a proporcionarle y obtener placer. Es lo de «enrollarse» con alguien sin llegar a la penetración. Ver *petting*. Se llaman también preámbulos, prolegómenos... todos apuntan a que el acto principal (coito) viene luego. A lo largo de todo el libro se explica su carácter imprescindible: activan la lubricación, favorecen la distensión de la vagina, erotizan cada zona —si se aborda, claro—, van construyendo gradualmente el ambiente de sensualidad que incrementa el deseo, etc. En el propio Kamasutra se especifica su importancia especialmente para la mujer y aconseja que para cada unión sexual, el hombre debe emplear los medios que juzgue convenientes «o sea, que del mismo modo que para hacer el pan se precisa preparar la pasta, así también hay que preparar a la esposa para la relación sexual, si se quiere que ella también obtenga la plena satisfacción». Por la diferente respuesta sexual del hombre y de la mujer, somos nosotras quienes más los necesitamos, lo que en absoluto significa que nos estén haciendo un favor: ellos se lo pasan exactamente igual de bien. En resumen, mejor ir poco a poco, ya que siempre es mucho mejor que nos pidan más a que se aparten con asco o con horror. Otra cosa: cuando la gente evoca con nostalgia a sus grandes amantes o noches de pasión absoluta, no suelen mencionar haberse tirado a alguien que trabaja en el Circo del Sol... las acrobacias caducan pronto en la memoria. La resistencia en la cama tampoco va de ser el más rápido haciendo el mete-saca, ni de que te perforen hasta desprenderte el útero de una embestida mal dada. Al revés, la clave del juego es dedicarse a fondo a estimular a la pareja. Que el guiso se haga a fuego muy, muy lento, para darle, una vez en ebullición, un buen golpe de calor de unos pocos minutos... No sólo lo digo yo. Me avala la cifra del sexólogo Alfred Kinsey, que publicó que el 92 % de las mujeres que recibía al menos veinte minutos de estimulación previa alcanzaba el orgasmo. Ah, y no hay un orden predeterminado (primero besar, luego tocar aquí, después chupar allá...). En esta historia, es un error pensar que hay un planteamiento, un nudo y un desenlace (y más grave aún es creerte que «ya has leído esto antes», porque cada persona es única y distinta).

Prepucio: en los hombres no circuncidados, es la funda de piel retráctil que recubre la cabeza del pene; si se echa hacia atrás bruscamente, duele. Ver el capítulo «Anatomía básica», donde se explica también lo que es la fimosis.

Preservativo: método anticonceptivo y de profilaxis frente a determinadas ETS. Los hay de dos tipos, según se coloquen en el pene o sobre la vagina. Se fabrican en látex y en poliuretano. Para utilizarlo correctamente ha de ponerse cuando el pene está en erección y, tras la eyaculación, agarrarlo de la base antes de retirarse, para evitar que pueda quedar dentro y el semen se salga en el interior de la vagina/ano —tanto si la finalidad es contraceptiva como para evitar contagios, y tanto en relaciones sexuales hetero como gays—. Ver el capítulo «Anticonceptivos».

Priapismo: viene de Priapus, nombre del dios varón y fértil en la mitología clásica, ese que nos apunta con su falo amenazante y que vemos reproducido en estatuillas y tótems. Se trata de un tipo de disfunción puntual que consiste en una erección persistente e indeseada. Los cuerpos cavernosos del pene comienzan a llenarse de sangre como en una erección normal pero, después de un estímulo o actividad sexual, la sangre no vuelve a salir y la erección no desaparece, a diferencia de lo que ocurre en una erección normal. Si pasado el tiempo que cada uno entiende como «normal», el pene no retorna al estado de flaccidez, se dé o no dolor, no hay pero que valga: hay que ir a Urgencias, que nadie sienta vergüenza de llegar empalmado, o, de lo contrario, las consecuencias sobre la futura capacidad de erección pueden ser graves.

Progesterona: hormona sexual cuyas funciones se asocian con la fertilidad femenina. Actúa acondicionando el endometrio para alojar al óvulo fecundado y que éste se desarrolle. Cuando su tasa desciende durante el ciclo menstrual, el endometrio se desprende y se produce la menstruación. Influye también en el correcto desarrollo de las mamas.

Promiscuidad: si hay una pregunta estúpida que se puede formular a tu amante cuando aún estás en la cama —aparte, claro está, de «¿cómo decías que te llamas?»—, sería la de «¿con cuántos te has acostado?» La sociedad se estructura a raíz de una serie de normas cuyos tentáculos se cuelan en la intimidad del dormitorio. Aquí y ahora, las familias se conforman por sólo dos personas. Sin embargo, en otros países, donde se permite la poligamia, nadie criticaría a un señor que tiene hasta cuatro esposas, siempre que a todas las pueda mantener y ofrezca a cada una lo mismo que a las otras. La promiscuidad atañe a la forma de ejercer cada uno su sexualidad, a la cantidad de parejas sexuales que frecuenta bien de modo simultáneo —no se refiere al sexo en grupo ni a las orgías, sino a que sean durante la misma época—, bien de forma sucesiva, y sea estando soltero o, de tener una relación, a espaldas de su pareja (siéndole sexualmente infiel) o de un modo consensuado (parejas abiertas). Nuevamente, se da un caso de machismo lingüístico; el término, cuando se aplica a la mujer, infiere crítica e insulto. Ser tildada de «promiscua» comporta cierto tinte de reprobación moral ya que, históricamente, las religiones la consideraban un pecado (porque iba contra la castidad, una tendencia muy arraigada que propició incluso el diseño de unos cinturones ideales, con llave y todo), ponía en peligro la certeza de la filiación (el tema económico era el verdadero motivo: una vez que el pueblo llano alcanzó el derecho de acceder a la propiedad, garantizar la paternidad y verificar el linaje se exigía para adjudicar la herencia, alcanzar la sucesión en títulos nobiliarios, etc.) y amenazaba la institución monógama preferida por excelencia: el matrimonio.

Con independencia de valoraciones morales, evitar la promiscuidad es, junto con el uso de preservativo y la advertencia de no compartir agujas y jeringuillas, la tercera medida para reducir el riesgo de contraer ETS y sida. Las autoridades sanitarias aconsejan que lo ideal es tener un compañero estable (que sepas que no ha tenido riesgo de contagiarse). Cuanto menor es el número, menor es el riesgo, pero deben ser parejas que a su vez no tengan relaciones con muchos otros compañeros (ellos citan a «prostitutas, chaperos, gigolós... o personas que se inyecten drogas», y yo añadiría a pescaderos, modelos, taquilleras, actores, tenistas, músicos, gasolineros, discjockeys, pintores, periodistas, abogados, peluqueros, fruteros, electricistas... ¿me explico?). Si bien la cantidad de parejas sexuales es directamente proporcional al riesgo que se asume, no es menos cierto que no importa con cuántos te acuestes —es un decir...— sino que siempre utilices protección. El contagio puede darse con una sola relación mantenida con una sola persona. No es menos peligroso un hombre que ha estado con seis mujeres que otro que se ha acostado con mil, si el de mil siempre «se plastificó» y el de seis lo hizo a pelo tres de las seis ocasiones. Otro asunto relacionado sería el de la «integridad» de las personas con pareja estable y supuestamente fieles que luego rompen esa palabra y se tiran a quien sea, y el riesgo de mantener relaciones sin protección con estos sujetos —y sujetas, por supuesto—, basándonos en la prometida fidelidad... Espero que se entienda el mensaje. No hago apología de la promiscuidad.

Próstata: glándula masculina que se encuentra frente al recto, bajo la vejiga y la uretra, con forma de castaña, y que se encarga de segregar un líquido que se mezcla y expulsa junto al esperma en el momento de la eyaculación. Lamentablemente más mencionada como causa de cáncer que como punto P (es el segundo tipo de cáncer más frecuente, por lo que conviene realizar revisiones periódicas a partir de los 50 años, lo que incluye, además de ecografía, un posible tacto rectal). En efecto, se trata del equivalente al punto G femenino. Para acariciarla se puede penetrar por vía anal o estimularla «desde fuera», tocando con el pulgar hasta localizar el hueco que hay en el tramo del perineo, desde el ano hasta el escroto. Ver los apartados «Sexo anal» y «Masturbación masculina».

Prostitución: actividad profesional desarrollada por hombres y mujeres que consiste en intercambiar servicios sexuales por dinero. Serían personas «prepago». Si se toma la palabra «dinero» en sentido amplio, dentro de la prostitución podemos incluir a quienes obtienen casa, coche, joyas, ascensos, ropa y complementos carísimos, drogas, viajes, etc., por «dejarse querer» (señoritas y caballeros en régimen de tarifa plana), que define a un buen grupo de la población (sí, incluyo a muchos «felizmente casados», a quienes debe de darles reparo autodefinirse como profesionales del sexo):

Desde 1995 ejercer la prostitución es legal en España, pero es ilegal fomentarla o lucrarse con ella. 400.000 personas ejercen la prostitución en España. 360.000 son mujeres y el resto, hombres y transexuales. 3.600 son los clubes de alterne y burdeles donde trabaja más de la mitad de las prostitutas. El resto lo hace en calles, plazas, parques, pisos y polígonos industriales. Existen 2.900 establecimientos de alto nivel, pero sólo un centenar es de auténtico lujo. La prostitución mueve 18.000 millones de euros al año en España. La trata de prostitutas es la actividad que más dinero negro genera dentro de la economía sumergida. 2.880 millones de euros recaudaría anualmente Hacienda si la actividad fuera regulada y los clientes pagaran con factura. 1.124 millones de euros ingresaría la tesorería si las prostitutas se dieran de alta en la Seguridad Social. 123 euros aproximadamente es lo que gana una prostituta al día en España. 9 de cada 10 prostitutas son extranjeras. El 60 % son latinoamericanas. 30 euros es el promedio que cobra una prostituta por tener sexo en la calle. El 50 % de las personas que ejercen la prostitución en Europa lo hace voluntariamente. El 5 % son víctimas del tráfico de personas; el 3,5 % son menores vendidas por sus familias; el 1 % son secuestradas. Del 39 % restante, poco se sabe. Todo esto según la INTERPOL. El 70 % de los españoles cree que debería regularizarse la prostitución.[34]

PT141: es el nombre de lo que, sin duda, va a hacer que se reescriban muchas de las teorías sobre sexualidad. Aunque todo lo que he encontrado ha sido en Internet, me parece fácil prever que este estudio de la Universidad de Concordia va a convertirse en un fenómeno social. Lo novedoso del fármaco es que afecta al deseo: es un chute —se inhala— que va directo a la sangre y que activa la libido. Se la denomina la Viagra femenina, pero no es exacto pues el PT141 va más allá, por lo que leo, sirve tanto para hombres como para mujeres y no interactúa con otros fármacos, ni con tabaco o alcohol. Afirman que no provoca efectos secundarios (en ellas son síntomas suaves, como náuseas, dolor de cabeza y congestión nasal). Al actuar directamente sobre el cerebro erradica el riesgo cardiovascular, y también por ello se nota el efecto en el deseo, porque no implica que se desvíe sangre al pene, sino que libera en la mente las ganas de sexo, con erecciones espontáneas y, en la mujer, provoca que gocen de un despertar de la libido. Además, la erección y el rendimiento sexual durante la penetración mejoran y hace efecto de inmediato. Hay algo más sobre este fármaco en el apartado sobre «Impotencia o gatillazo».

34. Datos extraídos del libro *Los amos de la prostitución*, de Joan Cantarero, Ediciones B.

Pubococcígea, musculatura: se utilizan las siglas PC para denominar los músculos del interior de la vagina y los que controlan el movimiento del pene. Intervienen en la respuesta a la estimulación sexual. Las leves contracciones de esta musculatura preceden a la lubricación, continúan durante la fase de meseta (manteniendo la lubricación e intensificando el placer) y desencadenan contracciones involuntarias y frecuentes —éstas mucho más fuertes— durante el orgasmo. En la zona del perineo se localizan varios músculos. Dos de ellos son los llamados «pélvicos»: el pubococcígeo, que tanto en hombres como en mujeres recorre la pelvis partiendo del hueso púbico hasta el coxis; y el bulbocavernoso (bulboclitorideo en la mujer), situado por encima y que con un recorrido en forma de ocho va rodeando la uretra, el perineo y el ano. Esta rama sensitiva del nervio recibe los estímulos de la zona del clítoris, los labios, la parte inferior de la vagina y el ano. Cuando se produce el orgasmo, ambos músculos se contraen y sufren espasmos de forma involuntaria. Sin embargo, de modo voluntario, también podemos localizarlos y emplearlos —como cuando evitamos mearnos encima: los estamos contrayendo—. Son claves en este libro y más en tu vida sexual, lee despacio *Kegel, ejercicios de*, el apartado sobre la «Masturbación femenina» y el capítulo «El orgasmo».

Pubertad: se asocia al despegue de la vida, especialmente de la sexual, que viene provocada por el cambio físico rápido y evidente que los chicos y chicas suelen experimentar entre los 10 y 20 años (especialmente sería entre los 12 y los 15, pero la OMS no concreta). A ellas les viene la regla, a ellos les cambia la voz; les crece vello, pegan un estirón, se llenan de acné, etc. Se debe al desarrollo de los caracteres sexuales secundarios.

Puerperio: es el período comprendido entre el parto y la regularización del ciclo menstrual de la madre y dura de 40 a 45 días. En estos días el cuerpo «vuelve a su ser», los órganos recuperan su tamaño y su ubicación, quedando tal y como son, deshaciendo las alteraciones que producen la gestación y el parto. Después, durante quince o veinte días, se suceden los llamados «entuertos», contracciones espontáneas del útero para reducirse hasta su medida original y terminar de expulsar las secreciones vaginales y restos de placenta (loquios: se trata de flujo vaginal sanguinolento a consecuencia del parto, pero que va, con el paso de los días, haciéndose normal y aclarándose hasta salir blanquecino).

Regla: período, ver *menstruación*.

Reich, Wilhelm: fue un médico austríaco (1897-1957). Inicialmente un colaborador de Freud, quien le consideró su «discípulo más brillante», aunque maduró y dio un cambio bastante apreciable en cuanto a sus teorías sobre el psicoanálisis. Reich, de modo recíproco, mostró gran entusiasmo por las teorías de Freud, en especial en lo relativo a la sexualidad. Aunque en eso Freud no fue demasiado original, ya que médicos como Richard von Krafft-Ebing llevaban muchos años haciendo investigaciones antes que él sobre el tema. Para Reich el sexo y el trabajo entretienen una relación bioenergética donde «la salud mental de una persona se puede medir por su potencial orgásmico». Según él, un individuo psíquicamente sano disfruta del sexo libremente, sin traumas o inhibiciones, y una persona neurótica no. Las personas no neuróticas manifestaban lo que él llamó «reflejo de orgasmo», consistente en el movimiento involuntario, incontrolable y repetido de la cadera a la hora de la descarga orgásmica. Para él, los tratamientos psicoanalíticos convencionales de la época eran muy poco eficaces porque el paciente tiene miedo a romper sus bloqueos, a relajarse, a dejarse llevar. Inventó el Análisis Caracteriológico: antes de pretender llegar al centro del problema de la psique del paciente mediante charlas, la misión de Reich consistía en derribar las barreras que bloqueaban su libre flujo de energía. Esto lo consiguió aplicando otro principio descubierto por él que afirmaba: «La psique de una persona y su musculatura voluntaria son funcionalmente equivalentes.» Esto quiere decir que los bloqueos psíquicos se corresponden a contracciones musculares crónicas. Reich mantenía contacto físico con los pacientes, los abrazaba, retorcía y estiraba hasta que rompían a llorar o vomitaban, liberándose. Finalmente, Reich percibió que los patrones musculares se podían explicar desde el punto de vista de una energía vital (que más tarde llamaría «energía orgánica») que recorre el cuerpo. Aquí Reich redescubrió para Occidente el concepto de *chi* (también llamado *baraka, vril*) ampliamente extendido en Oriente y las sociedades herméticas.

En su segunda etapa, se adhirió a las ideas marxistas y se afilió al Partido Comunista. A partir de entonces, su trabajo se orientó hacia la búsqueda de una síntesis entre el materialismo dialéctico y el psicoanálisis. Se destacan en este período sus obras *La revolución sexual* y *psicología de masas del fascismo*. Reich postuló el viraje hacia la metapsicología iniciado por Freud a partir de su obra *Más allá del principio del placer* (1920). Para Reich la mayor parte de la población sufre patologías mentales y vive en condiciones de fuerte represión sexual. Reich considera que el dominio de una clase social sobre otra necesita que la mayor parte de la población sufra una atrofia en su vida sexual.

En su tercera etapa (muy criticada, considerada un puro delirio por sus detractores) sus estudios se centraron en el «orgón», palabra que combina «organismo» y «orgasmo». Para Reich, el orgón es la energía vital de todo organismo, es la fuerza motora del reflejo del orgasmo. Además, es de color azul, medible y omnipresente. Toda materia viva es creada y produce esta energía. El objetivo de Reich era hacer fluir la energía en el cuerpo de sus pacientes. Enfermedades como el cáncer, para él no eran más que acumulaciones de orgones negativos, por lo que experimentó con enfermos terminales de cáncer creyendo que podía ayudarlos. Reich afirmó que la coraza corporal se encuentra dividida en siete áreas o sectores. Estos sectores forman bandas alrededor del cuerpo en su área, y en esa banda se estanca la energía. En orden céfalo-caudal las áreas son las siguientes: Ojos, Boca, Cuello, Pecho, Plexo Solar, Cintura o Pelvis, y Genitales. Reich debía analizar estas áreas en cada individuo y ayudarle a desbloquearlas para que la energía o el orgón pudiese fluir nuevamente. El desbloqueo era realizado mediante masaje, movimiento, sonidos y ejercicios.

Expulsado de los círculos comunistas y de la escuela psicoanalítica por lo radical de sus planteamientos, perseguido por los fascistas en Alemania por su libro *Psicología de masas del fascismo* y, finalmente, juzgado en Estados Unidos, donde fue diagnosticado como esquizofrénico progresivo y donde lanzaron sus manuscritos a la hoguera en el Incinerador Gansevoort de Nueva York el 23 de octubre de 1956 (craso error), Reich murió en la cárcel un año después de un ataque al corazón, un día antes de apelar su sentencia.

Respuesta sexual humana: ver el capítulo «El orgasmo», donde se tratan las fases por las que las personas atraviesan desde el nivel base de excitación o inicio del deseo, que son aspectos muy particulares, hasta el orgasmo, con sus connotaciones y alteraciones físicas: las reacciones del cuerpo hasta lograr el clímax y justo después, comunes en todo el mundo.

Rinding/Gibbing: una práctica sexual parafílica, entre escatológica y potencialmente peligrosa, que consiste en provocar arcadas para desatar contracciones vaginales y movimientos a ritmo de los vómitos.

Sadomasoquismo: cuando el placer se obtiene mediante el dolor, sea infligiéndoselo a otro o recibiéndolo. También se vincula a la disciplina. Es muy frecuente que del sadomasoquismo sólo tengamos la vaga idea de gente con fustas y vestida de cuero negro, y sea esa parcelita la que nos atraiga: utilizar una máscara o una cadena de perro un día... Pero hay más. Su nombre viene del autor polaco del s. XIX, Leopold von Sacher-Masoch. En nuestra cultura el dolor, sea físico o psíquico, se tiende a evitar, bien a base de fármacos, bien, sencillamente, negándolo. Sin ánimo de hacer apología del sufrimiento es incuestionable que, tanto para evolucionar y madurar como para sentir determinadas emociones, el dolor ha de experimentarse. Cuando alguien a quien queremos fallece se produce el duelo. Sufrimos lo indecible y, por más psicofármacos que traguemos para pasar el trago, al cesar su efecto, esa pérdida será igual de dolorosa, sólo lo disfrazamos o camuflamos su intensidad. Habremos de consumir cada gota de ese dolor a base de atravesar cada una de sus conocidas fases (no por esquematizadas menos duras) de negación, ira, negociación, depresión y aceptación. El dolor que persigue el sadomasoquismo se asocia al erotismo (por eso no se considera crueldad, que sería hacer daño sin una finalidad concreta), a ser o sentirse fuente de dolor o de placer. A los sadomasoquistas les produce satisfacción experimentar con objetos que, en su uso cotidiano, jamás proporcionarían placer sexual, o intentan

excitarse en circunstancias muy lejanas a lo «erótico» en su acepción más común.

Dentro del cine X, las prácticas del BD/SM (*Bondage*-Dominación/Sadismo-Masoquismo) se clasifican en función de su dureza. Así, el «blando», B/D, incluye los azotes, los pellizcos leves, el *bondage* (ataduras con cuerdas), la colocación de pinzas en los pechos y las lavativas. El «duro», S/M, incorpora castigos con objetos punzantes o a elevada temperatura, ahogamiento y estrangulación, potros de tortura, colocación de aparatos de succión o poleas de peso en los genitales, penetración con el puño *(fistfucking)*, con el pie *(footfucking)*, uso de electrodos sobre los genitales con aplicación de descargas eléctricas, escatología, etc. El S/M está prohibido en Estados Unidos (tanto la producción como la difusión de películas), mientras que en Japón y en Alemania se encuentran los principales productores. Aunque últimamente se fabrican en materiales y colores distintos, el cuero negro preside la ristra de objetos asociados: máscaras, caretas, fustas, látigos, esposas, pantalones, corsés, botas...

En general, todos, en determinado momento o aspecto de la personalidad, incorporamos rasgos sádicos o masoquistas que bien pueden permanecer latentes (en un plano inconsciente o de fantasía) o manifestarse en actos o actitudes concretas. Las prácticas sadomasoquistas, con lo que conllevan en cuanto a parafernalia estética, juguetes, etc., y psicológica de dominación, sumisión, y demás, sólo suponen un problema cuando llegan a ser una obsesión y se convierten en el único modo de poder alcanzar un orgasmo, rechazando o impidiendo el disfrute con las relaciones sexuales de otro estilo e incapacitando a estas personas para sentir un enamoramiento por nadie. Las parejas que combinan un sádico (el que causa dolor físico o psíquico y eso es lo que le pone) con un masoquista (el que se excita cuando le castigan, le pegan o le hacen daño) se compenetran puesto que cada uno obtiene el tipo de placer que le excita. Todos contentos (obviamente, entre adultos que consienten).

Semen: ver *esperma*.

Sesenta y nueve: para algunos, la única cifra mágica pese a que no sea el número que haga bingo. Dentro de las distintas posiciones sexuales, ésta implica dar placer oral recíproca y simultáneamente. La idea es colocar la cara frente a los genitales del otro, de modo que sea accesible con la boca (lengua, labios) e, incluso, con las manos. Esto se hace, bien colocándose ambos de lado, echados, o uno de los dos sobre el otro. Si quieres darle un punto acrobático a tu vida, prueba a hacerlo de pie: el que sea más grande, que agarre al otro, sosteniéndolo cabeza abajo. El único inconveniente sería la facilidad con la que nos despistamos cuando lo que estamos sintiendo gracias a la lengua del otro nos encanta, y nos desconcentramos de la tarea o nos dedicamos a cumplir sin demasiada entrega. Si sucede esto, mejor turnarse e ir combinando sexo oral con caricias: que mientras una practica una felación, el otro puede acariciar la vagina con la mano o viceversa: cunnilingus de él con masturbación de ella. Como se trata de una variante de sexo oral, deberías echar un vistazo al apartado específico.

Sexo oral: consiste en la estimulación sexual empleando la boca (los labios, la lengua, los dientes con suavidad...). Ver el apartado específico sobre «Sexo oral», la definición de *Felación*, *Cunnilingus* y *Sesenta y nueve*.

Sexo seguro: se da cuando el riesgo de contraer ETS o VIH mediante las relaciones sexuales es escaso, bien porque las prácticas son de bajo o nulo riesgo (cuando ambos están sanos o si alguno o los dos no lo están pero sólo se besan, acarician y masturban con la mano mutuamente, sin entrar en contacto con los fluidos genitales) o bien porque se emplea preservativo.

Sexualidad: es una dimensión humana que involucra todo nuestro ser. Todo nuestro ser es sexuado, esto significa que podemos obtener placer de cualquiera de sus partes, desde la piel hasta los genitales incluyendo, desde luego, el cerebro, las emociones, los tímpanos... Mientras que «sexo» sirve para definir y distinguir a los seres femeninos de los masculinos, con diferencias celulares, morfológicas, fisiológicas y psicológicas, «sexualidad» trasciende a los meros órganos genitales. La sexualidad y la reproducción no son lo mismo ni tienen, necesariamente, que ir ligadas. Podemos disfrutar ampliamente de la sexualidad con independencia de la facultad de procrear y podemos también decidir libremente el momento de tener un hijo. Cada persona vive y entiende la sexualidad de un modo propio, dependiendo de la etapa que atraviese, de sus circunstancias, de la formación que haya recibido, de sus creencias, de su modo de pensar y de sentir... Las vivencias personales y la educación sexual determinan nuestra sexualidad. La OMS definió la sexualidad sana como «La aptitud para disfrutar de la actividad sexual y reproductiva, amoldándose a criterios de ética social y personal. La ausencia de temores, de sentimientos de vergüenza, de culpabilidad, de creencias infundadas y de otros factores psicológicos que inhiban la reactividad sexual o perturben las relaciones sexuales». Este concepto fue desarrollado por Wilhelm Reich, el primer estudioso del orgasmo, que expuso ya en su época los efectos negativos de la sociedad sexualmente represora sobre el individuo. Su idea ya incorporaba todos los aspectos del ser humano: corporal, emocional, intelectual y social. Una sexualidad sana es la que fomenta el desarrollo del individuo, potencia su personalidad, su relación con los otros y el amor. La sexualidad es una fuente de placer y de satisfacción del deseo sexual, una forma de comunicación y de expresar afectividad, una manera de descubrirse a uno mismo y al otro.

Sida: acrónimo de Síndrome de Inmunodeficiencia Adquirida. Enfermedad causada por el virus de la inmunodeficiencia humana (VIH) por el que el organismo pierde su capacidad de defenderse contra las enfermedades, que terminan debilitándolo hasta causarle la muerte.

El VIH se transmite mediante el contacto sexual, contacto con sangre, hemoderivados u otros líquidos corporales, y por contagio materno (al feto durante el embarazo, en el parto y por la leche materna: las mujeres VIH positivas no deben amamantar a sus hijos). No existen pruebas de que se transmita por contactos casuales o familiares (besar, estrechar la mano, tocar a un enfermo, etc.), ni por picaduras de insectos como los mosquitos. Casi todas las ETS se curan, una excepción es el sida, aunque puede retrasarse la aparición de la enfermedad y mejorar la calidad de vida con el tratamiento. Si bien hoy por hoy no tiene cura, los retrovirales la han convertido en una enfermedad crónica. Su contagio puede venir por vía sexual, por lo que se recomienda practicar sexo seguro y utilizar preservativos (que alguien sea «majo» no certifica que una relación sexual con él no sea potencialmente mortal, un rato de placer no debería justificar que nadie se juegue la vida), y por vía sanguínea, por lo que los drogadictos por vía intravenosa no deben compartir agujas ni jeringuillas.

Sífilis: la sífilis es una ETS infecciosa crónica producida por una bacteria. Que sea crónica implica que puede curarse con tratamiento pero que puede contraerse de nuevo, el cuerpo no se hace inmune. La sífilis, como el sida, puede transmitirse por vía sanguínea o de la madre embarazada a su hijo en el útero o durante el parto. Si durante los primeros meses de gestación se detecta la infección y se sigue el tratamiento es posible la curación de la madre y del feto. Ciertos casos de ETS pueden afectar a la garganta o a la boca, y éstas pueden ser una vía de contagio. Las úlceras de sífilis —denominadas chancro sifilítico— desaparecen sin tratamiento, pero si el paciente no acude al médico y la enfermedad no se ha curado, ésta continúa su evolución: el germen pasa a la sangre y la infección continúa dando graves complicaciones, infectando seriamente el corazón, el cerebro y la médula espinal. Además, la mujer gestante con sífilis puede transmitirla al feto a través de la placenta, produciendo aborto, muerte intraútero, afecciones óseas, oculares, nerviosas, etc. Tras la úlcera, viene una fase de fiebre, nódulos y manchas cutáneas, con posibles complicaciones: ceguera, parálisis, etc. La última fase conlleva daños graves, pérdida de coordinación de las extremidades y lesiones en órganos vitales: el cerebro, los ojos, la médula espinal, etc., llegando incluso a causar la muerte.

Síndrome: se define como un conjunto de síntomas. Éstos pueden o no ser negativos y provocar o no enfermedad. A veces implica simplemente determinadas sensaciones físicas y cognitivas. He seleccionado unos cuantos, muy «de moda», que pueden determinar una relación si uno de los dos los sufre: Peter Pan, Wendy, Narciso, Don Juan...

Síndrome premenstrual: obviamente lo padecen las mujeres que tienen la regla. Se refiere a los síntomas físicos y psíquicos que se manifiestan entre siete y diez días antes del período y generalmente desaparecen con el inicio de éste o poco después. Son tantos y tan contradictorios entre una mujer y otra que, como ellos se quejan a veces, «no hay quien os entienda». Pues bien, aparte de bromas sexistas y ridículos anuncios de compresas (¿saben los guionistas lo gracioso que nos suena a nosotras eso de «me encanta ser mujer», cuando andas inflamada y desangrándote por los pasillos del metro a las ocho de la mañana, soportando un dolor de ovarios que baja hasta el tobillo y sube hasta las amígdalas?), el síndrome premenstrual merecería un epígrafe que bien podría titularse: «los mil y un síntomas», que van desde los afectivos y emocionales (tristeza, ansiedad, cólera, inestabilidad, irritabilidad, apatía, crisis de llanto o desesperación) a los físicos, asociados al dolor (cefalea, mastalgia o dolor en las mamas, y dolores músculo-esqueléticos), así como afecciones en el sistema circulatorio (retención de líquidos y la consiguiente ganancia de peso, edemas, pesadez), y otros (náuseas, palpitaciones, sofocos). También el apetito se puede ver alterado, con anorexia o ansias de comida. A nivel cognitivo, puede presentarse disminución de la concentración, indecisión, hipersensibilidad o incluso paranoia e ideación autolítica (ideas para autolesionarse). Insomnio, hipersomnia (somnolencia), fatiga, letargia, que pueden determinar aislamiento social y menor eficacia en el trabajo. Dermatológicamente se produce acné, pelo seco o graso. Y en el plano conductual disminución de la motivación y del control de los impulsos.

El SPM afecta al 75 % de las mujeres en edad reproductiva.

Contra el SPM ayuda practicar ejercicio, seguir una dieta que nos permita comer cinco veces al día en pequeñas cantidades para mantener equilibrados los niveles de glucosa en sangre, evitar los alimentos y bebidas excitantes (café y refrescos a base de cafeína, cacao, chocolate, té, etc.), el alcohol y la sal, incluir suplementos vitamínicos (la vitamina E disminuye el dolor de cabeza, el insomnio, la depresión, el ansia por comer o la fatiga; la vitamina B6 combate las dolencias mamarias, la depresión y la ansiedad), minerales, de calcio y magnesio, y hormonales. Como es obvio, el SPM se vincula a la ovulación, si ésta se elimina tomando anticonceptivos orales (la píldora), muerto el perro... También la progesterona, por vía oral o vaginal, mejora el SPM.

Single: anglicismo que vale su peso en oro porque designa al colectivo compuesto por todo ser que no esté emparejado en la franja de edad de los 25 a los 65; se trata, sin duda, de un potente nicho de mercado. Es una palabra que huye de la connotación negativa de «soltera» o «divorciado», y que añade a los demás recuperados de las filas de otros estados civiles (separados, viudos, etc.). Agrupa a todo el que se maneja por la vida sin pareja estable, sea de modo transitorio, sea para los restos. No cabe generalizar acerca de la forma de vivir la sexualidad de los *singles*, ya que depende, por supuesto, de cada persona. Lo que sí es cierto, dado que potencialmente son consumidores, es que se han organizado empresas especializadas en ponerles en contacto (desde las webs que prometen encontrar tu «media naranja» —a ver cuándo alguien valiente se atreve a decir que «somos naranjas completas» todos y todas, cada uno y cada una...—, se ha creado todo un sistema de citas para polvos esporádicos, agencias de viajes, excursiones y cruceros de toda índole, quedadas en discotecas, bares y demás, para que los *singles* se muevan, contacten, se apareen, se lo gasten, vamos. Desde luego, más ameno que matricularte en un MBA que no quieres hacer y que no te puedes casi permitir, sólo para poder conocer gente que aún sigue soltera, ya es.

Sling o columpio: en realidad alude en inglés a «colgar» y se utiliza para designar a esa especie de pañuelo con el que se lleva a los bebés, bien al frente, bien a la espalda. Su vinculación y finalidad sexual está en la acepción de *sling* como balancín, casi un columpio, compuesto por un rectángulo de cuero con cadenas en los extremos que pende de un soporte. Se asocia a las parafernalias fetichistas y del BD/SM. Una persona se coloca sobre él, boca arriba o boca abajo, y su pareja, de pie, lo balancea *ad gustum*, penetrando por vagina, ano o boca con el pene, con un dildo o con una mano (*fisting*).

Sodomía: penetración anal. Tiene un tinte de reprobación, asociándose comúnmente a ciertas parafilias. Por su etimología, la ciudad de Sodoma (casi indisolublemente unida a Gomorra) fue la que Dios mandó destruir por su depravación, castigando los actos de violación (pero no precisamente homosexuales). En el cine X las escenas de sexo anal se suelen pagar mejor que una simple masturbación o un lésbico. Mientras que no todas las actrices están dispuestas a practicarlo, hay otras bien expertas en penetraciones anales múltiples. En cualquier caso exige una preparación previa y la tarea de iluminar se complica. En Estados Unidos no todas las productoras incluyen escenas de *backdoor*, realizándose incluso versiones con esta práctica sólo para su distribución en Europa. Ver qué es, cómo prepararse y cómo hacer sexo anal, en su apartado.

Spanking: «¡Contesta!: ¿Has sido malo?» Toca hablar de disciplina de la buena, inglesa para más señas. Nuevamente un anglicismo bautiza una práctica sexual. Esta especialidad, que el día 8 de agosto celebra su Día Mundial, tiene que ver con la afición por los azotes en el culo. El *spanking* es para quienes piensan que cabe juntar en una misma frase «amor» y «placer» con «dolor» y «castigo corporal», y que entre mayores de edad que consienten, dar o recibir cachetadas con la mano desnuda, con regla, palmeta, látigo, fusta o con vara, a palo seco o combinado con *bondage*, es cuestión de arte y dosificación. Hay numerosas referencias, de texto y pictóricas, de un Aristóteles a cuatro patas, amarrado con bridas en la boca y cabalgado por Filis —una mujer muy influyente sobre Alejandro Magno—, que alcanzaba el orgasmo recibiendo azotes fuertes en las nalgas... Un matiz: los azotes genitales sólo deben darlos personas con experiencia. Una mayor intensidad del dolor —que provoca descargas de adrenalina en quien los recibe, de ahí la excitación— no se alcanza pegando cada vez más fuerte, sino más deprisa, con rápidos giros cortos de muñeca. Hay partes que deben quedar excluidas de los golpes por su extrema sensibilidad (glande, clítoris). El juego se establece entre dos posiciones: las *spankees* son quienes reciben —se les ata, se les coloca sobre una mesa, contra una pared o de rodillas— y los *spankers*, los que azotan. Roles de sumisión/ dominio aparentemente (sólo aparentemente) muy bien establecidos, porque esos azotes eróticos consensuados entre adultos obedecen a un deseo de ser golpeado: en realidad en el SM/BD es la *spankee* la que marca los límites de lo que está pasando. Para que la situación no se descontrole —si el dolor deja de ser bien recibido—, se pactan palabras clave que, de ser pronunciadas, harán que el otro cese. No hay *spankers* femeninas. Si es una mujer la que pega los azotes, se la considera siempre «Ama» o «dómina» y al hombre «sumiso» o «esclavo». Sin etiquetarse como aficionadas al *spanking*, muchas parejas participan de ciertos guiños de esta disciplina: ¿cuántas mujeres no disfrutan de una «palmadita» en el trasero bien dada en determinado momento de la relación sexual? (si se da cuando ella está muy excitada puede desencadenar el orgasmo). Un mundo, sin duda, cuyos secretos no están excesivamente divulgados.

Striptease: cuando quitarse la ropa se convierte en un arte, en una herramienta de seducción, ya sea en el círculo de lo privado o en plan profesional (los hay que se ganan muy bien la vida con ello). Puede ser muy erótica la combinación de ciertos elementos: gestos y movimientos seductores, música, determinada iluminación y cierta lencería *sexy*... Desde luego, no todo el mundo se plantea montar un *show* con la barra, la boa, las plumas y el tanga dorado de lamé o disfrazarse de policía; pero sí, sin duda, hacer un *striptease* como juego para el dormitorio. Cada año se hace más natural apuntarse a cursos de *striptease* que imparten *sex shops* y academias de baile, por aquello de no hacer el ridículo ante la pareja (y hasta por adelgazar).

Supuración uretral: la ITS masculina más frecuente. Consiste en la aparición de supuración por la uretra. Puede ser indicativo de una infección sexual producida por varios gérmenes, siendo los más comunes los gonococos, las clamidias o el ureaplasma y, según cuál sea el causante de la infección, variará la sintomatología. En general, el paciente con una uretritis se queja de que le sale pus por el pene y tiene molestias al orinar. El diagnóstico se hace tras una toma de la supuración que se analiza con el fin de instaurar el tratamiento específico, según sea el germen que la está produciendo. Si se ha hecho un diagnóstico precoz y correcto y se ha llevado bien el tratamiento, en la mayoría de los casos se cura sin secuelas. Siempre hay que hacer un control analítico de curación. Si la enfermedad no se trata, o se medica mal, pueden surgir graves complicaciones tales como esterilidad, por estrechamiento de la uretra, o inflamación de próstata, vesículas seminales, testículos, vejiga... etc.

Swingers/swinging: viene del inglés *swinging*, «columpiarse». Quienes se rigen por el *lifestyle*, como se conoce también al «ambiente liberal», tienen un código de honor y requisitos previos que los convierten en una tribu homogénea, muy cerrada y, por supuesto, muy «liberal». Son mujeres y hombres predispuestos a hacer intercambios de parejas, a la práctica sexual en grupo y todas las variantes de éstas. De modo casi clandestino, a través de la web o convocando discretamente a otros aficionados, se organizan fiestas de intercambio donde participan parejas que son seleccionadas (sí, a veces hay una especie de *casting* previo; para poder ir has de ser admitido, preseleccionan por foto). En algunas se fijan reglas concretas (por ejemplo, que sólo ellas puedan realizar contactos bisexuales). Normalmente, se establece la prohibición de consumo de drogas y se exige el uso de preservativo. Para un *swinger* el placer se obtiene en el ejercicio de una libertad sexual que traspasa los límites convencionales de la fidelidad o de la unicidad. Lo peligroso es practicar estos intercambios en etapas de la relación que hagan que ésta se resienta (hay que estar preparado mental y emocionalmente para contemplar a tu parienta o a tu marido disfrutando con otra y que no te asalte la duda o te dé un ataque de celos...). A ver, que lo de «te amo tanto que te comparto» no lo tenemos todos tan asimilado... La candalagnia o candaulismo es la parafilia que designa la excitación que se produce al ver a la pareja copulando con otra persona, como en el triolismo. El *swinging* proporciona contactos que se entienden meramente sexuales, no tiene que ver con sentimientos, y se realizan con entera aceptación de todas las partes. La variante *light*, el *Soft Swing*, implica que una pareja incluya a un tercero en besos, caricias y sexo oral, mientras que el *Full Swap*, o intercambio total, se refiere a la penetración con un tercero, sea un individuo u otra pareja. Evidentemente, se trata de uno más de los cambios que ha traído la transformación acelerada del modelo tradicional de relación de pareja. Se han establecido nuevas modalidades de acuerdo, bien porque ya no funciona la promesa de fidelidad hasta la muerte, bien porque el rol sumiso y pasivo de la mujer que tolera resignada la multiplicidad sexual del hombre ya no se sostiene.

Testículos: son los órganos masculinos a cargo de la producción de hormonas sexuales y del semen. Llamados «pelotas», «huevos», «bolas», etc., se encuentran en la bolsa escrotal, suspendidos fuera del organismo. Extremadamente sensibles, tanto si se acarician con la lengua o con la mano, como si se estrujan o machacan de un golpe, la reacción no se hace esperar.

Testosterona: es la hormona sexual masculina y que determina la masculinidad (no, no me he repetido). Aunque se encuentra en ambos sexos, en ellos se presenta con mayor peso específico y en mayor cantidad (lo que explica su mayor agresividad y musculatura). Tanto en hombres como en mujeres es la responsable del apetito sexual —cuando su tasa es baja, la libido cae— y, ya desde los primeros meses de desarrollo fetal, contribuye a la formación de las gónadas del feto. En ellos afecta a su rápido desarrollo muscular, al crecimiento, a la calvicie, etc., y en ellas se relaciona con el humor, la libido. Se dispara en la pubertad, originando los caracteres sexuales secundarios del varón: cambio de voz, nacimiento del vello, de la barba y aumento del tamaño de los órganos sexuales.

Tiña inguinal o dermatofitosis: infección que afecta a la zona de las ingles causada por un hongo, *Tinea cruris*, similar al pie de atleta. Se manifiesta con picores y debe ser tratada por un médico, pues podría tratarse de otra cosa. Normalmente se prescribe una crema o un *spray* que lo elimina en dos semanas. Se debe extremar la higiene (jabones neutros, sin olores ni desodorantes que irritan), cambiar diariamente la ropa interior (¿y cuándo no?), prefiriendo la de algodón y el modelo *boxer*, evitar el uso de toallas húmedas y secar bien después de la ducha diaria.

Traje de saliva: nada que ver con los trajes de cemento propios de bandas de mafiosos y bastante lejos de toda conexión con la alta costura, aunque, si te lo hacen con maña, subes bien alto. Ver el apartado «Sexo oral».

Transexualidad: casi todos los testimonios de personas transexuales coinciden en una afirmación: son personas que se sienten de un sexo, pero que están atrapadas en un cuerpo del opuesto. Cuando sucede que la genitalidad biológica no coincide con la personalidad y la psique de la persona, muchas veces se opta por la cirugía de reasignación genital. Hoy, en España, para poder modificar el nombre en la documentación oficial, adecuándolo a la identidad de la persona transexual, no se exige el paso por el quirófano (que puede ser traumático, además de peligroso y, en ocasiones, cuando la persona no siente conflicto con su genitalidad, resulta innecesario o casi una mutilación). Para el tema burocrático basta un informe psicológico y que se acredite haber seguido un tratamiento hormonal por un período de dos años. Ver abajo más información y distinción del concepto de travestismo.

Travestismo: afición por disfrazarse o utilizar ropa del sexo opuesto. A muchos hombres (y a sus parejas, novias, esposas) les divierte vestirse de mujer durante veladas eróticas, se incorpora a la relación como un fetiche. Otra manifestación consiste en el cambio de rol: cuando se maquillan, se arreglan con ropa de chica y se comportan como tal durante cierto tiempo —con conocimiento de su pareja o en secreto—. La ginemimetofilia designa una parafilia en la que la excitación sólo se producirá si la pareja es un travestí.

Una cosa: travestí y transexual son dos cosas distintas. Hay que tener claro que travestismo es utilizar la vestimenta y complementos socialmente delimitados para el sexo opuesto (por frivolizar: es el gusto por disfrazarse de mujer siendo un hombre y viceversa). Ser transexual no tiene nada que ver. La transexualidad es el nada fácil camino que siguen personas que nacen con un cuerpo que no se corresponde con su verdadera identidad. La mayoría rechaza los genitales con los que ha nacido. Por ejemplo, un chico se siente mujer o una chica se siente hombre. Viven atrapados en un cuerpo de mujer, hasta que un día, deciden dar el «primer» paso, que bien puede ser vestirse conforme se sienten, o maquillarse, o raparse la melena, o empezar un tratamiento hormonal. Nacer transexual implica la discordancia entre identidad sexual de una persona (el cómo se siente) y su genitalidad biológica (los órganos que le «han tocado» en suerte al nacer). Muchas veces las personas transexuales precisan cirugía de reasignación genital. La gente se conduce y juzga a la persona transexual movida por prejuicios, no me cabe duda, porque una decisión de tal envergadura no puede llevarse a cabo por capricho, porque hay que tener un buen par de... para cortarse el... Es una cuestión de necesidad absoluta motivada por el hecho de que la persona no llega a «entender» o a aceptar esos genitales y necesita imperiosamente adecuarlos a quien su mente le dice que es. Hay casos de transexuales que, en principio, querrían reasignar sus órganos sexuales, pero luego se aceptan a sí mismos con los genitales con los que nacieron y pasan a ser parte de su cuerpo masculino o femenino y ya no los perciben como del sexo opuesto. Rehúsan operarse por razones de salud, o de edad, o porque piensan que a lo mejor no van a obtener satisfacción sexual, o por mitos acerca de la cirugía, o porque resulta muy caro o, sencillamente, porque no les da la gana..., porque es una decisión propia. Leía hace poco que la operación en el caso del transexual masculino —de las personas nacidas biológicamente mujeres que inician su transición hacia hombres— no está suficientemente perfeccionada. El objetivo sería formar un pene, y hay dos técnicas. Una, a base de la reconstrucción del clítoris, pero que no es funcional a la hora de la penetración. Erecta, porque es el propio clítoris que, después de tratamientos hormonales se hiperdesarrolla. Luego está la otra, que se denomina la «técnica del colgajo», que suele emplear musculatura del brazo, con la que se realiza un injerto. En términos de sensibilidad, esta última cirugía logra unos resultados menos satisfactorios que la primera y por ello muchos chicos no se operan. En el caso de transexuales feminizantes, es más sencillo. Evidentemente, siempre es más difícil «crear» donde no hay que quitar y «profundizar» hasta formar una vagina y construir un clítoris y unos labios con tejido del glande y del pene respectivamente. Con la entrada en vigor de la Ley de Identidad de Género, el 17 de marzo de 2007, en España las personas transexuales pueden modificar la referencia del nombre y sexo en sus documentos, como el DNI, sin necesidad de someterse a una operación genital y sin procedimiento judicial. Como requisito para ello se pide un dictamen psicológico donde se le haya diagnosticado disforia de género y haber recibido tratamiento hormonal durante al menos dos años para acomodar sus características físicas a las correspondientes al sexo reclamado.

Úlceras genitales: dentro de las ITS más frecuentes se encuentran las úlceras genitales, sin duda, en la lista de cosas que nadie se pide para Reyes... Casi siempre, pasada una semana del contacto sexual infeccioso y no más de cuatro, aparecen en los genitales una o varias úlceras (llagas) que pueden ser dolorosas o no y que en algunos casos se acompañan de ganglios en la ingle. Las causas de estas úlceras son gérmenes de distintos tipos. Cuando las heridas son duras e indoloras a menudo es una sífilis. Si son dolorosas y sangrantes frecuentemente será un chancro blando. La presencia de lesiones vesiculares, como bolsitas de agua que posteriormente se rompen dejando erosiones en la piel, indicará que se trata de un herpes genital. En este caso, las lesiones desaparecerán tras el tratamiento y podrán volver a aparecer sin necesidad de un nuevo contacto sexual. Es pues una infección recidivante (que reaparece). Los varones se quejarán de la aparición de una o varias úlceras en el pene o en los testículos. En las mujeres las lesiones pasan desapercibidas en ocasiones, debido a que pueden aparecer en el interior de la vagina, no dando molestias en muchos de los casos. Estas lesiones aparecen también en la boca, después de las relaciones sexuales urogenitales. El examen médico, junto con el análisis de sangre y una toma de la secreción de la úlcera, permitirán un diagnóstico correcto. Como en la mayoría de las ITS, el diagnóstico y el tratamiento precoz, con el consiguiente control de curación, terminarán con la infección sin secuelas. En el caso del herpes genital no habrá un tratamiento curativo, pero sí se podrá disminuir la aparición de nuevos brotes y aliviar la sintomatología. Asimismo, la mujer deberá hacerse una citología anual para controlar una posible degeneración de las células del cuello de útero. En la sífilis, durante los primeros meses de embarazo, si se detecta la infección y se instaura el tratamiento, es posible la curación de la madre y del feto. Sobre las posibles complicaciones de las úlceras de sífilis, si el paciente no acude al médico, desaparecen sin tratamiento, pero no han curado. El germen pasa a la sangre y la infección continúa dando graves complicaciones, infectando seriamente el corazón, el cerebro y la médula espinal. Además, la mujer gestante con sífilis puede transmitirla al feto a través de la placenta, produciendo aborto, muerte intraútero, afecciones óseas, oculares, nerviosas, etc. El herpes genital puede dar complicaciones. Hay un aumento de la aparición del cáncer de cuello de útero en las pacientes que lo han padecido.

Uretra: conducto por el que se expulsa la orina desde la vejiga. En los hombres, este canal sirve también para la salida del semen.

Urolagnia: ver *lluvia dorada*.

Útero: órgano femenino donde se produce la gestación. En él, el feto se desarrolla desde la fecundación del óvulo hasta el parto. Protegido, caliente y aislado, dentro de la barriga de la madre es donde mejor se está, no en vano hay casi que sacar al niño a la fuerza y, a lo largo de la vida, quizá como reminiscencia inconsciente, muchos adultos adoptan la posición fetal para dormir. El cuello del útero o cérvix cuenta con terminaciones nerviosas, lo que lleva a muchas mujeres al orgasmo mediante penetraciones profundas. A través del cuello ascienden los espermatozoides y, si hay un óvulo fértil, se realizará la fecundación.

Vagina: el término latino se traduce como vaina, estuche o funda. Es el órgano donde se introduce el pene durante el coito. Desde fuera, la vulva sólo permite ver el orificio de entrada de este conducto que se extiende hacia dentro del cuerpo de la mujer y termina en el cérvix. Sus dimensiones varían según las razas, son de unos 8 a 12 cm de largo y unos 3 cm de ancho, aunque es elástica, lo que permite que pueda efectuarse el coito con penes de casi cualquier tamaño y que el bebé pueda salir a través de ella en el momento del parto. Aunque se trata de un órgano delicado, apenas cuenta con terminaciones nerviosas y éstas se concentran en el tercio más cercano al exterior. Los puntos más sensibles son la entrada, el punto G, el punto A y el cérvix, justo al fondo del todo. Esta zona, junto con el clítoris y el punto G, sería donde se concentra el mayor número de terminaciones nerviosas. Se oye hablar de la «flora vaginal», se trata de microorganismos que la limpian de modo natural y que la protegen. Cuando se leen los resultados de una citología asusta ver la presencia de bacilos de Doderlein, por ejemplo (ahí es cuando te da un paro cardíaco creyendo que «has pillado algo». No, son «normales» y confieren el carácter ácido al líquido vaginal, que sirve para salvaguardar la vagina de infecciones). La forma de la vagina es como un saco estrecho que se dobla sobre sí. Está permanentemente lubricada por las glándulas de Bartolino, lo que facilita la entrada del pene y, de no ser así —por cambios hormonales, nerviosismo, falta de excitación u otra causa—, la sequedad se puede solucionar con lubricación artificial. Ver el capítulo «Anatomía básica».

Vaginismo: disfunción sexual que sufren las mujeres cuando se produce un espasmo involuntario de los músculos que rodean la vagina, lo que hace que ésta se cierre, dificultando, haciendo doloroso o impidiendo el coito. Los motivos pueden ser de tipo psicológico: miedo al sexo, a la penetración, a su pareja, etc., o rechazo inconsciente por alguna situación traumática del pasado (abusos, etc.). Dado que la contracción de los músculos cierra el orificio de la vagina, se puede desistir del coito y dedicarse tranquilamente a acariciar y besar el resto de su cuerpo y la misma vulva, pudiendo alcanzar el orgasmo con estimulación del clítoris. Las parejas de quienes tengan vaginismo deberían procurar relajarlas y que se «olviden» de ese mal trago. Lo mismo que se necesita paciencia en casos de disfunciones eréctiles o de gatillazos, sucede en este caso. Se trata de algo involuntario y quizá se solucione por sí solo, o con cierto reaprendizaje de ella en solitario.

Vasectomía: método anticonceptivo quirúrgico, definitivo y permanente —aunque puede revertirse—, que consiste en cortar y cerrar los conductos que comunican los testículos con el pene y por

los cuales circula el semen, impidiendo que pueda dejar embarazada a una mujer. No afecta a la virilidad ni a la libido: los testículos
no se tocan. La cirugía la practica un urólogo y se hace con anestesia local. Ver el capítulo «Anticonceptivos».

Viagra: las pastilla azul más famosa del mundo. Fármaco que se
administra por vía oral para la disfunción eréctil cuyo principio activo es el sidenafilo. Necesita receta. Ver el apartado «Cirugía íntima masculina».

Vibrador: ver *dildo*. Aparato con motor a pilas o a la red, generalmente con forma de pene, que se utiliza para la estimulación
sexual: exterior, la zona de la vulva, perineo y ano, e interior, intro-
duciéndose por vía anal o vaginal. Cada vez más sofisticados, los
hay hasta con mando a distancia, que permiten incluso juegos de
pareja que uno se lo introduzca y el otro decida cuándo lo enciende
y con qué potencia. Ver el apartado «Juguetes eróticos».

VIH: Virus de Inmunodeficiencia Adquirida, causa del sida.

Violación: es un delito —acto tipificado y penado— que constituye un ataque contra la libertad sexual de las personas. Consiste en
obtener con violencia o intimidación (amenazas, coacciones) el acceso carnal: penetración del pene o de un objeto en boca, vagina o
ano de la víctima, y cuando la víctima es un varón: el tocamiento de
su pene o forzarle al contacto con los órganos sexuales del agresor,
ya sea con la boca o la mano. El delito de abuso sexual y el de violación se diferencian en la circunstancia de la penetración. Ese acceso
carnal —vaginal, anal u oral— que media en la violación no concu-
rre en el de abuso. Los demás elementos de falta de consentimiento, ataque a la libertad sexual, etc., son comunes. Sería constitutivo
de delito todo acto sexual llevado a cabo cuando el otro no ha consentido: sea contra su voluntad o bien cuando la víctima sea un menor o un incapaz que no puede prestar tal consentimiento. Atención: lo que determina que sea un delito no es que haya un coito
con violencia, sino que no sea consentido. Muchos adultos consen-
súan sus prácticas sexuales dentro de lo que se puede considerar
doloroso, incómodo, «perverso», «brutal». No hay delito si ambos

están de acuerdo. En los delitos de abusos sexuales y violación, lo que se castiga es que se fuerce a otro a realizar un contacto sexual no consentido (sería delito también si te penetran o te fuerzan a otra práctica sexual habiéndote drogado o mientras duermes, porque no estás en condiciones de consentirlo). Otro asunto que se debe dejar claro, de una vez por todas, es el tema de «la resistencia», la oposición que se espera de la víctima. La jurisprudencia ha evolucionado (parte de la sociedad, machista, quizá no tanto), y se ha pasado de exigir poco menos que una resistencia heroica —que heredaba esa cultura de «se merece lo que le ha pasado (la violación) por ir por ahí provocando»—, a pedírsele simplemente una oposición firme y razonable. Con el tiempo, se ha llegado a comprender que no es exigible de la víctima que arriesgue su vida cuando, muchas veces, es consciente de que la violación resulta inevitable y sabe que si encima lucha, probablemente el agresor se ensañe y sea aún peor, o la mate.

Virgen: persona que no ha mantenido relaciones sexuales con penetración. Por educación, incluso el lenguaje condiciona este «estado» por el que casi todas las culturas han mostrado cierto interés, especialmente por la primera vez de la mujer. En la mujer se habla de «pérdida de la virginidad», que equivale a una especie de tragedia o a un evento de tal gravedad que exige pensárselo mucho, muchísimo, habida cuenta que en según qué mentalidades, sólo se puede una casar con uno y acostarse con ese mismo, siempre tras la boda, hasta la sepultura; un drama, vamos. Se identifica la virginidad con la pureza y en determinadas sociedades se convierte en una «garantía» y en un trofeo (el libro *Memorias de una geisha*, de Arthur Golden, publicado en 1997, relata la subasta del himen de una *maiko*, la pugna económica entre varios acaudalados hombres de negocios. Ver *himen*, donde se explica un poco el significado de la subasta del himen o *mizuage*, un rito asociado con las *geishas*). Dos cosas: la primera vez puede no doler en absoluto y además, no siempre se sangra, no hay por qué cuestionar lo que la chica te cuenta. Puede ser verdad que seas el primero y que, por suerte para todos, no haya hemorragia ni dolor. Y en ellos, por lo de «cuantas más mejor y más machote», dejar de serlo es un mero trámite que se ha vaciado de emociones hasta el punto de encomendar a una «profesional» que se ocupe de la faena de «estrenar» al chaval. Craso error, porque acumulará la tensión de la «primera vez» con la de estar con una perfecta extraña... y a saber en qué condiciones (que no siempre acuden a sitios de lujo precisamente). No tengo nada en contra del oficio pero, si se puede elegir, y hoy día se puede, nada mejor que hacerlo con alguien que te gusta, con todo el cariño, con todas las ganas, la ternura y la entrega de los sentimientos de verdad. Ya vendrán las proezas, las superposturas y demás. Con preservativo, eso sí. Con la cultura actual y la promiscuidad que impera, que te llamen «virgen» es casi un insulto (sí, en la definición de promiscuidad también afirmo que es un insulto que te llamen «promiscua», pero así se entiende con ejemplos concretos que hasta el lenguaje nos mete mucha caña a las chicas), aunque, paradójicamente, coexisten de modo paralelo ciertas etnias y religiones que exigen la virginidad de la mujer hasta el matrimonio. En las sociedades romana y china también se realizaba en la noche de bodas este rito de mostrar la «sábana manchada». En el apartado sobre «Cirugía íntima femenina» se trata la himenoplastia, una intervención por la que un cirujano plástico reconstruye el himen. Personalmente, encuentro que convierten la ceremonia de «desflorar» a la novia (eso de mostrar a todos los presentes la sangre que ha de manchar un pañuelo de seda que una experta introduce en su vagina) en un atentado contra el derecho a la intimidad e, incluso, dudo que no vaya también contra la integridad física de la chica. De nuevo, colisión entre vivir conforme a una cultura y a unas costumbres y derechos fundamentales.

Virus del papiloma humano (VPH): es una ETS que puede desencadenar serios problemas, incluso el cáncer. Ver *condilomas o verrugas genitales*.

Voyeur o **voyeurismo**: los mirones obtienen placer y excitación al contemplar, observar, vigilar a otras personas que están desnudas o desnudándose y mientras se lo montan. Dicen que todo el mundo es un poco *voyeur*, aunque parece que el hombre es especialmente más sensible a la excitación sexual por vía de estímulos visuales: viendo una película porno, o fotos eróticas, o a alguien *sexy* por la calle. Como parafilia, el voyeurismo implica sustituir el sexo con una pareja por la simple observación de extraños en las actitudes descritas. Un *voyeur* suele conformarse con mirar, no necesita al objeto de sus miradas para el sexo, ya que esa contemplación le sirve para masturbarse —en ese momento o después, al recordarlo—. Media un abismo entre el encanto de ver a tu pareja sin ropa o haciendo algo erótico para ti, o el morbo que puntualmente puede darnos encontrar por accidente a alguien desnudo, y el voyeurismo patológico, que es un acto de robo de la intimidad de otros, no consentido y que, por añadidura, se convierte en la única manera de excitación de quien lo practica (llegado el caso, necesitaría terapia sexual y psicológica seguramente).

Vulva: son los genitales externos de la mujer, los que se pueden ver. Los labios, el monte de Venus, el clítoris. Ver el capítulo «Anatomía básica».

Zonas erógenas: ver el capítulo específico.

Zoofilia: no designa la afición por visitar zoológicos, precisamente, sino la realización de actos sexuales con animales. El género pornográfico *pets* se produce casi en la clandestinidad y con «actores» desconocidos. Algún productor de cine X me explicaba que sólo personas en situaciones económicas de extremada necesidad o con ciertas drogodependencias se prestan a filmar algo así. Como excepciones, Cicciolina y Linda Lovelace; esta última, antes de hacerse tan famosa en *Garganta profunda*, grabó, inducida por Check Traynor, cortos clandestinos donde mantenía relaciones sexuales con un perro. Para este tipo de cintas se han utilizado especialmente perros, pero en las que yo vi aparecían una cabra en una escena y un burro en otra. También las hay con caballos y toros, a los que las mujeres practican felaciones, o incluso penetraciones (con la dificultad y esfuerzo físico que implica), anguilas y serpientes (se introducen al animal vivo por la vagina). Los primeros testimonios gráficos de esta parafilia aparecen en los años treinta, en unos cortometrajes mexicanos (*Rin Tin Tin Mexicano* o *El perro masajista*). En la década de los setenta, fue Dinamarca el primer país en amparar legalmente películas con escenas de sexo con animales. Admito que las dos únicas cintas de zoofilia que he visionado me hicieron vomitar. Así lo publiqué en mi primer libro, y lo corroboro cada vez que navegando por Internet me topo con esta basura. Probablemente contemplar la extracción de veinticinco metros de cadena del interior de una vagina o la introducción de un dildo de treinta centímetros de diámetro por un ano humano me parezca «una barbaridad», pero ante adultos que consienten, poco puedo decir. Sin embargo, en las producciones zoofílicas, el asunto es distinto. Aquí el animal es parte activa sin poder prestar su consentimiento —los animales no tienen capacidad para ello— y además, se les fuerza. Viendo la peli, me percaté de que de no sujetar al perro éste saldría corriendo, que los arañazos y marcas que dejaba sobre la espalda de una tipa —ojo, que no empleo en ningún caso el término «actriz»—, que si no estaba drogada lo parecía, se explican porque estaba asustado y hacía por retirarse... Seguramente quienes menos aman a los animales sean los que les obligan a practicar un sexo que instintivamente rechazan, sólo para poder filmarlo y ganar dinero con degenerados que lo demandan. Fuera ya de la pornografía, es indudable que quienes practican sexo con animales necesitan un psiquiatra. Todos los estudios coinciden en que la soledad, el aislamiento y la falta de habilidades sociales propician este acercamiento hacia los animales que, desde luego, son mucho menos conflictivos y perversos que los humanos.

Fuentes

Ablación: Wikipedia, The Center for Reproductive Rights Plan de Prevención y Erradicación de la Mutilación Genital Femenina en Wajid. Mujeres en red. Centro de Información de las Naciones Unidas para España. Afrol News.

Aborto natural: *elbebe.com*

Adicción al amor: Psiquiatra Carlos Sirvent, director del programa de Formación en Adicciones y fundador del Instituto Spiral. La web *ahige.org*

Castración química: Datos de la web *adeguello.net*

Joyería íntima: *erotiza.com*

Masturbación: *enfemenino.com, comomasturbarse.com Revista de Derecho Privado de México, juridicas.unam.mx.htm* Artículo de Isabel Salama, «El arte de amar». *Isabelsalama.com*

Métodos anticonceptivos: *Sexualidad y juventud: Guía educativa para un sexo más seguro.* La web *sexologia.org bibliotecavirtual.clacso.org.ar*

Mito de Narciso: Historias recogidas en *www.analitica.com* y en *www.cepvi.com.* Ana Muñoz, psicóloga, directora de *Cepvi.com*

PT141: *www.pt141.com* y *www.buypt141.co.uk/es/pt141_viagra forwomen.htm*

Reiki y aceites esenciales: Contenido espiritual: Gamal Abdul (Egipto). Entrevista: Sabine Heimen (Alemania). Traducción: Rosa M. Prieto (España). Regalado por Gamal Abdul a *www. esenciassagradas.com*

Sexo tántrico: *ecovisiones.cl/taller/tantrismo.htm* y *mujeraldia. com*

Síndrome premenstrual: Datos ofrecidos en *www.webdelamujer.com* y *www.nlm.nih.gov/medlineplus/spanish*

Viagra: *viagra.com*

Wikipedia: como herramienta básica para sobrevivir en este siglo.

Y además:

Afrodisíacos naturales: Roberto Carlos Rodríguez, *Afrodisíacos naturales*, Edimat libros, 1999.

Anomalías sexuales: Ganon, J., Simon, W. (eds), *Sexual Deviance*, Harper & Rox, Nueva York, 1967.

Coitus interruptus: Family Health International (FHI), 2007.

Feromonas: Patrick Süskind, *El perfume*.

La píldora y la píldora poscoital: información basada en datos de Schering España, S.A.

Dr. Dan Kiley, *El Complejo de Wendy*, Javier Vergara Editor, 1985.

Sylvia de Béjar, *Tu sexo es tuyo*, Planeta, 2007.

Shere Hite, *Shere Hite responde a las cartas de los jóvenes sobre el sexo*, La esfera de los libros, 2006.

Pilar Cristóbal, *Prácticas poco usuales del sexo*, La esfera de los libros, 2002.

Askmen.com, *Del bar a la cama*, Ediciones B, 2007.

Kristen M. Lagarte, *Feng Shui en el trabajo*, Ediciones Obelisco, 1999.

Casto Escópico, *Sólo para adultos. Historia del Cine X*, La Máscara, 1996.

Osho, *Tantra, Espiritualidad y Sexo*, Arkano Books, 1995.

Elizabeth Landers y Vicky Mainzer, *Las cosas absolutamente predecibles que hacen los hombres infieles*, Debolsillo, 2007.

Tracey Cox, *Hot sex. How to do it*, Bantam Books, 1998.

Kama Sutra, Ediciones Petronio, 1974.

Paloma Aznar «Vampirella», *Sex Toys*, Ilustraciones de Lau, Vértigo Publishers.

Joan Cantarero, *Los amos de la prostitución*, Ediciones B.

Impotencia: International Journal of Impotence Research.

Paul Brecher, *Los secretos de la energía corporal*, Taschen, 2004.

C.W. Leadbeater, *Los Chakras*, Editorial EDAF, 2001.

Liz Simpson, *El libro completo de los chakras*, Gaia Books Limited, 1999.

ITS: Sexualidad y juventud: Guía educativa para un sexo más seguro

Orgasmo fingido: Susan Crain Bakos, *Dear superlady of Sex,* St Martin's Press, Nueva York, 1990, p. 89.

Emma Taylor y Lorelei Sharkey, *El Big Bang*, Océano, 2004.

Orgasmo y eyaculación: Miriam Stoppard, *The Magic of Sex*, Allen & Unwin, 1991.

Richard von Krafft-Ebing, *Psychopathia Sexualis, 69 historias de casos*, Editorial La Máscara, 2000.

Parafilias: Diccionario de Perversiones y Parafilias.

Publicado por Javier Moya Suárez en *hmmm*, su weblog, el 20 de octubre de 2006. *javimoya.com/ blog/diccionario-de-perversiones-y-parafilias/*

Más información:

carlosserrano.blogdiario.com/1161245160/catalogo-de-perversiones-(1 % AAparte)/musolari.blogia.com/2005/012001-perversiones-i-.php

Barbara Keesling, *The Good Girl's Guide to Bad Girl Sex: An Indispensable Guide to Pleasure and Seduction.*

—, *How to Make Love All Night (and Drive a Woman Wild).*

—, *Super Sexual Orgasm: A Woman's Guide to Guaranteed Satisfaction.*

Jenna Jameson con Neil Strauss, *Cómo hacer el amor igual que una estrella de porno*, Heterodoxia, Martínez Roca, 2005.

Régine Dumay, *Cómo hacer bien el amor a un hombre*, Plaza y Janés, 1986.

—, *Cómo hacer bien el amor a una mujer*, Plaza y Janés, 1986.

Tracey Cox, *Hot relationships*, Bantan Books, 2000.

Josep Tomás, *El pene. El mejor amigo del hombre*. Santillana, 2006.

Agradecimientos

A Mario Tascón, responsable de que yo vuelva a creer un poquito en el mercado laboral español. Gracias, Mario, por tu voto de confianza, por la oportunidad, por darme la caña y dejarme pescar (y pecar...).

A Javier Moya, porque encargándome el blog de sexo de *Eva al desnudo*, apostando por mí en *elpais.com*, se me ha abierto todo un universo. Gracias, Javi, porque has hecho posibles tantas cosas...

A D. Silverio Fernández-Polanco, de Adara Estudio Jurídico, por supervisar los fragmentos de implicación legal. Gracias, Silverio, por un apoyo que trasciende lo profesional desde hace años ya.

Al doctor Federico Mayo, cirujano plástico y miembro numerario de la Sociedad Española de Cirugía Plástica, Reparadora y Estética, por su colaboración.

A Guillermo Hernaiz, por creer en mí. Gracias, *Sensei*, por darme tanta cancha.

A Iñigo García Ureta, mi editor, por darme nada más y nada menos que un esqueleto, amén de mil arreglos. Y por apoyarme y por escucharme. Ciertas cosas no las paga ningún sueldo...

A Antonio Pasagali, por las sugerencias, por leerme, por soportar mi incontinencia verbal.

A Salvador Diago, porque es la mano (amiga) que mece la cuna. Gracias por estar ahí.

Ilustradores

Berto Martínez. Su indiscutible talento ya fue acompañante de lujo y un valor añadido a mi primer libro. En éste, además de sus dos más que evocadoras imágenes, ha impulsado la colaboración artística de los demás ilustradores. Cada vez que le cito me emociono porque, que existan personas como él, tan generosas y tan positivas, me conmueve. Gracias, Berto, porque siempre confías en mí. Gracias por estar siempre que te necesito. Gracias por tu apoyo sin condiciones.

Lau, con ese estilo fresco y dulce... Pasan los años y seguimos cruzándonos, incluso en Japón. Tus ilustraciones son dos regalos maravillosos. Sin duda, las muñecas sexuales y los juegos eróticos, vistos por ti, se cargan de una incitante sutilidad. Gracias por tu esfuerzo creativo y por echarme una mano siempre.

Carmen García Huerta, quien, en plena reinvención profesional y artística, ha permitido a sus flamantes muñecas contonearse y pervertirse por estas páginas. Gracias por regalarme tu mirada *sexy* y refinada sobre las situaciones más eróticas.

Nani Serrano. Cuando abrí el *e-mail* con tu tremenda ilustración sobre cibersexo, entre sutil y profanadora, me quedé con una sonrisa grabada durante media hora... Y esa guapísima chica rodeada de cuernos y de toros... Muchísimas gracias.

Damián A. Pissara, con esas imágenes entre fotográficas y dibujadas que arañan en la semiinconsciencia, lo oscuro, lo íntimo... Gracias por tus pinceladas de genuino morbo.

Ray Caesar, uno de los grandes, ese formidable señor con quien contacté un buen día, fascinada por su obra, esas imágenes sobrecogedoras que recrean su imaginario tan personal como fascinante, y de quien me he hecho amiga vía *e-mail*. Lo más sorprendente es que aún no me ha dicho que no a nada...

Arturo Elena, sus mujeres son el amor. Igual de hermosas e imposibles. Deseo y provocación, curvas y delirio. Gracias por esa lujosa, *fashionista* y sugerente invitación al pecado.

Kaik y sus croquis de última hora... Gracias, Quique, porque con tu generosidad me has salvado (literariamente) el culo... Esas muñecas triunfarán, son la semilla de todo un *sexual movement*.

A todos, gracias por formar parte de algo tan importante para mí.

Nota legal

Este libro está realizado solamente con fines divulgativos para adultos. Su información no debe ser usada para el diagnóstico o tratamiento de enfermedades o problemas de salud. Del mismo modo ha de interpretarse la información facilitada sobre algunos de los métodos anticonceptivos que existen en la actualidad y que se mencionan. Tanto si tienes dudas o sospechas de que puedes tener algún problema relacionado con tu sexualidad, como si has de decidir sobre cuál es el sistema de planificación de tu vida reproductiva idóneo para ti y tu pareja, consulta siempre a un profesional de la salud. Este libro no pretende ser, en ningún caso, un sustituto del médico.

Para mayor información sobre la autora:
www.evaroy.com